MODERN EUROPE,
1789–PRESENT

MODERN EUROPE, 1789–PRESENT

ASA BRIGGS AND PATRICIA CLAVIN

Second Edition

PEARSON
Longman

London • New York • Toronto • Sydney • Tokyo • Singapore
Hong Kong • Cape Town • Madrid • Paris • Amsterdam • Munich • Milan

PEARSON EDUCATION LIMITED

Head Office:
Edinburgh Gate
Harlow CM20 2JE
Tel: +44 (0)1279 623623
Fax: +44 (0)1279 431059

London Office:
128 Long Acre
London WC2E 9AN
Tel: +44 (0)20 7447 2000
Fax: +44 (0)20 7447 2170
Website: www.history-minds.com

First edition 1997
Second edition published in Great Britain in 2003

ISBN 0 582 77260 5

British Library Cataloguing in Publication Data
A CIP catalogue record for this book can be obtained from the British Library

Library of Congress Cataloging in Publication Data
A CIP catalog record for this book can be obtained from the Library of Congress

10 9 8 7 6 5 4 3 2 1

Set in 10.5/12pt Bembo by Graphicraft Limited, Hong Kong
Printed and bound in Malaysia

The Publishers' policy is to use paper manufactured from sustainable forests.

CONTENTS

CONTENTS

ACKNOWLEDGEMENTS

The publishers are grateful to the following for permission to reproduce copyright material:

Map 7 redrawn from *The Twentieth Century World: An International History, Fourth Edition*, copyright 1996, 2000 by William R. Keylor, published and reprinted by permission of Oxford University Press, Inc. (Keylor, W. R. 2000).

In some instances we have been unable to trace the owners of copyright material, and we would appreciate any information that would enable us to do so.

PREFACE

This is a fully revised and extended edition of a history first published in 1997. Already by then Europe and the world had changed greatly since the then terminal date of the history, the bicentennial year of the French Revolution, 1989. This new edition takes the story forward into a new century and a new millennium when the history of Europe is inextricably entangled with the history of the world. It is not only the last chapters that have been substantially re-written. Significant changes have been made to the earlier chapters. Perspectives have changed. New knowledge is available.

It remains as true in 2002 as it was in 1997 that it is dangerous to see everything in the past leading up inexorably to the present. Yet it has become more obvious since then that in the light of a changing and uncertain present aspects of the past that had previously been neglected or forgotten acquire new interest and relevance. In the preface to the first edition it was rightly stated that the 'facts' of geography can never be separated from the 'facts' of history, though both were transformed in the period covered in this volume as a result of unprecedented population growth, urbanization, industrialization, innovative technology and new communications processes. Society and culture have changed and are still changing as much as the economy. The importance of diplomacy in international relations is as great, however, in the twenty-first century as it was in the earlier chapters of this volume.

The period as a whole is a strategic period in European history. It was only after the French Revolution that what one writer, Pim de Boer, has called 'a distinct self-reflective idea of Europe with a history and meaning of its own' took shape. The new phenomenon of the nation state was at the centre both of events and of the study of history, a study which was based largely on newly opened national archives. Nation building became a major theme. It is impossible to separate Britain from the story. What British politicians, writers, artists and travellers felt and wrote about 'Europe' in the past adds depth as well as variety to current news commentary. The European Union reflects past experiences as well as carrying new opportunities and new hopes and new fears. Yet within the Union there are regional as well as national differences, and these affect both attitudes and policies.

As in the first edition, footnotes have been deliberately kept to a minimum, but the bibliography, highly selective though it must be, contains not only the names of books and authors on whom our text depends and to whom we are both indebted, but the names of books and authors to whom readers should turn in order to pursue study independently. Some authors reach conclusions different from our own. That adds to the fascination of history. So, too, do differing versions of the character of the personalities involved, even of the role of personality itself.

As joint authors we have discussed each chapter at different stages of our research and writing. We have each written sections of the final text, but we are jointly responsible for the shape and scope of the volume as a whole. We would like to express our thanks to the many librarians without whose help we could have never have produced either the old or the new edition, to anonymous readers of the text for their valuable comments, and to our editor, Heather McCallum. We would also like to thank, as we did in our first preface, Andrew McLennan for his dedication – and patience – while the first edition was being written. We are sure that he will appreciate the publication of this new edition in circumstances which are different for all of us.

Asa Briggs
Patricia Clavin
April 2002

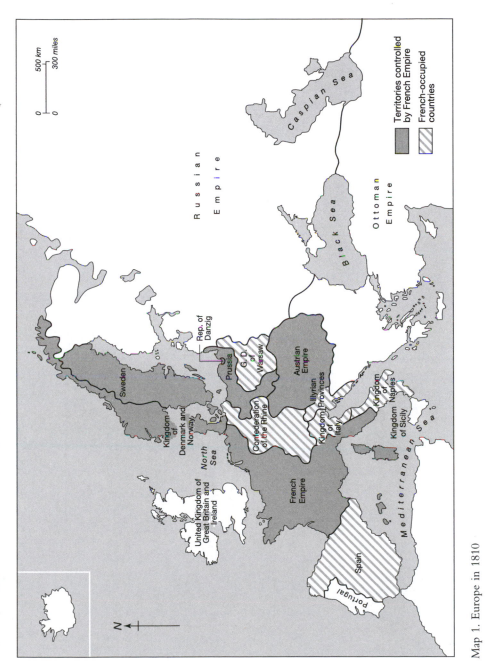

Map 1. Europe in 1810

Source: After Davies, N. (1996) *Europe, A History* (pub. Oxford and New York: Oxford University Press).

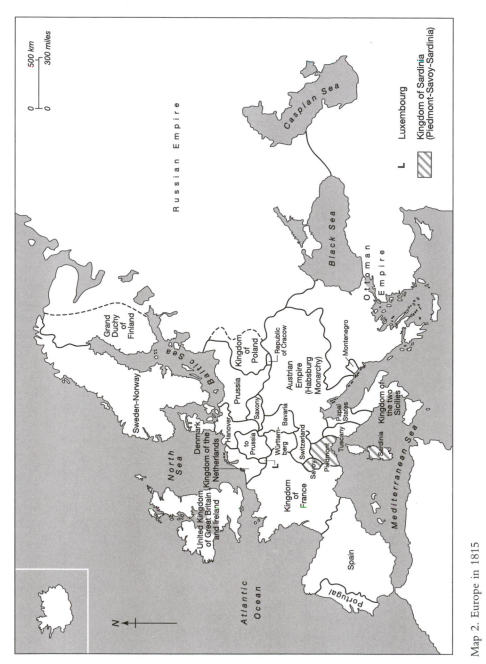

Map 2. Europe in 1815

Source: After Davies, N. (1996) *Europe, A History* (pub. Oxford and New York: Oxford University Press).

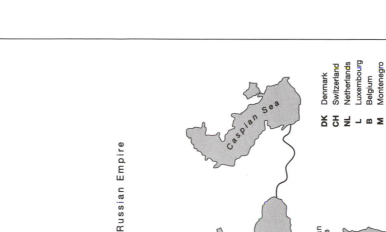

Map 3. Europe in 1914

Source: After Davies, N. (1996) *Europe, A History* (pub. Oxford and New York: Oxford University Press).

Map 4. The End of Imperial Europe, 1917–22

Source: After Davies, N. (1996) *Europe, A History* (pub. Oxford and New York: Oxford University Press).

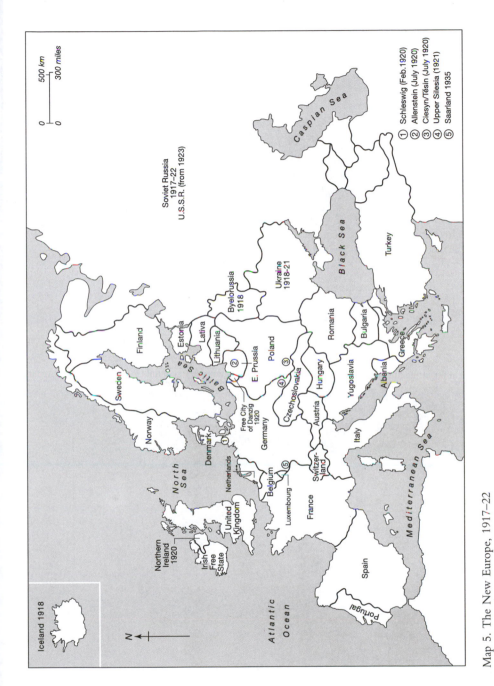

Map 5. The New Europe, 1917–22

Source: After Davies, N. (1996) *Europe, A History* (pub. Oxford and New York: Oxford University Press).

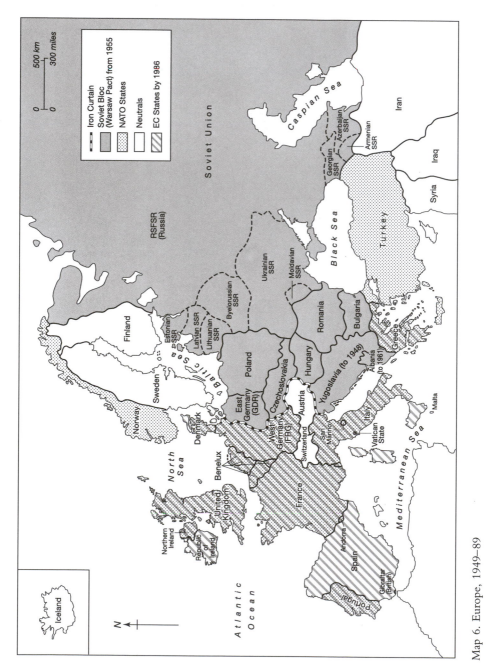

Map 6. Europe, 1949–89

Source: After Davies, N. (1996) *Europe, A History* (pub. Oxford and New York: Oxford University Press).

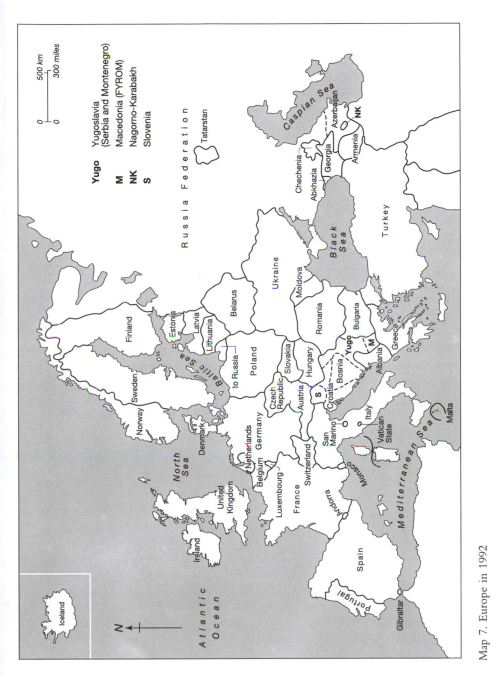

Map 7. Europe in 1992

Source: After map from *Twentieth Century World: An International History, Fourth Edition* by William R. Keylor, copyright 1996, 2000 by William R. Keylor. Used by permission of Oxford University Press, Inc.

Chapter 1

REVOLUTION AND EMPIRE: EXPERIENCE AND IMPACT, 1789–1815

CHANGE AND REVOLUTION: OLD AND NEW

There was so much change, most of it unprecedented, during the second half of the eighteenth century that both then and since most people have regarded this period in human history as the great divide between past and present. This, they have said, was the true beginning of 'modern times'. Looking backwards, the French nobleman, Alexis de Tocqueville, one of the shrewdest of political and social commentators, could 'find no parallel' in history. 'The past [had] ceased to throw its light upon the future.'

In the early twenty-first century, after the world has experienced further bursts of unprecedented change, much of it packed into the last 30 years, such a view of late-eighteenth-century change can be challenged. With the help of hindsight we can now identify continuities in thought, behaviour and institutions. The past did influence the future. We have also introduced the terms 'post-modern' and 'post-industrial' into our vocabulary to widen the perspectives. Yet the word 'revolution' still carries with it dramatic force. And this is true whether it is applied to late-eighteenth-century politics and society in France, in population by far the largest state in Europe (27 million in 1789, seven million more than in 1700), or to industrialization in Britain, a country with a third the population of France but with an unprecedented burst of economic growth in the last decades of the eighteenth century.

The word 'revolution' has been applied also to what happened in America following the American Declaration of Independence in 1776 (the year of Adam Smith's *Wealth of Nations* and of a large new James Watt steam engine, named not inappropriately 'Parliament Engine'). During the American War Frenchmen, including members of the French nobility, fought the British on American soil. The winning of American independence, a victory in which France shared, although at burdening financial cost, in effect bankruptcy, humiliated Britain, but it did not hold back striking industrial growth. As for the American political changes, some American historians have claimed that 'in the modern sense of the word it was hardly a revolution at all'.[1] There was, however, a new republic, and with it a commitment of the American people to the 'pursuit of happiness'. There was also the authority of a written constitution, drafted at Philadelphia in 1787.

Historians can learn much from changes in the meaning of words, indeed from the history of language as a whole. Originally the word 'revolution' had been an astronomical term applied to the regular round of the stars in their courses; and even after it came to be employed in political discussion during the seventeenth century it was usually implied that as a result of revolution the proper order of things, perverted by men in power, would be restored. You would move back to where you began. It was Tocqueville again who wrote of the beginning of the French Revolution in 1789 that 'one might have believed that the aim of the coming revolution was not the overthrow of the old regime but its restoration'. Nonetheless, after 1789 the word 'revolution' never meant quite the same again.

Whatever continuities there were between pre-revolutionary Europe and Europe after 1789 there was a very special sense of newness. Maximilien-Isidore Robespierre, revolutionary of revolutionaries, wrote to his brother in the summer of 1789 that France had produced 'in a few days greater events than the whole previous history of mankind', while across the Channel the leader of the English Whigs, Charles James Fox, described the fall of the Bastille as 'much the greatest event that ever happened in the history of the world'. In the new world of industry the pioneering English potter Josiah Wedgwood believed that 'the wonderful revolution' had 'thrown the world off its hinges', and in the old world of the Muses poets as different as William Blake and Samuel Taylor Coleridge joined in the chorus, along with Johann Wolfgang Goethe and Friedrich von Schiller in Germany. For William Wordsworth, aged 19, this was

> . . . a time when Europe was rejoiced,
> France standing on the top of golden hours
> And human nature seeming born again.

What could be newer than that?

The leading ideological opponent of the Revolution, Edmund Burke, born in Ireland, clearly appreciated the newness of what had happened as much as the revolutionaries themselves and those who sympathized with them. As early as 1790 he described the Revolution as a 'novelty', a deliberate break with history, not its culmination. For him it had nothing in common, therefore, with the 'glorious' English Revolution of 1688, the centenary of which had been celebrated in London just before the French revolution began. Nor had it much in common, he believed, with the American Revolution. Unlike foreign sympathizers with the French Revolution, many of whom, like Coleridge and Wordsworth, changed their minds about it later in the light of later events in France, Burke from the start saw pattern in the events: revolution was a cycle, not a sequence. It began with anti-absolutist abstractions and it would end with revolutionary absolutism and war.

The Revolution hinged (Wedgwood's word) on far more than the fate of a well-intentioned king, Louis XVI, who had ascended the throne of France in 1774. Yet it was only after the creation of a new French republic in September 1792 and the guillotining of the King on 21 January 1793 that revolutionary novelty was fully and self-consciously proclaimed to the world in a new republican calendar which was adopted by the National Convention on 5 October 1793, two weeks before the execution of Queen Marie Antoinette. Year I was now stated to have begun on 22 September 1792, and in future within each year the months still were to be redivided also. There were still to be 12 of them, but they were now all to be of thirty days.

Their 'republican' names, originally designated as 'first', 'second' and so on, like the names of streets in the grid pattern of American cities, were subsequently chosen by a specially appointed Commission neither from history nor from myth but from nature, nature as peasants, not as the *bourgeoisie*, were thought to understand it. The first, *Vendémiaire*, was the month of the vintage, the last, *Fructidor*, the month of fruit. The second, *Brumaire*, was the month of mist. *Germinal* was the month of seeding, *Floréal* the month of blossom, and *Thermidor*, the tenth month, the month of heat. Each month was divided into three *décades*, each of ten days. The Christian Sunday totally disappeared, as did Christian holy days. A new cult of Reason, grounded in eighteenth-century philosophy, displaced Christianity. The five days left over after the reorganization of the months were republican festival days dedicated to Virtue, Talent, Labour, Ideas and Rewards. In leap years the extra day, now to be the last day of the year, was to be called Revolution Day.

The calendar itself lasted only until 1805, ten years before the fall of Napoleon Bonaparte, born in the island of Corsica in 1769, who rose to power in revolutionary France as a soldier. He had begun his political career in 1799 as First Consul, a republican title with classical echoes, and five years later he crowned himself hereditary Emperor in a religious ceremony with the Pope in attendance. Christianity had not disappeared. Nor had industrialization disposed of an hierarchical order in Britain, despite the fact that British industrialists, like French revolutionaries, were fascinated by the concept of 'newness' and charged the word 'invention' with magnetic force. Matthew Boulton, James Watt's partner, took pride in dealing in 'novelties' before he sold steam power; and Birmingham, his city, which had no counterpart in France, was later said to represent, as other new industrial cities did, a system of life constructed according to 'wholly new principles'.

It was the spread of industrialization rather than the appearance of a revolutionary calendar in France that changed for ever the sense of time. The lives of the workers, who included children, were now regulated by the factory hooter. Work started early and went on late. Monday was called Saint Monday because it was a day when, in face of tough discipline, as tough as that in Napoleon's armies, workers might take a day off. In a further phase of industrialization there were to be battles between employers and workers about hours as well as wages. More generally 'time frameworks' were to change too. Faster coaches pulled by horses introduced 'time tables' before the age of the steam locomotive and the use of standard railway time. Foreigners often complained of the English mania for 'saving time'. Yet speed was to attract people in most countries, whatever their history.

Critics of what came to be called 'the industrial revolution' objected to the power of the machine and the monotonous routines of industrial labour, while critics of the French Revolution believed that what was happening throughout the revolutionary sequence or cycle that ended with Napoleon's defeat at Waterloo in 1815 could better be explained in terms of nature than of history – or, as later critics were to do, of theatre. They compared it with a storm or more dramatically with a torrent or a stream of lava, and it was with relief, therefore, if with premature confidence, that the *Quarterly Review* in London in 1814 could claim that 'the volcano is now extinguished; and we may approach the crater with perfect security'. That was before the final historical twist when Napoleon escaped from the island of Elba and lived to fight again.

In this respect political change in France was completely different from the economic and industrial change in Britain to which the label 'industrial revolution' was first attached in 1827 by a French economist, Adolphe Blanqui. Comparing the social and political changes that had happened in France during the 1780s and 1790s with the social and economic changes that took place in Britain, he could point to Georges Jacques Danton on one side of the Channel and Watt on the other. A French historian of a later generation, Paul Mantoux, writing in 1906, spoke of what happened in Britain in the late-eighteenth century as 'one of the most important moments in modern history, the consequences of which have affected the whole civilized world and are still transforming it and shaping it under our eyes'.[2]

Blanqui was living at a time when most knowledgeable Europeans were arguing that it was the economic strength of Britain, based on the exploitation of coal and iron, the invention of new machinery and the harnessing of new forms of power, that had accounted for victory in the long wars against the French Revolution and Napoleon which had lasted with short breaks from 1793 to 1815. Some Englishmen disagreed. They attributed success not to industrial – or financial – strength but to 'moral strength', to Protestantism, or, in Burkean language, to the excellence of an institutional 'inheritance' of parliamentary monarchy and the rule of law. Two systems were thus being compared – the British, which appealed to history, and the French, which in the course of revolution had tried to dispose of it. Yet even within this interpretation, which purported to explain why 'free born Englishmen' had not staged a political revolution, it was relevant to ask why there had been no industrial revolution in France.

Many reasons were found. The French social system, it was argued, was more rigid, despite the development of new wealth in the eighteenth century, much of it derived from the Caribbean as was much new British wealth; it permitted the creation of new noblemen with their origins in trade, but it did not favour entrepreneurs seeking new markets for new products. Capital was easily diverted from 'useful' projects to 'luxuries'. Income was spent conspicuously, not productively. Quality was preferred to quantity. Unlettered English mechanics produced machines: French artisans used their ingenuity in producing gadgets, like mechanical toys. The really large French textiles factory, which had been in existence for nearly a 100 years, produced tapestries. Manchester dealt in cotton: Lyons in silk. Wedgwood's 'Etruria', centre of the Potteries, was a very different place from Sèvres, home of French porcelain, as he himself recognized. English workmen were more adaptable and more mobile: Scottish workmen were more thrifty and ambitious. Protestants accounted for only 2 to 3 per cent of the French population, and Protestant seventeenth-century exiles from France, Huguenots, had stimulated British industry. British raw materials were more accessible – coal was conveniently located near the seaports: iron could be imported as well as smelted at home. And if roads were better in France, Britain had twice as many canals in 1800 – after a canal boom which anticipated the railway boom a generation later.

Industrialization, like political revolution, is best explained in terms of complex interactions, most of them at the regional level, rather than lists of causes and effects. In fact, while most eighteenth-century British industrialization was highly regionalized, leaving large parts of the country untouched, the French economy in the 1780s included more industrial elements in it than the first historians of the industrial revolution, including their own, suggested. There were entrepreneurs in France, and there were several substantial plants, including a spinning factory at Nantes that employed 4,000 workers. At Chaillot, near Paris, steam engines were being produced. There were small industrial regions in the east, like that round Mulhouse. If French coal production was only 10 per cent of that in Britain, cast iron production was actually greater in France than in Britain during the 1780s.

There was, however, one other critical economic difference. While both countries had already benefited from what came to be called (misleadingly) 'commercial revolutions', based on sugar and slaves, which increased the wealth of both countries in the eighteenth century, France, unlike Britain, underwent no 'agricultural revolution', an equally misleading term yet a convenient label for significant improvements in farming, the most important branch of economic activity in both countries. British improvements involved more effective use of land; new techniques of food production, widely publicized; systematic rotation of crops; the use of winter crops for fodder; expansion of cereal production, crucial for a growing population of men, women, children – and horses; and more careful breeding and rearing of bigger and better livestock.

In summarizing and extolling their own achievements in industry as well as in agriculture the British preferred, before and after the French Revolution, to use the older word 'improvement', a fashionable word in the eighteenth century on both sides of the Atlantic, to the word 'revolution'; and it was not until the 1880s, just before the centenary of the French Revolution was celebrated (the Eiffel Tower was its monument), that the term 'industrial revolution' passed into general currency in Britain.[3] By then it had become obvious that there could be no reversibility in industrial change. You could no more go back from an industrial society to a pre-industrial society than you could control the movements of the stars. It was easier, indeed, to attempt political restoration after a revolution than to set the clock back economically.

By the year 1889 the French Revolution and the British industrial revolution, separate in their origins, seemed to some commentators to be directly related to each other in their consequences. Factories and barricades were part of the same stage sets. The members of a new industrial 'proletariat' (in reality a divided, not united, labour force, divided by religion as well as by occupation) were thought of as carriers of continuing revolution. Particularly in the judgement of socialists, like German-born Karl Marx, the *bourgeois* revolution against feudalism as he saw it, which had been staged in France in 1789, would be followed, as industrialization extended, by proletarian revolutions that would destroy capitalism and (ultimately) usher in a 'classless society'. Such kinds of interpretation, which were to influence French thought and action more than British, were to be challenged in the late-twentieth century in the light not only of experience, particularly the experience of rise and fall of the Soviet Union, committed to Marxist theory, but of a deeper study of the nature of the two revolutions themselves. Yet there were significant similarities about both revolutions.

The first, as we have noted, was universalism, part of the rhetoric of both. The world was invited to proclaim human rights: the Declaration of the Rights of Man and Citizen of the summer of 1789 was a declaration of human rights, not just a charter for Frenchmen. It was not only France which was separating itself from the past, the world was being invited to separate itself too. Tom Paine, Burke's most effective and best-selling critic, was made a citizen of France and represented Calais in its National Assembly. There was universalism too in the 'industrial revolution' which could not be confined to Britain. Meanwhile, steam power, the newest form of power in use, could be deemed as universal as the power of ideas.

> Engine of Watt! unrivall'd in thy sway.
> Compared with thine what is the tyrant's power?
> His might destroys, while thine creates and saves,
> Thy triumphs live, like fruit and flowers.

In this case, however, not everyone found steam power so beneficent. There were, indeed, alternative universalist verses written in which steam – and machinery – figured as tyrants. The really ruthless king, steam, was served by 'a priesthood' who were 'turning blood to gold'.

The second similarity was that each revolution carried with it a sense of being 'unfinished'. This was obvious in relation to the industrial revolution, for it was inherently unlikely that techniques invented by Englishmen during the last decades of the eighteenth century would remain 'up-to-date'. The hand-made would become standardized: steam would give way to electricity. Prometheus had been unbound.[4] It was unlikely too that parts of the world with far greater natural resources at their disposal than Britain – America and Germany, for example – would allow Britain to maintain an industrial lead based on priority in invention.

The 'unfinished' element in the French Revolution was rather more complex. There were Frenchmen who would have liked to 'finish' the revolution at one particular point – 1789, before the fall of the Bastille, Paris's old prison, a great symbolic event; 1791, when the first revolutionary programme, including the overthrow of 'feudalism', was complete; 1795, after the exhaustion of 'the Terror' during which revolutionaries fought revolutionaries; or 1799, before the accession to full power of Napoleon. Yet there were others who wanted revolution to continue much further, even to become a 'permanent revolution'. For the mid-nineteenth-century French socialist Pierre Josèphe Proudhon, who coined the phrase 'all property is theft', there was 'only one revolution, selfsame and perpetual'. It was seeking to achieve not only political freedom but economic equality.

A very different writer, the German philosopher of history Georg Wilhelm Friedrich Hegel, whose theories influenced Marx as much as the theories of British political economists, was deeply impressed by the French Revolution as a manifestation of the human spirit. 'World history', he began his lectures in the University of Berlin in the 1820s, was 'nothing else but the development of human freedom', and the French Revolution was a triumph of right. 'Never since the sun has stood in the heaven and the planets moved about it', he added, using an astronomical analogy, 'had it been seen that man relies on his head, that is on thought, and builds reality correspondingly.' Such a philosophy was to culminate in a belief in historical necessity. For Marx also there was necessity in the outcome, although he substituted materialism for idealism in his own post-Hegelian analysis as he brought the industrial revolution as well as the French Revolution into the human story.

Such views did not go unassailed. Just as the French revolutionaries never won a unanimous vote of confidence, nor did the philosophies of Hegel or Marx. What both men did – in the welter and aftermath of revolution – was to turn history into a key subject, in Marx's case into a call for political action from below. When their influence appeared to have come to an end with the dissolution of the Soviet Union in 1991 it seemed to some observers that history itself had come to an end.

LONG-TERM: SHORT-TERM

Looking backwards rather than forwards, continuities are plain enough. The cult of freedom and the sense of citizenship predated the French Revolution. The exploitation of steam power did not start with Watt, who had taken out his first patent for a steam engine 20 years before the fall of the Bastille. An 'atmospheric' engine had been produced in the 1680s, and a steam pump in 1698. Watt's most talented predecessor, Thomas Newcomen, who died in 1729, had invented an engine in 1712 which pumped water from the tin mines of Cornwall: Watt's achievement was to make steam power move machines. A process for smelting iron ore with coke had been devised by Abraham Darby at Coalbrookdale in 1709.

Both things and ideas have pedigrees; and great events, like those between 1776 and 1815, were not complete in themselves on either side of the Channel. Likewise, when what appeared to be new language was used, it was often not for the first time. There had been talk even of 'revolution', particularly a revolution in government, in France and other countries of Europe long before 1789, particularly in the decade before Louis XVI became King of France in 1774. The historian Albert Sorel, who wrote a magisterial, if dated, eight-volume history of *Europe and the French Revolution*, published between 1885 and 1904, quoted one interesting specific example of the use of the word in 1751 – used with fear rather than with hope – when the writer remarked gloomily that he was 'very far from thinking that we are entering upon an age of reason: indeed, it would not take much to convince me that Europe is threatened by some catastrophic revolution'.

Trust in reason had been the core belief of the eighteenth-century 'Enlightenment', a term which, unlike the term 'industrial revolution', was used at the time by contemporaries; and the spokesmen of the Enlightenment, the *philosophes*, constituted a republic long before the establishment through revolution of a French republic, one and indivisible, in 1792. Although they were no more of one mind than the revolutionaries were to be, they shared a common outlook – unwillingness to take accepted principles for granted; interest in exploring the fields of what we would eventually separate out as politics, law, criminology, economics, administration, sociology, psychology and religion; hostility to ignorance and to superstition, which they identified with the Church; and the will (and ability) to circulate information and knowledge. The fact that the most famous (and the wittiest) of the *philosophes*, François-Marie Arouet Voltaire, talked not of a republic but of his own church, consisting of 'brothers' and 'faithful', was a testimony to its power.

In questioning 'authority' the *philosophes* freely used abstract nouns like 'reason', 'freedom', 'happiness', 'utility' and 'progress'. Nonetheless, they were equally interested in practical policies that were being pursued or might be pursued by rulers or their governments, an interest expressed in one of their great collective achievements, an 18-volume *Encyclopédie*, the first volume of which appeared in 1751. 'Everything must be examined', its editors, Denis Diderot and Jean le Rond d'Alembert, wrote. 'Everything must be shaken up without exception and without circumspection.' The full title of the work was *Encyclopédie ou Dictionaire Raisonné*.

The work covered almost every aspect of human thought and action, including 'technology', a new word of the late-eighteenth century, as was the word 'industry' in its modern sense. Hitherto it had been used to describe a human quality, hard work. Now it came to describe a branch (later the word 'sector' would be used) of the economy. The word 'constitution' was taking on a new significance also. Voltaire wrote the article on 'Men of Letters' (*Gens de Lettres*) in the *Encyclopédie*; and it was 'men of letters', for Voltaire a new nobility, who did much to develop a new vocabulary, with d'Alembert appointed Perpetual Secretary of the prestigious French Academy, guardian of the French language, in 1772.

The idea of an *Encyclopédie* had been suggested to the French by an earlier English encyclopedia, and throughout the century literary and philosophical communications between France and England (and later with Scotland) were of great importance in changing people's minds and in widening their horizons. There was a cosmopolitanism about most *philosophes*, and Edinburgh and Geneva, not Paris, were centres of Enlightenment thought. Voltaire had stayed in England as a young man; the Baron de Montesquieu, the most reflective of the *philosophes*, took the unwritten British constitution as his model; the French Physiocrats, who were anxiously concerned with the economic fortunes of eighteenth-century France, joined the Scottish philosopher Adam Smith in sharply criticizing the 'system of mercantilism' which in Smith's phrase could be traced back to 'Mr. Colbert, a famous minister of Louis XIV'.

Neither the Physiocrats nor Smith, whose *Inquiry into the Nature and Causes of the Wealth of Nations* was to have immense influence in shaping debates on what came to be called economic policy, clearly foresaw the revolutionary outcome of their own century, including the industrial revolution. They looked at society from above, not from below. So, too, did the French *philosophes*, most of whom put their trust in rulers rather than people as promoters of change. Diderot claimed in 1770 that 'the happiest government would be that of a just and enlightened despot'; and even Jean-Jacques Rousseau, who stands out on his own and whose theory of the 'general will' was to provide a justification of popular power, left a place for a legislator. The earlier *philosophes* were as famous for their correspondence – in French – with 'enlightened' monarchs as for their pamphlets and books. Even Jeremy Bentham, the British utilitarian thinker, who considered 'the greatest happiness of the greatest number' to be the criterion of government, put his trust at first in princes and corresponded with Catherine II (deemed 'the great') of Russia. Spannning the whole period covered in this chapter, he lived long enough to demand (and to witness) major political changes in Britain. Catherine, born in 1729, lived just long enough – until 1795 – to be able to condemn the French Revolution.

The *philosophes*, concerned as they were with prejudice and tolerance, and with 'progress' and 'civilization', were at pains to distinguish between an 'age of Enlightenment' and an 'enlightened age', recognizing that, however enlightened they themselves might be as individuals, they were surrounded by a darkness which was only slowly being dispersed. A French observer noted in

1750 how people living a 100 miles from Paris could be a century away from it in 'their modes of thinking and acting'. It was not surprising, therefore, that most of the *philosophes* believed that change would come from above, though they knew too that the kind of 'reason' that even the most 'enlightened' of monarchs would choose to follow would be 'reason of state' (*raison d'état*) which it was for them (and not for *philosophes*) to define.

The other and very different forces, economic and psychological, that influenced not 'the great' but 'little people' (*les petits*), a high proportion of whom were illiterate, included hunger, contempt and rage. The dark side of the Paris scene – and the contrasts within it – was unforgettably depicted in the pages of Nicolas Restif de la Bretonne's *Les Nuits de Paris*, published between 1788 and 1794. They described 'all the actual facts' which Restif had witnessed on nightly tours around the great city, 'the assemblage of luxury, commerce, mud, the Opera, girls, imprudence, urbanity, debauchery, courtesy, swindling, and all the advantages and abuse of city life'. Not surprisingly, in high literary circles Restif was judged to be 'the Rousseau of the gutter'.

The pursuit of self-interest, like social curiosity, was a force that could be understood on both sides of the Channel. Members of what the British called 'the middle ranks of society' and what the French called the *bourgeoisie* could be stirred by aspiration and ambition that might lead them either into economic or political activity. Lawyers could be as aspiring as merchants. They could easily be shocked too by scandals in high places, vividly described in *libelles* circulated underground and in pamphlets printed and sold openly in London's Paternoster Row. They had a more immediate and potent influence than the ideas of the *philosophes*.

'THE' REVOLUTION

Restif, who vividly chronicled the trial of Louis XVI and the guillotining of Marie Antoinette, was as disturbed as Burke was by the bloodiness of the revolutionary sequence which began ironically not with the revolt of the poor but with the revolt of the nobility.

The origins of the French Revolution – and it goes down to history as *the* Revolution – are to be found before 1789 in the impulses, often contradictory, and in the conflicts, often bitter, within an 'old regime' which was facing what were proving to be intractable financial difficulties. (France's Controller General of Finances, the Baron de Turgot, had warned King Louis XVI before France entered the American War that 'the first gunshot would drive the state into bankruptcy'.) The general financial and economic position in 1788 and 1789 was worse. Bad harvests in 1787 and 1788 raised the price of bread, in some places doubling it, while urban unemployment rose. The poor were on the brink of starvation. Grievances multiplied. Agriculture accounted for three-quarters of the French national product, and when it languished, the country was under stress. The weather had its own drama on the eve of the Revolution. A storm which swept across France on 13 July 1788 carried with it hailstones big enough to kill men and animals as well as to destroy crops.

The timing of the sequence of political events that led up to the Revolution, many with their own drama and, unlike the weather, with their own rhetoric, was directly related to France's complex financial problems, and these ranged from accounting procedures in peace and war, to tax distribution and collection (all taxes were 'farmed out' to collectors, the most lucrative form of farming), to powers of borrowing and public credit. Lawyers, an important element in France's vocal *bourgeoisie*, were at the centre of the economic and political argument as they were to be after the Revolution began. Nevertheless, the discontents of the poor, including poor peasants, could not be left out of the social and political equations. Arthur Young, England's indefatigable spokesman of agricultural improvement, who travelled extensively in France, stated at the time that the financial 'deficit would not have produced the Revolution had it not been for the price of bread'.

Between 1787 and 1789 one step led to another through a series of moves and counter-moves that later proved to have been an escalation. The first was the failure in 1787 of an attempt by the King's Controller General to raise revenue through a nominated 'Assembly of Notables'. The aristocrats present there would not support a radical proposal to introduce a tax on all landowners irrespective of rank, and in May 1787 the Chamber was dismissed. Privilege had proved entrenched and unbudgeable even though the financial crisis continued and would, indeed, be bound to continue until tax burdens were reallotted. As one of the King's previous financial advisers, the Swiss banker Jacques Necker, had fully appreciated before being dismissed in 1781, it was 'a real monstrosity in the eyes of reason', the eighteenth-century litmus test, that sections of the aristocracy (nobility) avoided taxation, that the clergy (the leaders of which, archbishops and bishops, were appointed by the King) were exempt, and that heavy indirect taxation (including a tax on salt) fell on the poor.

As a result of the impasse in 1787 and of further (but not new) constitutional conflicts between the King's ministers and the *Parlement* of Paris and other provincial *Parlements*, ancient bodies with legal powers and privileges which they conceived of as checks on absolute government, no alternative was found to summoning the Estates-General in 1789. This also was an ancient body, representative, not legal, consisting of three separate Estates – clergy, nobility and commonalty – and it had not met since 1614. Archbishop de Brienne, now the King's Principal Minister (a title not used since 1726), who had wrestled with the *Parlements*, summoned the Estates in August 1788 in the same week as the bankrupt French Treasury suspended all payments. By the end of the month Necker, a Protestant who was given no grand title like Brienne's, agreed to serve again temporarily, and Brienne resigned.

The *Parlement* of Paris decreed that when the Estates-General met they should follow all the ancient formalized rituals of state, just as Louis XVI had followed all the sacred coronation rituals when he was crowned at Reims Cathedral. Before they met, however, political developments had taken place which made the rituals seem archaic. The *Parlements* themselves in their constitutional struggles with Louis XVI's ministers had already been driven to using new language – 'citizens' for 'subjects', for example, and even the term 'the rights of man': they had claimed to be 'guardians of the people's liberties'. Now between August 1788 and May 1789 speakers (and writers) in a vigorous public debate drew on a variety of sources, new as well as old, in order to focus on fundamental questions concerning privileges, rights and constitutions.

No fewer than 752 pamphlets and other printed papers were published between September and December 1788, and 2,639 during the first four months of 1789. Opinions counted as much as interests. So too did violence which was generated not by the debate but by popular discontent, much of it peasant discontent. There were riots in places as far apart as Rennes in Brittany and Grenoble in Dauphiné. Thenceforth an interplay of opinion, interest and violence was to be at the heart of the story.

The spring elections for the Estates-General confirmed what was already clear – that neither the nobility nor the *Parlements* would be in any position themselves to dictate the future course of events. Every man on the tax rolls and over the age of 25 had the right to vote; and while nobles elected nobles and clergy elected clergy, the Third Estate, granted double the representation of the other two Estates, 648 deputies, was in direct contact with by far the largest constituencies. The various representatives of each Estate collected from their constituents written declarations of grievances, *cahiers des doléances*, which contained both general points, some based on precedent, some on recent political writing, and very specific grievances which multiplied during the months before the Estates-General met. The chosen representatives of the Third Estate were neither occupationally nor socially representative of the constituencies they served: they included 166 lawyers, 85 merchants, and 278 men holding various kinds of government post.

In Paris itself, where a far broader section of the population than this was to play an active and controversial role in the unfolding of events, there were two days of rioting in the Faubourg St Antoine in April 1789 (with 25 deaths and three subsequent executions). In this case the enemy was not the King, but local politicians and manufacturers who favoured lower wage scales. Workers from the same *faubourg* were to play a leading part in the destruction of the Bastille only a few months later.

This was to be remembered as a more portentous event than the opening on 5 May 1789 in pomp and ceremony of the Estates-General, preceded by a religious service of dedication. Yet it was immediately after the opening, which started with a dull speech by Necker (the King dropped off to sleep), that the Third Estate at once asserted its special role. It conceived of itself not in traditional terms as an Estate of the realm but rather as the voice of the nation, and it refused to sit alone or to vote separately. Its claim had been advanced in speeches and in print before the Estates-General met, notably in one of the most widely read and discussed pamphlets of the period, *What is the Third Estate?* Its author, a clergyman, the Abbé Sièyes, the son of a postal employee, was to play one of the biggest parts in the forcing of political events later in the year. 'Today', Sièyes wrote in his pamphlet, 'the Third Estate is everything, the nobility but a word.'

Just how language, verbal and visual, is related to action is one of the most fascinating issues raised by events between 1789 and 1795. In 1788 a memorandum from the municipal officers of Nantes had already stated simply that 'the Third Estate cultivates the fields, constructs and mans the vessels of commerce, sustains and directs manufactures, nourishes and vivifies the kingdom. It is time that a great people count for something.' Later spoken language was to become far more declamatory. To what extent declamation was effective was itself a matter of debate. Jean-Josèphe Mounier, one of the speakers in the debates of May 1789 about constitutional rights, asked once 'What do words matter when they do not change things?', to which an Assemblyman of different persuasion replied tersely, 'Ideas are clarified when words are explained'. Later revolutionaries believed instead that words would carry their greatest force when they were designed not to clarify or to explain, but to inspire and to move men to action.

Talks in May (with spectators present) led to no agreement, and on 10 June the Third Estate deliberately forced the pace when it carried by 493 votes to 41 a motion proposed by Sièyes that if the other two Estates did not agree to assemble together it would proceed alone. A further motion, declaring itself a 'National Assembly', was carried a week later by 491 votes to 89, and two days after that the clergy decided by a narrow majority to join the Assembly. And now came the first of what were to be recalled later as the *beaux moments* in a drawn-out revolutionary sequence. On 20 June, when the members of the Assembly reached their hall of meeting they found the doors locked and guarded by soldiers, and posters on the wall announcing an unscheduled 'royal session' for the next week. Instead of leaving quietly they adjourned to an adjoining tennis court (where 'royal tennis' was played), and all but one of them took a solemn oath not to disperse until 'the constitution of the realm had been established and strengthened on solid foundations'.

The will of the members was tested when at the postponed 'royal session' the King insisted in what was otherwise a conciliatory speech that the Estates should continue to meet separately and that they should now withdraw to their separate meeting places. The Tennis Court oath stood firm. In a phrase of the Comte de Mirabeau, who had been a member of the Society of Thirty, a small group of noblemen (and others) who were opposed to privilege, nothing but bayonets would now force the National Assembly to move. They were not used, and on 27 June, after much argument behind the scenes, Louis wrote to the Presidents of the first two Estates ordering them to join the National Assembly. When he and the Queen appeared on a balcony they were cheered by the crowds. Arthur Young believed that the revolution was now over.

Instead it was beginning, and Paris, not Versailles, soon became the place of action. Dissension at court, movements of royal troops round the city and the dismissal of Necker on 11 July – he was ordered to leave the country – suggested that the will of the people was being imperilled and that the National Assembly, which four days earlier had changed its name to National Constituent Assembly, would be dissolved. And these ominous moves came at the end of a week when the Assembly had been discussing not the constitution but the price of bread. There was an immediate furore in what was now a restless and unruly Paris when the news reached there. A 'citizens' militia' had already been formed to protect property, but it was not able to 'contain the people's fury'. As one of its members stated, 'it was not the moment to reason with them'. He was right.

To understand the changing position of the King and the subsequent dispositions of the revolutionary leaders, it is essential to study the attitudes and reactions of people whose names have not passed into the history books. Such a study has revolutionized the historiography of the French Revolution. In the beginning historians used general terms, like 'the people': now they consider particular people in particular places. Named or unnamed, it was people without power, not the members of the National Assembly, who now pushed the Revolution further forward by storming and destroying the Bastille on 14 July. Eighty-three lives were lost, among them that of its aristocratic commander who had tried to blow it up rather than hand over the keys. He was spat upon and beaten up as he was marched through the streets before being brutally killed. His severed head was then carried on a pike through the crowds.

There had been only seven prisoners inside the Bastille at the time – Louis himself had wanted to pull it down in 1784 – but the scale of the disturbance – and its character – proved (and there was more than symbolism in this) both that violence was endemic and that the King could no longer rely on his own troops. On 15 July the Duc de la Rochefoucauld-Liancourt is said to have told him, 'Sire, this is not a riot but a revolution'. He had found the right word. What was happening now was new. The King gave orders that his troops surrounding Paris should disperse. And three days later, in what was another symbolic event, he met representatives of a new Paris municipal government (with a mayor, a new title) and accepted from them a tricolour cockade.

There were some cries of 'Our king, our father', but Louis XVI himself was silent. He recalled Necker and confirmed the appointment of the Marquis de la Lafayette as commander of the citizens' militia, now called the National Guard. Lafayette, an aristocrat, had been one of the French heroes of the American War, and had named his first son, born in 1780, George Washington. He had sent a piece of the stone from the demolished Bastille across the Atlantic to Washington. Already, however, he (and Washington) were well aware that the French Revolution was following a different course from the American. In 1791, still only 31 years old, Lafayette was to counsel Louis

XVI to leave Paris for Rouen and raise the royal banners there, and a year later he was to flee from France himself when the monarchy was overthrown and to be imprisoned in an Austrian gaol. That was round the corner.

The physical demolition of the Bastille by the crowds was followed by a burst of demolition of old institutions by the National Assembly, a positive achievement, not a symbolic act, the most important of all the achievements of the Revolution. Yet it was achieved against a background of physical violence outside as well as inside Paris. Thus, on 19 July the manor house of an unpopular landlord at Quincey in Franche Comté was destroyed in a huge explosion. Peasant disturbances, creating what Georges Lefebvre, one of the greatest French historians of the Revolution, identified as *la Grand Peur* (the great fear), now reached their peak. In the midst of panic, however, there was hope. The peasants had been aroused by a belief that their condition would be radically altered, and afraid as they now were that they were going to be cheated by the nobility, they moved to take the law into their own hands, often, at first, to shouts of 'Long Live the King!'

It was in an atmosphere of exalted enthusiasm that on 4 August 1789 the Assembly decreed 'the entire abolition of the feudal system' and with it the structure of local and provincial administration, on lines that had not been discussed when the Estates-General was called. Old scores were now settled. Privileges were renounced, sometimes with abandon. The full implications of what was done took time to work out, although the first codification followed a week later. The 'peasant revolution' did not treat all peasants alike. Some were able to buy land at low prices and, once freed from the burdens of feudal dues and tithes, went on to prosper, often becoming politically conservative in the process. Others remained landless, poor and dissatisfied.

No government could ignore the peasants, although government was subject to more immediate pressures from inside Paris, where events moved more speedily than events in Versailles. They were driven mainly not by the poorest of the poor, but by 'the little people' – artisans, small manufacturers, retail shopkeepers, café keepers, barbers and small booksellers. The defiant word most commonly used to describe them, *sans culottes*, referred to clothes: the *sans culottes* wore the long trousers of the working man instead of the knee breeches of the aristocrat. What brought revolutionary *sans culottes* together was not their occupation or their income, but revolutionary activism: they had a sense of fraternity and of solidarity, the solidarity of citizenship that was positively set out in the Declaration of the Rights of Man and the Citizen which was adopted by the National Assembly on 27 August. 'Men are born free and remain equal in rights' read Article I. 'Social distinctions may be based only upon general usefulness.' The source of 'all sovereignty resides essentially in the nation' read Article III. Nine of the 17 Articles referred to 'the rule of law'.

The language was clear, but while it was being enunciated the most urgent question for most Parisians was still the price of bread, and this was demonstrated on 5 October 1789 when insurgents, caring little for the rule of law, stormed the *Hotel de Ville*, and a large crowd of women, who assembled at street markets, marched through rain from Paris to Versailles asking for food. They also demanded that the King, who had hitherto been unwilling, should give his unqualified support to everything that had been so far decreed in the name of the Revolution since 17 July. He did, after more court discussion, and on the following day, accompanied by Lafayette, who had arrived with 20,000 National Guardsmen, and wagons containing wheat and flour, he and his family moved in the wake of the crowds in mud and rain from the seclusion of Versailles to the Tuileries Palace in Paris which Louis XIV had abandoned a century before. Many members of the National Assembly, most of them shaken by what had happened, moved with them to a turbulent city which was brightly illuminated for the occasion, ready to welcome 'the baker, the baker's wife and the baker's boy'.

The subsequent unfolding of the French Revolution involved far more than the fate of a king. It is a revolution, therefore, which at all its stages, and in particular at all its turning points, requires to be studied in detail. Historians of the revolution disagree about the dates of both phases and turning points. Most of them, however, agree about the importance of geography and have drawn distinctions between countryside and cities and between provinces and Paris, a city with its own local differences. In places it was honeycombed with 'popular clubs', eagerly discussing revolutionary goals and tactics, forming revolutionary patrols, and carrying out other revolutionary tasks. Sizeable groups of activists believed that government had a duty to regulate prices, particularly the price of bread. Their political economy was their own from the start, very different from that of Smith or the Physiocrats and calculated to alarm *bourgeois* revolutionaries both in the Assembly and in the French provinces.

Outside Paris there were different chronologies as there were in Paris itself. In some provinces, where the Revolution had little initial hold, dedicated revolutionaries tightened their sense of mission after October 1789, and that added to the violence. From now onwards, indeed, there was, in fact, more than one revolution, with counter-revolutions. There were new regional boundaries also, for in 1789 *départements* took the place of the old provinces. Federation was the order of the day. A *Fête de la Fedération* was held in 1790 on the anniversary of the destruction of the Bastille.

Insurrectionary politics depended on more than constitutional debate, but it was the results of debate which made violence inevitable. The abolition of feudalism had won widespread acclaim. The next key decision of the National Assembly in November 1789 to expropriate Church property (along with Crown lands) did not. The reason for taking it was primarily financial: inevitably the Assembly had to concern itself with finance as the King's ministers had been forced to concern themselves before 1788. The situation had deteriorated, for even those people who had previously paid taxes were doing their best to evade them. Confiscated Church property was to provide security for a new revolutionary currency in paper money, *assignats*, first introduced in December 1789.

Further decisions, bound to perpetuate division inside France, were taken in February 1790, when the contemplative Church orders were abolished, and in July 1790 when a 'Civil Constitution of the Clergy' was promulgated. Parish priests were now to be elected by citizens gathered in local assemblies, and bishops by electors in departments. They were all to become paid officials of the state, and no papal messages could be circulated in France except with the permission of the government. In November the clergy were further required to take an oath. All who refused were to be dismissed and replaced. Large numbers of bishops and clergy, including members of the National Assembly, refused to accept the oath, and the Pope condemned it on 13 April 1791.

The numbers who refused to take it varied, however, according to region. In the Vendeé in the west, in Brittany, in Normandy, in Flanders and in Alsace, fewer than one in five accepted it: in the Var the percentage accepting was 96. The first signs of counter-revolution had been conspiracies: the newest signs now were mass uprisings with a popular base. *Emigrés* had already left France – the first of them, led by the Comte d'Artois, the King's brother, as early as July 1789 – and had prepared for civil war and foreign invasion in the name of the royal family and the aristocracy. Now the civil war acquired a genuine momentum within France itself as the counter-revolution was strengthened at the base. In many places – and the regional pattern varied in this too – the counter-revolutionaries formed their own National Guards.

The flight of the King from his Parisian palace to Varennes, near the French frontier, on 21 June 1791 – he and his wife travelled in disguise – brought this phase of the Revolution to a climax; and as he was led back to Paris as a prisoner on the evening of 25 June 1791 he is said to have muttered 'There is no longer a king in France'. What then seemed to him to be fragile connecting threads between the present and the past of France had been finally cut. It was a climax for the French people also. They now had to choose (if under duress) whether or not they favoured the Revolution. The Constituent Assembly imputed the King's flight to conspirators who had misled him, but there were large-scale demonstrations of militant Parisians, roused by a militant press, demanding a new form of republican government. Lafayette succeeded in putting the first big demonstration down, and at the Champs de Mars around 50 people were killed and others wounded on 17 July, but emigration from France continued on a bigger scale and on 13 September the King reluctantly accepted a new single-chamber constitution which curtailed all his powers.

Protracted discussions going back to 1789 – and earlier – about what kind of a constitution France should adopt, some of them carried on inside committees, had involved debate about what links there could be between past and future. What was a constitution? Was there an 'old constitution' to restore or should a new constitution be devised? Should the preparation of a constitution precede or follow the drafting of a bill of rights? What should be the position of the monarch? Now the answers to such key questions, some of which had never been put to the vote, seemed to have settled themselves; and the Constituent Assembly was replaced by a new Legislative Assembly chosen on a restricted franchise in elections held at the end of August 1791.

Half of its members were lawyers, and it was within this body that distinct political groupings, not yet political parties, emerged, one of them a *Girondin* group led by Jacques Pierre Brissot, another a *Jacobin* group, named after a Paris club with over 1,000 members and over a 1,000 affiliated societies. The name 'Girondin' referred to the department of the Gironde in south-west France, with Bordeaux as its capital, from which many of its members came. Whatever their allegiances, the delegates to the Convention had to pay attention to the very varied views of their own constituents. There were large numbers of Frenchmen who detested the breakdown of order and the extremism of the social and political views which they could hear expressed around them in Paris. They were as suspicious of Paris as the *sans culottes* of Paris were suspicious of bankers or big businessmen.

By vetoing two important decrees of the Assembly, however, as the new constitution permitted him to do, Louis showed that he was still not a cipher. He even gained a measure of initiative as news arrived that *emigrés* armies were massing in Germany near the French frontier, and he was loudly cheered on 14 December 1791 when he told the Assembly that he had issued an ultimatum to the Prince-Archbishop of Trier telling him that France would declare war unless all *emigré* activity was prohibited in his territory. The Prince-Archbishop obeyed. So, too, did the Elector of Mainz.

There was nothing revolutionary about this ultimatum, for in the eighteenth century it had been taken for granted that war, the organized use of armed force by one state against another, was justifiable in terms of *raison d'état*. Nonetheless, when the Comte de Vergennes, Louis XVI's last foreign minister before the Revolution, had signed a commercial treaty with Britain in 1786 and a treaty with Russia in 1787, he had stated categorically, 'it is no longer the time for conquests' ('*Ce n'est plus le temps de conquêtes*') and the National Assembly had made a 'Declaration of Peace to the World' in August 1791 at a time when a few foreign enemies of the Revolution, like Gustavus II of Sweden (soon to be assassinated, not by a revolutionary but by a nobleman), were already preaching a crusade.

REVOLUTION, WAR AND 'THE TERROR'

Once begun, war, a new element in the revolutionary situation, further revolutionized the revolution. In a phrase of Friedrich Engels, Marx's friend and collaborator, all the subsequent 'pulsations' of the Revolution depended upon it. Yet more than revolution was affected. The role of the state was to be affected too. As James Madison, fourth President of the United States, understood it, 'war is the matter of executive aggrandizement'. There were inevitable financial consequences. In France inflation was already a problem before the war began. The value of the *assignat* in 1793 was a quarter of what it had been two years before.

War enthusiasm had been stirred in France in 1791, and it intensified after the Austrian Emperor Leopold announced that troops would march if Mainz and Trier were forced to capitulate. On 25 January 1792 Louis was told to inform his royal brother-in-law that war with the Habsburg Empire would ensue unless he declared his peaceful intentions. When Louis responded less toughly in his note than the Assembly wished there was yet another crisis and threats were made to impeach both him and the Queen. Again Louis changed his mind, dismissed his now unpopular ministers, and on 20 April formed a new government, which was nominated by the Girondins, and declared war on the King of Hungary and Bohemia. Leopold had died on 1 March, and his successor, Franz, had not yet been made Holy Roman Emperor.

Brissot and his Girondin group believed that war might unify France and even preserve constitutional monarchy, and the declaration received a rapturous welcome in some revolutionary circles. Only seven deputies in the Assembly voted against it. 'Here is the crisis of the universe', one patriot proclaimed, 'God [had] disentangled the primitive chaos.' Now 'free men are Gods on earth' and a 'holy war' would be embarked upon by 'free men' and 'patriots'.

Unfortunately for Brissot, a war that was begun with such eloquent words and such mixed motives was to prove disastrous for himself and for his group and, not least, for the King. After initial defeats in which the French armies did not behave like the 'armed missionaries' that active citizens wished them to be (although one French general suspected of treason was murdered by his own troops), foreign armies entered France, and on 18 May all foreigners in France were placed under surveillance. Girondin ministers were dismissed, and on 20 June an angry group entered the royal apartments in the Tuileries.

At this point Louis held his own and donned the red cap of liberty to drink the health of the nation. But the anti-revolutionary leader, the Duke of Brunswick, issued a manifesto on 25 July 1792 threatening the direst of consequences if the royal family were harmed. This quickened revolutionary resolve, and the Tuileries Palace was stormed again on 10 August. This time 400 people were killed in the bloodiest of the revolutionary *journées* and the King's Swiss Guard was massacred. At the end of the struggle the members of the royal family were transported as prisoners to the Temple.

For a time a Paris Commune, noisily seeking vengeance, seemed more in charge of events than the Legislative Assembly and after the fall of Languy to the Prussian Army and later Verdun, only 200 miles from Paris, in September 1792, a panicky crowd broke into the prisons of Paris and killed over a 1,000 'enemies of the Revolution'. In the same month, after a citizen army had been hastily mobilized, the news arrived on 20 September of the first French victory at Valmy, and two days later the republic was proclaimed. The King, long since resigned to his fate, was interrogated (after a bitter debate as to whether he needed to be) and with the barest majority in favour, one, was guillotined in what is now Paris's Place de la Concorde on 21 January 1793.

The republic was proclaimed by a new National Convention which had been elected in the heat of the summer and which first met on the very day of Valmy. Like the Legislative Assembly, it was primarily *bourgeois* in its composition, with lawyers still predominating, and it included among its 749 deputies 200 who had belonged to the former body. There were also among them 83 members of the former Constituent Assembly. It was a younger body, however, and it included several ex-nobles at one end of the social spectrum and artisans at the other. Within it political groupings were tightened. Confronting the Girondins were the *Montagnard*, the Mountain, so called because its members sat on the upper tiers of the Chamber. Again they were not political parties, and there was a group of Paris deputies who often worked closely together. Members independent of both groups were called 'The Plain'.

With the guillotining of the king the revolution reached a stage which Burke deemed inevitable. It had begun with revolutionaries fighting 'enemies of the people'. It now went on, as revolutions were to do later, with revolutionaries fighting each other. Some early enthusiasts for the Revolution, like Burke's bitter critic, Paine, who had been chosen as a member of the new Convention, were now to spend time in gaol. (Paine spent his time there writing *The Age of Reason*.) Others were to go to the guillotine. Whether or not the first phase of the Revolution had fully succeeded in its purpose of providing 'liberty' – and it certainly broke many chains – the mood of the latest phase, which was to worsen throughout 1793 and 1794, made a mockery of 'fraternity'. Useful measures that were passed, like the introduction of the metric system of weights and measures or, in a different field, the prohibition of imprisonment for debt, were overshadowed by revolutionary events.

The war, which went through many twists and turns, had its own logic too, as relentless as that of the Revolution itself. Men had to be mobilized, resources had to be found. The first war news was good after Valmy, and subsequent victories took French armies into Belgium, Germany and, in the south, Nice. One city seized was Frankfurt. On 16 November 1792 the River Scheldt was declared open to all nations, and three days later France offered support to any people rising against its own government.

Britain was alienated by the first of these moves and the French Ambassador was asked to leave London. In reply France declared war against Britain and the United Provinces on 1 February 1793. France now faced not a combination of Austria and Prussia but a 'First Coalition', which included Britain, the United Provinces and Spain; and the tide of war seemed to have turned again when in March 1793 Austrian troops entered the southern Netherlands and the French General Dumouriez was defeated decisively at Neerwinden. In the following month Spanish troops besieged Perpignan, and in July French royalists handed over the great naval port of Toulon to an Anglo-Spanish fleet. Supporters of the royalist cause were most numerous in the Vendée region, where there was now a bloody guerilla war. There was treachery too at the front. After his defeat, Dumouriez asked for an armistice and tried to march his troops back to Paris to liberate the Queen and declare the Dauphin Louis XVII. When they refused, he defected to the Austrians. Lafayette too crossed the lines.

In such circumstances 'terror' became an inevitable part of the continuing revolutionary sequence. So also did tightened organization. It was in the testing difficult month of March 1793 that a Revolutionary Tribunal was created and that zealous *représentants-en-mission* were dispatched to each of the armies with orders to mobilize the nation for war. To turn all Frenchmen as rapidly as possible into soldiers meant that *élan* now counted for more than discipline. The new French national anthem, a hymn to brotherhood and war, first sung in the Rhineland, caught the mood: '*Aux armes, citoyens!*' Yet citizens needed food as well as arms, and in Paris rising food prices led the Paris Commune to decide to fix the price of bread by subsidizing grocers.

Every move in war mobilization had a political dimension to it, beginning in April with the setting up of a Committee of Public Safety which, during the course of 1793, acquired a parallel Committee of General Security handling police functions. It had behind it a revolutionary momentum, and at the end of the following month National Guardsmen surrounded the Tuileries when the National Convention met there. Three exciting days followed from 30 May to 2 June when 29 Girondin members of the Convention, who had been increasingly under attack from the Paris *sans culottes*, were expelled, a move that provoked anti-Montagnard revolts in parts of the provinces. Some of the expelled escaped from Paris: others, including Brissot, were guillotined. Any citizen advocating a 'spirit of moderation' was suspect. The food problem was not solved, however, and a death penalty for hoarding was decreed on 26 July.

One day later, Robespierre, whose revolutionary experience stretched back to his membership of the Estates-General, joined the Committee of Public Safety, which Danton, another lawyer and hitherto its dominating personality, had left on the 10th. (The members of the Committee were subject to monthly re-election.) A new democratic constitution for the nation, based on a unicameral legislature with annual elections and male universal suffrage, was promulgated on 10 August, and four days later a tough and efficient expert in what would now be called war logistics, Lazare Carnot, six years older than Danton and five years older than Robespierre, was made a member of the Committee of Public Safety: he was soon to be hailed as 'organizer of victory'. By the end of August a *levée en masse* of all single men from 18 to 25 years old had been decreed: 'until the enemies of France shall have been chased off the territory of the Republic, every French person must stand ready to serve and support our armed forces'.

Because of revolutionary upheaval the democratic constitution never came into effect. In September 1793, another cruel month, continuing popular disturbances led the National Convention (under pressure from the Paris Commune) to carry a *Maximum Général* Law which controlled the price not only of food but of other goods and services. In the same month a comprehensive Law of Suspects was passed which empowered watch committees, set up earlier in the year, to arrest citizens who either by their conduct, their contacts, their words or their writings, showed themselves to be supporters of tyranny or of federalism or to be enemies of liberty.

The *levée en masse*, with a target of a million men, did come into force, backed by the enthusiasm of Paris *sans culottes* organized in sections (there were 48 of them, each sending two representatives to the Paris Commune) and by the militancy of provincial *armées revolutionnaires* which have been described by Richard Cobb, a historian who knew how to bring the past back to life, as 'the most original and characteristic of the many spontaneous institutional creations of the Terror'. Among their tasks was the policing of food supplies, among their delights blasphemous attacks on priests and the pillaging of church silver. From October 1793 onwards, therefore, the Convention was as much at the mercy of forces beyond its control as the King had been. It remained in existence for its allotted three-year span, but 120 of its members were under arrest for various periods of time and another 74 were executed.

The scale of 'the Terror', which reached its peak under Robespierre, may have been exaggerated then and, more so, later, but certainly in 1793 and 1794 there were no fewer than 14,000 executions by guillotine, a revolutionary instrument which, like the steam engine in Britain, had its own rhetoric. Indeed, while the Terror lasted the guillotine, invented by Dr Guillotin in 1789 as a humanitarian instrument of death, painless and efficient – heads would 'fly off in the twinkling of an eye' – took the place of the cap of liberty as an image of revolution. 'Traitors look at this and tremble', ran one inscription attached to a picture of it. 'It will still be active while all of you have lost your lives.'

Most of those who lost their lives, the majority of them outside Paris, were not well-known figures, and the agents who sent them to death, often assisted by informers, were often little known too. It was not merely the guillotine which was employed. Ninety priests were disposed of in 1793 by sinking them in the River Loire, tied like animals, in a dilapidated barge with holes. As for the leaders of the Revolution during this period of the Terror, there have been profound disagreements between specialized historians concerning their personalities and their alignments, with Danton and Robespierre subject to almost perpetual review.

To the outstanding French radical historian of the Third Republic, Alphonse Aulard, writing a great four-volume political history of the Revolution at the beginning of the twentieth century, Danton was the hero, a man of intelligence, courage and realism, struggling for a 'democratic republic', and his guillotining in March 1794 was the great tragedy of revolution. (On going to his death he is reported to have said 'Show my head to the people, they do not see the like every day'.) To some later historians, however, Danton seemed to be paying the penalty for opportunism, even for venality.

Robespierre has been even more criticized from both right and left. He had served in the Assembly before he became a member of the Convention and the Committee of Public Safety, and originally he opposed the war. A French nineteenth-century historian/politician, Adolphe Thiers, described him as 'one of the most odious beings that could have borne absolute rule over men' and the great British historian of the French Revolution, Thomas Carlyle, who began his study of it by examining a folio of portraits of the revolutionaries, called him more poetically, but equally damningly, 'acrid, implacable, impotent, dull-drawling, barren as the Harmattan wind'.

There is no doubt, however, that Robespierre dominated the scene, if he could not always control events, between October 1793 and July 1794. Eloquence was his main weapon. 'Democracy', he maintained, 'is the only form of state in which all the individuals composing it can call [their state] their own country.' 'The French', he went on, 'are the first people in the world to establish a true democracy [he also called it a 'republic of virtue'] by calling all men to enjoy equality and the fullness of civic rights.' To achieve and to maintain a 'republic of virtue', 'false' revolutionaries were the ones who had to be destroyed, with the guillotine serving as 'the scythe of equality'.

The 'moderates' went first — Brissot and the Girondins, defiantly singing the *Marseillaise* as they made their way to the guillotine. The 'ultras' on the left went next, including J. R. Hébert, the most outspoken Parisian journalist, and the 'indulgents', those who, like Danton, wanted to relax the procedures of 'the Terror', went last — last, that is, except for Robespierre himself and the young St Just, 'the angel of the Terror', who were guillotined in July 1794 (10 Thermidor, Year II), a month which claimed 1,400 victims. The peak of 3,500 had been reached in January 1794. St Just had suggested that moneys confiscated from 'suspects' should be distributed among poor citizens.

The forces which ultimately destroyed Robespierre constituted a curious and temporary domestic coalition, less tightly bound together, indeed, than the First Coalition that had been formed by Europe's great powers to fight the French revolutionary armies. The centralization of authority in France was one source of anger, active dechristianization another: Robespierre, who believed that he was building a temple of liberty while Frenchmen were still 'scarred' by the fetters of servitude, wished to nationalize the cult of the Supreme Being. For 'the people', however, — and for the great French romantic historian, Jules Michelet — these were the 'very life-blood, inspiration and driving force of the revolution'[5] — economic grievances, studied more carefully since Michelet wrote, were usually paramount. The further depreciation of the *assignat* added to hunger in Paris not only because prices rose (despite the *Maximum*) but because peasants held back food.

The Terror phase ended in 1794 in a kind of stalemate: after the fall and guillotining of Robespierre there was yet another group who contemplated restoring the monarchy with a boy of nine, Louis XVII. (He died in prison on 8 June 1795.) Within a few weeks it was clear that the 'revolutionary storm' had spent itself, and the Convention went on to reduce the powers of the Committee of Public Safety, abolish the Revolutionary Tribunal and the Law of Suspects, close the Jacobin Club, the main stronghold of Robespierre, reinstate the surviving Girondins, free many political prisoners, restore freedom of worship and abandon the system of controlled prices and state intervention in the working of the economy.

There were protests from the left, particularly about the last of these moves, and in May 1795 (Prairial, Year III) 'ultras' invaded the meetings of the Convention. In the past, such invasions might have been decisive. Now they were put down by force, and many of the surviving Jacobin activists were sent to jail or guillotined. Force was used also to put down the 'White Terror' and an *emigré* invasion in the south. The Convention went on to draft a new and far from democratic constitution, known as the Constitution of the Year III. An Executive Directory was to be established, a five-man Board, to be elected indirectly by the Legislature which would consist of two chambers – the Five Hundred and 'the Senators' or 'Ancients'. The constitution set out 'duties' of citizens as well as rights. It also stated firmly that 'it is upon the maintenance of property . . . that the social order rests'.

There were protests against such an approach, including a conservative protest in October 1795, backed by royalists, which was dispersed with a whiff of Bonaparte's grapeshot before the Convention came to an end in the same month. A year later, with the Directory in power, a premeditated left-wing plot of a contrasting kind, led by 'Gracchus' Babeuf – who called himself a 'Communist', was put down also. Babeuf – who during his career had both collected and catalogued archives and destroyed them (he burnt seigneurial archives in an effort to protect the peasants of Picardy) – was responsible for an eloquent *Manifesto des Egaux* ('Manifesto of the Equals'). This was to be as famous after his death as it was when he was plotting to put its ideas into practice. The plot was handled gently. When it was crushed only Babeuf himself and one of his fellow conspirators were sentenced to death.

'Royalism' was not crushed, however, and at further elections in 1797 only 11 members of the old Convention were elected and many royalists were returned. The Directory was losing its grip, and there was ample evidence of corruption and profiteering. Not surprisingly, therefore, there was a *coup d'état* in September 1797 in which three of the Directors combined with Bonaparte to get rid of the other two, along with 200 members of the legislative chambers. This was a republican *coup*, and it was followed two years later in October 1799 with a further coup (Brumaire, Year VIII) which brought Napoleon to power as one of three Consuls. He was believed to be a steadfast defender of the Revolution. Sièyes, who devised the new constitution, was another.

FROM WAR TO NAPOLEON AND THROUGH NAPOLEON TO PEACE

The Directory had flirted with the generals as the revolutionary war continued, although it was never clear about how to deal with them once power was moving in their direction. Bonaparte, the most remarkable of them, knew how to deal with them himself, and it is now possible, while recognizing his strong family sense, to simply call him Napoleon. Jacques Louis David, born in 1748, had painted for Louis XVI. He now revelled in his responsibilities as painter to Napoleon. His 'Napoleon Crossing the Alps' is perhaps his most striking painting.

Napoleon was the rare kind of man whose career raises every kind of question concerning the role of the individual – and, in particular, 'the great man' or 'hero' – in history. The Russian novelist Leo Tolstoy in his novel *War and Peace* suggested that ultimately Napoleon may have been a 'puppet': 'the more powerful a man appears to be the more he is a slave of history'. That was a late view. Further back in time, as early as 1784, the year when Napoleon entered his military school, the German philosopher Immanuel Kant had forecast that a legislator of outstanding genius might arise who would do for human society what great scientific thinkers had done for the study of the physical universe in the past. 'Nature [had] brought forth a Kepler, who reduced the eccentric orbits of the planets to an orderly formula in unexpected fashion, and a Newton who clarified the universal principles governing the natural order.' Might not Napoleon be this man, a new kind of genius?

When a later German philosopher, Hegel, saw Napoleon ride through Jena in 1806 after one of his great victories he considered him Reason personified. The remark throws more light on Hegel than on Napoleon, for 'history' could be approached in a quite different way from his. The nineteenth-century French politician/historian François Guizot may have simplified it in his own way, however, when he stated that if the Revolution had been a violent way of breaking out of the old regime, Napoleon offered a violent way of breaking out of the Revolution.

Napoleon had studied the *philosophes*, but he believed in his own destiny rather than other people's theories. He had no great plan in mind. 'I am a fragment of rock launched into space', he once said in one of the memorable phrases that he produced in great quantities. Revolutionary war helped to prepare the way for him to fulfil his own destinies, and it was because of the Revolution that he was able to prove his remarkable capacity to win the devotion of his troops. 'Every step of the Great Nation is marked by blessings!', one of his Italian broadsheets ran. 'Happy is the citizen who is part of it. Happy is he who can say about our great men: these are my friends, my brothers!' It was because of the Revolution too that despite the fact that his troops lived off the land that they conquered Napoleon could win the support of influential sections of the local population. He was more than a conqueror.

Within a year Napoleon brought Piedmont/Sardinia to heel and drove the Austrians out of their province of Lombardy, and within weeks of the *coup d'état* of September 1797 he was able to secure a peace treaty with Austria at Campo-Formio which established the 'revolutionary Cisalpine republic' in northern Italy, the first of his 'satellite states', and ratified the acquisition of the left bank of the Rhine by France. Yet by the same treaty the Austrians acquired the republic of Venice and the Illyrian coast, so that the French, who at that stage had alienated large numbers of Italians by their behaviour as occupiers, seemed to be taking away other people's freedom while offering it to the world.

It was the world, not Europe, that inspired Napoleon's next military moves. In his youth he had once described Europe disparagingly as a 'molehill'. Now he turned across the Mediterranean to Egypt, and even though his Egyptian expedition was in effect an adventurous substitute for a direct campaign against island Britain it had a romance of its own. Having enjoyed what he later called 'the most beautiful time of my life because it was the most ideal', Napoleon returned to France in October 1799 a hero – and that despite the fact that the annihilation of the French fleet off Egypt in the Battle of Aboukir on the Nile in July 1798 had made his ambition to find lasting fame in the east impossible to follow through.

The demonstration of superior British naval power was to be repeated more than once during the long wars which were to be interrupted only once before 1815 at the Peace of Amiens in 1802; and the British admiral responsible for Britain's naval victory, Horatio Nelson, was himself to become a British popular hero in the future: London's main square, Trafalgar Square, named after Nelson's final victory, was to house his column on which was placed his statue. Napoleon, who continued to dream of distant conquests, even of India, rested his fortunes on war on land (outside as well as inside Europe) – and war was never to be the same again after his time. It was through war too that Napoleon would eventually lose all that he had won.

All this was in the glass in 1798. Nevertheless, Napoleon's elevation to the First Consulship for France, a new title with a Roman resonance, was less the result of any plotting on his own part than of the plotting of others. He went on to form a government of his own choosing which took the form of a Council of State in which no single minister had any authority independent of his own will. It was, however, broad-based in composition, including Lucien Bonaparte, his brother, as Minister of the Interior; Charles Maurice de Talleyrand, a highly talented and highly flexible aristocrat, Bishop of Autun from 1789 to 1791, who had already been both revolutionary and *emigré*, as Minister of Foreign Affairs; Josèphe Fouché, a veteran of 'the Terror', as Minister of Police; and Martin Gaudin, an able accountant, as Minister of Finance. The chemistry of the mix was curious but potent. The generals were now brought under control to leave the way clear for Napoleon to make his own moves. He was now ensconced in the Tuileries, and Burke's prophecy had been fulfilled that 'the officers of the army will remain mutinous for some time and full of faction until some general who understands the art of conciliating the soldiery . . . shall draw the eyes of all men upon himself'. A very different Englishman, Jeremy Bentham, who had been made an honorary French citizen, cast his vote for Napoleon in 1799.

Before there could be any European peace, the necessity for which Napoleon himself saw – indeed, he now promised it to France – further victories had to be won, for within 14 months of Campo-Formio Austria had abrogated its treaty with France and a new Second Coalition, which included both Russia and Britain, pushed the French backwards towards their 'natural' frontiers. The coalition was in a position to bring twice as many men into the field as France, and it was a Russian General Aleksandr Suvorov, born in 1730, whose victories in Italy destroyed all Napoleon's work there. Russian troops even entered Switzerland, which in April 1798 the French had converted into a Helvetic Republic. (At the same time the city state of Geneva had been annexed.)

Fortunately for Napoleon, Paul, the new Emperor of Russia, who had succeeded Catherine the Great, was dissatisfied with the conduct of his allies, particularly Austria, and, leaving the Second Coalition, which lacked any unified strategy, he recalled his troops by the end of 1799. In the new situation Napoleon went on to defeat the Austrians (by a slender margin) at Marengo in June 1800 and later in December at Hohenlinden. A new peace treaty at Lunéville in February 1801 did more than confirm Campo-Formio. The Austrians now recognized the Batavian, Helvetic, Cisalpine and Ligurian Republics and French annexation of the left bank of the Rhine. In the following month, by the Treaty of Aranjuez, a new kingdom of Etruria and a new Republic of Lucca were established in Italy, and Naples ceded the island of Elba to France. Not surprisingly – with Prussia neutralized and with Russia now friendly – Napoleon went on to settle minor disputes with smaller European countries during the early months of 1801. He also made a concordat with the new Pope, Pius VII, in April, and secured Louisiana from Spain.

Only Britain now remained hostile, and once again Napoleon had luck on his side when William Pitt, who had come to power controversially as a King's man, resigned the office of Prime Minister which he had held since 1784 in February 1801. Pitt remained a royal servant to the end, refusing to thwart George III's wishes on Ireland, where the French had launched an unsuccessful invasion in 1798, even though he had come to the conclusion that the King's refusal to allow the civil and political emancipation of Roman Catholics was wrong. Pitt's successor – Addington – lacked both his experience and his ability. He benefited from the fact, however, as Pitt had done, that by the beginning of the nineteenth century former friends of the Revolution, including Wordsworth, had become disillusioned with it, and few of them (William Hazlitt was an exception) had much sympathy with Napoleon.

Whatever the currents of opinion and whoever was Prime Minister, official British attitudes towards France and towards Napoleon were basically simple and consistent. France was an ancient rival, in the beginnings of the rivalry far stronger than England; and, going back no further than the reign of Louis XIV, Britain had had to struggle to prevent French domination of Europe. Yet fighting on land was desirable only when it was deemed necessary, as it had been when the French declared the navigation of the Scheldt open in 1792. Thereafter, fighting by sea to check French power in Europe and to guarantee British power overseas was essential. For Pitt, such an analysis, which he was to set out clearly in 1804, meant far more than any counter-revolutionary ideology. Burke was a political opponent of Pitt, not a supporter, when he had written his *Reflections on the French Revolution* in 1791. It was French policy in the Low Countries that led to Pitt's involvement in the First Coalition. And it was there at Waterloo near Brussels that the last battle against Napoleon was to be fought and won.

There was a brief spell of Napoleonic peace after Britain signed the Peace of Amiens in March 1802 which tacitly conceded French supremacy in Europe while recognizing all British gains outside Europe. (The British negotiator, Cornwallis, had been Viceroy in Ireland, Governor-General in India and commander of the British troops at Yorktown in the American War of Independence.) What was missing from the settlement was a treaty of commerce, and without this – as its British critics complained from the beginning – Article I, promising peace and friendship between Britain and France, was a piece of hypocrisy. Yet there was a desire for peace in both countries, and Napoleon, for the moment, was satisfied. 'At Amiens', he explained later, 'I had achieved the moral conquest of Europe.'

JUDGING NAPOLEON

The word 'moral' begs all the questions, as, indeed, do Napoleon's policies inside France. *Napoleon: For and Against* was the title of a remarkable book by a Dutch historian, P. M. Geyl, published in 1946. 'We have finished with the romance of the revolution', Napoleon himself remarked in another of his many dangerously memorable aphorisms, 'we must now begin its history.' As First Consul and, after August 1802, Consul for life, he consolidated much of the work of the French Revolution.

This was the necessary foundation of the power of Napoleon's state, and some of his work, though not all of it was to last. A new civil code of law was promulgated by his Council of State in 1804: experts had set to work on it in 1800 and it was completed under the Empire after he himself had taken the chair at 36 of its 84 sessions. The 1801 concordat with the Pope recognized Catholicism as the predominant religion in France, but the system of treating the clergy as paid servants of the state was retained. A comprehensive reform of local government involved the appointment of 'prefects' to each *département*: they obeyed central orders, and were committed to administrative reform.

Napoleon did not believe in universal free instruction, but the new kind of high schools he sponsored – the *lycées*, first created in 1802 – survived his regime as did the prefects. So, too, did the *Polytechnique*, an older educational institution for an elite, which was renamed in 1795. Napoleon's educational policy, directed by a 'University of France' which served as a Ministry of

Instruction, was more concerned with ladders than with floors or ceilings. (The real educational reformer of the period, Johann Heinrich Pestalozzi, was working neither in France nor Britain but in Switzerland.) The same approach was reflected too in Napoleon's creation of the new Order of the *Légion d'Honneur* in 1802. In the light of this, Napoleon's decision to become Emperor, announced in December 1804, surprised neither his friends, who were already vying with each other to acquire titles and to attend his court, nor his enemies, revolutionary or royalist, although it caused the great German musician Ludwig van Beethoven, one year younger than Napoleon – they had never met – to strike out his dedication of the 'Eroica' symphony to him.

Napoleon himself believed always in his own stagecraft, and having induced the Pope to attend his imperial coronation service he took care at the most solemn moment in a ceremony that was drenched in history to place his new crown on his head with no papal – or other – assistance. He had already played with the insignia and sword of Charlemagne and had even held court at Charlemagne's capital, Aachen. The 'Enlightenment' did not count at all in this web of ambition and fantasy. Yet both before and after he became Emperor Napoleon was in a sense carrying the policy of 'enlightened absolutism' to its logical conclusion, seeking to unify French administrative procedures and to give the country an efficient new order. This was a process that was bound to be marked both by successes and failures. Before lifting Charlemagne's sword he had always worn a revolutionary mask, and, having lifted it, he continued to win far more support from below – from peasantry and *bourgeoisie* – than an 'enlightened despot' like the Habsburg Emperor Josef II had ever been able to secure as a hereditary ruler.

There was, nonetheless, a sacrifice of freedom in France before as well as after 1804. As early as January 1800 as many as 60 Parisian newspapers were suppressed, and seven years later all but eight of the 33 theatres in Paris were closed. One of the several English biographers of Napoleon, Herbert Butterfield, who paid eloquent tribute to Napoleon's reforms in 1939, pointed out also that he generated an apparatus 'more dreadful' than that of ancient feudalisms and ill-jointed dynastic systems.

Napoleon knew this, but he was always conscious of his lack of 'legitimacy'. As a German historian, Fritz Hartung, has written, the Napoleonic empire 'lacked inner security'. There was an obviously 'ill-jointed' dynastic element in Napoleon's own policies. He placed on satellite thrones members of his own family, thought of by members of old royal families as upstarts, and in 1810 he divorced his wife, the childless Josephine, to marry Marie Louise, the daughter of the Habsburg Emperor. He himself had already humiliated the Habsburgs more than once, but he was never secure enough to ignore them. Moreover, he was aware of ominous continuities. Like many Holy Roman Emperors before him, he was thinking as much of Italy as of Germany. When Marie Louise produced him the much-wanted child, the child was named 'King of Rome': even in his cradle the child was called 'the King' by his devoted father.

Napoleon's passage from Consul for life to hereditary Emperor was never a difficult one, although on the way it involved the mock trial by a staged military court of the young Bourbon prince, the Duc d'Enghien, heir to the throne, who was accused of conspiracy. The death sentence pronounced on him meant that Napoleon, like the revolutionaries before him, had now spilt royal blood. It was in such a manner that he moved to his throne. Yet there was a real throne to ascend, and an Irish visitor to his court could claim that it was much greater in splendour than the old court of France. More of those attending it came from outside the ranks of the nobility than those who attended the court of Louis XVI.

Napoleon appreciated royal as well as revolutionary continuities. Thus, when he went to the Cathedral of Notre Dame to celebrate the Concordat with the Pope before he became Emperor, he wore the Regent Diamond which Louis XVI had worn at the opening of the Estates-General in 1789. Some of his Chamberlains had attended on Louis XVI. The artist Isabey, who had painted miniatures of Marie Antoinette's ladies, now produced drawings for the Emperor and designed efficient costumes. There was to be forward continuity too. Napoleon's official architect, Pierre Fontaine, was to serve future kings Louis XVIII, Charles X – and Louis Philippe.

Outside the court Napoleon looked to the future in many ways. He believed in natural science and encouraged it: an official report of 1808 on the progress of the mathematical and physical sciences since 1789 acknowledged what had been achieved and what might still be done. He found it easier to talk to engineers than to artists, and greatly improved the roads and bridges of France and the Empire. He was particularly proud of the mountain roads across the Alpine passes which linked France to Italy. He also reconstructed the *corniche* road along the southern Mediterranean coast, linking Nice with Genoa. It was that road which he had followed in 1796 when he first invaded Italy at the invitation of the Directory.

Napoleon's limitations as an 'enlightened' ruler were displayed most strikingly in his commercial and economic policy. A Bank of France was founded in 1800, which three years later was given the monopoly of issuing banknotes, and the system of collecting taxes was, at last, tightened up, but there was no French income tax while across the Channel, Pitt, a financial reformer, had introduced one. Napoleon believed in solvency, but it was only because he could extract funds from occupied countries that he did not need to raise taxes inside France until 1813. He never accepted any of the arguments in favour of free trade, and when the British proposed to return to the low tariffs of 1786 after signing the Peace of Amiens, which lasted for scarcely more than a year – continued British retention of the island of Malta was the pretext for the rupture – he refused. Yet he allowed corn to be exported to Britain to make up for deficiencies in domestic supplies even when the two countries were at war and he was preparing an invasion of England. His 'continental system', introduced in 1807, was an attempt to close the whole of Europe to the British, but British ships used a variety of devices, including sailing under foreign flags, smuggling, and straight bribery, in order to break the system. Their own attempts through Orders in Council to check international traffic and to search neutral ships on the seas – this was after Pitt's death in 1806 – provided a pretext for the United States to declare war on Britain in 1812, but the war was as inconclusive as the Treaty of Ghent which brought it to an end. It had none of the excitement for France of the War of American Independence.

Napoleon clearly recognized the importance of industry, particularly when it had a technological base, and succeeded in encouraging the production of substitute materials for materials that he could not import: thus, he welcomed a new chemical process for making soda from salt. He was aware also of developments in the textiles industry, and in 1806 the state acquired the patent of the new Jacquard loom which perpetuated French superiority in silk manufacturing. As a result there was enough French industrial expansion to worry British manufacturers, many of whom objected strongly to the Orders in Council. Yet French industrial development, which lacked adequate momentum from below, fell far short of an 'industrial revolution', and did not affect iron production. Nor did it help Napoleon that there were signs of serious strain in the British economy in 1811 and 1812, stimulating radical ideas both among employers and workers. The British combination of industrial and maritime strength proved vastly superior to anything the French could offer.

FROM TRAFALGAR TO WATERLOO

The 'continental system', which broke down in 1813, was not a new idea of Napoleon. Nor were many of the particular schemes which formed part of the Napoleonic Empire. Indeed, there was no grand Napoleonic design in foreign affairs. Issues were taken up one by one, and there was an underlying restlessness, culminating in overextension. Having failed to invade England, in 1804 he turned back to Italy. Having become Emperor, he could scarcely keep the title 'President of the Cisalpine Republic', but when he chose the new title 'King of Italy' (he was crowned at Milan in May 1805) the choice not unnaturally provoked the reactionary King of Naples as well as the Emperor of Austria, who saw the title as an undermining of the Treaty of Lunéville. In August 1805 Britain, Austria, and Russia formed the Third Coalition, and the armies which Napoleon had hoped would invade Britain were now rushed across Europe to defeat the Austrians at Ulm and the Austrians and Russians at Austerlitz. These were great victories, but 1805 was also the year of the Battle of Trafalgar. Nelson was killed in it but only one-third of the ships of France and its ally Spain ever regained their harbours.

Trafalgar was fought on 21 October, Austerlitz on 2 December. The Treaty of Presburg, which followed, was humiliating to the Austrians, for they were not only forced to recognize Napoleon's titles but to cede to him Venice and the Dalmatian coast. Territories were soon being disposed of thoughtlessly – often under threats or to keep promises – and after the Tyrol had been handed over by Austria to Max Josef, King of Bavaria, at Presburg, the Duchy of Berg and Cleves was handed to Napoleon's brother-in-law, Joachim Murat. In 1806 the kingdom of Naples was assigned to his brother Josèphe and a new principality, Neuchatel in Switzerland, was created for General Berthier. Meanwhile, the Dutch were forced under threat of annexation to accept as King another brother of Napoleon, Louis.

Those parts of the Presburg settlement that related to Germany, particularly the end of the Holy Roman Empire and the creation of a Confederation of the Rhine, succeeded in irritating the Prussians who had previously been neutral, and their irritation was not appeased by the handing over to them of Hanover, a territory ruled by the British royal family, which since 1714 had called itself 'Hanoverian'. Prussia went to war, therefore, in 1806, only to be routed by Napoleon himself at Jena and by one of his generals at Auerstadt. Two weeks after Jena (14 October) there were French soldiers, led by Napoleon, in Berlin, sharpening their swords, it was said, on the statue of Friedrich II. Russia proved more difficult. The costly battle of Eylau was indecisive, but victory at Friedland on 14 June 1807 forced the Russians to ask for an armistice, and they were treated on 7 July to one of the most fascinating events of the whole Napoleonic period – a private meeting between Napoleon and the Emperor Alexander I at Tilsit.

The two men seemed for a moment to be settling there the fate of the whole of Europe. They reached compromises on Prussia, allowing the King to retain his throne, and on Turkey, casting aside without scruple an old Turkish-French alliance and sharing Turkish spoils. A grand duchy of Warsaw was created, and Napoleon's brother Jerome became King of Westphalia. As far as Britain was concerned, however, they could do nothing except prepare the way for an anti-British alliance which was signed in secret later in the year. The two rulers hoped to bring into the struggle all the small maritime countries, including Portugal, Denmark and Sweden, in a kind of crusade in reverse, to create a system of 'federated states', in Napoleon's phrase 'a true French empire'. But their hopes were dashed when a British force took the initiative and in September 1807 bombarded Copenhagen: an earlier British force had bombarded it in April 1801, and now within two months of Tilsit all that remained of the Danish fleet, the biggest of Europe's 'minor fleets', was in British hands. A familiar pattern was now repeating itself – command of the land by the French; command of the seas by the British.

The Tilsit agreements between France and Russia were no more likely to last than the Treaty of Presburg with Austria. Yet Napoleon began to consider himself above all moral law and ultimately invincible. Thus, when the Portuguese refused to close their ports to British ships – and Portugal was England's oldest ally – he made a secret pact with Spain to dismember Portugal which he invaded in October 1807. Lisbon was duly occupied by General Junot's troops, but by showing an ignorant insensitivity both to Portuguese and to Spanish interests and susceptibilities Napoleon soon faced popular revolt in the Iberian peninsula. Disposing of the Bourbons and offering the Spanish throne to his brother Josèphe in the summer of 1808 – Murat was called upon to take his place in Naples – had not been a solution, and he himself was to comment later that it was 'the Spanish ulcer' that 'destroyed me'.

It was in the Iberian peninsula, not in the Low Countries, that British land power – not, this time, sea power – drained Napoleon's strength. The British General Arthur Wellesley – an Irishman who through war was to become Duke of Wellington – followed a highly effective strategy. It was in the Iberian peninsula, too, that the persistence and scale of popular resistance proved that not everyone without power in Europe was willing to respond to Napoleon's propaganda of revolution. Elsewhere in Europe, as far east as Poland, where his policies were bound in the long run to provoke Alexander I, Napoleon's armies carried a message which could attract both *bourgeois* and peasant backing, but the most support that he could get in Spain came from limited sections of the *bourgeoisie*. Meanwhile, in Spain there was a rallying of the great powers that still remained hostile to him. Austria declared war on France in April 1809, three months after Madrid had capitulated to Napoleon.

It was not a decisive decision, for Napoleon won the Battle of Wagram in July 1809, and after occupying Vienna the Habsburgs were forced to cede territories. There was now another redrawing, therefore, of the map of Italy and Germany. There was one new element, however, in the Napoleonic victory. It ended with wedding bells. The Emperor Napoleon married Marie Louise, the daughter of the man who had been Holy Roman Emperor, Franz I. Napoleon's court now moved on to Dresden, the capital of the kingdom of Saxony, where acting as host, the warrior Emperor was attended both by Franz I and by the King of Prussia. His armies were now moving towards the Russian border. Napoleon said later that Destiny led him eastwards, but this was his greatest mistake and the cause of his final undoing. His armies were huge and included thousands of soldiers from many parts of Napoleonic Europe as well as France: there were Austrians and Prussians among them, and Franz I would have liked to join them.

Dresden, one of the most beautiful cities in Europe, provided a good vantage point. The boundaries of direct French rule now stretched from south of the Pyrenees to the Baltic Sea and from the North Sea to the Dalmatian coast, and within this huge, if sprawling, area there were other great cities as large, as important and as different as Amsterdam, Barcelona, Hamburg, Florence and Rome. Yet this was not enough for Napoleon, and all was to melt away as his soldiers struggled in Russia in 1812 and 1813, actually entering Moscow in September 1812 only to see it burning – on the orders of the Russian commander.

The winter retreat from Moscow was terrifying. During this period, Prince Clemens von Metternich, the Austrian Chancellor, a Rhinelander by birth who had served as Ambassador in Paris, offered Napoleon prospects of a peace settlement that would have guaranteed France's 'natural frontiers' – the Rhine, the Alps and the Pyrenees. Indeed, as far as France was concerned, the map of Europe would have returned to what it had been in the first year of the Directory, with France still controlling Belgium, the left bank of the Rhine and Nice-Savoy. Napoleon refused. The Empire meant more to him than France, and hegemony meant more than settlement.

His end was as dramatic as his beginning. In October 1813 a new Fourth Coalition, which included Austria, Russia, Prussia and Britain, defeated Napoleon near Leipzig – still far away from the natural boundaries of France – in a battle which acquired the name of the Battle of the Nations. No fewer than 50,000 French lives were lost. Napoleon won further victories against Prussia, but Paris surrendered to the Allies at the end of March 1814, and Napoleon abdicated two weeks later. He was exiled to the tiny island of Elba in his native Mediterranean – an island far smaller than Corsica, where he had begun – and this, but for Napoleon, might have been the end of the story. Instead, he broke free, landed on the south coast of France and set out to rally Frenchmen to his cause again. The Allies had restored a Bourbon, Louis XVIII, a brother of Louis XVI, to the French throne, but he was no more capable of countering Napoleon's magic than the surviving democratic revolutionaries had been in 1799. In 1815 Napoleon had to emphasize his own commitment to the Revolution as he had done in 1799: 'I am not a military despot but the peasants' emperor. I represent the people of France.'

It was not France which counted in 1815, however, but Europe; and at Waterloo on 17 June British, Prussian, Austrian, Dutch and Belgian forces were together on the winning side, with the Duke of Wellington commanding 67,000 soldiers of whom 24,000 were British. Napoleon had 74,000, and there were 17,000 French casualties. Four days later Napoleon abdicated for a second time, surrendering – and it seemed part of a predestined fate – to the commander of a British warship. He was exiled to St Helena, a small island in the South Atlantic, and died there in 1821, still only 51 years of age. His captors refused to give him books or letters addressed to the Emperor Napoleon: they settled for General Bonaparte instead. Napoleon spent much of his time weaving myths about what he had done, what he had wanted to do, and what he might have done. There was one lingering regret. 'I asked for twenty years and destiny gave me only thirteen.'

SOCIAL ACCOUNTING: GAINS AND LOSSES

Historians have written about the Revolution and Napoleon – and the industrial revolution – from vantage points very different from that of Dresden, the centre of which was to be destroyed by a different allied coalition in 1945, or of Waterloo, just outside Brussels, where a European Commission was to issue orders for Europe in the late-twentieth century. Revolutionary change affects different people and different groups, whatever their country, in different ways: to some it means death, to others power. To some it means deprivation, to others liberation, to still more confusion.

If you were an aristocrat in France after 1790 – and survived the guillotine – you would be conscious, above all else, of the loss of privilege. Life would never be the same again even if you returned home. If you were a French lawyer in 1789, you would sense new opportunities, as Robespierre did. Merit could take you far ahead in 'a career open to the talents'. If you were a French peasant you would most likely, but not necessarily, have gained economically from revolutionary decrees, and some peasants did extremely well when feudal privileges were abolished. If you were a soldier your chances of being killed or wounded were high. Estimates of casualties vary from a half to three quarters of a million. If you survived, however, you would have seen more of Europe than most Frenchmen before or since. If you were a *sans culottes*, one of the very poor, you would be in some doubt in 1800 after ten years of revolution, much of it violent, whether you were better-off or not, although 15 years later you might feel that you had been when you lived in the Paris of Napoleon, complete with its court.

There had been brief times during the Revolution when revolutionary decrees had favoured the *sans culottes*, and there had been revolutionaries like the young and fiery St Just, who had claimed that 'the unfortunate' (*les malheureux*) were 'the power of the world' (*la puissance de la terre*), a cry to be echoed in the twentieth century by Franz Fanon born in the French Carribean in the island of Martinique. This was not far from Haiti where Toussaint l'Ouverture had led a black revolution. When Napoleon reimposed slavery, Toussaint rebelled against the French, and after he was captured was taken to France where he died in prison in 1803.

There were counterparts of the *sans culottes* in all European countries, just as there were aristocrats and lawyers, and lawyers did well in Britain too, but it was Britain that set out on a path to emancipate slaves, taking a unilateral decision to do so in 1807. Religion was a compelling factor in the decision. William Wilberforce, a Member of Parliament who had supported Pitt, led the campaign. He had written ten years earlier that his only 'solid hopes for the well-being of my country repose not so much on our armies, not so much in the wisdom of her rulers nor in the spirit of her people, as on the persuasion that she still contains many who in a degenerate age – Wilberforce abhorred revolution – love and obey the Gospel of Christ.'[6]

Wilberforce did not mention the economic factor, but the English poet and biographer Robert Southey, who had originally supported the French Revolution, did. 'Two causes and only two will rouse a peasantry to rebellion', he believed, 'intolerable oppression, or religious zeal either for the right faith or the wrong', but 'a manufacturing poor is more easily instigated into revolt'. 'If the manufacturing system continues to be extended, increasingly as it necessarily does [it did not] the number, the misery, and the depravity of the poor, I believe that revolution inevitably must come, and in its most fearful shape.'[7]

In the light of such comment, the French Revolution and the British industrial revolution can be compared in similar fashion – in terms of their effects on different groups of people (rich and poor: aristocrats, peasants and *bourgeoisie*) and on different parts of the country. In Britain you could either glory as a manufacturer in the new power of steam, comparing it with horse power – and profit from it – or, if you were an industrial worker in a new cotton mill, feel a sharp loss of personal independence even when you were materially better-off. Could you be better-off and still unfree? America led the way in raising such questions and in opening up new possibilities before Europe did. 'Happiness' depended on the answers.

The effects of industrialization were always as debatable as the effects of the French Revolution, even though no-one could doubt the unparalleled increase in both output and exports. Between 1765–74 and 1795–1804 annual exports of iron almost doubled (with fluctuations) and exports of cotton rose from £236,000 to £5,371,000. The great nineteenth-century Whig historian Thomas Babington Macaulay, who approved of the results of the French Revolution while deploring its violence, considered Southey's preference for 'rose-bushes and poor rates' over 'steam engines and independence' was sentimental. There was nothing sentimental in a positive verdict on the French Revolution of 1814 – delivered before Waterloo – that 'the Revolution substituted a system more conformable with justice and better suited to our times. It substituted law in the place of arbitrary will, equality in place of privilege; delivered men from the distinction of classes, the land from the barriers of provinces, trade from the shackle of corporations ... agriculture from feudal subjection and the aggression of tithes, property from the impediment of entails, and brought everything to the condition of one state, one system of law, one people.'[8]

This was measured language – if the last sentence raised fundamental questions about the role of the state which was far stronger in France than in Britain. And much of the language relating to industrial change was measured too in a way that Southey's judgements were not. Statistics provided one mode of measurement, as Napoleon himself recognized. More frequently, however, political revolutionaries dealt in words more enthusiastically than in figures, and most of the language of the French Revolution was as highly coloured as the events themselves. One problem with statistics concerned their selectivity: crucial figures might be missing. Another problem was how to interpret them. There was to be a vigorous twentieth-century debate on the standard of living during the first decades of industrialization.

Most sections of the labour force, notably handloom weavers, were worse off, catastrophically so. Most skilled workers – and there was a demand for new skills – were better-off. The situation varied from region to region, and within one region, like industrial Lancashire, from place to place. Distribution facilities were limited and local prices varied. Other evidence, qualitative and not quantitative in character, must be taken into account in any assessment of standards of life. And the qualitative evidence relates too to the effects of industrialization on the community and on the environment. Moreover, no account of the industrial revolution is complete either that does not consider its impact on women and children's work and on the structure of the family.

The shift from domestic work to factory work, associated with the rise of steam power, turned both women and children into wage earners who were paid less than men and were employed for that reason. Yet there were more domestic servants than cotton workers, and Lancashire (and later parts of the West Riding of Yorkshire) were special cases. In France women figured prominently in the heroic mythology of the Revolution, playing the major role in the march to Versailles on 5 October 1789, and, as Charles Dickens observed in his novel *A Tale of Two Cities* (1859), knitting and plotting while husbands and lovers killed. (Charlotte Corday passed into history by murdering the militant revolutionary J. P. Marat in his bath.) Yet women's clubs in Paris were dissolved in 1793, and from 1795 onwards women were not admitted unaccompanied into the spectators' gallery at National Assemblies.

While the Revolution had promised political participation for all, it excluded females from public life on biological, not on political, grounds – their physical constitution. War, of course, revolutionary or counter-revolutionary, strengthened the supportive role of women. While their husbands and children were away they had to cope. They were frequently left to run businesses also. In the Catholic provinces they were frequently the main defenders of the old faith. In Bordeaux, for example, when a brave female member of the Fumel family, owners of the great vineyard at Haut Brion, who had been imprisoned on religious charges, went to the guillotine before her father, she immediately became a martyr figure. So, too, did Marie Antoinette.

More historical research is needed on the history of gender in years of revolution, just as it was, until recently on the history of the unremembered country poor. They were hit by indirect taxation and were never free from deprivation. In 'bad years' when harvests failed or employment ceased (the two were interconnected) they experienced complete destitution. Their 'annals' were recorded at the time, mainly by others, in the proceedings of the law courts, the logs of hospitals and mortuaries, the reports of the local clergy and of managers of charities and occasionally in official inquiries. They were not a homogeneous group either in France or in Britain. Some were perpetually poor, some, particularly the young, were highly mobile in their search for food and employment. Some became beggars. In Russia and other parts of eastern Europe many were unemancipated slaves. As 'serfs' they were tied to a system that in the nineteenth century came to seem anachronistic.

In Britain, Sir Frederick Eden produced an invaluable book *The State of the Poor* in 1794, noting how the country poor were often victims of land enclosure carried through Parliament which changed their lives as much as it changed the landscape. And it was Arthur Young who, for all his trust in agricultural improvement, which preceded industrialization, recorded how commoners bemoaned that 'all I know is, I had a cow and an Act of Parliament has taken it from me'. Some of them fought hard – and continued to fight hard – for their customary rights, but they succumbed to the power of property. (In Scotland, where there were great estates, this was even stronger.) Meanwhile, through revolution the French peasantry, 80 per cent of the population, had secured new rights, but they were an even less homo-geneous group than the titled nobility to whom before 1789 they were expected to defer without question. One in five of them was already a labourer before the Revolution. In England there were few independent producers: 'yeomen' owned no more than 10 per cent of the land in the last decade of the century. There were, however, substantial tenant farmers, some of them keenly interested in new farming techniques, as were many of the 'squires' who owned the land, and indeed, some of the members of the aristocracy. King George III himself did not dislike being called 'Farmer George'.

The English did not usually employ the term 'nobility', a term which was defined by law in most European countries, particularly in the east and which applied to a particularly large section of the population in Spain. The Prussians had a powerful entrenched nobility, the *Junkers*, on whose service to the state the kings of Prussia depended. In Britain the term 'aristocracy' was preferred, and some aristocrats profited substantially from industrial interests. Others married into trade, if not on the scale that some contemporaries suggested. They all recognized that even as far as land ownership was concerned they were not the only men of influence. The 'squires', small country gentlemen, some of them of independent views, shared their local social and political power. They were magistrates and sometimes owned Church 'livings', and it was they rather than the aristocrats who were most suspicious in England of the new men of wealth who emerged in the City of London and in the new industrial districts, many of them wishing for nothing more than to become squires themselves. It was the squires too who took greatest pride in the defeat of Napoleon. He represented everything that they most detested.

Notes

1. D. Boorstin, *The Genius of American Politics* (1953), p.68.
2. P. Mantoux, *The Industrial Revolution in the Eighteenth Century* (1928) p.21.
3. Its chief populariser was A. Toynbee, *Lectures on the Industrial Revolution in England* (1884).
4. This image was used as a book title by D. S. Landes, *The Unbound Prometheus: Technological Change and Industrial Development in Western Europe from 1750 to the Present* (1969).
5. J. Michelet, *Historie de la Revolution Française* (1940, 2. Vol. Edn.), Vol. I, p.218. The first edition published between 1847 and 1853, was in seven volumes.
6. W. Wilberforce, *A Practical View of the Prevailing Religious System of Professed Christians in the Higher and Middle Classes of this Country Constrasted with Real Christianity* (1797), p.489.
7. R. Southey, *Letters from England* (1984 edn., with an introduction by Jack Simmons), p.375.
8. This judgement of Francois Mignet is quoted by S. Mellon, *The Political Uses of History* (1958), p.14.

Chapter 2

ORDER AND MOVEMENT, 1815–1848

RESTORATION: IDEA OR REALITY?

After the huge upheavals throughout Europe between 1789 and 1815 nothing could be quite the same again. The experience of revolution and war had gone so deep and had been shared by so many people, if unequally, that it could not be forgotten easily. Not everyone wanted to forget, however. Indeed, even before his death in 1821, Napoleon became a legend that still had the power to move men. In his *Memorial* which he wrote on St Helena, he blamed everyone else for his defeat, as he already had done in the Hundred Days, and claimed that had he been victorious Europe would have been a 'federation of free peoples' grouped in eternal peace around an enlightened France. 'There seems to have been something in the air of St Helena', an English politician wrote later in the century, 'that blighted exact truth.' And when Napoleon, who had seldom been concerned with 'exact truth', chose in his last years to depict himself both as a revolutionary and a liberal, those aspects of his career which did not fit into the picture were conveniently neglected.

Revolutionaries and liberals were to be found in most countries in post-Napoleonic Europe, both groups believing that the work begun in 1789 should continue. The former were often professional in their outlook and uninhibited in their methods. The latter sought to retain the positive gains in human freedom achieved as a result of 1789 while at the same time avoiding 'revolutionary excesses': they put their trust not in conspiracy but in 'constitutionalism'.

An Italian, Filippo Buonarroti, emerged as *the* professional revolutionary of this period, living in a world of spies and *agents provocateurs*. Born a nobleman in Tuscany in 1761, he had been an admirer first of Robespierre and then of Babeuf, and he attracted disciples and followers in countries from Poland to Italy, Belgium to Spain. Another professional, Auguste Blanqui, born much later in 1805, was in love with revolution. He divided his fellow conspirators into Years, Seasons, Months, Weeks and Days, sticking in that respect at least to the pre-Revolutionary calendar. But the name of his leader was Sunday.

There was nothing 'liberal' about such activity, yet the word 'liberal', including Liberal with a capital L, was now passing into daily politics in several European countries. An early example of its use comes from Spain, where it referred to supporters of an unimplemented constitution of 1812. Southey in 1816 referred to the *liberales*, and four years later in Paris *Libérals* were being contrasted with Ultras. In 1822 a periodical appeared in London with the title *The Liberal*; and later in the decade 'liberal minded' members of Lord Liverpool's Conservative government, which had first taken office in 1812, were being singled out from the rest. It was not until the 1860s, however, that the word passed into general use in Britain, the 'mother of parliaments', when the Liberal Party was identified with one man, William Ewart Gladstone, born in Liverpool in 1809, and in 1848 Gladstone was still a Conservative.

Political parties were still in an embryonic stage in 1848, although between 1832 and 1846 Sir Robert Peel, the Conservative leader whom Gladstone supported, built up a parliamentary party which broke up on the issue of the repeal of protective duties on corn. It was through the later development of political parties with a base outside parliaments as well as inside them, that 'liberalism' in a variety of versions, backed by a newspaper and periodical press, became a major political force. For some liberals, those, for example, who lived in Europe's great ports, economic liberty through free trade seemed a more urgent cause than political freedom – or rather the two were thought inextricable. Metropolitan liberals focused on constitutions, assemblies and freedom of speech.

In the interim, before political parties emerged that could function freely and continuously, the politics of protest depended on riots in countries without liberal constitutions and on platform agitations and pressure groups in countries which possessed them. In Britain, as in France, urban protests were most likely in years when bad harvests and unemployment coincided. In the words of William Cobbett, an English radical who was in no sense a liberal but who had spent a formative period of his life in America, it was difficult to agitate on a full stomach. The advice had universal applicability. At the same time, there were some liberals who were as afraid of pressure from below – either from towns or countryside – as they were of authority from above.

Rural discontent usually took unsophisticated forms, including arson, even in England; and in continental Europe, where peasants accepted toil and poverty as facts of life, they were more difficult to draw into public protest than townsfolk were. Moreover, when they were so drawn, they usually sought for redress at the local level. Their religion, a popular religion, whether Catholic, Protestant or Orthodox, was a source of consolation to them, and in France most peasants were now a conservative force. Nevertheless, peasant *mafiosi* in Sicily entered the streets of Palermo in 1820 to fight for home rule, and village labourers frightened Earl Grey's reforming Whig government before and after the Reform Act of 1832.

The years that followed the end of the Napoleonic Wars were particularly bleak throughout most parts of Europe, as the late 1820s were to be, serving to prove that peace was as hard as war. In France in 1816 the harvest was so poor that large quantities of grain had to be shipped from England, and there were fears of bad harvests in both countries in 1818 that pushed up the price of bread. There was heavy urban unemployment too. In 1817, when huge radical meetings were being organized in Britain's new industrial cities, the authorities of the ancient industrial city of Lyons, as subject to fluctuations of the trade cycle as any British city, were also reporting 'meetings, plots and movements'. Only half the silk looms in the city were in operation. Two years later, when a large crowd gathered in Manchester in August 1819 to petition for parliamentary reform, the yeomanry charged the crowds, killing 11 people and injuring 400. Waterloo had been followed by Peterloo. One of the members of Lord Liverpool's government that responded by passing Six Acts seeking to suppress freedom of the press and free assembly was Lord Castlereagh, a key figure in the devising of the post-Napoleonic settlement.

For the time being, Europe in 1815 after Napoleon's fall was in the hands of men who wanted to restore rather than to change. Looking back, Revolution and Empire seemed for them like adventures that had at last been brought – very properly but at real cost – to a close. Respect for legitimately constituted authority and for the social hierarchy that sustained it now had to be restored, they believed, along with the rulers who returned to their kingdoms, some of them small rulers to small kingdoms. It was a critic of Rousseau, Ludwig von Haller, a Swiss writer not a Frenchman, who wrote in 1816 that 'the legitimate monarchs have been restored to their thrones, and we are likewise going to restore to its throne legitimate science, the science which serves the sovereign master, and whose truth is confirmed by the whole universe'.

This was the logic of the situation as it appeared to those participants and observers who used pre-revolutionary language. Yet anti-revolutionism, like revolution or Bonapartism (the *ism* of the legend) or nationalism (a new phenomenon), was often expressed in highly romantic language, tinged with sentiment. The philosophers of 'restoration' included a number who looked back nostalgically to times before both the French Revolution and the industrial revolution, before the Enlightenment, even before the Reformation. They placed their emphasis on the need to recover an organic social order, based on duties, not on rights; on unity of thought and of morals, not on variety of opinions or behaviour; on religious faith, not on 'the march of intellect'. René de Chateaubriand, who had served briefly as a diplomat under Napoleon, had already written in his *Génie du Christianisme* (1802) of the 'sublime Christian mysteries' as 'the archetypes of the system of man and the world'. For him Napoleon had 'bewitched' French youth by 'the miracles wrought through his arms' and had taught Frenchmen to 'worship brute force'.

THE TASK OF RESTORATION

While the five leading statesmen who set about 'restoring Europe' in 1815 were of different temperaments and persuasions, they shared distaste for revolution and the sense that it had to be suppressed. None of them, moreover, needed nostalgia to prop them up. With the exception of Castlereagh, who had been British Foreign Secretary since 1812, most of them had had direct contact with Napoleon and had been prepared, not only at times of defeat, to make deals with him. At Tilsit, the Russian Emperor Alexander I had tried to settle the fate of Europe with him on a covered barge on the River Niemen decorated with two sets of imperial eagles. Metternich, the Habsburg foreign minister since 1809; while serving earlier as an ambassador at Napoleon's court appreciated the fact that Napoleon 'marched right to his goal without lingering for matters which he treated as secondary', but he had not been taken in by appearances. He had found the Emperor 'short, squat' and 'careless' in 'the way he held himself while he attempted to appear imposing'.

Essentially Metternich, who was to be Austrian Chancellor as well as foreign minister from 1821 to 1848, was a man of the eighteenth century who appreciated Voltaire: 'I reason about everything and on every occasion', he once said. Well-connected, he always thought in European terms. He was happier speaking French than German. He detested revolution, but he had no illusions concerning the permanence of the restoration, of which he was sometimes described as 'the rock'. Instead he was determined to preserve it for as long as was humanly possible. 'Fate', he said, 'has laid upon me the duty of restraining as far as my powers will allow, a generation whose destiny seems to be that of losing itself upon the slope which will surely lead to its ruin.'

Revolutions were never 'the work of great masses of the people', Metternich told Alexander in 1820: they were stirred up by 'the agitated classes', small groups of ambitious men, among them 'paid state officials, men of letters, lawyers, and individuals charged with public education'. The lawyers were, in his view, the most dangerous. In 1819 he used the murder of an anti-liberal writer August von Kotzebue by a mentally unbalanced theology student as the occasion for drafting the repressive Carlsbad Decrees which outlawed demonstrations, imposed a stringent press censorship, and rigidly controlled appointments to universities and what was taught in them.

Castlereagh, four years older than Metternich, would not have questioned either Metternich's diagnosis or his remedies. He too was 'bound by history and by tradition', and was well to the right in British politics (left/right terms were beginning to be used). As acting Chief Secretary for Ireland he had been responsible for the suppression of the French-aided rebellion of 1798 and for the Act of Union between Britain and Ireland in 1800. Like Metternich, he was suspicious of 'abstract and speculative' ideas and wanted more than all else a European period of 'repose'.

By contrast, Alexander I had many large and mystical ideas of his own, which became larger and more mystical the older he grew. In 1804 he had been in correspondence with William Pitt, Castlereagh's mentor, proposing to him a vague but high-sounding scheme for universal peace, based on a grouping of states, in effect a European government, that would be committed to the end of feudalism and to the introduction of constitutional rule. Pitt's reply ignored this vision and proposed instead a post-war settlement with guarantees that would be based on the principles of the balance of power. A decade later, in 1814 and 1815, Alexander retained a vision of Europe, still wishing to establish himself as its arbiter but arguing now that what was necessary was a new system of authority. He still preferred the idea of 'reconstructing' Europe to 'restoring' the *status quo*, and he was trusted neither by Metternich nor by Castlereagh. He had a number of advisers, however, from different backgrounds, who played a part in postwar negotiations, among them Count Nesselrode of German descent and Pozzo di Borgo, born, like Napoleon, in Corsica.

Friedrich Wilhelm III of Prussia had been interested in 'reforms' while Napoleon controlled the future of Germany, and his minister Baron Karl Stein had set out 'to do from above what the French have done from below'. In 14 months of office he emancipated serfs and inaugurated land reforms. He was forced to flee from Berlin, however, in 1808, and five years later when Friederich Wilhelm appealed to his fellow countrymen to re-enter the battle against Napoleon in 1813.

When European peace came he promised an extension of 'representative government', but he now did nothing to move even modestly in that direction, listening instead both to Metternich and to Alexander. His then chief minister, Karl August Hardenberg, who remained close to him until his death in 1822, now showed little sign of his earlier radicalism when he had been working with Stein. In 1819 he backed the King in supporting the Carlsbad Decrees, and it was in Prussia's capital city, Berlin, that the great founder of its university, Wilhelm von Humboldt, whose idealistic approach to higher education was to sway generations beyond his own in many countries outside Germany, now resigned in disgust.

THE SETTLEMENT

Before Metternich took over the role of supervising post-Napoleonic Europe Castlereagh played a major part in trying to bind together in a Quadruple Alliance the four main wartime allies who had been involved in the four wartime coalitions, and before the final defeat of Napoleon they had signed a 20-year treaty at Chaumont in March 1814 in which they all agreed to work closely together. There was a further proviso looking beyond the territorial settlement itself. The great powers would hold a series of peacetime meetings to consult upon matters of common interest. This would have been enough for Castlereagh and Metternich; Alexander, however, wanted something more high-sounding, not a compact that would rest on *raison d'état* but a declaration of principle based on those 'sublime truths' that were enshrined in Christianity ('justice', 'Christian charity' and 'peace'). He sought a 'Holy Alliance' of monarchs, whom he described as 'fathers of families', to guarantee a Christian order 'in the name of the Most Sacred and Indivisible Trinity'.

'The course *formerly* adopted by the Powers in their mutual relations had to be *fundamentally* changed', Alexander urged in the first draft of his alliance. 'It was *urgent* to replace it with an order of things based on the exalted truths of the eternal religion of our Saviour.' After the Emperor of Austria read his draft he is said to have remarked that he did not know whether to discuss the proposals in his Council of Ministers or in the confessional, and Castlereagh described Alexander's final document as a 'piece of sublime mysticism and nonsense'. Not surprisingly, the Sultan of the Ottoman Empire was the only ruler of a European realm who was not asked to join in; and while Britain's Regent, the future George IV, expressed sympathy he did not sign.

The first difficult task of the peacemakers was practical, not ideological – to restore thrones, states and boundaries. The thrones came first because the legitimacy of hereditary rulership had been challenged both by the revolutionary regicides in France and by the clan kingmaking of Napoleon. Restoration of the states came second, because these were the territorial units over which rulers exercised authority. The peacemakers unanimously rejected what they held to be dangerous ideas concerning the sovereignty of the people. Restoration of the boundaries came third, although it was recognized that they could not be restored just as they had been. The map of Europe had changed so many times between 1792 and 1815 – often with the active connivance of surviving rulers from the 'old regime' – that it was necessary to look closely at what seemed to be basic geographical facts.

These were soon to change substantially with the coming of railways and the creation of a new communications system. Metternich, however, began with the geographical situation of the great powers as it was. 'France [which he significantly put first] and Russia have but a single frontier and this hardly vulnerable. The Rhine with its triple line of fortresses ensures the repose of France; a frightful climate makes the Niemen a no less safe frontier for Russia. Austria and Prussia find themselves exposed on all sides to attack by their neighbouring powers. Continuously menaced by the preponderance of these two powers, Austria and Prussia can find tranquillity only in a wise and measured policy, in relations of goodwill and among each other and with their neighbours.'

The great powers had reached preliminary agreement earlier in the first Treaty of Paris (May 1814) after Napoleon had been dispatched to Elba. By then they had also settled a number of basic issues relating to the peace arrangements, including: the restoration of France to its 'ancient frontiers', the 1792 boundaries; the enlargement of Holland to include Belgium (the Austrian Netherlands before 1792) and Luxembourg; the independence of Switzerland; the division of Italy into independent states; the restoration of Spain, like France, to Bourbon rule; and the establishment of a confederated

Germany. Saxony, which had remained an ally of Napoleon to the last, and partitioned Poland, where Napoleon had figured not as an aggressor but as a restorer, were deliberately not mentioned in this first Treaty.

Within this broad framework there was, indeed, scope for considerable disagreement, even among the Big Four, whose representatives met privately in Metternich's apartments almost every day during the Congress of Vienna which gathered together on 1 November 1814. It was a large and glittering congress, attended not only by representatives from every state but from many organizations that now would be considered 'non-governmental'. Secret diplomacy went on behind the scenes on difficult topics, among them relations with defeated France which was represented at Vienna with great diplomatic and social skill by the 60-year-old Talleyrand, the man everyone knew. He could do nothing, however, to prevent (even had he wished to do so) British colonial gains during the revolutionary and Napoleonic wars from being taken into account as they had been in eighteenth-century treaties, like the Treaty of Paris in 1763 which ended the Seven Years War and which left Bourbon France seeking revenge. As far as Britain was concerned, the emphasis in 1815, as during the wars themselves, was not on acquisition of territory but on command of the oceans and the bases which would make this possible.

The Vienna settlement, discussion of which was interrupted by Napoleon's flight from Elba and the Hundred Days, was finally signed in June 1815. It was the most far-reaching agreement that had been reached in Europe since the Treaty of Westphalia in 1648. A very loose German confederation of 39 states (the *Deutscher Bund*) was to be presided over by Austria, and although it was never to develop a corporate sense of its own it was a creation of long-term importance for the future of Germany. At the same time, Austria was given direct control of lands in Italy that were to be of critical importance to the future of Italy. Lombardy and Venetia were annexed and Austrian princes were handed key Italian duchies, Modena and Parma. There were now eight separate states in Italy.

Metternich thus ensured through the terms of the German and Italian peace 'settlements' that he and the multinational Empire which was controlled from Vienna would be at the heart of the new European order so long as he lasted. Yet only one element in that order was long to outlast him: Switzerland was not only granted independence but neutrality. The 'old regime' in Switzerland was not restored in its entirety. Formerly subject districts, like Geneva and the Valais, now became confederate cantons. The settlement allowed for the expansion of trade and industry, but it too was to change in 1846 through Swiss crisis and war two years before Metternich's own fall.[1]

Prussia, which was as anxious to protect the new *status quo* as Metternich was, received (after critical secret sessions) 40 per cent of Saxony and was also granted strategic lands on the Rhine and the Napoleonic Duchy of Westphalia as a defensive bulwark against France, eventually enabling it to emerge as a champion of Germany against France. This was long after both Friedrich Wilhelm III and Metternich had disappeared from the scene. The immediate effect was a doubling of Prussia's population. Berlin, however, was in the east, not all that far from Russia and it was still a city of imperial residence, which only after 1848 began its transformation into a city of perpetual movement. Goethe, living in Weimar, visited it only once. Beyond Prussia, the other 39 German states, had different geographic orientations as well as a range of very different rulers. They each had also their own cultural as well as dynastic histories.

Between disunited Germany and comparatively united France the old principality of Liäge was arbitrarily merged with the former Austrian Netherlands and 'given' to Holland as compensation for its loss to Britain of Dutch colonies in South Africa. This was a settlement that could not last. In the east Russia was allowed to reconstitute part of the old Polish kingdom as a new but dependent Kingdom of Poland (a move which required Prussia to hand back the Warsaw region). It was not until after another protracted twentieth-century war that an independent Poland appeared on the map.

There were all kinds of compensation arrangements in 1815 of which this was one. Thus, when Austria secured the Italian duchies it lost its Belgian territories, and in the north Sweden 'gave' Finland to Russia and in return, as already agreed, 'received' Norway from Denmark. In Italy, where, as in Germany, the Habsburgs made substantial but in the long run dangerous gains, Vittore Emmanuele I, King of Piedmont-Sardinia, sporting an *ancien regime* peruke and pigtail, returned to Turin. Greeting his 'good and faithful subjects', he assured them that they would 'find themselves once more under the dominion of those beloved Princes, who have brought them happiness and glory for so many centuries', and offered them all the benefits of absolute government, although conscription was abolished and taxation reduced. As one item in the deal he received part of Savoy and Genoa which for centuries before French occupation had been an independent republic and which had been liberated by a British officer, William Cavendish Bentinck. In other parts of Italy the Grand Duke of Tuscany returned to Florence; the Pope, Pius VII (Pope from 1800 to 1823) returned to Rome (and the Papal States that straddled Italy); and Fernando IV, King of Naples – now renamed Fernando I, King of the Two Sicilies – was restored to his old throne: this, however, was only after he had signed a permanent defensive alliance with Austria.

Britain, so heavily and continuously committed to wartime coalitions, secured what it chose to seek. Command of the oceans was strengthened by scattered gains – Cape Colony in South Africa (a key position until the building of the Suez Canal, but a future cause of political conflict in both the nineteenth and the twentieth centuries), Ceylon, Mauritius, French islands in the West Indies, and – nearer home – Heligoland (off the German coast) and Malta, a Mediterranean shuttlecock during the Napoleonic Wars. Britain also secured agreements for the opening of certain rivers to navigation and a general condemnation of the slave trade, which was an insistent demand by influential British pressure groups that were represented at Vienna.

Unlike the other great powers present at Vienna, Britain was a country where pressures could register through Parliament and where policies of all kinds, however liberal, were open to debate. Castlereagh knew that all his actions would be subject to popular scrutiny and even to scurrilous attack at home. Cartoonists would be at work as well as journalists – and poets, among them Shelley, who in a famous poem, which had nothing to do with Vienna, described meeting 'murder on the way', wearing 'a mask like Castlereagh'. Although Castlereagh did not approve of the Holy Alliance, his political enemies in Britain drew no distinctions between the four-power treaty and the 'ideological' pact.

One participant in the Congress, Friedrich von Gentz, translator of Burke as well as secretary to Metternich, left a highly critical account of its work. Placed as he had been at the heart of the intriguing, he claimed that nothing had been achieved at Vienna except 'restorations which had already been effected by arms, agreements between the great powers which were of little value for the preservation of Europe, quite arbitrary alterations in the possessions of the smaller states'. There had been 'no act of a higher nature, no great measure for public order or the general good which might compensate humanity for its long suffering or pacify it for the future'.

This verdict has been reviewed many times in the light of subsequent experience, particularly the experience of the two world wars in the twentieth century, the first of which was followed by a controversial 'settlement' that was to last for only 20 years, and the second, a settlement in instalments, out of which emerged the United Nations Organization along with a 'cold war' beginning almost immediately after the 'hot' war had ended. Judgements have varied. Woodrow Wilson as American President at the end of the First World War set out at Versailles to devise a settlement on opposing lines which Harold Nicolson as a young diplomat present there criticized as strongly as Gentz criticized Vienna. Henry Kissinger, a later American Secretary of State during the Cold War years, who as a young historian had made a detailed and sympathetic historical study of the personalities at Vienna, praised the men who made the settlement for ushering in the longest period of peace in Europe that it had ever known. Moreover, he argued, it relied less on power to maintain itself than any other settlement would have done.

Undoubtedly the 1815 settlement secured a general balance of forces in Europe that survived local crises in particular places, including Italy and Spain, and one important change in the map of Europe, the creation of a new and independent Kingdom of Belgium in 1830. Within the overall balance there was to be an important place for defeated, though now royalist, Bourbon France, a very different place from that to be set aside for defeated Germany either in 1919 or in 1945. France had been forced to cease to be gigantic, it was observed, in order that it might be great. Depriving it of revolutionary and Napoleonic conquests did not mean destroying the country, and it was by its own choice that it changed its regime in 1830.

Even after Napoleon had escaped from Elba and the settlement had to be reconsidered, it did not become vindictive. Slices of Savoy and Flanders, which France had retained under the first settlement, were now to be handed over to its neighbours along with lands in Germany and a fortress in Alsace; in addition, France was held responsible for a limited indemnity and for Allied occupation costs. The new settlement, signed in November 1815 in a second Treaty of Paris, brought an even greater element of justice in that countless art objects looted by the French during the Napoleonic Wars now had to be returned to their rightful owners.

The weaknesses of the settlement, which included such novel features as an international Commission for the River Rhine, were that it left a number of future trouble spots on the map and that it created new ones. Moreover, while 'Germany' and 'Italy' were kept in place – divided – until 1848, thereafter they were to upset the balance. The settlement also ignored one area that had been of diplomatic and military importance immediately before the revolutionary wars began and which was to bring many future troubles in the nineteenth century: the east of Europe and the Ottoman Empire. There was no Commission for the River Danube.

THE 'CONGRESS SYSTEM'

Many problems became apparent soon after the initial period of peacemaking was over, and were not resolved during 1818 when the Quadruple Alliance became a Quintuple Alliance with the inclusion of France. This was a logical step which Talleyrand, always present at the right time, encouraged the other great powers to take. Yet, as he knew, France had interests and claims of its own within a 'Congress System', and these could now be expressed at the various congresses which met to monitor the postwar European order.

The five great powers who were now monitoring peace were the same great five who had dominated the European scene before 1789, but their interrelationships had changed after Britain had emerged from the revolutionary and Napoleonic wars with greater wealth at home and with access to far greater wealth in the world outside Europe than any other great power. At the same time Habsburg resources in relation to Habsburg commitments were inadequate to give Metternich the financial security he required in order to play the role in Europe that he felt necessary.

How wise he was to play it in the way that he did remains a matter of debate. The Habsburg Empire sprawled over many regions, and to suppress both liberalism and nationalism everywhere within it was a daunting task. Soldiers in his own armies, inadequately funded and difficult to reform, spoke many languages, including Magyar, Serb and Italian. To draw too much attention to this fact, however, violated military 'honour', a supreme virtue in Vienna. Politics from below could not always be suppressed, and Lord Palmerston, then British Foreign Secretary, told the Austrian Ambassador in

London long after 'the system' had broken down that Metternich's approach to European questions was 'repressing and suffocating'. Immobility was not conservatism, and it would 'lead to an explosion just as certainly as would a boiler that was hermetically sealed and deprived of an outlet for steam'.

While the 'Congress System' was new and untried, the four European congresses held between 1815 and 1822 already made it clear, first, that the wartime Allies (with Britain on the periphery and Austria at the centre) had different standpoints in peacetime and, second, that it was misleading to claim without qualifications that an old world had been 'restored'. There were far too many signs of a new world in the making. From the start Castlereagh, while unsympathetic to that world, saw the difficulties of policing any European order, Christian or not, while Metternich rejected attempts by the Tsar to create an international army to guarantee the boundaries and existing governments of Europe. Yet when risings broke out in Naples and Spain against reactionary monarchist regimes, Metternich was deeply shocked by what he thought of in non-historical terms as 'earthquakes', 'volcanic eruptions', 'plague' or 'cancer'. He is said to have used eight such metaphors to describe society.

In the case of Naples, where, as in other parts of Italy, Metternich always encouraged ministerial attempts to improve domestic administration, he felt bound to act without resorting to metaphor. A secret treaty between Austria and Naples (one of several such treaties) provided for Vienna to receive a full supply of intelligence, and it was with the reluctant concurrence of Britain and the enthusiastic backing of Russia (which wished to join in the intervention) that an Austrian army entered Naples in 1821 and crushed a Neapolitan revolt as quickly as it had begun. There was, in fact, little local support for the Army leaders who had led the revolt and who had resisted the idea of a separate new constitution for Sicily. In consequence Fernando I returned to his throne. The financial cost to Austria was high: it necessitated a large loan and, in order to get it, a speedy part repayment of an earlier British loan, and it led to a substantial budget deficit.

Even before Austrian interventions in Naples and in the Kingdom of Piedmont-Sardinia, where rebels had plotted to depose Vittore Emmanuele I and introduce a new constitution, the 'Congress System' was in difficulties. At the very first conference at Aachen in 1818 Castlereagh had been told by his government to avoid 'continental entanglements' except that of keeping France in check; and in November 1820 at the time of the Congress of Troppau, at which he was not present, he objected strongly – and publicly – to a protocol drawn up to meet Alexander's wishes. It stated that states which had undergone a change of government, due to revolution, and which as a result threatened other states would cease to be 'members of the European Alliance', adding that 'if, owing to such alterations immediate danger threatened other states, the powers bind themselves, by peaceful means, or if need be by arms, to bring back the guilty state into the bosom of the Great Alliance'.

At the subsequent Congress of Laibach (January 1821) it was clear that there would be no compromise between Britain's position on the one hand and Austria's and Prussia's on the other, although one Austrian diplomat described Castlereagh's reactions as being like those of 'a great lover of music at church who wishes to applaud but dare not'. Before the next Congress, which was held at Verona in October 1822, at which all five of the great powers were present, Castlereagh had committed suicide (his reasons were private), and his more forthright successor, George Canning, reiterated in stronger language than had ever been used before Britain's complete refusal to take part in Allied intervention in the second area of disturbance, Spain, where rebels were asking for the acceptance of an abortive constitution drafted in 1812.

When French troops moved into Spain in 1823, with the support of Austria and Russia, the 'Congress System' was clearly at an end. There was a plaintive note, therefore, to Castlereagh's remarks to King George IV in his last interview with him four days before his suicide. 'Sir, it is necessary to say goodbye to Europe; you and I alone know it and have saved it: no one after me understands the affairs of the Continent.' This, he knew, was an old continent, with significant differences, economic, social, political and, not least religious, between west and east and north and south. There was also a central Europe, still not clearly thought of as such, stretching from the Baltic to the Dalmatian coast, about which he knew little. Even the twenty-first century retains 'an overlapping network of family resemblances in the way things look and the way things are done'.[2] There are resemblances which derived from Habsburg history long before Metternich.

SIGNS OF CHANGE

What became abundantly clear between 1822 and 1830 was that there were different interpretations of what 'Europe' meant. This was because of a continuing sense of movement. Indeed, there were years when the word 'movement' was passing, like the word 'liberal', into the late eighteenth-century vocabulary as naturally as the term 'revolution' had passed into it during the late-eighteenth century. Used vaguely in relation not only to the diffusion of liberal ideas and opinions but to the advance of nationalism, the word 'movement' was employed less vaguely in relation to new organizations and new political groupings, and strictly literally in relation to 'the movement of peoples' which was to become a major theme in twentieth and early twenty-first century history. In industrializing Britain the words 'labour movement' were used as early as 1828. By then, forming part of it, there were trade unions, cooperative societies and socialist organizations.

Belonging to a movement by choice carried with it new commitments and new loyalties. The movement might either be open and public or secret. The former used pamphlets and posters, the latter relied on oaths and rituals. The most famous of the post-1815 secret movements, engaged in plots rather than in campaigns, was that of the *Carbonari* (rural charcoal burners), founded in Naples in 1810. 'Apprentices' in its French counterpart, the *Charbonnerie*, were initiated in a mock trial of Jesus, and dedicated themselves to Faith, Hope and Charity.

Another group, with lodges scattered everywhere, was Buonarroti's League of Sublime and Perfect Masters, with their headquarters in Turin. There was a Greek society also, the *Hetairia Philike*, which linked Greek sympathizers in various cities of the Balkans. Some counter-revolutionaries attributed the French Revolution itself to a conspiracy, Masonic in origin; while anti-Semitism, endemic in various forms throughout Europe, generated deeply disturbing theories of conspiracy across the centuries. In Russia there was a distinctive twist to revolutionary conspiracy. On the death of Alexander I in December 1825 there was a misunderstanding about who should succeed him, and as the throne remained vacant for three weeks sections of the Army rebelled at St Petersburg, demanding the summoning of a national assembly. When Nicholas I, Alexander's younger son, succeeded to the throne as his father had intended, the so-called Decembrist Revolt was crushed with great severity, with four of its leaders being executed and 120 exiled to Siberia. The new Emperor, not a title used inside the Russian Empire itself, was haunted for the rest of his life by the spectre of revolution.

France itself remained a centre of political conflict. Yet the Bourbon kings – Louis XVIII, twice restored, and his reactionary brother Charles X (the former Comte d'Artois, who succeeded Louis in 1824) – had to take account less of movements than of an ambiguous but to them inhibiting Constitutional Charter which had been drawn up in 1814 by a committee of former ministers, senators and deputies of the Empire: it guaranteed the land settlement of the Revolution, retained Napoleon's administrative and educational system, and provided for parliamentary government. Only the preamble, which stated that the Charter was the monarch's 'gift to France', belonged unequivocally to the *ancien régime*. Although the parliamentary franchise was severely restricted in 1822 – there were only 100,000 voters out of a population of 29 million – Charles X himself made the first moves that led to his downfall by trying to evade all the provisions of the Charter. French opposition, whether organized in small clandestine groups meeting in secret or expressed openly in newspapers and in a Society of the Friends of the Freedom of the Press, could never be quelled, let alone crushed.

Nor could it in Spain, where the Bourbon Ferdinand VII sought to follow in the footsteps of his uncle, Ferdinand I, King of the Two Sicilies, and tried ruthlessly to stamp out 'liberalism' through royal or 'white' Terror. One of Ferdinand I's chief ministers once said that 'the first servant of the Crown should be the executioner'. Yet the King of the Two Sicilies did not have at his command enough executioners to maintain uncontested order, and civil disturbances followed his death in 1825. An all-out victory against 'liberalism' was even more out of the question in Portugal, where John's elder son, John

IV, having returned from Brazil, swore to uphold a liberal constitution adopted in 1820, and faced an absolutist revolt in 1824 after Brazil declared its full independence in 1822 with John's elder son Pedro as emperor. Civil war in Portugal followed at once. There were many twists and turns – including the return of Pedro from Brazil in 1831 who fought his brother the absolutist Miguel, but John's daughter, Maria II, who ascended the throne in 1834, eventually won the struggle in 1847 with the support of the liberals.

During the 1820s the issue of freedom was at stake not only in Spain and Portugal but in the east of Europe, where it was often to be threatened in the future. And once again rifts were revealed between Britain and the other four great powers. There were also new diplomatic complexities, including a temporary isolation of Austria. After 1815 two revolts began against the very loosely exercised imperial control of the Ottoman Turks. The first was in Serbia where two rival families, the Karadjordjevič and the Obrenovič, struggled for power, Milos Obrenovič, devious, cruel and illerate, who had declared himself hereditary ruler in 1817, secured Serbian autonomy from the Ottoman Empire in 1830. His success attracted relatively little attention outside the Balkans. By contrast, the movement for Greek independence attracted as much attention in Europe as the Spanish Civil War was to do during the 1930s.

In 1821 Greek rebels wrested the ancient Pelopponese from the Turks with deceptive ease and speed, and the Turks retaliated at once with savage reprisals against Greeks both in Turkey and in the Mediterranean islands. The Greek Patriarch and three archbishops were hanged in their ecclesiastical vestments in Constantinople, the centre of the Greek Orthodox Church, and as many as 30,000 people were killed or enslaved on the predominantly Greek island of Chios not far from the Turkish mainland. This was the beginning of a protracted struggle that continued for most of the 1820s. The Greeks, who had the American constitution in mind when they assembled in Epidaurus in 1822 to draft their own, secured immense public backing in all countries from 'Phil-hellenes' – writers, poets, politicians and rulers, like Ludwig of Bavaria, who sent an army brigade. Even Charles X had Phil-hellene sympathies.

The leaders of the romantic movement found a hero in the poet Lord Byron, England's 'brightest genius' and 'Greece's noblest friend', and leapt enthusiastically to the defence of what they took to be the greatest of causes. (One British supporter, Colonel, later Earl, Stanhope was described by Byron as 'the typographical colonel' because he equipped Greeks not only with arms but with a printing press.) Byron died of fever in Greece in 1824. Despite such European backing, the Greeks seemed to be in danger of total collapse in 1827. With Athens besieged, they then elected as President for seven years Capo d'Istria, who had been one of Alexander's advisers at the Congress of Vienna.

Even if Metternich had not been in power, Austria and Russia would have been bound to disagree on the Greek question. Indeed, differences of interest and outlook on all east European questions were to remain, if often 'put on ice', into the twenty-first century. During the 1820s Russian leaders, committed neither to the classical world nor to Greek liberalism but to the Orthodox Church, had begun giving help to the Greek rebels even while they were urging joint European action against all rebels everywhere, but Metternich, considering the Greek rebels to be no different from rebels in Naples or Spain, was determined at the very least to prevent any inter-state action on their behalf.

The blow to him came in April 1826, when Nicholas I entered into an agreement with Britain to impose mediation upon the belligerents in order to secure an autonomous Greece under the nominal suzerainty of the Ottoman Empire. In July 1827 France associated itself with the new agreement, bringing about an interesting – although temporary – alignment of the great powers who were to be in alliance again in 1914 when the First World War broke out. The climax of this phase came when a British admiral annihilated the Turkish fleet at Navarino in October 1827, the greatest Turkish disaster at sea since Lepanto in 1571.

Nevertheless, it did not seem to be in British interests then, or later in the nineteenth century, for the Ottoman Empire to be carved up and destroyed (although Charles X of France dreamed of doing so); and the Duke of Wellington, who after Canning's death in 1827 succeeded him as Prime Minister in 1828, actually apologized to the Sultan as 'an old ally'. British fears seemed justified when the Russians advanced against the Turks on land and in August 1829 reached Adrianople, the nearest they had ever been to Constantinople. Yet Nicholas halted. He had no desire to destroy the Ottoman Empire, preferring to keep it weak – and by the Treaty of Adrianople obtained a financial indemnity from the Turks who pledged that they would not impair Christian rights, which were to be under Russia's protection. By a later London agreement, signed by Britain and France, Greece secured not only autonomy but independence. It was to become a kingdom rather than a republic, but it was only after protracted negotiations involving different possible names that Otto, the son of the Phil-hellene King of Bavaria, ascended the Greek throne.

The significance of the Greek revolt did not lie primarily in the field of diplomacy. Metternich had been isolated, if only for the time being, and Britain and France (for different reasons and not for the last time) had revealed their own special interest in what was happening in Constantinople. Far more important, however, the Greek revolt had mobilized the kind of popular support, including support from the peasantry, that Metternich most feared. It had ended too with the recognition of a new country that took its place on the map not just as a state but as a nation state. The fact that the new nation acquired a dynastic monarch in 1833 did not minimize the extent of the change as far as Europe was concerned, although it was to complicate future Greek politics both in the nineteenth and twentieth centuries. Europe would move ahead, not stand still or, as some hoped, return to the past.

The statesman who best understood this was Canning. Like his predecessor Castlereagh, he was a conservative, although he favoured Catholic emancipation, the granting of civil rights to British Roman Catholics, for long a controversial measure, but he knew that Europe – and the world – must change. 'Canning soars', Metternich complained, 'I walk. He rises into a region uninhabited by men. I keep on the level of human things.' (Canning called Metternich 'the greatest rogue and liar on the Continent, perhaps in the civilized world'.) Metternich was wrong in feeling that Canning was out of touch with reality. As Member of Parliament for Liverpool, his British opposite number was very much in touch with the hard issues of British trade and with the industry which increasingly sustained it. He was unwilling to subordinate British interest to the fears of a conservative concert of powers. 'Every country for itself and God for us all' was one of his mottoes. And, unlike Castlereagh, he had to deal with places outside Europe as well as on the continent.

The Spanish colonial territories in South America were in revolt against Madrid during the revolutionary and Napoleonic wars, and civil wars raged there in waves from 1812 to 1820. Byron sympathized with the liberationist cause there before he turned to Greece. There were dramatic events in the struggle too, like the crossing of the high Andes by 'the Liberator', Simon Bolivar, to create a republic of Venezuela in 1819, the year of Peterloo. It was of importance, therefore, that in 1825 and 1826 Canning did not hesitate to give his full support to the rebels, calling 'the New World into existence', as he put it in one of his famous phrases, 'to redress the balance of the old'.

This was 1776 in reverse, and Canning won great popularity in Latin America for his stand, which was shared by many Englishmen. Bolivar's dreams of a union of peoples were shattered, however, by 1830 when he died unpopular and reviled. After falling from power he was to declare that 'he who sows a revolution ploughs the sea'.

THE REVOLUTIONS OF 1830: CHALLENGING THE *STATUS QUO*

No such memorable aphorisms were pronounced in 1830 when Europe was swept by a revolutionary wave, although the French dramatist and poet Victor Hugo, whose political output was to be as prolific as that of Voltaire, chose appropriate and for him unusually concise words when he described the French Revolution of 1830 as 'a revolution stopped half-way'. There would have been no revolution at all in France in 1830, however, had it not been for Charles X's desire to make his regime even more authoritarian than it had been. Supported by extreme right-wing politicians, he invited trouble when he asked one of their number, the Comte de Polignac, who had been serving as French Ambassador in London, to become Prime Minister in

August 1829. Polignac had been one of two members of the Chamber who had refused to take the Oath to the Charter of 1814, and the result of the royal *coup d'état* was direct confrontation. 'On the one side is the Court', one Paris newspaper put it, 'on the other the nation.' This newspaper, the *Globe*, was a new one. It belonged to Louis Adolphe Thiers, a young liberal politician (and later both historian and suppressor of revolution), who was supported – or patronized – by Talleyrand.

Charles X was subsequently disposed of with very little bloodshed in a July Revolution in Paris that was engineered mainly by the disgruntled *bourgeoisie* under the tricolour flag, supported by crowds of workmen willing, if necessary, to go to the barricades. The outcome, however, was not a new revolutionary republic but a constitutional monarchy, with Louis Philippe, the new monarch, designated 'King of the French' not 'King of France'. At the same time the 1814 Charter was revised and identified explicitly as a contract between King and People.

Louis Philippe was the son of 'Equality Philip' (*Philippe Egalité*) who had conspired against Louis XVI but had subsequently been guillotined. He had fought as a young man at Valmy, the defensive battle of the Revolution in 1792, and at a critical moment in the July Revolution he now appeared on the same platform as Lafayette, whom some revolutionaries had wished to see appointed as President. There were many historical echoes in all this, although they were echoes that stirred controversies as much as they brought back memories. The celebration of Bastille Day was revived. So, too, was the tricolour flag. But liberty caps were taboo, and after liberty trees had been planted in 1830 and 1831 the planting stopped on the orders of Louis Philippe's first conservative prime minister.

The immediate consequences of the Revolution were more striking outside France than inside, and they might have been sweeping had Louis Philippe been willing to place himself at the head of revolutionary forces in Europe. He was not. As a result events everywhere took their own course. Austria and Prussia remained quiet – for financial reasons Austria could take no action to intervene in events in France – but there was a violent uprising in Brunswick where the ducal palace went up in flames. (There were historical echoes for France too in the name Brunswick.) 'For fifteen years it seemed as if the eternal generative power of the world's history [had been] paralysed', a German liberal wrote years later. 'And then three days sufficed to overturn one throne, and make all the others tremble.'

The first throne to tremble was that of Holland. A successful revolt in Brussels in August 1830 fittingly followed a demonstration after an opera which had an anti-authoritarian plot. (Opera frequently served political purposes in the nineteenth century.) A provisional Belgian government demanded independence, and the Dutch King, William I, who had insisted on making the Dutch language the official language of the whole of his kingdom, was unable to re-establish his authority. The Holy Alliance now seemed to have tumbled. 'Bold ardent hopes' sprang up 'like trees with golden fruit', according to the young German romantic poet, Heinrich Heine, a Jew who moved to exile in Paris in 1831. He had been disappointed when he visited 'materialistic' England a few years earlier as an admirer of Canning. 'Don't send a poet to England', he advised. For Heine it was Paris that was 'the new Jerusalem' and the River Rhine was the River Jordan 'which divides the land of freedom from the land of the Philistines'.

Nonetheless, Heine's fruits had also begun to appear even in Germany before he left it, for liberal constitutions were adopted in several German states, including Saxony, Hanover and Hesse-Cassel, and in May 1832 over 20,000 people from all parts of Germany held a festival at Hambach in the Palatinate at which the tricolour flag was hoisted. Toasts were drunk too to the sovereignty of the people and the brotherhood of nations. In the previous year the tricolour had even flown in Birmingham when Britain was in the throes of a protracted political and constitutional crisis centred on the passing of a parliamentary reform bill, which extended the franchise to a large section of the middle classes. The Whig Prime Minister, Earl Grey, who succeeded Wellington in 1830, believed rightly that political adaptability at the top was required to canalize popular pressure from below. By increasing the electorate by almost a half, the Act would hitch the 'middle ranks of society' to the constitution.

There were further fierce, if less successful, struggles for political and constitutional change elsewhere, with more evidence of repression than of reform. Before further German demonstrations were crushed in 1832 and 1833 – Metternich succeeded in getting the German Diet to carry Six Articles banning political associations and popular meetings – there had been a terrifying revolutionary *débacle* in Poland. The Poles had risen against the Russians in November 1830, but the Polish nobility had made no attempt to win the support of the peasants, and there were fierce divisions among them between 'whites' and 'reds'. When in September 1831 the Russians were able to re-enter Warsaw their revenge was swift. An ordnance of 1833 declared Poland in a 'state of war': it authorized the death or imprisonment of thousands of patriotic Poles, the seizure of Polish lands, the closing of universities, and the military policing of Warsaw. Nearly 10,000 *emigrés* left Poland, most of them travelling to France. Some were to make their way to America, a route followed by thousands later in the century.

The fact that Belgium could secure its independence while Poland was crushed, and that the British could carry a Reform Act through Parliament in 1832 while German states were being warned to accept decisions of the Diet without question, were signs of increasingly sharp and now obvious divisions between the east and west of Europe. The Belgian conflict did not end with the Treaty of London in December 1830, which guaranteed Belgium independence and, a month later, its neutrality. (Talleyrand was the French signatory, and Lord Palmerston, the ex-Canningite Foreign Secretary, the British.) In subsequent divisions, however – about who should be King and where the frontiers should be set – Britain and France drew closer together, standing out as 'liberal' powers arrayed against 'conservative' powers Austria, Prussia and Russia, the so-called 'Northern Courts'.

In Holy Alliance terminology Louis Philippe was no better than a 'king of the barricades'. Yet this was not the judgement of Palmerston, who (with breaks) was to serve as British Foreign Secretary for more years than any other. He welcomed the fact that Louis Philippe preferred entente with Britain to the all-out support for other European revolutions which some of his own supporters were demanding. The King of the French even put on one side the idea of a French ruler of Belgium, his son the Duc de Nemours, and accepted the nomination of Leopold of Saxe-Coburg, uncle of the British Queen, Victoria, who was to come to the throne in 1837. When the King of Holland refused to accept the new arrangements in Belgium, a French army and a British fleet moved together to force him to do so. The new Belgian constitution – with Leopold as 'King of the Belgians' – now constituted a new liberal model, more up-to-date than the American. It was to be widely studied. A royal matchmaker, Leopold reigned until 1865.

The French and British also worked closely together in Portugal and in Spain in 1834, signing a Quadruple Alliance which Metternich, who tried to split them, was anxious should not take on any ideological significance. And in Egypt too in 1833 they supported reconciliation between the Sultan and Mehemet Ali, an intelligent and ambitious rebel, Albanian by origin, who was de facto ruler of Egypt. Once again their interest was not ideological: it lay not in the strenuous efforts of Mehemet Ali to reform Egyptian politics and administration but in the diplomatic and military implications of his en-lightened activities on Constantinople. The main problem there was the role of Russia, and in their combination they were no more successful in protecting the Sultan against the Tsar than they were in safeguarding the independence of Poland. By the Treaty of Unkiar Skelessi in 1833 Russia secured Turkey's agreement to close the strategic Dardanelles to all foreign ships. It was in the same year that Nicholas I described Metternich as his 'chief' and that Metternich 'acquitted' Russia of any aggressive views with regard to the Ottoman Empire. When a second crisis centred on Mehemet Ali's move into Syria in 1839 Britain and France took up different positions, and Palmerston himself worked in cooperation with Metternich to secure the Straits Treaty of 1841 which reversed Unkiar Skelessi (and isolated France).

Meanwhile, Russia had joined with Austria and Turkey in policies of repression in eastern Europe, in Germany and in Italy. After the *Deutscher Bund* had passed its Six Articles, joint commissions were established to monitor all subversive activity and to adjudicate in disputes about constitutions. Nicholas I, along with the rulers of Austria and Prussia, signed the Convention of Münchengratz (October 1833) which recognized the right of any sovereign threatened by revolt (as in the Holy Alliance of 1815) to summon Austria, Prussia and Russia to his aid. 'So long as the union of the three monarchs lasts', said Metternich, 'there will be a chance of safety in the world.' Thereafter until the 1840s Metternich's unflinching determination to maintain 'safety' proved stronger than any desire on the part of the British or French governments to support liberal regimes. The main interest of Palmerston, indeed, was not to change the European balance but to maintain as effective an 'equilibrium' as possible.

In Italy, after Austrian-backed rulers were driven out of Modena and Parma in largely uncoordinated moves in 1831 and after provisional governments had been set up in Bologna and the Papal States, leaving only Lazio under papal rule, the Austrian army had no difficulty in restoring order. Louis Philippe sent 'an army of observation' to Ancona, where it remained until 1838, but it played no part in the subsequent unfolding of events.

NATION AND CLASS

A more interesting development had taken place in 1831, when Giuseppe Mazzini, born in 1805, the year of Austerlitz and Trafalgar, founded Young Italy on French soil at Marseilles. Mazzini, a dedicated advocate of nationalism as a liberal and a liberating force throughout Europe, was influenced by other writers, but he always struck his own notes, and he enrolled more than 60,000 Italian supporters, all under 40 years of age, before he embarked on a bigger but related project to create a Young Europe.

Time was to prove that Mazzini was neither an effective nor a realistic politician: he allowed neither for the strength of alternative ideologies nor for localism and apathy, very strong in Italy both in 1830 and later; and he sacrificed more friends than he converted enemies. Yet he made his presence felt with small publicized raids, even when they turned into fiascos, like a crossing from Switzerland into Savoy in 1834; and his ideology of liberal nationalism deserves to be given pride of place at the opposite end of the political spectrum from 'safety in the world'. It has to be sharply distinguished also from nationalist philosophies that involved chauvinist aggression and the unleashing of the will to dominate. For Mazzini different nationalisms were complementary, not competitive.

There were problems, however, in Mazzini's conception of 'national mission'. He did not believe in Irish nationalism and he was unimpressed by all versions of nationalism different from his own. After reading the writings of the exiled Polish poet Adam Mickiewicz, who lived in Paris, but always thought that Poland, the 'Christ among the nations', might have as its mission the demonstration of national redemption through suffering, Mazzini continued to give 'primacy' to Italy in relation to the remaking of Europe: 'the destiny of Italy is that of the world', 'God's word among the nations'. Not all French nationalists agreed. Whatever Louis Philippe and his ministers might say about the limits of French foreign policy, there were many Frenchmen – not all of them Bonapartists – who believed that it was France that had a special duty to act as 'the pilot of the ship of humanity'. No one believed this more strongly than Victor Hugo.

In Germany 'nationalism' took a different form. It was identified with trust in the *Volk*, a word very different in derivation and orientation from the French words *peuple* and *nation* (with Italian and Spanish equivalents), which were now bracketed together by definition. J. G. Herder, the first German philosopher of nationalism, who died in 1803, thought in terms not of national power but of national cultures based on a shared language. Nationalism, he believed, would appeal to young people seeking 'unity of spirit'. As it subsequently developed, German nationalism appealed to the unsophisticated young more than to the meditative old and to the heart as much as to the mind. Throughout its development the word 'reason' became suspect. The young, it was appreciated, might live long enough to see Germany actually converted from a geographical expression (as Metternich thought of it) or a cluster of historical associations and loyalties (as Friedrich Wilhelm III thought of it) into a nation state appearing on the European map.

Where its borders would be drawn was not clear. Friedrich Ludwig Jahn, who encouraged the postwar youth movement to adopt a black, gold and red flag for a new Germany, thought that the state should be a big state – including Switzerland, the Netherlands and Denmark – and have its own capital, Teutonia. Nor was he alone in this. Others were prepared to include all the Habsburg lands. Prophets could evade the issue. Heinrich Laube, who prophesied the end of nationalities and the coming of a new European republic in the first part of his *Das Junge Europe* (1833), had changed his mind when he wrote the second part in 1838. The German nation now came first.

Nationalism was a movement which emerged in the immediate postwar years when distinctions between different kinds of 'movements' were not being closely drawn. Later, however, they were, particularly after the word 'class' came to be used more widely, replacing, though not at once and not universally, the old language of ranks, orders and degrees. In Prussia, indeed, and even earlier in some of the smaller German states, representation through local Estates was restored after 1815 and in most parts of Germany power remained with the nobility, entrenched in an upper Estate, as it had been in France before 1789. There was a gulf between them and the merchant 'middle classes', strong in the Rhineland. Both in Germany and in Italy as well as in France the words *bourgeois* and *bourgeoisie* had a long history, leading back to the medieval city. It was to prove awkward, however, that in the German language *burgerlich* meant both *bourgeois* and 'civil': there was no distinction, therefore, between *bourgeois* society and civil society. And this could lead to confusion – then and in the late-twentieth century when the term 'civil society' was revived in political debate.

Such terms were used far less often in Britain, where pragmatism prevailed in the pursuit both of domestic and of foreign policy, but it was in Britain that a new entrepreneurial employer class emerged, proud of its energy and its will to innovate, and looking for profits, not for fees or rents. It was of this class that Marx and Engels, sons of well-to-do families of converted Jews living in the Rhineland, were thinking most when in exile in Britain they looked to a revolutionary future. They were to set out their forecasts in unforgettable language in a *Communist Manifesto*, written in six weeks and published in London in 1848. Drafted by Marx, although Engels contributed facts, money and ideas, it bore on its title page words which were to become famous, 'Workers of the World Unite'. They were to claim later (and far more systematically) that past, present and future could be approached 'scientifically' – as could revolution itself. Out of facts and ideas derived from the German philosophical dialectic of Hegel, from French histories of the 'class struggle', and from British political economy, particularly the labour theory of value of the English political economist David Ricardo, they forged a new synthesis.

Classes developed through movement, through economic change more than through political change, and their identities, often blurred at the edges, were established neither by law nor by custom. They were articulated through common experiences, including 'combination', and through conflict. It is more dangerous, however, to generalize about 'classes', as Marx and Engels often did, even 'ruling classes', some of whom were very suspicious of all forms of movement, than it is to generalize about bureaucracy, whoever the rulers were. A close look at both the working class in the making and the *bourgeoisie* during these years directs attention as much to occupational and regional group variation within each class as to incipient or imminent class solidarity. In continental Europe the small-town *bourgeoisie*, entrenched and often traditionalist, could be comfortable, even deferential, in its own local communities, which were sharply distinguished from new industrial cities; its members were by no means attached in any obvious way to the cause of political movement.

Nor at a different level were shopkeepers (some serving the aristocracy), merchants (some very wealthy), industrialists (still a small group numerically, but some of them rich), and bankers, the greatest of whom constituted an ambitious *haute bourgeoisie* which might, like the Rothschilds, operate through a network of international links. The founder of the House, as it was called, Mayer Anselm Rothschilds born in Frankfurt in 1743, established moneylending branches in continental Europe and England (one son settled in Naples). Solomon in Vienna was on good terms with Metternich. As Metternich well knew, the Rothschilds were less attached to general causes than lawyers or 'intellectuals', the latter a term little used in Britain.

British university students, unlike their European counterparts, for the most part stayed out of political movements. In continental Europe they were vocal representatives of a new generation. So too were poets, who in France and Germany might be stronger advocates of 'movement' than railway promoters. Alphonse Marie Louis de Lamartine, who was to play a key role in the French Revolution of 1848, wrote to a friend 11 years earlier that 'the only road to power' lay 'in identifying oneself with the very spirit of a victorious movement at a time when no one can gainsay you'. Deciding on the right movement was, as the young Marx appreciated, perhaps the biggest of all the decisions that revolutionaries had to take.

Only in Britain, Belgium and parts of Germany and Austria was there an industrial labour force employed in mines, workshops, mills and factories during the 1830s and 1940s that was big enough to count politically, and even there the 'force' was largely localized in industrial regions. Handicraft rather than machine production remained the dominant form of manufacturing employment in most countries, and during the 1840s there were always handicraft workers in France, Germany and Austria who behaved like Luddites in Britain a generation before, destroying machines that seemed to be taking away their employment. Everywhere, despite urban growth, more workers laboured on the land than in the towns and cities, and even in Britain it was not until the year 1851 that the urban population exceeded the rural.

Nonetheless, it did not require industrialization – and most of it was still small-scale even in Britain – for the *bourgeoisie* to assert its claims against the aristocracy or for socialist ideas to emerge in towns and cities. It was because of the sense of continuing revolution, hated though it was by substantial sections of the *bourgeoisie*, that socialist manifestos were drafted. 'Labour had arrived before capital was ready for it.' In France itself, where industrial progress was relatively slow after 1815, there was a profusion of socialist ideas, many of them propounded by intellectuals who knew the inside of libraries better than the insides of factories. Indeed, the word 'socialism' in its modern sense was invented in France.

The views of the socialists, most of whom Marx dismissed as 'utopian', diverged. Christian socialists looked back to Jesus as the first of the *sans culottes*. Louis Blanc, who published his *L'Organisation du Travail* (The Organisation of Labour) in 1839, believed in using the power of the state to control the market. Charles Fourrier and his disciples canvassed the creation of socialist communities, *phalanges*, as did the British cooperator Robert Owen, who used very different, and less bizarre, language.

St Simon and his followers, who in the 1820s used the word 'masses' as well as the word 'classes', thereby pointing to a further new social scenario, believed in the necessity of industrialization. Past society had been a military society in which warriors had been supported by priests. Future society would depend on enterprise, not on force or reverence. St Simon's opinions evolved, and as they evolved they strongly influenced thinkers outside as well as inside France. Auguste Comte, founder of 'positivism', had followers everywhere, believing that 'the determination of the future' should be 'the direct aim of political science, as in the case of other positive sciences.' Marx too conceived of his task explicitly not as that of 'trying to bring some kind of utopian system into being', but 'of consciously participating in an historical process by which society is being transformed before our very eyes'.

FACTS AND *ISMS*

The sense of there being a 'system' or complementary or competitive 'systems' was strengthened between 1830 and 1848, although there were some thinkers and writers, like the socialist Pierre Josèphe Proudhon, who distrusted all dogmas, and the Danish Christian philosopher Sören Kierkegaard who resisted all systems. Many of the systems were treated as *isms* by their antagonists if not always by their proponents. 'Romanticism', 'Capitalism', 'Socialism', 'Utopianism', 'Liberalism' and 'Positivism' provide six of the leading examples. Most of the proponents of each system looked to the future, as the last of the eighteenth-century *philosophes* of the Enlightenment, the Marquis de Condorcet, had done. Believing in the perfectibility of man, he offered the readers of his *Esquisse*, a 'Historical Picture of the Progress of the Human Spirit', published posthumously in 1795, a vision of the human race emancipated from its shackles and consequently released from the empire of fate. But Condorcet did not tread that path himself. He was gaoled by the Jacobins during the Terror, and after writing his book died in prison, probably by suicide, before he could be sent to the guillotine.

St Simon, who completed a new *Encyclopédie*, was in line with Condorcet in setting his golden age in the future, not in the past. And Marx too envisaged a 'classless society' and the withering away of the state after the class war had been won by the proletariat. The French Liberal Catholic the Abbé Lamennais, a French liberal Catholic, put Church before State and dreamed in 1832 of converting the Pope to liberal Catholicism. His journal was called *L'Avenir* ('The Future'), and his pamphlets, which stressed the need for unselfishness and justice, were very widely read.

Influencing all political development then and into the 1840s were far-reaching structural changes – urban growth; industrialization; and, above all, new communications patterns. A 'railway age' had been ushered in when a line between Manchester and Liverpool was opened in 1830 (Wellington was present at the opening), and by 1838, the year when Russia built its first railway, there were almost 500 miles in operation in Britain. From the start, railways were symbols of movement (and speed), stimulating the imagination even more than the steam power that moved the locomotives. But they were far more than symbols. They reduced transport costs, opened up markets and created an unprecedented demand for coal and iron. Both freight and ideas were carried by railway and soon after its introduction by telegraph, a new invention with which they were quickly associated. Small countries could benefit from railways as well as countries with great spaces. In the middle of the 1830s Belgium was ahead of Britain in having evolved a 'railway policy', and the line from Brussels to Malines carried more passengers in its first year than all the railways in Britain.

It was to facilitate and increase the volume of movement of freight across customs barriers that Prussia, not Austria, took the lead in 1828 in creating a *Zollverein* ('Customs Union') built on a Prussian tariff of 1818 which was soon to be a matter of concern to Metternich who saw it as a 'state within a state' but who knew that Austrian industries were then not sufficiently advanced to participate in it. The *Zollverein* was subsequently expanded in size and scope until in 1834 it included 18 states in central and southern Germany with a population of 23 million and a total area of 112,000 square miles. Its political advantages to Prussia were small: its economic advantages to Prussians substantial. By eliminating internal customs barriers it widened German markets and by sheltering its members behind the Prussian tariff of 1818 it restricted imports of manufactured goods from other parts of Europe: the duty on them was 10 per cent *ad valorem*. Fear of German economic competition from the *Zollverein* was expressed in the British Parliament in the late 1830s, and while the first administrator of the *Zollverein* was a Prussian admirer of Adam Smith, in Prussia a strong protectionist strand prevailed in Georg Friedrich List's *The National System of Political Economy* (1844). List had been an exile in America, where British free trade views never commanded universal assent.

America figured in European history in a variety of different ways between 1815 and 1848, but mainly because it too was both a symbol of open movement and a real place to which real people moved. It was people, however, not governments, who determined the pattern of overseas emigration, sometimes under the pressure of fear of their own governments; and every year in order to find new hope in a new land large numbers of people crossed the oceans, an increasing proportion by steam ship, often suffering great hardship on the way. Emigration from Britain alone rose from about 57,000 in 1830 to 90,000 in 1840 and 280,000 in 1850. The emigrants were drawn by more than dreams. The hard facts of daily life in Europe during the 1830s and 1840s drove some of the most enterprising people to seek to better their condition, and such betterment was certainly more than a dream. 'Now father', one British emigrant wrote home in 1848 after reaching Australia, 'I think this is the Promised Land.'

Many moved from the countryside, some from the great cities. By 1848, 47 towns in Europe had a population greater than 100,000 – 28 of them in industrializing Britain – and all were centres of problems even while they were also centres of local pride, often expressed in rivalry with other cities. Industrial Manchester became the shock city of the age, and every social observer or critic who wanted to see how society was developing thought it necessary either to learn about it or preferably to visit it. Everywhere conditions in industrial centres and bulging capital cities received far more attention from social commentators than villages and country estates, although social conditions were often bad there also.

The hardest of all the European facts, perhaps, were those of the Great Famine which affected Ireland and large parts of eastern Europe too in the mid-1840s. By the end of the Irish famine the Irish population had decreased by a third. This was a grim reminder that the main check on the optimism of Condorcet was the pressure of population on resources. It was not so much Condorcet's own fate in the Paris of the French Revolution that made his vision seem unduly optimistic, but the critique of it written by the English clergyman and political economist Thomas Malthus, whose *Essay on the Principle of Population* was first published anonymously in 1798: it was to go through many later editions in expanded form, beginning with a two-volume edition of 1803 under his own name. The first essay began as a refutation of Condorcet and of the English social philosopher William Godwin.

Malthus's view that population always rises faster (geometrically) than the means of subsistence (rising arithmetically) had a continuing influence far outside anti-revolutionary circles. Until 1750 Europe's population had grown slowly as it had done during the previous century. From 1750 onwards, however, when there were 120 to 140 million Europeans, the rate of growth began to accelerate, and by the time that Malthus wrote there were between 180 and 190 million. Growth was to continue in even more spectacular fashion – but not evenly – throughout the nineteenth century, with the population of France – and no one foresaw this – growing less than that of any other European country. Famine had nothing to do with that. Nor had another of Malthus's checks on population growth – 'moral restraint'. Demographers look for other explanations as they examine the age of marriage, family size, and, above all, nutritional factors influencing death rates. The facts of demographic change began to be collected in dicennial census returns during the early nineteenth century – Sweden had led the way before the century began, and the first British census was taken in 1801.

The urge to collect statistics, which had been described in the *Encyclopaedia Britannica* in 1797 as a word 'recently introduced' from Germany, was apparent everywhere, particularly, perhaps, in Britain and France. Statistical facts took the form both of official statistics in documents like the great British 'blue books' (the reports of committees of inquiry) and of unofficial statistics collected by social investigators and voluntary societies. They were statistics relating to public health or to population – still rising in Europe despite emigration and reaching over 260 million by 1848, 75 million more than in 1800 – but also to industrial production, trade, public health, literacy and, not least, crime. One common use of the word 'classes' related not to economics but to morals. The perception that there were 'dangerous classes', particularly in the great cities, was shared across national frontiers. So too – and the concept was refined later – was the sense of the existence of a distinct 'criminal class'.

The health statistics were particularly important, for it was through the analysis of differential mortality rates (different death rates in different regions of a country or even in different parts of the same city) that statisticians with a social purpose came to the crucial conclusion that it would be possible to eliminate some local and regional differences if proper social policies were pursued. Faced not only with endemic diseases, like typhus, which were related to poverty, but epidemic diseases, particularly cholera, which struck people from all classes (including one of Louis Philippe's prime ministers), they talked boldly of challenging Fate by deliberately altering people's chances of life and death through the public provision of better water supply and sewage systems. This was not a dream, as it might have been in the eighteenth century, but an intention that could now be fulfilled (with the help of engineers even more than of doctors). Supplying clean water – and there were large parts of Europe where this was not assured – preceded the large-scale manufacture and distribution of cheap soap.

Meanwhile, the supply of statistics increased annually. In France, social investigators related health to housing and housing to crime. It was to take many more decades to achieve by public policy an improvement in housing conditions that conservatives, believing in the family and the home, favoured even more than radicals. It was less easy to deal with housing issues – jerry building, overcrowding, and lack of necessary domestic amenities – than it was to deal with collective measures to improve public health. Sewers came before bathrooms. In 1829 Louis Villermé was one of the founders of the *Annales d'hygiène publique et du médicine légale*, the first regular journal in the world to concentrate on problems of public health. 'The pursuit of statistical enquiries', the tenth Report of the Statistical Society of London claimed in 1844, 'has already made such progress . . . as henceforth to be a necessity of the age, and one of its most honourable characteristics.'

Not all commentators on social change put their trust in statistics. The quest to collect them was sometimes satirized, sometimes described as a fad. For some novelists and poets social problems were better explored through literature than through statistical tables. They preferred to focus imaginatively on human experience. Fortunately, there were some statisticians who could push forward imaginatively into difficult issues of social analysis. For example, the Belgian statistician Adolphe Quetelet, who loved to explore 'laws of large numbers', examined probabilities as well as aggregates and rates of change and, for good or ill, introduced the notion of 'the average man'.

Few of the social investigators of the 1830s or 1840s were socialists. Indeed in England, Edwin Chadwick, Bentham's last secretary, was associated in the public mind not only with public health reform (the first British Public Health Act was passed in 1848) but with the earlier introduction of a controversial new Poor Law in 1834 which was also based on Benthamite postulates. Debates on how to deal with the poor were paralleled in other countries and were often bitter. They had been common in the late-eighteenth century. The 1834 Act, therefore, was a European landmark. By abolishing all outdoor relief for the poor and forcing them into 'workhouses', it was believed, individuals would become more self-reliant, public money would be saved and the care of the poor, previously associated with charity, would be systematized. Conditions for the inmates of the workhouses were to be made deliberately worse than those in the worst forms of alternative employment. Not surprisingly, the poor compared the workhouses with Bastilles and their own conditions with those of black slaves.

Opposition to the Poor Law of 1834 in Britain played a major part in triggering off the great protest movement of Chartism, the first specifically large-scale working-class movement in Europe, as Marx and Engels recognized. Another element in the snowballing protest was the demand for legislative limitation of factory working hours for women and children, still a major element in the labour force, particularly in the textile industry (the hare among the tortoises in the industrial race). A substantial instalment of factory reform was achieved in Britain in 1847, one year after the repeal of the corn laws, with some of the corn law repealers opposing the reform on the grounds that by extending the scope of factory inspectors it constituted governmental interference with industry. This was a relatively new political alignment. So, too, was rural aristocratic interest in the conditions of the urban poor as expressed, for example, by England's seventh Earl of Shaftesbury, an Evangelical reformer who was also a Tory. In Prussia too there were strong paternalistic strains in the aristorcracy, and in 1839 a factory law was introduced (if not fully enforced) prohibiting the employment of children under nine years old and restricting the working day of children aged between 9 and 16.

Politics centring on the improvement of public health, on social intervention in factories and on measures to deal with pauperism – a serious problem in all countries, industrial or not – were 'social politics', and for many people without the right to vote at elections, and for some who had this right, this was the kind of politics that really mattered. It was complex, not simple, politics. The British Chartists, who drafted their key document, the Charter, in 1838, started with facts – the facts of a limited franchise and a grim 'condition of England' – but they had their dreams also, dreams of converting the British Parliament into a People's Parliament based on an electoral system with manhood suffrage, voting by ballot, annual elections, and no property qualifications for members. When their parliamentary reforms had been achieved there would be roast beef on every man's table.

When the Chartists began to agitate during a severe business depression, the most serious depression since the industrial revolution, the first important measure of parliamentary reform had already been carried in Britain. This, indeed, afforded the Chartists with one of their main arguments: they were only asking Parliament, they said, to grant the working classes what had already been granted to the middle classes by the Whigs in the Reform Act of 1832. Yet neither the Whigs nor their opponent Peel, the son of a rich cotton manufacturer, who accepted the implications of the 1832 Act and who won a general election under the new franchise in 1841, had any sympathy with Chartist demands. The Chartists were to prove the strength of the new working-class presence in British life – for the propertied classes a source of fear – but they seldom, if ever, threatened revolution. Many of them believed in the motto 'peaceably if we may, forcefully if we must', but there was little well-organized physical force in Chartist politics. Nor – until it was too late, in 1848 – was there a real junction between Chartists and disgruntled Irishmen, chafing against the 1800 Act of Union with Britain. The fact that the most popular Chartist leader, Feargus O'Connor, was himself Irish did not make for a Chartist-Irish alliance, since O'Connor was distrusted by (and himself distrusted) Daniel O'Connell, the Irish leader in Parliament.

From 1841 to 1846 Peel carried out a programme of major reforms – including tax reforms, strengthening of the banking system and in 1846 the repeal of the corn laws – that laid the foundations for the security and prosperity of mid-nineteenth-century Britain. For Richard Cobden, founder of the British Anti-Corn Law League, which carried out an efficient extra-parliamentary campaign, Peel had come to represent 'the idea of the age'. Yet Peel did not think in these terms, and carried repeal only at the expense of dividing his own Conservative Party, through his efforts one of the first parliamentary parties in Europe to have an organized base in the constituencies. Now a large section of it, including the squirearchy, turned against him. It was rallied by the brilliant rhetoric of Benjamin Disraeli, a young politician in the making, for whom being a Jew (if a Christian Jew) was only a handicap to overcome. More important, therefore, than any social alliance in the British politics of the 1840s was a political rupture.

What happened in 1846 had long-term political consequences of great importance. The Whigs, a predominantly aristocratic party with a 'tail' of Protestant dissenters (or nonconformists), political radicals, Irishmen and ex-Canningites like Palmerston, now, after Peel's death (by accident) in 1850 were gradually able to assimilate 'Peelites', of whom Gladstone was one, and thereby dominate British politics for more than a quarter-century. Yet *Whiggery*, not an *ism*, lost its power for during the mid-Victorian period there was to be a gradual transformation of British party politics that started at the grass-roots level and culminated in the emergence of a new kind of liberal party.

The facts of British politics, which permitted such important adaptations, contrasted sharply with the facts of French politics in the reign of Louis Philippe, 'the July monarchy'. The 'Citizen' King admired Britain, as did one of his most able ministers, the Protestant François Guizot, who believed in economic progress and parliamentary government. Yet there was still no industrial revolution in France and committed republicans continued to look back to the Constituent Assembly, to the Convention or to Napoleon, about whom songs were sung and whose body was brought back to Paris in 1840 and interred in imposing surroundings in the Invalides.

The red flag flew in the streets of Paris at the funeral of the radical General Lamarque (a cholera victim) in 1832, and there was a serious working-class insurrection in industrial Lyons in November 1831 when the local garrison was driven out of the city.[3] Five years later black flags were carried through the streets by marching silk weavers. This was the year when the first popular French daily newspaper *La Presse* was launched. Seven years later the radical newspaper *Le Réforme* was founded. Nonetheless, plots, assassinations and insurrections did not greatly disturb parliamentary politics between 1830 and 1848. Reform bills were introduced but defeated, and the opposition was always divided. There were no fewer than 17 different governments holding office between 1830 and 1840.

Louis Philippe, ambitious and determined to rule as well as to reign, had few Napoleonic qualities and was the inevitable target of satirists and cartoonists. The most famous cartoon of him, often reproduced, showed him as a pear: the most revealing showed him wearing city clothes over a suit of armour. He loved restoring palaces, but he accepted a civil list of Fr. 12 million instead of Charles X's Fr. 32 million. The Chamber as a whole was subject to satire too. Only one out of every 200,000 Frenchmen could vote, as against one out of 30 in Britain after the Reform Act of 1832.

It was generally recognized, moreover, that many French deputies – perhaps most – put their own private interests before those of the nation. So, too, did ministers: two of them were involved, for example, in an attempt to rig the salt market. While the British carried free trade, the French continued to pursue the protectionist measures of the Restoration; and while the British not only enjoyed a railway boom but actually built railways, the French mainly talked about them and speculated in them. There were only 1,200 miles of railway track in France in 1848, less than a quarter of the British mileage. (And, an equally pertinent comparison, there were by then far more railways in Germany than in France.)

In exile after 1848, Guizot, who had not hesitated to use the police to 'muzzle the country' in his last spell in office, wrote a flattering biography of Peel: his own accomplishments were less lasting. Nor was the motto with which the Louis Philippe regime came to be associated, *Enrichissez Vous* ('get rich'), which is said to have been devised by Guizot himself, calculated to make for acceptable leadership in a period of social tension. In 1840 a republican publicist claimed that seven million out of eight million of the 'active population', the *menu peuple*, were potential revolutionaries because of the poverty of their lives. The great French novelist, Honoré de Balzac, much admired by Marx, caught the distinctive atmosphere of the period. Some of his descriptions had a photographic character about them appropriate to a country that had displayed photography for the first time in 1839.

In Paris, unlike the rest of France growing rapidly in population, the financial and social scene was often hectic. It was the centre of finance, trade, administration and communication, and there was no comparable centre either of activity or of authority. The provinces, rural and urban, were more set in their ways. Speculation was frowned upon, and there was more fear of disaster than display of entrepreneurial drive, more grumbling about usury than effort to widen the provision of necessary credit. 'We are staunch conservatives', Guizot wrote to the French Ambassador in Rome in 1846. 'It is the first and natural responsibility of governments. We are all the more staunch conservatives because our country has been through a series of revolutions.' It was only in retrospect that it could be claimed that while Britain had avoided revolution, France was moving towards one.

Nevertheless, one of Louis Philippe's most unwise remarks was a comment he made in January 1848 to General von Radowitz, the plenipotentiary of the King of Prussia, 'Tell your master that there are two things that cannot happen again in France – one is revolution, the other is war', for in the same month Tocqueville made a prophetic speech in the French Chamber in which he warned that there was trouble ahead. (He used the word 'storm' not 'revolution'.) 'It is true that there is no visible sign of disorder, but that is because the disorder is deep down in people's hearts. The ultimate reason for a man's losing authority is because he is not fit to hold it.' The speech was greeted with laughter.

The timing of the collapse of the French monarchy has been directly related to a serious worsening of the economic situation in 1847 following the same bad harvest (of corn and potatoes) in 1846 that provided the occasion for the Irish famine and for Britain's repeal of the corn laws. Grain prices rose to new heights in May 1847. Political factors were more directly relevant, however, than economic facts. What was felt in many political circles to be the 'real character' of Louis Philippe's regime was exposed in a series of scandals involving prominent figures in the news. In 1847 and 1848, therefore, there were two kinds of relevant social politics, the social politics of the deprived poor and of the grumbling *bourgeoisie* and the social politics of High Society. 'There is great disquiet in Paris', the *Gazette de la France* reported on 16 January 1848. 'The funds are falling every day. In politics people have stopped being reasonable.'

There had also been a royal excursion into dynastic diplomacy in France that had brought friction with Britain. The King wanted Queen Isabella of Spain to marry one of his sons, and in 1847 and 1848 he seemed to be pressing this plan to a successful conclusion. Palmerston, back in power as British Foreign Secretary after the collapse of Peel's government, now used the occasion to rouse British opinion against the French regime. Under Peel, the entente cordiale of the early 1830s had been extended, Queen Victoria had visited France twice, and Louis Philippe had been received at Windsor, much to the annoyance of the rulers of Austria, Russia and Prussia. But Palmerston, who had broken the entente once before (on Mehemet Ali and the Turkish question in 1840) before Peel returned to power, did not scruple to break it again: he even communicated to some of Guizot's political opponents (Thiers, who had held government posts in 1836, 1840 and 1848, was prominent among them) political documents calculated to compromise the French government.

The end was not premeditated. A series of well attended 'reform banquets', *bourgeois* demonstrations in favour of an extension of the franchise, spread from Paris to the provinces in 1847 and 1848; and when it became clear that neither the King nor Guizot had any intention of yielding to pressure (as Grey was said by his opponents to have done) protest stiffened. While the socialist Louis Blanc declaimed that the 'phantom of revolution' was present at every feast, the romantic poet Alphonse de Lamartine, sometimes described as 'the French Byron', chose more appropriate language to describe the situation when he spoke of a 'revolution of contempt'. The press, particularly *La Réforme* and *Le National*, played a key role at this time even when it merely reported.

At the banquets toasts to the 'King of the French People' were proposed before the speeches, but there were also toasts to 'the improvement in the conditions of the working class'. From the outset 'real' revolutionaries were in a minority, but on 22 February 1848 after the banning of a banquet rioting broke out in Paris with students joining forces with artisans at newly erected barricades. On the following day after sections of the National Guard had joined the rioters, the King dismissed Guizot and tried to replace him first by Comte Molé and then by Thiers before losing confidence in himself, abdicating, and fleeing in disguise to Britain on 24 February. A majority in the French Chamber probably would have accepted his nine-year-old grandson as his successor, but the Paris crowds, invading the Assembly, ensured that with the help of the radical press this would not be the solution. Simultaneously, a republic was proclaimed in the Paris Town Hall. Lamartine, given charge of foreign affairs, extolled the spirit of freedom rising from the ruins of a 'retrograde regime', and in language as dated as that of the Holy Alliance in 1815 asserted the 'sublime mystery of universal sovereignty'.

THE SPRINGTIME OF LIBERTY:
THE DAWN OF THE REVOLUTIONS OF 1848

The February Revolution in France and the consequent inauguration of the French Second Republic heralded a whole series of further revolutions that swept the capital cities of Europe, including Vienna and Berlin, during the exceptionally beautiful spring of 1848. There was even a massive Chartist demonstration in London on 10 April 1848 when the Chartists were joined for the first time by supporters of Young Ireland, an Irish nationalist group that had sprung into prominence after O'Connell's death in 1847. The accent there and elsewhere was on youth.

The new provisional government of the French Second Republic, heterogeneous in make-up, included a former opposition politician, Alexandre Ledru-Rollin, at the key Ministry of the Interior, Lamartine at the Ministry of Foreign Affairs, and Blanc, who insisted that the revolution should proclaim the right to work as well as the right to vote. In addition to fixing elections by universal suffrage for early April – this meant an increase in the electorate from 25,000 to nine million – the provisional government also set up 'national workshops' in Paris to provide labour for the unemployed. On paper the 'right to work' was guaranteed, while the length of the working day was reduced by one hour. Meanwhile, great caution was shown in dealings with revolutionaries abroad, who looked to Paris for leadership, while in phrases, at least, the provisional government saluted 'the great European republic', a federation of free peoples.

Such phrases were not needed to stir citizens of other countries into action. Before the February Revolution began, a short civil war in Switzerland had ended in the victory of the liberal over the Roman Catholic cantons – with Metternich having been unable to intervene – and Switzerland now emerged as a federal state. There had also been a January revolt at Palermo in Sicily, the poorest part of Italy, against Ferdinand II of Naples, who was forced to offer a liberal constitution for the whole of his kingdom based on the French constitution of 1830 in the hope, unrealized, that this would stop the Sicilians from pressing for independence. There was a victory for 'constitutionalism' in Germany too, in Baden, where the liberal leader demanded the immediate summoning of a German national Parliament.

There had been several signs before 1848 both in Italy and in Germany that liberalism was at last in the ascendant. Indeed, a liberal-sounding Pope, Pius IX, had been elected in 1846 against expectations, and his papal reign began with an amnesty, a loosening of controls on the press and the creation of a state council of lawyers to advise him on foreign affairs. Decisions were taken too to build railway lines in the Papal States and to create a telegraph system. Pius's liberalism was not to prove durable, but at that time he seemed to echo the hopes of Vincenzo Gioberti, an eloquent Italian advocate of an Italian confederation of princes under the presidency of the Pope; and when in 1847 Metternich ordered Austrian troops to occupy the papal city of Ferrara Pius circularized the great powers in protest, and Carlo Alberto, King of Piedmont-Sardinia, offered to assist the Pope with troops. Metternich withdrew from Ferrara in December 1847. Piedmont-Sardinia would obviously have a crucial part to play in any moves towards Italian unification, and on 8 February 1848 Carlo Alberto I announced a draft new constitution which incorporated a bicameral parliament, elected on a limited franchise, and a citizens' militia.

For liberalism and nationalism to triumph either in Italy or in Germany it was just as essential that there should be a revolution in the multinational Austrian Empire and that Metternich should be removed from the European stage as it was that there should be a revolution in France. It was in Budapest rather than in Vienna, however, that the chain of events began that was to lead to Metternich's fall. On 3 March, Lajos Kossuth, who was to emerge as one of the heroes of 1848 (and then as one of the victims), delivered an impassioned speech to the Hungarian Diet – consisting only of the nobility, a huge group in Hungary, one in 20 of the population – demanding an end to absolutism and to centralized bureaucracy. 'Unnatural political systems', he told his fellow members, 'sometimes have a long life, for it takes a long time to exhaust people's patience. But some of these political systems do not grow stronger as they grow older, and there comes a moment when it would be dangerous to extend their life.'

These were well chosen words, and on 6 March petitions were circulating in Vienna also demanding free institutions and a free press. The fall of Metternich was accomplished and announced in Vienna on a bright spring day a week later, when – after skirmishes in the streets and arguments behind closed doors in which Metternich urged resistance – he was dismissed by the Emperor and left the country to join Guizot in London. They were soon to meet on the steps of the British Museum.

A strictly pertinent question to ask is 'Did the revolutions of 1848 cause the fall of Metternich or did the fall of Metternich cause the revolutions?'[4]

The feeble-minded Austrian Emperor Ferdinand, who himself was to abdicate later in the year (his abdication had been discussed in 1847), was willing to step down to protect the dynasty, although he was unaware of the full ramifications of Metternich's fall. Equally unaware were those sections of the nobility who pressed for Metternich to go, believing that he had surrounded himself with a 'forest of bayonets'. There were, indeed, some people, including the poet Franz Grillparzer, who considered that Metternich should have retired long before, after the death of the Emperor Franz I in 1835. Yet no-one had acted to get rid of him then or later. Now the Emperor in his capacity as King of Hungary accepted what on paper were far-reaching reforms, and that too was to have ramifications of which few were aware.

Once in exile – and it proved a brief one – Metternich, turned to autobiography, like other exiles, and blamed in public the nobility, Hungarian, Italian, Austrian, as he had previously blamed them in private. 'To the list of symptoms of a sick, degenerate age', he wrote in 1850, 'belongs the completely false position which the nobility all too often adopts. It was they nearly everywhere who lent a hand to the confusion that was being prepared.' He had less to say of a financial crisis in Vienna, near bankruptcy, which had led him to appeal to the Rothschilds for urgent help in 1847. 'If the devil fetches me', he told Solomon Rothschild, 'he will fetch you too.'

Students – and their professors, hitherto quiet – were among the most active in the street-fighting in Vienna which preceded Metternich's fall, as were craft and factory workers who, like French and British workers, were feeling the strains of the economic depression: large numbers were unemployed. And when it came to the crunch Metternich had a surprisingly small police force at his disposal in the streets – only a 1,000, far fewer than Louis Philippe – with a municipal guard of 14,000 men. It was a newly formed civil guard and a student legion that now assumed control. Significantly there were no demands for a republic, but a new government, led by Count Kolowrat, who had worked (sometimes disloyally) with Metternich, promised freedom of the press and the convocation of delegates from the provincial Estates to frame a new constitution.

There were many different and contradictory elements in the subsequent disturbances (liberal, nationalist, peasant and, not least, anti-Semitic) inside the sprawling Habsburg Empire; and soon the great cities of Prague, Budapest, Milan and Venetia were all in the grip of revolutionary fever. By the end of March Hungary had passed the so called 'March laws', accepted by Ferdinand, that could have transformed the country from a feudal into a modern state. They proclaimed equality before the law, abolished censorship of the press and took away from the nobility (this was the one sacrifice they made) their exemption from taxation. In Milan, with a population of 200,000, successful street-rioting (18–23 March), passing down to history as 'the Five Days of Milan', forced the veteran Austrian general Count Josef Radetzky, who had fought against Napoleon, to leave the city with his 13,000 troops. 'The whole country', he told Vienna, was in revolt. In Venice (there was no direct connection between events in the two cities), Daniele Manin, who had been imprisoned in January for urging moderate constitutional reforms, proclaimed a restored republic after a city crowd had raided a medieval armoury and the Opera House in search of weapons.

In Piedmont-Sardinia reformers turned for help to Carlo Alberto, untrusted in his own country and outside, but who now acted on the advice of his chief minister Count Camillo de Cavour, who a year earlier had founded a newspaper, *Il Risorgimento*, to work for a liberal, but monarchical Italy. For Cavour 'the supreme hour of the Piedmontese monarchy now had struck'. 'The state would be lost if we did not fight'. In consequence, troops under Carlo Alberto's command arrived in Milan on 26 March after Radetzky had already withdrawn, proclaiming that 'the destinies of Italy are maturing and a happier future is opening up for those who bravely stand up for their rights against the oppressor'. He was unsuccessful. Neither a liberal nor a romantic, he fell from power in 1849 after his armies were defeated by the Austrians first at Custozza in July 1848 and next at Novara in March 1949. He had learnt by then that the Lombards of Milan were unhappy about being incorporated in a Piedmontese-Sardinian monarchy governed from Turin.

In Germany, where there was an upsurge of enthusiasm, there were demands everywhere in February and March for the freedom of the press and for constitutional government; and the Diet of the *Deutscher Bund*, meeting in Frankfurt, with a changed composition, cheerfully adopted the black, gold and red flag of Germany. The idea of a national parliament which would include representatives of each German state was successfully canvassed, and on 31 March a 'Pre-Parliament' (*Vorparlament*), the first relatively representative national assembly in Germany, met, also in Frankfurt, to work out the arrangements.

Excitement was high when on 18 May the members of the new Parliament walked in solemn procession to the Paulskirche with church bells ringing and cannon roaring. They included some of the outstanding lawyers, judges, writers, professors, and artists in the various German states, among them Jahn, the poet Ernst Moritz Arndt, the Roman Catholic leader Bishop Ketteler, and the historian Friedrich Christoph Dahlmann, who had been dismissed from his chair at Göttingen University when the reactionary British Duke of Cumberland arrived in Hanover as King in 1837. Dahlmann's *Political Dictionary* and his later study *Politics* had focused on the need for a strong state. To him the state was as natural an institution as the family.

None of this German development would have been possible had not the situation changed in Vienna as well as in Paris. For the time being the Habsburgs were in no position to intervene outside the borders of their Empire, and many members of the Austrian delegation to the Frankfurt Parliament arrived late. Yet there were even bigger changes in the Prussian capital, Berlin, than there were in Vienna. Friedrich Wilhelm IV, who had come to the throne in 1840, had vacillated before 1848 between liberalism and authoritarianism, and now he continued to vacillate in 1848 itself. Willing to reform the *Deutscher Bund*, as advised by his personal friend, General Radowitz, grandson of a Roman Catholic Croatian officer, he had been prepared early in 1848 to summon a congress of German princes in Dresden. Because of the fall of Metternich, who appeared in Dresden on the appointed day on his way to exile, this congress never met.

Berliners discussed the rapidly changing situation in beer gardens, while the citizens of Frankfurt discussed it, like Parisians, in cafes and clubs. There had been 'hunger riots' in 1847. Now there were none, but tension rose in Berlin on 16 March when news of Metternich's fall arrived, and two days later the King issued a proclamation lifting censorship and promising constitutional reforms in Prussia and in the *Bund*. He was cheered by his subjects, but by the end of the day the cheers had turned into groans and the laughter into tears. As crowds of people poured into the squares round his royal palace, the presence of visibly intimidating royal troops created alarm, and after two shots were unintentionally fired by his soldiers, there was fierce fighting in which workers from Berlin's craft guilds were prominent. Some of his subjects took to the barricades, some were taken prisoner or killed.

Now it was the turn of his officers to groan, for on the following morning a sad King, romantic at heart but tantalizingly vacillating in behaviour, issued a new proclamation declaring that while his subjects had been misled he offered them forgiveness and a withdrawal of all troops. As a result he was now compelled to pay his respects to the corpses of some of his subjects killed in the fighting and to appoint a new government headed by a liberal merchant from the Rhineland who felt it was necessary to declare (however vaguely) that 'from now on Prussia will merge into Germany'. At such moments the King was as 'defenceless', wrote the American minister in Berlin, as 'the poorest malefactor of the prisons'.

Later in the spring of 1848, on 22 May, four days after the opening of the Frankfurt Parliament, in which there was only one peasant and not a single industrial worker, the new Prussian National Assembly with a more varied social composition, including peasants, met in Berlin, a still deeply disturbed city over which civil guards could not exercise adequate control. The King spent most of the summer at Potsdam, surrounded by aristocratic conservative friends ('the *Kamarilla*') and well disciplined royal troops. It was unlikely, therefore, that the first gains of an exhilarating 'springtime of liberty' would now be consolidated.

There were to be surprises for many people in many countries in the sequences of events that followed and which are discussed in the next chapter. What already stood out, however, was that the Europe that had been opened up in 1848 after decades of 'order' was unlikely to last. The 1848 revolutions were urban rather than rural and were usually led by 'intellectuals' whose objectives diverged. They had little political experience. Moreover, the workers who took part in them were for the most part not factory workers but journeymen, artisans and small masters, a very different labour force from the industrial proletariat to which Marx and Engels had appealed in the *Communist Manifesto*, published in 1848.

Even in Britain, where there were more organised factory workers than in any other European country, it was not the strength of the working class which was demonstrated in the spring of 1848, but the strength of the middle classes. It did not need elaborate military precautions organized by Wellington or a host of special constables (among them the future Napoleon III, then living in London) to save the city from revolution on the day of Kennington Common. Most of the Chartists did not want one. When Lady Palmerston, wife of Britain's Foreign Secretary, wrote to a friend giving her what she called 'private' details of 'our revolution' she concluded cheerfully, 'I am sure that it is fortunate that the whole thing has occurred, as it has shown the good spirit of our middle classes'.[5]

After April 1848, it still remained to be seen whether social peace in continental Europe would hold. Rulers had shown themselves reluctant to use force to suppress disturbances in the spring of 1848, and some of them, like Friedrich Wilhelm, had yielded even more readily than Louis Philippe. Would government, changed in composition and direction by revolution, act in the same way? Most of the new governments feared social disorder, rural and urban, as much as they hoped for change. So far, at the end of spring there were refugees, but no political prisoners. Would this always be so? Two of the refugees, the German radicals Friedrich Hecker and Gustav von Struve, had attempted a republican coup in Baden while the Pre-Parliament was discussing elections. It was totally ineffective, and both men made away across the Atlantic to the United States.

It was particularly ominous for revolutionaries that throughout the spring of 1848 Russia, where there were many rural but no urban disturbances, was waiting in the wings. Nicholas I had immediately mobilized a large army to support any possible victims of French aggression in February 1848. And although the European situation changed completely after the fall of Metternich and the revolution in Berlin, the great Russian Army – as liberals and nationalists everywhere knew – was still on the alert.

Notes

1. C. Hughes (ed.) *Switzerland and Europe: Essays and Reflections by J. R. Salis* (1971) pp.32–4.
2. Noel Malcom, review of N. Davies and H. Moorhouse, *Microcosm: Portrait of a Central European City* (2002), in *The Sunday Telegraph*, 31, March 2002.
3. For its significance see A. Briggs, 'Social Structure and Politics in Birmingham and Lyons, 1825–1848', in *Collected Essays*, vol. I (1985) pp.231–3.
4. A. Sked, *The Decline and Fall of the Habsburg Empire, 1815–1918* (1989) p.41.
5. Quoted by C. R. Fay, *Huskisson and His Age* (1951), pp.137–8.

Chapter 3

NATION BUILDING, 1848–1878

THE REVOLUTIONS OF 1848 AND THEIR 'LESSONS'

The mere fact of revolution carried with it great excitement in 1848 as it had done in 1789. An entrenched social and political order had collapsed. To everyone who had chafed under that order 'the March days' were days of unparalleled freedom and seemed to offer a future dispensation full of promise. Nonetheless, in every country, too, there were people who thought that Europe was suffering from March madness. There was general agreement on only one point – that the adjective *vormärzlich* ('before March'), like the adjective 'pre-war' in the years after 1918 or 1945, referred to days which were beyond recall.

One former German radical, David Friedrich Strauss, had complained as early as April 1848 that he had lived more happily in pre-revolutionary times, able to devote himself to 'true theory' without bothering himself about how to apply it. That was one individual's response. Another, not dissimilar, was the novelist Adalbert Stifter's in Vienna. The revolution had shown that 'people who are possessed by powerful desires and urges' were not to be trusted. People who promised 'to overwhelm you with immeasurable freedom' were 'mostly men corrupted by the power of their emotions'. These were very different responses from that contained in a Paris placard of March 1848 which read 'When only counter-revolution has had the right to speak for half a century, is it too much to give perhaps a year to liberty?' A contrasting response on the part of large numbers of people during and after the springtime of liberty, not usually put into words, had nothing to do with 'theory' or with past experience. They preferred to put their trust in individual self-help and their own material betterment rather than in communal revolutionary fervour.

Each revolutionary situation had its own history with tangled strands, confusing alignments and contrasting personalities, but there were elements that were common to them all, including ultimate disillusionment. For the twentieth-century American historian Bernadotte Schmitt 1848 was a 'terminus', while for the British historian G. M. Trevelyan, disappointed rather than disillusioned, it was 'the turning point at which modern history failed to turn'.[1] The liberal forces in which Trevelyan, descendant of Macaulay, believed had failed to take charge of events. In June 1848 France, which had led the way to revolution, had provided the first evidence of the despair that could accompany 'reaction', and by the end of 1848 revolutionary causes were in danger everywhere. It was not until 1849, however, that the revolutionary fires were finally put out in Germany and in central Europe. The Russians then played the role of firemen in a way that they had not been allowed to play the part of policemen after 1815. Authority had triumphed.

Both sides learned lessons from 1848 and 1849. 'Authority' learnt what it meant to have to prevaricate and to yield: for a time, as the King of Prussia put it, it had been forced to crawl on its stomach. 'Never allow that to happen again' was his lesson. The revolutionaries, who before 1848 had learnt most of what they knew from books – it was books, indeed, which had done the talking – learnt less, perhaps, from experience; and, divided as they always had been, they now gave way to others. But for new revolutionaries it was not simply that new chapters had been added to old books: the whole text required substantial revision. A major theme for the future was to be the national unification of Germany and Italy, not achieved in 1848. How could that be accomplished?

There seemed to be three main sets of lessons to be learnt from 1848 and the year that followed, although not everyone drew the same lessons and there were divisions inside the revolutionary and counter-revolutionary camps as well as between them. The first concerned the dynamics of social class; and in that connection what had happened in France was the main, though not the sole, source of instruction. A second theme was related to the interplay of nationalisms, far more intricate than either nationalists or anti-nationalists had realized before 1848; and the third was the role of force in politics and in nation building, a subject which nationalists had increasingly begun to talk about in 1848 and 1849 while their opponents acted, driven by fear more than hope. There were two other themes that concerned all three sets of lessons – the relationship between monarchy and 'parliamentarianism' (which in future was to involve far more than the granting or withdrawal of constitutions) and the development of the apparatus, including the military apparatus, of the state.

THE DYNAMICS OF CLASS

Events between March 1848 and June 1849 revealed more about the dynamics of class within different social and political frames than the *Communist Manifesto* had done – first in France, then in Germany. Even in Britain, where there was no revolution, the Chartists continued to argue fiercely about class conflict and cooperation, political leadership and education even after the European revolutions had been put down. In France, which was always the subject of special study for Marx and for Engels, antagonism between Parisian workers, most of them untouched by the industrial revolution, and *bourgeoisie* (likewise untouched) was apparent almost from the start; and 'socialization' claims, which sounded as revolutionary in liberal London as they did in aristocratic Vienna, rang alarm bells in Paris itself. 'The population of our kings in overalls grows larger day by day', wrote one of the alarmed.

The republicans had promised elections in France as soon as they came to power, yet whatever the alarms, when these took place – with universal male suffrage – in April 1848, before the spring was over, the outcome showed that there were real limits both to revolutionary zeal and to social commitment. Of the new deputies in the French Chamber 165 had sat in the previous Chamber under Louis Philippe. Monarchists far outnumbered radicals, and there were only 30 'workingmen'. Even in Paris itself only 12 socialists were elected. In total, out of 876 seats, radicals and socialists won only 100 in a poll of 84 per cent. When Frenchmen went to the ballot box, ownership of property and the desire to protect it provided 'a sort of fraternity' which had nothing to do with equality.

Paris demonstrators in the streets, fearing the outcome, had tried to have the elections postponed, and true to the traditions of 1789, they were not prepared to abide by a national electoral verdict. As a result the revolution from below went on, and there were street disturbances in May when a new revolutionary government, backed by Blanqui, was proclaimed in the Hotel de Ville. The National Guard came into action against the revolutionaries when they burst into the Chamber and made many arrests. The showdown came in the following month. The existence of the national workshops, designed to provide labour for the poor, had sharply divided opinion on class lines, and one of the people arrested in May had been Louis Blanc. To their critics the workshops were 'temptations to idleness' (and disorder); to their defenders they were the only guarantee of the 'first vow of the Republic to provide bread every day for all its children by proclaiming the universal right to work'. The threat by the government to close them – or to run them down – triggered insurrection. Trees were chopped down and barricades built on 22 and 23 June.

The mood was very different from that of the March days, when trees of liberty were being planted everywhere; and when a soldier fresh from Algeria, General Cavaignac, acting on behalf of the national government, ruthlessly put down all disturbances, he was helped in his task by the predominantly *bourgeois* National Guard. A siege was declared on 24 June, and in a civil war in the Paris streets on that day and the next more Parisians were said to have been killed than in the whole of the revolutionary sequence that began in 1789. The outcome of the 'dreadful blood letting' was never in any doubt. Cavaignac, with the help of French recruits from the provinces, broke all workers' resistance, with the Faubourg St Antoine being the last place to fall.

In November 1848 a new republican constitution was drafted which made no mention of the right to work and which entrusted executive power to a president to be directly elected by the people. He was not to be Cavaignac, however, the hero of the *bourgeoisie* in the 'June days' and now the 'order' candidate, but Prince Louis Napoleon, nephew of the hero of heroes during what in retrospect most Frenchmen were now considering to be the most heroic age of French history. Cavaignac came in second in the elections, held in December, receiving only 1,442,302 votes as against Louis Napoleon's 5,534,520. The most radical candidate polled only 36,920, and Lamartine, the romantic hero of February, received only 17,910.

Louis Napoleon was new to French politics (two earlier conspiratorial attempts at intrusion had failed), and his opponents, large numbers of whom were members of the second popular assembly to be elected in the year, judged him to be shallow and 'trivial'. Obviously, however, he had received large-scale support from many different quarters. Peasants, who had made great gains in the first French Revolution, turned to him not only because they were totally opposed in 1848 to the idea of continuing social revolution but because liberal republicanism meant little to them. Working-class votes were even easier to explain. Why should any Parisian worker have voted for Cavaignac? It was as a conciliator, with a legendary name, standing above class and party, that Louis Napoleon made his first appeal to France. What had moved him personally from within was different – burning belief in his family inheritance and in his personal destiny. 'I am sure', he had exclaimed in 1842, 'that the shade of the Emperor protects and blesses me.'

What happened in France by the end of 1848 was very different, therefore, from what revolutionaries and non-revolutionaries alike had expected to happen at the beginning of the revolutionary sequence. With hindsight, there had never been any chance that disgruntled workers concentrated in Paris and large cities would win lasting gains (least of all, the right to work) in the economic, social and political circumstances of 1848. They would have to learn to organize – and to fight – in a different way – through trade unions and political parties – and even then the results of their struggles were to be limited. Republicans – and they came in different varieties – had had little real chance either. The events of the year had shown that under the prevailing circumstances the introduction of universal suffrage would not necessarily be followed by the coming to power of a democratic republican government. This was a political lesson which was to be repeated many times in the future. Napoleon, indeed, was quick to see that national plebiscites could reinforce his personal authority. For Proudhon universal suffrage was counter-revolution.

Napoleon's success was bound to create uneasiness in other parts of Europe where older forms of authority were restored. Yet some of the same lessons could be drawn out from the revolutionary sequence in Austria which had interesting features of its own. In Austria, unlike France, revolution was a novelty. In Austria also, again unlike France, there was not one nation but many. The first achievements of an all Austrian Parliament (*Reichstag*), which met in July 1848, chosen not by universal suffrage but by indirect election –

it included many members of the lower *bourgeoisie* and peasantry (some of them illiterate) – were impressive, recalling those of the French Revolution of 1789. In particular, in months of continuing economic difficulty, it had carried through by early September, with the endorsement of the Emperor, emancipation of the peasants on grounds of principle – their human rights – thereby completing the work of Josef II in the eighteenth century.

Thereby, too, of course, it satisfied large sections of the peasantry in the same way as the French peasantry had been satisfied in 1789, while at the same time – and this differed from what happened then – granted landlords compensation for losses of historic rights. As a consequence, the militant revolutionary movement in Vienna, a precocious city movement led by professors, students and artisans, with little support in the countryside or in the *Reichstag*, was left to struggle on its own after the late summer of 1848. The demand for public works to eliminate unemployment provoked the same responses and problems in Vienna as in Paris, following earlier disturbances in Prague and Budapest, aggravated when the wages of those engaged in public works were cut, there was street-fighting, the so-called 'Battle of the Prater', on 23 August.

October was the critical month in the Austrian capital. The Habsburg court, which had fled to Innsbruck in May and returned briefly in August, now had to flee from the city for a second time, leaving it in the hands of committed revolutionaries who strongly opposed the decision of the Austrian government to declare open war on Kossuth's Hungarian revolution. On 6 October, when an Austrian battalion was due to move into Hungary, rails were unbolted at the Northern Station and telegraph wires cut. On the same day the Minister of War was murdered and the arsenal attacked. Yet authority, brutal military authority under the direction of Prince Windischgrätz, triumphed in Vienna as it had done in Paris. Martial law was proclaimed at the end of October 1848, political clubs were suppressed, the freedom of the press was abolished, and the students' organizations and the National Guard (in Vienna still a revolutionary force) were dissolved.

Three weeks after 'the fall of Vienna', Austria had both a new emperor who was to reign for 68 years, and a new prime minister, the brother-in-law of Windischgrätz, Prince von Schwarzenberg. Member of a powerful old family, he had been elected to the *Reichstag* and was intelligent enough to appraise the strengths and limitations of the revolutionary movement. It was he who persuaded Emperor Ferdinand to abdicate in favour of the 18-year-old Franz Josef. The Schwarzenberg ministry included some liberals, and the *Reichstag*, which was engaged in drafting a constitution, continued to sit and debate, not in Vienna, however, but in the small Moravian town of Kremsier.

The task would have been challenging in any circumstances. As things were, it was impossible. Yet the *Reichstag* was bold enough to introduce into the first draft of its constitution a clause, which it soon had to drop, stating that 'all sovereignty proceeds from the people'. It also decreed that the Emperor's ministers were to be responsible to Parliament. Other paragraphs in the constitution included the abolition of titles of nobility, the introduction of civil marriage, and, of key importance in the imperial situation, a statement that all peoples of the Empire (Hungary and Lombardy-Venetia were excluded for constitutional reasons) were equal in rights. 'Each people has an inviolable right to present its nationality in general and its language in particular. The equality of rights in the school, administration and public life of every language in local usage is guaranteed by the state.'

There were divisions in the *Reichstag* on some of these proposals which were far too radical to be acceptable to the Emperor or his ministers, and in March 1849 Schwarzenberg's Minister of the Interior informed the Kremsier deputies that the *Reichstag* had been dissolved. Although he also told them at the same time that the Emperor had approved a new constitution 'by God's grace', this constitution too was never to be implemented. Karl Kübeck, head of the Treasury under Metternich and a representative of Austria in the Frankfurt Parliament, advised the Emperor to return to the pre-March *status quo*, and on the last day of 1851 yet a third constitution was swept aside. Instead, Kübeck was to head a commission to examine all the laws passed since March 1848 to ensure that everything of a liberal kind would be eliminated. Schwarzenberg, who would have been prepared to work within a parliamentary system but did not object to personal rule by the Emperor, died on 5 April 1852. The only main substantial reform that was to last after 1852 was the emancipation of the peasantry.

In Berlin the failure of the Vienna revolution stirred the King of Prussia to action. He had already been roused when the newly appointed Prussian National Assembly, meeting in Berlin, had voted in favour of the abolition of aristocratic titles and of dropping the words 'by the grace of God' from his own royal title. On 2 November he appointed a new prime minister, a cavalry officer, Count Brandenburg, and a week later (in face of protests from the Assembly which called for a tax strike) he moved the meeting place of the Assembly from Berlin to the provincial town of Brandenburg. Two days later, a state of siege was declared throughout Prussia. Finally, the Assembly was dissolved on 5 December and a new constitution was imposed emphasizing the divine right of the monarch, leaving the control of the executive in the hands of the King, treating the Army as a separate establishment in the state, and creating a two-chamber parliament which favoured big landowners. The lower house was to be elected by universal suffrage, but since voters were divided into three groups according to the amount of taxes that they paid the constitution consolidated property interests. At the same time the Civil Guard was disbanded and the political clubs were closed. The freedom of the press too was restricted.

Then and later Friedrich Wilhelm was totally opposed to the view which had been expressed by a leading speaker in the Frankfurt Parliament that 'we derive our authority [for framing a constitution] from the sovereignty of the nation'. And when the Frankfurt Parliament, now placed in an awkward position because of the restoration of monarchical authority both in Berlin and Vienna, decided in March 1849 (by a majority, with almost as many abstentions as votes) to offer Friedrich Wilhelm the crown of a new Germany he refused it. He was 'deeply moved' by the offer, he told a deputation from Frankfurt – and it had made him turn his eye towards 'the King of Kings' – but in a considered statement made later he turned not to the King of Kings but to his fellow German kings and princes, pointing out that he had earlier made 'explicit and solemn promises' that he would 'gain the voluntary assent of the crowned heads, princes and free states of Germany' in any move towards 'German unity'. More vividly, he stated in private that an imperial crown presented him by the rump of the Parliament, described by Friedrich Wilhelm as a 'dog collar' that would make him 'a serf of the revolution of 1848'.

It was of critical importance in German history that Friedrich Wilhelm made no attempt after this to take advantage of the fact that no fewer than 28 of the existing German governments, beginning with Baden, declared their willingness to approve of the election of the King of Prussia as German Emperor within a German constitution decided upon by the Frankfurt Parliament. He would not accept such a constitution from a divided Parliament, the very existence of which he now disapproved. By April 1849 any hope of German unification under Prussian leadership (with liberal support) had disappeared. Instead, Prussian troops helped to suppress revolutionary disturbances in April and May in Baden, Bavaria and Saxony.

The fate of the Frankfurt Parliament was now sealed. From beginning to end it had no executive responsibilities, and to the very end it failed to develop organized formal groupings along the lines of political parties which might have given a focus to its decisions. The largest moderate liberal grouping favoured a limited suffrage, but most of the moderates abandoned the Parliament during the disturbed months of April and May 1849. The delegates from the Habsburg Empire withdrew *en bloc*, and the King of Prussia ordered that all the Prussian deputies should follow them. The rump of the Parliament, 136 in all, described by Friedrich Wilhelm as being 'in league with the terrorists' who took part in the scattered Spring uprisings, now moved on to Stuttgart where they were eventually to be forcibly dispersed by soldiers from Württemberg in June 1849. By then there were some liberals in Germany as well as conservatives who had concluded, as Friedrich Wilhelm had done, that the Parliament had urged the unity of Germany as a pretence. The rump of its members had really been fighting 'the battle of godlessness, perjury and theft'.

THE INTERPLAY OF NATIONALISMS

The liberalism or radicalism of the Frankfurt Parliament in face of authoritarian power, particularly when it was left as a rump, stood out less at the time and stands out less in retrospect than its nationalism. It became almost immediately apparent after the Parliament met that one of the major problems confronting it was deciding which Germans it should exclude from the orbit of geographical unification and which non-Germans it should incorporate. Of the Habsburg Empire's 36 million subjects, fewer than 6 million were German-speaking, most of them Roman Catholic, while of Prussia's 16 million, most of them Protestant, there were 14 million German speakers. A 'big Germany' (*Gross Deutschland*), which would include the German-speaking areas of Austria, would involve the disruption, if not the dissolution, of the Habsburg Empire: a 'little Germany' (*Klein Deutschland*) would involve not only giving a preponderant share of power to Prussia within a new Germany, but leaving large numbers of German-speakers outside the German borders.

Some Germans always believed that it was an advantage to their cause that the Habsburgs as Germans ruled non-Germans, and there were few people in Austrian politics and government who believed that the Habsburgs should surrender their non-German areas. At the same time, there were some Germans who believed that Germany was not a territorial but a metaphysical concept: anyone of German stock and language owed allegiance first and foremost to the German Fatherland, which had its roots deep in the past, as had a cluster of revered Fatherlands. Many Germans, not only in Bavaria, but in Hanover, Saxony and Württenberg, each with its own rulers and its own traditions, were resistant then as later to the idea of an overarching German nation.[2]

Practical as well as metaphysical or historical problems dogged the Frankfurt Parliament just as they dogged the Habsburg court. What was to happen, for example, to the large number of Poles who lived in Prussia? If Poles were still prepared to remain subjects of the King of Prussia – and many Prussians in 1848 were far more willing to acknowledge Polish linguistic and cultural claims than the Russians were – they were not prepared to be submerged in a German nation state. The members of the Frankfurt Parliament held a wide variety of views concerning the 'Polish question', ranging from those who wished to undo the injustice of the three Polish partitions of the eighteenth century to those who wished to prevent the establishment of an independent Polish state. Initially the pro-Poles were in the majority, but opinion shifted later. And when at last open fighting broke out between Germans and Poles in Posen, the Prussian-controlled districts of Poland, German national solidarity triumphed over support for Polish nationalism and over a cosmopolitan belief in the complementarity of different national causes.

There were awkward issues also in relation to Denmark. Many chauvinistic speeches were made in the Frankfurt Parliament about Germans and Danes as, indeed, there were about Germans and Czechs. There was even contemptuous general talk of 'puny nationalities' (*Nationalitäten*) attempting 'to found their own lives in our midst and live like parasites to destroy ours'. The Czech politician and historian Frantisek Palacky had made it clear from the outset that Czechs did not wish to be represented in the Frankfurt Parliament: in words that became famous, 'If the Austrian state did not exist', he told the Parliament, 'we should have to create it in the interests of Europe.' Just 500 years before the revolutions of 1848 the University of Prague had been founded as a German university. Now Bohemia looked in the future to a multinational Habsburg Empire, to be reorganized on a federal basis, an outcome never to be realized then or later.

Within the Habsburg Empire there had long been a persistent tendency on the part of the authorities to play off one nationality against another, and in 1848 there was considerable confusion as to who or what could be called 'revolutionary' or 'counter-revolutionary'. This was largely because the Hungarian revolution, successful in its first phase because the Emperor as King of Hungary accepted its demands, seemed to carry with it not a social threat but a threat to the 'submerged nationalities' of the Habsburg Empire, among them Croats, Czechs, Slovaks and Ruthenians: all of these were represented in Hungary itself. Kossuth himself supported Magyar hegemony in Hungary, and when a new national assembly met in July 1848 the Croats rebelled against it. The Hungarian Diet had decided that all candidates for election should speak Magyar (Latin had hitherto been the official language) and that the older Diets of Croatia and Transylvania should disappear.

Already by then events in Prague had followed a pattern of revolution and reaction. A Congress of Slavs convoked by the Czechs in Prague on 2 June 1848 and presided over by Palacky was conceived of by him as a deliberate counterpoise both to the Hungarian and to the Frankfurt Parliaments. Yet this Congress too revealed a remarkable number of inter-Slav tensions – between Czechs and Slovaks, for example, and between Czechs and Poles – with the Poles being well disposed to the Magyars and far less well disposed to the Czechs. The Congress carried a resolution that a 'general Congress of European Nations' should be summoned 'for the discussion of all international questions', but there was never any question of this. Instead, an uprising in Prague, which began on the day that the Congress ended, and which was led by the same kind of combination of workers and students active in Vienna, was put down in five days by Austrian troops.

The suppression of the Hungarian revolution followed, although it took far longer than five days and went through many different phases. In September 1848 the Emperor, who now wished to see the March Laws revoked, declared war on the revolutionary Hungarian regime, provoking the further autumn disturbances in Vienna, and Windischgrätz entered Budapest on 5 January 1849. In February 1849 the Austrian Army defeated the Hungarians at Kapolna, and when the Austrian *Reichstag* was dissolved in the next week the new unitary constitution that was promulgated took no account of Hungarian or Czech demands for a federal system in the Habsburg territories.

As a result, Hungary, abandoning the Habsburgs for the first time, declared its independence in April 1849, making Kossuth Supreme Governor, only to fall – after initial victories, valiant resistance, complex manoeuvres and Russian intervention – in August 1849. (One castle held out until November.) For several years the Magyars remained under martial law, administered by

German officials sent from Vienna. Kossuth, who had buried the Hungarian crown near the frontier, fled to Turkey, and later visited London, where he was given a hero's welcome, but he was not received by Britain's Foreign Secretary, Palmerston. He also visited the United States which by the end of the nineteenth century was to house millions of immigrants from different ethnic groups in central Europe and the Balkans. There were to be more of them in some cases than there were in their own capital cities.

To sum up, the second lesson of 1848 and 1849 was that nationalism had revealed itself as a force making for conflict and even for confusion rather than for liberation. Leaving Germany on one side, it was apparent in the light of Magyar and Slav experience alone that a new *international* order based on coexisting nations would involve just as many conflicts of interest as the older dynastic order seeking after a 'balance of power'. The same lesson had been taught further east, too, in the Ottoman Empire, where risings had broken out in Bucharest, capital of Wallachia, where an independent government was set up in June 1848 proclaiming the unity of Wallachians, Moldavians and Transylvanians as free Romanians. There were deep divisions, linguistic and cultural, between Magyars on the one side and Wallachians and Moldavians, speaking a Latin language, as there were between German minorities living in these lands and the rest. And when Nicholas I gave aid to the Sultan to suppress the Romanian revolt it was the fraternity of the great dynasties not of the revolutionaries that was demonstrated to the world.

'The year 1848', wrote Sir Lewis Namier, the distinguished twentieth-century British historian of Polish extraction, marked 'for good or evil the opening of an era of linguistic nationalism, shaping mass personalities and producing their inevitable conflicts'.[3] And while the term 'mass personalities' begs questions, 'linguistic nationalism', often reinforced by religion, was to become an increasingly strong force after 1848–49. Nevertheless, rooted prejudice was more dangerous to the future of Europe than the language in which it was expressed, and rooted prejudice could be revealed even when the languages were the same. In May 1848, for example, a French Army officer reported that French navvies working on the Dunkirk railway line had 'attacked Belgian workers, who after collecting their pay, returned home'.

In Italy, where lovers of the language were cultivated, often learned people, and where, whatever the dialects, it was largely one language that was being read, local and regional differences (as well as imperfect communications) kept apart people who spoke varieties of Italian: many of whom still did not consider themselves to be 'Italians'. There were massive problems, national and non-national, in fighting for principle as Carlo Alberto's minister Cavour fully appreciated. Carlo Alberto's defeat at Novara by Austrian forces led by Josef von Radetzky in March 1849 forced him to recognize Austrian authority in Lombardy and Venetia and to pay a large indemnity to Vienna. He also abdicated, little lamented, to spend the rest of his life in Portugal, which was to become a home for many later royal refugees. He was succeeded by his son, Vittore Emmanuele. Radetzky went on to become

Governor-General and Military Commander of Lombardy and Venetia until he retired in 1857.

In the meantime, a short-lived Republic of Rome had come and gone, and Pope Pius IX, who was to become one of the most implacable enemies of all versions of liberalism, outside as well as inside Italy, had been restored to power by the new Napoleon. There seemed to be little principle here on the French side, at least, for it was to Napoleon that many Italian nationalists had looked for support. French troops sent to Rome met with brave resistance from guerrillas led by Giuseppe Garibaldi, one of the greatest guerrilla fighters in history, but the resistance failed and the French were to stay in Rome, continuing to protect the Pope until the Franco-German War of 1870 and Napoleon's fall. For a brief moment Mazzini, who earlier in his life had solemnly maintained that 'the worship of principle' had begun, had been a 'Triumvir' in the Republic of Rome which had been proclaimed on 9 February 1849 by a Constituent Assembly elected by universal suffrage. After 1849 he was never to hold any kind of power again.

THE ROLE OF FORCE

The third lesson of 1848 and 1849 was that force had triumphed over principle in battle as well as at the barricades. *Einheit, Freiheit und Macht* (Unity, Freedom and Power) had been a German slogan in 1848: now the emphasis was to shift to *Macht*. It was in Germany too that the term *Realpolitik*, the politics of power, was invented, and that the greatest military theorist of the nineteenth century, the Prussian Karl von Clausewitz, was to exert major influence, inspiring long after his death Helmuth von Moltke, Chief of the Prussian General Staff from 1858 to 1888 in a new phase of German history. Moltke placed the works of Clausewitz on a par with Homer and with the Bible. Clausewitz had joined the Prussian Army in 1792 and within a year had been pitched into battle against the French. His military experience, however, was not entirely Prussian. He learned from the French how important it was to involve the whole nation in war, and he learned too from a spell with the Russian Army. He had fought at Borodino and had watched Moscow burn before taking part in the Battle of Waterloo. It was experience as well as 'science' that led Clausewitz, to conclude that 'true military spirit is to be found only in an army that maintains its cohesion under the most murderous fire, that cannot be shaken by imaginary fears and resists well-founded ones with all its might; that proud of its victories, will not lose the strength to obey orders and its respect and trust for its officers even in defeat; [and] whose physical power, like the muscles of an athlete, has been steeled by training in privation and effort'. This is what he taught in long sentences as Director of the German Military School in Berlin from 1818 to 1830.

The Prussian Army sought to achieve such resolution of spirit, but it was in economic rather than military matters that Prussia rather than Austria had taken the lead in German affairs before 1848 through the activities of the *Zollverein*. (See above p.62) In the words of a British observer in 1840, this 'brought the sentiment of German nationality out of the regions of hope and fancy into those of positive and material interests'. The fact that the customs union excluded Austria did not mean that the rulers of Prussia, far more powerful in military terms than any other state, had a free hand. Indeed, in 1849 in politics and diplomacy Austria retained primacy in 1849 once the vacuum created by Metternich's dismissal had been filled by Schwarzenberg.

One man who hoped that Prussia could have taken the lead, General Josef von Radowitz, a friend of Friedrich Wilhelm, failed in his plans to control a newly founded federation of German states, the Erfurt Union, for Schwarzenberg shrewdly bided his time, and agreed on what was called an 'Interim', during which both Prussia and Austria would jointly supervise the affairs of Germany. Once the 'Interim' expired, however, on 1 May 1850, with order re-established in the Habsburg Empire, he succeeded in restoring the old Diet of the *Deutscher Bund* as it had been before 1848. There had been tense moments when Austria and Prussia were on opposite sides in relation to troop movements in the duchies of Schleswig-Holstein and Hesse, but it was Prussia that backed down.

Radowitz lost his power and was dispatched to London as Prussian Ambassador, and in November 1850 the Prussians reached an agreement with Austria at Olmütz by which they dropped their independent policies and virtually accepted Austrian leadership in German affairs. Finally in May 1851 a three-year treaty was signed between the two countries that was manifestly one-sided in character. Prussia guaranteed Austrian power in Italy, but there was no corresponding guarantee of Prussian power in the Rhineland. Only in economic matters was Prussian primacy still assured. The *Zollverein* held firm against Austrian attempts to dilute it, and in 1853 it was renewed for another 12 years. In the longer term Austria, weaker economically, was not able to sustain its primacy in German political affairs which had been reinstated in 1849 and 1850, but it required war, not diplomacy, for Prussia to secure it – a short, sharp war which, according to the rules of Clausewitz, was 'the continuation of policy'.

The language of power had been heard in 1848 and 1849, and from the left, not from the conservatives. 'If I knew that the unity and future greatness of Germany had to be attained through a temporary renunciation of all the freedoms', a liberal deputy had declared in February 1849, 'I should be the first to submit to such a dictatorship.' (The declaration complemented the famous phrase of Ludwig Ühland, one of Germany's most popular poets, a month earlier: 'No head will shine forth over Germany that is not anointed by a full drop of democratic oil.') When the Prussians were forced by Austrian (and significantly, Russian) pressure to withdraw from southern Denmark, where they had intervened in 1848 and 1849 to support 'Germans' living in Schleswig-Holstein, it was the radical members of the Frankfurt Parliament who protested most strongly about the affront to German 'national spirit' and 'military honour'.

The man who found the successful way to German unification was not a radical but a conservative, Otto von Bismarck, the son of a *Junker* landowner in Prussia, although he was not to become President of the Prussian Ministry until 1862. Born in 1815, the year of Waterloo, he first came to prominence as a politician at the time of the 1848 revolutions. After hearing that Friedrich Wilhelm IV could not sleep because of worrying about the revolution, Bismarck commented simply that 'a king must be able to sleep'. Yet Bismarck himself often found it difficult to sleep. The most sensitive and the most volatile of conservatives was a man of nerves as well as of iron.

Bismarck stands out in retrospect as the main architect of German unification, more fully described below (p.102), and he followed subtle and devious policies before and after achieving it using individuals. The kind of unification that he achieved in 1871 did not imply centralization except in diplomatic and military matters. Germany then (as now) retained within it a high degree of regional and local initiative. Bismarck's greatest skill was displayed in using individuals and groups for his own ends, selecting and discarding them when they had ceased to fit his purposes. Serving Prussian kings, as he did, he had no illusions about their personal limitations, particularly their dependence on their relatives. He was well aware of the limitations of dynastic diplomacy in a Europe networked by royal marriages, although he knew how to exploit it.

So far as serving 'Germany' was concerned, Bismarck always put the interest of Prussia first. 'What the devil do I care about the petty [German] states?' he once asked 'My only concern is to safeguard and increase the power of Prussia.' 'The only healthy basis of a large state which differentiates it essentially from a petty state, is state egoism and not romanticism, and it is unworthy of a great state to fight for that which is not connected with its own interest.'[4] This was a classic expression of *Realpolitik*. It had nothing in common with the liberal German nationalism of the Frankfurt Parliament, even when that nationalism demanded the use of force. 'Germany', Bismarck consistently maintained, 'does not look to Prussia's liberalism, she looks to her power . . . Since the treaties of Vienna our frontiers have been ill-designed for a body politic. The great questions of our time will be decided not by speeches and resolutions of majorities, but by blood and iron.'

Bismarck achieved power in 1862 after roughly attacking 'the chatterers' who were incapable, he said, of ruling Prussia. In foreign politics, in particular, they were 'children'. Foreign politics always interested him profoundly, not least when he served as Prussian representative on the revived *Deutscher Bund* from 1851 to 1858. He went on to serve as Ambassador to Russia from 1858 to 1862 and for a few months in 1862 as Ambassador to Paris, learning from the new Napoleon. He learned from these useful experiences how to deal with Russia and how to assess Napoleon in a decade of change. Both countries played a key part in his thinking about the international scene, while Britain came a low third.

His relations with Austria were even more central to his planning, how-ever, for there could be no German unification unless Prussia replaced Austria as the main influence inside Germany. Frustrated by what he described in 1852 as the 'measureless ambition' of the Austrians, he was prepared to wage what he thought of as a 'necessary' war between Prussia and Austria in 1866 to settle the issue of supremacy in 'Germany'. Yet he wanted a strong Austria, not a weak one, and he attached supreme importance to maintaining long-term Austro-German ties.

Ties with France, so important to German politicians after 1945, played no part in his vision. He wished to balance forces in Europe, not to integrate it. He believed also – and correctly – that since France encouraged, even repres-ented, forces of movement in Europe, Prussia could benefit from this disposi-tion so long as Napoleon III reigned in Paris. For Bismarck the period since 1852 was a 'transitional' period in European history which ended in 1870 with the second of his 'necessary' wars – and that was how he described them – this time between France and Prussia. It can be claimed, however, that in 1870 he unified Germany to defeat France rather than defeated France to unify Germany.[5]

DIPLOMACY AND WAR

During the transitional period, which in economic terms was a period of boom rather than transition, there were, in fact, many signs of international change which Bismarck surveyed from various vantage points after 1852. At the beginning of the 1850s Schwarzenberg's policy of tightening Austria's hold on the smaller south German states and isolating Prussia politically and diplo-matically by retaining the goodwill of Russia seemed to be highly successful. The middle German states were suspicious of Prussian ambitions, and Russia, the saviour of Habsburg interests in 1849, continued its vigilance. 'No one needs a strong and powerful Austria more than I do', Tsar Nicholas I had told the mother of Franz Josef, the young Austrian Emperor, in December 1848.

Economics had nothing to do with such calculations. Nor had it much to do with Bismarck's own calculations. Yet in the background between 1852 and 1870 – and sometimes in the foreground – was economic growth, broken with business crises in 1857 and 1867. Agriculture flourished, indus-try burgeoned. Railways remained symbols of change as well as its agents. So, too, was the Great Exhibition of 1851 held in an impressive Crystal Palace in London, where different countries, 'all the nations', including Germany and France, brought their multiple products for display. 'Work' was honoured: in what in Britain became thought of not as a 'transition period' of social equipoise but as the 'mid-Victorian years', it became a gospel. So too did 'the gospel of peace', although in the year 1851 Napoleon, who considered himself a man of destiny, extended his power by a *coup d'etat*, ratified by a referendum, and within the decade after 1851 France and Britain, with both

Prussia and Austria on the sidelines, went to war with Russia, the first war of the 'great powers', all of them so identified, since 1815.

It was Russia, the saviour of Habsburg interests in 1848 and 1849, that was to be at the forefront of European diplomacy after 1851, and having avoided revolution in 1848 was to be drawn into war in 1854. The danger points in the European balance were at the geographical edges of the continent – in the north Schleswig-Holstein, historic key to the Baltic, and in the south the Ottoman Empire, thought of by Nicholas I (and others) as 'the sick man of Europe'. And after the complex question of Schleswig-Holstein was apparently settled (if uneasily) in May 1852 by the Treaty of London, which determined the succession to the Danish throne and recognized Danish authority in the two duchies (while allowing Holstein to continue to be represented in the *Deutscher Bund*), attention moved eastwards.

Napoleon, who was proclaimed Emperor (after a plebiscite) in 1852, rightly believed that a strong policy in eastern Europe and an alliance with Britain would give his regime the security and prestige that it required, while substantial sections of British opinion, roused by the press, believed even more than British governments that vital British interests were threatened by Russia.

All this was around the corner before the Crimean War, bitterly opposed by Cobden, broke out in 1854. Its immediate causes, some of them lying outside Europe, were more complex than its consequences. Control of the so-called 'holy places', religious sites in and near Jerusalem, which was to figure even more prominently in early twenty-first-century politics, became a matter of dispute between France and Russia, and when in 1852 the Ottoman government allowed Roman Catholics equal rights with Greek Orthodox Christians (and full control of the Church of the Nativity in Bethlehem) Russia put strong pressure on the Sultan, moving troops to the borders of Moldavia and Wallachia, the future Romania, sending a commission to Constantinople to demand Russian rights to protect Orthodox Christians everywhere, and proposing to the British Ambassador there a scheme to partition Turkish territories. When the commission, headed by Prince Menshikov, failed, Moldavia and Wallachia were occupied, provoking popular as well as governmental protests in both Britain and France. After Austrian attempts to avert war failed, Turkey declared war on Russia in October 1853, and in March 1854 Britain and France declared war on Russia: for the first time in centuries they were on the same side.

War lasted long enough in the Crimea to reveal military and administrative ineptitude on both sides. The losses in men were substantial, more than in any other war between 1815 and 1914 (300,000 Russians, 100,000 French and 60,000 British), with more deaths from sickness, particularly typhus, than from battle, and with cholera, which had added to the problems of Europe during the aftermath of revolution, once again proving impossible to control. Florence Nightingale, 'the lady of the lamp', who organized the nursing of the British sick, the wounded and the dying, became a national heroine.

Russia, which had neither heroines nor heroes, took the initiative in seeking to end the war not through a change of government (there was one such change in Britain) but through a change of tsar. In March 1855 Nicholas died and was succeeded by Alexander II who, faced with threats that Austria might enter the war, made peace overtures before the full strength – or weakness – of either side had been fully tested. Nevertheless, as the British historian A. J. P. Taylor noted, for all the ineptitude and confusion, of the five invasions of Russia in the nineteenth and twentieth centuries (1812, 1854, 1916–18, 1919–20 and 1941) this was by far the most successful.

Paradoxically, the Peace of Paris, which followed in 1856, prepared the way for a future understanding between France and Russia – as Bismarck, watching from the sidelines, recognized. 'You wish to change in part the Treaty of Paris', Napoleon could write to Alexander II in 1858, adding that he too 'would change in part the treaties of 1815.' The two treaties were, indeed, closely related. By the terms of the 1856 peace, which neutralized the Black Sea and checked Russia's freedom to intimidate Constantinople, the free navigation of the Danube was achieved. At the same time the Ottoman Empire was admitted to 'the Public Law and System of Europe', the 'concert', from which the Sultan had been excluded in 1815. The idea of such a 'concert' had survived the failure of the regular Congress System devised in 1815, and a 'Declaration respecting Maritime Law' was agreed upon by the great powers represented at Paris.

Napoleon emerged from the Crimean War with his prestige greatly increased, while Britain, shaken in victory, became aware of the problems that had to be faced by a 'liberal state at war' (with militant anti-Russian radical groups pressing for a more comprehensive victory). Piedmont-Sardinia, which had joined Britain and France in an alliance which strengthened its claims to be considered a power on the European stage, gained, if not territorially, from being present at the Congress of Paris. Russia lost in territory as well as in prestige, being forced to cede parts of Bessarabia to the Turkish province of Moldavia, the core of the future Romania. The Ottoman Empire was propped up but not strengthened. Indeed, the Sultan agreed to grant a substantial degree of delegated authority not only to Moldavia and Wallachia but to Serbia which was to secure its full independence in 1878. (Turkish garrisons in Belgrade were withdrawn in 1867.) There was ample scope, therefore, for intensified Balkan rivalries between Austria and Russia after 1856, and at many times these were to prove stronger than counter-revolutionary community of interest.

In time Bismarck was able to put the memories of the Crimean War to good account. And he was able to put economics to good account also. Austria suffered economically as a result of the Crimean War, and throughout the 1850s it was losing ground every year to Prussia and to the *Zollverein*. In the very year that Bismarck came to power, 1862, a trade treaty between Prussia and France destroyed any continuing hope of Austria ever being able to join the Prussian-led economic grouping. Politically some of the smaller German states might wish to look to Vienna: economically they did not. The

Austrian economy was technologically backward. Prussian economic growth was significant before the iron in what came to be called Bismarck's 'blood and iron' policy was fully forged. As late as 1860 France was still producing more pig iron than Germany. Significantly the most striking portent of Prussian economic power was military – the rise of Krupp and the German armaments industry. At the Great Exhibition of 1851 in London, while the gospel of peace was sung, Alfred Krupps had displayed a huge gun – and the biggest ever block of steel.

In retrospect there seems to have been an unfolding logic behind Bismarck's sophisticated diplomacy, backed by growing military power, between 1862 and 1871, the year when Wilhelm I, who succeeded Friedrich Wilhelm IV in 1861 as King of Prussia, was crowned German Emperor. He had served as Regent since 1857 after the Emperor became incapacitated; and although deeply conservative he believed strongly in Prussia's mission to unify Germany. Nevertheless, as in the case of the 'revolutionary logic' of the 1790s or of the years 1848 and 1849, what happened thereafter was not premeditated or worked out according to plan, Bismarck, who secured power for domestic rather than diplomatic reasons in 1862, called in as prime minister to defeat the Prussian Parliament, thought primarily in terms of the present, making use of its fluidity in all his calculations. 'When I have been asked whether I was pro-Russian or pro-Western powers', he wrote in a letter of 1857, 'I have always answered I am Prussian, and my ideal in foreign politics is . . . independence of decision reached without pressure or aversion from attraction to other states and their rulers . . . I would see our troops fire on French, English or Austrians with equal satisfaction.'

Before Bismarck acquired the power in 1862 to exploit or to fashion events, the position of Austria and France had completely changed. This was a result of the unification of Italy, and it was this change of position that made his policies during the 1860s possible. The chronology was important. As late as 1860 the Prussian Prince Regent told Napoleon III that he did not expect to live to see German unification, and when he was crowned King of Prussia at Königsberg neither he nor Bismarck could have foreseen that he would be crowned Emperor of Germany nine years later not in Germany but at Versailles. Nor was that to be the end of the story. There was to be a French revenge for Versailles after the First World War in 1918 when the Hohenzollerns lost their throne, and following the Second World War when Königsberg was to be turned into a Russian city.

ITALIAN UNIFICATION

The key figure in the Italian context was the Prime Minister of Piedmont-Sardinia, Camillo di Cavour, five years older than Bismarck, who entered parliamentary politics in Turin in June 1848, and who became Prime Minister in 1852, ten years before Bismarck. Like Bismarck, he made full use of the increased fluidity of European diplomacy, seeking to achieve the possible. He was prepared, therefore, to use treaties, battles and back-stairs intrigues to achieve his purposes. Although he edited *Il Risorgimento*, he despised 'frenetic, ferocious and absurd' revolutionaries, and once said that he would willingly use them as manure for his sugar beet.

Cavour was the younger son of a nobleman, and his mother, French by origin, had lived in Switzerland. He himself wrote French more easily than Italian, and with his European perspectives was well aware of all the problems of what he once called 'our poor peninsula'. He even described Italian unification as 'nonsense'. For him, indeed, it was essentially a by-product of the struggle for independence and of a series of exceptional and unforeseen events inside Italy from which he could profit. He knew that there were other personalities involved in the process of unification besides himself and that for some of them unification was the goal. In some respects he had more in common in his general outlook with Peel and with Guizot, both of whom he admired, than with Bismarck. Moreover, many of his policies were necessarily concerned with issues derived from an earlier age than that of Bismarck. Thus, he dissolved half the monasteries in Piedmont-Sardinia as an enlightened despot might have done, and supported the abolition of ecclesiastical courts which had survived in their original form in Italy but nowhere else in Europe.

With a very different agenda in mind, he also shared Peel's ideas on free trade, the need for economic progress (including agricultural improvement), and the importance of forestalling 'general political and social upheaval'. He had visited Britain in 1835, when he was greatly impressed by industrial Birmingham and commercial Liverpool, where he saw a workhouse and caught a train for Manchester. Railways, he recognized, were symbols of prosperity. As late as 1859 half the railways in Italy were in Piedmont-Sardinia.

The British minister in Turin, who greatly admired Cavour's work and helped him to achieve his objectives, called him 'a financier who has Adam Smith at his fingers' ends, not a conqueror who aims at debt and empire'. But this was to underestimate Cavour's diplomatic subtlety and the range of his preoccupations. They were never exclusively economic; and if he was uninterested in empire himself, he could not ignore the existence of the Habsburg Empire. Independence meant primarily independence from Austria which had a different role to play in Italy – with a different history behind it – from the role that it played in Germany. Cavour could talk naturally of 'the barbarians' from outside, 'encamped' as they were in Lombardy, who oppressed Italy. Even had he wished to do so, Bismarck could never have employed the same kind of language about the Austrians in Germany. He had to be content with taking off his jacket when he talked to their envoys and ostentatiously smoking cigars in their presence.

The movement of Italian politics and the achievement of Italian unification in two stages – 1861 and 1870 – depended on many people in many places, outside Italy as well as inside it. Cavour had no sympathy with those Italian revolutionaries like Mazzini, who renamed his followers 'the Party of Action' in 1853; and when in that year Mazzini and his followers tried to organize a republican revolution in Milan, Cavour attacked them openly and for doing so was thanked by the Austrians. Nonetheless, after 1856 he courted the National Society, the main agency of the Italian *Risorgimento*, even though it was led by and included radical Italians whose views about social politics and Italian unification were different from his own, and it was a triumph for him when the Society began to refer to Vittore Emmanuele as King of Italy. Cavour described Daniele Manin, one of its leaders, as 'always a little Utopian', but he realized shrewdly that even such utopianism might on 'a practical occasion' be 'useful'.

He then proceeded by a different route to show that he was just as anxious to get rid of the Austrians as Mazzini was. Looking around for allies, he recognized realistically from the outset that Italy would have to win French support above all else, and when in 1855 he deliberately chose to embroil Italy in Crimean War politics, he did so fearing that Austria might join the war first. At the end of the war he had useful discussions with Napoleon III at the Congress of Paris, which were followed up at Plombières in the summer of 1858.

By the so-called pact of Plombières (a secret pact, details of which were not disclosed by Cavour to his cabinet) Napoleon accepted 'the principle of nationality' and declared that he would join in a war to drive Austria out of Lombardy and Venetia. This would be a repeat performance, of course, of the achievement of Napoleon I, and there was another Napoleonic repeat in that Napoleon III and Cavour agreed that a marriage would be arranged between a middle-aged cousin of Napoleon, Jerome, and Vittore Emmanuele's 15-year-old daughter. The most cynical aspect of the deal – a demonstration of the bargaining aspect of Cavour's *Realpolitik* – was that Piedmont-Sardinia would cede Savoy and Nice to France. The informal agreement at Plombières was turned into a formal treaty in January 1859. A Franco-Russian understanding followed. Russia would accept change in Italy, and France would support Russia in overturning the still recent decisions of the Congress of Paris to close the Black Sea.

It was left to Cavour to find an occasion for war. At first this seemed difficult, since there was pressure even from friendly countries, like Britain, for a European settlement of 'the Italian question' without recourse to war. (Palmerston had always recognized the need for a secure Austria, not least in the excitements of 1848 and 1849.) But in the course of a 'war scare', something that was to become a familiar event in the years before 1914, the Austrians conveniently played into Cavour's hands, as they (and in 1870 the French) were later to play into Bismarck's hands. When Cavour mobilized the relatively small army of Piedmont-Sardinia in March 1859, the Austrians retaliated in April by mobilizing their own far bigger one; and when they went even further and in April 1859 sent an ultimatum to Piedmont-Sardinia demanding Italian 'disarmament' within three days, Cavour rejected the ultimatum and Napoleon III, as promised, marched into Italy.

The war did not go entirely according to plan, for Napoleon was no Bismarck. Yet it lasted only for six weeks, and the two bloody and costly Franco-Italian victories at Magenta and Solferino were decisive. Railways were brought into use in the warfare, and it was out of the carnage of Solferino that the Red Cross was born: a Swiss observer on the battlefield, Jean-Henri Dunant, had been appalled by the treatment of the wounded on both sides. The peace did not go according to plan either, for Napoleon in a characteristically sudden switch of tactics made overtures to the Austrians before Cavour wished, and, unknown to him, agreed in secret talks with Franz Josef at Villa-Franca to leave Venetia and the central Italian duchies in Austrian hands. Only Lombardy was to be given up. Napoleon also proposed an Italian confederation with the Pope as President and with Austria as a member. A deeply shocked Cavour resigned after as stormy a scene with his king as any that Bismarck ever had with his.

But the wheel of fortune had not stopped turning, and a few months after the pact of Villa-Franca Cavour was back in office again and Piedmont-Sardinia had doubled its size, incorporating not only Lombardy but the three central Italian duchies and part of the papal territories. Moreover, a changed British government – there was a general election in 1859 – had made it clear in public that it would not allow these Italian moves to be resisted. Palmerston, the British Prime Minister from 1859 to 1865, and his Foreign Secretary, Lord John Russell, were so passionately pro-Italian at this crucial moment in Italian history that they were nicknamed 'the two old Italian masters'. Gladstone, the future leader of British liberalism, who had served under Peel but had joined Palmerston's government as Chancellor of the Exchequer, was equally pro-Italian. Italy contributed directly to his political development as a popular politician.

The expansion of Piedmont-Sardinia took place in separate phases. After Villa-Franca constituent assemblies in Parma, Modena, Tuscany and the Romagna formed an alliance with a common army and turned to Piedmont-Sardinia for leadership. Cavour returned to power, confident of British support, and when Napoleon also (in another volte-face) accepted this total modification of the terms of Villa-Franca, Cavour declared himself willing to allow Nice and Savoy to pass to the French. And this they duly did after French troops had moved in not to wage a campaign but to arrange a plebiscite.

Cavour was still not the only character on the stage, however, and at first he was deeply alarmed, not enthused, by what was happening further south in Italy. Two months after Napoleon secured Nice and Savoy, Garibaldi and a 1,000 Redshirts – soon to become even more famous throughout Europe than Garibaldi's heroic defenders of Rome in 1849 – landed in distant Sicily, where there had been a popular uprising against the King of Naples. The 'thousand' (there were actually 1,088 men and one woman, the largest single group among them from Lombardy) soon captured the city of Palermo, and within three months crossed the strategic Straits of Messina and moved on to the Italian mainland. On 7 September they entered the city of Naples and paused before marching on Rome.

Such spectacular success was far more dazzling than anything that had happened in northern Italy, and it was happily achieved, moreover, without deviousness. Garibaldi had little use for diplomacy; indeed, before landing in Sicily he had contemplated as an alternative a landing in Nice, his birthplace, to thwart the French. His actions – in the name of 'Vittore Emmanuele and Italy' – were certainly too spectacular and too direct for Cavour, who at this critical moment in time needed every resource of *Realpolitik* to decide what to do. He had been strongly opposed to Garibaldi's expedition, but he had been unable either to prevent it or publicly to criticize its outcome: 'the ministry could not have lasted', he wrote later, 'if it had tried to stop Garibaldi'. Writing privately six days after the Sicilian landing he noted that 'if the Sicilian insurrection is crushed we shall say nothing: if it succeeds we shall intervene in the name of humanity and order'.

Afraid of Garibaldi's impulsive spontaneity, of his natural radicalism, and of his immense prestige, Cavour made a number of moves to check him before finding the move that worked. Knowing that there would be serious international implications if Garibaldi's troops entered Rome – for Napoleon III, as self-appointed defender of the Pope, might intervene and might on this occasion be backed by Austria – Cavour concluded that what was necessary was a still more spectacular triumph than Garibaldi's. He had to make news. And he succeeded. On the day that Garibaldi entered Naples, Cavour sent an ultimatum of his own to the French-protected Papal States. Claiming that the Pope was incapable of controlling revolutionary movements in his territories, Cavour sent in his own troops, and on 18 September, at Castelfidaro, the Piedmontese defeated a Papal army that was commanded by a royalist French general who was a bitter opponent of Napoleon. Bypassing Rome, they moved towards Naples and there they converged with Garibaldi's troops who had defeated a Bourbon army of 30,000 at Volturno. Vittore Emmanuele and Garibaldi now rode together into the city of Naples.

The great powers had not been able to intervene directly in this story, although Britain, in particular, approved of its outcome, and Cavour had coordinated beforehand (very cynically) this boldest of moves with Napoleon, whose troops stood in the way of Rome. The whole of Italy except Venetia and the area immediately round Rome was now under the physical control of Piedmont-Sardinia.

Garibaldi's 'irregulars' were soon disbanded without fuss, and the great hero went away to live (quietly Cavour hoped) in an island off Sardinia. Plebiscites which were held on the basis of universal adult male suffrage in Naples, Sicily, and the captured Papal territories, confirmed the wishes of the inhabitants to become subjects of Vittore Emmanuele (they were not given the choice of voting to belong to independent kingdoms), and the 1848

Constitution of Piedmont-Sardinia, which Carlo Alberto had granted to his subjects, was now extended to the new kingdom of Italy. Vittore Emmanuele II, who had made many moves of his own during this extraordinary sequence, was proclaimed King, and Cavour became the first prime minister. The first national Parliament met at Turin in March 1861. Only around 2 per cent of the population, however, had the vote. This was not a plebiscitary assembly, and from the start it faced serious problems in seeking to determine the extent of administrative decentralization.

The word 'national' begged many questions, just as did the inevitable choice of Turin, the capital of Piedmont-Sardinia, as the national capital. There were enormous regional differences – economic, social and cultural – between north and south, and in many of the cities also, old and new, there were differences between 'clericals' and 'anti-clericals' and 'respectable' politicians and radical revolutionaries. Vittore Emmanuele refused to call himself Vittore Emmanuele I, while one surviving federalist deputy asked in the first national parliamentary debate why Milan, Florence and Naples should be ruled from Turin. There were troubles in Naples almost immediately after the union. Pro-Bourbon riots were one manifestation of discontent. Another was the so-called 'brigands' war' in which large numbers of civilian lives were lost through peasant disturbances. And there was another moment of drama further north when in 1862 Garibaldi failed to seize Rome (*O Roma, o Morte*: 'Rome or death') with an army of volunteers who were checked at Aspromonte not by the French but by Italian troops. By then Cavour was dead, a victim of 'fever' (probably malaria) at the age of 51. He had already stated publicly in March 1861 that Rome, the key to Italy, should become Italy's capital. Now he suddenly disappeared from the stage when he was at the very centre of it.

There were to be more tensions in the new but still impoverished kingdom of Italy than there were in the prosperous new German Empire, as ministers who claimed to be as dedicated to Cavour's memory as the Peelites were to Peel's memory in Britain tried to hold the country together. Yet the prime minister who succeeded him came not from Piedmont-Sardinia but from Tuscany, and Turin was temporarily to give way as a capital to Florence. The man who now moved into the centre of the European stage was Bismarck, who achieved power in 1862 by ensuring that it was possible for his king to govern by himself without depending on Parliament. Taxes were raised to support a substantial military budget – and collected – without Parliament approving of them. Bismarck, contemptuous of liberalism (though prepared to use even that) had the right personal qualities to counter the liberal watchword of 'a people's army behind Parliament' with the King's watchword 'a disciplined army that is also the people in arms, behind the King, the warlord'. The Austro-Hungarian envoy to Britain, Count Karolyi, fully approved. 'If democracy is suppressed inside Prussia, its damaging influence on the rest of Germany will also be crippled.'

GERMAN UNIFICATION

In making it possible to employ the Prussian Army effectively as an instrument of policy, Bismarck, who wished any wars in which it was engaged to be short, had to avoid the creation of foreign alliances or coalitions that would stand in his way. The first critical year for him was 1863, when a Polish revolt began after Russia had tried to draft urban Poles into the army. Following the revolt, Russia suppressed all remaining Polish liberties and even the old name 'Kingdom of Poland' disappeared. Bismarck won Russian good will by dismissing all the protests of Prussian liberals in favour of Poland, and was equally brusque with the Prussian Crown Prince when he protested too. In the same year Bismarck began a series of moves on his northern borders which were to place him in a position whereby he could successfully go to war against Austria in 1866.

When King Frederick of Denmark died in November 1863, the question was raised again of who should rule the southern Danish/German duchies of Schleswig and Holstein, and a German pretender appeared, Friedrich of Augustenberg, who proclaimed himself Duke of Schleswig-Holstein. Bismarck avoided European intervention in the dispute – partly by skill, partly by accident – and after successful military intervention, authorized by the German *Bundestag*, he reached a settlement, by which, ignoring Friedrich, the King of Denmark renounced all his rights in the Duchies of Schleswig and Holstein to the King of Prussia and the Emperor of Austria. In 1865 by the Convention of Gastein it was agreed, and this was clearly transitional, that Austria would occupy one duchy – Holstein – and Prussia the other – Schleswig. The presence of Austria in distant Holstein, a predominantly German duchy, would give future grounds for Prussian manoeuvre.

No European congress was called despite the fact that both Prussia and Austria had defied the recently signed Treaty of London, and this seemed to have proved Bismarck's powers of calculation. In London itself Palmerston, who had made promises to the Danes and who claimed that he was one of the few people who understood the Schleswig-Holstein issue, won no support for any British intervention from his cabinet or from the Queen. Meanwhile France and Italy were won over by Bismarck: two months after Gastein he visited Napoleon and had friendly talks with him at Biarritz. Throughout, Russia, already won over, gave no support to the Danes. In 1860 *The Times* in London had derided Prussia for 'always leaning on someone, always getting someone to help her, never willing to help herself; always ready to deliberate, never to decide; present in congresses, but absent in battles'. Now the tables had been turned, and there was no 'concert'.

Already there was Prussian revenge for Olmütz. When the Austrian Emperor travelled to Frankfurt to present to the German princes a plan for a five-man German directorate under his own leadership and a new German Diet composed of representatives from the German state diets, Bismarck persuaded the King of Prussia not to attend. The Emperor was welcomed by *Gross Deutschland* politicians and was received with cheering crowds, but his plan had no chance of success. Instead, Bismarck put forward a far more popular plan in July 1866, proposing the abolition of the Diet and the summoning of a German Assembly to draft a new constitution. It would then create a new German parliament to be elected by universal suffrage. Bismarck's object, of course, was to outbid Austria, not to give the German people a share in their government, but it was difficult, once his plan had been published, for liberals to oppose it. Ex-members of the Frankfurt Parliament, in particular, could scarcely find reasons for protest. Bismarck had already won the support of the nationalists of 1848 when he invaded Schleswig-Holstein: they had protested sharply in 1848, when Prussian troops had been withdrawn.

Secret diplomacy counted for more than public appeals, important though the latter were in Bismarckian tactics. Behind the scenes he quietly won the support both of Piedmont-Sardinia (which, after all, had been at war with Austria in 1859) and of France (Piedmont's ally in that struggle) in the eventuality of Prussian military action against Austria. 'Prussia and France', he flatteringly told Napoleon at Biarritz in 1865, 'are the two nations of Europe whose interests are most nearly identical.' In securing promises of French neutrality in a war between Prussia and Austria the possibilities of an under-standing between France and Austria – with so many eighteenth-century echoes – were effectively discounted. And in Schleswig-Holstein, as he had hoped, he found ample material with which to provoke Vienna, even though the Austrians had successfully set out to be moderate and conciliatory. There was no formal declaration of war in 1866, but it was Austria that broke off diplomatic relations with Prussia on 12 June, declared the *Bundestag* at an end on 14 June and invaded Saxony on 15 June. The Italians, seeking to profit from the war, made a local declaration, and were quickly defeated on 24 June at Custozza, scene of their earlier defeat. Austria, however, did not benefit from this victory. Instead, on 3 July, its army was routed at Sadowa. The Prussian Army, well drilled and well armed, made the most effective use possible of superior weapons and, not least, of railways and telegraphs as instruments of mobilization and deployment. The war lasted only seven weeks.

Had the war gone badly, Bismarck would not have scrupled to call on Magyar, Polish, Czech and Croat resistance groups in a struggle against Austria; and it was significant, perhaps, that the final treaty was signed in Prague. Yet he did not seek a vindictive peace, and he told his Minister of the Interior to work hard so that Berlin newspapers did not demand one. He believed that he would need Austrian 'strength' in the future – a somewhat dangerous belief, given ample evidence of increasing Austrian weakness – and he had to argue with his own king to get his way, as he had earlier been forced to argue with him about Schleswig-Holstein. Whatever the news-papers might have said, the peace would have been far more severe had Wilhelm I determined it.

The Peace of Prague on 23 August in effect excluded Austria from both Germany and Italy, and in the following year the Magyars gained full control of their own internal affairs. A Dual Monarchy was set up by which Franz Josef, dividing his territories at the River Leithe, a small tributary of the Danube, became simultaneously Emperor of Austria and King of Hungary. This *Ausgleich* (compromise) set up two parliaments with two chief ministers, but foreign policy, the Army and fiscal policy (a tariff) were common to both. Liberals in Vienna, who had provided a Prime Minister for the Habsburgs between 1840 and 1865, Anton von Schmerling, who had once served as chairman of the Frankfurt Parliament, supported the change which brought with it parliamentary government and guarantees of civil liberties. Hungarians, happy with the complicated arrangement – although there were to be difficulties later in the century – had a prime minister Count Gyula Andrassy – exiled from his homeland between the fall of Kossuth and the year 1857. He was to become Foreign Minister in 1871, serving until 1879.

The dual monarchy did not and could not quell the claims of other 'nationalities' in the Empire, and when these were vigorously put forward directly or indirectly they made it difficult for ministers to govern firmly either in Vienna or Budapest. Andrassy himself was irrevocably opposed to Slav groups which sought varying degrees of autonomy, and in 1879 signed an Austrian-German alliance which survived until the end of the First World War. (See below, p.119) So long as the Habsburg empire itself survived, Czech, Polish, Slovak and Croat ministers continued to fashion their own identities, inevitably drawing Europe as a whole into their conflicts. Bargains had to be made in the interests not only of conciliation but of executive action. In the process Europe lost.

That was future history. At the end of Bismarck's first necessary war the North German Federation was moving along different lines. The King of Prussia became President and Commander-in-Chief, and it was in effect a greater Prussia. Neither the king nor Bismarck wished it, however, to centralize all aspects of government and life. Much that mattered could be determined far away from Berlin. Those north German states that had opposed Prussia during the war were annexed, except Saxony, but other German states, particularly Bavaria, retained a different set of traditions and remained in existence within their old boundaries. In Prussia itself Bismarck won a political victory when after years of obstruction moderate liberals in the *Landtag* now voted for an Indemnity Bill which indemnified the government from responsibility for the previous four years of unauthorized public expenditure. Bismarck was victorious in the new Germany too when he refused to make himself legally responsible to the *Reichstag*. In a new *Bundesrat*, where representatives still voted under mandate, as in the old Federal Diet, the fact that a two-thirds majority was required ensured Prussian power, and in a new *Reichstag*, elected by universal suffrage, popular power was restricted: there was to be no annual budget for it to discuss and ratify.

The age of Metternich had been left far behind. Inside Europe, thanks to Bismarck's diplomatic skills, as great as those of Metternich, and Prussian economic and military power, which was to grow throughout the decade, the work of the counter-revolution of 1848–50 and the Vienna settlement that preceded it had now been undone. The age of Palmerston (who died in 1865) had been left far behind also. Britain, indeed, did no more during the Austro-Prussian War than it had done during the Schleswig-Holstein crisis. It was preoccupied with its own affairs.

THE FRANCO-PRUSSIAN WAR
AND THE GERMAN EMPIRE

Bismarck's next 'necessary' war, that against France in 1870, had its immediate origins, as had so many previous European crises, in the issue of the Spanish succession. The Spanish Queen, Isabella, whose marriage had been a diplomatic issue just before the fall of Louis Philippe, was driven into exile in 1868 following a successful revolution; and a constituent Spanish assembly offered the vacant throne to a reluctant member of the Prussian royal family, Leopold of Hohenzollern. Bismarck encouraged Leopold to accept and in 1869 was secretly spending money in Spain to ensure Spanish backing. The French government, inflamed by an excited press, became increasingly hostile to Leopold's candidature, and the Prussian press too fanned the flames in 1870 as the British press had fanned the flames before, during, and after the Crimean War.

The active role of Bismarck in stirring up intrigue and excitement was very cleverly thought through, for he knew that in France there was never any shortage of combustible material. Napoleon was always interested in possible deals, and when with Bismarck's encouragement he showed himself willing to contemplate French territorial gains in Belgium and Luxembourg he was falling into Bismarck's trap. There were many people in Europe in 1870 – not least in London – who saw Napoleon, not Bismarck, as the main threat to peace. Bismarck was even attempting behind the scenes to win the support of Mazzini for this interpretation.

Faced with French protests about the Hohenzollern candidature, Wilhelm I was prepared to back down, and Leopold subsequently withdrew his name (for the second time). The crisis, however, was not solved. The French government foolishly went on to ask for further guarantees. When Wilhelm refused – Bismarck was manoeuvring very cleverly behind the scenes, as became known years later, going so far as to manipulate the wording of a royal telegram – it was France, described in its press as 'insulted', that declared war on 19 July 1870. Once again Bismarck had so organized affairs that it was not he but his opponents who were made to take the initiative: he was able to tell the German Parliament 17 years later – with no one to contradict him – that Napoleon had 'launched into the war' because he had 'believed that it would strengthen his rule at home'.

Once again the Prussian victory, achieved at Sedan on 2 September, was swift, if not immediately decisive, and this seemed to justify all the tactics employed. Napoleon's empire had collapsed within two months, and a new and more powerful Empire came into existence in 1871, when Wilhelm was proclaimed German Emperor in the Hall of Mirrors at Versailles on 18 January 1871. Britain and Russia both stayed on the side-lines, as did Franz Josef, with whom Napoleon had had abortive treaty discussions following Sadowa.

Whatever the future power of myth, the capitulation of France in 1871 demonstrated that, imperial or republican, France no longer possessed the great advantages in Europe that it had fewer than a 100 years before. Its population in 1870 was five million less than the 39 million in the united Germany that Bismarck created, and it was Germany that experienced large-scale industrialization after 1870, not France. The new Germany was a triumph both of blood and of iron.[6] Money played its part, too, however, for it proved necessary to persuade the King of Bavaria to join the new German Empire by bribing him with money acquired from the King of Hanover after the annexation of his kingdom in 1866.

After victory Bismarck demanded from defeated France a large financial indemnity as well as the cession of the provinces of Alsace and Lorraine, the latter rich in minerals. This cession, urged on Bismarck by his king, by generals and by popular pressure inside Germany, was a mistake. Even in 1848, when the Frankfurt Parliament was rallying Germans everywhere, no one had suggested that there should be delegates from Alsace-Lorraine, and after 1870 the issue was to bedevil future Franco-German relations down to the First World War of the twentieth century. After 1870 Bismarck professed that Germany was 'satiated' and that his only interest was peace. Here, however, was oversatiation and a 'cause of war'.

There were also flaws in the new imperial structure, in this case most of them quite deliberately put there by Bismarck himself to stem 'democracy'. No elected representatives of the German people were present at Versailles when Wilhelm I was crowned (there was to be no hint of the gutter this time), and although the new German constitution, like that of 1867, was based on universal suffrage, it was clear from the start that the relationship between Chancellor (Bismarck) and the new Emperor would continue to be more significant than the relationship between Chancellor and *Reichstag*. The personal relationship began less triumphantly than appeared on the surface, for in the words of the Crown Prince of Prussia there were 'sobs and tears' before the coronation. Wilhelm had to be persuaded tactfully by King Ludwig of Bavaria to accept the new Crown, and it required Bismarck's insistence to force him to call himself 'German Emperor' and not 'Emperor of Germany', a controversial title given the existing German states.

Bismarck's insistence demonstrated, if it needed to be demonstrated, that he held the same views on the constitution after 1871 as he had held before 1870. Given the importance of the Army, there was to be no *annual* debate on the military estimates which accounted for 90 per cent of government expenditure. The government could be outvoted in the *Reichstag*, made up of political parties, but the Chancellor of the *Reichstag* had to be a Prussian, and all ministers were responsible only to the Emperor. After 1870 the Prussian system of administration was introduced throughout the imperial institutions of the new confederal Germany, ensuring that while there was to be no democracy there would always be a bureaucracy. It was difficult within the new constitution, therefore, to envisage how any movement towards a 'constitutional government' resting on a greater degree of individual freedom and responsibility would be possible; and the system, which at the same time allowed for initiative and devolution in the internal affairs of the states, was to survive his own fall from power in 1890. Thereafter, as the German economy boomed, it was to create impasses in German domestic politics that were to have disastrous consequences.

The biggest difficulty in 1871 – in national terms – was a different one. So many Germans were left outside the new Empire (a *Klein Deutschland*) that the Austrian poet Franz Grillparzer could say, 'you think you have created an empire, when all you have really done is destroyed a nation'. Likewise, many non-Germans were left within the new boundaries: nearly three million Poles, for example, lived in West Prussia and Posen. Those Germans who were left outside the new frontiers could become dangerously radical – a threat to the peace that Bismarck, having unified Germany, now wished to maintain. In 1873, like Metternich before him, he encouraged the Emperors of Austria, Germany and Russia to sign a Three Kings' Pact to work in concert and resist revolutionary ideas. It was a more formidable task than Metternich had faced. Ethnic relations within the Habsburg Empire were often to reach boiling point, and it was equally ominous that German intellectuals inside the German Empire – even intellectuals who were suspicious of Bismarck – could rally to the defence of Germans living outside. Pan-Germanism was to increase its appeal after Bismarck disappeared from the scene.

Because of the way in which the Empire was made, there were immediate difficulties in getting the new imperial symbols right. At first, for example, there was not even a new German national flag or a national anthem. (By contrast Britain's 'God Save the King' – or Queen – had been written in 1745.) It was not until 1892 that an imperial tricolour was devised of black, white and red (the black and white colours of Prussia were dominant); and even then, this flag, like many of the other emblems, was never popular in Bavaria. *Deutschland Über Alles* (its music had originally been composed by Haydn for the Habsburg Emperor) was sung frequently as a kind of national anthem during the 1890s. So, too, was *Die Wacht am Rhein*, a nationalist song that reiterated and emphasized all the old enmities between Germany and France.

In 1871 Bismarck believed that a 'satiated' Germany had nothing to gain from a new war, yet nationalism, often inflamed by the press, a force growing in importance, still pointed towards new wars rather than towards new harmonies. Moreover, inside the country strident nationalists could also exploit, as they often did, anti-Semitism, present long before 1871, anti-Catholicism and anti-socialism. The writing on the wall was beginning to be plain before Bismarck completed his work. 'Nationality', wrote the British historian Lord Acton in 1862, 'does not aim either at liberty or prosperity, both of which it sacrifices to the imperative necessity of making the nation the mould and measure of the state.' Four years later Emile de Laveleye, who knew as much about French nationalism as German, commented despairingly that 'nationalism . . . mocks at treaties, tramples on historic rights, puts diplomacy in disarray . . . and tomorrow perhaps will unleash a cursed war'.

Acton was writing as a liberal Roman Catholic, and the Roman Catholic Church was itself directly affected by the political changes that took place in Europe in 1870. The destruction of the temporal power of the Papacy was made possible by the grace of Bismarck, for Italy was able to profit from the Franco-German War of 1870 and Napoleon III's withdrawal of French troops from Rome enabled Italians by themselves to seize the city and turn it, as Cavour himself had wished, into Italy's capital. It had been by Bismarck's grace too that Italy had secured Venetia by the Treaty of Prague in 1866 after Italian forces had been defeated by the Austrians at Custozza. The two unified states owed much to each other.

1870 AND BEYOND

By a coincidence, when the political and military crisis of 1870 was at its height, the Pope had summoned to Rome a Vatican Council from 'the whole of Christendom' which proclaimed the dogma of papal infallibility in *ex cathedra* spiritual pronouncements, a dogma which the historian Acton, like many German theologians, the Bavarian Johann von Dollinger prominent among them, found difficult to justify. Dollinger's *Der Papst und die Konzil* (1869) was described as 'the severest attack on the Holy See in a thousand years'. Already in 1864 Pius IX had attacked liberalism of every kind (and with it socialism and, broadest of all, belief in 'modern civilization') in a *Syllabus of Errors*.

After 1870, bereft of temporal power, which it could never regain, the Church was to become involved in disputes in many European countries, not least Germany and Italy, and it was not until a new Pope, Leo XIII, was elected in 1879 that the Papacy regained any capacity to manoeuvre and to adapt. Leo XIII was a completely different kind of Pope from Pius X. In two encyclical *Libertas* (1888) and *Rerum Novarum* (1891), he acknowledged the more positive aspects of liberalism, condemned unrestrained capitalism, and urged states to promote the social welfare of their subjects.

Such promotion was never the main preoccupation of the Italian state which kept him a prisoner. Cavour's successors were adept at political man-oeuvring, but even after a widening of the parliamentary franchise in 1882 – before then there was a high income qualification, and the electorate was only 600,000 – social objectives counted for little. While drawing on the myths of the *Risorgimento* they did not want nationalism to be converted into continuing revolution, and they were unwilling to change the *status quo*. It was only after Mazzini was dead, in 1872, that a statue was erected in his memory. Some of his last thoughts on the new regime were that having sought to evoke the soul of Italy, all that he now saw before him was its corpse. Few Germans would have been so depressed or so frank. Garibaldi fared better: the personal relics of his campaigns had become museum relics of the *Risorgimento* in his lifetime.

Agostino De Pretis, who became left-wing Prime Minister in 1876, was a Lombard by birth with a Mazzinian past. He had accepted the House of Savoy, however, and had served in a ministry led by Urbano Raltazzi who died in 1873. In office as Prime Minister for 11 years until his death in 1887 perfected a system he called *trasformismo*, taking your political opponents into your orbit, whatever political labels they attached to themselves, a system associated in retrospect with Cavour whom De Pretis had opposed. The system did not change in 1887 when De Pretis died and gave way to his Sicilian rival Francesco Crispi, in youth a republican who had been one of Garibaldi's Thousand in 1860. In office Crispi venerated Bismarck and pushed Italy into expensive and unsuccessful colonial ventures in Africa. Following in the wake of Bismarck, he reduced the powers of Parliament and its independence.

In 1877 on a visit to London Crispi had met Gladstone, who had sharply criticized the old Bourbon regime in Naples when it was not fashionable to do so and had once described the unification of Italy as 'among the greatest marvels of our time'. Yet under Crispi, who died in 1901, there were no signs that it was such a marvel. In the twentieth century it was to be claimed by the highly intelligent Italian Marxist, Antonio Gramsci, that the most important feature of the *Risorgimento* had been a 'missing revolution' (*rivoluzione mancata*).

In Germany, less bedevilled by endemic regional poverty and by parliamentary squabbling, there were quite different political problems, and the Bismarckian era, which lasted until 1890, was a distinctive era of unchallenged power, with a strong belief in the nation's future. There were problems, however, in the rate and scale of industrialization in a society with an agrarian base and an authoritarian government. German industrialization took place in very different circumstances from industrialization in late-eighteenth century Britain. Yet like industrialization at all times and in all places it was an uneven process. Bismarckian Germany after 1870 did not enter a period of exceptional prosperity. Economic crisis in 1873 brought to an end a 'promoters' boom' and the economy limped through the later 1870s.

The German experience was not unique, but it had special features. The 1873 crisis followed three years of hectic business promotion in Berlin, fuelled by a large French war indemnity. It was a landmark date in Germany which figures far less prominently in British history, although it affected France and

Austria as well. It followed three years of falling prices, including the price of land, and falling rates of profits not only in Berlin but in Europe as a whole.

One reaction to this new conjunction of circumstances was protection, and even in Britain, still the world's largest trading nation, where the gospel of free trade retained its hold, protectionist voices could be heard, rising it was said 'as if from the tomb'. France returned to protection soon after the fall of Napoleon III. So did Russia, and in Germany protection was the key to Bismarck's domestic politics during the last decade of his power. In 1879 he introduced a tariff in the 'national interest' not only on agricultural products (this satisfied the Junkers) but on iron and steel (which satisfied West German industralists). In so doing he was able to raise revenue which would be outside the control of the constituent German states. And he met with only limited opposition.

Britain remained attached to free trade until after the First World War (see below, p.242), but this was not the only difference between Germany and Britain. In Germany the state actively fostered industrialization, as did the banks. Meanwhile – and partly as a result – large organizations flourished, including the chemical industry, were scientifically based, and science was taught in institutions strongly supported by local, regional and national government, including the great Charlottenberg Technische Hochschule, set up in 1879. Germans recognized that their capacity to compete with other countries, particularly Britain, depended both on research and on education, and that only by competitive drive could there be a widening of markets. The Potash Syndicate, founded in 1881, aimed deliberately at the exploitation of new foreign outlets, and in 1910 the state insisted on its further continuation.

In trade too the *Deutsche Bank*, founded in 1870, was encouraged by the state to extend German 'spheres of influence' abroad. As Germany climbed higher in what was already thought of as an international league table, Germany and Britain inevitably became economic rivals. Although each was a good customer of the other, the rivalry was a new factor in international relations which received more and more public attention both in Germany and in Britain just before and just after the fall of Bismarck. There was particular publicity for the fact that Germany's commercial fleet, one of the smallest in Europe in 1879, came second only to that of Britain by the end of the century.

Economic progress did not foster a more democratic government as it had done, state by stage, in Britain. On coming to power in 1862, Bismarck had been strongly opposed by liberals, but from the mid-1860s down to 1879 he relied on the parliamentary support of the majority of 'National Liberals' among them. Their liberalism had little in common with Gladstonian liberalism and their efforts to explore the implications of parliamentary government were limited and belated. As one of them put it, 'the time for ideals is past, and the duty of politicians is to ask not for what is desirable, but for what is attainable'. More positively, they supported Bismarck's attack on Roman Catholic privileges (and 'clericalism') in the so called *Kulturkampf* (struggle of cultures) of the early 1870s, when a new Centre Party emerged in 1871 to defend the Church. Some of the National Liberals would even have been prepared to support his open move towards protection in 1879.

Unwilling to trust them, Bismarck made a *volte-face* in 1879 when he made his peace with the Centre Party, but he could not trust its Roman Catholic leaders either. Nor, had he done so, could they have provided him with a parliamentary majority. Yet once he had secured his tariff in 1879 his description of the National Liberals, now divided, were as his cutting descriptions of the members of the Frankfurt Parliament 30 years had been. They were, he once said, 'the gentlemen whom our sun does not warm and whom our rain does not moisten'. By making them appear disloyal not only to their Emperor but to their country, Bismarck ensured that they suffered heavy defeats at the election of 1881 from which they never recovered. The liberals were in decline in Austria at the same time, and Franz Josef used his influence against them at the elections of 1879. Never again in the nineteenth century did they achieve a majority in Parliament.

Bismarck's moves towards seeking support from conservative groups, who, above all else, were alarmed at the spectre of socialism, may well have accelerated the growth inside Germany of social democracy, a new force distrusted by most liberals just as much as – if not more than – by conservatives. Bismarck tried to buy himself out of danger on this front by introducing sickness insurance in 1883, accident insurance in 1884 and old age pensions in 1889, the first statesman in Europe to follow this social policy. He could claim, as some German conservatives and professors of political economy asserted, that 'protection of the rights of labour' was one of the necessary forms of protection, fully in line with the traditions of German history going back to the Middle Ages. He could also claim that, like agricultural protection, it was in the national interest.

Long before the 1880s Bismarck had revealed that his own instincts were paternalistic, and like Disraeli in Britain he was willing to make sizeable bids for working-class support. Thus, as early as the 1860s, he had held secret talks with one of the first independent German socialist leaders, Ferdinand Lassalle. Bismarck could not prevent the rise of German social democracy, which adopted Marxist or near-Marxist programmes, but he made it as difficult as he could for the socialists to rely on German mass support. They nonetheless created at Eisenach in 1869 what later became the most powerful Social Democratic party in Europe. They were divided in their attitudes towards the Franco-Prussian War of 1870, with the followers of Ferdinand Lassalle supporting it, and August Bebel, a Prussian, and Wilhelm Liebknecht, a follower of Marx, opposing it, but they united again in 1875 – with a new political platform, the 'Gotha Programme'. In 1871 Bebel had been the only Social Democrat in the *Reichstag*: in 1877, however, the party won 12 seats and attracted 9 per cent of the total German vote.

It was in these circumstances that in 1878 Bismarck carried an anti-socialist law providing for the dissolution of all social democratic, socialist and Communist associations. It also included clauses threatening printers, booksellers and innkeepers with loss of licences if they collided with the law. As a result many Social Democratic institutions, including newspaper and publishing firms, went out of business and the powerful German trade unions, although not affiliated to the party, were affected too. Between 1878 and 1890, when the law was repealed after Bismarck's fall, 900 persons were expelled from their homes and about 1,500 imprisoned. Nonetheless, whatever Bismarck did either by way of repression or 'social insurance' he could not stop the advance of social democracy. The Social Democratic vote fell by a quarter in 1881, but was larger in 1884 than in 1878 and more than tripled in 1890.

Within the new German nation a largely insulated Social Democrat subculture took shape, always under the scrutiny of the Police. The Erfurt Programme (1891) was explicitly Marxist (although there were fierce disputes about what Marxist theory and tactics were correct), and because the party was kept out of power it retained a belief in revolution without being prepared to make one[7], it became the largest socialist party in the world, which in the words of a party ideologist in 1893 was 'a revolutionary party, but not a party that makes revolutionaries'.

Unlike his opposite numbers in most other European countries, Bismarck was never a party leader, drawing his supporters out and encouraging them to participate in power. He made no effort to educate his countrymen, whether they opposed or supported him, and when he had to make constitutional statements fell back on unqualified support for the monarchy. This was to prove his own political undoing when a new German emperor, Wilhelm II, took over in 1890. Young, ambitious and more in tune with the restless mood of the new and richer Germany which had taken shape between 1871 and 1890, Wilhelm was determined to make his own policies. The Chancellor had to go, and Germany entered a new phase, dangerous and wayward, in its history.

What remained was a national ideology which Germans had fostered in place of liberalism. Bismarck spoke the language of duty, but many German exponents of national power expressed their ideology in language that could veer between sentimentality and totalitarianism. For the National Liberal Professor Heinrich von Treitschke, the worst sin of the state was feebleness and its highest moral duty was to increase its power. Only great and powerful states deserved to exist. It was the sociologist Max Weber, however, 30 years younger than Treitschke, who emphasized most strongly that unification in 1871 was a beginning for Germans and not an end. In his inaugural lecture delivered at Freiburg University in 1895 he demanded that Germany should become a world power. Unless unification became the 'starting point for a German *Weltmachtpolitik*', 1871 would seem like 'a youthful folly, which the nation committed in its declining days and would have been better dispensed with because of its expense'.

NATIONS AND EMPIRES

No account of nation building in the nineteenth century would be complete if it dealt only with Germany and Italy or even with those two countries and the multinational Habsburg Empire. Nationalism was a force in all parts of Europe, associated in many instances (as in Austria-Hungary and, above all, the Ottoman Empire) with partition more than with unification. It was also associated, however, with dreams of huge national territories on a new map of Europe, including a revived Poland that would cross the existing frontiers of three dynastic empires. This chapter ends with a new map of eastern and central Europe drawn up after yet another European Congress, fittingly held in Berlin, the city where Bismarck grappled with the domestic and foreign problems of the German empire.

Nationalism within this context was associated with language and with religious differences, but before turning to eastern and central Europe it is useful to consider how it expressed itself in other parts of Europe in a period very different from the late 1840s and the early 1850s. In the west of Europe was Ireland, an agrarian and largely Roman Catholic appendancy of a Protestant and increasingly industrial Britain (with Irish industrialization concentrated in the Protestant north). There were people of Irish origin scattered throughout the British Empire and Irishmen serving in the British forces, but Ireland's representatives in the Westminster Parliament remained hostile to the Act of Union, the existence of which was reaffirmed in 1886 when the Liberal Party split on the issue. A 'Home Rule' Irish Party had been founded in 1870 which in 1878 chose Charles Stewart Parnell as its leader. He remained in that position until 1889 when his political career was ruined in a much publicized divorce case. In a different part of Europe's west, Belgium, Flemish nationalists, both Roman Catholics and Protestants, demanded the extended use of the Flemish language in the Army, in courts, in schools. The University of Ghent, founded in 1816, was a centre of Flemish studies.

In the north of Europe was Norway, an independent-minded community of farmers and fishermen, largely Protestant and still tied to Sweden by the settlement of 1815 in which it had been treated as a pawn. The Norwegians adopted and fostered their own national language, *Landsmaal*, had their own Parliament (*Storting*) and after constitutional disputes secured their own control over ministers (but not over foreign policy) in 1884. In Finland there was a growing demand for the teaching of Finnish in schools – most educated Finns had Swedish as their first language – and during the reign of Alexander I officials and courts were required to accept documents and pleas in the Finnish language. The Finnish philosopher/statesman Johan Wilhelm Snellman (1806–1881) was a more effective politician than Parnell, and in 1878 Finland secured its own conscript army. There was to be a backlash between 1900 and 1901, however, when the army was disbanded and 'Russification' was imposed.

The Russians had been drawn deeply into Slav politics between the 1850s and the 1890s. It was not a coincidence that in 1867, the year of the foundation of the Dual Monarchy, the second Pan-Slav Conference was held in Moscow. Yet Pan-Slavism in its later phases was an imperialist rather than a nationalist movement and could be identified with reactionary philosophy and policymaking. Danilevski's *Russia and Europe* (1869), which went through five editions before the end of the century, not only unabashedly proclaimed Slav superiority but extolled Russia's 'special mission'.

Relations between different Slav communities were as complex as their relations with the empires of which they formed a part, as had been demonstrated before 1867 at the Slav Congress in Prague in 1848. Slavs lived in large numbers inside the boundaries of the Habsburg and the Ottoman Empire, but there were other submerged nationalities, including often sizeable 'pockets' of German-speakers who had migrated across the centuries. The different minorities within the Ottoman Empire, some of whom had been converted to Islam, enjoyed varying and fluctuating degrees of autonomy and cultural expression. 'Massacres' made news, but there was usually a high degree of tolerance, not least to Jews – and Gypsies – both to be tragic victims of twentieth-century racist nationalism grounded not in empire but in prejudice. Turkey too was to have a nationalist movement, the Young Turks. Confronting an autocratic Sultan, Abdul Hamid II, 'Abdul the Damned', who ruled from 1876 to 1908, the 'Young Turks' secured from him the setting up of a parliamentary system in 1907 before deposing him and replacing him with his younger brother Mohammed V.

Russian nationalism was itself a powerful, if latent, force within an expanding Russian Empire. Alexander II's emancipation of the peasants in 1861, however, without a revolution, did not turn them into a politically conscious force at the base of society. They were no longer forced to provide dues in cash, kind or labour to owners, but they had to pay redemption money, often borrowing it from the state. They held their land not as private property but as a share in the collective property of the village community (the *mir*). They were not free to move to the towns. The sense of Russia being distinctive in Europe in its institutional frame was strong, although land problems were common to most parts of eastern Europe, particularly as population grew.

In most, but not all, of Europe, great power rivalry influenced patterns of allegiance and of aspiration. The Irish had something in common with the Poles, but they were not subject to influences from three directions – Austria, Russia and Prussia – as were the Poles. Nor, for all the religious differences, were there any places outside the Balkans where local populations included both Christians (of various sorts) and Muslims. It was not until after the First World War – and then not completely – that the map of Europe began to show most of its boundaries as national boundaries, and even then it was to reflect imperfectly, as any map must, the distribution of 'nationalities', some of whom thought in terms of bigger affiliations, 'Pan-Slav', Pan-German or 'Pan-Scandinavist'.

The nineteenth-century developments within the Habsburg Empire (itself appealing to history) were always revealing, for within its extensive frontiers nationalism, including German nationalism, could express itself at the same time in pure and in perverted form. When Hungary secured equal rights in 1867 and the Empire became a Dual Monarchy (Franz Josef was crowned with the crown of St Stephen in Budapest), there were some Hungarians, as there had always been some Austrian Germans, who hoped that moderate policies would be followed towards the other national minorities. Yet most Hungarian nationalists cared little for such considerations. Their intensely proud nationalism reached its nineteenth-century climax in 1896 with the celebration of the 'millennium' of Magyar power on the Danube.

The position of the Czechs was often equivocal. After the founding of the Dual Monarchy they were unable to secure similar arrangements in Bohemia, and they went into total opposition to centralizing 'liberal' administrations in Vienna from 1867 to 1879. One Austrian politician, Edvard Taafe, born into a noble family with Irish origins and a friend of Franz Josef, who served him for more years than any other Austrian politician, wished to favour them, but he did not become Prime Minister until 1879 after the Congress of Berlin.

CRISIS AND CONGRESS

The crisis of 1875 to 1878 was the most testing of all the so-called Near Eastern crises, largely because Russia threw all its weight behind the creation of a new big Bulgaria, carved out of the disintegrating Ottoman Empire. The politically active Slav-speaking Bulgars had pushed demands for increased use of their language since the 1860s, and in 1870 the Sultan, pressed by Russia, had recognized the ecclesiastical authority of the Patriach of Bulgaria as head of a Bulgar Church which no longer accepted the authority of the Patriarch in Constantinople.

In 1875 mountain revolts in the Ottoman provinces of Bosnia and Herzegovina adjacent to the Austro-Hungarian border triggered off this crisis. They were occasioned by a bad harvest in 1874 which drove peasants to flee from Turkish tax collectors, and as revolt spread it drew in volunteers from Serbia, Croatia, Slavonia, Slovenia and even Russia. There were also Garibaldists from Italy. Many peasants were killed, and the roads were crowded with large numbers of refugees; more than 100,000 left Bosnia in conditions of great hardship.

A subsequent uprising which followed in 1876 in the Bulgarian provinces of the Ottoman Empire, was put down savagely, and as news spread the principalities of Serbia and Montenegro declared war on the Ottoman Empire, having agreed beforehand that Serbia would annex Bosnia and Montenegro Herzegovina. Serbia was quickly defeated, but Montenegro held its own, and the crisis reached its climax when on 24 April 1877 Russia declared war on the Ottoman Empire, backed by Pan-Slavs who were as much opposed to the Austrian Empire as they were to the Ottoman Empire. The campaign was not well handled, but it ended in disaster for Turkey. The

Russians entered Sofia in January 1878, and as they swept forward to Constantinople, the Turks sued for peace.

In March 1878 the Treaty of San Stefano, in effect dictated by Russia, was signed between them. Romania, Serbia and Montenegro were recognized as completely independent national states, and an enormous new principality of Bulgaria was created, reaching from the Black Sea to the mountains of Albania. It even included a stretch of the Aegean coast. This was a Pan-Slav peace, although it divided the Slavs against each other and left Bosnia and Herzegovina under Turkish suzerainty.

The crisis, unlike most previous Balkan crises, could not be 'localized' in scope. It stirred and divided foreign public opinion at the same time as it provoked conflicting foreign policies in Europe's major capitals, with the main divisions of opinion about what was happening and how to respond to it appearing in the country farthest away from the action, Britain. There the liberal Gladstone emerged from retirement to support the Bulgarians. Thundering against Turkish atrocities, he drew on – or rather was driven by – popular liberal enthusiasm expressed at huge public meetings and demonstrations. Gladstone knew little of the Bulgarians, but then he knew even less of the Afghans when in 1879 he urged a large and enthusiastic popular audience in Scotland to 'remember that the sanctity of life in the hill villages of Afghanistan, among the winter snows, is as inviolable in the eye of Almighty God as can be your own'. Moral and political principle 'passes over the whole surface of the earth and embraces the meanest along with the greatest in its unmeasured scope'.

The Conservative Prime Minister during the years of crisis, Disraeli, as highly suspicious of Gladstone as of Russian designs in the Balkans and further afield – and afraid of Russia gaining access to the Mediterranean through the Black Sea – tried to eschew all moralizing. Britain's interests mattered just as much to him as German interests did to Bismarck. The Austrian government was divided even before San Stefano about what their interests were. Should they become involved with Russia in the partition of the Ottoman Empire? Should they resist a further growth of Russian power on its borders? Should they take independent action? Even before decisions had to be taken, it was apparent that earlier agreement reached between Austria, Russia and Germany (the Three Emperors' League) to resist revolution and to maintain the *status quo* was a broken reed.

As a bilateral peace San Stefano went too far to be acceptable to the other great powers. Indeed, in February 1878, before it was signed, Disraeli had ordered a British fleet to sail through the Dardanelles and anchor off Constantinople. He was determined to demonstrate Britain's interest in the survival of the Ottoman Empire. And after the signing of the treaty in March 1878, Austria proposed, with British support, that it be referred to a congress of the great powers. The Russians had to give way, and the Congress was held at Berlin during June and July 1878, with Bismarck willingly offering to play the part of honest broker. Unharassed by any expressions of free public opinion inside his own country, he was unwilling to give Russia a free hand against Austria; and in 1879, when the crisis was over, his support of Austria was to be enshrined in a dual alliance of the utmost long-term significance. Yet in 1877 he had taken no steps to restrain Russia from attacking the Ottoman Empire, and in a famous speech, contrasting in content and style with Gladstone's great speeches on this issue, he argued that 'the Eastern question' involved 'no German interest which would be worth the bones of a single Pomeranian grenadier'.

Attended by the chief ministers of the great powers, including Disraeli from London and Andrassy from Vienna, the Congress of Berlin, presided over by Bismarck, was the last glittering gathering associated with what came to be thought of after the First World War of the twentieth century as the 'old' European diplomacy, the diplomacy in which Bismarck excelled. Essentially, the Congress was a 'carve-up'. The Ottoman Empire was 'saved' and its integrity guaranteed, but it lost most of its European territories to new national states. As at San Stefano, Romania, Serbia and Montenegro were recognized as independent, but the big Bulgaria was split into three. One part became an autonomous principality; the second became an Ottoman province under a Christian Governor; and the third, Macedonia, was handed back to the Sultan. In 1885 the first and second portions were to become united under a German – and not a Slav – King of Bulgaria, Ferdinand, a younger son of the Prince of Saxe-Coburg and a grandson of Louis Philippe. Bosnia and Herzegovina, treated as one, were handed to Austria for occupation and administration, and Britain received Cyprus, a dangerous legacy.

The Habsburgs expected to be welcomed in Bosnia, and sent the news of the decision of the Congress to Sarajevo by telegram ten days before it was printed in the newspapers of Europe's capital cities. They were not welcomed. Religion came into the reckoning when a green Islamic flag was flown outside the Sarajevo mosque, and it was only after victory in battle at Klokoti near Vitez and an assault, house by house, on Sarajevo that they won control. The troops had been commanded by a Croat nobleman. There were some Austrians who had opposed the occupation, fearing that it would be dangerous to add millions of Slavs to their large ethnic minority, and the new provinces were neither added to Hungary nor kept by the Austrian government in Vienna. They became Crown lands, administered through the Minister of Finance.

There was little to enthuse about in Vienna. In London, however, there seemed to be. British jingoism in 1878 ('we don't want to fight, but by jingo if we do') showed that Britain was not immune to nationalist fever, although the jingoists were subject to fierce internal criticism. Disraeli exploited the jingoism when he talked of bringing back from Berlin 'peace with honour'. The Italians could never make that claim. They secured no territorial gains, and when the Italian delegate boasted on his return to Rome that he had kept 'clean hands' he was mobbed by his compatriots and thrown out of office.

The new Balkan nations, each of which moved quickly to develop all the familiar apparatus of nationalism – anthems, flags, schools and barracks – were not satisfied nations. Romania, which lost Bessarabia to Russia (only a part of the Russian share of the final carve-up), actually had fewer Romanians within its new borders than within its old, and Romanian eyes were turning longingly towards possible territorial gains in Hungarian Transylvania. Serbia, which aspired to become the Piedmont-Sardinia of the Balkans, was now confronted with increased Austrian dominion over fellow Serbs living within the boundaries of occupied Bosnia and Herzegovina. Bulgarians, who had been dazzled with the prospect of a big Bulgaria, saw their territories dismembered in the very year when they had been put together. Not surprisingly, therefore, the Balkans began to be thought of as 'the cockpit of Europe'. They were also, however (to use another contemporary metaphor), a 'cauldron', and out of the cauldron further trouble for the rest of Europe, ill-informed as it was, was still to come.

Not all the problems were ethnic or religious, although Croatia was devotedly Roman Catholic and Serbia equally devotedly Orthodox. Ownership of land remained contentious. In 1876 the Turks had allowed serfs to free themselves by paying an indemnity, and many did so, but Austrian attempts to improve agriculture (without introducing a major land reform) were little appreciated. Serbia, dependent on Austria-Hungary for trade, resented Austrian economic and political power, and many of its citizens dreamed of a greater Serbia.

For the American historian and analyst of nationalism, Carlton J. H. Hayes, all that Berlin had done was to substitute for one sick man (the Ottoman Empire) half-a-dozen maniacs: 'For the Congress of Berlin drove the Balkan peoples mad.'[8] It is an inadequate and incomplete final verdict, but it points to another important conclusion. Insofar as there was madness in changing Europe, it would require more than *Realpolitik* to control it.

Notes

1. G. M. Trevelyan, *Manin and the Venetian Revolution of 1848* (1923) pp.vii–viii. A.J.P. Taylor took up and sharpened the phrase (A.J.P. Taylor, *A Personal History* (1983) p.190).
2. A. Green, *Fatherlands: State Building and Nationhood in Nineteenth-Century Germany* (2001).
3. See L. B. Namier, *Personalities and Powers* (1955).
4. Quoted in D. Hargreaves (ed.), *Bismarck and German Unification* (1991) pp.23, 32.
5. A.J.P. Taylor, *The Struggle for the Mastery of Europe, 1848–1918* (1954), p.82.
6. A Roman Catholic critic of Bismarck, Edmund Jörg, feared after the victory of 1871 that the 'humanity and civilization of the nineteenth century will give way in its final third to a new iron age'. H. Böhme, *Die Reichsgründung* (1967) p.26.
7. The story is told briefly in G. Lichtheim, *Marxism* (1961) pp.259ff.
8. See C. J. H. Hayes, *Essays on Nationalism* (1928) ch. 5, 'Nationalism and International War'.

Chapter 4

RIVALRY AND INTERDEPENDENCE, 1871–1914

'THE CAUSES OF WAR'

As was fully revealed during the 1870s, there were many contradictory forces inside and outside Europe during the 43 years of European hegemony that separated the founding of the German Empire in 1871 from the outbreak of the First World War in 1914, a European war that became a world war. It was fashionable, indeed, during and after that war to look back and identify these contradictory forces, domestic and international, as 'causes' of the war, distributing blame. More recently the word 'fuse' has replaced 'causes', with one American historian, Laurence Lafore, writing of the war's 'long fuse'.[1] Just as the period began, Disraeli predicted what the future might be like when he told Parliament in 1871 that the war between France and Germany was 'no common war like the Crimean War, the Italian War or the Austro-Prussian War. It represented a greater political event than the French Revolution last century', adding percipiently that he did not say 'a greater or a great, social event'. 'You have a new world, new influences at work, and unknown objects and dangers with which to cope.'

One identifiable force in the 'new world' around the turn of the century, militarism, was not new. It had never been confined to one country or group of countries, and in some places it had the force of a religion. Now it was intensified, and Disraeli's great opponent, Gladstone, saw it as the biggest danger in an unpredictable future. (Plutocracy, the role of wealth, was for him another). Militarists strutted. Brightly uniformed men on horseback were proud of their rank and of their code of honour, but most ominously they were proud too of their weaponry. It was placed on display not only on parades but at international exhibitions. There was a 300 per cent increase in the level of armaments, military and naval, in Europe between 1870 and 1914, made possible not only by decisions taken by political leaders but by the increasing wealth and advancing technology associated with industrialization.

Another force was autocracy, which was prominent on each side during the First World War when the Russian Empire was pitted against the Habsburg Empire. In Vienna liberalism and populism had checked it. In Russia Tsarist authority went unchecked before 1905 except by assassination. Three attempts were made to assassinate Alexander II before he was killed by an anarchist's bomb in 1881. When the first Russian socialist party came into existence in 1883 it was organized not in Russia but in Switzerland, and when revolution came in 1905 in circumstances which the exiled revolutionaries did not plan or foresee, they arrived too late to influence events. Seventy thousand people were arrested and 15,000 people killed before the revolution was put down. As a consequence the Tsar summoned a national assembly (the *Duma*) which met in April 1906, but dissolved it after two months. Three more such assemblies met before 1914, but they achieved little.

Autocracy was prominent in Germany too, where, if anachronistically, industrialization was accompanied by a 'neo-absolutist culture of the court' to which 'military brass' had special access. The annual cost of the court was more than the cost of the Reich Chancellor and his Chancellery, the Reich Justice Department, the Foreign Office (including the whole diplomatic corps) and the Colonial Office put together. The office of the Senior Marshal of the Court had an establishment of nearly 500 persons.[2]

A third force was imperialism, which usually referred to empires outside Europe rather than within it and to the fierce rivalry in distant lands to gain profit as well as power. For 'realistic' politicians, particularly in Germany, imperial policies seemed capable of diverting attention from internal social conflicts. Fürst Bernhard von Bülow, who took over the Foreign Ministry in an important ministerial reshuffle in 1897 and was soon to become Chancellor, wrote in retirement in 1914, in a widely read book, that *Weltpolitik* (a world policy) was 'the true antidote against social democracy'.

A fourth force, more contentious and more difficult to pin down, was moral disintegration, whether expressed in demagogic leadership or in mass hysteria. 'The popular imagination is by no means a thing to be left out of account when calculating political probabilities', a writer in a popular journal, *Science Siftings*, stated in 1897. The word 'masses' came into increasing use during that decade and the next in Germany, France, Austria and Britain, where there was more talk of *Masspsychosen*, the psychology of the masses, than of 'popular imagination'. One of its manifestations was anti-Semitism. Jews became scapegoats in Berlin, Vienna, Moscow and Paris. And attacks on them contributed to the unleashing of forces that it was difficult to keep under control. In a much publicized study, *The Crowd*, the French sociologist Gustave le Bon shifted attention from individuals to what he called 'a collective mind'. One of his key phrases was 'social contagion'.

Militarism, imperialism, autocracy and social contagion were all related to each other in the work of the English liberal writer, J. A. Hobson, who influenced the Russian Marxist Lenin, born Vladimir Ulyanov. Lenin shared his views on imperialism, in particular, and came to believe that successful revolution would come through war, as it eventually did in Russia in 1917. In searching for the 'causes' of war, however, most people looked no further than what a German under-secretary of state called (in August 1914, the month when European war broke out, called 'this d . . . d system of alliances, the curse of modern times'. In October 1916 the American President Woodrow Wilson, whose country was outside the system, blamed the war upon 'a concatenation of alliances and treaties, a complicated network of intrigue and espionage which unerringly caught the entire family in its meshes'. The fact that the network had been developed to a considerable degree in secrecy was for Wilson an additional factor responsible. 'Leaks' of secret information, some of them deliberate, had served as a weapon of diplomacy. So, too, had code-breaking and other forms of military and naval intelligence. They assumed greater importance between 1890 and 1914.

The origins of the European treaty system lay far back in time, although it was under Bismarck – who worked in terms of options, preferences for deals with particular countries or groups of countries according to the circumstances of the case – that the system was in his view perfected, as an instrument of peace between 1871 and his fall from power in 1890. Already, before the founding of the German Empire Bismarck had proved himself a master of treaty-making, using resourcefully both open and secret treaties as best suited his purpose. And after 1871, when he proclaimed the German Empire a 'satisfied' power, he was determined to use treaties, as Metternich had tried to do, in order to keep other powers in order. His skill was unmistakable. So, too, was the military power that lay behind its deployment and which he had demonstrated before 1870 that he was prepared to use. In addition to knowing exactly what he wanted, he had a keen sense of exactly how far he dared go in order to get it.

Nevertheless, the Bismarckian peace was a peace in which rivalries and conflicts were exploited rather than eliminated, and Bismarck himself had no commanding sense of European interest. Sometimes his exploitation involved a degree of subtlety and subterfuge that generated new misunderstandings, not least in his own country. He himself remained prone to nightmares. If inside Europe there was often fear on the part of rulers, officials and large sections of the public, particularly fear of social revolution, there was always fear inside Bismarck himself.

It could be the fact that he was no longer at the helm, of course, that caused the subsequent hardening of the European alliance system into rigid blocs after 1890 when he was succeeded by lesser men than himself. His immediate successor, Georg Caprivi, who was a loyal servant of the new Emperor, Wilhelm II, fell into this category. Yet he and other men who succeeded him thought in terms of options as Bismarck had done, treating war as a legitimate continuation of policy. A favourite word in their vocabulary was 'sphere of interest', used in relation both to Europe and, just as frequently, to the world. Britain was already a world power in 1871. Indeed, it had been one since the eighteenth century, and over a long period of time it had identified its own 'spheres of influence', extending the notion in the late-nineteenth century to include what Lord Rosebery, a Liberal imperialist, called 'precautionary' zones that other powers might claim. Germany, which was not a world power in 1871, developed a conscious thrust to become one only after the fall of Bismarck in 1890. Many Germans from different backgrounds felt that Britain should lose its dominant role.

There was intellectual as well as economic backing for Wilhelm's professed desire to wield a world trident. The economist and economic historian Gustav Schmoller predicted in 1890 that the great world empires of the twentieth century would be Germany, Russia, Britain, the United States and, thereafter, possibly China. Europe, he and others claimed, was too small and crowded. Expansion was necessary. Moreover, within Europe many Germans perceived of their country as 'encircled'. After 1897 its leaders wished to break through – and out. And this inevitably implied confronting Britain.

THE ALLIANCE SYSTEM

While Bismarck was in office, he worked out relevant power equations with conspicuous care and set them out later in his *Gedanken und Erinnerungen* (*Reflections and Reminiscences*). They can be set out simply in diagrammatic form, and in the tables that follow — represents an alliance; ...... an agreement or entente; - - - a commitment to remain neutral if one of the allied parties is at war; and + + + + and a commitment to co-operate over imperial issues. Arrows pointing ← or → represent which power an alliance or entente was directed against, and a vertical line | shows which powers were isolated in the pattern.

Bismarck's favourite preference was for mutual understanding among three great powers – Austria, Russia and Germany – with a fourth, Italy, added when necessary. The 'triple alliance of monarchical powers' as he called it in his *Gedanken* left defeated France and neutral Britain in isolation, and it was important for Bismarck that they should never work closely together over a significant period of time. He described the fourth power in his equations as 'monarchical Italy'. The adjective 'monarchical' mattered to him. He did not refer to Britain as 'monarchical Britain', but couched his preference for his 'triple alliance' in terms of the common threat to all three of an 'anti-monarchical development either sinking slowly or moving by leaps and bounds' into 'social republic'. He realized his purpose in the League of the Three Emperors (*Dreikaiserbund*) of 1873, knowing clearly that Austria-Hungary and Russia had divergent interests, particularly in the Balkans, but showing little concern himself for 'the fragments of nations which peopled the peninsula'.

Table 1

Britain   Germany ———— Russia ———— Austria ++++++ Italy

France

Bismarck's preference for a 'common understanding' between the three monarchies had been shared by Metternich when he was in power in Vienna, but there was one new force in Europe which had not been present in Metternich's time – the Workers' International which Marx and Engels monitored and sought to control.

Even before the 'Eastern crisis' of 1875 to 1878 exposed the problems inherent in this alliance, Bismarck had engineered or exploited a Franco-German 'war scare' that drove both Russia, inside his alliance system, and Britain, outside it, into common protests. 'Is war in sight?' a German newspaper headline asked after the French had passed a law in 1875 adding a fourth battalion to each regiment of the Army. The idea of a 'preventive' war by Germany so soon after 1870 was anathema both to London and St Petersburg.

It was not so much a combination of Britain and Russia that Bismarck most feared, but a combination of Tsarist Russia and Republican France, and after the Congress of Berlin in 1878, when he played the part of broker, Bismarck's nightmares grew more frequent, for he realized that Russia had become an aggrieved as well as an 'unsatisfied' power: it could gain something from change, as France had done under the now deposed Napoleon III. What the Russians most wanted – access to the Mediterranean through the Black Sea – could scarcely be secured peacefully: the Tsar was disposed to look upon what happened there as an enforcement of a European coalition against Russia under the leadership of Bismarck himself. Among Bismarck's nightmares was an unlikely Prussian isolation; and it was in the aftermath of the Congress of Berlin that he decided – in spite of bitter opposition from his Emperor, an uncle of the Tsar – to seek a Dual Alliance with Austria-Hungary.

Table 2

Britain	Germany	Russia
France	Italy	Austria

The result was a comprehensive treaty which Andrassy, the Habsburg negotiator, well judging Bismarck's fears, insisted should contain very specific clauses. The first clause stated that if either one of the two contracting parties, 'contrary to their hope' and against 'their loyal desire', should be attacked by Russia, the other party would go to its assistance with its 'whole strength'. The second clause, covering attack by any other power, pledged 'benevolent neutrality' at the least, unless Russia supported the other power 'either by active participation or by military measures which constitute a menace to the party attacked'.

The Dual Alliance between Germany and Austria, defensive though it was in its origin and intent, proved to be far more lasting than any other nineteenth-century treaty. Concluded originally for a period of five years (Bismarck watched the dates of the expiry of treaties as keenly as Americans watched dates of presidential elections), the Alliance was renewed in 1883 and in

1902, and it lasted until the collapse of the Habsburg Empire in 1918. It was, indeed, the prop of the pre-war alliance system which developed into a confrontation of alliances; and by drawing Germany into Austro-Hungarian politics in the Balkans – Germany had other interests of its own there, particularly economic – it contributed directly to the war of 1914–18. Bismarck, however, certainly did not see future dangers in this way. Nor did the Marquess of Salisbury, British Foreign Secretary in 1879, who hailed news of the Alliance from the Austro-Hungarian government as 'good tidings of great joy'. For Bismarck, it would be necessary to supplement the Alliance with further treaties – if possible, with the Tsar, to whom, at the Emperor's insistence, details of the treaty were sent secretly.

Before further agreement with Russia, a revived Three Emperors' League was recreated in 1881. Differences between Britain and Russia in the Near East and Asia had predisposed Russia to sign it. The treaty was to be brought into operation in the first instance for three years. This time Bismarck had to win over the Austro-Hungarians. Germany and Austria-Hungary agreed that they would not assist Britain against Russia (the names of the countries were not spelled out), and Russia agreed to remain neutral in a war between France and Germany or between Italy and Austria-Hungary. Attached clauses stipulated in some detail the policies that Austria-Hungary and Russia would follow. The new League, far more formal and specific in its arrangements than the old League, was kept a secret from the other powers. It was renewed in 1884, and when it came to an end in 1887 (in the same year as other Bismarckian treaties) the implications were serious.

The arrangement reached in 1881 represented the best that Bismarck could obtain. And he soon had a supplementary agreement, at first sight of a remarkable kind. One year after the signing of the Three Emperors' League, a secret Triple Alliance, described as such was signed between Italy, Germany and Austria-Hungary, with five years' duration.

Table 3

This alliance left Britain isolated, although such isolation was thought of by Salisbury as 'splendid isolation'.

The Italians, so recently within the orbit of Vienna, naturally would have preferred an alliance with Germany alone, but Bismarck insisted on Habsburg participation. This time particular countries were named in what was a purely defensive treaty. 'In case Italy without direct provocation on her part should be attacked by France for any reason whatsoever, the two other contracting parties shall be bound to lend help and assistance with all their forces to the party attacked.' Vienna did not insist on Italian help against a Russian attack.

The Italian negotiator had already refused to promise military assistance to Germany against an attack from France.

Bismarck had no illusions about Italian military power, but the value of the Triple Alliance to him was obvious. Just as the League of the Three Emperors kept Russia apart from France, so the Italian Alliance kept Italy aloof from France and lessened the chances of what to Bismarck would have been an unnecessary conflict between Italy and Austria-Hungary. Meanwhile, the two smaller powers, Serbia and Romania, both at this stage anxious, if for different reasons, to keep aloof from Russia, secretly moved into the German–Austro-Hungarian orbit in 1881 and 1883 – the former through a ten-year alliance with Austria in 1881 and the latter through a five-year alliance with both Austria and Germany in 1883.

In 1884 Bismarck showed the range and resilience of his diplomacy when he co-operated closely with France, deliberately forced Britain into isolation, and secured the first colonial gains for Germany in Africa.

Table 4

British isolation was always possible in the nineteenth century, and sometimes the British themselves, like Salisbury, thought of it as 'splendid'. There was nothing splendid for Britain, however, about this particular isolation in 1884. Gladstone, a politician for whom Bismarck had no respect, was now Prime Minister and 1884, a year of mounting domestic tension and national humiliation was an *annus horribilis* in Gladstone's political career. Far away in the Sudan General Charles Gordon, whom Gladstone had dispatched there, met his lonely death.

The alignments of 1884 were short-lived, however, and by 1887 Bismarck was preferring a quite different option as far as Britain and France were concerned. A 'Mediterranean agreement' reached between Austria, Italy and Britain, now with Salisbury as Prime Minister, was designed to preserve the *status quo* in the Mediterranean, Adriatic, Aegean and Black Seas and to provide a barrier against both Russia and France.

Table 5

There was a bonus for Bismarck. The signing of the agreement persuaded the Italians to renew the Triple Alliance (albeit in changed form). There were two main reasons why Bismarck was anxious to secure its renewal even though in its new form it allowed for changes in the *status quo* for the benefit of two of the three partners. In France a new nationalist Minister of War, General Boulanger, Bonapartist in his sympathies and an 'apostle of revenge', seemed to be threatening the peace, and in Russia there was a clamorous agitation against the renewal of the Three Emperors' League on the grounds that it limited Russian freedom to manoeuvre in the Balkans. Earlier there had been tension in Vienna and Budapest, and Bismarck had to tell Vienna that if Austria-Hungary attacked or provoked Russia it would be doing so on its own risk and that Germany would not come to its aid under the 1879 treaty.

The year 1887 was as dangerous for Bismarck as the year 1884 had been propitious, although he secured from a newly elected Reichstag an increase in the size of the German Army which had been denied him a year earlier. He now felt it essential to secure an agreement with Russia, which he did in June – in a secret Reinsurance Treaty, signed in the month that the Three Emperors' League expired and one month after France (very fortunately for him) dropped Boulanger from office. By this treaty, which few knew about or suspected, Germany was assured of Russian neutrality if attacked by France, and Russia was assured of German neutrality if attacked by Austria or Great Britain.

Table 6

The Reinsurance Treaty was not incompatible with the Dual Alliance of 1879, but it required great nerve on Bismarck's part to maintain both it and the Dual Alliance at the same time. This was not Bismarck's favourite prefer- ence, for it pledged Germany to recognize Russia's historic rights in the Balkans and its 'preponderant and decisive influence' in Bulgaria. Yet it was the most acceptable treaty in the circumstances, and it seemed effective enough to continue to ward off the dangers of a Franco-Russian alliance.

With great difficulty the treaty stood up to the strains of a year when Russia, still deeply embroiled in Bulgarian politics, rearmed along the German and Hungarian frontiers. Bismarck had to resort to other diplomatic and economic moves, such as restricting Russian credit in Germany and publishing the text of the 1879 Dual Alliance to show how deeply committed Germany was to the support of Austria. 'We Germans fear God and nothing else in the world' was his message to Europe. He was right to direct attention to the brute fact that in the last resort German diplomacy rested on superior power.

Bismarck's own position as juggler-in-chief, however, was limited through- out the whole period from 1871 to 1890 in one crucial way. Unless he were backed by the Emperor, he would be nobody. This was the key relationship within the constitution of the German Empire, and Bismarck himself had so fashioned it. Before the Reinsurance Treaty came up for renewal in 1890 not only had Franco-Russian economic and military relations drawn a little closer

(German withdrawal of credits was followed by Russian borrowing and purchase of military equipment in France), but the 91-year-old Emperor, Wilhelm I, with whom Bismarck had often quarrelled, but who had always yielded on major matters to Bismarck, however reluctantly, was dead. His first successor in 1888, Friedrich, liberal in his sympathies and married to Queen Victoria's daughter, reigned for only three months; his second successor, Wilhelm II, was barely 31 (Bismarck was now nearing 75), and he was to reign until his deposition in 1918 after Germany's defeat in the First World War.

A new Reichstag, elected in 1890, reduced Bismarck's parliamentary support – the National Liberals lost 57 seats, and the Conservatives lost 24. By itself, however, this would not have mattered. Bismarck had bold plans for calling new elections and, if need be, for introducing martial law and amending the constitution. What did matter was that Wilhelm II, who had begun by admiring Bismarck, did not like this approach. He feared not only that Bismarck would lead the country into civil war but that he would establish his own dictatorship for ever. 'It was a question whether the Hohenzollern dynasty or the Bismarck dynasty should rule.' After weeks of growing disagreement following the elections, Wilhelm demanded Bismarck's resignation on 17 March, and nine days later the two men had their last meeting. 'I am as miserable as if I had again lost my grandfather', Wilhelm wrote to a relative. But he ended with the words 'Full steam ahead'.

It was of special importance at this point that the chief official in the German Foreign Office, Friedrich von Holstein, had long opposed the Reinsurance Treaty, which was due for renewal, on the grounds that it was incompatible with the Dual Alliance. The Emperor was willing to renew the treaty, but Holstein was able to persuade Bismarck's successor, Caprivi, a soldier with no previous diplomatic experience, that the Bismarckian system was too complicated. For Holstein it seemed irrelevant that the Russians with a pro-German Foreign Minister wished to renew the treaty. A more open foreign policy would be desirable, one that would involve not only a loyal understanding with Austria but increasing friendship with Britain.

The Reinsurance Treaty was not renewed, therefore, and while Wilhelm expressed continued desire for Russian friendship, a bilateral Anglo-German agreement was signed in July, involving an exchange of the island of Heligoland (which the British had held since 1795) for colonial territory held by the Germans in Africa (Zanzibar and Uganda). In May 1891 the Triple Alliance with Austria and Italy was renewed for 12 years. And when British ships paid a ceremonial visit to Venice and Fiume in June 1891 – in the same year Wilhelm visited London – there was much talk that the Triple Alliance would turn into a Quadruple Alliance with Britain as the fourth party.

Table 7

It did not need a Bismarck or a diagram to deduce what would happen next given the fears of isolation and the trust in the power of alliances that characterized this period of European history. Yet there were strong reasons why Russia and France should not join together. There were Frenchmen, committed to the cause of revolution, who feared any association with the most 'reactionary power' in Europe, and even more there were Russians who thought that the French Republic not only had 'revolutionary heart' but that it was notoriously undependable.

The first moves towards the Franco-Russian alliance were more dramatic than consequential. Thus, the Tsar listened bareheaded to the playing of the Marseillaise when French warships visited Kronstadt in July 1891. Eventually, however, in December 1893 (after the Germans had carried a new Army Bill and the French had been embroiled with the British in the colonial politics of the Far East) a secret Franco-Russian convention was signed. 'If France is attacked by Germany', the first clause read, 'or by Italy supported by Germany, Russia shall employ all her available forces to fight Germany.' The second clause dealt with the Triple Alliance: if the Triple Alliance powers mobilized, Russia and France would mobilize too, and the Treaty would remain in force for as long as the Triple Alliance lasted.

In the first instance, the signing of this new treaty, which was to become the second cornerstone of the early twentieth-century alliance system, did not harden the European power blocs. They still remained side by side, not face to face. This was largely because Britain never joined any alliance with Germany, Austria, and Italy – either in the early or the late-1890s, but partly also because in 1897 Franz Josef, on a visit to St Petersburg, agreed with the Tsar to co-operate to maintain the *status quo* in the Balkans and the Straits. It was as important a feature of this agreement that Austria–Hungary and Russia should restrain their own 'satellites', the new nation states formed throught the break-up of the Ottoman Empire, as that they themselves should remain in agreement.

As far as Britain was concerned, it was often easy during the 1890s for all the European powers together – Triple Alliance, France and Russia – to line up against it on colonial issues and they could act bilaterally too. Thus, in 1894 Germany supported France in blocking an African land deal between Britain and the Congo Free State, an enterprise in central Africa under the personal control of King Leopold of the Belgians; and a year later, to the irritation of the British government, Germany, Russia and France intervened to check Japan after it had defeated China and went on to acquire bases for themselves on the Chinese mainland.

Almost every year there was some such episode. In 1896 Wilhelm sent a congratulatory telegram to President Kruger, the head of the Boer Republic of the Transvaal, after the failure of the Jameson Raid (a freebooter raid by white settlers of British descent in South Africa that was staged with the connivance of Joseph Chamberlain, Britain's energetic and ambitious Colonial Secretary). When Britain went to war with the Boers in 1899 and soon became involved in a messy and surprisingly protracted conflict – a big power against a small one – most European countries expressed sympathy for the Boers. Both the French and German press revelled in anti-British diatribes and cartoons. It proved possible, however, for the British to survive the disapproval of foreign governments as well as of newspapers since they were secure in their command of the seas. Sea power was as vital in underpinning Britain's 'isolation' as Germany's land power was in underpinning the alliance system to which it belonged. Neither now thought in terms of a 'concert of Europe' as Gladstone always set out to do.

THE POLITICS OF EMPIRE

Before considering by what stages the European alliance system hardened after 1900 – and sea rivalry was to play an important part in drawing Britain into a hardening system – it is necessary to consider in more detail the politics of late-nineteenth-century empire. These were even more complex than the politics of Europe and cannot be summed up in diagrams. Decisions were made not only in European foreign offices but on the spot, miles away, and many people were involved in making them. Pressures came from missionaries preaching the gospel and adventurers dealing in gold and guns. Communications were improving, but were still slow. Orders could arrive too late.

Until the end of the 1860s the word 'imperialism' – one of many *isms* of the late-nineteenth century – had been used mainly with reference to the France of Napoleon III. It was not until 1869 that a British writer drew attention in a magazine to what he called 'imperialism in its best sense', by which he meant 'the consciousness that it is sometimes a binding duty to perform highly irksome or offensive tasks such as the defence of Canada or the government of Ireland'.

Profit was not mentioned in this statement, although there was clearly money to be made out of foreign investment whether in territories controlled directly by European countries or in other countries open to 'informal empire', the empire of development and trade. The statement concentrated also on white settlement, whereas most of the 'colonial gains' between 1869 and 1900 were in the Tropics.

These were the years of the so-called 'partition of Africa' and of struggles for peace in Asia and the Pacific. They were years, too, however, when two great powers outside Europe were emerging – the United States and Japan. In 1898 the United States by its victories over Spain and the occupation of Cuba and Puerto Rico and by the annexation of the Philippine Islands and Hawaii began a process of imperial expansion of its own, and in 1904 Japan issued an ultimatum to Russia in February 1904 and opened what were proved to be highly successful hostilities without a declaration of war. (See below p.137) The treaty which ended the war was signed not in Europe but in the United States.

Western European states became involved in China between the end of the Russo-Japanese war and 1900, as we have seen, securing concessions and creating coastal enclaves for themselves. It was in other parts of the world, however, that they made great territorial gains. From 1870 to 1910 colonial powers annexed over 11 million square miles of territory. The British Empire alone increased its territory by a half and its population by a third during the last three decades of the nineteenth century although anti-imperialist governments were sometimes in power in London. (Gladstone never approved of imperial expansion.) Likewise, France, where the imperialists never had their own way, added 3.5 million square miles of territory during the last two decades of the nineteenth century. One prime minister, Jules Ferry, who held office from 1883 to 1885, was a particularly active and vocal colonizer who extended French power in Indo-China and fell from office after a military reverse in far-off Tonkin (northern Vietnam). Germany too added 1 million square miles. Bismarck had once stated that his map of Europe was in Africa, and he loved to dissipate or to divert dangerous rivalries inside Europe by encouraging distant competition. Yet it was he who began German colonial expansion.

Others, more committed to it than Bismarck, and with all the rhetoric of empire at their disposal, could follow expansion through to the point where it excited fear in Britain. Meanwhile, the old empires of Spain and Holland continued to exist on the map – the latter growing in wealth, if not in size, the former losing valuable territory – and the old empire of Portugal grew both in size and wealth. Italy took part with little success in imperial competition (it failed in 1896 to establish power in Ethiopia), and Belgians, nominally without any empire, managed Leopold's Congo State until it was left to them in his will in 1889. Reverses in Africa led to the resignation of Crispi in 1896, and Leopold's ruthless policies came under attack in Belgium itself as well as abroad.

Statistics of territories gained or of private and public wealth tell only a part of the imperial story which was usually told at the time in non-statistical terms – in maps, in adventure stories, in travel books, in popular songs, and in rousing speeches on flag-draped platforms. Imperialism shared some of the same folklore as nationalism, for it always had its heroes and its myths. And like nationalism it could claim that the world was being partitioned not so much between competing but between complementary imperialisms, each with its own 'mission'. Sometimes, indeed, the different imperialisms could come together, united in the cause of 'civilization' and 'progress'.

British spokesmen usually drew a sharp distinction between themselves, along with their 'kith and kin', and the 'natives' or 'aborigines' whom they conquered or controlled. In the first case – Canada and Australia were obvious examples – settlers, among them waves of new immigrants, acquired substantial independence during the last half of the nineteenth century. The federal government of Australia dates back to 1900. In the second case there was talk of 'burden', but there could also be exhilaration. There was also a will to 'get things straight'. 'We find by practical experience', wrote Sir Francis Younghusband, explorer of Central Asia (where British and Russian interests clashed in what was sometimes called 'the great game'), 'that the affairs of the world will not work while there is disorder about.'

So many people were involved in 'imperialist' adventures, at so many levels of activity and in so many places, that it is difficult to generalize. In Africa, a scene of rivalry, there was a general sense of a 'dark continent' being explored and exploited, whereas in Asia, 'strange and mysterious', there were old religions and old cultures that could never be ignored. In 1837 when Queen Victoria ascended the throne European settlements in Africa were patches on the coast. By the time of her death in 1901 only two independent states remained in Africa – Ethiopia and the tiny republic of Liberia. Victoria was proud of her title of Empress of India, bestowed upon her at the instigation of Disraeli on 1 January 1877, and 20 years later she was even more proud of the presence of her 'Indian' and other 'native' subjects in the celebrations of her Diamond Jubilee in London. (The new adjective 'diamond' for a sixtieth jubilee came from Africa.)

By the last decade of the nineteenth century the question of 'the Far East', a composite term which reflects European dominance in the world, was brought to the fore not so much by direct European expansion as by the rise of an Asian power, Japan, which had already taken over much of the apparatus of European nationalism. (In 1880 the German bandmaster of British troops at Yokohama had been invited to set the words of a ninth-century hymn to music in order to provide a national anthem.)

Japan was also in the first stages of an industrial revolution that was supported by the power of the state and which was to transform the whole basis of its power in the twentieth century. In 1894–95, following a short Sino-Japanese war that demonstrated both Japanese strength and Chinese weakness, the Japanese went on to make territorial and other gains for themselves. By the Treaty of Shimonoseki, 17 April 1895, China and Japan recognized the independence of Korea, the territory at issue in the war, and Formosa, Port Arthur and a Chinese peninsula were ceded to Japan. In face of Russian, French and German protests – Britain abstained – Port Arthur and the peninsula were handed back to China, but a huge Japanese indemnity was imposed on China. Was the Chinese Empire the Ottoman Empire of the Far East? France, Russia and Germany made gains for themselves in 1895, but before the century ended the anti-foreign Boxer Rebellion in China alarmed European countries and the United States more than anything that had happened in Japan. By 1908 China was to have a draft constitution – something that the Sultans had never been prepared to do much about in Constantinople – and in 1912 it was to become a republic.

Looking at the 'imperializing' world as a whole – Africa, Asia, and the Pacific – the people involved in the intricate processes of expansion included explorers (Leopold, a latter-day *conquistador*, launched his African project at an international geographical congress in Brussels in 1876); missionaries of all denominations, spreading the gospel and with the gospel or gospels much else besides, including education; emigrants, acquiring new homes, far from their places of birth, along with new lifestyles; businessmen, big and small, seeking new raw materials (as different as rubber, minerals, and vegetable oils) or new outlets for manufactured goods; contractors, builders, architects and engineers erecting cities, harbours and railways; soldiers, fighting in what were called, often misleadingly, 'small wars'; and administrators, also big and small, with some big enough to be called – and to think of themselves in Napoleonic terms as – 'pro-consuls'. Such were the big three British pro-consuls of the late-nineteenth and early-twentieth-century empire: Evelyn Baring, first Earl of Cromer in Egypt, a country that linked Africa and the Ottoman Empire (as Napoleon, the first of the consuls, had known); George Curzon, the first Marquess Curzon in Persia and India; and Alfred, first Viscount Milner, a new recruit to the aristocracy, in South Africa.

The place of profit in imperial story is not easy to assess, although it was given a central place in theories of 'imperialism' that were developed on a Marxist basis by Lenin in the twentieth century. For him, after reading the English Liberal economist J. A. Hobson, the mainspring of imperialism was to be found not in trade but in investment. Colonies offered new outlets for capital, and capital invested overseas could bring higher returns than capital invested at home; it could also provide employment and raise domestic standards of living. There would be competition for markets, however, and Lenin claimed that the age of imperialism, which followed naturally and inexorably from the age of European capitalism, would lead to war.

The explanation Lenin offered was no more comprehensive than Marx's explanation of capitalism as an inevitable source of revolution, an explanation which in the late-nineteenth century and early twentieth century was being 'revised', particularly by Marxists in Germany and by Fabian socialists in Britain. (Many of the latter had not read Marx.) There are many examples of colonial expansion that can be explained only in non-economic terms. Nor was it the case that investment followed the flag. A relatively small share of British capital in the late nineteenth century went to the new territories painted red on the map, except South Africa. A far bigger share went to Latin America, especially Argentina, which in the process accumulated large foreign debts as it was to do in the early twenty-first century. In Europe itself Norway, with an oceanborne commerce exceeded only by that of Britain and Germany, had no empire. Until 1905 it was not even a nation state when it split away from Sweden, and chose as its king a Danish prince.

The place of politics and government in the story of empire is as difficult to assess in general terms as the economics of empire, for the pursuit of empire often went on without break as governments changed. Meanwhile any government could always be faced with colonial *faits accomplis*, miles away, which it could not foresee or control. There were also many different and sometimes conflicting motives among 'imperialists' in European political parties and cabinets. Some thought of colonial territories providing outlets for surplus population. This, indeed, was a favourite conservative argument, advanced by people who had no connections with trade or investment.

Others thought of power or prestige. Again this was conservative thinking, natural to men like Disraeli or Bismarck, although they were both clever enough to exploit it rather than to share it. Ferry in the defeated France of the 1870s made much of *esprit* and *élan*: he also argued, whenever he was talking of places as far apart as Tunis and Tonkin, that if France did not create a new empire, it would 'descend from the first rank [of power] to the third or fourth'. Later in the century, Joseph Chamberlain, whose radical background in Birmingham civic politics made him think in terms of action, treated empire as 'underdeveloped estate'.

Even after Chamberlain had broken with Gladstone and the Liberal Party on the Irish issue in 1886, the surviving Liberal Party remained divided between Liberal Imperialists ('Limps') and other Liberals who were categorized by their opponents as 'Little Englanders'. There were ambivalences, too, as well as contradictions – all present in Cecil Rhodes, who arrived in South Africa (on grounds of ill health) in 1870, the year when diamonds were discovered in Kimberley, and who amassed a fortune from diamond production and trade and was Prime Minister of Cape Colony from 1890 to 1896. Rhodes was interested in everything imperial – money, power, development, welfare, education – yet he admired Irish nationalism and gave money to Parnell. In Africa he was for the most part sympathetic to black Africans. He died in 1902 and by his will he founded scholarships at Oxford for students from the Empire, the United States and Germany.

The effect of non-European rivalries on European politics varied from year to year stood out, with some particular rivalries hitting the headlines. By any standards, however, the years from 1884 to 1885 and from 1904 to 1905, stood out. The former were years when the great powers met at Berlin to consider Africa, the first and last time that they did so. (The United States was one of them.) It was an impressive conference which coined the term 'sphere of influence' and which agreed, with little concern for African sensibilities, that the powers could, in effect, acquire African territories by possession, provided that they respected the claims of other countries and notified them of what they were doing. These were the years when Leopold's Congo State was recognized (suppression of slavery was made a condition) and when Bismarck made his 'bid for colonies'. Hitherto he had condemned 'our colonial jingos'. Now he found no difficulty in choosing the right language: 'colonies would mean the winning of new markets for German industries, the expansion of trade and a new field for German activity, civilization and capital' (in that order). New Guinea was involved as well as Africa, and after its non-Dutch territories had been partitioned between Germany and Britain, the Germans went on to acquire Samoa (not without argument) and gave Bismarck's name to an archipelago in the Pacific.

And all this did not exhaust the themes of 1884 and 1885. There was trouble for the British in India to the north-west and to the north-east. There was great alarm in Calcutta and London in 1884 when the Russians occupied Merv, a Turcoman centre that was only 200 miles from what was believed to be one of the key points on the road to India, Herat. To the east, when the King of Burma offered railway and other economic concessions to the French in 1885, the British sent him an ultimatum, captured him, and annexed Burma to India on 1 January 1886.

Other years of incident between 1884 to 1885 and 1904 to 1905 were 1896, 1897 and 1898. The first was the year not only of the Jameson Raid, but of the British conquest of the kingdom of the Ashanti on what was called the Gold Coast, in 1960 to become the republic of Ghana; of the French subjugation of Madagascar; and of the rout of the Italians by the Ethiopians at Adowa (a rare example of the defeat of a would-be colonial power at the hands of a non-European opponent). It was the year, too, when a French Army officer, Jean Marchand, was given orders to march into the Sudan, where the British General Horatio Kitchener had just defeated a native Sudanese army at Omdurman. (One of the young British officers present there was Winston Churchill.) Marchand declined to obey Kitchener's request to retire, and the impasse was reported back to Europe.

What happened next was felt later to have been of great significance, of more significance than it was. The French, represented by a new foreign minister, Théophile Delcassé, agreed to retire from the Sudan, and a more general agreement, reducing friction, was subsequently signed by the French and British in 1899. This was seen later as the beginning of a Franco–British *rapprochement*, which was to move through an entente cordiale in 1904 to a full Franco–British alliance during the First World War, although as late as 1900 a Franco–Russian military convention was still envisaging war with Britain.

Characteristically, the entente, signed by Delcassé, merely liquidated over-seas rivalries: no mention of Europe was made in it. Characteristically, too, Britain's first move out of isolationism (just when the Boer War was coming to an end) had already been made – an alliance not with a European power, but with Japan – in January 1902. In other circumstances and with other politicians this might have been an alliance between Germany, Britain and Japan, for at the time the Germans were interested in such an agreement. As it was, however, Japan benefited from the bilateral alliance when it went to war with Russia in February 1904. It was to go on to annex Korea in 1910. Meanwhile, Britain too was to become further estranged from Germany in drawing closer to France between 1904 and 1914. Wilhelm was fascinated by a *Weltpolitik* backed by sea power, as was recommended to him by some of his advisers, notably Admiral Alfred von Tirpitz, and Delcassé believed quite simply that Germany was France's 'hereditary enemy'.

WORLD INTERDEPENDENCE

Talk of friends and enemies among nations was becoming just as common-place in the late-nineteenth century as talk of the need for competition between them, and the language of competition itself was influenced as much by biology as by economics. Charles Darwin's theories, advanced in *On the Origin of Species* (1859), one of the 'great books' not only of the nineteenth century, but of all time, became a key text for a wide variety of people who believed in the 'survival of the fittest' as a social concept, vulgarizing it in the process. There were other social evolutionists, notably the British writer Herbert Spencer, who provided ammunition. Some 'social Darwinists' were, to use a later pejorative adjective, blatantly 'racist', and talked of the survival of 'inferior' and 'superior' races among nations. There was ample scope to justify the triumph of the strong over the weak. Bernhard Heinrich von Bülow, who became German Chancellor in 1900 – only the third Chancellor after Bismarck – was convinced that there was no such thing as permanent peace, nor should there be: 'War is an essential element of God's scheme of the world.'

Yet at the very time that such language was most fashionable – it was often nasty, and it was never profound – the facts of economics, if not all of its theories, were pointing to an unprecedented degree of world interdependence. Never before had the economic ties binding different countries together been so close or so essential to the daily well-being of millions of people as they were in the quarter of a century before 1914. However much talk there might be once the First World War started of the need to move away in the future from pre-war *International Anarchy*, the title of a book by G. Lowes Dickinson published in 1926, during the 1920s there was always contrasting talk, whenever economics was mentioned, of getting back to pre-war 'normalcy'.

The interdependence rested, however, on European dominance and on a system of economic specialization developed to meet European interests. The first countries to industrialize in the Western world were now the richest – Britain, Belgium, Germany, France – but their industrialization had depended on imports from overseas. Cotton had led the way and linked the interests of the still economically-backward plantations of the American south, with their slave workers, to the mills of one of the most economically-advanced regions of the world, industrial Lancashire with its confident factory owners and operatives and its busy commercial exchanges. Other textiles followed. By 1914 half the world's supplies of wool were coming from Australia and New Zealand, new lands of white settlement that were almost exclusively British (English, Scots, Welsh and Irish) in composition and background. It was ominous, however, that the number of textile spindles in Japan, only 13,000 in 1880, by 1914 was 2,287,000.

The great change during the last years of the century was the increasing dependence of Europe on non-European parts of the world for food as well as for raw materials for industry. The mid-West plains of the United States provided wheat (the value of United States exports of wheat increased more than 20 times between 1850 and 1914, although France and Germany did their best behind trade barriers to maintain their own production); Argentina provided meat (refrigerated ships, first introduced in the 1870s, made this trade possible); the West Indies provided sugar (although continental European countries produced larger quantities of sugar from beet); New Zealand provided lamb and dairy products; West Africa provided cocoa and vegetable oils; India (and to a lesser extent China) provided tea; and Brazil provided coffee (64 per cent of Germany's coffee imports in 1914 came from Brazil).

These are only representative statistics, partial in their range of reference, and, like the statistics of empire, they tell only a part of the story. Alongside the maps painted in imperial colours in the new school atlases must always be set the maps of trade and communications. And alongside the chronologies of treaties and battles should be set the chronologies of trade cycles, most of them international in character – some short-term, with peaks and troughs in output, employment, prices, and incomes, and some long-term, covering movements of rising and falling prices (and innovation trends) over a whole generation.

It is important to note that the general price level, which had been rising through the middle decades of the century, was falling between the mid-1870s and the mid-1890s, with different consequences for different economic and social groups. Talk of a 'great depression', general in scope, was, as has been noted, completely misplaced. Low interest rates favoured particular forms of investment, and while profit margins narrowed, the real income of employed wage earners increased and their standards of living improved as their hours of work shortened. The term *belle époque* was a label attached to the last years of the age in France. Yet in bad years, however, like 1902 and 1907, many industrial workers in all countries, including France – and service workers like dockers, the most 'casual' of all labourers – were thrown out of employment.

The role of Britain, still the world's greatest trading nation, which had passed the peak of its industrial supremacy by 1970, was crucial to the working of the international system, even more crucial than the role of Bismarck's Germany was to the working of the post-1870 alliance system. In 1914 Britain was the only European country that was selling more goods outside Europe than inside it. It was also the world's greatest importer, banker and provider of business services (such as insurance). Behind the pound sterling was gold, and it was Britain's role as a free-trading country with a dominating interest in the world's commodity markets and a highly flexible money market that allowed the gold standard to operate as automatically as possible, free from intervention by governments. The Bank of England was a private institution. The apparent automatism of this system, which relied on tacit understandings rather than formal rules, contrasted with the contrivance of the political system and, even more, of the diplomatic system. Meanwhile, Britain exported capital as well as manufactures to the rest of the world: 43 per cent of the world's foreign investment in 1914 was British when the share of Germany was only 13 per cent and that of the United States only 8 per cent.

The extent of interdependence was apparent in Europe itself. Half the total recorded trade of the world was made up of the exports and imports of seven

European countries. Germany was Britain's main industrial rival inside Europe (the theme of a fascinating book, *Made in Germany* by Edward Williams, published in 1896), but Britain, Europe's largest producer and exporter of coal, was Germany's best customer, and Germany came second only to India as a customer for British goods. British coal was being burned in Berlin when war broke out in 1914 At the same time, German sheet steel was being used to make ships for the British Navy, and in France the building of blast furnaces was going ahead in 1914 with the help of German capital. Germany was forging ahead of Britain in the production of steel (with the United States far ahead of both), in the use of electricity, and in industrial productivity. There was also a flourishing chemicals industry.

The Austrian economist Josef Schumpeter saw the so-called 'great depression' years as a period of entrepreneurial drive, backed in Germany by the banks, noting the power of German industry to combine to create large organizations, in sharp contrast with the small-scale organizations which had emerged during the early years of British industrialization. Competition in industry was restricted, and industrial cartels were formed both to fix prices and to control production. In Britain the implications of technological obsolescence, though pointed out by critics and in the press, were not fully appreciated. Nor were deficiencies in the educational system, which at the highest level seemed to spurn not only technology but all forms of money making.

Russia, despite its political backwardness, came into the picture too. With an unprecedentedly high economic growth rate, the revenues of the state were to double between 1908 and 1914 as were the number of banks. A cartel of electrical industries (the *elektroprovd*) was formed in 1912. Foreign capital, much of it German, played a major part in this development, although between 1900 and 1914 as a proportion of total Russian investment it fell from a half to a fifth.

There were a few powerful international trusts and cartels that cut across national boundaries, 'carving up' national shares by formulae that they devised for themselves, and in global context – the word 'global' was still not used in its contemporary sense – the division of the world into 'green' (agricultural) and 'black' (industrial) regions was accompanied, as it was in Europe, by a division inside countries between 'rich' and 'poor'. It was easy to think of both divisions as works of nature rather than as human dispensations. Nevertheless, while expectations were limited, they were rising with the rise in the standard of living of a larger section of the population than ever before. There was an increase in leisure too.

In Europe itself there were marked differences in the standard of living from Palermo to Milan, from Milan to Luxembourg and from Luxembourg to Lübeck. Nor did intervention by the state, whatever the reasoning behind it (welfare or power) necessarily make things better. Bureaucracy frustrated and intimidated. Social compensations, while deemed necessary, were uneasy. Thus, German landowners benefited from agricultural protection, but German workers suffered. Finally, while international horizons were changing. Europe dominated international trade, but the United States was forging ahead in production, benefiting from enormous reserves of materials, a huge home market, and an advanced labour-saving technology. In new industries – such as the automobile industry, to be as much of a key industry in the twentieth century as railways had been in the nineteenth – the United States very quickly established a lead that was never lost.

The Japanese industrial revolution proved also that industrialization was in no sense a monopoly of white peoples. Japan was closest in political relations to Britain after the signing of the Anglo-Japanese Treaty, but it was Germany rather than Britain that provided models of economic development, and it was competition from Japan that was to break the world power of British textiles manufacturing, the original pioneering industry of Britain's industrial revolution. Yet this was still around the corner, for in 1914 no less than 80 per cent of the huge output of the British cotton textiles industry was being exported. (India, whose own pre-industrial revolution textiles industry had been finally destroyed by British competition, was taking no less than 40 to 45 per cent of the whole.)

No account of interdependence would be complete without bringing in communications. Without railways and steamships (supplanting sail in the 1870s and 1880s) the unprecedented expansion in output and trade could never have taken place. Nor could the growth of the coal, iron and steel industries. Brazil got its first railway in 1854, the same year as Australia, Argentina in 1857, and South Africa in 1860. Rails and locomotives were often exported from Europe, from Britain in particular. But in the last quarter of the nineteenth century North America, crossed for the first time by rail, recognized the importance of physical communications in the 30 or 40 years before the coming of the automobile, which subsequently changed everything. The transportation phase of what came in the 1960s to be described as a 'communications revolution' was a necessary phase, as was the development of the banking system for economic integration. In Britain the implications of technological obsolescence, though pointed out by critics and in the press, were not fully appreciated.

Out of transportation other forms of communication developed, beginning with the telegraph, patented in Britain in 1837. The British, with their scattered Empire, were carriers of the telegraph during the 1850s and 1860s, and it was in London that in 1851 Baron Reuter, born in Hesse Cassel, created his huge news agency based on telegraphy not carrier pigeons. The telephone, however, invented in Canada in 1876 by a Scottish immigrant, Alexander Graham Bell, was exploited far more effectively in Canada and in the United States than in Europe. Wireless, an invention of the 1890s, following in the wake of X-rays, was thought of at first as a substitute for communication by wire – Morse Code, dots and dashes, not words, invented by an American Samuel Morse, was its language – just as the automobile (a luxury product invented not in Britain but in France and Germany) was at first thought of as a horseless carriage. The aeroplane was still a dream, although it was a dream that enthusiasts believed would come true.

News of inventions which gave enormous, if often highly risky, opportunities to entrepreneurs, were international in their origins and development, Guglielmo Marconi, who arrived in London in 1896 with a package of wireless devices was Italian; Gottlieb Daimler, who pioneered the car and the internal combustion engine, was German (he built the first petrol engine in 1883); the Wright brothers, who flew the first powered aeroplane in 1903, were American. It was not until the second half of the twentieth century that people were to talk of a 'communications revolution', of 'media of communication', and of electronic 'global networks'. Yet, by the middle of the nineteenth century, the laying of the great transcontinental cables was already heralded as a way of uniting the world through science, and by the 1890s there was an increasing emphasis on the possibilities of further enhancement of human interchange, particularly at international exhibitions, through 'wonderful new inventions'.

It was not only to be business or government that was to benefit. Everyone, it was forecast, would gain, for the home would be penetrated as well as the factory or the office, now equipped with typewriters as well as telephones. Meanwhile, the daily newspaper, which made its way into the home along with the products that were advertised in it, would not have been able to provide the news that it did from all corners of the world had it not been for the telegraph, which in the words of Britain's last Victorian prime minister, Salisbury, a Conservative, 'combined together almost at one moment . . . the opinions of the whole intelligent world with respect to everything that is passing at that time upon the face of the world'.

Once again, it is important not to idealize. The telegraph could be used to twist diplomacy, as Bismarck used the Ems telegram from the Emperor on the eve of the Franco-German War of 1870, and the newspaper could be used to exploit prejudice as much as to spread facts. Even when the press was not controlled by government it could heighten tension behind the scenes, as it did at the time of Fashoda. Mass circulation was the object. The year 1896 saw the founding of Alfred Harmsworth's cheap *Daily Mail* in London which by 1900 had a circulation of over a million. This was also the year when Paris and London held their first cinema shows. By 1900 the *Daily Mail*, which trumpeted every new invention, had a circulation of over a million.

By 1900 *Le Petit Parisien* was selling 800,000 copies, and *Berliner Morgenpost* was read by over half a million people. All these newspapers had far more to say of 'crises' and of 'rivalries' than of interdependence. And Marconi displayed his wireless not only to the Post Office but the British and Italian navies and armies. By the end of the century his newly founded company, which made no profits in the first 12 years of its life, had a German rival, the Telefunken Company which had the backing of Werner von Siemens and of the German government and court.

FROM CRISES TO WAR

In retrospect, it is easy to overemphasize those aspects both of European technology and of European diplomacy between 1904 and 1914 that pointed towards the First World War. There were, in fact, intimations of a later concern for peace. Among the Nobel Prizes, funded after his death through the will of Alfred Nobel, inventor of dynamite, there was a Nobel Peace Prize which in 1905 was won by the Austrian novelist Baroness Bertha von Suttner who had persuaded Nobel to endow it: her book *Die Waffen Nieder* ('Lay Down your Arms') went through 37 editions between 1889 and 1905.

More questions of contention were settled by arbitration during the last 20 years of the nineteenth century than during the previous 80 years, and there were over a 100 such arbitrations between 1904 and 1914. The article on arbitration in the eleventh edition of the *Encyclopaedia Britannica* (1910) stated optimistically that 'with the help of world-wide Press, public opinion can always be brought to bear on any state that seeks to evade its moral duty'. Unfortunately there was no consensus on what 'moral duty' meant. It was a concept too large for the lawyers, more so, indeed, than *raison d'état* had been a century before. Nor did it even carry the weight more recently attached to the term 'concert of Europe', by 1900 out of fashion, or to the later term 'international community' still not in.

Towards the end of the nineteenth century, in 1898, six years before the Russo-Japanese war, Nicholas II circulated to diplomats in St Petersburg an imperial rescript stating that 'the preservation of peace has become an objective of national policy', and a Peace Conference opened at the Hague, capital of Holland, on his birthday in 1899. Salisbury publicly – and rightly – said that it should not be taken 'too seriously' and Wilhelm in Berlin described it as 'utopian'. In fact, it adopted a number of 'rules of war' and strengthened the position of the Red Cross, as did a second Hague Convention in 1907. Nothing was done, however, to secure disarmament, as Nicholas had hoped (if only for economic reasons). Indeed, many of the people who attended the convention were in their own countries powerful advocates of increased expenditure on armaments – among them the British Admiral, Sir John Fisher, and the German military expert, Colonel Schwarzhoff, who told the conference bluntly that he did not see why Germany should be expected to restrict its military power because other countries could not afford to compete.

The United States had among its representatives Captain Alfred Mahan, author of a classic study of naval power, published in 1890, which explained how essential sea power was to national prosperity, an argument reiterated ten years later by the German geographer Friedrich Ratzel who urged Germany to 'be strong on the seas to fulfil her mission in the world'. Not surprisingly, therefore, the naval armaments race between Britain and Germany, the latter seeking always to catch up, was now to speed up. One year before Nicholas produced his imperial rescript, Germany passed a new Navy Law announcing its intention to build a battle fleet. Without it, maintained Tirpitz, the initiator of the new policy, Germany would be 'a mollusc without a shell'. Navy Laws passed in 1898 and 1900 equipped Germany to take limited action in the North Sea, but not to challenge Britain on the oceans of the world. Thereafter, as questions of relative naval strength hit press headlines, there was no issue more calculated to disturb British policymakers and British public opinion. The launch of HMS *Dreadnaught* in 1906 enormously enhanced the fighting power of the British Navy. The first big gunship, she made obsolete all existing battleships.

In military strength Germany was far ahead. As early as 1894 Count Alfred von Schlieffen produced the first version of his battle plans to prevent the two new allies France and Russia from meeting on German soil. It was based on a lightning attack on France through Luxembourg and Holland. A further version was agreed upon in 1905, but this version of the battle plan was amended in 1911. Instead of invading Holland, German forces would move through Liège and across Belgium. By then the German military leaders were deeply concerned about the growing military strength of Russia, and the *Reichstag* agreed to the biggest increase ever in the German Army (to be financed from a wealth tax).

The Russians themselves had not demonstrated strength, either naval or military in the first of the great twentieth-century 'crises' which was of particular interest to Britain. Thereafter, Russian power considered almost legendary before the Russo-Japanese war, could be – and was – judged critically but the effect was to turn Russia back from the Far East to Europe. It was not in Europe, however, that the treaty ending the war was signed but at Portsmouth, New Hampshire in the United States, in August 1905 – itself a marked departure from nineteeth-century patterns of diplomacy. The Peace recognized Japan's permanent interest in Korea, not dissimilar, it was judged, to Britain's interest in Egypt: a Japanese Governor was appointed in Seoul, and in 1910 the whole of Korea was annexed by Japan.

The Russo-Japanese War was watched with varying degrees of concern in France, Germany and Britain. Russian imperial rule had never before looked more shaky than it did in 1905. The regime had been shocked by assassinations, but there had been no revolution. Now in 1905 a revolution that anticipated a later revolution, that of 1917, began with an incident on 'Bloody Sunday', 22 January, that brought to the surface all the many manifestations of unrest which had never before converged. A large and powerful crowd, led by an Orthodox priest, Father Gapon, was shot down on the orders of the Tsar after demanding the summoning of an assembly based on universal suffrage, land reform and an eight-hour day. Revolt spread to the countryside and to the ports as peasants attacked manor houses and sailors mutinied.

Taken by surprise, the socialist leaders in exile, Lenin and Trotsky (Lev Bronstein), who were to lead the revolution in 1917, returned to Russia, but not before there had been a wave of strikes and a mutiny on the battleship *Potemkin* which has passed into myth as well as into history. When they arrived in late November they created a Soviet in St Petersburg which was brutally crushed after 50 days of life, as were other peasant and workers' uprisings. The failure of the revolutionaries seemed decisive, but the authorities showed little intelligence or imagination in the aftermath of the disturbances. Although they made 'concessions' and a Manifesto of October 30th promised freedom of speech, meeting and association and a wide franchise and although in elections for the first *Duma* (Parliament) reformers won a majority, the Duma was dismissed by the Emperor after only three months of existence. A second *Duma* was to be called in 1907, but in the meantime Russian governments had switched their eyes westwards after the Peace of Portsmouth blocked any thought of further Russian expansion in the East. This drew Russia back again into Balkan politics.

The switch took some time, however, and meanwhile there had been a second crisis in 1905, which stood out as 'a turning point in the diplomatic history of modern Europe'. An entente cordiale between Britain and France was reached in 1904 – an entente, not an alliance – which settled longstanding colonial differences and included an understanding that in two of the north African territories in the Ottoman Empire, France would take no further steps to hinder British activity in Egypt and Britain would take no further steps to hinder any French activity in Morocco. The German government, which had never believed that an entente of this kind between Britain and France was possible (it still seemed possible to some Germans that Britain could be drawn into an alliance with Germany), was determined to test it. Wilhelm, who was *en route* for a Mediterranean cruise in March 1905, was induced to disembark at Tangier in Morocco and pay his respects to the Sultan, thereby providing an opportunity both for a naval demonstration and for a declaration of German interest in the affairs of Morocco not only on economic grounds, but to maintain prestige.

This was a dangerous form of counterstroke that was likely from the start to be counterproductive, and when the idea was first proposed by Bülow and Holstein, Wilhelm himself did not like it. He was right to have had doubts, for the main effect of his declaration, which hit the headlines, was to strengthen the entente. First, however, there was a pyrrhic victory. When Germany demanded that France should agree to submit the Moroccan question to an international conference, the French government, fearing war, accepted the demand, and Delcassé resigned in protest. Not surprisingly, he became a national hero. Also not surprisingly, when the international conference was held at Algeçiras in Spain in 1906, all countries except Austria supported the French case. Italy, which by a treaty with France in 1900 had recognized French interest in Morocco in return for French support of Italian interest in Tripoli, stood by this arrangement, although still a member of the Triple Alliance. Another supporter of France was the United States. Britain and France were drawn closer together. The least of all the surprises was that Holstein resigned.

The following year, the full implications of the Moroccan counterstroke became apparent when Britain, after long negotiations, reached an agreement with Russia designed to reduce frictions. Like the 'entente cordiale' it dealt directly only with issues outside Europe, but, given the existence of the Franco-Russian Alliance, it had obvious European implications, and the French naturally gave it their full support. The agreement partitioned Persia into 'spheres of influence' and recognized Britain's interests in the Persian Gulf, Afghanistan's neutrality was to be respected, and Tibet was to be treated as a buffer state. Nothing was said about the old issue of contention between Britain and Russia – the 'Eastern Question' – except that the territorial integrity of the Ottoman Empire was guaranteed and that the British promised their goodwill if at a later date there were to be international discussions about the Black Sea and the Straits. The opening of Constantinople to Russian warships was a Russian objective that had always been opposed by Britain from the days of William Pitt.

Wilhelm had every reason to be disturbed by this arrangement. He had, in fact, signed a short-lived alliance with the Tsar at Bjîrko in 1905, which failed – on the surface at least – because it was pushed too far and too fast. Before the Russian-British agreement was reached, Holstein had talked (not for the first time) of German 'encirclement' (*Einkreisungspolitik*). Now Wilhelm became conscious of his own imminent isolation: 'A nice outlook. We must bargain the future of the Franco-Russian Alliance, the Anglo-French entente, and an Anglo-Russian entente, with Spain, Italy and Portugal as secondary satellites.' Isolation was the wrong word, however. There remained the defensive 1879 Alliance with Austria which had never been designed to be exclusive. Between 1907 and 1914, however, it was to drag Europe into the worst war in its history.

Table 8

The significance of the alliance was soon tested in what came to be called the 'Bosnian ordeal' of 1908–09 which had its origins in 1903 when the Obrenovic dynasty was overthrown in Belgrade, and their old rivals, the Karageorgenics, brutally seized power. The balance had changed, and in 1906 Austria-Hungary, fearful that Serbia was following in the path of national resistance that Italy had pursued earlier in the nineteenth century, imposed import duties on Serbia's main export, pigs, beginning what became known as the 'Pig War'. When two years later the Young Turks disposed of the Sultan Abdul-Hamid II, the last Ottoman Sultan (he was to die in confinement in 1918), an opportunity was provided for taking other measures and the Habsburg Foreign Minister, Baron Aloys von Aehrenthal, who took office in 1906, announced the full annexation of Bosnia-Herzegovina on 5 April 1908, a step that Franz Josef had always wished to take. By the terms of the Treaty of Berlin in 1878, Austria had been empowered to 'occupy and administer' the

Turkish provinces of Bosnia and Herzegovina, and one of the confidential stipulations in the Three Emperors' League agreement of 1881 had been that Austria-Hungary reserved 'the right to annex the provinces at whatever moment she shall deem opportune'. Nonetheless, the news of the annexation without preliminary warning in October 1908 shocked not only Serbia, as Aehrenthal had intended it to do, but Russia, which he had not intended to do. Russia now offered support to Serbia which wished to take over the provinces itself.

Tension mounted, but peace was preserved after the Russian Foreign Minister, Alexander Izvolsky, who had been engaged in earlier talks with Aehrenthal, advised Serbia to 'remain quiet . . . and . . . do nothing which could provoke Austria and provide an opportunity for annihilating Serbia'. As a result the Austro-Hungarian and Turkish governments signed an agreement in February 1909 under the terms of which Austria-Hungary acquired full rights over Bosnia, withdrew from the Sanjak of Novi-Bazar, the strip of land that divided Serbia from Montenegro, guaranteed full freedom of religion for Bosnian Muslims, and paid an indemnity to Turkey. But even then the crisis continued for several months.

The fact that there was no European war in 1909 offered no guarantee that war on such an issue could be avoided in the future since the only reason why Russia ultimately did not press the issue was that Germany backed Austria without qualification. Wilhelm had disliked the annexation, which he heard of as a *fait accompli* and which seemed to undo nearly 20 years of increasingly close German co-operation with the Ottoman Empire, part of a *Drang Nach Osten*, which included the German-backed building of a railway from Berlin to Baghdad. Yet as the crisis continued Germany gave Austria a *carte blanche* and sent to Russia what was in effect an ultimatum stating that, like Serbia, it should accept the annexation without question. Izvolsky concluded that he had no alternative but to give in. Any possibility of a revival of the Three Emperors' League, which Aehrenthal had thought possible, was now lost for ever.

This time there was not even a pyrrhic victory for Germany. Wilhelm had stood by his ally 'in shining armour', as he put it, but it was his ally who had chosen the issue and who had led Germany along. And Austria, unbacked by Britain, almost immediately signed a secret treaty with Bulgaria, a further threat to Balkan stability. Russia quickly recovered from any diplomatic humiliation and increased its armaments programme (ironically drawing on the German armaments industry), and Serbia, which had to sign a humiliating declaration that it would 'modify the direction of its present policy towards Austria-Hungary, and live in future on good neighbourly terms', waited for revenge. France became increasingly suspicious of German policy, and Britain augmented its programme of naval construction.

Before two new Balkan wars further disturbed relations between empires and nations in 1912 there was a second Moroccan crisis, again directly focused on Germany and France. A Berber rebellion in Morocco in 1911 provided the excuse for France to send an expedition to occupy Fez, the Moroccan capital, and this in turn provided the excuse for Germany to send a battleship, the *Panther*, to the Moroccan port of Agadir to protect German nationals. (There were none in Agadir, although a year earlier the French had arrested three German deserters from the French Foreign Legion at Casablanca.) The ensuing crisis lasted for several months as the Germans put pressure on the French to offer the French Congo as 'compensation' for recognition of their claims in Morocco. The French government then in power was keen to reach a bilateral understanding with Germany, but the British on this occasion were more anti-German than the French.

It was a Welsh Liberal leader, an opponent of the Boer war but a future Prime Minister during the First World War, David Lloyd George, who caught the mood. He had hitherto been known as an advocate of friendship with Germany and, as Chancellor of the Exchequer, an opponent of heavy British naval expenditure on giant Dreadnoughts. Now in a widely reported speech he declared that 'peace at any price would be a humiliation intolerable for a great country like ours to endure'. When all that the Germans could secure from the French in an agreement of November 1911 was the handing over of small sections of the French Congo in return for recognition of the French protectorate over Morocco, it was their turn to feel humiliated. And as they blamed Britain more than France, Tirpitz used the crisis to try to gain support for an enlarged naval programme.

It was during this crisis that details of military and naval co-operation between France and Britain in case of war were settled. Moreover, since the French government had seemed too willing to reach a political accommodation with Germany, it was replaced by a 'patriotic' government headed by Raymond Poincaré. Finally there was an Italian epilogue to the crisis that led almost immediately to a broader war. Seeing the weakness of the Ottoman Empire in Africa, Italy declared war on Turkey in September 1911 and landed troops in Tripoli. The Turks soon ran into difficulties, and the war spread from Africa to the Dodecanese Islands.

When the beleaguered Turks closed the Straits, Russia protested, triggering off a new Balkan crisis that was to lead directly to a further war, with Serbia, watching with envy Italian advances in Tripolitania, Cyrenaica and the Mediterranean, once more a key player in the scenario. In March 1912 it joined in alliance with Bulgaria and later Greece, setting out to share the spoils in a partition of the Turkish Balkans. Serbia was to gain lands on the Adriatic, part of a greater Serbia; Bulgaria was to acquire Macedonia; and Greece was to take Salonika. It was a fourth small country, more influential in politics, largely for dynastic reasons, than its smallness suggested, mountainous Montenegro, adjacent to Serbia, that declared war on Turkey on 8 October 1912, with the immediate consequence of forcing the Turks to make peace with Italy. Its further consequence was to alarm both Austria-Hungary, fearful of Serbian aggrandizement, and Russia, fearful that Bulgaria would take possession of Constantinople.

It was not a league of Balkan Powers, however, but the great powers of Europe that worked out a settlement in London in May 1913. They even drew closer together in the process. And they did not intervene when a second Balkan war started almost at once over the division of the spoils. A bigger Bulgaria attacked both Serbia and Greece, Romania attacked Bulgaria, and the Ottoman Empire recovered Adrianople. Nor did the great powers intervene in the Peace of Bucharest, arrived at by the Balkan states themselves, which forced Bulgaria to disgorge almost all its gains of the first war.

Gains made by Serbia, which seemed yet again to be playing the part of the Piedmont of the Balkans, angered Austria-Hungary, and when the Serbs contemplated a further move into Albania, Austria-Hungary secured German backing. In October 1913 Wilhelm promised Field-Marshal Conrad von Hötzendorf, who with a short break in 1911 had been Austrian Chief of Staff since 1906, that if Austria marched against Serbia (Hötzendorf had been pressing for this since January) he would go along with him, 'ready to draw the sabre if ever your action makes it necessary'. Nor would he be the only one. In March 1913, Germany had introduced its new Army Bill designed to put it ahead of Russia in the following year. The Russians responded by increasing their own forces, with a target of an extra 40 per cent by 1917, thus clashing not only with Austria-Hungary but with Germany, which now sent a military mission to Constantinople.

'Russo-Prussian relations are dead once and for all', Wilhelm recorded in an excited minute that would have shocked Bismarck. 'We have become enemies.' The sense that Russia was growing stronger each year gave weight to the military judgement that if Germany did not go to war in 1914 it would not be able to stand up to a conflict that was now inevitable. Early in that year the Austrians decided to start military manoeuvres in Bosnia, knowing that they would provoke the Serbs.

The final crisis began on 28 June 1914 when the heir to the Habsburg thrones, Archduke Franz Ferdinand, and his wife were assassinated by a Bosnian Serb, Gavrilo Princip, member of a secret society dedicated to the liberation of Croats and Serbs from Bosnian rule, at Sarajevo, a city where several other assassins were lying in wait. Hötzendorf did not want to delay for the results of a judicial inquiry. Berchtold and the Austrian and Hungarian Prime Ministers did. Wilhelm asked no questions. He wanted to act. 'Now or never.' The treaty of 1879 stood. For Hötzendorf it was a matter of principle or rather of principles, two of which were in sharp conflict: 'the maintenance of Austria as a conglomerate of various nationalities . . . and the rise of independent national states claiming their ethnic territories from Austria-Hungary'. Serb activities had brought this conflict to a head.

The German Chancellor, Theobald von Bethmann-Hollweg, who had succeeded his political leader Bülow, in 1909 with little knowledge of foreign affairs, was fully aware in 1914 of the implications of his actions, backed by Wilhelm, when he promised full support to Vienna on 5 July, but the government in Budapest needed persuasion. It was not until 19 July, therefore, that a ten-point ultimatum to Serbia was agreed upon and presented to Belgrade on 23 July with the demand for a reply within 48 hours. This was nearly four weeks after the assassination. Another different reason for the delay was an already planned three-day visit to Russia by the French President, Raymond Poincaré, elected on 13 July, which started on 20 July and consolidated Franco-Russian relations.

When the Serbs asked for more time to reply, they were abruptly reminded that they were living in 'the age of railways, telegraphs and telephone'; and when they failed to accept all ten points the Habsburg Empire declared war on 28 July. For Germany, well armed and ready with imposing war plans in the west and in the east, this was the moment to strike. Days mattered now, even hours. Once Russia mobilized, which it began to do slowly before the Serbian reply was received, the Germans wanted to start what they believed would be a short war as quickly as possible.

Thereafter the treaty system moved into gear in the hot summer of 1914 – Triple Alliance versus Triple Entente – although there was a final exchange of dynastic telegrams between Wilhelm and Nicholas II, cousins soon to be at war, and abortive efforts by Sir Edward Grey, Britain's Foreign Secretary, to call for a conference. On 1 August Germany declared war on Russia, and France mobilized. On 2 August the Germans presented an ultimatum to Belgium, which was immediately rejected, and two days later crossed the Belgian frontier. On that same day, 4 August, Britain declared war on Germany. That there was little regret among the peoples, and in most countries even great enthusiasm, requires a different kind of explanation from that given in books of diplomatic history or in the memoirs of foreign ministers and generals. The next chapter, therefore, which is concerned not with days or years, but with long-term social and cultural processes, inevitably interrupts the chronological narrative.

Notes

1. L. Lafore, *The Long Fuse: An Interpretation of the Origins of World War I* (1965). Compare Lafore's *An Interpretation of the Origins of World War II* (1970).
2. J. C. Röhl, *The Kaiser and His Court* (1995), ch. 5.

Chapter 5

MODERNITY

_____

THE SENSE OF HISTORY: FACT, FICTION, MYTH

Modern history, which takes many different forms, was born in the nineteenth century, a century when, despite changes of mood – and of scholarship – historical explanation was employed in most discussions of change, revolutionary or, to use a key word of the century, evolutionary. Not all history was tied to fact. For the French poet and professor, Paul Valéry, born in 1871, who brought science into the reckoning, history was, therefore, 'the most dangerous product which the chemistry of the intellect has ever evolved'.[1] History was a subject of fiction – of historical novels – but some history in textbooks was fiction, and even more of it myth, a word with a complex history that at the beginning of the century was associated with fable.

Behind the various nineteenth-century *isms*, most of them introduced in earlier chapters of this history, *isms* like classicism and romanticism, capitalism and socialism that made their way into every language, was the desire to identify forces of change. Since one *ism*, 'nationalism', as we have seen, rested on language and on myth; and since the First World War, the subject of the next chapter, was the climax of a period when nationalism played a large part in shaping popular consciousness, myth, along with national stereotypes must be given as much attention as fact in any explanation of why war came. In order to understand what was happening it is necessary, therefore, to turn to historians (and anthropologists, sociologists and psychologists) as much as to philosophers, to scientists, a new nineteenth-century word, and to technologists, a descriptive word little used. Nevertheless, all these too were re-shaping the human environment inside and outside Europe.

A renowned Italian liberal historian, Benedetto Croce, born in 1866, who lived through stirring years of twentieth-century history and survived the Second World War, argued forcibly that after the year 1871, the period covered in the last chapter, there had been a profound change in 'the public spirit of Europe', directly associated, he thought, with the unification of Germany and Italy. And other historians have extended his argument by identifying a profound change in attitudes and perception, tracing back to this period, which links nineteenth and twentieth centuries, the origins of 'a modern movement' expressed alike in literature, painting, music and architecture.

It was not, however, the only period covered in this History when contemporaries felt a sense of profound change and attached to it the adjective 'modern'. In the mid-eighteenth century, just before this History begins, there had been an equally strong sense of change and the word 'modern' was used then, if always with a reference back to the 'ancient world' both for comparison and for example. Greece and Rome, which figured prominently in linguistic and historical education, were always in mind. Change was already thought of as more than intellectual, but in 1759 d'Alembert, joint editor of the *Encyclopédie*, product of the Enlightenment, in dealing with change concentrated on 'a very remarkable change in our ideas' that was taking place, 'one of such rapidity that it seems to promise a greater change to come'. When it did come after 1789, the subject of the first chapter of this History, it was not quite of the kind that d'Alembert and most of his fellow writers of 'the enlightenment' expected.

By 1789 there had been further significant changes in tastes as well as in ideas. There were new reactions, including reactions to 'Nature' and new assessments of 'human nature'. What was artificial (or trivial) became suspect. The 'picturesque' and the 'sublime' were viewed in new ways – mountains, moors, tombs and ruins. The 'sentimental man' was held up for approval. So, too, was Rousseau's 'noble savage'. Bernardin de St Pierre's *Paul et Virginie* (1788), an exotic island idyll, suggests, as Rousseau did, that tragedy follows from contact with European 'civilization'. More than 20 years earlier, James Macpherson's *Poems of Ossian* (1762) had recalled a mythic Celtic twilight. 'We call back', he stated in his preface, 'the years that have rolled away'.

Recall went with novelty, and the two were not then treated as opposites. Indeed, for all the dwelling on the past in Ossian's poems, the poems themselves were inventions. Public reaction to them, like reaction to 'novels' (the very name 'novel' is linked with the sense of the new), is of interest to cultural historians who seek to uncover feelings as well as to trace ideas. There have always been novels deemed by contemporaries to be particularly 'significant', like Rousseau's *La Nouvelle Héloïse* (1761) and Goethe's *Werther* (1774), fiction to be set alongside autobiographies like Rousseau's *Confessions* (1781). To extend the range, the English historian Edward Gibbon's *Autobiography*, published in 1796 in edited form two years after his death, should also be considered. His *Decline and Fall of the Roman Empire*, completed in 1788, was described by Madame Necker as a bridge that carried the reader from the ancient to the modern.

The eighteenth and early-nineteenth century novelists themselves could be as interested in evidence as Gibbon was – he used long footnotes – and it is of more than symbolic interest that the British novelist Henry Mackenzie, author of *The Man of Feeling* (1771), used the device of an incomplete bundle of papers discovered after the event to introduce one of his plots. Sir Walter

Scott, too, historian as well as novelist, uncovered all kinds of historical evidence in his Waverley novels, at first published anonymously, the first of them in 1814, and throughout the nineteenth century there were other genres that brought history directly back to life, particularly biographies, often focusing on 'great men', some of them treated as 'heroes'. These usually rested on the evidence of letters, diaries and autobiographies, and it is of interest, therefore, that when another Scots writer (and prophet), Carlyle, devoted to heroes who created his own highly distinctive literary style, began his massive work on the French Revolution, it was to prints and portraits of the revolutionary leaders that he first turned.

CULTURAL HISTORY

Through cultural history, which incorporates the history of art and music as well as of literature, and, not least, the history of history, we approach what came to be thought of as the sub-branches of history, political, social, economic, diplomatic and military, in a way that enables us to understand more clearly the processes of change. It provides new insights, for example, into the structures and dynamics of politics, the processes of class formation, the economics of enterprise and of corporate culture and systems of military conscription and military promotion. In dealing with any of these sub-branches statistics by themselves, as we have seen a major nineteenth-century pre-occupation, are never enough even when they are examined comparatively. They register material progress, singled out at the time as the main feature of a century when belief in progress was an article of faith, but they were often unreliable, and, as we have seen, they meant little to those contemporaries who did not believe in progress. It was not just Carlyle who drew on other kinds of impressionistic evidence, much of it equally unreliable. Cultural historians have examined a far wider range of historical evidence than statistics or, indeed, the evidence of the written (or spoken) word. They have turned for witnesses of past times to objects, ranging from buildings to the furniture and other objects inside them and from medals, commemorating great events, to 'tokens', at some times and in some places paid to workers in lieu of coins, to banknotes, which could take the place of coins, to company share certificates, some of them worthless from the start, and, not least, to the multiple forms that people had to fill in, if not as often as they were required to do in the late-twentieth century. Ephemera, objects that were thrown away and their wrappings, have been collected and examined also. Waste as well as wealth has become part of history.

On the basis of exploration, cultural historians have drawn distinctions between 'high' and 'low' culture – or cultures – and particular attention has been paid to 'consumer culture' which has been traced back to the eighteenth century. Folklore too has been recorded and sifted. Bound up as it is with myth, it predated commercialised 'mass culture'. Yet an examination of 'high culture' rightly comes first in relation to the eighteenth century and most of the nineteenth. There were great names in history as well as great events. A figure from the past, Shakespeare, stood out in what came to be thought of during this period as 'literature': he was translated into many languages as was Scott. In music Beethoven quickly stood out as a genius: he himself never doubted it. And for Ernst Hoffmann, early-nineteenth-century composer, romantic painter and music critic as well as writer, whose tales were to be set to music, popular music, by the mid-nineteenth-century opera composer, Jacques Offenbach, the music that Beethoven composed did far more than close eyes to strife and war. It 'set in motion the lever of fear, of awe, of horror, of suffering' and awoke 'the infinite longing which is the essence of romanticism'.

In art, which during the course of the nineteenth century acquired a market, there was an early distinction between 'classical' and 'romantic'. David, who had painted for Louis XVI before he made his way through the Revolution and revelled in his new responsibilities as 'painter to the Government' of Napoleon, provides a contrast with Eugène Delacroix, born half a century after him. David chose a 'classical' style, as did many French revolutionaries (see above, p.25) whatever the subject of his paintings. Two of the best known of them are *The Death of Socrates*, a classical topic, and *Marat Assassinated*, the most topical of subjects. (He also sketched Marie Antoinette on her way to the guillotine.) Delacroix, reputed to be an illegitimate son of Talleyrand, painted huge romantic canvasses, including many that dealt with revolutionary upthrust, among them *Liberty Guiding the People*, painted in 1831.

Many of the greatest poets and writers of the late eighteenth and early nineteenth century defy the easy application of labels like 'classical' and 'romantic' Goethe, for example, who created the suffering young romantic 'hero' Werther – Napoleon took a copy of *Werther* with him on his Egyptian campaign – admired classical forms and was critical of many aspects of romanticism which he did not hesitate to condemn. 'The most impetuous painter', he wrote as early as 1781, 'has no right to daub any more than the fiercest musician should strike wrong notes.' In 1805 he complained at an art exhibition in his city of Weimar that 'feeling' was being exalted 'over mind and spirit'.

One great painter who is difficult to fit into any *schema* is the Spaniard Francisco José de Goya, born in 1746, three years before Goethe, and, like him, living deep into the nineteenth century. His early work was rococo, the style which neo-classical artists considered trivial. His dark and mysterious etchings, *Disasters of War*, suggested by the Napoleonic invasion of Spain – so different in style from his earlier paintings, including his satirical works – are among the outstanding artistic triumphs of a period in which superimposed official order was often no more than a façade. When Goya returned to his villa at the age of 70 he chose to decorate it with paintings that had subjects like 'Saturn devouring his children' and 'the Witches Sabbath'.

These were the kind of subjects that appealed most to some of the German romantics, and it was German romantics who saluted the nineteenth century at its very beginning as a new dawn. In a theatrical piece, *Canonical Way of the Old and New Century*, performed on 1 January 1801, A. W. Schlegel, older of two brothers who set out between 1798 and 1800 to define romanticism, claimed that the parent of the nineteenth century was not the eighteenth century, an old hag, but Genius wedded to Liberty. And in his pageant the withered old hag was carried off to Hell by the Devil, a familiar romantic character.

THE SENSE OF A CENTURY

The nineteenth century for most contemporaries was the first century to have a unique number attached to it. Historians have subsequently divided it into three parts – between early, middle and late, with the late century beginning, for most of them in 1871, where Croce put it. More recently they have treated it as a 'long century', which started in 1815 with the fall of Napoleon and ended in 1914 with the outbreak of the First World War.

Schlegel believed, as Croce was to believe, that history was 'the self-consciousness of a nation' and much play was made of the terms 'self' and 'self-consciousness' from the beginning of the century. Thus, Carlyle, writing a generation after Schlegel – and it may be more instinctive to think in terms of generations than of centuries – believed that 'never since the beginning of time' had there been so self-conscious a society' as that to which he belonged. The spirit of the age (*Zeitgeist*) was frequently invoked throughout the century although there was never any agreement about what was representative of it. The self-consciously modern English poet Alfred Lord Tennyson, born in 1809, added to the list of current *isms* '19th Centuryism', 'if you will admit such a word'.[2] Across the Channel *dixneuvièmité* was often extolled, and while the great French novelist Stendhal, who died in 1842, described his century as *triste*, the poet Victor Hugo, apologist of romanticism, who lived from 1802 to 1885, conceived of it in terms of triumph. As a young man he had dismissed all eighteenth-century rules of taste and style, including the dramatic unities on the stage of time and place. He had also extolled Genius as the Schlegels had done.

Towards the end of the century, when the term '*fin-de-siècle*', originating in France, had come into use, the English biologist A. R. Wallace, who had anticipated Charles Darwin in what he wrote about 'evolution', called the century 'wonderful'. For all its 'failures' – 'militarism, the curse of civilization', 'the demon of greed', and 'the plunder of the earth', it had had huge 'successes'. There had been only seven inventions of the first rank 'in all preceding time'. In the nineteenth century there were 13.[3] Wallace was not an unqualified believer in progress. Nor were socialists, whatever their variety. For the English novelist, H. G. Wells, Fabian and writer among other novels of science fiction, the century had been for himself 'an age of relatively good fortune, an age of immense but temporary opportunity', but his contemporaries had been overtaken by power, by possessions and great new freedoms, and unable to make any civilized use of them whatever. At best the century had been 'a hasty, trial experiment, a gigantic experiment of the most slovenly and wasteful kind'.[4]

At different points in the century, early, middle and late, there was a sense of malaise on the part of many writers and artists, some of them less interested in politics than Wells or near the beginning of the century Shelley and Byron. Thus, the French romantic poet Alfred de Musset, who lived from 1810 to 1857, wrote in 1835 his *Confession d'un Enfant du Siècle* of the pain of living a 'life of love' in the nineteenth century. The love he had in mind was George Sand, a pen-name for Amandine Dupin, who had a tumultuous love affair not only with de Musset but with the Polish pianist, Frédéric Chopin. (Her first novel, *Indiana* (1832), was a plea for women's independence.) Musset believed in a *mal du siècle*, and in the middle years of the century a greater French romantic poet, Charles Baudelaire, wrote *Fleurs du Mal* (1857). Towards the end of the century the British writer and playwright Oscar Wilde, who in 1891 wrote an essay *The Soul of Man under Socialism*, described himself as one of 'those upon whom the ends of the world are come'. 'Fin du Siècle', exclaimed his character Dorian Gray, subject of another of his books of 1891. 'Fin du globe' was his hostess's reply. For Gray life was 'a great disappointment'.

Most of the characters mentioned in the previous paragraph were romantic writers, and the prefixes early, middle and late have been applied to such writers as often – and as eloquently – as to their century. For the great French novelist Stendhal, another pen name, romanticism (and he used the *ism*) could be defined as simply (if as inadequately) as Hugo defined it. It was 'at any time the art of the day', while 'classicism was the art of the day before'. After attending the first night of Hugo's *Hernani* (1830) Stendhal wrote briskly 'champagne and *Hernani* did not suit me at all'.

Few twentieth-century critics have found romanticism as easy to define as Stendhal or Hugo, and many of their definitions, some of them contradictory, have attempted to cover writers, artists and musicians as diverse as Wordsworth and Byron, Schubert and Verdi. The main difficulty in placing romanticism in history is, however, 'less that of finding a definition than of finding one's way through the mass of definitions that have already been put forward'.[5] As far as the characters are concerned, each one followed his own course within his own society and culture, with some like Byron and Verdi establishing an international reputation that has lasted. In Britain Wordsworth, revolutionary in his youth, became Poet Laureate in 1843 on the death of his friend, Robert Southey, who had then been even more revolutionary than he was. In the mid-Victorian years Wordsworth was paid literary – and popular – tribute for his ability to make his readers 'feel'. He not only cast a spell, he gave spiritual comfort.

Comfort, a word more usually associated in the nineteenth century with material comfort, did not usually figure in what was described as 'the romantic quest', pursued through light and shadow, carrying with it moments both of desire and guilt, accomplishment and regret, ecstasy and agony, melancholy (ennui) and elation. Above all, there was always a sense of the unattainable. *Sehnsucht* (longing), a key word in the romantic vocabulary, belonged to the night as well as to the day. Dreams were a regular item in the romantic vocabulary. De Musset's best-known lyrical poems were called *Les Nuits*. In Britain William Morris, poet as well as craftsman, described himself as 'dreamer of dreams, born out of my due time'. That was in 1868 before he crossed what he called a 'river of fire' and set out to be a socialist revolutionary.

Morris, like John Ruskin before him, was ill-at-ease in his century. Scornful of machine-dominated and steam-driven industry he dismissed contemptuously the pride of modern civilization:

> Was it all to end in a counting-house on the top of a cinder heap, with Podsnap's drawing room in the offing, and Whig committee doling out champagne to the rich and margarine to the poor in such convenient proportions as would make all men contented together, though the pleasure of the eye was gone from the world and the place of Homer was taken by Huxley.[6]

T. H. Huxley was the main spokesman of nineteenth-century science. Podsnap was a character created by Charles Dickens, one of a cluster of great Victorian novelists, England's 'special correspondent for posterity', as Honoré de Balzac was for France.

Dickens's Podsnap appeared in his brilliant novel *Our Mutual Friend* (1865) which focused on the rubbish heaps of nineteenth-century civilization. A stock English type, self-assured and complacent, he was incapable of speaking except in platitudes. Other countries were a 'mistake'. 'Painful discussions' were to be avoided. Podsnap had a remarkable ability to evade or to dismiss as 'disagreeables' all unpleasant realities: 'it is not for me . . . to impugn the workings of Providence'. Morris demanded action, not satire. If all were not to end in 'a counting house at the top of a cinder heap' there would have to be collective action, and for there to be collective action there would have to be collective 'hope'. That he found in socialism, although in his utopian romance *News from Nowhere* (1891) he looked back to the middle ages, as he did in his earlier *Dream of John Ball* (1886). There were many other critics of the nineteenth century who looked back to the thirteenth, like Carlyle and Ruskin who treated medieval 'Gothic' as the highest form of 'organic architecture' and Viollet-le-Duc in France, who restored cathedrals and castles.

In retrospect, the nineteenth century, which had no single architectural style just as it had no single philosophy – eclecticism was dominant in the middle years of the century – was no single person's century. Nor was it a century of consensus. Argument prevailed. The currents of change could often direct people into whirlpools or over waterfalls. Pursuing what to contemporaries was a favourite metaphor, there were watersheds too and sometimes 'meetings of the waters'. For all the power of nationalism the currents were seldom simply national. Nor for all the appeal of socialism (or revulsion against it) were they driven entirely by 'class'. Ideas (or styles) might be born in Germany or France or Britain and make their way everywhere, sometimes strangely transformed in the process. When Marxism was 'revised', always controversially, there were common features in different countries. Pamphlets as well as books could be quickly translated. Newspapers had foreign correspondents.

This was a century of travel too, and of travel on a far bigger scale and far more commercially organized than the aristocratic 'grand tours' of the eighteenth century. Thomas Cook, pioneer of the guided tour, founded his travel agency in 1841. The German Karl Baedecker, like the English publisher, John Murray, had pioneered guidebooks in the two decades before his death in 1859. Switzerland and the French Riviera were on a new tourist map long before the century ended. Italy always had been, and was to be in the future. In the early twentieth century picture postcards, stamped with one of the most interesting new inventions of the nineteenth century, the postage stamp (1840), made their way across Europe.

THE SHOCK OF THE NEW

At times 'fashion' seemed to have dictated the process of change. Yet in every generation there were to be writers like the young French poet Arthur Rimbaud, born in 1854, who hailed what was new for reasons which had nothing to do with fashion. 'Let us ask the poet for the new in ideas and forms', he wrote: it was he who would 'arrive at the unknown'. Rimbaud, who published his first volume of poems while he was still at school and composed little of importance after the age of 19, claimed that a poet makes himself a seer 'by a long and rational disordering of the senses. He consumes all the poisons in him and keeps only their quintessences. This is an unspeakable torture during which he needs all his faith and superhuman strength, and during which he becomes the great patient, the great criminal, the great accursed – and the great learned one among men.' Samuel Taylor Coleridge, poet and philosopher, had put it differently when in relating excitement in the discovery of the new to the years of youth he had written of discovering 'the charm of novelty' in the 'things of every day', 'a feeling analogous to the supernatural by awakening the mind's attention from the lethargy of custom'.

'Not to be new in these days is to be nothing', wrote an English literary critic in 1893, and the shock of the new was to be a source both of thrill and of puzzlement then and in the early-twentieth century. The first great exhibition of impressionist paintings in Paris in 1874 shocked and puzzled without necessarily thrilling viewers who were disturbed by the sight on canvas of a world perceived momentarily by the senses'. One of the characters in a novel by Emile Zola (1840–1902), a realist writer, who knew exactly how to shock his readers, said of impressionist artists, who held six exhibitions between 1874 and 1886, that their art 'contradicted all the regular habits of the eye'; and even viewers who accepted impressionist ways of depicting water or flowers hesitated when they saw paintings of landscapes or locomotives, like Claude Monet's great painting of Paris's St. Lazare railway station.

They were to hold six more exhibitions before 1886, with one critic calling their second exhibition a disaster, second only in magnitude to a recent fire at Charles Garnier's Paris Opera House, work on which had started in 1861. It was one of the most famous buildings of the century. Opera, often bound up in politics, was one of the delights of the century. Alongside Verdi, who died in 1901, must be set Richard Wagner (1813–1883), who founded the Festival Theatre in Bayreuth in 1872. His *Ring*, written over a period of years, is one of the great masterpieces of the nineteenth century, transcending it as it delves deeply into the psychology of love, trust, hate, power and redemption. Wagner broke with traditional opera, seeking to depict in one work of art a complete unity of words and music, performance and production. He laid the foundation stone of his new opera house in Bayreuth on his 59th birthday with a performance of Beethoven's Ninth (Choral) Symphony. Bayreuth became a place of pilgrimage, for Wagner had disciples commit his 'music of the future'. But he had enemies too.

ANTI-SEMITISM

One element in Wagner – and one episode in Zola's life – must be taken into account in assessing the century. Wagner's anti-Semitism contrasts sharply with Zola's attack on the anti-Semites who in France fuelled the excitements of what was called 'the Dreyfus case'. The term 'anti-Semitism' seems to have been introduced into modern usage by an Austrian journalist Wilhelm Marr who in 1879 founded the League of Anti-Semites, but long before that elements of anti-Semitism were to be found in most European countries, in some countries in central and Eastern Europe, taking virulent populist form. It was in Germany, however, that Houston Stewart Chamberlain, who lived long enough – until 1923 – to heil a then powerless Hitler, advanced an Aryan racialist philosophy that took hold. Treating the Jews as 'mongrels', he claimed that interbreeding with Jews would destroy European civilization. 'Judaism' and 'Germandom' were irrevocably opposed. Without irony, however, he dedicated his most famous book to the Jewish Rector of Vienna University with whom he had studied.

All versions of anti-Semitism were current in Vienna, a city which influenced Hitler before 1914. One text, later exposed as a forgery, that carried influence, the *Protocols of the Learned Elders of Zion*, which first appeared in short form in 1903 in a Russian newspaper, purported to present the minutes of secret meetings of leading Jews planning to take over the world. Russia, the scene of anti-Jewish pogroms, made its own contribution both to anti-Semitism and to Jewish aspirations for a land of their own. In retrospect Theodor Herzl's Zionism, proclaimed in Vienna, was the most decisive historic response to anti-Semitism with far-reaching twentieth-century consequences.[7] His book *Jewish State* (1896) launched Zionism, and he became the first president of the World Zionist Organization in 1897. He died in 1904 ten years before the First World War when the British government committed itself in 'the Balfour Declaration' of 1917 to support for Jewish 'national self-determination' in Palestine.

Herzl had been influenced by the Dreyfus case, a complex French case that went through different phases, stole the headlines, a legal case at the heart of which was the claim to justice. In December 1894 a court martial found Captain Dreyfus guilty of treason – passing on secret information to Germany – and dispatched him to a French penal settlement in Central America, known aptly as Devil's Island. Before the sentence was finally cleared in 1906 – after more than one trial – the handling of the case, a matter of high politics, revealed the intensity of anti-Semitism in right-wing Roman Catholic circles, the distance between the French army and the French public, and, above all, the role of propaganda in the Press and especially in cartoons. It was not only Zola who hit the headlines with his famous cry *'J'accuse'*. The French socialist leader Jean Jaurès (1859–1914) was a prominent intellectual as well as political leader. In 1904 he founded the newspaper *L'Humanité*. A fighter for international peace, he was assassinated on 31 July 1914 a few days before the outbreak of the First World War.

CITY AND METROPOLIS:
PARIS, BERLIN, LONDON, VIENNA

Paris, centre of arts and politics, was a city which figured prominently in all the phases of history examined in this volume. But other cities figure too, some of them provincial industrial cities of a new kind in history, like Manchester or Düsseldorf, some national capitals. The most striking feature of population growth in the nineteenth century was the growth of cities. Already by 1851 around half of the people in England and Wales lived in towns of more than 10,000 people. By 1891 the comparative figure was 71 per cent. During the last decade of the century the urban population of Germany surpassed the rural for the first time. In France this did not happen until after the First World War, but the population of Paris, long a European metropolis, increased from half-a-million in 1800 to well over three millions in 1900. It was by then seven times as large as Lyons, France's second city which had had a pre-nineteenth-century industrial base.

Many capital cities, the focus of the state in the eighteenth as they were to be in the nineteenth century, had industrial areas by the end of the nineteenth century. Vienna was one. It was physically transformed after its seventeenth-century fortifications were demolished in 1859 and a spacious *Ringstrasse* was opened six years later – building went on until the 1880s – with new public buildings, including a university, museums and galleries, on each side of it. The industrial area was located near the Danube. At the end of the nineteenth century Otto Wagner, author of *Die Großstadt* (1911), produced a plan for the whole city in which tramways and railways played a major part. The city had been the centre of an imposing international exhibition held in the Prater in 1873 on the 25th anniversary of Franz Josef's succession. It had left as a legacy a huge Ferris wheel, which, like Paris's Eiffel Tower (1889) became a lasting city landmark.

Berlin, the Prussian capital and after 1871 the capital of the German Empire, was even more dramatically transformed than Vienna between the revolutions of 1848 and 1905, when its population had leapt from 400,000 to 2 million. There too a transportation system was essential for the development of its trade and industries and in new suburbs which between 1870 and the 1890s grew more quickly than the older parts of the city. Berlin, which also created in 1910 a huge 'amusement park', Lunapark, was a city in constant motion, for one observer a 'nowhere city', a city that was 'always becoming and never is'.[8]

Paris, by contrast, was a city with a past, revolutionary as well as imperial, that without a Lunapark, attracted tourists who never journeyed anywhere else. For the German poet Heinrich Heine, who settled there in 1830, it was 'really France: the latter is only the countryside around the capital'. It too was physically transformed during the reign of Napoleon III. Baron Georges Haussmann, a French Protestant of Alsatian origins, whom Napoleon made Prefect of the Seine in 1853, worked to plan, creating huge boulevards converging at the Place de l'Étoile. One of the most impressive of his planned streets was the Avenue de l'Opéra. Behind the boulevards and avenues the narrow streets of old Paris remained. In the north-eastern suburbs there was 'industry'. There growth was 'haphazard' and transportation lagged. It was not until 1900 that work on the Metropolitan underground, first discussed in the 1870s, was begun. It did not extend to the suburbs.

Most European cities went through physical transformations too. Brussels, Rome, Stockholm, Barcelona, Madrid all felt the influence of Haussmann. Yet among all the capital cities it was London, with no Haussmann to replan it – and with no Ring – that grew most remarkably, although there was a marked decline in the rate of population growth during the 1880s. It had long been difficult to say where London ended. The old city of London, the financial capital of the world, was small in area: 'Greater London', as it was first called at the census of 1881, was vast, and even earlier it had been described as a 'world city'. Meanwhile, the number of inhabitants of smaller capital cities soared. In Copenhagen, for example, they increased nearly five fold between 1800 and 1914. In Budapest they rose from 50,000 to nearly a million.

There, and, indeed, in all cities, it was the processes of growth that most fascinated contemporaries along with the social relationships that differentiated cities from villages. One British writer compared the processes with the growth of a coral reef: another invented the ugly word 'conurbation' to describe the built-up areas which surrounded them. One such area was the German Ruhr, an industrial spread which had no centre and no unified administration.

As far as the relationships were concerned, the most interesting late-nineteenth-century sociological writing was German. Ferdinand Tönnies drew sharp distinctions between face-to-face relationships in the village and anonymous aggregation in cities in his widely quoted book *Gemeinschaft und Gesellschaft*, published in Leipzig, a city of music and of industry, in 1887. And not far away in Dresden, old capital of Saxony, a great city exhibition was held in 1903 at which 128 German Cities, large and small, old and new were represented. The participants were discussing urban services and town planning, more advanced in Germany than in most other European countries. Nevertheless, there was a sense of foreboding, particularly in Germany, about the future of the city. 'Great agglomerations' would generate increased social disorder. As Tönnies, politically progressive, put it:

> The masses [a term increasingly in use] became conscious of [their] social position through . . . education in schools and through newspapers. They proceed from class consciousness to class struggle. This class struggle may destroy society and the state which it is its purpose to reform.

Another German writer Georg Simmel, living in Berlin, foresaw a different danger in his *Die Großstadt* (1903). People got lost in large cities: 'one nowhere feels as lonely and lost as in the metropolitan crowd'.[9]

Cities figured, even prominently, and both in fiction, particularly short stories, and in the daily and weekly press and treatises and surveys. London's *Daily Mail* has already been mentioned. In Berlin, which has been described as a 'world city', the *Berliner Morgenpost* (1898) was an overnight success, following in the wake of, but highly competitive with, the *Berliner Lokal-Anzeiger* (1883), distributed at first free of charge. They were indispensable reading, the former, like the *Daily Mail*, offering its readers 'something new'. In 1904 a mid-day and afternoon paper *BZ am Mittag*, sold on the streets, paid particular attention to sport which was becoming increasingly commercialized as 'spectator sport' in the years between 1900 and 1914. The media were to transform it in the later twentieth century. By then it had become religion.

One of the most innovatory and successful of all media developments before 1900 was launched neither in London nor in Berlin but in Budapest. A Hungarian inventor, Theodore Puskas, who had worked for the Edison Company, inaugurated in 1893 telephone news (including financial news) and entertainment (including music) programmes which offered subscribers what in retrospect was the world's first broadcasting system, Telefon Hirmondo. It also broadcast (the word was not used) 'linguistic lectures' in English, French and Italian.

SCIENCE AND TECHNOLOGY

Thomas Alva Edison, American inventor, had more than 1,000 patents to his name, ranging from the electric light bulb to the kinetoscope which transmitted pictures, but he never thought in media terms. His business interests stretched everywhere, particularly Europe, but few, if any, of his inventions, depended directly on 'pure' science. Nor did most of the 'discoveries' on display at a series of great international exhibitions, the first of which took place in London's Crystal Palace in 1851, four years after Edison was born. Some of the inventions on display, including the most ingenious, had no future. Others were to change ways of work and of life. 'Palaces of Industry' in Paris and Vienna proudly proclaimed the new, exploiting special effects as eagerly as they were to be exploited in late-twentieth-century cinema. In particular, they made the most of electrical power. Electricity, which had figured prominently at a Paris Exposition of 1889, was dominant at the great Paris Exposition of 1900 which stands out in retrospect, as it did at the time, as the climax of what many observers interested in science conceived of as a 'wonderful century'.

All the great exhibitions were photographed: all were seen too through tinted spectacles in an 'Age of Spectacles' which produced thousands of pairs of spectacles, thought of increasingly as 'common things' for the first time in history. (How did people manage without them before?) It is not easy to fit the story of spectacles or of photography into the scientific history set out, for example, in a collection of essays, *The Progress of the Century*, published in 1901, where it was possible for spectacles to be left out completely and for the writer on physics to describe 'the development and the art of photography' as 'not of the first importance', while admitting that it had 'contributed much to the pleasure of life'. Yet photography expressed what the international exhibition sequence proclaimed – the union of science and art. The first Impressionist Exhibition was held in a photographer's studio, and photography, culminating in moving pictures, influenced more than any other nineteenth-century invention both artists' and popular perceptions of the world.

Photography was a nineteenth-century invention with a long pre-history, conceived of both as science and art. The first fixed photographs, 'heliographs' or 'sun drawings', had been taken in France during the 1820s. It was not until 1839, however, that Louis Daguerre, like so many men of his century a born impresario, demonstrated his photographic processes in Paris, and later in the same year in London, Henry Fox Talbot displayed his first 'photogenic drawings', 'calotypes', for 'lovers of science and nature' at the Royal Society. Daguerre had presented his first 'daguerreotype' to the Curator of the Louvre gallery in Paris.

During the decades that followed, photography was employed in many different settings from photographers' studios (portrait photography became an industry) to houses and gardens, theatres, hospitals and prisons and even during the Crimean War to military tents. It was a photographer born in

Germany but a naturalized Frenchman, Edouard Baldus, who took pictures of places on the route of Victoria and Albert's visit to Napoleon III in 1855, when they visited the first of Paris's international Expositions, and of the railway from Paris to Marseilles opened by the Emperor in the same year.

By the end of the century the camera, like spectacles, was coming to be thought of as a 'common thing'. The box camera, with a branded name, Kodak ('branding' of products was now becoming more general), was introduced from the United States in 1888. Already the first moving pictures had been taken in 1872, and in 1896 the Lumière brothers exhibited moving pictures in Paris and in London. It was not until the twentieth century, however, that the cinema captured a regular mass audience, directly through Hollywood influencing the relationship between Europe and the United States.

The year 1896 was an *annus mirabilis* because it was then that in London Alfred Harmsworth founded the *Daily Mail*, a truly popular half-penny newspaper, that a young Italian inventor Guglielmo Marconi arrived with a bundle of wireless devices (there was no thought of broadcasting), that the first motor rally to Brighton took place (Harmsworth was an automobile enthusiast), and that far away from London the first modern Olympic Games were held in Athens. Sport, with its own history, laws, like cinema, to play a major role in twentieth-century history.

For the scientific experts, who produced *Progress of the Century*, 'serious science' was best represented by chemistry, the science which had most directly affected daily life and which Valéry had directly related to history. Physics, a new word, seemed less 'relevant' as a subject, although, before Einstein, there were great nineteenth-century physicists like Michael Faraday, James Clerk Maxwell and Herman von Helmholz, who did not break with Newtonian principles, but pursued their implications. Without the work of Heinrich Hertz and other physicists French, Russian and British, who were examining the nature of radio waves, there would have been no Marconi.

In chemistry the work of the great German chemist Justus von Liebig (1803–1873) had been influential in improving public health as it had been in transforming agriculture and food processing, while the great French chemist Louis Pasteur (1822–1895) influenced the preparation both of milk and wine as steps in the development of bacteriology, a science that changed the basis of the understanding of disease. A Pasteur Institute was founded in Paris in 1888.

Other branches of theoretical chemistry made advances, too, both through classification and through experiment. There was a place in the atomic table, first set out by the Russian chemist Dmitri Mendeleyev (1834–1907) in 1872, for chemical elements which had not yet been discovered. Three of them were discovered in his lifetime. By the end of the century it seemed 'obvious', Professor William Ramsay wrote in 1901, 'that the nation which possesses the most competent chemists, theoretical and practical, is destined to succeed in the competition with other nations for commercial supremacy and all its concomitant advantages'.

This was on the eve of a revolution in physics, although there was little intimation then that physics – theoretical, experimental and applied – would become the major science of the first half of the twentieth century, culminating in the harnessing of the split atom during the Second World War. The laws of thermodynamics had been enunciated in the nineteenth century *after* the invention of the steam engine, which depended on them, but it was long after Albert Einstein, breaking from Newton, published his special theory of relativity in 1903, that there were practical consequences. Already, by 1901 a prominent physicist could salute 'the great and rapidly increasing number of well-organized and splendidly equipped laboratories in which original research is systematically planned and carried out'.[10]

The advance of science in the nineteenth century, he claimed, had hitherto been 'more or less a guerrilla war against ignorance'. Now in an age when warfare itself seemed to be becoming more 'scientific', the research war in science was to be organized through campaigns in which teams would be involved as well as individuals. The participants were to be professionals, too, for while discovery in geology and 'natural history' earlier in the century had often been the work of 'amateurs', some of them 'gentlemen', some self-taught, laboratory science, passing far beyond observation and classification, required a professional base. This was first provided in Germany, although it had been in Britain that the Cambridge philosopher William Whewell, inventor in 1840 of the word 'scientist' (and the word of 'physicist'), foresaw the shape of things to come when he described 'the tendency of the sciences . . . to an increasing proclivity of separation and dismemberment. The mathematician turns away from the chemist; the chemist from the naturalist; the mathematician, left to himself, divides himself into a pure mathematician and a mixed mathematician, who soon part company.'

Nonetheless, in Britain, both in the provinces and in London, great emphasis was placed on publicizing science through lectures and demonstrations and through the opening of museums, and there was stimulating argument about the place of science and classical studies in the curriculum. There was also a noisy debate about evolution after the publication of Charles Darwin's book *On the Origin of Species* in 1859. Darwinian biology was even more controversial than geology which had already dramatically lengthened the span of the Earth's history and disturbed beliefs in the *Book of Genesis*. *The Origin of Species* was one of the 'great books' not only of the nineteenth century but of all time, although it was an essentially nineteenth-century work and could have been written in no other century. It had a nineteenth-century centrality too. Marx, nine years younger than Darwin, emerging from a completely different background and with a sharply contrasting personality, wished to dedicate his huge treatise on political economy, *Das Kapital*, the first volume of which appeared in 1867, to the English scientist. 'Darwin has interested us in the history of Nature's technology', Marx wrote. 'Does not the history of the productive organs of man, of organs that are the material basis of all social organization, deserve equal attention?'

When Darwin died in 1882 he was buried, although a religious agnostic, in Westminster Abbey, proof of the authority of a new 'scientific priesthood' as one scientist called it. For the liberal John Morley 'the Darwinian creed' (itself a religious term) 'runs through all the best thought [he did not add the worst thought] of our time. It tinges our unformed public notions; it reappears in a hundred disguises in works on law and history; in political speeches and religious discourses . . . If we try to think ourselves away from it we must think ourselves entirely away from our age.'

Yet not all nineteenth-century evolutionist writing was a by-product of *On the Origin of Species*. Much of it developed independently. Indeed, the idea of evolution had a long pedigree, and the literature of the period, including the poetry – Alfred Tennyson's *In Memoriam* was an example – was full of references to it. Ideas interconnect. So do pedigrees. If there had not been a transformation in the study of geology, there could have been no Darwinian achievement in biology leading ultimately to a new appreciation of Man's place in the long process of evolution. Darwin, like Marx, was looking for 'laws', but he saw 'grandeur' also in a view of life that started with 'the war of nature' and ended with 'the most exalted object which we are capable of conceiving, the production of higher animals' – including humans. That Man was not set apart from the animal kingdom – and this was the theme of Darwin's *Descent of Man* (1871) – seemed to Darwin's admirers to be 'the grand and special discovery of natural science in our generation'. It was not, however, to be the end of the story.

Nor was it ever the whole of the nineteenth-century story. Jean Baptiste de Lamarck, who had died in 1829, continued to exert an influence even though Darwin had set out to repudiate him. He had coined the noun 'biology' and after him others coined the adjective 'Lamarckian'. Herbert Spencer (1820–1903), a writer who extended what were essentially Lamarckian laws of evolution, 'sure, inflexible and ever active', to cover all spheres of existence, was the first person to use the phrase 'survival of the fittest'. (Darwin talked of 'natural selection'.) 'Social Darwinism', many versions of which would have offended Darwin as much as many versions of Marxism would have offended Marx, used the idea of a 'war of nature' to apply also to the world of men. There was a competitive struggle which the fittest would and should win.

Spencer, like Comte, to whom he owed no debt, never lacked confidence in his own judgements, but Tennyson, English Poet Laureate from 1850 to 1892, a self-consciously 'modern poet', changed his attitudes towards science as some of his contemporaries did. It is interesting to compare two poems of his, *Locksley Hall* (1842) and *Locksley Hall Revisited* (1882). In the first of them, like Victor Hugo in France, he put his faith in science: 'Science moves but slowly, creeping on from point to point.' And while he was more clearly aware than some of his contemporaries of the needs and demands of a 'hungry people', he had – again, like Hugo – great confidence in the future:

For I doubt not through the ages one increasing purpose runs,
And the thoughts of men are widened with the process of the suns.

By the 1880s Tennyson was less sure about science and more afraid of 'the power of Demos' than disturbed by the needs and demands of a 'hungry people'. And he was pessimistic rather than optimistic about the future:

Gone the cry of 'Forward, Forward,' lost within a growing gloom;
Lost or only heard in silence from the silence of the tomb.

This was more than the gloominess of old age. Despite the advance in education and in literacy there was doubt about direction. It was during the 1870s, when agnosticism and relativism were winning new adherents, that Morley talked of the air in Britain being full of missiles. 'Those who dwell in the tower of ancient faiths look about them in constant apprehension, misgiving and wonder . . . All is doubt, hesitation and shivering expectancy.'

Values were changing too, and in Britain, where 'Victorianism' had seemed so strong in the middle years of the century there were rebel voices like those of Oscar Wilde and George Bernard Shaw, both claiming that it was not the 'respectable poor' who were most worthy of care on the part of charity or the state, it was axiomatic that 'the virtues of the poor are readily admitted and are much to be regretted. The best among the poor are never grateful. They are ungrateful, discontented, disobedient, and rebellious. They are quite right to be so.' Both Wilde and Shaw used the stage as a place for argument as well as for entertainment.

There were many different kinds of rebels, with two types standing out: aesthetes, like Wilde, savouring every aspect of experience, particularly the forbidden and the bizarre; and 'primitives', seeking a simpler and less 'artificial' life than that offered through advancing science and technology. Most of the latter read the poems of the American Walt Whitman and enjoyed the paintings of Paul Gauguin with their South Sea themes. Many, like Edward Carpenter, were willing to reject all accepted conventions. Women rebels were prominent, too, asserting rights that had been unclaimed a few decades before. The idea of the 'new woman' was as influential during the *fin de siècle* years as the idea of 'new art'. Indeed, the adjective 'new' became increasingly popular as the century grew old.

Even in the middle years of the century behind the great new boulevards of Paris there lay the courtyards and garrets of *Bohemia*, a place not on the map that was known in every language. '*La Bohème*', 'ideal, free, pleasurable', unconventional, anti-bourgeois. In most European capital cities there was also a Bohemia, a clustering of artists and writers seeking to escape both from conventions and from commerce. Much that was to be thought of as 'modern European' was born in Europe's Bohemias. And some of the people who contributed most to the making of what has been called 'the modern European mind' had lived there before 1870 when the great break in European consciousness was said to have occurred.

MODERNITY

The concept of 'modernity', which has a long history, can confuse as much as the concept of romanticism when it is used to describe as wide a range of cultural expressions as the stagecraft of Henrik Ibsen (1828–1906) and the symbolism of the French poet Stéphane Mallarmé. Yet Mallarmé's poem *L'Après Midi d'un Faune*, published in 1887, was not only set to music by Claude Debussy but became a famous stage ballet presented by Sergei Diaghilev who founded the *Ballet Russe* in Paris in 1909. There was a passion for Russian dancing, music, art and literature at this time, and it was a Russian-born musician, Igor Stravinsky (1882–1971), who ushered in the twentieth century in 1911 when his shattering musical composition – noisy, rhythmic, 'primitive' – *Sacré du Printemps* ('The Rite of Spring') was performed in Paris.

Of the intervening year, 1910, the English 'Bloomsbury' novelist Virginia Woolf was to make the startling statement in 1924 (after the shock of the First World War) that 'on or about December 1910 human character' changed. It was then that a controversial Post-Impressionist Exhibition was shown in London where most British viewers saw for the first time paintings by Vincent Van Gogh, and Paul Gauguin, bringing into Europe the sights of the South Seas.

'Modernity' worked through a series of connections between arts and between countries; and if Paris was a centre, so too, in the years before 1914 was Vienna, home not only of Sigmund Freud but of the musicians Richard Strauss, Gustav Mahler, Arnold Schoenberg, Alban Berg and Anton von Webern; of the poet and librettist Hugo von Hofmannstal; of the novelists Karl Kraus and Robert Musil; of the painters Gustav Klimt and Oscar Kokoschka; and of the philosopher Ludwig Wittgenstein. These are all key names in every dictionary of modernist biography, spanning nineteenth and twentieth centuries.

Berlin and Munich were other key centres, the former 'making up in "modernity" for what it lacked in antiquity', the latter the cradle of German 'expressionism'. It was there in 1908 that Wilhelm Worringer, a proponent of 'abstraction', followed in the wake of Madame de Stael early in the century by seeking to explain the differences between 'northern' and 'classical' and 'Oriental' art. It was there too that Wassily Kandinski, a Russian-born pioneer of abstract painting, moved in 1897. Between 1910 and 1914 he produced his series of *Improvisations* and *Compositions* the first known examples of purely abstract work in twentieth-century art.

Much of the 'modern movement' has been described – and was, indeed, so described at the time – in terms of *isms*, however misleading they can be. Symbolism was the first, with a symbolist manifesto, published in 1886. The Symbolists rejected both impressionism and realism, and, like Wagner, often expressed themselves in myths. Paul Verlaine wrote a sonnet called '*Parsifal*', the title of Wagner's great opera, first performed in 1882. 'Futurism' was proclaimed in 1909 in one of the most famous of manifestos, the first of several, written by the Italian poet Filippo Marinetti (1876–1944). One of its objects was to make a 'clean sweep' of 'all stale and threadbare subject matter in order to express the vortex of modern life – a life of steel, fever, pride and headlong speed'.

There was no similar manifesto of cubism, although the poet Guillaume Apollinaire, who introduced Pablo Picasso (1881–1973), born in Spain, to Georges Braque in 1907, did much to diffuse knowledge of it (and of African art). Cubists, whose works had changed in style by 1912, set out to show objects as they are known to be rather than as they look at a particular moment.

Between and across the *isms*, connections can be traced back before and after 'symbolism' through *art nouveau* (called, in Klimt's Vienna *Sezession*); through *fin de siècle* 'decadence' – comprehensively condemned in one of the most discussed books of the 1890s, Max Nordau's *Degeneration* (1892); through opera beyond Wagner (from Strauss's *Salome* to Berg's *Wozzek*); through literature (from Ibsen to James Joyce); and through philosophy (from Friedrich Wilhelm Nietzsche (1844–1900) to Ludwig Wittgenstein); and they can be traced geographically too. *Art nouveau* was developed in Scotland (Charles Rennie Mackintosh), Belgium (Henry van der Velde and Victor Horta), France (René Lalique), Finland and other countries; and when Strauss turned Wilde's play *Salomé* into an opera in 1905 (the play had been performed in Berlin two years earlier) this was 'a bridge' which joined the England of Wilde and Aubrey Beardsley, who illustrated *Salomé*, with the Austria-Hungary of Klimt.

There was a great flowering of Scandinavian culture at this time, related in part to nationalism. Julian Christian Sibelius, born in Finland in 1865, composer of seven symphonies, composed his symphonic poem *Finlandia* in 1900. There were also cross-linkages there between the arts. Thus, the musician Edvard Grieg composed the music for Ibsen's symbolic verse drama *Peer Gynt* (1867) converted into an opera. One of the greatest expressionist painters was the Norwegian Edvard Munch (1863–1944), who frightened himself as much as the people who looked at his pictures: one of the most famous of them (1893) was called '*The Scream*'. There was a link here with Ibsen: pure emotion was expressed 'in the raw state'. Meanwhile, a later Swedish playwright and novelist, August Strindberg (1849–1912), bitter and at times obsessive, employed experimental expressionist techniques that influenced twentieth-century theatre. His derogatory attitudes towards women scarcely qualified him, however, to be a prophet of a new century which was to end with a further feminist upsurge.

There was symbolism in Ibsen as his last plays – *The Master Builder* and *John Gabriel Borkman* – bring out; and within France itself in Zola's 'realist' novels. (Zola was a member of a Wagner society in Marseilles as was the French post-impressionist painter Paul Cézanne (1839–1906). And in the background both of symbolism and of realism were changing attitudes towards both time and place. They had been changing throughout the nineteenth century, but before time was unmoored in the twentieth, it was regulated. 'Standard time' was settled in 1884 when representatives of 25 countries met in Washington and established Greenwich as the zero meridian and divided the world into time zones. The system was slowly accepted between 1884 and 1900, with surviving exceptions like St Petersburg that retained their own time.

Individuals had their own time, too, and 'modern literature' made much of them. The American philosopher William James invented the term 'stream of consciousness' in 1890. Marcel Proust (1891–1922) played with time in his great modern novel *A la Recherche du Temps Perdu* ('Remembrance of Things Past'), the first volume of which appeared in 1913. So, differently, did James Joyce (1882–1941), the Irish novelist in exile in France, whose *Ulysses*, considered to be one of the most important of modern novels, appeared in 1922. Set in Dublin, a very different city from Paris or London, it was banned in Britain (and in the United States). Preoccupation with time and space was apparent too in the work of painters – and sculptors. Thus, the French painter Marcel Duchamp (1887–1968) described his *Nude Descending the Stairs* (1913) as 'an organization of kinetic elements, and expression of time and space through the abstract presentation of motion'.

This sounded completely new, yet 'modernity', self-conscious as it became, was not a new concept during the late-nineteenth century nor even during the 1860s and 1870s. It has been traced back to the Renaissance, Stendhal's favourite period, and even to the fall of ancient Rome, the period when Oxford and Cambridge Universities deemed 'modern Europe' to have begun. It was during the last years of the nineteenth century, however, and the first decade of the twentieth, that old senses of perspective and purpose were most under attack. Not only were the classics pushed into the background, even for the educated, becoming 'dead languages' – Greek before Latin – but the Bible lost its power of reference for both educated and non-educated, the latter now being drawn into compulsory school education. It was then, in a period of increasing secularization that Marx and Wagner were admitted into a select group of 'modern' thinkers: Marx because his ideas were still active and were to be in the shaping of twentieth-century history and Wagner because he had written what was hailed as 'the music of the future'. There was a place also among the moderns for the German philosopher of 'pessimism', Arthur Schopenhauer, although he died in 1860, and for the French poet Baudelaire, who was read more after his death in 1867 than before.

Nietzsche proclaimed that 'God is dead'. Nietzsche, who had begun by admiring Wagner – his first book, *The Birth of Tragedy*, was dedicated to him – intuitive and anti-intellectual, stood out because he was at war not only with the purposive nineteenth century but with all the Christian centuries that had preceded it, dwelling on 'the feeling of power in man, the will to power, power itself'. Insisting that the positive passions which had to be released included pride, joy, health, sex, enmity and war, he proclaimed an *Übermensch* or 'Superman' who would impose his will on the weak and worthless. Nietzsche, whose last book was called *Nietzsche Contra Wagner*, did not care that he had many enemies, including all systematizers: 'I mistrust all systematizers and I avoid them. The will to system is a lack of integrity.'

Freud, different in background, temperament, ideas, intuitions and talent, had his place too because he explored the unconscious, revealing 'the night side of nature and the soul' that had been. His *Interpretation of Dreams* was one of the last books of the century. 'These wishes in our unconscious', he wrote, 'ever on the alert . . . remind one of the legendary titans.' 'In the unconscious nothing can be brought to an end, nothing is past or forgotten.' Yet Freud, who influenced literature and art as well as psychology and psychiatry (psycho-analysis), was to live long enough to explore *Civilisation and its Discontents* (1930), where he suggested that the repression of desire that was essential to the existence of civilized society made happiness virtually impossible.

As the third key figure, the Norwegian prophet of modernity, Ibsen, saluted along with Wagner by George Bernard Shaw, was renowned throughout Europe during the last decades of the nineteenth century for his treatment of drama as social criticism, seeking to expose the errors both of convention and superstition. In particular, he was offended by the morality of 'respectability' (a key word of the nineteenth century): Nietzsche described the norms of respectable morality as 'the herd instinct in the individual'. For its critics the conformities that went with it rested inevitably on repression. One of Charles Dickens's characters, Podsnap, said that there should be nothing in any book unfit for the reading of any 'young person', nothing that should bring a blush to that person's cheek. Sex had to be kept a secret in the mid-century middle-class home, and outside the home as much was made in Scandinavia as in Britain of the need for 'purity' in thought and deed.

One of the people who influenced Ibsen most, the Danish critic Georg Brandes, gave a lecture in 1871 that Ibsen hailed precisely because it placed 'a yawning gap between yesterday and today', adding that anything was better than the existing state of affairs. There were other 'yawning gaps' in what had once seemed the safe structure of social life. Ibsen, who dwelt on the influence of the personal past on the lives of his characters, was aware also of the significance in mid-century morality of a 'double standard' in prescribing the behaviour of men and women. The 'manly man' was expected to behave in ways quite inappropriate to the chaste 'womanly woman', and the much cherished 'sanctity of the home', based on a family ideal in most European countries, was maintained in practice by the coexistence of widespread prosti-tution, regulated in most countries through licensed brothels.

It is always difficult to generalize about attitudes towards sex or about sexual behaviour, not only because there is much that is hidden away from outside scrutiny but because there are both individual and class differences. There is no doubt, however, about the existence in nineteenth-century Europe of many forms of repression, and of the complex reactions of 'modernists' to what were their current values. Some were homosexuals, others libertines, some solitaries. The fact that 'the working classes' seemed to have kept free from some of the shibboleths of *bourgeois* morality encouraged some of the modern rebels to seek an alliance with them, curiously similar, though for different reasons, to that which the positivists, the followers of Auguste Comte, had sought. Comte had set out to establish 'laws': many of the rebels put their trust in 'will'.

There were obvious cultural and social contradictions. Thus, romantic love, idealized in prose and poetry, particularly in the middle years of the century, was as much in sharp contrast with the competitive drive which sustained the private enterprise economy in its progress towards increasing industrialization as it was to dynastic and aristocratic approaches to family strategy. In mid-century middle-class circles the home, presided over by *pater familias*, was conceived of, therefore, as a place of release from the business pressures of daily life, above all a place of peace. 'The family', it was claimed in Britain in 1874, 'is the unit upon which a constitutional government has been raised which is the admiration and envy of mankind . . . The husband and wife, however poor, returning home from whatever occupations or harassing engagements, have found there *their* dominion, *their* repose, their compensation for many a care . . . There has been a sanctity about this.'

The problem, of course, was, as all 'realist commentators' were forced to note – and this was a link between 'realism' and 'modernism' – that all homes were not like this. Ibsen, in particular, dwelt on the tendency for husbands to treat wives and even children as property, at best as dolls in dolls' houses, and in most countries, north or south, east or west, women were slow to secure their own property rights or (if they could divorce at all) to free themselves from their husbands on grounds of cruelty or desertion. Despite increasing pressure for women's rights, the husband remained 'the lord of creation' until the end of the nineteenth century, presiding over what were usually large nineteenth-century families. Children were present in such large numbers that the one Victorian maxim about them which is still remembered is 'little children should be seen and not heard'. Child mortality was high, and the death of young children was a common experience. For Christians such children were often thought of as 'angels', but while popular Christianity thrived during the last years of the nineteenth century, large numbers of people, who had never heard of Nietzsche, found religion no consolation.

'Modern' writers, like the novelist Samuel Butler in Britain, were fascinated by the implications (sometimes 'unconscious') of authoritarian family relationships. So, too, of course, was Freud. Preoccupation with the 'unconscious' was growing throughout the period, as Stuart Hughes demonstrated in his study *Consciousness and Society*, and there was no preoccupation more calculated to erode the basic liberal and positivist philosophies of the mid-nineteenth century. Significantly, however, Freud himself, emerging from a *bourgeois* background in the Vienna of the late Habsburg Empire, retained a liberal belief in toleration and a positivist faith in science.

The 'well-ordered home' whether in Vienna or London required an ample supply of regimented domestic servants, and, despite occasional press publicity to the contrary, they remained in ample supply (if at rising cost) until the First World War. In all countries families were divided in status according to whether or not they employed domestic servants and if they did, how many. Working-class homes with no servants could be 'respectable' – even if by then this was bleak praise – but they could not be more. The mid-nineteenth-century middle-class household had to be full of things too, and before 1914 there was change here – as there was in the size of families: middle-class families were falling in size before the size of working-class families fell.

It was another sign of 'modernity' when fullness of possessions within the home began to be called clutter during the 1880s and 1890s. During the early-nineteenth century eighteenth-century objects had been relegated to attics or to cellars: they seemed too simple and balanced in design, and in house building too there was a sharp reaction against 'monotonous' Georgian canons of taste. It was an even greater sign of change when the design of the houses themselves began to change during the 1900s, particularly in Germany. Mid-century taste-makers, a motley crew, given unparalleled opportunities when eighteenth-century rules were cast aside, now changed their advice. As many 'new things' made their way into the home, there was a further reaction against the mid-century predilection for solid, preferably highly decorated, furniture that was designed to last. Permanence was what 'modernists' most despised. There was ample scope, however, for luxury. The quest for wealth and for material progress did not cease as the doubts and anxieties of the philosophers and artists multiplied. Nor did the advance of socialism which accompanied the great burst of European economic development.

During the first decade of the twentieth century, when attempts were made to measure the extent of 'poverty in the midst of plenty', there was far more willingness on the part of the rich to spend ostentatiously (at the table or the shoot, in the country or in the town) than there had been during the middle years of the nineteenth century. Plutocracy mingled with aristocracy. Edwardian Britain tried hard not to be Victorian in spirit. It did not help that 'scandals' were publicized, as they were in Wilhelmine Germany, a society full of social contradictions. The most famous was the case of Moltke vs. Harden which involved six trials, the first of them in 1907: they exposed a network of homosexual relationships in the Army and in the Emperor's immediate entourage.

There was political ambivalence in the self-consciously modern society and culture, for some modernists turned more and more to the revolutionary left and some to the radical right. One French critic of reason, Georges Sorel, who owed much to Marx, managed – and he was not alone in this – to look both ways. In rejecting the liberalism of the ballot box and demanding direct action through general strikes, Sorel was searching for 'myths of action'. There was a disturbing preoccupation with violence, domestic and international on the very eve of the 'Great War' of 1914–18, which so transformed history. Thus, a young British philosopher, Bertrand Russell, who was keenly interested in mathematics and the new sciences, was writing of the 'barbaric stratum of human nature, unsatisfied in action', finding 'an outlet in imagination'. Russell did not have long to wait for the action; and he did not like it when it came.

Notes ·

1. Quoted in E. Bruley and E. A. Dance, *A History of Europe* (1960), p.9.
2. Quoted in G. Tillotson, *A View of Victorian Literature* (1978), p.1.
3. A. R. Wallace, *The Wonderful Century* (1898), p.2.
4. See L. R. Furst, *Romanticism* (1968) for the range of definitions.
5. For changes in the use of the term, see L. R. Furst, *Romanticism and Revolt* (1967).
6. Quoted in A. Briggs, *William Morris: Selected Writings and Designs* (1962), p.13.
7. See C. E. Schorske, *Fin de Siècle Vienna, Politics and Culture* (1980).
8. Quoted in P. Firtzsche, *Reading Berlin 1900* (1996), p.7.
9. Quoted in A. Lees, *Cities Perceived, Urban Society in European and American Thought, 1820–1940* (1985), p.172, p.164.
10. See E. N. Hiebert, 'The Transformation of Physics', in M. Teich and R. Porter (eds), *Fin de Siècle and its Legacy* (1990), ch.12.

Chapter 6

A EUROPEAN CIVIL WAR,
1914–1918

‘Germany has declared war on Russia – (went) swimming in the after-noon.’ So it was that the Czech author Franz Kafka recorded the outbreak of the First World War in the hot first week of August 1914. His phlegmatic diary entry was in marked contrast to the jingoistic reactions to the declaration of war in most European capitals. Crowds gathered in Berlin, St Petersburg, Vienna, London and Paris during the final days of the Sarajevo crisis, cheering the escalation of international tension and the likely imminence of war. Berlin newspaper vans carrying *The Tägliche Rundschau* were stormed by crowds anxious for news of the Serbian response to Austria-Hungary's ultimatum, and Serbia's rejection of the Austrian demands was greeted with jubilant cries in Berliner dialect: ‘*Et jeht los!*’ (it's on). During the weekend crisis of 1–2 August 1914 almost 2,000 emergency marriages were performed in Berlin, and when the Rector of Kiel University made an impassioned address on the declaration of war, almost the entire male student body enlisted.

Peering beneath the surface of the crowds' behaviour, historians have unearthed different emotions from mass enthusiasm for war, including feelings of fear, panic and even simple curiosity. Whether motivated by the desire to preserve the present (Britain? Austria-Hungary?), to restore tarnished honour (France? Turkey? Russia?) or to create a glorious future (Germany? Serbia? Italy?), citizens, subjects and governments alike appeared eager to wage war. Cross frontier ties were wrenched apart and the international socialist brother-hood was broken when the majority of socialists, including the powerful French and German parties, decided to support their own national governments rather than honour anti-war pledges made to one another. The enthusi-asm for war can be explained in part – but only in part – by the popular conviction that the war would be over in a matter of months. Many war strategists were less confident there would be a quick resolution to the conflict, yet at the same time they could not see how the state would be able to finance a long war – they failed to anticipate large-scale borrowing by the state both from their own people and from overseas. (Taxation was to play a relatively small role in financing the war.) There was also ample military evidence from the Crimean War, the American Civil War and the Boer War, which indicated that a major conflagration would involve long, drawn out and bitter fighting. This miscalculation was to change Europe for ever. Fifty-one months and nine million deaths later the war was over, in time for Christmas 1918, not Christmas 1914, as had been widely predicted.

THE DAWN OF 'TOTAL WAR'

By 5 August 1914 Britain, in proclaimed defence of Belgian neutrality and, more significantly in fear of German hegemony in Europe, had joined France, Russia, Germany, Serbia and Austria-Hungary at war. It thus became the first major conflict since the Napoleonic wars which involved all the major European countries. They had been split into opposing camps of Central and Entente or Allied powers during more than a decade of diplomacy. During the course of the war, however, while Germany's new ally, Turkey, and Russia's old protégé Bulgaria fought alongside the armies of the Central alliance, Japan and the United States joined the side of the Entente, alongside Italy (after the 1915 Treaty of London), to be followed by a number of independent states in Latin America, by China and by Siam (later in the century called Thailand). Some of these powers, like Italy, entered the war because participation in the conflict seemed less dangerous than neutrality. The entry of the non-European nations, particularly Japan and the United States, had an important long-term effect for Europe. The entry of the United States was to shift the balance of power away from the European nations in the twentieth-century world.

Soldiers from distant imperial lands were heavily involved in the war: Senegalese and Zouaves served in the French army, Indians in the British army. Subject peoples also made an important contribution to the Romanov and Habsburg armies, while Poles and Danes fought for the German army. Despite this vibrant ethnic mix, the conflict for the most part, and especially in its beginnings, was a European Civil War, waged between countries which were either industrialized or on the way to being so. Paradoxically, it was because of the nature of European industrialization that military planners were led to believe that there would be a quick end to the war, typified by Prussia's nineteenth-century victories over Austria and France. The military believed that railways would move men quickly to the front, machine guns would create a powerful offensive force, and mighty ships and artillery would overwhelm the enemy. Speed of attack was the key to the German Schlieffen Plan on which the beginning of the war hinged, with its stress on a quick strike to be followed by a decisive victory on the Western Front, and a turning East to confront the large and cumbersome Russian force, the plan promised dramatic action. For Alfred von Schlieffen 'the whole of Germany must throw itself upon *one* enemy, the strongest, most powerful, most danger-ous enemy and that can only be France.' Instead, the nature of the industry behind the war ensured that it would become a bloody and protracted conflict in which success along the Western Front was to be measured in inches rather than in miles.

Europe's economic growth, which had fashioned the most prosperous and privileged continent in the world, also created both the wealth and organizational potential to raise large armies that could be supplied on a massive scale with industrial products. Meanwhile, individuals could contribute more in taxes towards the cost of waging war and endure greater reductions in living standards long before being reduced to subsistence level. Industrial and social progress in itself determined that the war would be a protracted conflict lasting over four years. No country had the freedom to wage war as it had been claimed.

It was the large-scale development of Europe's heavy industries (metal, engineering, chemical and power) especially after 1870, that had helped to secure European economic dominance, which could now be applied in warfare. The quantity of military hardware in Europe increased by around 300 per cent from 1870 to 1914 and Europe's powers could now kill one another far more efficiently. There were also many more Europeans to do the killing. In 1800 the five main belligerents (Britain, Germany, Austria–Hungary, France and Russia) had a combined population of around 98.8 million; by 1910 this had risen to 355.5 million. In 1914 the universal weapon of the infantry was the rapid fire rifle with a magazine of six to eight rounds. Refined machine guns, too, had enhanced killing power. Innovation in the chemical industry had finally replaced the black gunpowder used for centuries with high explosives containing nitro-glycerine, developed by the chemist Alfred Nobel in 1866.

Already by September 1914 Britain and France were buying liquid chlorine to produce poisonous gas, and the technology of chemical warfare developed quickly from chlorine to phosgene and mustard gases. The Germans were the first to use gas extensively and methodically. Flamethrowers and trench mortars were other German innovations in the field of battle. Denounced by 'the Tommies' (British forces) for their 'barbarism', the 'Boches' were also quicker than the French and the British to exploit sophisticated new devices like tanks and submarines, although the former were first made and deployed by the British in 1916, while German engineers had transformed a seventeenth-century Dutch concept of an underwater craft by the inclusion of the diesel internal combustion engine in 1906. Large German airships, Zeppelins, named after their inventor Count Ferdinand von Zeppelin, were used to threaten London where the first attack came in June 1915.

Nevertheless, it would be a mistake to see the war as an entirely modern conflict. Seasoned methods of warfare continued, coexisting uneasily with the new. 'Old-fashioned' forms of transport – donkeys, mules, horses, particularly horses – were still essential, although the hundreds of thousands of men in cavalry divisions waited in vain for the decisive encounter which had characterized European warfare in the Napoleonic era. In the twentieth-century experience of war, however, cavalry was consigned mostly to the less glamorous role of intelligence gathering and horses to transport and supply. Military pride often stubbornly resisted change, even in the uniforms of war. To protect their troops in combat the British had already changed their uniforms to khaki and the Germans had moved from Prussian blue to field grey, but in 1914 the French army still wore the same blue coats, red kepi and red trousers which they had worn in 1830. Making the French soldier less conspicuous on the field of battle would undoubtedly have saved lives, but as the *Écho de Paris* reported, to banish the red trousers was 'contrary to French taste and military function'. The final verdict came from France's Minister for War: 'Eliminate the red trousers? . . . Never! *Le pantalon rouge, c'est la France!*'

During the first months of the conflict, Germany, well prepared, appeared to take the initiative in its choice of methods, tactics and instruments of war. But as the war continued and the resources of an entire nation had to be mobilized in what came to be called an age of 'total war', a phrase popularized by the German General Erich von Ludendorff in the 1920s, this lead was lost. It was the underlying economic strength, social cohesion and political stability of each nation and its allies, alongside the support or opposition of the United States, that were crucial in determining the 'winners' and the 'losers'. For the United States this was to be World War One, to be followed up and contrasted with World War Two.

HOW TO WAGE WAR?

The Schlieffen Plan failed when French and British troops halted the initial German advance from Belgium to Paris, and by November 1914 the mobile war had shuddered to a halt with troops of the Allied and Central powers dug in behind trenches stretching across Northern France. Technological developments had already determined that the war, contrary to expectation, would be largely a defensive one, although until 1917 most politicians and strategists did not abandon the hope that one successful offensive could turn the conflict in their favour. Meanwhile, European governments were slow to develop strategies to fight a long war as they were to do during the Second World War. They extended their control over their human resources, men (for the army), women (for factory and field), only in a haphazard and short-term fashion, if at all. Austria–Hungary, the Ottoman Empire and Russia, paid the ultimate price of the failure to manage their 'war economies' – not simply defeat but political revolution.

The evolution of British policy towards the war provides a typical example of how the conflict surpassed the expectations of politicians, military personnel and ordinary people alike. When the British, Liberal governments decided to fight in the summer of 1914, its immediate objectives were to restore Belgian neutrality and to prevent France and Russia from succumbing to the domination of the Central Powers. Yet separated from Continental Europe, as they were by 'the English Channel', the British were as suspicious from the start of the long-term ambitions of their fellow allies as they were of their enemies.

Nineteenth-century experience had taught British governments to be wary of Russian expansionism in the East (the Crimean War, imperial rivalry in Asia) and of French colonialism in the south and east. The British government wanted any future peace settlement, therefore, to secure not only a Germany that would be tamed, but that Russia and France would not become so strong as to threaten the British Empire.

The question was posed inevitably, as it had been during wars against Napoleon, as to whether Britain could offer greater assistance to its allies by limiting the size of its own army and supplying the Allies with money and equipment *or* by raising a large conscript army which would demonstrate that Britain had not abandoned its allies. The British Isles, with its large empire to back them, seemed to have a greater range of strategic options than other Entente powers, another choice being whether to concentrate their military effort on initiatives on the Western or the Eastern Front.

Like the Central powers, 'the Allies' of the Entente worked together at a number of levels – military, political, naval and economic. Britain assumed that the main burden of the land war would fall on France and Russia, with troops from the BEF (British Expeditionary Force) making a limited contribution. Britain's role in the war effort would be to employ its great naval power to impose a naval blockade on the Central powers while providing financial support to its allies as it had against revolutionary France and Napoleon. 'Maximum victory' was to be achieved at 'minimum cost'. Already by December 1914, it was clear that such a strategy was wildly unrealistic. France and Russia were unable to fight without large-scale military assistance, and the Russians already joked caustically that the British were prepared to fight to the last Russian. So it was that by December 1914 British and later Imperial troops (including Canadians, Australians, New Zealanders and Indians), became bogged down on the Western Front. The first months of the war were enough to shatter any illusions that the conflict would find a speedy resolution.

THE COURSE OF THE WAR

Losses in the first phases of the war set the pattern, for already by the end of 1914 France and Germany had sustained around 600,000 wounded or missing soldiers with over 300,000 dead in the 'battle of the frontiers', and nearly every family in both countries had suffered some bereavement. There were logistical problems also – ammunition and shell shortages – and grave concern about long-term food provision for the civilian population. Added to these difficulties came growing awareness of the terrible reality of trench warfare. Endless rain – the heaviest December rainfall since 1876 – turned the field of battle into an impassable, muddy swamp. Water pumps, hose pipes, shovels and pick-axes became as important as guns and ammunition in the struggle for survival.

The horrors of trench warfare continued until the end and left abiding memories. The first battle of the Marne (September 1914), the battle of Ypres (April – May 1915), the struggle for Verdun (February – November 1916), the battle of the Somme (June – November 1916) and the recapture of the fortifications of Verdun by the French in December 1916, all took place within a remarkably small band of territory. The battle of the Somme and the third battle of the Ypres campaign, Passchendaele (1917), stand out equally for their bloodiness and for their futility. Gains were small and the cost of life was very high both in officers and in 'men'. Death came by bullet, shrapnel, gas, high explosive shell and, at Passchendaele, by drowning in mud: the very name seemed to convey the image. Meanwhile, in the air, the first combats might lead to death, but they brought out feats of individual daring that produced the only contrasting images, those of blue skies and intrepid 'aces', like the Prussian aristocrat Manfred von Richthofen.

Away from the Western Front, Russian defeats at Tannenberg (in August 1914, where the Germans took over 100,000 Russians prisoners), in the region of the Masurian Lakes (November – December 1914), and in the winter campaign in the Carpathian mountains were the prelude to what was to follow. It was on the Eastern Front that German Generals, Ludendorff and Paul von Hindenburg, important actors in the post-war history of Germany, established their military reputations. Then the Ottoman Empire entered the war.

The Turkish decision to join the Central Powers on 31 October 1914 also directed attention away from the Western Front. It was taken after the Young Turks had rejected a belated proposal from Britain, France and Russia at the end of August to guarantee the Ottoman Empire from attack in return for Turkish neutrality. A German military mission, sent out to Constantinople in 1913, had laid the foundations for a German-Turkish alliance, and the British Naval Mission, already there, for a number of reasons had lost its authority. Following the British interception of a Turkish torpedo boat, which contained German soldiers, at the mouth of the Dardanelles, the vessel was ordered to go back to Turkey, but the German soldier commanding fortifications closed the Dardanelles straits. The closing of free passage of the Dardanelles was itself a *casus belli*, but it was not until 30 October that the British, Russian and French ambassadors in Constantinople delivered a 12-hour ultimatum to the Young Turks. When it went unanswered, war began. Turkey lost most of its European, and some of its non-European, possessions before 1914, and by the end of the war it had lost what remained, thereby, in the long run, creating new territorial boundaries for the Middle East in the twentieth century – Palestine, Syria, Iraq, Saudi Arabia, Yemen. Yet in the short term, Turkish intervention added greatly to the problems of the Allied powers. The closing of the Dardanelles prevented Allied provisions from reaching Russian lines and factories. For Britain Turkish involvement also threatened the oil-fields of the Middle East, and Muslim insurrections in Mesopotamia, Persia and Afghanistan posed a grave potential threat to the British Empire.

After Anglo-French efforts on the Western front were trapped in a bloody stalemate, the British decided controversially to launch a naval assault on the Dardanelles, with the enthusiastic backing of Winston Churchill, then First Lord of the Admiralty, and in April 1915 an Imperial army landed on the Gallipoli peninsula. The failure of the first assault prompted a second landing at Suvla Bay in August, but all to no avail. After weeks of indecision and at a high cost in ships and life – particularly amongst Australian and New Zealand forces – the Allied troops were driven into the sea and forced to withdraw. Early in 1915, therefore, the Allies, in the words of Lord Kitchener, Secretary of State for War, had recognized that 'unfortunately we had to make war as we must, not as we should like to'. By 1915, Britain, like France and Russia before it, had now raised a large conscript army, and after military setbacks at Neuve Chappelle, Festubert, Arras and Loos on the Western Front, the Entente powers finally recognized the need for a common plan. Notwithstanding this, the year 1916 proved as bleak for the Allies as 1915 had been. They held firm under a young General, Henri Philippe Pétain, against a concentrated and determined assault by the Germans, now led by General Erich von Falkenhayn at Verdun, but in the battles both sides sustained losses of around 800,000 men.

The war in Eastern Europe remained far more mobile than the war in the West, if only because the thin railway network reduced the ability of the belligerents to bring up reserves quickly to resist attack. In October 1914, for example, it took the Russians one month to transport 18 divisions from East of Cracow to south of Warsaw. Comparable troop movements on the western front took a matter of days. Strategically, however, the east did not differ greatly from the west since troops on the offensive invariably ran ahead of their communications, supplies and reserves, and defenders could easily assemble their reserves to counter attack.

The offensive staged at Lake Narotch in March 1916 was typical of the inept efforts of the old Russian army (as distinct from the 'new' army led by 'sensible technicians' which emerged in the summer of 1916). Launched in the spring (18 March 1916), soldiers faced alternating heavy-frost and thaw which turned road and field from ice to morass. This made the movement of heavy equipment impossible, shooting difficult and camouflage awkward: 20. Corps was sited in marshy ground, easily visible to German artillery. The Germans also had good intelligence of the offensive two weeks before it began. The Russians lost over 100,000 men, as well as 12,000 men who died of frost bite. The Germans lost 20,000.

This typically horrendous defeat condemned the Russian army to passivity. Russian generals argued that if the effort and resources of this campaign could not bring success, then only a mammoth increase in their supply of shells could. Even the brilliance of General Aleksei Brusilov could not rescue the Russian war effort. The Brusilov offensive, launched 4 June 1916, was the most successful campaign of the imperial army in the war when, for once the bravery of the Russian soldier was matched by sufficient support in equipment, food, co-ordinated leadership and communications to offer the possibility of conquest. But the momentum was not sustained and by the following month the advance had faltered. Thereafter, the Central powers recaptured Galicia, the Habsburg territory of Poland, which had been lost in July, and in September 1916 the Germans took Riga.

By 1916 more nations European had joined the war: Italy, Bulgaria, Greece and Romania. Japan also entered the war in 1916 not to influence events in Europe, but to eliminate the German naval threat, to extend its influence into China (especially Manchuria), and to spend more money on armaments which pleased those who had ambitions for Japan's role as a world power. Hopes receded of the 'one great offensive' which would create a turning point in the conflict, and instead, the war became one of attrition, the last resort of a paralysed strategy. Resources were severely strained, and the Allies, under increasing pressure from within, as were the Central powers, were saved by the entry of the United States in April 1917. The United States, with its seemingly boundless supply of commodities, manufactures, loans and ultimately men, was the only country which could break the stalemate in the European war.

MEN IN TRENCHES

For the men battling in the trenches, the war brought horrors far beyond the imagination of politicians in the hot summer of 1914. What lingered in the mind as the 'Great War' helped fix the standard imagery of mass warfare until the deployment of atomic weapons some 30 years later. Networks of inter-connected trenches, uncut barbed wire and grenades, 'deafening artillery barrages', long lines of attacking men 'going over the top', moving as if in slow motion to be confronted by machine gun fire, men on the attack were left almost entirely defenceless. For a British soldier Germans appeared to 'fall like shooting gallery targets'; a German machine gunner depicted an Entente attack:

> The officers went in front. . . . I noticed one of them walking calmly, carrying a walking stick. When we started firing we just had to load and reload. They went down in their hundreds. You didn't have to aim, we just fired into them.

There were other horrors. On taking over one waterlogged trench, a Frenchman quipped, 'It'll be all right so long as the U-boats don't torpedo us'. Terrible mutilations of comrades in arms were common. So were de-composing corpses. Soldiers attempted to cover rotting bodies with dirt, but sometimes bits of corpses would find their way into sandbags – arms and hands were known to unexpectedly pop out from burst bags. Decaying bodies also attracted lice and rats the size of cats. Poison gas attacks were the only way of killing the vermin, although, of course, this had the unfortunate side effect of killing men too. For men on the front dirt and filth were constant companions. A spell of trench duty normally consisted of three to four days and nights in the support trenches. This was followed by a similar length of time in the reserve before men returned to the front, and only here could they wash, change and rest. For those troops behind the front line the principal feature of the war was boredom. Not surprisingly, there was a loosening of public morality. In 1914 soldiers were warned off wine, women and song, but by 1915 brothels were a standard component of base camps.

The gulf between officers and other ranks did not diminish to any substantial degree on either side during the course of the war. Europe's pre-war armies, with an officer class recruited from the traditional elites, and the regular rank and file often drawn from the lowest members of society, were not especially representative of society as a whole. Even when the patriotic rush to enlist was followed by conscription, 'class-orientated' structures survived. This was even, in part, true of the Russian Imperial Army when it became the Red Army under Lev (Leon) Trotsky's leadership in 1918. The status and privilege of officers were marked in many different ways: better food, cleaner dugouts, segregated eating places and cinemas, separate brothels, and longer periods of leave. For the British the distance between the Western Front and 'Blighty' was not great – an officer on leave could breakfast in the trenches and dine in his London club – but the psychological distance was immense.

With all the hardship and inequalities of trench life, the terrible sacrifice demanded of millions of men across Europe and the obvious confusion over what each nation was fighting for, why did the soldiers continue to fight? Unlike the ideologically driven Second World War (the fight for liberal democracy and freedom on the part of the Allies; the fulfilment of national destiny on the part of the Axis powers) and the Cold War ('Communism' versus 'Freedom'), the First World War lacked any substantial ideological thrust apart from nationalism and the sense of sacrifice. By the end of the war the great majority of soldiers involved in the struggle of mass armies were not professional but armies of relatively poorly trained volunteers and conscripts, many of the latter even unused to wearing uniforms. Military discipline was not intolerably harsh, although desertion remained punishable by death and the label 'conscientious objection' carried with it considerable social stigmas.

Amongst the German and British troops, aside from a relatively minor incident at the British base camp at Étaples, soldiers remained remarkably loyal until the end. In Austria, however, there was confessed war weariness, and in the French lines there were widespread mutinies in 1917 after a series of disastrous and futile offensives. Between April and June 1917 there were 250 collective acts of indiscipline, involving almost two-thirds of the French army. The Belgian army suffered large-scale desertions in the same year, with over 5,000 men abandoning their posts in 1917. Italian troops, too, deserted in their droves in the autumn of that year. As in Russia, which in political turmoil experienced the most dramatic breakdown in military discipline, soldiers' protests centred on basic grievances – the quality of food, the cost of tobacco and the regularity of leave. Objections rested, therefore, on the poor administration of the war, not on the war itself. Perhaps, as was often suggested, the reality of life in the trenches helped to dull the senses and to suppress seemingly futile questions, while menial work – digging latrines, cleaning equipment, preparing rations – meant that there was little time for contemplation.

It would be wrong to suggest that soldiers were 'bludgeoned' into submission. Once the passion of patriotism had cooled, there still remained a sense of 'duty', *'devoir'*, *'pflicht'*, along with a gritty determination to see the conflict through, thereby making sense of the sacrifices that had already been made. There could also be outstanding courage in 'going over the top'. But it is a small wonder that, given the appalling conditions which soldiers on all sides endured, more men did not emerge from the war brutalized and alienated. Some were proud of their medals, some of their promotion to higher rank. However, some never reached positions of power again. There were other soldiers who were inspired to depict the 'pity of it all' and to recreate in prose after the war ended the appalling conditions soldiers had suffered. A later generation of writers argued that the road to the Holocaust began in the dehumanized slaughter of the First World War.

WAR AT SEA

Before the outbreak of the war, Britain's position as the pre-eminent world power and the attempts of Germany to achieve a similar *Weltmacht* status, had resulted in a spectacular naval rivalry between the two nations, and popular interest in naval rivalry did not end in 1914. The British public awaited a second Trafalgar when the upstart German Navy would be rapidly defeated by a Royal Navy superior in numbers and imbued with a fighting spirit honed by generations of naval supremacy. But public opinion was to be disappointed. Although the Royal Navy had superiority in numbers – in August 1914 it had 24 Dreadnoughts with 11 building while Germany had only 15 with 6 building – it failed to win a decisive victory against the German High Seas Fleet, and the war at sea settled into a similar pattern of attrition and stalemate as the war on mainland Europe.

At Jutland in the North Sea (31 May – 1 June 1916), the only significant sea battle in the war where firing was over a range of 16,000 yards – at Trafalgar it had been at 200 yards – the Royal Navy was not unequivocally victorious, for Britain lost more men and ships than the Germans. Set in a different perspective, however, Jutland was a victory for the Allies. Thereafter, the High Seas Fleet remained in harbour where its morale collapsed and its sailors eventually mutinied. The German Fleet was finally scuppered at Scapa Flow, Scotland in November 1918.

In the war of attrition at sea, which entailed blockading supplies to the Central powers and providing convoy support for Allied merchant shipping, the Royal Navy was undoubtedly successful, but Germany was innovative and bold in its employment of submarines or U (*Untersee*) -boats – a form of operations largely unforeseen by the British – until Admiral Jellicoe's opposition to the convoy system was finally overcome in 1917. Although Germany had only 39 submarines during the first months of the war, their operational importance, and the fact that they were cheaper to build than surface craft, meant they soon came to dominate naval strategy. Britain's change to a convoy system came just in time, for between 1914 and 1916 over one million tonnes of shipping had been lost, and with the final onslaught of unrestricted German submarine warfare in 1917 Britain's situation became critical. One in four ships coming to Britain was being sunk and only nine weeks' of grain supplies were left in the country. Even after the war Western Europe's fishing industry continued to suffer the effects of the U-boat campaign: in some waters it became impossible to trawl for fish because of the large number of wrecks on the ocean floor.

WHY CONTINUE TO FIGHT?

Given the apparent deadlock in military operations until 1917 and the terrible sacrifice of life and resources, it was perhaps surprising that governments in Europe did not make a more concerted effort for a negotiated settlement to bring an end to the war, as American statesmen, like Colonel E. M. House, wished. The first step to any negotiated peace, or even to initiate 'talks about talks' would have been for each belligerent to clearly identify what it was fighting for – its war aims, *buts de guerre*, *Kriegsziele*. But these aims were inherently difficult to define and, as the war continued, their range was widened. This can clearly be seen in the evolution of German war aims from 1914–16, a period when the Central powers generally held the initiative in the land war. In 1914 German war aims had been formulated on the basis of establishing the security of the German Reich. This was a difficult enough concept to specify, but by 1915, with German territorial expansion into Eastern Europe (especially Poland), there was talk of a Central European Customs Union or *Mitteleuropa*.

The more territory Germany and Austria-Hungary occupied, the grander their war aims – and they were not the same – became. By 1915 in Germany, as elsewhere, there developed an imposing, unofficial movement strongly opposed to a compromise peace and firmly in favour of sweeping annexations. This lobby included German princes, and Conservative, Free Conservative and National Liberal politicians. In the same year a 'Petition of the Intellectuals' calling for 'the most ruthless humiliation of England' (*sic*) was signed by, among others, 352 university professors. A competing, anti-annexationist petition boasted only 141 names. Thereafter, there was little hope of the Entente powers or of the United States facilitating a negotiated peace.

The most interesting secret attempt was that made through dynastic diplomacy by the last Habsburg Emperor Karl, who came to the throne in

1916, to seek a general compromise peace in the spring of 1917. The move came to nothing, however, and damage was done to the Habsburgs when in 1918 – and much had changed by then – George Clemenceau, a radical who had become Prime Minister of France in 1917, divulged details of the attempt.

The war aims of the Entente powers, before and after Clemenceau and Lloyd-George, were no easier to define. Britain, France, Russia, Italy and Japan had been rivals in the past and were likely to be so in the future. Within the alliance, therefore, each ally hoped to profit from the war to stake out its own position. There were also differences within countries as well as between them. There were people in Britain who shared the American President Woodrow Wilson's approach to a peace that would be liberal in 'tone' and national in its approach to communities and boundaries. For instance, Lord Lansdowne, a former conservative Foreign Secretary and Minister without Portfolio in Britain's coalition government, called for a 'realistic balance sheet approach to war aims' in which war aims would be balanced against the tremendous human cost of the war, but he quickly was denounced by cabinet colleagues who asserted that 'only cranks, cowards and philosophers' would consider peace before the enemy had been crushed. In Russia, too, the Tsarina was well-known to be entirely opposed to a compromise peace.

The same view also predominated in the French cabinets of René Viviani (1914–1915) and Aristide Briand (1915–1917), although political tensions in France erupted in 1917 when Socialists in the short-lived cabinet of Alexandre Ribot demanded that the French government negotiate with fellow Socialists across Europe for peace. It was a demand strongly and successfully denounced by the French Right. It was only in 1917, with Lloyd George and Clemenceau now in power, that Britain and France were finally able to spell out their broader war aims before embarking on a further reassessment when Russia collapsed in revolution and the United States, where there had been ample discussion of war aims, entered the war. Wilson's Fourteen Points were first unveiled to the US Congress on 8 January 1918.

As the bloody fighting continued, it also became clear that European war aims were moving further apart. Indeed, like the alliances which increasingly had divided Europe irrevocably before the war, war aims could become barriers to peace and not the means by which peace could be negotiated. Equally destructive to hopes of bringing the war to an end was the inclination of governments to behave like addicted gamblers with an 'in for a penny in for a pound' mentality. Once the war was under way, they became entangled in a web of 'incremental commitment': they had to decide whether to launch the next offensive in the hope that this would create a decisive breakthrough and secure victory, or whether to cut their losses and negotiate peace. War served to deaden governmental sensibilities, and it was easier to sacrifice the *next* 50,000 lives after the first had been lost. It was only when the carnage ceased and wartime passions cooled that the benefits of victory appeared out of all proportion to the cost of war.

THE CHURCHES AND WAR

In August 1917 the Vatican also attempted in vain to bring an end to the war with the publication of a peace note from Pope Benedict XV. Aside from the obvious humanitarian concern behind this gesture, the Roman Catholic Church wanted to terminate a war which had set Catholic against Catholic and undermined the Vatican's authority over its congregations. In Italy, in particular, the Catholic church became an indispensable prop to a weak state fighting an unpopular war.

Organized religion across Europe had been seriously damaged – 'crippled' was the appropriate word used generations later – by the unprecedented enthusiasm with which many ministers greeted the war, often urging their parishioners to further slaughter. As Pastor Phillips, a German Lutheran clergyman exhorted, 'Put more steel into your blood! German women and the mothers of fallen heroes must also not tolerate a sentimental attitude towards the war'. At a more practical level war broke the continuity of local service by laymen in church and chapel. Some laymen never returned to what before the war had been regular commitments.

In the short run, death and suffering in family circumstances might encourage spiritual concern, but it undermined the church's spiritual influence. The association of organized religion with other traditional forms of authority – the military, the imperial monarchy – was significantly undermined in a conflict which to poets and artists everywhere appeared to banish God's benevolence from Europe. For the English painter, Paul Nash, 'no glimmer of God's hand is seen anywhere'.

The churches of Europe had already been under threat before 1914, both from intellectual and social changes – the increasing urbanization of society; the movement of population; the growing tolerance within Europe of non-Christian ideas; new approaches to both sciences and the scriptures. Now there were new challenges, particularly to local parish priests. Some of them responded by serving at the battlefront, with open air mass becoming a regular feature of army life. Others took the lead in organizing relief work – exchanges of sick or wounded prisoners, the repatriation of displaced civilians – and in local initiatives on the home front. In Italy, for instance, Catholic Action founded rural banks, Catholic newspapers and promoted peasant co-operatives. Some of the war's many casualties flocked to Portugal in the hope of solace and recovery after a vision of Fatima in 1917.

Two further challenges to the Church – Communism and extreme nationalism – were also significantly strengthened in the course of the First World War. Communists who were to seize power in Russia in 1917 had long seen religion as the 'opiate' of the masses, the means by which the poor and destitute remained passive under the oppression of society's middle and upper classes. Now they saw it as an obstacle to the success of their cause. Extreme nationalists totally rejected Christian teaching that all men and women are equally children of God and asserted that some peoples were clearly superior.

Each of these creeds were to pose organized religion with important challenges in the decades which followed the war, creating new justifications for the persecution of Christians.

THE UNITED STATES ENTERS THE WAR

The entry of the United States on the side of the Allies won their war. In 1914 the American people, who included large numbers of first generation immigrants, had treated the war in Europe as an outbreak of madness, and even as late as 1916 North American involvement on the side of the Entente powers was far from a foregone conclusion. Some American statesmen, like Secretary of State William Jennings Bryan, believed that the United States had a distinct world role, based on its unique history, which entailed that it should remain aloof from European conflict in order to pursue an impartial, mediating role between the warring parties.

Yet between 1914 and 1917 there was a gradual build-up of American support for the Entente, generated, in part, by the cultural sympathy between the United States, Britain and France. They were all democracies, and they had many interests in common. France was an old ally, Britons spoke the same language. Before the war, Britain and France had been important trading partners for the United States, and after 1915, they became important debtors. There were barriers, however, to going beyond sympathy. The Royal Navy had violated American 'freedom of the seas', as it had during the wars against Napoleon; both Britain and France had empires; British policy in Ireland, especially in the aftermath of the Easter Rising (Dublin, 1916), alienated the American Irish; and leaving Britain and France on one side, Russia was an autocracy. Moreover, there was a strong German element in American life. One-fifth of 'American stock' derived from Germany and Austria-Hungary. It was German conduct of the war, particularly German submarine activity – the sinking of the 'Lusitania' (4 May 1915) with 124 American deaths and the 'Sussex' (24 March 1916) – that turned public opinion against Germany.

Mexico also figured in preparing opinion for war. In January 1917 the newly appointed German Foreign Minister, Arthur Zimmermann, authorized Germany's diplomatic representative in Mexico to propose a Mexican alliance with Germany should the United States declare war on the Central Powers, offering such incentives as the return of Mexican territory lost to Texas in 1848. British naval intelligence intercepted Zimmermann's telegram. What the telegram said threatened what had become the traditional commitment of the United States to withstand European intervention in the affairs of the American continent. This German intervention in the American continent, followed by the Central powers' resumption of unrestricted submarine warfare on 1 February 1917, and the abdication of Nicholas II of Russia, certainly increased the likelihood of American involvement.

In the end, it was a desire to play an effective, if not pivotal, role in the formulation of the peace settlement which caused the Democrat President Wilson to abandon his pacifist principles in the spring of 1917 and to enter the war on the side of the Entente (6 April 1917). The war, he told the Senate, was a conflict between two incompatible systems of government.[1] This was an ideological message. For a large section of the American public the war became a holy crusade.

GOVERNMENTS AND PEOPLES

As well as irrevocably altering the lives of the veterans of the battlefields or the ocean ways, the war also had a profound effect upon those who remained behind. Some of the effects might seem trivial. Some were irreversible. In Belgium, Northern and Eastern France, not only were families divided, but property was destroyed or requisitioned by the occupying Germans. Belgium, occupied for over 50 months, was starved by a British blockade, and families struggled to find sufficient food to survive. The calorific shortfall of the average civilian was over 56 per cent, whereas in Britain it was 3.5 per cent. When the industrial town of Lille was finally liberated most homes were said to be without a mattress.

It remains hard to quantify how much social and political change was attributable to the war or how far the war merely accelerated trends which were apparent before 1914. Some change was unplanned. Other change followed from the marshalling of national resources on an unprecedented scale. Every man, woman and sometimes child, it was now felt, had to be put to good use. Politicians, in consequence, found themselves taking on new administrative and social responsibilities far beyond their peacetime activities: they organized manpower, industrial production and distribution, rationed food, made agreements with organized labour, attempted to control public access to information, distributed propaganda, borrowed money and in the process imposed taxes on society at unprecedentedly high levels.

The most immediate challenge to government in the winter of 1914 was to muster sufficient numbers of men to fill the ranks of rapidly expanding armies, and then to organize enough manpower (women, the redistribution of workers from non-essential to essential industries) to maintain vital wartime industrial production. Within a matter of months, a large pool of unemployed labour had been absorbed and governments across Europe were faced with acute labour shortages. European society was dramatically changed by this search for labour. Those in work became more prosperous, as did those who owned factories – the industrial dynasties of Thyssen, Krupp and Vickers, for example – while the fortunes of Europe's landed classes were under threat. Businessmen were also recruited into government both in Britain and Germany, although the transformation from politicians into managers of a sometimes effective war machine was never complete.

Nor did it happen overnight. In Britain, Lloyd-George was deeply involved in the process.

One such businessman who was successfully recruited to serve his government was the German Walther Rathenau, heir to one of the biggest concerns in Europe, the *Allgemeine Elektrizitäts Gesellschaft* (AEG), with ambitions as a writer, philosopher and social thinker. Appointed as head of the *Kreigsrohstoffabteilung* (war materials administration) to tackle Germany's desperate shortage of raw materials – by October 1914 Germany's food and fuel reserves were almost entirely exhausted – Rathenau created hundreds of 'war companies' to manage all the materials essential to the war effort. Tough measures for civilians followed and the German people began to suffer deprivations which did not affect Britain for another two years. By March 1915 Rathenau had returned to his business interests, although he played an important, if short-lived, role in the Weimar Republic founded after the war.

While Rathenau's wartime accomplishment was important, his writings, notably in *Von kommenden Dinge*, published in Berlin in 1918, also foreshadowed the development of European governments in the later twentieth century. Rathenau exhorted that the economic and social life of society ought to be ordered to 'equalise' property and income. To some observers, Rathenau's ideas were akin to revolutionary Communism, but others recognized the positive role that he assigned to industry in opening up access to education and culture. His system, which sought to moderate the manifest evils of capitalism, presaged aspects of state corporatism which emerged in Europe after 1945.

In democracies like France and Britain, party political rivalries often surfaced when the war went particularly badly or was judged to be going badly, while authoritarian governments, like Germany, Austria-Hungary and Russia, found themselves riven by constitutional and ethnic rivalries, as well as by party politics, even before it was sensed that defeat was at hand. In a three-step evolution during the course of the war governments often passed through a first 'honeymoon' period of 'business as usual' into a period when problems were encountered that the state had never envisaged in 1914, and from then into a third stage when, threatened by subversion or revolution, it was necessary to promise post-war 'reconstruction'.

In a 'war of attrition' which came to be a 'war of exhaustion' each government was forced to borrow money and to tax its subjects more than ever before. France borrowed heavily from Britain ($3,000 billion) and the United States ($4,000 billion), and Britain borrowed from the United States ($4,700 billion), while allies like Canada, New Zealand and Russia borrowed from Britain and France ($11,600 billion). Germany and Austria-Hungary relied less on international credit and had little choice but to extend the tax burden, particularly to war profits: in 1917 profit tax was fixed at 60 per cent. Moreover, all nations issued government bonds (by 1918 the German Imperial debt was 156.1 billion marks; it had been 5.4 billion marks in 1914) and printed money with insufficient reserves in order to pay for the war effort.

Financing the war had important implications for the long-term health of Europe's economy, but even during the war when price controls were widely introduced, most countries experienced considerable inflation causing serious hardship. In France the wholesale price index rose from 100 in 1913 to 340 in 1918; over the same period the German price index rose to 415, Britain's to 227 and Italy's to 409. In Russia prices rose by around 500 per cent as wages, though rising by some 100 per cent from 1914 to 1918, failed to keep pace. The origins of the hyperinflation that rocked much of Central and Eastern Europe after 1918 began in the war.

The magnitude of social upheaval varied across Europe, and on the whole the challenge was managed more effectively in Britain and France than in Germany, Austria-Hungary and Russia. On 8 August 1914, for example, the French government introduced a rent freeze and acted to help families deprived of their principal breadwinner by granting a family allowance of 1.25 francs a day. Everywhere the food situation became a critical index of the success or failure of the war effort. In Germany it was commonly said that 'When Old Bill's [the Kaiser's] lady wife queues for spuds, then the war will be over'. It was often women, young and old, who took the responsibility for feeding their families. In Britain the War Office even produced silent films designed to show families how to make supplies of food and soap go further. In Vienna, by contrast, where there was no attempt to develop a social policy, poor families had to forage from dumps and collect firewood from the Wienerwald where, by the end of the war, there was precious little 'picking wood' left on the ground of the forest.

Government intervention had its paradoxes. For example, at a time when millions of lives were lost in senseless battle, working classes in Britain and France found their standard of living enhanced and their health improved. This was largely because they were able to earn more. In Germany, Austria-Hungary and Russia, by contrast, food shortages amongst the urban population were a considerable problem throughout the war. Germany in its encircled and blockaded position introduced *ersatz* bread made of potatoes and later turnips in October 1914, and ration cards for bread, fats, milk and meat were compulsory by early 1915. Meanwhile, German agriculture went into a steady decline, with vital manpower carted off to the front, and the farmers who remained behind had their best horses requisitioned by the army, were forced to slaughter their pigs, and were allocated insufficient fodder for their surviving animals. When the 1916 harvest fell below official expectations by over a million tons, it was clear that Germany's arable land was also suffering the effects of extensive over-cultivation. Even requisitions from newly conquered territories (areas of Poland, Romania and the Ukraine, for example), and imports from Austria and neutrals such as Holland and Denmark could not make good this shortfall.

In Austria-Hungary food was also in short supply. Fighting in the eastern half of the empire, Czech and Croat nationalist resistance, and the decision by the Magyar owners of large estates in Hungary to keep large quantities of grain to feed their animals all worked substantially to reduce grain supplies. In Italy, too, which entered the war in May 1915, farmers' incomes decreased and levels of production declined: over two and a half million peasants and labourers had been taken into the army, leaving only older men, women and adolescents to till the fields. French farmers, by contrast, began to enjoy an increase in their profits, despite a fall in the overall levels of production, from the increased prices their goods could command, and some of them even took the opportunity to improve their equipment or animal stock.

In Europe's towns and cities the dislocation caused by the war was felt more directly. Food and accommodation rose considerably in price, but, as we have seen, working-class labour was in unprecedented demand, enhancing both working-class ability to consume and political power. This was reflected in the changing size, character and strength of bargaining power of many trade unions, some of which, however, like the Genoese and Viennese munitions workers' unions, were ill-equipped to cope. There was a serious shortage of union officials, as the unions found themselves flooded by new workers and they were no longer dominated by skilled artisans. In cities like renamed Petrograd, Milan, Turin and Berlin, radicalised workers in the munitions industries sometimes seized control of their factories, against explicit union directives, to make their grievances known. Through the 'Hindenburg Plan'(*Hilfdienstgesetz*), passed in 1916, German trade unions had already markedly increased their authority to hire and discipline German labour under the watchful eye of the German military.

For large sections of Europe's middle classes the impact of the war was disastrous. Families living on unearned incomes, members of the liberal professions, the dwindling numbers of craftsmen and even civil servants, were badly affected by the consequences of the war. When 'heads' of the family were called up for military service, they often left their families very badly provided for as their social status and pride often prevented them from claiming allowances which were now available. The perception that the working class were doing considerably better out of the war than the middle class was particularly strong in Germany.

Despite the equalizing power of death on the battlefield, the perceived gains made by Germany's working class encouraged the birth of the *Dolchstoss* ('stab in the back') theory. As early as 1915 in a highly prophetic essay, the German sociologist Max Weber, warned that while

the prolongation of the war is entirely the result . . . of a fear of peace . . . To a far greater extent still . . . people are afraid of the domestic political consequences of the disillusionment that will inevitably set in, given the foolish expectations that have now run riot.

These 'foolish expectations' were to haunt post-war German politics.

In France, too, there was potential for future trouble. Members of the middle classes frequently served far longer spells of duty than their working class counterparts and, with their higher standards of education, they were

often subalterns of the reserve with an increased chance of becoming casualties. For the middle-class family the loss of the father often made it very
difficult for some to regain their social status once the war was over.

For all men returning home from the front, wherever they had been
serving, readjusting to peace and family life magnified many of the subtle
changes society had undergone in their absence. When the 'storm of steel'
finally stilled, disabled men struggled to survive on meagre disability pensions,
and some of the marriage vows hastily made in the heat of war were abrogated in peace. Fathers who felt their authority within the family damaged by
their absence, often battled, sometimes brutally, to reassert it over their children and wives. One man described his father thus:

> Of course he was sick from the war. He had had malaria, he had bouts of fever for
> the rest of his life, you know, and shivering fits. Actually he was pitiful, a pathetic
> figure. But the worse he felt, the more he played master and we were all the more
> afraid of him.

With the end of the war, an unprecedented number of veterans returned
home with a dramatic impact upon the public's perception of war. Europeans
were no longer confident with the Idea of Progress which had dominated the
nineteenth century. Instead, Europe had been plunged into an 'abyss of blood
and darkness'.

WOMEN AT WAR

The First World War appeared to revolutionize the place of women in
European society. Women, who were often 'invisible' in the political and
economic history of Europe at peace, made tangible political, economic and
social advances during, and especially after, the war. Much of this progress
was more apparent than real. It is clear that for some middle and upper class
women the war offered an excellent opportunity to escape the stuffy vacuum
of knitting, good works and polite conversation in which they had been
swaddled for much of the nineteenth century. As the inspirational nurse
Florence Nightingale reflected earlier, (prosperous) women often suffered
from 'the accumulation of nervous energy which has had nothing to do all
day . . . [making] women feel every night as if they are going mad.' The
contribution of some 'gentlewomen' to the war effort was more effective
than others. The bravery of nurse Edith Cavell shot by the Germans for
aiding British as well as German war wounded stood in marked contrast to
the activities of Lady Fanny Byron who sent a consignment of soccerballs
(bearing the inscription: 'simple mirth kept high courage alive') to the Western
front, being convinced that this 'manly' sport was the main foundation of the
British character.

Nursing the dying and wounded was the most immediate contribution
made by women across Europe to the war. In Britain the Queen Alexandra's
Imperial Nursing Service, for example, grew from a force of 463 trained

nurses in August 1914 to a force of 7,710 trained and 5,407 partially or untrained volunteers at the end of the war. In the brutal conditions of the battlefield it was a profession which demanded considerable courage. Before the invention of antiseptic paste, the dressings on bad headwounds had to be changed several times a day, yet even the high-speed butchery of the operating theatres did not extinguish the compassion and care of these, often poorly trained, nurses for their patients.

The war served to enhance the standard of living and health of working-class women employed in industry. They discovered that they could secure employment and command wages at levels undreamed of before the war. But they were still paid less than most male workers and employers often went to great lengths to avoid replacing a skilled man with a woman worker (a strategy warmly endorsed by trade unions). Women were employed in munitions production (called munitionettes in Britain) – in France women provided a quarter of all personnel in war factories and in Germany the proportion was even higher. The German Krupp arms factories which had employed 2,000 to 3,000 women before the war employed 28,000 women by 1918. In Russia, it is estimated that by 1917 women made up almost 44 per cent of the workforce. Other women were drawn into transportation, becoming bus conductors or working in railway stations and into farming, and into a variety of jobs where they had never been employed before, but very few occupations were feminized as a result.

During and especially after the war, women continued to be employed predominantly in nursing, domestic service, secretarial work and school teaching. In 1921 there were only 17 female solicitors in England and Wales, 49 architects and 41 civil engineers; in post-war Germany large numbers of working women were concentrated in unskilled industrial, agricultural and domestic work which was demanding in effort and carried with it lower status and income than ever before. These characteristics of women's employment remained unchanged for the next 30 years. Women's wages remained lower than their male-counterparts, they were not encouraged to acquire new skills, and when men returned from battle, the women were expected to return home to the hearth. However they served, women were regarded, first and foremost, as supports for their men-folk. Men were expected to kill and women were not. Only in Russia did a few hundred women join the army to fight alongside the men as part of a Provisional Government initiative to shame Russian soldiers into a more effective performance. Most famous among this group was Maria Bocharaeva's Batallion of Death.

To the vast majority of women, governments portrayed their war effort in propaganda terms: they should say goodbye, bear dead heroes' babies and browbeat men into joining the forces. Public 'concern' was also voiced that women earning money would upset the traditional 'male-centred' lines of authority within the family – the father as breadwinner with mother acting to reinforce his authority – but while families were often split up, family life continued much as before as eldest sons, uncles, grandfathers, stepped in to replace the absent father. Daughters also became more important: their duties now included waiting in queues for hours on end for potatoes, margarine and horsemeat. Many women did not expect recognition for their contribution to the war effort from their fellow men. Beneath a Kitchener poster in 'Red Clydeside' in Glasgow – YOUR KING AND COUNTRY NEEDS YOU – was scribbled:

> Your King and Country Need You,
> Ye hardy 'sons' of toil,
> But will your King and Country need you
> When they're sharing out the spoil?

The most obvious spoil which came to women in the aftermath of the war was the vote, but even here it is difficult to decide whether the women's war effort had contributed to this decision (taken by male politicians). In Britain and Germany, for example, the decisive battle had already been won before the war. By 1914 specious arguments that women were illogical; lacked talent, even common sense, and were unstable in opinion and allegiance largely had been refuted. By 1912 H. H. Asquith, then Britain's Liberal Prime Minister, although opposed to giving women the vote, had prepared his line of retreat into democratized women suffrage. In pre-war Germany women had become increasingly organized – the *Allgemeiner Deutscher Frauenverein* had over 12,000 members – and they were already an indispensable factor in industrial production (between 1882 and 1907 the female proportion of the manual labour force increased from 13.3 to 18.2 per cent, while in Britain women made up around 30 per cent of the manual labour force). In 1908 German women were granted the right to participate in political meetings and associations, and by 1913 the German writer, Gertrud Bäumer was confident that 'the state has come nearer to women, has become more alive and responsible to them'. In Norway, women's suffrage had been introduced with no reference to military matters.

It is clear, however, that the contribution of women to the war effort helped to reinforce changes in attitudes to female suffrage and the diminution of party divisions on the issue. This is most evident in France, where the academic lawyer and conservative politician, Joseph Barthélemy, was in no doubt by 1918 that the war had 'accomplished rapid and extraordinary progress for the cause of sex equality'. When the bill on women's suffrage came before the French Chamber of Deputies in January 1918, deputies both on the Left and Right of the political spectrum spoke in favour of enfranchising women on the same terms as men. Yet the bill was thrown out in 1922, when radical and socialist politicians got cold feet, fearing that women's votes would lead to clerical rule and the subversion of republican institutions, and it was not until 1945, after a second war, that French women were finally granted the vote.

Women certainly appeared more emancipated during the war, most obviously in the way they dressed. Many women wore trousers or uniform – they delighted in the their new found freedom of movement and pockets – but they were by no means emancipated from their central responsibility for raising the family. In France, for example, continuing concern over the declining birthrate led to propaganda efforts to encourage couples to have children and by December 1915 even feminist newspapers, like *Le Féminisme Intégral*, reversed its stance on such matters for fear of being branded unpatriotic and now urged its readers to provide 'children, lots of children to fill the gaps'.

Historians have not been able to agree whether the war altered how women understood themselves and perceived their position in society. 'Emancipation' was limited. As the social historian Susan Pedersen has demonstrated, the state's determination to 'relieve the minds' of its fighting men by providing separation allowance reinforced a notion of the man as 'head of the household' while the wife and children became 'dependants' for whom the husband – or in his absence the state – had to provide. In Britain, the development prompted the Leicester branch of the Women's Labour League to protest: 'for the hard-working wife to be called a "dependant" is offensive and even insulting'. And especially in Germany, Russia and France the advancement of such welfare provisions, coupled with the continued cultural emphasis on the family and the need for women to have children, left many women without an obvious role in society. The war had killed or maimed a large number of their husbands would-be husbands, and the sight of women partnering women at tea-dances in post-war Europe was a poignant reminder of this lost generation.

POLITICAL CHANGE

Some features of social, organizational and political change during the war were common to all countries. Others, however, were specific. There were obvious differences, for instance, between France and Britain. At the outbreak of war the French President, Poincaré, spoke in Paris of a *union sacrée* (sacred union) which bound the nation, needlessly provoked by German aggression, together in a common cause. This unity, which embraced statesmen across a broad political spectrum and most of French society, was also evident in Germany, Austria-Hungary and Russia. In Britain, however, there was less unity amongst British politicians than elsewhere in 1914, doubtless, in part, because the war did not automatically challenge British national security. Within the Liberal government, the Foreign Secretary Lord Grey, urged caution, fearing that 'we shall suffer more . . . than if we stand aside'. But the violation of Belgian neutrality and, more important, fear of a German-dominated Europe, created a pro-war majority. Anti-war minorities consisted largely of socialists who, unlike many socialists in both France and Germany, were not prepared to support war credits.

The long-term impact of the war on British politics was great. The Liberal Party which had held office since 1906, never regained power after the war. Divided over conscription and over the qualities required for wartime liberal leadership, it acquired a new leader in 1916, Lloyd George, who under political pressure and with press support, replaced Asquith as prime minister of a coalition government which now included Conservative and Labour members. Lloyd-George hastily established a small cabinet and set up new departments of shipping, food production, national service and labour. All this was designed to encourage 'efficiency'. Nonetheless, so long as military success continued to elude the Entente powers, the domestic situation was never stable, and in 1917 workers' unrest, already evident in 1916, broke out once more amongst engineering workers in Coventry, Sheffield and Liverpool. All in all, discontent on the home front was ominous but not serious, and in a 'Coupon election' Lloyd George's governing coalition won a massive victory.

Political life in France remained relatively stable until 1917 under the government of the *union sacrée*. By 1915 French life was restored to some semblance of normality, and Parisians, who had fled from their city in fear of the advancing Germans, returned. Theatres reopened, undaunted by Zeppelin raids, one of the new hazards of war. It was only when the war reached a critical phase in 1917 with the failure of the Nivelle offensive at Chemin des Dames, followed by mutinies in the French army, massive industrial unrest at home and the collapse of Russia, that co-operation within the *union sacrée* became strained. In secret sessions of Parliament, the ruling cabinet was severely criticized from both the Left and Right. On the Left, many socialists were now arguing that the war should be brought to an end by peaceful negotiation, while the Right denounced the Interior Minister Louis Malvy as a German agent and pressed for a more energetic prosecution of the struggle.

In November 1917, the 76-year-old Georges Clemenceau, nicknamed 'The Tiger', who had been an unremitting and sometimes unrealistic critic of French failure to score a decisive victory against the Germans, took office as Prime Minister. Given the new name *Père-la-Victoire* he immediately took a hard line against all his political opponents. Pacifists, declared guilty for seeking an end to the bloodshed, found themselves clapped in jail; while the socialists were bitterly denounced, particularly after a massive wave of strikes swept France in the spring of 1918. Clemenceau retained the loyalty of the army. Yet he was keen to limit the growing power of the military in French civilian life, and he set the tone of post-war politics in France.

In Germany, unlike France, the outcome of widespread industrial unrest in 1918 led to the collapse of the established political order, the abdication of Wilhelm II, and the creation of a democracy. Nonetheless, while the Socialists played an important role in the political history of the new Weimar Republic, they were never able to shake claims that the strikes they had launched at home had brought about their country's defeat. Germany's conservative leaders, like their military leaders, were able to assert, therefore, that Germany had been defeated by the Reds, rather than by the British and French. Industrial interests, too, increasingly came out on top before and after 1918, while national minorities also began to make substantial gains in return for agreeing to co-operate with the German war effort. As one Polish deputy boasted: 'the Foreign Office is as soft as prunes these days. It is willing to make concessions for us'.

It was not merely strikes which had contributed to a mood of defeat in Germany. The standard of living for ordinary Germans had deteriorated sharply – as it had in Italy – and young civilians were said to be dying from malnutrition before they had time to get to the front: it has been calculated that there were about 300,000 'excess deaths' among those aged between 15 and 19 from 1916 until the end of the war. Clearly, while imperial military forces were holding their own on the Eastern and Western fronts, imperial bureaucracy was losing the war at home. In 1917, after the failure of the so-called Hindenburg Programme designed to limit shortages of food and labour, grievances burst out into the open. The Kaiser had already begun to negotiate with leaders of Germany's burgeoning trade union movement when widespread strikes and food riots erupted in major cities. In a momentous 'Easter Message' of April 1917, he opened the way for greater post-war democracy, but the Russian Revolution and the International Socialists' Conference held in Stockholm in June 1917 – the short-lived attempt of Europe's Socialist International to forge a path to peace – precipitated further German unrest. While floundering cabinet ministers were sacked and replaced, society disintegrated into chaos. The administrative structures of Germany had proved incapable of coping with the demands of total warfare, and by 1918 no scheme – economic, political, or military – was effective enough to save the German Empire from defeat and dissolution.

During the first two years of war the Austro-Hungarian Emperor had succeeded in bringing together the Empire's different political parties, churches and people, but in 1916 there was a striking change in public sentiment. Following the lead of the Social Democrats, other opposition groups began to express doubts about the military leadership, and in July of that year a new Independence Party came into existence, led by Count Mihály Károly, the future President of the Hungarian Republic, which demanded internal political reforms and a peace without annexations.

Ironically, German propaganda did little to help its Central Power ally when it portrayed the war as a 'decisive struggle between Germandom and Slavdom'. This poisoned the Slav population relationships with the military authorities. There was opposition in Hungary also where industrial strife reached new heights in 1917, and in January 1918, a munition workers' strike in Vienna spilled over into Hungary, encouraging greater unrest, and infecting other national minorities. In the wake of defeat in 1918, all that remained for Emperor Karl's government was to dissolve the *Ausgleich* of 1867 and proclaim Austria and Hungary as two separate states on 11–12 November 1918.

RUSSIA IN REVOLUTION

In February 1917, the Russian Empire was the first imperial casualty of the war. After repeated military defeats and internal chaos, Nicholas II was forced to abdicate and for the next nine months, the ensuing leadership vacuum was filled by the dual regime of a Provisional Government created from the former Duma, first under Prince L'vov and then under Alexander Kerensky (from July 1917), and the Petrograd Soviet, a self-styled workers' council dominated by socialists. By October 1917 the Provisional Government, too, had failed to provide the Russian people with a military victory or with relief from massive food shortages, industrial disruption and calls for a redistribution of Russian land, and Russia succumbed to a Bolshevik revolution, followed by civil war.

The war alone was not responsible for the ruin of the Russian Empire. In July 1914, on the eve of war, following a strike at the Putilov armaments works, industrial unrest had swept the Russian capital and within days over 110,000 Petrograd workers were on strike. The visiting French President, Poincaré, had been greeted with the sight of Cossacks and police struggling to control demonstrators who were waving red flags, singing revolutionary songs, and intent on smashing their way to the centre of the capital. It took the suffering, deprivations and defeats of the war, however, to fuse the discontents of the Russian peasants, workers and middle classes, and it was because Nicholas lost the support of his armed forces that the Romanov dynasty perished. He had mustered an army of one million, ill-equipped men in 1914, but there were huge losses: between 7.2 – 8.5 million Russians were killed, missing or wounded.

As Mikhail Rodzianko, Chairman of the last Duma an elected, but power-less chamber, wrote of the February 1917 street protests:

> Unexpectedly for all, there erupted a soldier mutiny such as I have never seen. These, of course were not soldiers but *muzhiki* (peasants) taken directly from the plough. . . . In the crowd, all one could hear was 'Land and Freedom', 'Down with the Dynasty', 'Down with the Romanovs'.

When Nicholas abdicated in February 1917, in the same month his German born wife disappeared from the scene with him. She had been left in charge of the home front, with the disreputable monk and mystic, Grigorii Rasputin at her side, while Nicholas led his troops in battle. But Tsarina Alexandra Fedorovna was unable to appease mounting popular discontent with the Imperial government. In the month before the Tsar's abdication there were over 1,330 industrial strikes involving around 680,000 workers.

Writing in April 1917, Weber described what happened in Russia as the 'elimination' of an incapable monarch, not a revolution, and certainly for some members of the Provisional Government, the events of February merely marked a political transformation that did not challenge the existing social or economic order. The Kadet (liberal party) leader, Paul Milyukov, typified this view with his fervent belief that the Tsar had lost the throne through his inept conduct of the war. But such a view was not confined to the Russian liberals. Left-wing parties believed it too. The largest grouping was the Socialist Revolutionaries (SRs), while the Communists, divided by ideology, in 1903 formed two distinct groups: the majority or, in Russian, *Bolsheviki* Party and the minority or *Mensheviki* Party, although the Bolsheviks soon lost their numerical superiority.

In March 1917 the SRs, the Mensheviks and even some Bolsheviks, like the future leader of the party Jusip Stalin, at first supported the Provisional Government in its efforts to continue the Russian war effort. The SR's awaited a promised general election, while the Mensheviks co-operated with the Provisional Government because they were orthodox Marxists who postulated that Russia had to develop a larger working class before the time was ripe for a Marxist revolution. The Bolsheviks were different however. They had split from the orthodox Communist Party because they believed Russia could leap-frog the requirement of a large working-class base needed to effect a Communist revolution thanks to a dedicated but small vanguard of workers and, what the Bolsheviks claimed was the 'revolutionary nature' of the Russian peasantry.

Marx had argued that a Communist revolution in which an exploited, industrial working class would unite and revolt against its capitalist employers, thereby abolishing private property and in time create a 'classless society', was most likely to take place in countries that had a large working class, like Germany, Britain, Belgium and Holland. Indeed, for many Marxists the peasantry were a reactionary force. Hence the determination of the Russian Mensheviks to await the emergence of a Russian industrial proletariat with a revolutionary consciousness. But Lenin, leader of the Russian Bolshevik Party, was eager for power, although as always cloaking his political ambition in Marxist theory, determined that the new Bolshevik formula should be 'a revolutionary dictatorship of the proletariat and the poorest peasant'. He cleverly exploited the frustrations of the Russian peasantry, as well as those of the working class, in his quest for political control.

After Lenin's return from exile in April 1917, however, the Bolsheviks, revitalized and reorganized, now began openly to sing a different revolutionary tune to that of other political parties. Since his elder brother's execution for the attempted assassination of Alexander III in 1887 at the age of 19, Lenin had called himself a 'professional revolutionary'. For 30 years this St Petersburg trained lawyer and his similarly intellectual comrade leaders – men who later helped create the Soviet Union, like Nikolai Bukharin, Grigori Zinoviev, Karl Radek – had withstood imprisonment and exile in Siberia, London and Switzerland. Under Lenin's leadership the Bolsheviks developed a distinct programme of their own, promising 'Peace, Bread and Land' to Russia's workers and peasants. Driven by the profound conviction that 'history will not forgive us (the Bolsheviks) if we do not assume power', Lenin questioned whether Russia should continue to fight in the war. But it was not all plain sailing for the party. Despite the continued slaughter of Russian troops on the battlefield and the failure of the much publicized June offensive against the Germans, the Bolsheviks themselves were discredited when starving workers took once more to the streets of Petrograd in riots that became known as the 'July Days'. The Bolsheviks claimed these demonstrations were peaceful and spontaneous, but Soviet archives have revealed that the demonstrators' actions were orchestrated by the Bolsheviks planning a *coup d'état*. At the last minute Lenin lost his nerve and though Petrograd was there for the taking, the Provisional Government temporarily regained the initiative. As a result, Bolshevik fortunes plummeted as party members fled into hiding or were arrested by forces loyal to the Provisional Government.

There was an economic crisis too. Growing anarchy in the countryside had profound implications for life in Russia's towns and cities, and by July 1917 food supplies to the capital had become erratic – Voronezh some 300 miles east of Moscow, for example, only produced 30 per cent of the grain it had produced in 1916 – and prices were spiralling upwards. Starving workers now fled the towns for the countryside and as a consequence, industry continued to collapse.

Reflecting on his short-lived career as the fourth Russian Premier since the abdication of Nicholas, the Socialist Revolutionary Alexandr Kerensky, claimed that he had been undone by two plots of a very different kind. The first had been hatched by Lenin and by Ludendorff, the latter providing the sealed train used to transport Lenin from exile to ferment unrest at home, unrest on a scale undreamed of by the Germans. The second plot took place in August 1917 when Russia's Commander-in-Chief, Lavr Kornilov, marched on Petrograd in a counter-revolutionary attempt to impose martial law. Kornilov's rash act had dramatic consequences: Kerensky's authority collapsed, Russia's traditional conservative elites – judges, civil servants, priests and military officers – were discredited, the army was in disarray and the Bolsheviks were able to come out of hiding and pose as defenders of the February Revolution. Florence Farmborough, a field nurse from Britain, noted how uncertainty fostered despair amongst the soldiers: 'if only they had someone in whom they could put their trust . . . Whom were they to believe?'

The Bolsheviks certainly made a big effort to capture the trust of the Russian soldiers issuing their own army newspapers, *Soldiers' Pravda* and *Trench Pravda*, which urged disgruntled troopers to fraternize with the enemy along the Russian front. Authority and discipline began to collapse as servicemen formed their own soldiers' committees (soviets) and desertions from the front rose to unprecedented proportions. By then, the Petrograd Soviet, which in its Order Number One acquired control over Russian weapons and created soviets in all regiments, battalions, batteries and squadrons, was dominated by Bolsheviks and it was reinforced by its own Red Guard which numbered between 70,000 to 100,000. The Provisional Government was slow in calling a general election, and a Constituent Assembly, with a majority of SRs and Mensheviks met for the first – and it proved to be the last time – in November 1917. On the night of October 24–25 a Bolshevik coup in the Marrinsky Palace secured the support of a wider audience. Far from being a bloody, jacobin revolution, the Bolshevik revolution was a quiet affair. A deputy of the now defunct Provisional Government recorded his bewilderment when told an armed insurrection was under way: 'I laughed since the streets were absolutely quiet and there was no sign of any uprising.'

Once in control of the Russian capital, Lenin and his party needed to secure the support of the peasantry, numbering more than 100 million and by far the majority of the population, in order to provide a popular mass base to help them retain power. Embittered by years of redemption payments (payments to the government for land granted during their emancipation in 1861), they were also frustrated by a pattern of landholding which determined that the gentry still owned 47 per cent of the land. When the honeymoon of the February revolution passed, peasants began to demand action on the distribution of land and food, and only the Bolsheviks appeared to promise immediate answers. They alone promised to end privilege and to dismantle the existing social order. As one peasant–worker demanded in May 1917: 'All people, whether rich or poor, should be provided for; every person should receive his fair and equal ration from a committee so there is enough for everyone. . . . Everything should be declared public property.'[2] Peasant Soviets were created on an *ad hoc* basis across the former Russian empire and peasants began to seize land for themselves.

Having taken Petrograd in October 1917, Lenin declared a republic based on soviets, urban and rural, and set about arranging a peace with the Central Powers. In the belated elections for the Constituent Assembly, however, the Bolsheviks polled less than one quarter of the vote. Despite this election result the Bolsheviks kept a determined hold on power, and, in January 1918, though defeated in elections by the SRs and the Mensheviks, they dissolved the Constituent Assembly.

PEACE AND CIVIL WAR

After tense negotiations the Treaty of Brest-Litovsk, a separate peace, was signed on 3 March 1918, even though some Bolsheviks, like Bukharin and his 'Holy Group', had wanted to extend Russia's war effort into a marxist revolutionary war across Europe, The terms of Brest-Litovsk were harsh and made it all the more difficult for Lenin to peddle the treaty to comrades reluctant to lay down arms: Russia lost 27 per cent of its cultivated land (particularly damaging was the agreement that surplus food supplies from the fertile Ukraine be given to the central powers), 26 per cent of its population (some 55 million people), and 75 per cent of its iron and coal. Nonetheless, with peace to the West, Lenin could now concentrate on securing the Bolshevik revolution at home.

By July 1918, three months before the end of the war in the West, the Bolsheviks faced serious opposition from disgruntled SRs and Mensheviks unable to translate their electoral votes into political power, from traditional conservative and liberal elites and from the Allied troops now landing at Archangel and Siberia. British, French, American and Japanese troops became embroiled in what became a Russian civil war, albeit in limited numbers and to limited effect. There were a number of reasons why. For Britain, France and the United States, Ludendorff's punishing offensives in the West and the signs of an alliance of sorts between the Bolsheviks and the Germans threatened to halt their progress towards victory, especially as Germany's penetration of Russia undermined the Allied blockade. There was hostility towards a Bolshevik victory, especially in the United States, France and Japan – the latter also determined to use its intervention to establish a permanent base in Siberia.

In Russia severe food shortages continued throughout that year, and on 30 August there was an attempt on Lenin's life. The first months of the Bolshevik government, far from putting out the flames of social unrest, fanned an even greater conflagration. The economic policy of 'state capitalism' gave way to 'war Communism', based on grain seizures and complete nationalization, as the Bolshevik party embarked on a civil war which outstripped fighting on the Eastern Front in its savagery and brutality.

THE 'CREATION' OF POLAND

By returning Lenin to Russia, Germany had played an important role in the creation of the new Union of Soviet Republics. Likewise, when Germany transported Józef Pilsudski, the 'Prophet of Polish Independence' to Warsaw in November 1918, the collapsing Kaiserreich was also instrumental in forging the character of the new Polish Republic. When Europe was engulfed by war in 1914, Poland did not exist in any practical sense. Some 20 to 30 million people called themselves Poles, but they were imperial subjects of Germany, Austria-Hungary and Russia. The great Polish cities were similarly dispersed: Warsaw lay in Russia, Danzig (Gdańsk) in Prussia and Kraków in the Austro-Hungarian empire. It was because the belligerent powers needed to win and to retain Polish support for their war efforts that they revived the issue of an independent Poland. What role it would play was as contentious and unresolved as it had been in the nineteenth century.

As early as August 1914 the opening gambit to the Polish people had been offered by the Russians. The Poles were promised 'a reborn Poland . . . free in her own faith, language and self-rule' under the sceptre of the Tsar. From then until November 1918 various bids were made by Austria-Hungary, Germany (their bids were not the same) and, most notably, by Wilson in the thirteenth of his 14 points (January 1918) which called for a 'united, independent and autonomous Poland'. Meanwhile, the bitter and bloody fighting on Polish lands helped create both a sense of solidarity and political structures which Polish nationalists were able to exploit.

Poles, who had numbered 30.9 million in 1914 fought in the armies of Russia, Germany and Austria-Hungary, often against each other, and sustained over a million military casualties and a population decrease of 4.5 million people. But now Polish military and political organizations burgeoned on all sides, including the Polish National Committee under Roman Dmowski, based first in Lausanne and then in Paris, calling for Polish autonomy under Russia; the Polish Information Committee based in London; and the Polish Relief Committee with strong links to Polish-American groups in the United States of America. These groups, led by Dmowski, were the 'passivists' who hoped to achieve an independent Poland through diplomacy and co-operation with the Allied Powers. They stood in marked contrast to the 'activist' grouping led by General Pilsudski – he worked to make his Polish troops indispensable to the Austro-Hungarian military – which sought an independent Poland through the Central powers.

From August 1915 until November 1918 it was the German military authorities who ruled Warsaw. There was also a rudimentary Polish administration created by the region's Governor-General, General von Besler. The return of Pilsudski to Poland by the Germans forestalled, therefore, the implementation of the victorious Allies' plans for the rebirth of Poland. On 14 November 1918 Pilsudski was declared Chief of State of a nation without a frontier, government or constitution. Many Poles believed they had fought in the war for an independent Poland, and although this was erroneous, the sacrifice and courage of Polish soldiers and their families were instrumental in the years which followed, not only in the series of local wars (1918–1921) which defined the boundaries of Poland far more than the Paris Peace Conference, but in the struggle to maintain an independent Poland in the face of future German and Russian territorial ambitions.

Important, too, was the notion of a distinct and respected Polish culture in the establishment of the Polish state in the twentieth century, exemplified by the work of Nobel laureate Stefan Żeromski. In the famous verse of Edward Słoński, written on the eve of war, the sacrifice of blood and the notion of an immutable, common identity amongst all Poles, found popular expression:

> Now I see the vision clearly,
> Caring not that we both will be dead;
> For that which has not perished
> Shall rise from the blood we shed.

WRITERS AND THE WAR

Słoński was not alone among writers in hailing war in 1914. At first, many of them, like many artists, welcomed the outbreak of war as a revolt against the selfishness and greed of the pre-war world. In England the young romantic poet Rupert Brooke, who was never engaged in military action, could write:

> Now, God be thanked Who has matched us with His hour,
> And caught our youth, and wakened us from sleeping.

In Germany Thomas Mann greeted the war as a 'purification and release . . . and a mighty hope'. Other writers and poets as diverse as England's Thomas Hardy, Italy's Gabriele D'Annunzio and France's Charles Maurras (later leader of the right-wing group Action Française), welcomed the war as an opportunity to reassert national or imperial identity and the chance for adventure and heroism. As the German author Ernst Jünger recorded in his war diary, 'having grown up in an age of security we were all of us filled with longing for the unusual, for great risk . . . the war would give us that mighty, powerful, awesome experience'. Even Freud had not been immune to the atmosphere which surrounded him in the summer of 1914: for the first time in 30 years, he felt himself to be Austrian – 'All my libido is given to Austria'.

But for Freud and writers like the German Rainer Marie Rilke, this early enthusiasm was soon extinguished by a moral repugnance for the reality of the war. It was a rejection which found echoes amongst writers on the Left in Britain and France – George Bernard Shaw and Romain Rolland – where war soon lost its appeal in the eyes of younger generations. For many writers involved in military action, heroics gave way to disillusionment, even despondency. Prominent among them was the English poet Wilfred Owen, born in 1893, whose 'Anthem for Dead Youth' was written in 1917. Its opening line 'What passing bells for those who died as cattle' was to be remembered as long as Brooke's 'Now, God be thanked'. In France Henri Barbusse published a widely-read and acclaimed novel *Le Feu* (Under Fire) in 1916 that denounced war.

Soldiers and sailors' war-time letters, subject to censorship, concealed much that was going on, not least the bravery as well as the horror of war, and for this reason alone lyric poetry, a form of expression encouraged by the character of existence in the trenches, had a very special intensity. Freedom of expression depended not only on the level of government censorship but on propaganda which entered every home. In Vienna the satirist Karl Kraus's publication, *Die Fackel*, sought to highlight the incongruities and, whenever possible, the horrors of war against the welter of official propaganda. In 1916, for example, Kraus reported of children's essay titles at the Kaiser Karl Realschule: class Vb were given the choice of 'A walk during the holidays' or 'The latest methods of warfare' and class VIa were offered the choice of 'The main characters in Goethe's *Egmont*' or 'The intensification of U-boat warfare'. As the war went on cartoons and poster art became prominent as governments strove to 'educate' the public, and the industry spawned some surprising propaganda objects including Foch ashtrays, Hindenburg doilies and Kitchener beer mugs.

The most searing prose was published in the form of memoirs and novels not during but after the war. Erich Marie Remarque's *Im Westen Nichts Neues*, (*All Quiet on the Western Front*), Robert Graves's *Goodbye to All That*, and Ernest Hemingway's *A Farewell to Arms* all appeared in 1929. They recalled both the horror and the camaraderie of war while ex-servicemen's institutions, like the British Legion, the 'Association of Italian Volunteers' and the *Vaterländische Kampfverbände* (union of German activists), indicated that ex-servicemen were more concerned with the conditions of resettlement into civilian life than they were with sharing any common experience of military service. Critical accounts of warfare triggered a hostile response from many of those who had lost loved ones or who felt their nation discredited by 'cowardly' views. In particular, Remarque's novel and the German and Hollywood-produced films based on the book provoked demonstrations by right-wing political groups in Germany, where the German government banned the 1930 American film on the grounds it was anti-German. By contrast, Jünger's novels *In Stahlgewittern* (Storm of Steel), with its celebration of primitive violence, found a ready audience in Germany.

Meanwhile, the experience of women writers during the war was as varied as that of the men. Some, like St Clair Stobart, saw war and militarism 'as maleness run riot', while for others, like the volunteer nurses who cared for the wounded on the front (such as the 18 year old Scots nurse Mairi Chrisholm and her English colleague Baroness T'Serclaes known as 'The Heroines of Pervyse'), the war was an opportunity for adventure. The fact that they had not shared precisely the same stressful experiences during the war was later reflected in their writings. Women had no experience of trench life and while they risked death in munitions factories or as auxiliaries behind the lines, they did not have to endure hours of endless bombardment or the sight of friends blown apart before their eyes. As one German carpenter wrote to his wife in 1914:

> You know more about the war theatre than we, except that everything is painted in bright colours for you. Would that some of those propagandists and superpatriots could be in a position now to see the corpses . . . piled high.

Such a letter home was rare. Few soldiers wanted to cause futile unease at home, and if they tried to tell the truth, it was excised by company officers who censored all outgoing mail.

For the unprecedented numbers of war veterans returning home the sense of isolation and brutalization precipitated by their wartime experiences was oppressive. As Remarque's returning war veteran reflects in *All Quiet on the Western Front*: 'A terrible feeling of foreignness suddenly rises up in me. I cannot find my way back.' For some veterans it was easier to continue fighting – in Communist insurrections in Eastern Europe, in patriotic societies in Germany and Italy – than it was to face the realities of peace in 1918.

Notes

1. A. M. Schlesinger, *The Rise of Modern America, 1865–1951* (1957), p.266.
2. Quoted in O. Figes, *A People's Tragedy. The Russian Revolution, 1891–1924* (1996), p.506.

Chapter 7

A NEW ORDER? 1919–1929

Before the war Europe had comprised some 20 independent states (excluding Monaco and Andorra) of widely differing size. Six of them, as we have seen, were so-called 'great' powers with populations of more than 30 million people. The remaining countries all fell below the ten million mark with the exception of Spain (with its population of around 20 million). This was Europe's sole middle-ranking power. Only two of the twenty were republics – France and Switzerland: the remainder were all monarchies. But after the First World War much had changed. By 1919 the number of European states had risen to 26, and while the disintegration of Austria-Hungary had reduced the number of great powers to five, the number of middle-ranking powers was swelled by three new countries – Poland, Czechoslovakia and Yugoslavia. More dramatic was the decline of monarchy in Europe. Now only two of the five great powers remained monarchies, and all six of the new states set up as a consequence of the war, alongside a reformed Russia, Germany, Hungary, Austria and Turkey (now with just a toehold in Europe), lined up as republics.

The visions of two men now played a central role in the reshaping of postwar Europe. For Wilson, as for Lenin, the end of the First World War in Europe marked the beginning of a new age. Wilson believed he had set out principles of national self-determination and democracy which he trusted would bring peace, prosperity and greater democracy to Europe as a whole. In Russia, Lenin and his party cohorts set about consolidating the Bolshevik party's slender control and postponing any co-ordinated attempt at international revolution. Communists were largely left to make their own futures, while Wilson's vision inspired hopes for the future – from Poland in the East to Ireland in the West. Nevertheless, although 1919 brought much that was new to Europe – new nations, a new and more open diplomatic order, a striking extension of democracy – many old social, economic and diplomatic structures survived to interact uneasily with the new. Self-determination was sometimes at odds with ethnic nationalism, and within three years democracy was banished from Italy. The political and social fabric in nations as diverse as Britain, Germany, Spain, Poland, and Hungary became increasingly strained.

THE 'PRICE' OF WAR

Managing the peace was the most immediate problem which faced a war-weary Europe in 1919. The situation was different from that after the Second World War, for in 1918 few plans for the rehabilitation of post-war Europe had been drafted by the Allies – or by the Central powers; and although the continent had not been subjected to the horrors of saturation bombing and sweeping military campaigns across its length and breadth, the damage wrought by the war was substantial and affected every aspect of European society. The number of deaths and casualties was unprecedented. Historians calculate losses of between 9.4 and 11 million people, a figure which amounted to over one per cent of Europe's population in 1913. Expressed nationally, Germany lost 2,037,000 men, Russia 1,811,000, France 1,398,000, Austria-Hungary 1,100,000 and Britain 723,000. Only American casualties were substantially less, with 114,000 killed in action.

Nonetheless, Europe's population was to recover. In the West it rose from 170.2 million in 1920 to 189.9 million in 1940, although there was only slight growth in France and Austria, and a static population level in Ireland. In the East and South the statistics were even more impressive. In the former it rose between 1920 and 1940 by 84.4 million to 102.4 million in 1940, and in the latter from 68.6 million to 84.9 million. The impetus for the rise came from the continued popularity of marriage at an early age and continued improvements in nutrition and health-care. (Celibacy, partly because of the decline of organized religion, lost ground in the twentieth century). The decennial growth rate of the European population during the 1920s was 10.9 per cent despite massive overseas emigration, restricted by American immigration controls, first imposed in the 1890s.

It proved more difficult for many European governments to recover from the financial cost of the war than from the loss of life. The physical damage wrought by the war was concentrated in Northern France, Belgium and Western Russia. In all, some 15,000 square km of France were laid waste, and damage to French municipal, private and industrial buildings amounted to $17,000 million, a high proportion out of a world loss of $29,960 million. Much of the remaining physical damage wrought by war was concentrated in Western Russia, Poland and Belgium. In Belgium no aspect of life was left untouched by war. Four years of occupation and warfare on Belgian soil had brought industry to its knees. Here the Germans had gone so far as to partially dismantle Belgian factories and transfer the equipment to Germany.

The financial cost of the war was equally high. All the European belligerents had lost loans and bonds invested overseas when war broke out, and large debts to the United States had accumulated during the course of the war, in particular, by Britain and France, to fund their victory in Europe. And they themselves, in turn, had lent some of their own resources to subsidiary allies, like Australia and Canada. Before the First World War Britain had been the world's banker, the primary source of overseas investment capital, and

British banking and monetary pre-eminence, accompanied by the promotion of free trade, had helped to foster stability and growth in the international economy. After the First World War the United States replaced Britain as the world's greatest creditor nation, with an important, though different role from nineteenth-century and early twentieth-century Britain, in supporting the world economy.

The financial supremacy of the American economy was confirmed by the success of American technology, and with it American methods of industrial organization which generated both attraction and resistance in Europe. The term 'americanization' became synonymous with 'scientific' management and production, involving simplification, standardization, and time-and-motion studies of workers on assembly lines. The name of the American entrepreneur Henry Ford, an initiator of these practices, was equally well known on both sides of the Atlantic and in the Soviet Union, where he was greatly admired, as well as in the West. So, too, were his automobiles. Dubbed 'Ford the Conqueror' by the British press, the American tycoon who lived from 1863 to 1947 – and who had opposed US entry into the First World War – had big plans for Europe's post-war production and consumption of cars, many of which remained unfulfilled because of Europe's slow recovery from the war.

In 1919 few statesmen or businessmen appreciated the scale or, indeed, the nature of the economic consequences of the war. There were dreams of a return to normality or 'normalcy' as US President Calvin Coolidge, Wilson's Republican successor in 1923, famously mispronounced it. Yet a short European economic boom, fostered by pent-up consumer demand and heavy government spending on the replacement of war-damaged resources like ships and railways between 1919 and 1921 sent out the wrong signals. Once the smoke of this spending spurt had cleared, the problems of the British economy, in particular, loomed large. Some old industries had already begun to decline before the war, and after 1921 their decline was to continue for much of the remainder of the twentieth century. For the shipyards of Glasgow and Belfast, and the cotton mills of Lancashire, the days of prosperity and expansion were over. Heavy industry elsewhere in Western Europe, too, began to feel the pinch of decline. It was the United States which enjoyed a spectacular boom during the mid-1920s, which optimistic Americans felt, might last for ever.

THE PARIS PEACE CONFERENCE
AND THE TREATY OF VERSAILLES

By then the government of the United States had passed from the Democrats to the Republicans and Wilson's 'new age' in Europe had faded. His Fourteen Points aspired to a 'healing' and flexible European peace settlement and the abandonment of the sterile system of bilateral alliances and secret treaties (Points two, four and fourteen). The language was lofty, but when the

American President crossed the Atlantic to chair the proceedings at the Paris Peace Conference the rapturous welcome he received from the European public belied the hard bargaining that was to take place between the victorious powers, especially amongst the 'Big Four' – British Prime Minister Lloyd George, French and Italian Premiers Clemenceau and Vittorio Orlando and, of course, Wilson himself. To many it seemed that Clemenceau, with 'the face and figure of a Chinese Mandarin (according to American Secretary of State, Robert Lansing), dominated the Paris proceedings.

The Peace Conference proved a miserable affair for all concerned. The unwieldy, haphazard structure of Conference deliberations did little to soothe the discomfort of the delegates, many of whom suffered from the 'Paris Cold', a world wide influenza epidemic which killed more people than the war.

For John Maynard Keynes, the British economist who was present at the Peace Conference, the terms of the peace treaty signed with Germany at Versailles was 'a Peace which, if . . . carried into effect must impair yet further . . . the delicate, complicated organization already shaken and broken by war'. In a devastating and highly influential critique, *The Economic Conse-quences of Peace* (1919), written after he had resigned from the British delega-tion, he argued that the 'honest and intelligible' French policy to irreparably weaken Germany, which had gone uncurbed at Versailles, posed a tremend-ous future danger for the 'perpetual prize-fight' (a completely unWilsonian image) of European politics.

Keynes had a point. The spectacle of the Peace Conference had underlined Germany's status as a defeated power. The German government was not consulted during the negotiations, and only when the final draft of the settlement was completed were the Germans allowed to see the Treaty. They were then given 15 days to put their complaints in writing to the Allies before minor emendations were scratched in red ink onto the completed treaty. The German delegates to the Conference, Hermann Müller and Johannes Bell, had been humbled, therefore, before they signed the Treaty before an audience of 2,000 in the Hall of Mirrors of Louis XIV's magnifi-cent Versailles palace where Bismarck had humbled the French in 1871. The date was 28 June 1919, the fifth anniversary of the Sarajevo assassinations. Defenders of the Treaty argued that the treatment of the German delegates was no different from that which Prussia had inflicted upon France in 1871 or which Germany itself had imposed on Russia in 1918.

Nevertheless, despite this humiliating treatment, according to Harold Nicolson, a member of the British delegation at Paris, who wrote a vivid account of what happened, the 'forlorn and deathly pale' demeanour of the German delegates did not imply that Germany had been resoundingly defeated in 1918. Rather, the German people had accepted Wilson's Fourteen Points as the basis for armistice negotiations and the new German democratic government, known to history as the Weimar Republic, watched proceed-ings in Paris with mounting dismay. It was clear to all Germans that their country had not been treated as an equal, and it was small wonder then that the Peace came to be thought of as a '*diktat*' or '*Schandvertrag*' (treaty of shame). Instead of bringing peace to Europe, it provided a source of social, political and economic discontent for years to come.

Anti-German sentiment ran high in Britain and France in 1919, although there were differences on the two sides of the Channel. In both countries, sections of public opinion, stirred by a chauvinistic press, wanted to extract their pound of flesh from the German people. As Clemenceau put it, 'Our trials have created a profound feeling in this country about the reparation which is due to us; and it is not only a matter of material repairs: the need for moral redress is no less great'. Clemenceau, Lloyd George and even Wilson eventually appeared to respond to calls to 'Hang the Kaiser', but were saved the embarrassment of a public trial of the former German Emperor when the Dutch, neutral during the war, refused to hand over their unwanted guest. There were no such fortunate solutions to other issues in Paris. Even when French and British national interests coincided, they did not always match those of the United States. Moreover, if and when the Allies reached an agreement in the *ad hoc* muddle of committee meetings, their findings rarely, if at all, matched German aspirations for a just and honourable peace.

Arguably the hardest development for the German people to accept in 1919 was defeat in a conflict which, until the summer of 1918, they had believed they were winning. The terms of the peace were hard. Germany lost over 27,000 square miles of territory, containing about seven million people – about one-tenth of its pre-war territories – and its brief flirtation with Empire was cut with the loss of overseas imperial territories in Tanganyika and South West Africa. Closer to home, German territorial losses greatly modified the map of Europe. They included the return of Alsace-Lorraine to France and the creation of a strip of Western Prussia to provide a 'Polish corridor' to grant the new independent nation of Poland access to the sea. The former German Hansa trading city of Danzig at the end of the corridor was given the status of Free City, since Lloyd George balked at the notion of granting outright to the Poles German territory, especially a prosperous, cultured city with 90 per cent of its people German. To have handed it over to the 'primitive' Poles he felt, would have been like putting a 'watch in the paws of a monkey'.

These and some other new territorial arrangements, bitterly resented by Germans, appeared to them a gross violation of Wilson's Fourteen Points and of Allied promises that a democratic Germany would be treated fairly. The German peoples of Austria were not allowed to unite with Germany, and over three and a half million Sudeten Germans became part of the new Czechoslovakia. The French government would have gone further. It demanded an independent German Rhineland, for example, and it was only through Lloyd George's last minute pleading that plebiscites were held in the East Prussian districts of Allenstein and Marienwerder. As a result these territories were allowed to remain in Germany.

Allied demands for a reduction in German arms, though greeted with resentment by conservative elements in German society, met with little dissent

amongst the German population as a whole. The Rhineland was demilitarized, the army was reduced to 100,000 volunteers, and Germany was
deprived of a High Seas Fleet. These military injunctions, plus economically
motivated extractions, like the lease of the coal-rich Saarland to France for
15 years, did not provoke popular outrage in Germany to the same degree as
a hastily drafted 'war guilt' clause which placed the responsibility for the origins
of the war firmly on the shoulders of Germany and its Allies. The 'war guilt'
clause has been controversial ever since, providing employment for a legion
of historians, not least those first engaged by the German Foreign Ministry in
1919, in a strenuous effort to refute this Allied claim. Reparations were
equally controversial and the issues involved remained intricate long after
1919.

REPARATIONS AND WAR DEBTS

When Britain and France outlined their conditions for peace in 1918, they
made no mention of an indemnity – a payment to be made by Germany for
damages caused to the Allies during the war. During war-dominated election
campaigns, however, both Clemenceau and Lloyd George promised to 'make
Germany pay'. Significantly, the elections produced new Cabinets named
after the colour of military uniforms – in France in November 1919 the
Horizon Bleu, in Britain the Khaki government which took office in December 1918.

Of all the powers assembled in Versailles, the United States stood alone
in refusing to demand 'tribute' payments from Germany, but the Americans
were powerless to prevent their former Allies from demanding them. In the
years which followed, however, this moral stance rang increasingly hollow
when the United States itself continued to demand war debt payments on
loans granted to its Allies during the course of the war. Its refusal to recognize any link between Germany's ability to pay reparations and the capacity
of Britain and France to make war debt payments bedevilled foreign – as well
as economic and political – relations.

In 1919 France took a 'realistic' and flexible bargaining position on reparations. A careful assessment was made of Germany's capacity to pay, and its
government expressed willingness to reduce its demand significantly if the
United States agreed to guarantee French security. As negotiations wore on,
it became increasingly clear, however, that the United States would not
honour its earlier pledge to help construct a collective security pact that
would help to keep France safe. And this was the nub of the longer-term
problem. It was on the vexed questions of American involvement in Europe
and France's preoccupation with independent national security that the
Versailles settlement floundered. In the committee rooms of the Paris Peace
Conference and on the floors of the Congress and Senate of the United
States, it was obvious that most of the people involved in the bargaining were

not so much invigorated by Wilson's ideas of the future as burdened with the experiences of the past.

France's determination to secure reparations was born as much from a desire to rebuild its own economic base as from any impulse to ensure that Germany remained economically toothless. It did not. Indeed, some Britons and Americans argued that the requirement on the Germans to deliver both gold and goods to the victorious Allies as reparations would strengthen rather than weaken the German economy. The sticky problem in the Paris deliberations, once the principle of reparations had been accepted by the Big Four, was determining Germany's capacity to pay. For Britain and France the figure had to be large enough to satisfy promises made to the general public; for the United States the agreed sum had not to be so high as to starve an already emaciated Germany. After much foot dragging, a veneer of compromise was finally achieved with the creation of an inter-allied reparation commission to fix the final sum after an initial German payment of a thousand million pounds in gold.

Neither Britain, France nor the United States profited from the reparations saga. The European victors collected nothing like the specified reparation payments, while the United States was forced into concessions on war debts, forgoing much of the debts due to it: by 1930 it had waived 35 per cent of Britain's debts, 82 per cent of Italy's debt and 65 per cent of French and Belgian debts. But by then the economic situation had changed radically. At least such issues had proved open to modification and negotiation. A far greater test for Allied cohesion and aspirations for a 'healing, flexible peace' in 1919 came quickly with increased signs that the American Senate harboured profound misgivings about any American commitment to French security and to a new League of Nations which lay at the centre of Wilson's vision of the future.

THE LEAGUE OF NATIONS

The American President dreamed in 1919 of an organization which would safeguard international peace and serve as a forum for a more orderly management of the world's political, economic, financial and cultural affairs, but while he worked hard to foster European support for his idea, enthusiasm in the United States for such an international commitment soon began to wane. Increasingly fearful of repeated involvement in European squabbles and suspicious that the League would cripple America's cherished freedom to take independent action whenever and however it pleased, the American Senate, in November 1919, refused to ratify the Covenant of the new League which contained plans for a collective security arrangement: League members would step in to help one, or more, of its members if unjustly attacked. Without American support the plans collapsed and, in rejecting the League, the USA also failed to ratify the Peace of Versailles. For all his pains to secure agreement in

Paris and at home, Wilson, the idealist, had failed through the resistance of his fellow countrymen. He suffered a severe stroke and passed out of history.

The damage to European confidence in the United States was profound. The original Covenant of the League of Nations aspired to 'elasticity and security' in international relations. Now there was a knee-jerk reaction from France. During the 1920s France resolutely maintained that the Paris deliberations had determined the *status quo* in Europe. For security reasons it could not and should not be changed. Ironically, when by the 1930s France adopted a more conciliatory approach to German demands, Germany was under a new regime, that of Adolf Hitler whose dreams encompassed far more than a change in the *status quo*.

The difficulties for European peacemakers were stark after the effective withdrawal of American support for the peace settlement. They lacked the power, military or diplomatic, to enforce the Versailles peace terms. Moreover, when France did not win the much prized guarantee for its security from the Americans, this provided an opportunity for Britain to take a longed for step out of Europe. Although the British government remained committed to the security of France's borders with Germany, it became profoundly wary of becoming embroiled in French foreign policy and the Republic's network of so-called Little Entente alliances with Poland (1921 and 1925) Czechoslovakia (1925), Romania (1926) and Yugoslavia (1927). France had courted these alliances in an attempt, which proved forlorn, to contain any potential German ambitions of aggrandizement. Instead, the French government's decision to establish mutual guarantees of security with these struggling new powers, which had their own differences, only served to emphasize the potential mismatch in conflict between a French nation of 40 million people and a Germany of 65 million.

The dearth of military or diplomatic authority to support the peace became more dramatically apparent during the 1930s, but it was obvious as early as 1919–1920 that the League of Nations lacked the clout to provide sufficient economic aid to the emerging nations of Central and Eastern Europe. It was the Americans who stepped in, despite the abandonment of Wilson's vision. Flexing its new economic muscles, the American government created the American Relief Administration which supplied food to the value of $1,145 million, spearheaded by Herbert Hoover, a future Republican President of the United States. As 'Food Regulator of the world' Hoover was enthusiastic in his duties, but he was never above giving a political twist to American aid. Thus, he offered the carrot of food to capitalist Austria, while granting none to a Hungary which stood under threat of Communist domination by Béla Kun. His Relief Administration also arranged exchange deals which cut across wartime divisions: Austrian machines for Polish eggs and ham, Yugoslav wheat for Polish gasoline, and German coal for Polish potatoes.

Only by the mid-1920s did the League's Economic and Financial Organization have sufficient resources to make a genuine contribution to the prosperity of the region. Its efforts then on behalf of Europe's displaced communities and its collation of statistical data on healthcare, the level of social provision, working conditions and economic performance were useful as was its recruitment of expert advisers who developed extensive contacts with foreign governments, international institutions and centres of higher learning. (Such international networks were to become even more important during and after the Second World War.) Unfortunately for the League, the least successful of its activities was the most public, that of promoting international disarmament at large political gatherings held in Geneva.

While people across Europe looked to the League to rid Europe of the spectre of war, negotiations in the new Palais des Nations in the beautiful remote city of Geneva, set in neutral Switzerland, increasingly turned on the question of rearmament. It was argued that if stronger powers would not reduce their level of armament, then weaker powers, including countries defeated in the First World War, should be allowed to expand theirs. Meanwhile, France continued to build and stockpile weapons and refused to bow to international pressure to accede to German demands for treaty revision. According to the French Prime Minister, Edouard Herriot, who took office in 1924, France needed to rearm (thereby providing an excuse for other nations to follow suit) because 'my country has a dagger pointed at her breast, a centimetre from the heart . . . I cannot renounced the security of France.'

Even after the immediate post-war period of rehabilitation had ended, agricultural problems persisted. Europe's diverse agricultural community, which ranged from small tenant farmers in Spain and Italy to German landowners (*junkers*) who tilled larger estates, was in trouble during the 1920s. All farmers, including the British, were affected by the sharp drop in agricultural prices which had several causes. Amongst the most important was the opening of further huge new grain fields in America, Canada and Russia; more intensive use of farmland with the arrival of mechanised farm equipment, like tractors; and the mounting popularity of chemical fertilisers. Europe's population also grew more slowly, and its diet was changing too in favour of dairy over cereal produce. These challenges spelt trouble for Europe's farmers and for countries highly dependent on income from agriculture, most notably the new nations of Eastern Europe. Some countries confronted them successfully, however, notably Denmark.

THE SETTLEMENT IN CENTRAL AND EASTERN EUROPE

The Paris Peace Conference marked the beginning of a wider concept of Europe as the Empires of East and Central Europe, Ottoman, Habsburg, Romanov and Hohenzollerns gave way to new nations and new democracies. If there was a moment when the nineteenth-century 'principle of nationality', largely defined by language, triumphed, it was at the Paris Peace Conference. In creating new nations from old empires, Wilson's fifth point, that of self-determination – the right of 'nations' to choose their own form of government – was deemed crucial.

For the victorious nationalists themselves, leaders like Thomas Masaryk, the highly respected Slovak President of the new Czechoslovak republic, the creation of a jigsaw of new states in Eastern Europe was a victory against the 'Caesarism' of Europe's former empires. His hope, as idealistic as Wilson's, was that changes in frontiers would 'stimulate endeavours to bring a renascence and regeneration in ethics and culture'. The new states were broadly defined both as nation-states and as parliamentary democracies. For Masaryk this, too, offered an exciting opportunity for democracy. Indeed, he argued nobly that the nation of Czechoslovakia could only be preserved 'through freedom increasingly perfected'. Not all European nationalists shared this vision in 1919, however, any more than they had shared Mazzini's vision in the nineteenth century, and the link between nation-state and democracy in Eastern Europe, increasingly weathered by economic, social and political pressures in the years ahead, proved extremely short-lived.

At first, Britain and France had been uncertain as to whether they wished to destroy the old Habsburg Empire or merely to 'reform' it, but the swift disintegration of Austro-Hungarian rule, the threat of Communist insurrection – during 1918 troops were used over 50 times to restore civil order in Austria alone – and Wilson's determination to uphold the principle of national self-determination wherever possible, forced the Allies' hand. A radical revision of national borders in the Balkans followed: many of the boundaries 'fixed' at Versailles were decided by the more junior members of the Allied delegation. In Eastern Europe, where language, history and religion intermingled, each was an important feature of nationalism. Wilson's approach was, at best, problematic. Unlike *emigrés* to the United States who had 'chosen' to become American, in Eastern Europe an individual could not 'choose' to be Polish or Lithuanian or Serb or Bulgarian, he or she either was, or was not. Ironically, the application of 'self-determination' alongside strategic and economic considerations made an already complex task impossible. So, too, did the creation of states based on more than one 'nation', like Yugoslavia and, indeed, Czechoslovakia. Where to place them was a matter of controversy.

There were certainly clear 'winners' and 'losers' in the radical revision of national boundaries in central Europe and the Balkans. The treaties of Saint-Germain-en-Laye with Austria (signed 10 September 1919), Neuilly with Bulgaria (27 November 1919), Trianon with Hungary (4 June 1920), and Sèvres with Turkey (10 August 1920) marked out who they were. Germany and Russia lost territory too, and it was land taken from Russia which helped to create or re-define the national borders of Finland, Estonia, Latvia, Lithuania, Bessarabia and Poland. Germany contributed territory to the new Poland, while Austro-Hungarian land was incorporated into Romania, Czechoslovakia and Yugoslavia. Bulgaria, a late entrant into the war on the side of the Central powers, conceded territory to the new Yugoslavia, and although its territorial and population losses were small, they were felt acutely as a penalty because of the territorial expansion of neighbouring Romania and Yugoslavia.

Hungary, for centuries amongst the most stable powers in the region was arguably the most aggrieved. Its defeat in war cost it dear at the Paris Peace Conference. So, too, did its ethnic diversity. The punitive Treaty of Trianon left it with only 32.7 per cent of its pre-war territory and 41.6 per cent of its pre-war population. Nor was that all. To the Magyar people of Hungary the peace treaty appeared to endorse the dubious assumption that all non-Magyar people ought to be freed from the Magyar yoke. (The idea that the Slovaks, for example, might not want 'liberation' from Hungary was never taken seriously.) Yet, for all these losses, the Treaty of Trianon did not promote national homogeneity within the 'new' Hungary. Over 15 per cent of its peoples remained of non-Magyar descent. After Trianon Hungarians harboured a profound sense of injustice, and their governments were to vigorously follow revisionist policies which spelt trouble for the future.

It was not only the 'losers', however, who were appalled by the application of the peace settlement. For all Wilson's principles provinces and peoples were, in Nicolson's words, treated like 'pawns and chattels in a game'. The territorial settlements 'were based on mere adjustments and compromises between the rival claims of States'. Nicolson did not note, however, that the idea of forcibly moving peoples was rejected. Instead there were tensions and anomalies. Even the most apparent winners, the newly created states of Yugo(south)-Slavia and Czechoslovakia faced problems. Their boundaries were so arbitrary that quarrels were bound to follow, especially as these new nation-states contained the largest variety of different ethnic groups in Eastern Europe. Neither they nor the former wartime Allies were willing or able to protect the rights of all the different ethnic groups who resided within national borders. Some groups were numerically small, but it has been estimated that in 1930 around 52 per cent of Czechoslovak and 57 per cent of Yugoslav citizens belonged to 'minority' groups whether designated by nationality or religion.

So-called natural frontiers, like the sea or a mountain range, did receive attention, and Wilson ensured, for example, that Yugoslavia incorporated the Dalmatian coast. But this decision itself created problems. It frustrated Italian ambitions by breaking promises made to Italy in the Secret Treaty of London (1915) which had secured Italian intervention on the Allied side during the war. Orlando, the Italian prime minister and the only member of the 'Big Four' who took a sustained interest in arrangements relating to Eastern Europe, was so incensed that he stormed out of the Conference and returned to Rome. Yet while Italy could not annex the Dalmatian coast because it was not 'Italian', it was given the German-speaking territory of the South-Tyrol in the Dolomite Mountains for strategic reasons. Even in Poland where, as in Romania, the ethnic minorities were a smaller proportion of the total population (approximately 30 per cent for both nations in 1930), any such advantage was more than outweighed by the fact that it shared a common frontier with Germany and Russia. Moreover, during the inter-war period ethnic minorities in Poland were increasingly seen as 'Trojan horses' of these revisionist powers, with Poland's large Jewish population often cast as potential Communist agents.

The Paris Peace treaties went some way towards creating a new geographic order for Europe. They reduced by half the number of people living in Eastern and Central Europe under alien government. But the application of self-determination also fuelled the nationalism of the new nation-states in Eastern Europe, and not just among the dominant national groups – the Serbs in Yugoslavia, for instance. At the same time, the peace treaties did nothing to provide Europe's minorities with national outlets for their 'nationalism' and offered them even fewer guarantees of their rights.

Meanwhile, the stress on self-determination enhanced the determination of the former Central powers – notably Germany, Hungary and Bulgaria – to 'return' their minorities, like the Sudetenland Germans in Czechoslovakia, home to the 'fatherland'. Given the unwillingness of national groups to live in countries where they did not form the dominant nationality – and there were over 30 million of them – nationalism was to become increasingly inseparable from political ambitions. As early as 1919, on his return to Washington, Wilson told the Senate that when he had proclaimed that all nations had the right to self-determination, he had not known that some nationalities existed which were coming to him 'day after day having had their hopes raised' by what he had said. And in the immediate aftermath of the treaties, problems flared further in the east. The Allies saw the crumbling Ottoman empire, which over the centuries had left its mark – religious as well as political – on the European map, as the ideal territory with which to pacify resentful Greek and Italian delegates who believed they had been shabbily treated by their former Allies. But as Turkey retreated from Europe, an attack by an overwhelmingly Greek force at Smyrna (modern-day Izmir) on Turkey's Eastern coast in May 1919 served only to fuel anti-Greek and anti-Allied hostility – although the Italians and later the Americans opposed the Greek invasion – and precipitated a 'modern', nationalist revolt in Turkey itself which was led by Mustapha Kemal. The Sèvres peace settlement of 1920 for the former Ottoman Empire had already proved unworkable and was replaced by a new treaty, the Treaty of Lausanne, in July 1923. By then, the formidable task of trying to create an effective peace for Europe had taken longer than the prosecution of the seemingly endless war.

RUSSIAN CIVIL WAR AND PEACE, 1918–21

Boundaries in Eastern Europe were not determined solely by weary peace-makers in Versailles. The bloody civil war in Russia, which erupted in the summer of 1918, also helped define the borders of the Soviet Union and Poland. It was a war between the Bolshevik Red Guard and a White Guard composed of disparate political opponents, including former Imperial troops, which received military assistance from European, American and Japanese Allies.

After the conclusion of the Brest-Litovsk Treaty in March 1918 the Bolsheviks confronted three principal problems domestic: political opposition, which by July 1918 had taken up arms against the Bolsheviks; extending the Bolshevik revolution beyond Russia's urban centres, like Petrograd and Moscow; and determining the territorial boundaries of the new Soviet Republic and its policies towards non-Russian nationalities. This was a formidable challenge. The new Soviet Republic was in economic disarray, and the Red Guard, unlike its enemy, had to be built up almost from scratch by Trotsky who converted it from a relatively informal force of volunteers, to a highly disciplined and effective army recruited by rigorous conscription. The control of Red officers over their men was harsh: for Trotsky discipline could not 'possibly be maintained without revolvers'.

The Red Guard had a clear war aim: to establish a Soviet Republic. To achieve it, control of the railways and of the lines of communication and supply was essential, and as part of Trotsky's propaganda the Railwaymen's Union was told that: 'the future historian will most likely say "the railwaymen saved the revolution" or "the railwaymen ruined the revolution." ' By contrast, members of the White Guard were dispersed across Russia and fighting under a variety of Commanders, General Anton Denikin, Admiral Aleksandr Kolchak, General P. Wrangel and General I. Yudenich, who followed diverse, and sometimes conflicting, strategies and goals. The administrative hold of the disunited White forces on the surrounding countryside was weak. It was plagued, too, by a third force, the so-called 'Green Armies' – peasant and Cossack troops that gave allegiance to neither side, but were most active in the areas where the Whites were based.

The civil war, the mood of which was to be so evocatively captured in Boris Pasternak's novel *Doctor Zhivago* (repressed in Russia but published around the world in 1954), was hard and bloody for soldiers and civilians alike. Both sides resorted to terror in order to silence opponents and to requisition food, with important consequences for the victorious Soviet regime, which created the Cheka (a brutal commission dedicated to the struggle against counter-revolution). According to Bolshevik figures for European Russia, it shot around 9,000 persons without trial and arrested another 90,000 between January 1918 and July 1919 alone. By November 1920 the final Red offensive had successfully defeated Wrangel in the Crimea and a Red victory was assured. The British author, Arthur Ransome, who travelled in Russia during the civil war, described vividly the hasty evacuation of Wrangel's troops from the Crimea, leaving in their wake – to the mercy of the Red Army – 'portmanteaux, rifles, machine guns . . . undamaged tanks, undamaged aeroplanes' and Cossack troops.[1]

The intervention of France, Britain, the United States, Canada and Japan on the side of the White Guard was insufficient to provide practical aid to the Whites and merely helped to prolong the civil war. Ironically, it helped to unite Russians against them. 'Never had the Entente Powers been offered such a golden opportunity.' Denikin reflected, but as the war went on and '[practical] help was not forthcoming'. Foreigners trapped behind Red Army lines had an uncomfortable time. When Englishman Gerard Shelley, under house arrest in Moscow, demanded food from the Soviet authorities, he was told: 'If you don't like starving to death, dance! In any case, there will be one English dog less!' Foreign intervention also left a bitter legacy in international relations. The young Soviet Union continued to fear the intervention of the West in its foreign affairs.

This fear, however, was not enough to curb Bolshevik long-term ambitions to ferment Communist revolutions in other countries, and in 1919 they founded the Third Communist International or Comintern to promote world revolution on the Russian Communist model, ostensibly a direct descendant of the Second Communist International that dissolved in 1914 when international worker solidarity proved no match for nationalism. Under the leadership of its first President, Grigory Zinoviev, the Comintern was very much a creature of the Soviet Union, and although it comprised 44 Communist Parties and allied groups from more than 50 countries, the ideology and international agenda of the Russian Communist Party dominated its work and earned Communists around the world a reputation as traitors, a 'fifth column' that would take orders only from Moscow.

As the Communist tide receded in Europe after 1924, so, too did the power of the Comintern. Its decline was aided by the increased introversion of the Bolshevik party as it sought to recover from the Civil War. In the words of the General Secretary of the Communist Party from 1922 to 1953, Jusip Stalin, a Georgian born in 1879 whose real name was Dzhugashvili, its object now was to build 'Socialism in One Country'. Stalin had little interest in the Comintern beyond its use as a means to strengthen his personal power at home and abroad, and years later it was to be dissolved in 1943 at the request of Russia's allies in the Second World War. The enormous expansion of Soviet military power by then meant that he no longer had any need of the Comintern to realize his ambitions for the Soviet Union.

Nearly every facet of Bolshevik party life was changed by the tribulations of the civil war. The ruthless suppression of opposition outside the party and the increasingly undemocratic character of the party itself even under Lenin – elective party committees within the armed forces were abolished lock, stock and barrel, for example – were the price paid for a Bolshevik victory. The Bolshevik leaders underestimated the dangers of authoritarianism and centralism in their struggle for victory, and by failing to build institutional bulwarks against authoritarianism – such as freely elected national and local government organizations – pushed ahead a revolution which soon betrayed the workers and peasants that it was supposed to protect. In 1921, however, the brutal economic policy of War Communism was abandoned and succeeded in 1921 by the so-called New Economic Policy (NEP). This was a more liberal economic regime, but it was not to last.

Peace was sealed when Soviet Russia signed the Treaty of Riga with Poland on 18 March 1921. World war and civil war had cost Russia dear in life, material and territory. To its north-west, Finland, the Baltic states of Estonia, Latvia and Lithuania had all achieved independence from Russia by 1919 and had organized democratic elections by 1920, and elsewhere in the Soviet Union, the 'nationalities issue' presented the Bolsheviks with a continuing dilemma. The former Russian empire had ruled over a host of different ethnic groups, who included Ukrainians, Turks, Azheris, Siberian Yakuts and Buryats. How were they now to be treated? Lenin had cautiously endorsed the principle of self-determination as set out in a 'Declaration of the Rights of the Peoples of Russia' (15 November 1917), drafted by Stalin, then People's Commissar for Nationalities Affairs. Under the slogan 'National in Form, Socialist in Content' it provided an encouragement to minority self-consciousness yet denied ambitions to political nationalism and claims to autonomy.

For Marxists considerations of 'class' were always more important than national considerations, but the dangers inherent in working-class nationalism had become clear to the Bolsheviks when the Red Army marched into Poland in 1920 and Polish workers resisted the invasion. The experience was also to shape the Soviet Union's treatment of Poland after 1944.

Amongst the remaining ethnic groups within the former Russian empire, the Ukraine with its own form of recently created Soviet in March 1917 (the Rada) appeared to present the greatest separatist threat to the Bolsheviks. But the Ukraine remained within Lenin's Soviet republic largely because over half its population was Russian and because its peasants, as elsewhere, were more interested in acquiring land than regional autonomy; intellectuals often complained of their indifference to the nationalist message. In 1920 Mikhail Hrushevsky, the 'father' of Ukrainian nationalism and President of the Rada, was allowed to return from exile to lead the movement for Ukrainian cultural progress.

To the outside world, the most conclusive proof of the Bolshevik tolerance of national minorities, came with the formation of the Union of Socialist Soviet Republics (USSR) in December 1922 which appeared to allocate equal status to the Soviet republics of Russia, Transcaucasia, the Ukraine, and White Russia (Uzbek and Turkmenian joined in 1924, Tajikistan in 1929), and the new Soviet Constitution in July 1923 which established a Soviet of Nationalities. According to the historian Richard Pipes, however, the Bolsheviks' apparent commitment to minority rights quickly became mere 'window dressing' as the revolution and the imposition of Bolshevik control destroyed many religious and cultural institutions, and independent parties.

As the 1920s progressed, many ethnic groups found themselves worse off than they had been under Tsarist rule. Even the favoured ethnic groups of Byelorussia and the Ukraine, closest to the Russian borders, were repressed when the Bolsheviks realized that the nationalism they had encouraged could backfire against them; and after 1928 the demands of a new economic programme, launched by an increasingly powerful Stalin, very different from the relatively liberal regime of the NEP, put paid to the few remaining freedoms enjoyed by the USSR's minorities. Stalin's Five Year Plans demanded the collectivization (or industrialization) of Soviet agriculture and the massive build-up of heavy industry. Collective farms would feed industrial workers, heavy industry would provide machinery for agricultural workers to farm more efficiently. Marx had given no guidance to Communists as to how to plan an economy of the type that Stalin desired, so he implemented his own policies to make the USSR an industrial workers' state.

REVOLUTIONS IN GERMANY AND HUNGARY, 1918–19

Marxist analysis would have suggested that the first revolution during or just after the First World War would have taken place not in Russia but in Germany and there was a German 'revolution' in early November 1918, when the monarchy was replaced by democratic constituent assembly after mass, popular protest across the length and breadth of Germany – events which led German Communists, like Karl Liebknecht, to believe that it could lead to a total social revolution of the kind Marx had envisaged. Instead, although there were dramatic sequences of events, the outcome was quite different. Uprisings in a number of German cities were quickly put down. Instead of defeat, the existing capitalist order was re-invigorated by the crisis. Right-wing political groups and big business fought back. Capitalism became more concentrated and formed new, large-scale production and trading units. Out of a 'rationalization mania' came the great German mergers of Vereinigte Stahlwerke in 1926 (United Steel Works) and I. G. Farben (1925), a conglomeration of chemical producers. All this went further than Rathenau (see above p.183) had forecast.

In the chaos of defeat and abdication in the early winter of 1918, it came as a great relief to Frederich Ebert, the highly responsible leader of the German Socialists, when he was assured that the army would support the new German Republic. The once persecuted German Social Democratic Party (*Sozialdemokratische Partei Deutschlands*, SPD), with its Marxist roots, was now set to become the main party of government in 1919. Yet fear of 'class war' expressed by politicians like Gustav Stresemann, founder of the conservative *Deutsche Volkspartei* (the German Peoples' Party), stood in the way. So also did resistance to 'moderation' on the part of independent socialists and Communist Spartakists who were fired up by the Russian Bolshevik Revolution which they believed would become world-wide. Hungry workers organized self-appointed revolutionary factory councils, not only in Berlin, but in industrial centres outside Berlin, like Leipzig, and there were violent street protests in Bavaria, Thuringia and Saxony.

The effect of the street violence was different from that which had been anticipated. The badly organized *Spartakist* revolt in Berlin championed by

Liebknecht and his rather more reluctant conspirator, Rosa Luxemburg, met a bloody end. On the 11 January 1919, five days after it had begun, the murdered corpses of the two leaders were dumped in a canal in Berlin. A similar revolution fizzled out in Bavaria, where a short-lived ultra-democratic state founded by Kurt Eisner ended its fraught life with Eisner's assassination. The upsurge of street protest on the left prompted a response from the German right which, in the long run, was to seem more significant. In March 1920 came a 'putsch', the first major right-wing attempt to overthrow the new German constitutional order by force; and when the *Reichswehr* ignored government orders to fire on Walter Kapp and his armed, volunteer *Freikorps* supporters, men newly returned from the battle fronts, there was evidence of the tacit support that the right-wing 'boot-boys' appeared to enjoy amongst 'respectable' people and the authorities. Indeed, bungled revolutionary attempts from the right were treated more leniently than attempts from the left. Kapp's co-conspirator, General Walther von Lüttwitz, was merely retired on a military pension and an ex-corporal, the then unknown Adolf Hitler was also treated indulgently after his abortive Beer Hall putsch in Munich in 1923. Further north, in Germany's industrial heartland, the Ruhr, force had been ruthlessly employed to disperse a left-wing army of 50,000 volunteers in May and June 1920. The size of the army indicated the frustration and radicalization prevalent amongst sections of the German working class.

In the winter of 1918–19 left-wing revolutions had also erupted in Austria and Hungary. They were inspired by the example of the Bolshevik putsch in Petrograd and by the education in Marxism of captured soldiers of the former Imperial armies who had been interned in Russian prisoner of war camps on the Eastern front. In February 1919 amid considerable economic and military confusion, power in Hungary passed to one such Bolshevik educated prisoner-of-war, Béla Kun, who had returned to Hungary armed with Bolshevik funds and promises of assistance. General Jan Christian Smuts, a South African representative at the Paris Peace Conference despatched to Hungary, sensibly concluded that Hungarian Bolshevism 'was not a serious menace and cannot last'. He was right. Kun had been promised Russian support which did not materialize. He also advocated radical reforms, including nationalization rather than the redistribution of agricultural land, which were hugely unpopular in a country where more than half the population was engaged in agriculture and where many tenant farmers aspired to landowners themselves. An energetic Anti-God campaign and Kun's resort to organized terror against his opponents, orchestrated by his bloody-thirsty aide, Tibor Szamnelly, turned the tide against him, and by 1 August 1919 he and his associates had fled the country.

Further confusion followed. Kun was succeeded by a right-wing government under Admiral Horthy, and even after the professedly home-sick ex-Emperor Karl fruitlessly attempted to exploit the situation and to recover his throne by returning to Hungary in April 1921, rumours of a monarchist coup continued to bedevil Hungarian politics. In fact, Kun's 133-day Soviet-style republic had a far greater impact on Hungarian politics. As in Germany, a threat from the left had aroused an energetic response from new radical right-wing political groups who alleged Communists were intent on destroying both the nation and capitalism, and on throwing in their lot with the USSR. In reality, however, workers' protests were born of hunger, inflation and unemployment during the first winter of peace and revealed very little ideological commitment to an international marxist revolution across Europe (a conclusion Lenin himself reluctantly reached). The only exceptions to the trend were among leading party activists in Italy, France and Spain. Meanwhile, the spectre of a Communist revolution which would eliminate God as well as private property, continued to haunt the middle classes, sections of which had grown deeply hostile, not only to the left, but to the ideals of Liberal Democracy.

The magnitude of political violence in post-war Europe augured ill. There was a renewed upsurge in political assassinations in 1920–2, accompanied by an increase in overt anti-Semitism. (Many of the Communist revolutionaries were Jewish, which fuelled right-wing prejudice: Luxemburg, Liebknecht, Kun and Szamnelly amongst the most prominent.) In Germany, E. J. Gumbel, the author of *Zwei Jahre Mord* (*Two Years of Murder*, 1922), calculated that there had been 334 political murders from March 1919 until June 1921, 318 committed by the German right, 16 committed by the left. Prominent casualties included representatives of Liberal Democracy, the Catholic leader Matthias Erzberger and the Jewish economic organizer Rathenau.

THE SURVIVING EMPIRES: BRITAIN AND FRANCE

While the map of Europe was being redrawn, Britain, France, Germany, the Netherlands, Belgium and Portugal were also forced to reassess their imperial relations. Rivalry between the European empires, especially between those of Britain, France and Germany, had contributed to the mounting tension in Europe before 1914. After the war, Britain and France modified their imperial ties. The notion of a British Commonwealth, grouped around White Dominions like Australia and Canada, who had gone to Britain's assistance during the war, helped to release a weakened Britain from some of the burdens of empire. But Britain now also had to protect territories mandated by the League of Nations in the 'Middle East' and Africa, as the Paris Peace had also taken decisions which modified the maps of both these regions, as well as that of China.

Closer to home, the declaration of independence by the self-constituted Irish parliament, *Dail Eireann* (21 January 1919), marked a new stage, although by no means an end to the long history of troubled Anglo-Irish relations. The newly proclaimed republic launched an appeal for recognition by the powers assembled at the Paris Peace Conference; and by the end of 1919 the two 'nations' were effectively at war, although the British government did not admit that it was a war. The Irish Republican challenge, led by Michael Collins, Cathal Brugha, Eamon De Valera and Arthur Griffiths was determined, if often divided, and British forces in Ireland had to be increased in numbers. The Royal Irish Constabulary recruited amongst ex-soldiers in England – thereby establishing the notorious Black and Tans. Indeed, *The Times* newspaper suspected that government's use of force in Ireland, perhaps deliberately, would arouse a state of rebellion in which a settlement would be impossible.

Progress in the British Parliament on the Irish question was as troubled as the 'policing' activities of British forces within Ireland, but on 23 December 1920 the Government of Ireland Act became law, with the North partitioned off as a Unionist stronghold: the Protestants there were noisily enthusiastic in their loyalty to the United Kingdom. The war in the South continued until May 1922, when the Republic government in Dublin wrung substantial concessions from a reluctant British government. Educated opinion in Britain, reflecting a view widely held across Europe, had come to recognize that it was unfair to deny Irishmen and women independence from empire when it had been granted to miscellaneous Czechs, Poles and Slovaks in the peace settlements of 1919. The civil war was over, although for decades to come, masked gunmen continued to fight the war either in the name of Irish independence or of loyalty to the British Crown.

The First World War and, less significantly, the struggle for Irish independence, had taxed Britain's resources immeasurably, yet the British Empire or Commonwealth was larger after the First World War than at any other period in its history. It extended over almost 14 million square miles of the globe and contained a population of over 454 million. The only nation which could possibly hope to compete with Britain on such terms was China, and its population was still 123 million less than that of the British Empire. There were few changes in the pattern of colonial empire, and the idea that there existed a 'sacred trust' between the civilized peoples and the 'backward' natives remained dominant: it was even incorporated into the Covenant of the League of Nations. The ideology of empire gradually changed, however, with an increasing emphasis on the notion of 'responsibility' over that of 'power'. This was also true of French colonial relations, as Albert Sarraut, French Minister for the colonies and an important colonial theorist, argued in 1923: 'Colonizing France does not work only for itself . . . its efforts must be beneficial to the colonies as to itself, for there France assures economic betterment and human development.'

At home even Britain's 'established democracy' extended the franchise to men in 1918, enfranchising all men over 21, and all soldiers regardless of age; and in 1921 women over the age of thirty were finally granted the right to vote. But as quickly as the working classes of Europe were given the vote, they uncovered their continued political impotence on issues which immediately concerned them: the price and availability of food, the provision of adequate housing and unemployment.

Despite new legislation, like the Unemployment Insurance Act (1920) and the momentous Pensions Act (1925), there was increasing frustration when governments failed to support the ailing domestic economy, suffering from outmoded methods of production and a chronic loss of export markets. Even the short-lived, first (minority) Labour government of 1924 offered few new policies to tackle Britain's industrial difficulties. There had been large-scale industrial unrest every year since the end of the war, and on 3 May 1926 a miners' strike became a nine-day General Strike, so-called although it was never general. The fact that it was short-lived demonstrated that British Socialism, and indeed British politics as a whole, were dominated by moderate politicians determined to preserve British democracy and some form of capitalist system. Although not apparent at the time, the General Strike marked the end, not the beginning, of widespread social unrest.

FEMINISM AND SOCIETY

Communism was not the potentially revolutionary force in Europe after the First World War. At first, the extension of suffrage to many, but by no means all, women in Europe was regarded by some as an equally dangerous and destabilizing force as the appeal of Communism. Indeed, the Soviet Union's quick introduction of formal equality of the sexes in law, a 1918 Family Code and the legalization of abortion in 1920 appeared to signal a terrifying union of revolutionary forces. Yet within a few years measures supporting women's rights and calls for a new Soviet morality soon withered. Europe's first female government minister and, later, first female ambassador, Alexandra Kollontai fell out with Lenin in 1922 over how women might best be attracted to, and supported by, the Communist Party. By the end of the 1920s, the same shift away from a radical feminist agenda where women demanded legal equality, equal opportunities to work, the right to participate in politics at all levels, and access to contraception, abortion and sexual freedom, was apparent across Europe. It gave way to a more conservative ideology of 'social housekeeping' that emphasized the contribution women made to society as a whole through their traditional skills as mothers and housewives.

The problems generated after the First World War created a difficult context for feminism. The pressures of post-war inflation made everyone more conscious of class or interest group divisions than of gender divisions, and this, coupled with the widespread application of female suffrage in the aftermath of the war, worked to fragment the feminist movement. Women's politics were absorbed into mainstream political parties, and here, on a national level at least, women found it difficult to make their mark. Even in parties where women were well represented amongst the rank and file – in interwar Britain women made up half the total individual membership of the Labour Party and there were similar levels of female membership in the

German SPD – this was not fully expressed at the national level. Even in 1931, the high point of female representation, only one-and-a-half per cent of all Members of Parliament were women; in Germany female representation in the Reichstag averaged around 7 per cent throughout the 1920s. A variety of obstacles stood in the way. Local party organizations were reluctant to put women forward for national elections; nor were they encouraged by the party leadership to do so. At the same time, women were disillusioned by the day-to-day reality of party politics: endless debate in smoke-filled rooms, long-drawn out procedures, the patronizing tone adopted by their male colleagues.

In an effort to realize their own agenda women remained much more active at a local political level. This was especially important in France and Italy where women still did not have the vote. In 1923, the Fascist government of Benito Mussolini, in an effort to outmanoeuvre his political opponents, granted Italian women the vote in local elections for the first time, announcing the decision at a meeting of the International Alliance for Women's Suffrage held in Rome that May. But the step was mere window dressing as the government moved at the same time to undermine women's status and limit their contribution to Italian society. Mussolini's Minister for Education, Giovanni Gentile, for example, attempted to limit the number of women teachers, arguing they lacked the mental and moral vigour to educate men.

In France, where women were also denied the vote in national elections, they too were invited to serve on local councils. Local politics proved more attractive to them because they offered access to policymaking on issues of immediate concern to women, notably education, housing and healthcare. Moreover, in a further continuation of the activities that had characterized women's political and social activity during the nineteenth century, women remained active in a host of voluntary societies and pressure groups, and female membership of the League of Nations Union, an international supporters club for the work of the Geneva-based organization, was especially impressive. So, too, was women's work in pacifist organizations. They were motivated by a number of concerns: the experience of the First World War, the treatment of war veterans, and the desire to project to the wider world what they regarded as the special perspective offered by mothers. In Paris women could be found in no less than 144 different political associations, more than 25 of them declaredly working in pursuit of peace.

Taken together, however, the primary focus of women's political activity in the inter-war period centred on the family and the contribution of the family to the nation state. The great failure on the part of female political activists of every political hue was to make a direct connection between their work on a local level and social policies imposed at a national level relating to topics like unemployment and access to education. There was also a tendency to focus on women's *needs* rather than their *rights*. Not only did this dull the critical edge of inter-war feminism, it also made it very easy for women's demands to be appropriated and repackaged by fascist and authoritarian governments who were preoccupied with implementing family policies that related to national or racial well-being.

Debates about sexuality and procreation were especially prominent in the cultural and political life of Europe in the 1920s. The war loosened, if it did not liberate, attitudes towards sexuality. Before it around 19 per cent of European women had sex before marriage: between 1915 and 1925 the figure rose to 39 per cent. This change was welcomed and encouraged by artists, performers and left-wing radicals who called for a new honesty in sexual relations between men and women, and a more active policy on birth control, the simplification of divorce proceedings and even the legalization of homosexuality. But there was an inevitable counter reaction from those who saw a strong causal relationship between morality and a strong nation, and between morality and a strong Christian Church or Churches. Sex for them should only take place between married couples for the purpose of procreation, anything which deviated from this path – homosexuality, premarital sex, the use of contraceptives or abortion – should be corrected or prosecuted. Although this view found its clearest expression in policies implemented across authoritarian and fascist Europe in the 1930s, it already played an important role in shaping political debates and government policies in the democracies during the 1920s.

The division between radical and conservative groups was not always as clear-cut as it seemed. Some of Europe's staunchest advocates of contraception, like the pioneer of women's clinics in Britain, Marie Stopes, were also motivated by racial concerns. A distorted approach to Darwinian and post-Darwinian theories of evolutionist biology prompted demands from right-wing and left-wing quarters that the state take action to care for the physical and mental well-being of its people in order to ensure 'racial survival'. This strand of thought, known as Eugenics, called on the state to manage the reproduction of its citizens by encouraging 'biologically strong' couples to procreate by offering financial incentives to those with children and penalties for those without them. (In Germany a so-called 'batchelor tax' was introduced). Moreover, eugenicists argued, it was important for everyone in society to have access to contraception because a 'mentally unbalanced population' could result from the suppression of sexual needs. The eugenics movement had supporters in most countries and from every walk of life, but it was especially strong among sections of the middle classes. The ideas behind it were to provide the impetus for programmes of compulsory sterilization that targeted society's most vulnerable members.

The debate about contraception was influenced by concerns other than racial survival. Supporters of birth-control saw it as a major step to improving living conditions for society's poorest members. Lower birth rates would create a better material world for children, while marriages would be happier when freed from the fear of unwanted children. The German intellectual Julius Wolf argued that society should recognize the desire to procreate was not an instinct but a voluntary choice (an idea that was to make a big impact during the 1960s): most working-class men and women, he claimed, wanted access to contraception more for practical than for intellectual reasons. Advancements in healthcare for women meant that doctors were now able to tell women when it was unwise to have any more children, but they were prevented, whether by law, religious conviction or cultural mores, from giving advice on, or access to, contraception. That was why large numbers of women, desperate for advice, wrote to Marie Stopes, who had touched on the subject in her book *Married Love* (1918). Typical was the letter of Mrs E. B.: 'My first baby was born three years ago and the doctor advised me not to have any more children. But he did not give me the necessary advice as to how to avoid them.'[2] In the Weimar Republic it was claimed that over 875,000 illegal abortions were performed in 1925, rising to over a million abortions a year during the Great Depression.

ITALY: THE FIRST CASUALTY, 1919–24

During the first years of peace German, Hungarian, Austrian and Polish democracy had charted routes which were to be travelled with increasing frequency in European politics in the years that followed: an increasingly pronounced division between reformist socialists, prepared to co-operate with the existing democratic order and revolutionary Communists striving for a world-wide working-class revolution; a reliance on nationalism as a political force; the propensity to resort to street violence; and the decline of pre-war liberalism.

In Italy the level of street violence and the mounting confrontation between forces of the left and right established a pattern which was to be repeated elsewhere during the inter-war years. Before the war Italy's Premier, Giovanni Giolitti, an accomplished manipulator, had attempted to accommodate the left into the Liberal movement, but he failed to preserve the dominance of the Italian Liberal party. Just as the divided British Liberal party lost out to the Independent Labour Party and a new Labour Party after the war, so also in the wake of Italian post-war electoral reforms, which introduced universal male suffrage and proportional representation in 1919, the Liberals loss of votes to the radical left and to the increasingly troublesome *Partito Popolare Italiano*, (PPI, Italian Popular Party), the latter a curious blend of right, centre and left-wing Catholics, supported mainly by the small peasant proprietors and tenant farmers of Northern and Central Italy.

In November 1919 and again in May 1921, two successive Liberal Premiers, Nitti and Giolitti, called general elections to try to staunch the flow from the ranks of Liberal supporters into the parties of the left and right. But the Liberal Party was unable to resolve the tension between history and modernity, so well portrayed in paintings and posters. On a more practical level too, it faced a broad range of social and economic problems for which its leaders had no satisfactory answers: an economic crisis in the now seemingly superfluous munitions industry; urban unemployment; land hunger amongst peasants in the South; and high rents for tenant farmers in the North. Italy's middle classes went on to desert the Liberal party in droves, complaining bitterly that the tired old clichés of Liberal politics offered no new answers, and matters were made worse by Italy's soaring rate of inflation: the whole-sale price index (1913=100) rose from 413 in 1918 to 591 in 1920 wiping out salaries, pensions and savings. As in Germany three years later, white-collar workers were especially badly hit; middle-class fears of a Communist revolution increased as confidence in the existing political order diminished.

To add insult to already substantial injury, the treatment meted out to the Italian people by their Liberal coalition government was mirrored by the victors at Versailles. Prime Minister Orlando's inability to secure the territories promised to Italy in the Treaty of London rankled, especially amongst tens of thousands of ambitious, young officers, still intoxicated by the patriotic fervour uncorked by war. In 1915 Italian nationalists trusted that the First World War would cement a disparate people and create a truly united Italy, but post–war economic hardships and disappointment in Paris brought regional tensions to the fore once again. As the march of the flamboyant poet Gabriele D'Annunzio to take Fiume (September 1919) had revealed, there were plenty of eager, young Italian men ready to resolve their disagreements with the Italian government by force. The era of mass politics and of potentially disloyal military forces had descended upon Italy.

The extension of the electoral franchise, as in Germany and Hungary, had heightened the challenge to the dominant liberal democratic order, but while large numbers of working-class Italians swarmed to support the socialists – there were violent food riots in Central and Northern Italy and factory seizures in Piedmont – the newly formed Italian Communist Party and the peasants of the South turned to the PPI. Italy's ultimate political fate, like that of so many liberal democracies in inter-war Europe, turned on the arbiters of political power in late-nineteenth-century Europe: diverse members of the middle class, including industrialists and shop-owners along with tenant farmers, civil servants and businessmen. The King himself became increasingly frustrated with the inability of successive governments to contain mounting insurrectionist violence. The answer they all reached was ominous. Frustrated by the failure of the traditional Liberal parties, they turned to a journalist and former PSI (*Partito Socialista Italiano*) socialist, Benito Mussolini, who, after a highly successful career as the editor of the Socialist *Avanti!* newspaper, had impulsively broken with the PSI in 1914 in favour of an interventionist stance on the First World War. And by the end of the war, he had adopted an aggressive nationalist posture (and garb) as founder and leader of the *Fasci di Combattimento* (Fascists), offering land reform to the peasantry, and the abolition of the Senate and the summing of a new Constituent Assembly. None of these policies was new. What *was* new was the large number of armed gangs who roamed both rural and urban Italy, under the new banner of Fascism, recruiting most successfully in regional capitals. By 1921, Mussolini began to make electoral and financial capital from Italy's rising revolutionary violence, privately aware that his own squads had been contributing to the problem.

By the end of 1921 Italian fascism had already taken on its chameleon form: it promised to please all except Italy's socialists, who played into Mussolini's hands by creating a rival Communist Party with links to Moscow, a tremendous propaganda coup for the fascists. Pledged to break strikes, to discipline labour, to offer local political representation, and to end widespread public disorder, they presented Mussolini as a new, national leader, *Il Duce*, and in October 1922 the King invited him to join a coalition cabinet as Prime Minister. By May 1924 Mussolini faced allegations, made by a Socialist deputy, Giacomo Matteotti, that the last Italian elections were fraudulent, distorted by violence and torture. Mussolini was furious at Matteotti's efforts to discredit his 'respectability' and allegedly told his thugs, 'if you were not cowards, nobody would have the courage to make a speech like that.' On 10 June 1924 Matteotti disappeared and everyone rightly assumed that Mussolini's boot-boys had wanted to make good their earlier oversight by murdering him. Mussolini defused the crisis by sacking a number of his most unpopular henchmen, and with the opposition bitterly divided and public opinion apparently reluctant to blame him for Matteotti's murder, he maintained a clear majority in parliament. Rather than weaken the *Duce*, the Matteotti crisis had made Mussolini's position stronger and from now on he made promises which the 'conservative' middle classes wanted to hear: the freedom of the press would be curbed, opposition parties would be disciplined and Italy would be governed with efficiency.

The collapse of Italian democracy came far sooner than that of Germany – or Spain – despite the fact that Italy had been a victor in war, but certain elements of the Italian story were to be repeated later in the collapse of liberal democracy in those two countries, and also in the story of the more established democracies of France and Britain. Securing the vote had not solved the problems of the less privileged in society, while those groups who had been favoured within nineteenth-century political structures – the upper and middle classes – had grown fearful and resentful at the extension of the suffrage. Economic collapse in Europe at the end of the 1920s was to fan tensions throughout Europe. Meanwhile from January 1925 Italy embarked on a painful journey to a dubious goal: the fascist state, basing its authority on mass popular support. Mussolini brought the fascist squads under more rigorous control, the Fascist party's highest body, its 'Grand Council', was constitutionalized, and he himself assumed responsibility for the ministries of war, air and navy. Although most of the party's actions were the huff and puff of theatrical propaganda rather than the product of hard, clearly defined policies, Italian spirits were lifted in the early years of fascism with higher levels of employment, while admiring foreigners – and there were many of them – were impressed, they said, by the fact that trains ran on time.

The cultural dimension of Mussolini's regime is important in explaining its appeal since the movement made conscious efforts to legitimate itself in the eyes of the Italian public by drawing connections between Fascism and particular features of Italy's glorious past. Fascist symbols shamelessly echoed those of the Roman Empire and 'appropriate' anniversaries or events were celebrated with gusto. Typical were the celebrations held on 28 October 1930 to commemorate the anniversary of the March on Rome when massed ranks of Blackshirts and 'Representatives of National Strengths' – in an obvious echo of Roman legions – assembled and marched together in an impressive formation before the Palazzo Venezia in Rome. During the 1930s such oceanic assemblies became increasingly important to the public presentation of Italian fascism. Indeed, Mussolini boasted that he could summon a crowd just by ringing a bell.

PARALLELS?

In Spain the dictatorship of Primo De Rivera (1923–30), a man of 'immense optimism', was the Spanish answer to rising inflation and agrarian unrest. Farmers in Catalan Spain, as in Southern Italy, had grown to resent the traditional patterns of landholding which milked the labour of tenant farmers without enabling them to enjoy the rewards of owning their own land, while Southern Spanish agriculture, by contrast, was dominated by large estates (*latifundia*) run on a factory-style system which enabled employers to keep wages down to starvation level by means of huge reserves of unemployed labour. For Spanish peasants there were few alternatives to radical, anti-clerical political protest. With only 2 million workers employed in industry, urban migration was no real solution to Spain's heady rate of population growth at the turn of the twentieth century, and the country faced a grave political crisis.

De Rivera came to power, like Mussolini, on the shoulders of King and army and sought to guide Spain with a strong hand. But his authoritarian approach was clumsy and he alienated his strongest supporters on the right with his attempts at army reform and angered the left with his repressive measures against the Catalans. (He even banned the Catalan National dance, the *Sardana*.) Regional republican sentiment was stirred up. Worse unrest was to come.

Portugal, too, was hit by wave after wave of strikes in the mid-1920s, while worker anti-clericalism also provoked a reaction from the Portuguese right. Unlike Spain, Portugal was not riven by regional conflict and all the Portuguese spoke the same language. Yet there was widespread disenchantment with the democracy of the First Republic which had been inaugurated in 1910. At first, the declaration of the Republic had appeared to place Portugal at the vanguard of European politics – the only other republics were France and Switzerland – but its democracy soon faltered. There were 45 administrations between 1910 and 1926 each lasting on average four months; the national budget ran a consistent deficit, and the army and navy officer corps became increasingly involved in national politics influenced, in part, by the example of Primo De Rivera in Spain.

In 1926 a national revolution replaced the democratic republic with a military dictatorship. Yet social unrest continued and in early 1927 demonstrations and riots swept the country once more. In Oporto 80 people were killed, a further 100 lost their lives in Lisbon, and over 600 alleged troublemakers were exiled. The following year António de Oliveira Salazar, a Catholic Professor of Economics at Coimbra University, born in 1889, joined the dictatorship as Finance Minister. Influenced by Charles Maurras, leader of the *Action Française*, and by other French and Italian right-wing activists, Salazar was determined to bring Portugal's rampant budget deficit under control. He also wanted a corporate government that would act in the interests of all, not just the majority of individuals. To Salazar, 'man in isolation is an abstraction, a fiction mainly created under the erroneous principles during the last century'. He drew on Roman Catholic thought in reaching such conclusions.

Salazar's record as Portugal's financial supremo, his main source of strength, was impressive. During 1917–28 the budget deficit totalled 2,574,000 contos, yet in the next 11 years – which included the worst of the depression – he achieved a total surplus of 1,963,000 contos (then the equivalent of around £20 million). In initiatives which extended far beyond his portfolio as Finance Minister, and while other ministers were appointed and dismissed, he spent the budget surplus on public works, social assistance, rearmament, communications, ports, irrigation, hydro-electric schemes, and education. A widely respected financial dictator, overseas as well as at home, he also came to be regarded by the younger generation of nationalists and army officers as the answer to Portugal's political problems. As a result in July 1932 he became Prime Minister of Portugal (confusingly his official title was President of the Council of Ministers), a position which he was to hold until his health failed in the autumn of 1968. Yet, although his *Estado Novo* (New State) was similar in several respects to De Rivera's and later Franco's Spanish state, Iberian co-operation remained limited. During the Spanish Civil War Portugal was able to act as a clearing centre for Nazi supplies to Franco and to surrender Republican refugees to the nationalists, but Portuguese canniness in its relations reflected the old Portuguese proverb, 'Neither good winds, nor good marriages come from Spain'.

In Germany a new right, sometimes known as the 'extreme of the centre', received a powerful impetus for growth with the onset of an unprecedented hyper-inflationary crisis in 1923. Never before had the economy of an industrialized nation experienced such uncontrolled destruction of the value of money. The German mark was already in trouble in the summer of 1921, slipping to one-fiftieth of its 1914 value, and by the summer of 1923 the spiral of inflation reached its zenith. It was a good time for American tourists to visit Germany. Germans, however, despaired. In November 1923 one US dollar could buy 4,200 milliard marks. Inhabitants of both town and country began to abandon the mark in favour of direct bartering, swapping household items, like saucepans and furniture, for food. Families wallpapered rooms and fashioned kites from worthless mark notes. The impact of the crisis is best illustrated on a human level by the story of a young disabled woman who, when orphaned in the war, inherited some 112,000 marks. Within months her inheritance turned to worthless paper and she twice attempted suicide. In Berlin, Arnold Bauer, a theatre critic, recalled that 'there was an awareness of great poverty on the streets . . . people bought enough for one or two days – that was as far ahead as they could buy.'[3]

Much of the inflation had been generated by domestic economic difficulties as a consequence of the decision of the imperial government to finance its war effort by selling war bonds in preference to taxing the German people. A large domestic debt was accumulated which had to be paid back with interest, a burden compounded by Entente reparation demands and by social payments, for example the costs of demobilization and care for the wounded and widowed. Yet it was easier for the German government to tolerate and even generate inflation than to try to control it. Inflation depreciated the debts and, in the short term, enabled bills to be paid. But the human and political-economic cost was very high. The political, psychological and social impact of the inflation profoundly undermined support for the Weimar Republic.

The rest of the world sat up and took notice when, after Germany had failed to meet repeated French demands for reparation payments, French troops marched into Germany's industrial heartland, the Ruhr in January 1923. The French suspected that the Germans were deliberately trying to destroy their economy so that they would not have to pay reparations – there was some truth in this accusation – while the United States and Britain expressed outrage at France's deployment of black colonial troops on German soil. The German government won international sympathy. There was sympathy too for the German policy of passive resistance in the Ruhr, while a British cartoonist could flippantly refer to the 'ruhrnation of Germany'. Nonetheless, by the summer of 1923 the German government was forced to concede that 'we are sitting on a volcano and we are on the threshold of revolution unless we can ameliorate the situation'.

For most Germans, especially the middle classes, who saw their pensions, savings and salaries wiped out, the ordeal of hyper-inflation was not one they wished to repeat. As a result Germany developed a deep-seated fear of inflation that was to have profound consequences for German politics during the Great Depression when Chancellor Brüning (1930–2), believed he could not resort to inflationary methods to combat the depression. More immediately, the crisis shocks of 1923 enabled government to reduce wages by 18 per cent, a devastating blow for the artisan class. For traditional craftsmen – the carpenters and cabinetmakers of a former age – an industrialized, capitalist Germany, prone to crisis, appeared to offer no special place for them. Increasingly they, and groups like them, found refuge in nationalist, romantic movements, like the 'Militant League of Beggars', which harked back to a fictional age when the German race was 'pure' and the countryside unpolluted by greedy capitalists.

At first, such right-wing fringe movements, like their revolutionary Communist counterparts, posed no immediate threat to the Weimar Republic. But hyper-inflation, followed by the introduction of a new currency, exacerbated social and economic divisions within Germany and led to a loss of support for liberal, democratic and centre parties operating within it. The division between ostentatious rich and deprived poor grew more pronounced within the context of a 'modern' culture at its most vibrant – and tense – in Berlin. 'We needed very little sleep and were never tired', the celebrated German dramatist, Carl Zuckmayer wrote, 'Berlin tasted of the future and that is why we took all the crap and coldness'.

In 1924 Germany was saved by Gustav Stresemann and American dollars. Stresemann, the charismatic leader of the Deutsche Volkspartei (DVP), briefly became Chancellor in 1923–4, before becoming Foreign Minister, a post he occupied with considerable skill until his death in 1929. He put an end to passive resistance in the Ruhr and set about overseeing arrangements for a new currency – the *Rentenmark*. Though a nationalist, Stresemann was prepared to work with the Socialists – notably President Ebert – to restore stability to Germany. Indeed, in their efforts to resolve the Ruhr crisis, Ebert and Stresemann repeatedly resorted to Article 48 of the German constitution which enabled them to by-pass the Reichstag, suggesting that even amongst the defenders of German democracy, there was only a superficial commitment to the rigours of democratic politics.

Their efforts were also aided by Anglo-American hostility toward France after the Ruhr invasion, and most important of all, by a US $200 million loan granted in September 1924, under a new Dawes plan which enabled Weimar to begin again.

DANGER SIGNS: EASTERN EUROPE, 1920–28

The Dawes plan influenced the pattern of economic recovery in central and eastern Europe, where there had been many danger signs during the early 1920s. The chaos, destruction and dislocation in the states of Eastern Europe, both old and new, far outstripped those experienced in the West, and while by 1921 Finland, the Baltic states, Poland, Czechoslovakia, Austria, Hungary, Yugoslavia, Bulgaria and Romania had all held some form of relatively free democratic elections, there were formidable social divides between aristocrats and peasants, and business and trade were largely managed by minorities, notably Germans and Jews. Most of Eastern Europe's immediate post-war leaders were of peasant stock. Masaryk was the son of an ex-serf, the Bulgarian Agrarian Prime Minister from 1919 to 1923, Alexander Stambolisky was the son of peasant. So, too, was Engelbert Dollfuss, the Prime Minister of Austria from 1932 to 1934. Such peasant Prime Ministers helped to give Eastern European politics a populist character, moulded by romantic images of commonfolk and an intense nationalism. They were viewed with incredulity, however, if not hostility, by the old nobility who once held sway. A typical reaction was that of the Polish diplomat, Count Potocki, who described Poland's Prime Minister in 1919, Ignaz Paderewski, a concert pianist who had delighted President Wilson with his performances of Chopin, as 'a re-markable man . . . Do you know that he was born in one of my villages? And yet when I speak to him, I have absolutely the impression of conversing with an equal.'

The social legacies of the old empires contributed to the character of politics in Eastern Europe which could be divided into three, broadly defined, camps. First, there were supporters of the old nationalist movements, championed by men such as the Polish National Democrat Roman Dmowski, and characterised by bourgeois, conservative politics. Second, there were the new nationalists – led by Pilsudski in Poland, and Fan Noli in Albania, their numbers later swollen by a new 'radical right' which was even less interested than they in democratic niceties, and which borrowed from Italian Fascism and, subsequently, from German National Socialism. And finally, there were numerous peasant parties whose spokesmen argued that society should be governed in the interests of the peasant majority. This group were preoccupied with questions of land ownership and the rapidly declining prices fetched by agricultural produce.

These basic political distinctions were complicated by the large variety of languages, religions, histories and constitutions of the new nations. In Austria, Poland and the Baltic states, and to a lesser extent Czechoslovakia, the demo-cratic constitution was modelled on the Third Republic of France with its dominant legislature and weak executive. Yet even in Romania, Yugoslavia, Greece and Bulgaria, where the crown retained important powers, the political role of a parliament elected by universal suffrage became increasingly important. In most countries there was no experience of democracy, and strong support from overseas powers was absent. Instead, violence and instability became the hallmarks of politics. In Poland, for example, where civil war threatened and government changed hands 14 times from 1919 until Pilsudski launched a successful military coup in 1926, and in Bulgaria where the assassination of Stambolisky in 1923 demonstrated how fragile was the rule of law. In December 1928 King Alexander of Yugoslavia, a country riven by dissent over the constitution and the need for agricultural reform to provide improved living standards for the peasantry, who made up four-fifths of the population, announced that 'the (democratic) machine no longer works' and introduced a royal dictatorship. Romania, too, fell under complete control of its monarch, King Carol, from 1930 until his abdication in 1940, while in Albania, after bitter rivalry between Fan Noli of the progressive Popular Party and Ahmed Zogu, a local clan chieftain, democratic government fell to Zogu. A year later he heralded a Republic with himself as President. By 1928, having tired of this title, he proclaimed himself 'Zog I, King of the Albanians'.

Poland, Hungary, Bulgaria, Romania and Greece all experienced very high levels of inflation. Only Czechoslovakia in central Europe was spared. In the case of Poland and Hungary the problem was the same as that which engulfed the Weimar Republic. But the countries of Central and Eastern Europe had neither sufficient financial strength of their own, nor powerful banker friends overseas (like those of Germany) to secure the loans necessary to stabilize their currencies. Instead, the new Financial and Economic Organization of the League of Nations stepped in, helping all of them except Romania whose government decided, for reasons of national pride, that it did not want any foreign aid. This assistance marked the beginnings of a League commitment to promoting growth in the region which some countries subsequently achieved. Thus, between 1925 and 1929, the manufacturing sector grew by 48 per cent in Hungary, 36 per cent in Poland and 48 per cent in Romania. The growth levels looked impressive, but this was because these countries were starting from a low level of industrial development. Agriculture still remained much more important as a source of employment and wealth, and after the end of inflation competition from farmers in North America remained fierce, levels of productivity failed to improve and in some regions yields of the most important crops were down by as much as 13 per cent. The pattern of land ownership did not help. Many landholdings were too small to be viable. In Poland only 17 per cent of the peasant population owned farms adequate in size to earn a livelihood; in Yugoslavia two-thirds of farms measured under two hectares – the minimum necessary to sustain a family.

Eastern Europe's relations with the rest of Europe helped to shape its fate. By the end of the 1920s France's political, diplomatic and economic role in the region was increasingly challenged by German economic penetration and diplomatic involvement. Italy, too, laid claim to strong economic, cultural and political ties to the region. Far more menacing, however, was the rising popularity of new German political models, notably National Socialism, in the region. Despite its emphasis on free choice, democratic government required the creation of majorities to work effectively. Eastern Europe was bedevilled by too many conflicting and minority groups which governments were unable to contain. Only Czechoslovakia, with its relatively efficient economy, successful land reforms and strong executive, provided stable government during the 1920s, and even this rare success story, was dimmed by the economic crisis which swept Europe in 1929.

A SEMBLANCE OF STABILITY, 1925–28

Germany's continued interest in Eastern Europe was signalled by the Rapallo Treaty (April 1922) – ostensibly a Russo-German 'economic agreement' – which, at the cost of French hostility, broke the diplomatic isolation of Germany and the Soviet Union. The two outsiders of international politics established full diplomatic and consular ties and agreed to renounce all their debt claims on one another. Not only had they secured important economic markets and diplomatic contacts, they had thumbed their noses at their Western creditors, notably France. By 1924, however, Britain Italy and France had also granted *de jure* recognition to the USSR. (The USA was to recognize the Soviet government in 1933.)

In 1923 Franco-German relations, as we have seen, deteriorated further with the French invasion of the Ruhr, but many German politicians increasingly recognized that Germany would only grow stronger through co-operation with the West. Stresemann was the leading exponent of improved relations, especially with France. The crowning achievement of his career was the Treaty of Locarno, signed in December 1925 which proved his determination to use economic diplomacy and conciliation, rather than the assertive revisionism which had characterized Rapallo and the policy of passive resistance in the Ruhr, in order to effect a peaceful revision of the Versailles Treaty.

Stresemann's efforts were aided by the coincidence of a 'Cabinet of the left' in France. The French Foreign Minister, Aristide Briand, who had been Prime Minister from 1921 to 1922, shared Stresemann's view that European stability would be better served by incorporating Germany into the League of Nations and French security arrangements than by treating the German people as outcasts. In these circumstances the Treaty of Locarno, signed by Germany and France, and supported by Britain, was a landmark. It swept away the old distinction between 'Allied' and 'enemy' powers, Germany thus implicitly recognized the Versailles Treaty when it signed the Treaty of Locarno. French troops left the Ruhr, and the frontier between France and Germany was guaranteed with British support. The Treaty contained echoes of a 'European rhetoric' which was to resurface in Briand's diplomacy in 1930 and, with greater consequence, after 1945. For Stresemann 'everyone' was a citizen of Europe, 'pledged to the great cultural idea that finds expression in our continent'.

This approach was welcomed elsewhere. The Belgian government, ever anxious to promote international co-operation and European unity to guarantee its national security, called the Pact 'a decisive step towards the formation of the United States of Europe'. The optimistic signals of Locarno were confirmed in 1928 when Briand, once more French Prime Minister and the then US Secretary of State, Frank Kellogg, signed the Kellogg-Briand pact which outlawed war as an instrument of policy. To its critics, however, it amounted to little more than an 'international kiss', particularly when the United States, anxious to avoid any commitment to French security, invited all other independent powers to sign it; 65 powers eventually did so. The Soviet Union, however, remained excluded from this European reconciliation. As for Britain, it became as suspicious of French ambitions to revise Versailles as of Germany's revisionist rhetoric, and by 1928 the Royal Airforce had drafted plans for an attack on France should it violate Locarno.

Improved international relations at and after Locarno were enhanced, if not fostered, by the apparent recovery of the European economy. The Soviet NEP (New Economic Policy) encouraged the USSR to trade overseas after Lenin instructed that 'Communists must learn to trade', while in the West, the Dawes plan, an aid scheme for which its progenitor, Charles Dawes,

Coolidge's Vice-President received the Nobel Peace Prize in 1925, was followed by a massive infusion of American capital into Germany. The country received far more American money than it paid in reparations, and through the plan the USA was locked into the rise or fall of Europe's economy. Meanwhile, Belgium, Italy, Czechoslovakia, France and Yugoslavia all signed parallel new war debt schedules with the USA, and France, too, managed to bring runaway inflation under control in 1926. Many countries in Europe showed a determination to return to the gold standard, as Britain did in 1925. Its supporters believed that it would limit inflation, make trade easier, and remove uncertainty from the world's money markets. Yet there was considerable criticism of the return to gold in Britain, which had been carried through by Churchill, then Chancellor of the Exchequer, his critics complaining that this made British exports uncompetitive.

Elsewhere in Europe the levels of trade had increased to their pre-1914 level by the years after Locarno, with industrial products notably in much greater demand than agricultural output. Trade within and beyond Europe also benefited from the loosening of government economic controls, although the plight of Europe's farmers soon encouraged tariff walls to rise again. Many of the wartime economic controls were abolished in the rush to return to the freedom of pre-war business transactions, despite the fact that government interest in planning remained, notably in the Soviet Union, Germany, Hungary and Czechoslovakia.

Europe, to use the language of the time, appeared to have turned the corner, and although prosperity remained patchy, signs of optimism began to emerge. Material progress was evident as modern technology brought electric cookers, toasters and tinned food into the home, a more comfortable place than it had been in 1914. The Weimar government helped build almost two million new houses and there was an extensive public housing policy in Britain too.

With greater social security and more adequate educational provision, a 'modern' life seemed now more acceptable. It included more leisure, although much of it was used for escape. Hollywood, with many of its stars coming from Europe, influenced America-European relations as much as the Dawes Plan. Most people visited their local cinemas ('picture houses') at least once a week, and a large number of European countries, notably France, Germany, Italy and Britain, developed their own film industries. Radio, a new force in the 1920s, was organized on national lines, as were some of the large circulation, popular newspapers which, some claimed, contributed to the formation of a more democratic society. They provided not only news but entertainment and, not least advertising which promoted consumer booms.

FRAGILE FOUNDATIONS, 1929

The dislocation of the post-war decade liberated and promoted an unprecedented flourishing of artistic activity which reflected the uneasy coexistence of the modern and traditional. While the architect, Walter Gropius of The Bauhaus movement, excited by the challenge of urban life, was determined to design buildings that would 'avert mankind's enslavement by machine', conservative writers wrote urgently of the importance of the family and of tradition, and young men and women joined movements like the German *Wandervogel* to explore the countryside and sing folk songs. The boy scout movement, founded in Britain by Robert, later Lord, Baden Powell, a hero of the Boer War, became international. He founded 'girl guides' too and 'wolf cubs'.

Nevertheless, Europe's relative prosperity – like the fortunes of its youth – was fragile. The peace of 1919 had satisfied no one, Locarno did not reduce all the international tensions any more than prosperity reduced all internal tensions. Each European nation continued to jostle with its neighbours to assert its own national interest. France continued to regard Germany with a wary eye, and fresh anxieties surfaced after the death of Stresemann in October 1929. (It was reported that Paris received the news of his death 'as though the greatest living Frenchman had died'.) The French were suspicious too of Italian expansionist ambitions in Central and Eastern Europe, while British relations with France remained prone to misunderstanding and ill-will. In the relative prosperity of the 1920s this rivalry posed no threat.

Europe's economy also showed signs of potential weakness. Debt burdens were high, and much of the money owed was used unproductively. In Hungary in 1928, for example, more than 40 per cent of the foreign investment that flowed into Hungary went straight back out again to pay off existing debts. The same was true for 28 per cent of the foreign money entering Poland. More than finance was involved. Throughout the 1920s, before and after Locarno persistently large numbers of Europe's working class remained unemployed. Even in comparatively wealthy Britain unemployment never dropped below the level of one million and in Germany it averaged one-and-a-half million from 1926–9. The figures for Scandinavia were more dramatic. Between 1925 and 1929 in Norway, the state registered almost 20 per cent of workers as unemployed and in Denmark the figure was close to 19 per cent. (The real jobless figures were even higher.) The alleged beneficiaries of the 'new order', workers in employment, often perceived their new won freedoms as illusory. Working conditions were still poor, with most employees working 10–12 hours a day. Housing provision, too, remained inadequate, and in continental Europe – the term generally used in Britain – frustration with democracy was often translated into increased recruitment for the Communist Party.

A rising swell of support for the radical left was matched by a further rise of the 'new' right as disaffected elements in 'traditional' European society, the lower middle class, the artisans and the large landowners, turned to it to give vent to their discontent. In the 'revisionist' states of Germany, Hungary and Austria, in particular, democratic politics took a negative and destructive character, with politicians well able to criticize and destroy democratic politics but offering little constructive in its place. It was into this vacuum that the radical right, with Germany's National Socialists in the vanguard, were to fill with their own brand of 'revolution'. As the Earl of Birkenhead, a former Conservative minister and close friend of Churchill, prophetically cautioned in 1930:

> Will Germany's rancour die down with the flux of time or will some unforeseen and untoward incident upset the balance of power? Then Germany might stretch out a hand to clutch at Poland and all Europe once again will be dragged in.

By then the European economy had crashed. So, too, had the economy of the United States, which had enjoyed a huge boom between 1925 and 1929. Most American people had come to believe by 1929 that their new found prosperity was permanent and assured and their boundless optimism was reflected in a stock market boom of unprecedented dimensions. On 1 January 1925 the total value of all shares on the New York Stock Exchange was around $27 million.

Four years later, the value exceeded $67 million – an increase of over 250 per cent. When Herbert Hoover accepted the presidential nomination for the Republican party in 1928, he spoke for millions of Americans as he declared: 'We shall soon with the help of God be in sight of the day when poverty will be banished from all the nation.' Hoover would have done well to exercise greater caution. Within a year of his speech there were clear signs that all was not well in the American economy itself, and a Wall Street crash – on 'Black Thursday', 24 October 1929, almost 13 million shares changed hands at vastly reduced prices, shook American confidence to the core. The only diversion from the terrible news for the crowds amassed in front of the stock exchange on Wall Street was the spectacle of a would-be suicide balanced on a nearby skyscraper.

Notes

1. R. Hart-Davies (ed.), *The Autobiography of Arthur Ransome* (1976), p.299.
2. M. Stopes (ed.), *Mother England. A Contemporary History* (1929), p.24.
3. Quoted in A. Gill, *A Dance Between Flames. Berlin Between the Wars* (1993), p.256.

Chapter 8

GUNS AND BUTTER, 1929–1939

The Great Depression, a world slump unprecedented in scale, which followed the Wall Street Crash, left a profound impact upon European history. Its effects lingered on throughout the 1930s until Europe was engulfed by tragedy of a different order – the Second World War. There had been only a superficial economic recovery by then, for in 1937 the European economy began to turn down once more and its people were saved from further unemployment and deprivation only by an increase in expenditure on rearmament. It was poor consolation for the workers of Lille and Sheffield to find jobs in factories when it became increasingly clear that more military orders signified the likelihood of a European war which promised to be even more terrifying than the last.

As 'moderate' politicians struggled and failed between 1929 and 1933 to find effective answers to mass unemployment, in Germany, Britain and France there were dramatic political consequences. In Britain the Labour government elected in 1929 collapsed and a so-called National Government was set up under the same Prime Minister, James Ramsey MacDonald, treated as a traitor by his former colleagues. France, with a political system which failed to throw up a coalition government, endured 11 different cabinets in four years between 1932 and 1936. There were also numerous national budget crises.

'Bread and butter' issues came to dominate political argument. How could farmers secure a reasonable price for their produce in a world of falling prices? How could workers in Europe's cities find enough work to buy food? The depression disrupted diplomatic relations also as the severity of the world slump pushed countries to protect their national interest above all else through discrimination, tariffs and import quotas. The globe was divided into protected and warring trading blocs, and it was in an atmosphere of intense economic competition, sometimes between nations that shared diplomatic interests – like Britain, France and the USA – that German National Socialism, triumphant in 1933, Italian Fascism and Japanese Imperialism sought to extend their power. For Germany, Italy and Japan, taking pride in their peoples' 'racial superiority', economic nationalism was a step on the road to the creation of empires.

CAUSES OF THE GREAT DEPRESSION

The causes of the depression were complex. The European 'Slump', the term the Europeans used at the time, although the American 'Great Depression' has come to take its place in the history books, did not originate in the USA. But the shock of the Wall Street crash in stock and share prices immediately affected Europe adversely, just as American economic involvement had buoyed the European economy in the 1920s. At the most elementary level, the European economy had still not entirely adjusted to long-term, structural changes in the world economy wrought or accelerated by the First World War. There had been a considerable unemployment problem in Europe in the 1920s as it faced fierce economic competition not only from the United States but from Japan. Competition was aggravated by the growing uncompetitiveness of German, and to a lesser extent, British labour. From 1925 until 1930 real wages in Germany grew considerably, at a rate of 4.6 per cent per annum. Productivity did not. Among Britain's 'old industries' textiles faced as many problems as iron and steel, coal and shipbuilding. The official *History of Munitions*, published in 1922, described British manufacturers as 'behind other countries in research, plant and method . . . with competition becoming impossible'.

By early 1929 most policy-makers in Italy, France, Germany, Britain and some in the United States recognized that the upswing in the world economy had come to an end. Demand for machinery was falling. So too was demand for wines from France and for new housing in Britain. To the German-born economist Josef Schumpeter, fascinated by the coexistence of capitalism and socialism and by the relationship of both to democracy, the depression was both cyclical and structural. To the Russian-born economist Nikolai Kondratieff this was the end of a long economic cycle covering 50 years.

The causes of the initial downturn in prices and production in 1928/9 were not the same as the causes which led to the recession becoming the most protracted and profound economic depression of the twentieth century. There were four distinct elements in the situation – the loss of American investment in Europe; the collapse of world primary prices and the subsequent rise in trade protectionism; the clinging to the gold standard – Britain was the first power to abandon it in 1931, while France and Italy stuck by it until 1936; and the failure of politicians to promote international, as distinct from national, initiatives for economic recovery. As the shadows of depression fell across Europe each nation was determined to secure its own interests following what became known as 'beggar-thy-neighbour' policies.

American loans had helped to paper over some of the cracks in Europe's economy before 1929, and many politicians failed to appreciate fully the degree to which their national prosperity had become dependent on that of their European neighbours and the United States. They now became increasingly visible. The prosperity of Germany, of all the European powers, was dependent on a stream of American Dawes plan credit which stimulated not only German economic growth, but that of the central and eastern European nations around it, and the stream ominously began to dry up in 1928. The United States, whose intervention in the First World War had been decisive, now had a decisive and this time destructive impact on the whole of Europe after 1929.

It was ironic that American credit to Europe evaporated not because of economic weakness, but rather because of economic success in the USA. From 1924 to 1928 American investors had been drawn to Europe by high rates of interest, but by late 1928 it had become clear to them that they could make even more money by investing in the American stock market. The stream of gold began to converge on Wall Street in 1928 while credit became scarce in Europe. American overseas investment fell from $2,214 million in 1928 to $1,414 million in 1929 (in 1930 it was to fall to $363 million). In a vain attempt to retain foreign investment Germany, Britain, Italy, Hungary, Poland and Yugoslavia, among others increased their discount (interest) rates, but this was a step that made it more expensive for the weaker economic powers (as well as their own businessmen) to borrow money in London, Berlin and Paris to replace the loss of American credit. A dangerous chain reaction began.

THE EUROPEAN SLUMP, 1929–36

Different European countries hit economic rock bottom at different times over the next four years. The first misguided policy decision came in the United States where American bankers believed that Wall Street's melt-down had been triggered by too much cheap money (loans granted at a low rate of interest) sloshing around within the economy. This interference prompted the Federal Reserve Bank of New York to increase base lending rates making it more expensive to borrow money, an action which made the depression more severe as consumer demand and business investment now dried up altogether. The British economist Keynes, whose ideas were to influence economic policies after 1945 was in no doubt: 'the fall of investment . . . I find – and I find without doubt or reservation whatsoever – the whole explanation for the current state of affairs'. It was only as the depression progressed that the Americans and British, the world's largest financial powers, gradually reduced their interest rates and introduced a policy of cheap money, a policy which helped to revive industry and to stimulate demand.

Without American investment after 1929 Europe's banks became increasingly unstable. Representatives from Eastern and Central Europe – Germany, Poland, Austria, and Czechoslovakia – now came to London, instead of New York, in search of loans just at a time when Britain was least able to provide them. Matters came to a head in May 1931 when Austria's largest commercial bank, the Creditanstalt, collapsed. A banking crisis quickly followed in Germany.

European bankers were not the only businesses with problems, and as banks appeared unsafe, frightened Germans and Austrians began to withdraw investments and savings to hoard and, it was said, to hide them under beds and, it was said, in chamber-pots and tea-caddies. At the heart of Europe's difficulties lay the global collapse not in the prices of stocks and shares, but in primary prices (notably the price of wheat, meat, coal and steel). During the 1920s agricultural prices had already fallen between 20 per cent and 50 per cent. After October 1929 this trend continued and accelerated. With over 67 per cent of the world's active population still engaged in agriculture, falling prices spelt disaster and had several important consequences.

At the most obvious level European farmers became politically militant and began agitating anxiously for governments to address their plight. As a result, the governments of France, Germany and Spain, amongst others, began to modify and increase protectionist measures which were already in place in the 1920s, seeking to protect their disgruntled farmers behind walls of tariffs, export quotas, depreciated currencies and (sometimes bogus) sanitary regulations. In 1931 the Nazi publication *Der Deutsche Volkswirt* (*The German Economist*) wrote, in typically florid prose, of the 'bondage of tariffs tearing into the body of international trade', a sentiment difficult to challenge. German import duties soon increased by over 50 per cent, by 1932 French quotas covered more than 3,000 goods, and a small European country, Romania, imposed quotas on 80 per cent of its imports.

The most dramatic transition to protectionism took place in Britain. With the withdrawal in October 1931 of many of the Liberals in MacDonald's National Government, including his Chancellor of the Exchequer, Philip Snowden, and one of his few Labour colleagues to stay with him, the British government finally decided to abandon its historic promotion of free trade, and following the depreciation of sterling in September 1931, the government passed a series of tariff acts, including the General Tariff in April 1932 and the Imperial Protection Agreements signed in Ottawa in August of the same year. Yet the protectionism was limited. Imperial preference did not mean that the British had plans to make the Empire self-sufficient. By 1932 the mercantilist concept of an industrialized mother country linked to primary producer countries had become grossly anachronistic. The Dominions had begun to industrialize and would have resented such a paternal approach from Britain.

For frustrated national-imperialists in Germany and Italy, however, Britain's move towards Empire appeared to emphasize the inequality created by the Versailles Treaty between the *have* and *have not* powers, and a sense of injustice was compounded when nationalists in Germany and Italy surveyed the remainder of the globe during the Depression years. France fostered its imperial connections in North Africa and the 'B' mandate territories of Eastern Togoland and the Eastern Cameroons, while Japan established a protectorate in Manchuria in 1931, and the United States showed renewed commercial interest in Central and South America. Mussolini fantasized a

Second Roman Empire in the Mediterranean, while for Hitler, no more concerned with acquiring colonies than Bismarck, Germany's imperial destiny lay on its doorstep – the security of *Lebensraum* (living space) for the German people in Eastern Europe.

The division of Europe into exclusive trading blocs was compounded and accelerated by currency instability. This was all too apparent in the summer of 1931 when pressure increased on the pound sterling and the Labour government fell. The confidence of investors who owned large amounts of sterling began to evaporate amidst mounting political and economic uncertainty, and they began to convert their paper pounds into gold. Gold, in turn, began to drain from the Bank of England at an uncontrollable rate and, on the 20 September 1931, the Bank's Governor, Montagu Norman, announced that the British government had decided to float the pound. Sterling was no longer on the gold standard, and countries which had large reserves of sterling – Britain's Empire and Dominion partners, and Scandinavia – quickly floated their currencies too. Once Britain was off the gold standard, prices at home began to rise, but British exports became more competitive overseas.

While Britain declared that it had been 'forced' off gold, Franklin D. Roosevelt, who became President of the USA in 1933, deliberately chose to float the United States dollar as part of his New Deal recovery measures on which he had fought his Presidential campaign. By the end of the year the dollar had depreciated by around 40 per cent, American domestic prices had improved, and jobless figures had begun to fall. This American recovery helped sponsor a rally in the world economy as a whole. US citizens gradually regained their appetite for overseas imports, and it gradually became possible once more to borrow money for investment.

Abandoning the gold standard was not, then, the recipe for economic disaster which many critics believed it would be in the inter-war period. But there were still gold bloc nations (France, Italy, Poland, the Netherlands, and Switzerland among them), which stuck with the gold standard, their leaders believing that it had helped to generate prosperity in the 1920s and that to abandon it would destroy their economies. There were other countries, like Germany and Hungary which remained on the gold standard, while circumventing some of the 'golden rules' governing its operation, because they were terrified of encouraging inflation within their economies. Through the relative under-valuation of the French franc and the predominance of agriculture in France (unemployment was more easily concealed in the countryside), the depression came to France relatively late, and although by 1934 it had taken hold with a vengeance, it was only in 1936 that France finally devalued the franc, and then with bitter regret.

Italy, like France, proved a stalwart supporter of the gold bloc. For Mussolini the much vaunted 'Battle for the Lira' in 1927, had been more than a struggle to defeat 'the moral disgrace and economic disaster of a bankrupt lira'. According to him 'the fate of the regime' was 'tied to the fate of the lira'; a stabilized currency was a reflection of Italy's determination to achieve

Great Power status in economic and diplomatic terms. (The *Duce* also used stabilization to force through price and wage cuts for Italian workers.)

THE INTERNATIONAL AND NATIONAL RESPONSES, 1929–32

In the rush by politicians to preserve national economies, international efforts to revive the world economy were stillborn. Britain, France, Germany, Italy, Belgium, the Netherlands and Austria, among others, continued to express the need for international economic co-operation to tackle the rising levels of international protectionism and competitive currency depreciation, but in practice efforts at international co-operation were, all too frequently, stymied by domestic priorities.

After the failure of the 1927 Conference to tackle the growth of protectionism in Europe, the next concerted effort at international co-operation came in the depths of the depression with what was described as a 'momentous' Hoover Moratorium. In June 1931 President Hoover announced that Europe could postpone its debt payments to the United States for 12 months and this, in turn, enabled Britain and France to forego German reparations for that year. 'Momentous' or not the European economy failed to improve, and at a Lausanne Conference held in June 1932, German reparations were finally abolished and with them the hated 'war guilt' clause which had accompanied reparations in the Treaty of Versailles.

From the Lausanne Conference grew the initiative for a second World Economic Conference. This was an unprecedented gathering. Sixty-five nations came to deliberate the condition of the world economy in London's newly opened Geological Museum in the summer of 1933, but the Conference soured, rather than improved, the economic and diplomatic climate. Representatives were more anxious to preserve protectionist measures they had already introduced than to secure any loosening of international restrictions. Britain, for example, was anxious to preserve its tariff levels and the depreciated status of the pound, while the United States wanted the freedom to depreciate the dollar further. Many European delegates, particularly those from Eastern Europe, returned embittered, therefore, from London. Dependent as they were on the good offices of their larger European neighbours, the prognosis for them had been poor. The productivity of their farmers, the biggest element of their population and their economies, was far lower than that of west European farmers. In Bulgaria, for example, there were around 450,000 wooden ploughs to 250,000 made of iron in 1936 while Yugoslav and Romanian farmers spread 0.2 kilograms of fertilizer per hectare of land, their Dutch counterparts used 311 kilograms.

Eastern Europe, inextricably drawn as it was into the network of European financial relations, could find no help overseas during the 1930s. The League of Nations, which had proved a useful source of economic and financial help in the 1920s, was now ineffectual and the world's greatest financial powers – the United States, Britain and France also failed to provide economic support. As for Eastern Europe's powerful near neighbours, they were first pre-occupied with their own problems, but in time they came to threaten the very territorial integrity of Europe's newest nation states. In the wake of the depression, competition, not co-operation, became Europe's watchword, despite the fact that the symptoms of the slump were the same across Europe, no common approach to them emerged.

European governments chose national and generally ineffective policies to defeat the Great Depression. In the winter of 1929 their politicians could not foresee how serious it was to become, any more than they had been able to foresee the character of the First World War. Governments evolved and modified their economic policies as each new crisis unfolded. For all of them the experience of the 1920s helped to condition their response. Politicians were certainly not reluctant to get their hands dirty in managing the economy. In many European nations, including Sweden, Italy, Britain and Hungary, government intervention had increased greatly already during the 1920s, and even in Hungary, which had amongst the most liberal economic policy in the Balkans, there was strong pressure to extend government involvement. By 1931 the Hungarian state owned many large industrial enterprises like the Diósgyör iron and steel works, and the Nitrokemia gunpowder factory.

For some European governments the Depression revived notions of economic planning which had been hastily abandoned at the end of the First World War. In Germany, Italy, Hungary and Romania, for example, the metaphors of war returned with talk of industrial and agrarian 'fronts', 'shock' workers and recovery 'campaigns'. But despite greater levels of political economic management, strict financial orthodoxy prevailed, and in Germany the dominant fear was that the hyper-inflation of 1923 would return to destroy the economy. There were new ideas of what to do – in Sweden for example (see below p.246) – but in Britain Keynes, who produced a new theory of employment in 1936, was left to observe mass unemployment rather than to participate in reducing it. In Britain unemployment rose from 12 per cent in the 1920s to 15.4 per cent from 1930–38 while in Germany the jobless total was even more startling, reaching a peak of almost six million in 1932. After 1933 unemployment was reduced in Germany, Sweden, Italy and Hungary, partly through increases in government expenditure.

The Great Depression was a global crisis which left few unscathed, and unemployment was indiscriminate, hitting blue-collar, white-collar and professional groups alike. Many people found themselves out of work for three or even four years, with younger age groups hit disproportionately hard. Infant mortality began to rise and young men began to experience the negative, social and psychological effects of being 'out of work'. Widespread joblessness could have as devastating an effect on communities as on individuals. Jarrow in the North-East of England became a symbol. In Hamburg, almost half of all young men between the ages of 20 and 25 found themselves among the long-term unemployed. Even the Soviet Union, while proclaiming loudly that the depression sounded the death-knell of capitalism, found that its economy was not entirely insulated from the slump's devastating effects.

Mass unemployment contributed to political extremism in complex ways, but in many countries it was political parties to the far Left and Right who proved the main beneficiaries.

BRITAIN AND GERMANY: A CONTRAST

Britain's National Government, though headed by a former Labour Party politician and prime minister, MacDonald, was a product of the crisis. The ministers in Ramsay MacDonald's Labour government of 1929 to 1931, like their luckless socialist counterparts in Germany and France, had no new weapons to combat the economic slump. Nor did they agree on how to resolve the spending demands of social welfare provision, with existing budgetary methods of economic management. Jimmy Thomas, a trade unionist who was MacDonald's Minister for 'Unemployment', could do little to control it. When it became clear that the Labour government was to adopt cautious and conservative strategies to defeat the depression, Thomas' deputy, Sir Oswald Mosley, resigned from the government and the party to pursue a more sensationalist career in British politics becoming founder of a so-called 'New Party' and later the British Union of Fascists.

In the summer of 1931, while central European financial systems wobbled and sometimes crashed, Britain's political and economic problems reached fever pitch. Sir Clive Wigram, private secretary to George V, warned the King that 'We are sitting on top of a volcano'. The foreboding atmosphere was enhanced by an official report by the May Committee which pointed to serious problems in Britain's industry and finance, and estimated that by April 1932 the British government would be £120 million in the red. The committee urged the Labour government to increase taxes and introduce economies, largely by cutting unemployment benefit. It was the May Committee's call for reduced unemployment benefits that split the Labour party, leading MacDonald, after two visits to the King, to head a National Government composed of individuals rather than parties, as a temporary expedient to settle the financial crisis. Instead, events that summer heralded what were to be nine years of Conservative government beneath a National Government banner. In the long run the Labour Party recovered and consolidated its position in the years which followed the split, but in the short term the crisis was by no means over.

To observers overseas and at home it appeared that dramatic changes were afoot as Britain followed the depreciation of the pound with its series of tariff acts designed to protect British trade. The closest Britain ever came to a dramatic political upheaval, however, was on 15 September 1931 when

12,000 sailors refused to work after they heard that their pay was to be cut (the wage cuts were uneven: a 3.7 per cent reduction for lieutenant commanders, with up to a 13.6 per cent cut for unmarried Able-Bodied Seamen). Some fearful voices compared this incident at Invergordon to the Krondstadt rebellion in 1917 which had preceded the Russian Revolution, but the Depression never seriously threatened the stability of British political life.

After the depreciation of sterling in 1931 the British economy began to show tentative signs of revival, a recovery which was made all the more dramatic by the economic collapse which continued to grip Germany, France and the United States. Political extremes, like the National Unemployed Workers' Movement on the Left and Mosley's British Union of Fascists, were successful only in areas where unemployment remained high and British politics did not take an anti-democratic or revolutionary path. The country had a strong parliamentary tradition, sound financial and banking institutions, and a trust in the virtues of the British people. Indeed, there was a widespread feeling that British democracy was 'superior'. As MacDonald's successor as Prime Minister, the Conservative leader Stanley Baldwin, serving a second term, put it, England was 'the only country where parliamentary government has grown up, the only country . . . where it is flesh of our flesh and bone of our bone.'

It was in Germany, where parliamentary government could make no such claims, that liberal democracy faced its greatest test. Here, however, the Left was unequal to the challenge of the depression, but here, too, there were forces on the Right whose strength and character were not paralleled in Britain. In the spring of 1930 a Great Coalition, dominated by the SPD and led by Hermann Müller, failed to weather the economic storm, and the last SPD government of the Weimar period collapsed in the spring of 1930. Although the Left continued to command substantial support in the *Reichstag* – the KPD (German Communist Party) and the SPD together held more seats than the NSDAP in November 1932 – the SPD and KPD did not join forces to defeat the Right (the German Communists had been forbidden to do so by their Stalinist directors in Moscow). But, as in Britain and France, Germany's socialists were also impeded by their economic principles. As in Britain, they were wedded to balancing the national budget, which inevitably entailed cutting unemployment benefit and the pay of public employees.

Germany's budgetary difficulties had been made more acute by the expansion of German social security legislation in 1927. Whereas social expenditure had amounted to 19.3 per cent of all public expenditures in 1913, in 1930 it was 40.3 per cent. Successive German Chancellors were faced with the dilemma of ever rising unemployment benefit payments while their income from taxation was falling because of business failure and declining income tax yields. Consequentially, in March 1930, when unemployment stood at a new high of over three million and the Nazis had collected over 107 seats in the German Reichstag, a new Right-wing coalition under Heinrich Brüning took office. Chancellor Brüning quickly introduced draconian measures to rescue the German economy, rigorously cutting government expenditure, at the same raising levels of taxation. He seemed to have few policy alternatives given the German electorate's deep fear of inflation and the dearth of foreign investment available to Germany, but his inevitably harsh measures made him few friends within the German electorate.

Lower middle-class businessmen saw profits slump, salaried public employees saw their wages cut – the income of a petty bureaucrat earning 260 marks per month in 1927 was slashed to 202 marks by 1932 – farmers were unable to sell their produce, some industrialists went bankrupt, and the unemployment figures continued to rise. Every social class in Germany was affected. In order to distract hostility at home and hopefully provide an alternative remedy to Germany's economic downturn, Brüning began to pursue a vigorous foreign policy for the abolition of German reparation payments and modifications to the military restrictions imposed on Germany by the peace of Versailles, but in May 1931 matters grew even worse when there was a run on German banks. Large amounts of foreign and German money now fled Weimar and now there was even less money available for investment and loans. But, as was not the case in Britain or France in 1936, neither Brüning nor his successors as Chancellor Franz von Papen, Kurt von Schleicher in 1932 and Adolf Hitler in 1933, ever entertained the possibility of devaluing the Reichsmark for fear of the political repercussions. Indeed, currency devaluation had been outlawed by the 1924 Young Plan.

By early 1932 it was clear that Brüning's measures were having little effect. German unemployment had risen to six million, and one in five Germans was out of work. The year 1932 was a hungry and demoralizing year for many people and for the Weimar Republic a disastrous year as faith in it was further undermined by the activities of Germany's political elites – the army, the judiciary and landowners. As in Britain, it was centre liberal parties which lost out as the German political scene began to fragment with dire consequences. While in Britain the constitution held fast, in the Weimar republic the political constitution too began to fail.

Divisions in the business classes increased as Brüning's government introduced legislation to protect the small shop-owner, in response to harsher economic realities, German big business began to strengthen cartels to keep up prices. This move, in turn, was resented by those who had to pay more for their goods, notably other members of the middle classes and working classes. Big business, despite its reputation for actively assisting Hitler to power, was in reality a passive contributor to Hitler's success. True, it had no allegiance to Weimar and its representatives were prepared to tolerate and even support anti-democratic and anti-parliamentary rule, but businessmen did not automatically fly into the arms of the National Socialist Party.

German farmers also became divided in the harsh economic climate. The small peasant farmer grew indignant at the preferential treatment accorded to the Junkers (large Prussian landowners) and the trend towards small, specialized splinter parties – facilitated by Weimar's electoral system of proportional representation – accelerated during the first two years of the depression. Parties like the Christian-National Peasants and Farmers' Party, the Green Party, the German Peasants' Party and even the 'Militant League of Beggars', began to collect votes. And while German workers took to the streets demanding jobs, conservative groups began to claim that Germany stood under threat of imminent 'bolshevization'. Both the Communists and the Nazis, drawing on the sense of frustration and helplessness felt by disaffected young men, formed a number of paramilitary organizations that spied on, and intimidated their opponents.

Violence became endemic. The Red Front Fighters' League was banned by the German government in 1929, but continued as an underground group while the Proletarian Self-Defence Force was formed in 1930, boasting a secret, cell-based inner cadre similar to that deployed by the Bolsheviks in Russia before 1917. Police attempts to impose order in Communist-dominated areas in Germany's cities and towns were met by attacks from rooftop snipers, and ordinary policemen were frequently assassinated. In August 1931 three policemen were murdered outside the Babylon cinema near the Bülowplatz in Berlin. The Nazis were not above such attacks. While they preferred to direct their violence against Communists, Socialists, Jews and foreigners – they terrorized whole towns and city districts – they also waged personalized campaigns against particular individuals, like the vendetta pursued against the Berlin Police Chief Bernard 'Isidor' Weiss. The Nazi Sturm Abteiling (SA) or brownshirts as they were known because of the colour of their uniform shirts, demonstrated an alarming capacity for violence and cunning. They often staged attacks on their own offices, lashing out at their opponents to create the illusion that they were responding to Communist provocation. The German electorate was thus becoming radicalised, drawn to the political extremes of the right and left for an answer to economic distress, and more terrorized too. Civil war seemed imminent.

As Brüning found his political support wearing thin, he, like his predecessors, increasingly employed emergency decrees to avoid the need to secure a majority in the Reichstag. Thus, German democracy was being undermined already before Hitler came to power. In June 1932, when Papen became Chancellor, few mourned Brüning's parting. Even the Americans condemned him as 'ascetic, scholastic, fanatic and despotic', but neither Chancellor Papen nor his successor Schleicher remained in office for long. They could not muster sufficient support in the Reichstag to withstand 'no-confidence' votes now that the National Socialists and the Communists commanded over 50 per cent of the Reichstag. On 30 January 1933 the Nazi party came to power, therefore, and that at a time when their electoral support had actually been declining, and their party funds were running low.

Hitler proved to be the politician to square the circle of German interest group politics. He actively courted small peasant farmers, for instance, and within the first six months of holding office, the Nazis introduced protective measures to favour the peasant farming over export industry. He silenced businessmen with promises of German rearmament and threats of civil war if they failed to support the National Socialists. Germany was revived by lavish rhetoric. The subordination of labour to the state enabled employers to push down wage costs (they fell by around 24 per cent over the next four years), while much publicized public works schemes reduced unemployment. It is important to note, however, that Hitler did not abandon orthodox economics – the Reichsmark was not devalued and money supply was kept constrained. In its remarkable rise to power, the National Socialist Party had successfully harnessed what has been termed the 'coalition of no' with its promises of 'bread and work'.

Like Mussolini, Hitler was also able to rally Germany's youth to his cause. Both leaders were relatively young (Mussolini was 39 when he became Prime Minister, Adolf Hitler 44 years old when appointed Chancellor), and both seemed dynamic in temperament. They conducted their juvenile highly organized propaganda drives in an atmosphere of passion and violence, boasting that, in Mussolini's words, 'fascist ideas were the ideas of the age'.

THE SPECIAL CASE OF SWEDEN

Germany's economic recovery when it came under the Nazis had important implications for its trading partners, notably in Eastern Europe and Scandinavia. Eastern Europe was penetrated increasingly by German political ideas and economic policies, while the economies of Scandinavia, notably that of Sweden, benefited from Germany's revived appetite for raw materials. Swedish iron ore exports grew from 3 million tonnes in 1933 to 12.5 million tonnes in 1939 – over 70 per cent of this ore was shipped to Germany.

Sweden, the most industrialized Scandinavian economy, was exceptional in that it adopted less conventional, and more successful, policies for tackling the depression which attracted the interest of German and American economists at the time and historians ever since. Politicians listened to Swedish economists, notably Bertil Ohlin and Gunner Myrdal, who advocated greater state intervention and expenditure to stimulate demand, and their ideas were adopted with gusto by a 1932 coalition government dominated by the Social Democratic Party. This government and its economic policies marked a sharp break with the past orthodoxy, even on the part of Swedish Social Democrats, as the new finance minister, Ernst Wigfors, implemented radical and innovative recovery strategies. Sweden's tax burden was redistributed and the government's budget deficit was balanced over a number of years (around three to four) rather than year by year. This increased the amount of revenue available to the government, and the revenue was then ploughed back into the economy by public work projects and subsidised building schemes. Contemporary estimates suggest that around 40,000 jobs had been created by 1934/5. It took time for the benefits of these programmes to be felt.

Even in Sweden, where these policies, often described as 'Keynesian', had found a receptive audience, the benefits of currency depreciation, low interest rates, price stability and the recovery of German and British export markets (especially as the drive for rearmament accelerated) was as important as deficit spending to its economic recovery. Sweden's depression was undoubtedly serious, as the suicide of well-known industrialist Ivar Kreuger (March 1932) and a bitter labour strike (from April 1933 until February 1934) testified, but a stable political environment, an innovative policy response, its small, open economy and international recovery also contributed towards Sweden's exemplary recovery from the depression.

FRANCE, 1932–38

The same could not be said for France. Developments in Germany may have offered temporary benefits to the Swedes, but were viewed with mounting anxiety by the French, many of whom began to fear not only a resurgent Germany, but for the stability of liberal democracy within France itself. As we have seen, the French Republic was slower than Britain or Germany to feel the full impact of the Great Depression and its comparative good fortune earned it the nickname 'L'ile heureuse' (the fortunate island), but by 1932 the French economy was in obvious difficulties. As the depression began to bite, the political climate became increasingly unstable. Like Germany, France had introduced proportional representation after the First World War, and from 1932 onwards, its government became fragmented. There were varying shades of radicals, radical-socialists, socialists, conservatives and nationalists.

In June 1932 Edouard Herriot, a Radical, came to office. He lasted for six months, defeated over the issue of cutting national expenditure to balance the national budget and France's failure to meet its war debt payment to the United States; his successor Edouard Daladier, a radical socialist who had been a history lecturer at the Lycée Condorcet, lasted nine months. This pattern was to become typical in a political system which was hijacked by narrow coalitions focused on individuals like Herriot, Daladier and the radical Camille Chautemps. Although French democracy did not fall prey to anything as extreme as National Socialism, by early 1934 the Radical and Socialist parties were increasingly discredited by a series of political scandals and by their failure to initiate any effective policy to spare France from the worst effects of the depression.

Fascist movements began to flourish in France too. Popular right-wing, anti-semitic and nationalistic politicians found a ready audience amongst lower middle-class Frenchmen who feared marxism and resented the Third Republic which had allowed this 'fifth column' to grow. In 1934, some 370,000 people – set against 35,000 Communists – belonged to four separate French fascist movements (Action Française, the Légion, Jeunesses Patriotes and the Faisceau). The ideologies of French fascism were influenced by foreign fascist movements, but they had an older pedigree. Much of its anti-semitism dated back to the Dreyfus case, while anti-parliamentarianism and support for the army grew out of the conservative backlash to the liberalism and socialism prevalent in France in the late-nineteenth century.

In February of the same year bloody fighting broke out on the streets of Paris as right-wing demonstrators marched in protest against the new Radical government led by Daladier. People threw marbles under the hooves of horses, slashed horses' bellies with razor blades and tore up iron-railings from the streets. Two years – and several right-wing cabinets later – the French Left (Radicals, Socialists and Communists) finally united to defend the Republic, and in May 1936 the Popular Front, a coalition of left-wing parties, came to power although Communists did not join the cabinet. Drawing an important lesson from the fatal divisions amongst the German Left, French Communists and socialists had bound together to save France from increasingly subversive elements. The German remilitarization of the Rhineland and a physical assault on socialist leader Léon Blum by the Action Française in the early months of 1936 had reinforced the sense of danger to the Third Republic.

Under the leadership of Blum, born in 1872, a noted literary and drama critic and horseracing buff before entering politics as Secretary to Jaurès, the Popular Front introduced economic and social measures which were popular with French workers, but such economic recovery as there was came almost by accident when the Popular Front was forced to devalue the French Franc in September 1936 by around 25–33 per cent. Without a vigorous recovery programme, the devaluation had limited effect, although the election of the first declaredly socialist government stood out as a significant milestone in French political history. Nevertheless, in May 1937, the French economy took a tail spin and the Popular Front collapsed in disarray over whether it could afford to give French workers a 40-hour week. Blum was defeated by the conservative Senate's refusal to grant the extraordinary powers he required to carry through his economic programme and by the collapse of support among his Radical coalition supporters. 'I've had enough', he complained, 'All I have tried to do has been sabotaged.'

In France's political turmoil the role of the middle class, as in Germany, proved especially important. Indeed, middle-class Frenchmen who were most anxious that orthodox economic policy be followed to preserve the value of their pensions, savings and salaries. But while the position of farmers and big business was crucial in undermining Weimar, in France and Britain these strata of society remained essentially conservative and loyal to the existing political and constitutional order. When the 371st regiment of the French heavy artillery hatched an insurrectionist plot through their local branch of Action Française, the local police were rightly confident that it would not succeed 'because of the sincerely Republican spirit of the local population'.

CIVIL WAR IN SPAIN

France had come close to civil war in the 1920s and 1930s, but for Spain the election of a Popular Front government in 1936 was the catalyst for, not the antidote to, a bitter and bloody internal conflict. Spanish neutrality during the First World War had brought a much needed era of prosperity to a Spain, humiliated by defeat in the Spanish American War (1898), and impeded by relatively low levels of population growth and a predominantly agrarian economy. But the end of the 'Great War' had brought economic recession, as it had done across Europe, and with the coming of the Great Depression the relatively benign right-wing dictatorship of Primo de Rivera, which had lasted from 1923 to 1930, could not cope with the combination of events, and in 1931 the grip of the Spanish right on power loosened. 'We are', as King Alfonso XIII admitted, 'out of fashion'. He then hastily left Spain for exile.

Meanwhile, recession and the Great Depression had encouraged the growth of powerful movements on the Left. The Spanish socialist, *Partido Socialista Obrero Español* (PSOE), and its influential trade union, the *Unión General de Trabajores* (UGT) coexisted alongside the marxist *Partido Obrero de Unificación Marxista* (POUM) of which the English writer George Orwell became a member after the start of the Civil War, and the anarchist union, the *Confederación Nacional de Trabajo* (CNT) had all emerged with strong, though conflicting visions of Spain's future. As in France and Germany, the Spanish Left was split into revolutionary and reformist movements and these divisions were made yet more complex by anti-clerical and separatist tendencies, most notably the struggles for autonomy by Catalans and the Basques.

Spain became a Republic overnight and after five more years of frequent cabinet changes and a brief revival of the Right in 1933, the Popular Front – an alliance of Republicans, Socialists, Communists and anarchists – narrowly won a hard fought election in 1936. These years had witnessed the mass politicization of Spanish life, perhaps even more so than in Germany and France. But while rivalries and differences amongst the governing socialists grew more bitter, the 1936 victory galvanized the army to mount a military coup against the Republic. Of the three generals leading the coup, the youngest, Francisco Franco, came to dominate an alliance of the Right which included defenders of the Catholic Church and of Spanish unity, alongside conventional political parties: the *Confederación Española de Derechas Autónomas* (CEDA), the fascist *Falange* and the *Carlists* – the traditional Catholic and conservative party of Spain.

In the Civil War which followed, the Republic, at first, appeared to hold the stronger hand strategically and in the *matériel* at its disposal. But acrimonious feuding within the Popular Front became more divisive as the war proceeded. The Communists and the CNT on one side and POUM on the other, and they, too, began shooting at one another on the streets of Barcelona in 1937. The war had an international dimension from the start. Early German and Italian aid to Franco was vital in the first stages of the war. Franco's rebellion was launched from Morocco and German and Italian air power was of crucial importance to him in moving some 15,000 men from Morocco to Seville in only ten days. Such help continued until 1939. Of the Republic's potential allies, only the USSR came to its aid; France and Britain did not.

France wanted to help, but internal and British opposition quashed any move. For the British government, intervention on the side of the Popular Front was out of the question for fear of provoking a general European war. The Soviet Union's intervention was not always positive. Its unfair condemnation of POUM as 'Trotskyist' and the activities of its secret police (the GPU) in Spain fuelled divisions within the Popular Front. The International Brigade, perhaps the most widely publicised aspect of foreign assistance, so evocatively portrayed in George Orwell's *Homage to Catalonia* and André Malraux's *Days of Hope*, both published in 1938, never played a decisive role in the war although its losses were substantial: of the 20,000 volunteers, who joined it almost half were killed.

The Right, on the other hand, was in a stronger position to win a war which was widely reported throughout Europe. The army co-ordinated discipline and Franco united the various political groups by judicious use of the 'carrot and stick'. The most was made of their desire to defeat Communism, defend the Church and suppress regional aspirations. The help that they received from their 'friends' overseas was given publicity by both sides. Italian aid was far more plentiful than that of Germany and, at one point, almost 50,000 Italian soldiers were fighting in Spain. But Germany's contribution hit the headlines when the Luftwaffe's Condor Legion infamously attacked the small Basque town of Guernica on 26 April 1937. In a slaughter that was vividly commemorated in a great painting by Pablo Picasso, the town was destroyed and civilians were machine-gunned as they fled. This was the first time in European history that the devastating potential of air warfare was demonstrated. It seemed a terrifying foretaste of what a future war would hold in store.

In 1936 the Right had controlled a band of territory in the East stretching from Algeciras in the South to the Franco–Spanish border. Almost all of New Castile, Catalonia and the Basque territories were in the hands of the Republic. By the end of 1938, however, the advance of the Right on Catalonia had become a rout and by 1 April 1939 Franco's forces had engulfed New Castile and emerged victorious. Franco, who had been a puny, bullied schoolboy dubbed *cerillito* (little matchstick) by his classmates, had now become a ruthless political as well as military leader. His 1939 government appeared a somewhat old-fashioned, traditional dictatorship when set against the dynamic, new-style leaderships of Hitler and Mussolini. Yet he survived for nearly 40 years as ruler of Spain – one of the longest terms of one-man rule in modern European history – and his monolithic power rested on two foundations: the army and the catholic church. Spain, still a predominantly rural country in 1939, thus took a separate and isolated path from the remainder of Western Europe.

CENTRAL AND EASTERN EUROPE, 1929–38

Like Spain, Eastern Europe, too, was ravaged by the severe agricultural depression of the 1930s. In Poland, Romania and Bulgaria agricultural income collapsed by 50–60 per cent, and in Hungary it fell by 36 per cent. Industrial production was also reduced considerably: Czechoslovak and Austrian industrial output fell by over 40 per cent. In such circumstances the land-hunger, the widespread indebtedness and the low peasant incomes which had dogged political stability in the 1920s posed a threat to the maintenance of democracy which was soon beaten or on the retreat across the whole region, with the notable exception of industrialized Czechoslovakia.

Peasant parties found it difficult to promote through agricultural co-operatives more modern methods of farming, although some of their plans were grandiose like those of the agrarian premier of Bulgaria, Alexander Stambolisky, who dreamed of 'electrified' peasant villages, connected by a network of railways, each with a 'hall of popular culture' and silo store. Without Western investment or, indeed, Western markets, it was impossible to turn dreams into realities. Instead, a widespread adoption of autarkic economic policies was echoed in an increasingly inward-looking intolerance of ethnic minorities, especially the Jewish community with its popular association with *Finanzcapital* (financial–capitalism) and 'internationalism'.

By the mid-1930s most of Central and Eastern Europe had succumbed to authoritarian government. In Poland, after Pilsudski's death in 1935, his successors, a small group of old military associates known as the 'Government of Colonels', perpetuated his policies and encouraged popular nationalism with the dream of creating a 'Great Power Poland'. In contrast to the relative longevity of Pilsudski's reign, Hungary endured a succession of conservative, nationalist leaders – Count Gyula Károlyi, Gyula Gömbös, Kálmán Darányi and Béla Imrédy – each more nationalist than the last. When Imrédy took the helm in May 1938 he promptly introduced anti-semitic legislation into Hungary, supported German policy in Czechoslovakia and paved the way for Hungary to join the Anti-Comintern Pact in January 1939.

Austria, too, was racked by nationalist tensions – in 1934–35 there was even a movement dedicated to a Habsburg restoration – with the conservative countryside increasingly at odds with the Socialists in 'Red' Vienna. On 25 July 1934, Dollfuss, the Austrian Chancellor and head of the coalition of conservative parties, called the Fatherland Front, was murdered by members of an Austrian Nazi unit. Their *putsch* was unsuccessful, and Dollfuss's successor, Kurt von Schuschnigg, took the bold step of attempting to broaden the appeal of the Fatherland Front, reducing the powers of the *Heimwehr*, its 'homeguard', and even attempting to include in his government a token number of Social Democrats, members of a party which had been outlawed since 1934. Yet despite his determination that Austria 'remain independent', his country had neither the unity nor the strength to withstand the powerful alliance of Austrian and German Nazis. It was annexed (*The Anschluss*) to Germany on 11 March 1938, with the German Field Marshall, Hermann Göring, a Prussian expressing himself satisfied that 'the existence of Austria' was now 'past history'.

The Czechoslovak President, Thomas Masaryk, unlike his Austrian counterpart, took repressive action against pan-German nationalism as early as 1931.

But, although Nazism was outlawed, it regrouped into the *Sudetendeutsche Partei* (Sudeten German Party) led by Konrad Henlein. In secret, Henlein continued to foster links with Berlin while his party grew in electoral strength. In 1935 Czechoslovakia's non-German parties unanimously endorsed Masaryk's successor, Edvard Beneš, but such cross-party co-operation was rare, and the government faced mounting ethnic opposition, not only from Germans but also from Poles, Hungarian, Ruthenian and, most importantly, Slovak minorities who demanded independent republics. As Czechoslovak democracy became increasingly prone to intolerance towards its minorities, the political activities of these minorities, ethnic tensions described by the Germans as the 'authentic chemical process of disintegration', provided the Nazi government with an invaluable pretext to intervene in Czechoslovakian affairs.

Hitler's appointment as Chancellor in 1933 had sent shock waves across Central Europe. His government was determined to extend Germany's economic and strategic involvement and succeeded in doing so. For example, whereas in 1929 Germany imported 20 per cent of all Hungary's exports, by 1938 this proportion had risen to 41 per cent. Nor was this involvement necessarily unwelcome. In May 1934 King Alexander of Yugoslavia was reported to have complained that Yugoslavia was 'tired of being treated like a puppet by the French, and would gladly free themselves of the tutelage by a *rapprochement* with Germany'. The National Socialist movement itself provided an inspiration and model for fascist movements across the region, most significantly in Romania where the Iron Guard (*Gard de Fer*), with some 200,000 members and 25 per cent of the vote in 1937, was led by the young, handsome and charismatic Corneliu Codreanu (who was murdered by King Carol in 1936). In Hungary, the Arrow Cross movement came to dominate other far right-wing groups by the late 1930s, attracting at its peak more than one million members and between 25 and 45 per cent of the vote – the best fascist showing outside Germany in a (more or less) free election.

By contrast, neither Greece nor Bulgaria produced popular fascist movements in the 1930s, despite the pretensions of the Bulgarian Warriors (*Ratnitsi*) and Chain (*Zveno*) movements bidding for power, a fact which surprises many historians given the conditions in the region. Instead, trying economic, social and political conditions produced right-wing dictatorships under the King Boris in Bulgaria in 1934, and under General Theodoros Pangalos (1925–6) and, more significantly, General Ioannis Metaxas (1936–41) in Greece who was, ironically, leader of the Free Opinion Party.

COMMUNISM AND FASCISM, 1933–41

During the 1930s Europe became dominated by political leaders and groups with strong revolutionary aspirations. In the Soviet Union Stalin was determined to create 'Socialism in one country': visitors from Europe went out to see it. Beyond his insatiable greed for personal power, Comrade Stalin aspired to fulfil Lenin's dream of a Soviet Republic peopled with dedicated and educated working class citizens, and his record is set out below (see p.258). Elsewhere Marxist revolution was more usually a spectre than a dream. Fascist movements, which stretched from the Atlantic to the Baltic, were dedicated alternative 'revolutionary' vision, wherever they sprang up, and because of their large array historians and political scientists have faced substantial problems in defining what fascism was. In 1920 the word 'fascism' was known to very few people, far fewer than the word Communism. Even Mussolini placed fascism in quotation marks when he used it to describe an 'organized, concentrated, authoritarian democracy on a national basis'. Mussolini's definition would encompass the government of Franco's Spain, Dollfuss's Austria and Szálasi's in Hungary, yet although these groups were anti-communist, they made no real ideological contributions to fascism. Franco, for example, was more a military dictator in an old-fashioned sense than a fascist *Führer* in the Hitler mould. Salazar was a Roman Catholic professor.

Other movements, like National Socialism in Germany and the British Union of Fascists, actively sought to emulate Mussolini's movement, and each of them put their trust in, despite their differences, a charismatic leader who sought the complete conquest of power. Once in power, he would set out to establish the fullest control over all aspects of life, best achieved by the creation of a single party system. The leader of a fascist movement held a uniquely powerful position; a role which Mussolini and Hitler expounded on at length (*il Duce*: the *Führerprinzip*). In particular, they both cultivated a mystical, superhuman aura.

The Action Française, the NSDAP, the Italian Fascists, the Romanian Iron Guard and the Nordic Fascists shared some common features. Beyond an ideology which was strongly nationalist, anti-communist and anti-Marxist, they often attempted to appeal to all social groups while at the same time establishing elitist party structures. Party members, proudly attired in uniforms, joined a movement whose image was one of a tightly organized, semi-military machine. Yet their leaders could rapidly alter political policy, unfettered by party constitutional 'niceties'. This flexibility enabled Mussolini to make political compromises – with the monarchy, army, state bureaucracy, large landowners and Catholic church – and Hitler to abandon quietly the socialist elements of the National Socialist party programme to help secure the support of traditional conservative elites in business, the army and the judiciary.

Each movement also cultivated national, imperial and racial myths – German *Lebensraum* in the East, a second Roman Empire in the Mediterranean – and appealed to Europe's youth by promoting a cult of violence and action in preference to ordinary political discussions. The emergence of fascism has been closely identified with Europe's middle classes, the lower middle class in particular, but, of course, they were not the only social group to provide the fascists with a legitimate avenue to power. It was the Great Depression which offered them a mass audience. They were also successful amongst the working classes of Eastern Europe as the success of the Iron Guard in the Romanian elections of 1937 demonstrated, for its core supporters were members of the urban working class. In Scandinavia, on the other hand, the ideas of the Nordic racists, espoused by men like Hans Günther, with its pretensions to scientific objectivity, had greater success amongst the educated bourgeoisie.

Most recent studies of fascism have sought to differentiate between Fascism as a movement, as a set of ideas, and as a regime. This approach helps to distinguish, for example, between Italian Fascism on the one hand, and German National Socialism on the other. As far as ideas were concerned, the central role played by racism in general and anti-semitism in particular, was distinctive to National Socialism: it culminated in the holocaust. The key features of the ideology were hardly original – popular anti-semitism and crude Social Darwinism – but Hitler and his ideologists bound these together with especial violence, and racism played a central role in Nazism's foreign policy, notably in the delineation of friend and foe. The emergence of Nazism as a movement too was very different from that of Italian Fascism. It took the Nazis 13 long years of struggle and gradual growth before they achieved power; Mussolini's rise was much more rapid: he found himself holding the keys to office in under three short and eventful years. Nazism was a formidable political force with an extensive and well-organized paramilitary wing. Italian Fascism, by contrast, lacked such a large, coherent and loyal base of support for its authority. As a result, Mussolini's regime remained dependent upon the political support of traditional conservative powerbrokers, like the Church and the army. A further consequence of their very different paths to power was that when Hitler finally secured the Chancellorship in 1933 he had a clear notion of what his party wanted to achieve, and how to go about it (even if not all the fine details were planned). The early years of Mussolini's regime were not marked by a similar drive or by any clear sense of direction.

NAZISM, 1933–39

For Hitler, the door to unfettered political power opened when he was appointed Chancellor on the 30 January 1933; few people realized that once the National Socialists were in power it would take an earthquake to move them. Hitler was able to achieve legal access to the Chancellorship by forming a temporary alliance with the Conservative elites and the DNVP under Hugenberg. The day after Hitler's accession to power, Hugenberg is supposed to have remarked: 'I've just committed the greatest stupidity of my life; I have allied myself with the greatest demagogue in world history'.[1] Hugenberg was right.

While Hitler's opposition was divided in the wake of his appointment as Chancellor, the Reichstag fire (27 February 1933), another assault on National Socialism that was falsely blamed on the Communists, and Hitler's boot-boys stoked the atmosphere of terror. This enabled the NSDAP to pass the Enabling

Act on the 23 March 1933 and commence the process of *Gleichschaltung*: the 'co-ordination' of German society, bringing everything from bowling clubs to bee-keeping under National Socialist control. This was something that never took place in any other Fascist state. In the march toward total power, the NSDAP concentrated upon dissolving what remained of Weimar's constitution and creating a total 'leader' state. With this in view, it created party offices to be superimposed upon those of the state, like the NS Development Department which addressed issues of race, culture, agriculture and internal affairs. But, in reality, the Nazi state after 1933 was far from monolithic. Different bureaucratic structures came to rival and conflict with another, and Germany never became the completely totalitarian nation to which Hitler aspired. Some historians have even gone so far as to describe the National Socialist state as a 'chaos state'.

Hitler used the democratic process to achieve power. He then set about destroying it, and there was chaos in this too. As he had explained in 1930, 'the constitution only marks out the arena of battle, not the goal . . . once we possess the constitutional power, we will mould the state into the shape we hold suitable', and the acquiescence of Germany's administration and institutions in these changes certainly simplified Hitler's task. The veneer of legality which accompanied Hitler's revolution was complete when Hitler appointed himself 'supreme judge' in June 1934. Henceforth all magistrates and civil servants were required to take an oath of allegiance to the Führer. As part of the process, notions of equality before the law were replaced by a system of legal 'apartheid', and any crime could be defined as an 'illegal act' committed against what the Nazis called the 'National Community'. By this means a gypsy or Jew who had sexual relations with an 'Aryan' woman was guilty of a new crime, 'racial defilement'. That the Nazi party prized qualities such as ruthlessness, intolerance and an unquestioning obedience to party leaders did not solely result in a radical change in the relationship between the state and the judiciary, it also made the later adoption and implementation of racial extermination programmes much easier. The rule of law was no longer an ethical or moral restraint.

Hitler used violence, as well as the rule of law, to eliminate his opposition. At the end of January 1933, the National Socialists embarked upon a legal and physical attack, with the help of Ernst Röhm's SA (*Sturmabteilung*) against the German Communist Party. The SPD and the German trade-union movement were soon drawn into this oppressive net, and by 14 July the NSDAP remained the only legal party within Germany. For those with associations to parties on the left and centre of German politics, January 1933 marked the dawn of years of imprisonment, exile or fear of discovery – the endless, 'panicky fear' which pervades events in Anna Seghers' novel *The Seventh Cross*, published in 1943.

In all areas of German life, a Weimar institution was replaced by a National Socialist one. Trade Unions, for example, were smashed and workers now became members of the Labour Front (*Deutsches Arbeitsfront*: DAF); agricultural organizations 'chose' to dissolve themselves and were replaced by Walter Darré's agricultural marketing corporation, the National Food Estate (*Reichsnährstand*: RNS). The army was the only conservative group at this stage to maintain its independence from overt Nazi infiltration as the combination of legally orchestrated state power, grass roots terrorism and the acquiescence of Germany's conservatives had combined to ensure the destruction of all that Weimar had stood for.

Like Stalin, Hitler was also prepared to launch an attack on his own party faithful. In the Night of the Long Knives in June 1934 Hitler attacked the considerable influence of the SA to eliminate Röhm's personal power. Röhm, one of Hitler's most enthusiastic supporters from the early days, had no stomach for Hitler's compromises with Germany's conservative elites, and said so. But Hitler scorned Röhm's talk of a second revolution. At this stage, he was anxious to placate the German army, court international opinion and consolidate the gains of the first year in power. He had no qualms in having Röhm murdered and the SA purged.

The Nazis shamelessly propagandized every advance of their 'revolution'. Joseph Goebbels persuaded Hitler to give him control not only over the press, radio, films and theatres but over books, visual arts and music as well. Propaganda was a vital element of the social revolution which Hitler sought to engineer, a revolution whose muddled ideological vision sought to embrace all pure (*rassenrein*) Germans in a *Volksgemeinschaft* (a folk/people's community) based on racial superiority. The promotion of National Socialist 'culture' was part of the wider efforts of the regime to shape the identity and social experience of all Germans, with the ultimate ambition of establishing a German Empire that would last for a 1,000 years. Hitler fulfilled his promise of providing 'bread and work' to the German people, although his interest in a vibrant German economy was founded upon aggressive foreign policy ambitions. The Nazi government wanted economic recovery, greater autarky to avoid the danger of blockade and the re-creation of a broad military capacity for Germany. The economy was Hitler's fourth 'arm' for war – alongside a rebuilt navy, army and airforce. It was the importance of producing guns for Germany's racial struggle in Eastern Europe rather than any genuine interest in the welfare of the German worker which determined the increase in government investment and the creation of public work schemes.

Germany's youth came in for particular attention in Nazi propaganda as well as in Nazi education. According to Hitler, their parents were 'a lost generation', one which had acquired its values in a different, non-Nazi world. To this end new guidelines for schools were drafted to educate Germany's 'youth in the service of nationhood and state in the National Socialist Spirit'. Young men between the ages of 14 and 18 were expected to join the *Hitler Jugend* (Hitler Youth), while young women of the same age group were encouraged to participate in the *Bund der deutschen Mädchen* (League of German Girls). The German Young People and League of Young Girls catered to a younger age group of 10 to 14 year-olds. As Margarete Fischer, wife of the

German historian Fritz Fischer, recalled, the appeal of the *Bund der deutschen Mädchen* lay in activities like camping, hiking and singing: 'These girls I brought together found it terrific something of this kind was happening in the village. It wasn't like today where every village has a discothèque or swimming pool.'[2]

Nazi demands on young people did not diminish as they grew older. University students were to serve compulsory labour service, while universal military service was introduced in March 1935. Even more was expected of the SS (*Schutzstaffel*). This was the party's weapon of racial terror, and its head, Heinrich Himmler, aimed to create a new Nazi elite based on racial criteria, an explicitly anti-Christian ideology and unconditional obedience.

Women, too, had a particular place in Hitler's vision. In the blunt words of one party activist, the Nazi goals were: 'Produce babies and educate them according to Nazi party doctrine . . . Support men's activities in whatever roles the leadership deems necessary . . . maintain family-orientated values'. Like Mussolini, Hitler wanted women to produce future soldiers. But the Nazi vision for women was rife with contradictions. Hitler's attacks on the Catholic and Protestant Churches and Himmler's breeding schemes, which briefly appeared to sanction promiscuity for 3 million SS members in 1933, undermined Nazi statements on the sanctity of the German family.

The Nazis did not intend to banish women from the workforce. Rather, they wanted to rationalize the process of deciding which women should perform which functions: manufacturing goods or producing children. Even in peacetime the involvement of German women in the labour force increased, although the type of jobs open to women was predominantly low-skilled. In expanding the contribution of women to the national economy the Nazis went some way to modernizing the position of women in German society, but they always made it clear that docility was the only trait in women that counted.

At the heart of Hitler's world view (*Weltanschauung*) lay his anti-semitism. In 1933 the world received reports of Jews expelled from public service, of shops boycotted, of concentration camps, mass arrests and torture. During the following years Hitler's fanaticism and tireless anti-semitic propaganda acted as encouragement and sanction to the growing persecution of Jews, along with gypsies, beggars and homosexuals. At the Nuremberg Rally of 1935, Hitler dwelt on laws *inter alia* forbidding marriage or sexual relations outside marriage between Germans and Jews, and two years later he returned to the subject with a terrifying tirade. Agitation by the party rank-and-file in the summer and autumn of 1938, finally, exploded in the so-called Crystal night (*Kristallnacht*) pogrom of 9 – 10 November. Initiated by Goebbels in an attempt to curry Hitler's favour, the SA were given 'the freedom of the streets' in a wild night of terror. Two hundred synagogues were burned down, 91 Jews murdered and 7500 Jewish shops and business were destroyed. Germany's streets stank of schnapps from the ransacked shops as the SS arrested a further 26,000 Jews. Already earlier in 1937 some 17,000 Polish Jews living in Germany had been expelled.

Active resistance to Nazi terror amongst the German population remained sporadic, subdued by propaganda, the strength of state control and by the daily struggle to survive described by German journalist, Berndt Engelmann, in a play on political commentator Hannah Arendt's famous phrase, as the 'evil of banality'.[3] Virtually all gave their assent to Nazi rule. But while employment prospects for most had improved, the basis of Nazi economic success came partly by reducing the living standards of the working class – wages fell from 64 per cent to 57 per cent of national income between 1932 and 1938 as the production of guns took priority over that of butter.

STALINISM, 1927–39

In the Soviet Union, the ultimate target of Hitler's aggression, all citizens and those who belonged to the party were terrorized by a dictator's unbridled ambition before Germany and the Soviet Union went to war with each other. Like the Night of the Long Knives, in which Hitler rounded upon some of his most loyal and long-standing party cohorts, Stalin purged the Bolshevik party (the *Aktiv*), in his case using trials to dispose of them. He also carried out what has been called 'a reign of terror' against the ordinary Russian people (the *Narod*) – peasants and workers – during the period of collectivization and industrialization. After the chaos of the First Five Year Plan introduced in 1929, heavy industry continued to expand at the expense of Soviet agriculture (guns over wheat), 1932 saw a return to more sober economic planning in Stalin's drive for industrialization. The Second Five Year plan, instigated that year, was less ambitious than its predecessor, although his targets for industrial output remained characteristically unrealistic. It was that year that Stalin found that his self-styled industrial revolution for the Soviet Union sometimes threatened to run away from his control through the zeal of local party workers who were growing, in his words 'dizzy with success'.[4] The pace of industrialization had created earlier an acute labour shortage in 1930 and in order to prevent workers from abandoning their jobs and returning to the countryside, Stalin re-introduced wage differentials. The desire to 'consolidate', as the Communist party's new slogan demanded, was made more urgent by a famine which spread across the Soviet Union in 1933. Once again the conflict between the towns and villages, so characteristic of Russian history throughout the century, became overt as food grew scarce and the need to feed Soviet workers took priority.

Stalin continued to propagandize his role as protector of the proletariat, although he had already terrorized any opposition within it, and by the increasing involvement of the OGPU (the state's security services) and the army to enforce collectivization and to manage the enormous expansion of labour camps – and by tolerating corruption – he had lost any pretence to be creating a just and equal society. He himself conceded that the battle for industrialization had been Russia's true civil war. It has been estimated that some ten million people 'demographically disappeared' inside the Soviet Union between 1926 and 1939 and many estimates are now higher as more details emerge from the archives of the former Soviet Union. Recent research has highlighted the mass arrests of people living on the margins of society, pro-stitutes, beggars, wanderers, horse thieves and so-called 'religious sectarians' following a secret directive from the Politburo in July 1937.

Nevertheless, by 1934 life became more stable for Soviet working and peasant classes: the provision of housing, education and employment for men and women all improved, and in 1936 a new constitution for the Soviet Union, 'Stalin's Constitution' was ratified by an extraordinary Soviet Congress. It spelt out equality between races and sexes, and guaranteed each Soviet citizen the right to work, to welfare benefits, to education, and to housing. As a consequence, and for the first time, priests and former members of the White opposition of the Civil War were able to vote, although other political parties remained outlawed. For young men and women from even the lowest social classes, industrialization, the growth of the party machine, a govern-ment promoted drive to increase adult literacy, and open access to technical colleges and universities brought greater scope for advancement and a better life. The Kremlin launched a major propaganda campaign to promote family life and sexual abstinence after earlier legislation legalizing divorce and abor-tion resulted in almost one out of two marriages failing and three times as many abortions as live births in Moscow during 1934. But government support for 'family values', did not result in women being forced from the workplace.

Meanwhile, for the privileged members of the *Nomenclatura* (selected through a system by which the Communist Party approved of all appointments in the government and the economy), a new phase of the terror had already begun. During the 1920s Stalin had re-written the history of the revolution to make Lenin its sole architect with Stalin at his right hand, establishing a 'cult of personality' focused on Lenin which in turn enhanced his own mystique. All dissenting voices had been quelled in the name of Lenin's ban on factionalism of March 1921 and through Stalin's control of the Bolshevik party machine. While never describing his regime as 'Stalinist', he now engineered a bloody and unprecedented political 'revolution' against his own party members to secure his personal political power and the economic revolution he had already forced upon Soviet society.

Stalin's suspicions became obsessional and, in his boundless lust for power, purges within the Communist party swept away one million people between 1935 and 1939. For Eugenia Ginzburg, a model Communist and teacher, the reality of Stalin's brutality began to unfold with the murder of Sergei Kirov, Secretary of the General Committee, in November 1934. For her, and loyal party cadres like her, allegations against fellow Bolsheviks accused by Stalin 'must be true' because they were printed in *Pravda*. But by 1937, convicted of trumped up charges and imprisoned in solitary confinement by a 1930 statute, GULAG authorizing the Main Administration of the Labour Camps,

Eugenia had uncovered the true nature of Stalinism. Amongst her fellow prisoners were German and Italian Communists who had fled Hitler and Mussolini only to fall prey to the leader who had claimed to be their ally. She described the solitary cell in which she was imprisoned for almost 24 hours a day:

> I remember the anxiety of my whole body, the despair of my muscles as I paced out of my dwelling, five paces by three, five and a quarter if I took very short steps. One-two-three-four-five one way, turn on the toes not to waste an inch, one-two-three the other.[5]

By 1936 arbitrary arrest and execution without trial became commonplace and by the mid-1930s Labour camps contained six to eight million people. Rykov and later, and most famously, the exiled Trotsky, were murdered at Stalin's behest. But not all acts of terror took place behind closed doors. Spectacular show trials open to the public, and recorded on film, were held, like that of leading party intellectual and former leader Nikolai Bukharin. In May 1937, Trotsky in exile published *The Revolution Betrayed*, just as the trials of the old Bolsheviks entered full swing, noting that, 'the bureaucracy' for that was how he saw it, 'superstitiously fears whatever does not serve it directly, as well as whatever it does not understand.' Justice and truth had no place in these staged events where the defendants showed a suspicious willingness to confess. Even the Red Army, which had, like the NKVD and the Soviet Navy, greatly benefited from Stalin's policies during the first and second five year plans, found itself victim of Stalin's insatiable suspicion. In 1937 he executed the Soviet Union's leading military commanders for treason as a prelude to a drastic purge of the entire High Command and of the Russian Officer Corps – a purge which murdered three of the five Soviet Marshals, thirteen out of fifteen army commanders, and eight out of nine fleet admirals.

Of course, Stalin could not have been responsible for all the individual decisions of the purges, but he alone allowed the purges to assume such proportions – a charge supported by General Secretary Mikhail Gorbachev in 1987. The question of who was to blame for the terror – Stalin, local party officials, or the 'administrative-command system' – continue to be the subject of heated debate among historians. Indeed, Stalin often resorted to carefully calculated but equally brutal measures to ensure the loyalty of even his closest advisers. For instance, he arrested the wife of his personal secretary, A. N. Poskrebyshev, to ensure the latter's unswerving loyalty and allowed Poskrebyshev to remain a trusted servant until 1953.

It has been argued by 'new' historians of the Soviet Union that it was Stalin, and not Lenin, who created radically new and durable economic, political, social and cultural structures that lasted for more than 50 years. These structures embodied many paradoxes – the way the paternalistic Soviet state, for example, saw itself on a mission to 'civilize' peasants, women and backward ethnic groups by using terror against them – that characterized the

1930s as a whole. The market forces that brought the Wall Street Crash encouraged the state to become heavily involved, for the first time in peace, in the management of the economy and of society in ways that brought lasting benefits; a further paradox was the way that mass democracy in Europe had helped bring about governments that claimed to be totalitarian, commanding an absolute state authority. The decade had taught lessons that were to be vital in shaping the world after 1945, none more so than the interdependence of nations made clear by the Great Depression, yet the climate of competition generated by the economic crisis and the radical, new ideologies and leaders that came to power in the 1930s had brought Europe to the brink of a Second World War by September 1939.

Notes

1. L. E. Jones, 'The Greatest Stupidity of My Life: Alfred Hugenberg and the Formation of the Hitler Cabinet, January 1933', *Journal of Contemporary History*, Vol. 27, 1, 1992.
2. A. Ownings, *Frauen, German Women Recall the Third Reich* (1993), pp.8–9.
3. H. Arendt, Eichmann in Jerusalem. A Report On The Banality Of Evil (1963).
4. J. V. Stalin, *Problems with Leninism* (1955), p.755.
5. E. Ginzburg, *Into the Whirlwind* (1967), p.280.

Chapter 9

FROM EUROPEAN TO WORLD
WAR, 1933–1945

The Second World War falls in the chronological centre of twentieth-century European history, and understanding the origins, course and impact of a conflict that took some 55 million lives world-wide is central to any appreciation of the next 60 years of European history. After 1945 a new Europe was forced from the rubble of the old, but the origins of the war and its legacy played a crucial role in shaping its identity and future prospects. The Cold War and the European Union were but two of the most important outcomes of the conflict.

The events of 1936 dramatically encapsulate the changing nature of diplomatic relations within Europe, and between Europe and the remainder of the world. In this critical year, Hitler took the bold but calculated move of cancelling the Locarno treaties and remilitarizing the Rhineland, a vital step in a Four Year Plan implemented at the same time radically to remilitarize Germany. It gave a clear signal to those who were in any doubt – and there were many – that Hitler's diplomatic intentions stretched beyond the policy of revising Versailles. Returning German troops to the Rhineland was a calculated risk. Before the gamble Germany was at its most vulnerable to foreign intervention. After remilitarization Germany now had the economic and military base to make it a formidable foe.

But no European power was prepared to challenge Germany in 1936. Of Europe's 'great' powers, crucially France was the most vulnerable, deep in the throes of a profound political and economic crisis, and diplomatic co-operation within the League of Nations stood in tatters following the debacle of attempted sanctions against Mussolini after the Italian invasion of Abyssinia (October 1935 – May 1936). The approbation of the international community made little impact on a man who offered Italy the 'gospel . . . better to live for one day like a lion than a hundred years like a sheep.' Within Britain, which was politically stabile, there was strong pacifist sentiment and the government itself attached priority to the need to defend its world-wide Empire. The United States was preoccupied with domestic affairs, with pacifist and 'isolationist' sentiment running high in the 1936 Presidential elections. Economic and political issues also determined the response of Europe's remaining democracies to a new expansionist menace – six years of negotiation and then six months of mounting confrontation when war became 'unavoidable'.

THE AXIS POWERS

The future direction of world diplomacy was now set along a loosely established axis in an anti-Comintern pact spanning first Germany and Italy, and then broadened to include Japan. Facing these dictatorships were the 'democracies'. The pact created the spectre of full scale co-operation amongst the world's most ambitious and militaristic powers, although, in reality, the pact was never more than a loose understanding: Germany's co-operation with Japan was limited and inside Europe the fascist partnership of Mussolini and Hitler was fraught with conflicting objectives and interests. In 1934 Mussolini used his troops to defend Austria's territorial independence from Germany, but *Il Duce* grew to respect *Der Führer*, a man whom he had once considered neurotic and vulgar. By 1938 Mussolini was prepared to tolerate the invasion of Austria, and by shifting Italy's imperial ambitions southwards, he left Eastern Europe to German influence.

The war in Ethiopia (then called Abyssinia) was popular at home, reinvigorating Italian fascism and enhancing Mussolini's personal reputation, but it also proved costly and took its toll on Italy's military and economic resources. Nonetheless, successful intervention in the Spanish civil war and the invasion of Albania (1939) were one thing, involvement in a world war another. Mussolini's involvement in chairing negotiations over the future of Czechoslovakia in Munich in 1938 was an indication of his desire for peace. Even the so-called Pact of Steel, signed between the two powers in May 1939, did not make the Nazi-Fascist alliance completely binding. Italy did not enter the Second World War until the German invasion of France was about to reach its successful climax in 1940. Until then, Britain and the United States continued to harbour hopes that the Italians would abandon their neutrality and join the side of the 'democracies' as they had done, for a price, during the First World War.

The governments of Germany, Italy and Japan committed their peoples to war when their national interests – *Lebensraum* in Eastern Europe, the aggrandizement of the Italian Empire in North Africa, the search for raw materials (especially oil) and markets in the Far East – determined that no other course was available. Aside from ambition and militarism, these three powers believed that they were the 'have not' powers, denied the empires and status achieved by Britain, the United States and France. To Hitler 'the Englishman had reason to be proud' and German men and women did not. The military incursion and conquest of Manchuria in 1931, of Ethiopia in 1935 and Czechoslovakia in 1939, all illustrated Axis resentment. According to Axis rationale, economic collapse had come about by excessive dependence upon other nations and their raw materials. With the creation of empire this dependence would cease.

The net result of growing nationalism and imperial ambition was a sharp increase in rearmament. There was no country in Europe which did not begin to rearm in the 1930s, although the major arms race, as it had been at the start of the century, was once again between Britain, France and Germany. All had begun new rearmament programmes in 1936 and Germany's was by far the most ambitious. By 1938–39 the burden of producing armaments was so heavy – for Britain the expenditure on rearmament threatened a crisis of confidence in the pound sterling, in Germany consumer goods and food became increasingly scarce – that some historians have argued that by the end of 1939 waging war was the only alternative to widespread social unrest.

Hitler's foreign policy tactics, as well as the ambitions which under-pinned his foreign policy, have generated much heated debate amongst historians. They have largely rejected suggestions that Hitler's aggressive foreign policy was born simply of an 'unprincipled opportunism'. Despite the fact that changes to Hitler's diplomatic strategy sometimes surprised even his closest advisers – it is now clear that Hitler had four broad ambitions – the restoration of German military power; the expansion of German frontiers; the gathering together of Germany's *Volksdeutsche* (German people); and the creation of a German Empire to provide *Lebensraum*, (living space) in Eastern Europe which might possibly entail a racial war against the Soviet Union. It was possible for Hitler to hold 'principles', however repugnant these beliefs may seem, and at the same time be 'opportunistic' in their execution. Hitler doubtless seized the moment in timing the remilitarization of the Rhineland, but the need to rearm Germany for the racial conquest of Eastern Europe was a long-term, 'principled' consideration.

What was striking in Germany's foreign policy ambitions was the way that Hitler was able to place the 'revision' of Versailles at the forefront of Europe's diplomatic agenda. All Weimar's Chancellors had, to some degree, sought to revise the Versailles Treaty, be it by abolishing reparations or covertly training German troops inside the Soviet Union, but only Hitler succeeded in hijacking events to ensure that the 'German Question' became the world's foremost diplomatic consideration, even determining, to a degree, the conduct of British, French and American foreign policy towards Italy and Japan.

Why was Germany, relatively weak and demilitarized, in 1933, able to threaten not only European, but global peace by 1937–38? On the positive side Germany had a number of legitimate diplomatic grievances which Europe needed to redress. Indeed, the process of addressing them had already begun with the revision of the reparations in the 1920s. Far more important, however, were the 'negative' considerations which determined that Britain and France were unwilling and/or unable to resist Hitler after he seized the initiative until the magnitude of his ambitions became absolutely clear. In all these diplomatic discussions, as was so often the case, the smaller powers of Europe stood largely on the side lines while Britain and France bargained for their national and imperial integrity and for future peace. The Soviet Union, too, largely was excluded from this process with explosive results in 1939.

In the same way as Hitler had exploited Weimar's law and democracy in Weimar to overturn them, so too he exploited the language of Wilsonian liberalism, using lofty phrases like 'restitution' and 'repudiation', to attack the Versailles treaty. His attacks found a receptive audience, at home and abroad, amongst those who believed that Versailles had ensured the instability of Weimar or that French intransigence and rearmament had left Germany with little alternative but to rearm. In reality, the moral tenor of this argument was false: Versailles aspired to a fairer peace than that signed by Germany with Russia at Brest-Livtosk in 1918, while in the case of reparations, Prussia had demanded similar 'tributes' from France in 1870. Nor was Germany's sense of injustice unique: it was shared by others.

THE POLICY OF APPEASEMENT

Until 1938 Hitler consolidated the labours of Brüning and Papen, who, from 1930 to 1932, had worked to remove reparations and the 'war guilt' clause, by attacking the territorial and security arrangements of Versailles, and he remilitarized the Rhineland, achieved union or *Anschluss* with Austria in 1938, and began to move in on Czechoslovakia, while Britain and France appeared to do nothing. Nor, according to Hermann Göring, Commander in Chief of the German *Luftwaffe* (airforce) should these developments have been of any real concern to them. In December 1937, he informed a British visitor:

> You know of course what we are going to do. First we shall overrun Czechoslovakia, and then Danzig and then we shall fight the Russians. What I can't understand is why you British should object to this.[1]

To the Nazis it seemed clear: Britain and France already had empires and it was Germany's right to establish an empire in Eastern Europe.

French, American and especially British attempts to reach a negotiated settlement with Hitler have been called 'appeasement', a policy that affected notions of diplomacy in the same way that the First World War affected notions of war. Debased by over-use, it is still often used by today's politicians to denote a policy of weakness and capitulation. The realities of diplomacy are, and were, more complex. Appeasement – the skills of arbitration, negotiation and tackling each new problem as it arose – were tactics long associated with British diplomacy. On the whole, French and British leaders were not naïve, but dealt with each new crisis as it happened, and it was this which gave the 'democracies' the appearance of weakness, especially when Anglo-French efforts at arbitration were set against Hitler's bold initiatives. Britain and, after 1932 France, were prepared to make readjustments to the post-war settlement provided these revisions did not damage their national interests – although this was almost impossible in the case of France. They wanted to reach a settlement with Germany.

That Hitler's ambitions extended far beyond the revision of Versailles was only fully clear when he tore up the Munich agreement of 29 September

1938, whereby three million Sudeten Germans, formerly citizens of the Czech Republic, were incorporated into the Third Reich (Slovakia and the Capartho-Ukraine were also granted autonomy), and ordered German troops to invade the remaining rump of Czechoslovakia in March 1939. It was then obvious that 'appeasers', men like Chamberlain, Lord Halifax, his foreign secretary, and Georges Bonnet, French Foreign Minister, had failed to reach agreement with Hitler and in 1940 were identified as 'the Guilty Men' by a trio of radical journalists including the future leader of the British Labour Party, Michael Foot. It was also then that appeasement became a term of abuse. Britain and France had hoped desperately that the Munich agreement would be Hitler's final demand, a view that Hitler encouraged. They were certainly not persuaded by Nazi logic, but had to take pressing domestic and international difficulties into account when responding to Hitler's sequence of demands. The adjective 'guilty' is now dated.

THE WESTERN POWERS, 1933–39

Co-operation between Britain and France on military and diplomatic matters had never been easy. European 'harmony' in the later 1920s had been built on fragile foundations. Important issues remained unresolved and returned to plague relations in the 1930s: France's quest for security, the contradiction in Britain's obligations to the Empire and Europe, the diplomatic isolation of the United States and the relations and responsibilities of Western Europe to a 'new look' Eastern Europe.

Good Anglo-French bilateral relations became essential once it was apparent that the League of Nations was redundant, if not a liability, as an instrument of international co-operation. When League directives were ignored by Japan (over Manchuria 1931), Germany (over disarmament in 1933), and Italy (over Ethiopia in 1935), cynics had good reason to accuse the League of hypocritical moralizing about the *status quo*. According to the journalist Robert Dell, the League was 'a fraudulent institution betraying the confidence of the public' and he dubbed it 'the Geneva racket'.[2] European statesmen ignored the League when it suited them to, preferring to revert to the bilateral treaties so criticized by Wilson. The alliances between France and the Little Entente powers (see above p.231), were typical of such revived bilateralism, though these were alliances of unequals and by the late 1930s France was in no condition to help the powers of Eastern Europe. Conveniently for Hitler, France could barely help itself.

It was a sense of national 'weakness' accentuated by conflicting pressures on national policy, not the persuasiveness of Hitler's case, that determined Britain and France's response to his demands. France was weakened primarily by political strife as the late impact of the depression grew more severe and nowhere were the consequences of unstable domestic politics on international policy denoted more obviously than in France's reaction to Mussolini's invasion of Ethiopia in 1935.

The British were hostile to an Italian presence in North Africa, but France, at first, wanted to pursue a more conciliatory policy against the Italians in order to prise *Il Duce* away from *Der Führer*. France's reaction was surprising given that the Italian invasion threatened imperial routes to Algeria and North Africa, and that Italian propaganda and bribery was undermining the French Empire. Pierre Laval, the unfortunate French statesman who negoti- ated with Mussolini over Ethiopia quickly found himself isolated at home and abroad, a symbol of sullied patriotism and *facilité* – cheap appeasement. On the eve of the invasion, Mussolini boasted, 'I have reflected well; I have calculated all; I have weighed everything'. But the invasion was completed at no small cost to the Italians who had discounted the determination of the Ethiopians to resist European involvement in Africa. Nonetheless, Africa, once again, was trapped in the jaws of European rivalry, with Mussolini's greedy claim that 'if for others the Mediterranean is a route, for us Italians it is life'.

The failure of sanctions imposed through the League of Nations and Anglo- French disagreement only served to bring Mussolini closer to Hitler. Division amongst French politicians in 1936 grew when Hitler remilitarized the Rhineland and Belgium renounced its security treaty with France. The public withdrawal of Belgian confidence was a hard blow to a France already struggling under a caretaker government with widespread labour unrest. The prospect of German rearmament and the recently agreed Anglo-German Naval treaty (1935) which sanctioned the re-creation of a German Navy at a ratio of 35 to 100 British ships, seemed less damaging, but was still contradictory.

Nor did matters improve with the accession of the Popular Front govern- ment in France in 1936. Although domestic politics became more effective, France's foreign policy was still filled with contradiction. Blum, leader of the cabinet and a life-long pacifist, now argued that France's best hope of secur- ing peace was by preparing for war: France could produce peace abroad by a position of military and political strength at home. But when the Popular Front collapsed under a wave of strikes and currency depreciation in 1937, France appeared weaker, not stronger, for its efforts. Premier Chautemps succeeded Blum and Blum then succeeded Chautemps. By March 1938 the time had come for a new man and new measures, but when a veteran of 15 cabinets, Daladier, became Prime Minister and French politics shifted dramatically to the Right, France's relative diplomatic weakness continued.

Like many of the Socialists in Blum's Popular Front government, the Labour Party in Britain began to demand a more assertive, if not aggressive, policy towards European fascists and National Socialists in 1936. The decisive struggle was played out between the minority, pacifist wing of the party represented by party leader George Lansbury and those who saw Europe's fascists as murderers of working class men and women and wreckers of free trade unions, represented by Ernest Bevin, the most powerful trade union leader of the day and a future Labour Foreign Minister. At the 1935 Labour Party conference in Brighton, many agreed to abandon their long-standing hostility to the League of Nations as an agent of capitalist oppression and support sanctions against Europe's aggressors. Bevin's pragmatism had won the day. Lansbury resigned from the party leadership and was replaced by Clement Attlee, the future prime minister of the first Labour government. Seen in retrospect, this transition marked a watershed in the development of the Labour party.

'Peacenik' sentiment was evident, however, in the centre and right of politics during the mid-1930s and grew strength with grisly newsreel footage of the Spanish Civil War, particularly the bombing of Guernica, and later from news of Japan's invasion of China in 1937. In the 1930s, in sharp contrast to 1914, there were widespread horror stories of what a war against Germany would cost European citizens and subjects, fuelled, in many instances, by the experience of the First World War. Civilians feared mass gas attacks and civil unrest, culminating in Communist revolution and there was a particular alarm about large-scale bombing of civilians. All of these fears made public opinion hostile to the prospect of war. Amongst the most persistent rumours was the tale that in the first week of a German air offensive, Britain would suffer over 150,000 casualties. In reality Britain suffered less than 147,000 casualties from all forms of bombing in the *whole* of the Second World War.

THE MUNICH CRISIS, 1938

For France the best hope for peace appeared to be a strong Anglo-French entente. It was, however, an entente of unequals. France was dependent upon British military and material help, but could not provide such useful assistance to Britain. As a result, France had to tow the British line on the war in Ethiopia, the Anschluss and, perhaps most significantly of all, sign the Munich Agreement after repudiating its alliance with Czechoslovakia in July 1938 and informing the Czech Premier, Edvard Beneš, 'that France would not go to war for the Sudeten affair'. Constrained by coalition politics and the slow pace of rearmament at home, Daladier could do nothing to save Czechoslovakia – France's ally – from Hitler's demand that Czechoslovakia's three million Sudeten Germans join his greater Germany. In reality, Hitler was as anxious to lay hands on Czechoslovakia's raw materials (bauxite, oil and wheat) as to reunite the 3 million *Volksdeutsche* living on Czech soil. When, at a conference held in Munich, Beneš was forced to accept the cession of the Sudetenland to Germany with Chamberlain famously, and prematurely, branding it 'Peace in our time', there were other political repercussions. Thus, Hitler's move to annex the remainder of Czechoslovakia prompted Poland, in a desperate scramble to reinforce its own fragile security, to annex Teschen.

In September 1938 France, embattled by political division and economic weakness, had had little choice but to abandon its ally. Daladier found himself increasingly at odds with Bonnet, who remained willing to do deals with

Hitler, and by October, Daladier had reverted to a policy of *fermeté* (firmness) in French foreign policy and ordered a massive increase in rearmament spending, 93 billion francs against a 1937 level of 29 billion francs. Meanwhile, Britain, too, had shown itself unwilling to become enmeshed in a 'quarrel in a far-away country between people of whom we know nothing'. Stalin was not invited to the meeting in Munich, despite the fact that he had offered military help to Czechoslovakia. His efforts to build a front to resist Hitler came to naught. He had been ignored by all the parties to the Munich agreement.

The alarm with which the peoples of Western Europe regarded Hitler's foreign policy grew further when German troops invaded and occupied the remaining rump of what was once the Czechoslovakian Republic on 15 March 1939. It was now clear that Hitler's appetite for conquest extended further than revising Versailles, that his promises made in negotiation were worthless, and that Poland was the next target of German ambition. On 24 October 1938, only a few weeks after Munich, the Poles were informed by the Foreign Minister of the Reich, a former 'champagne salesman', Joachim von Ribbentrop, that it was now time to settle outstanding issues in German–Polish relations. In October 1938 German demands included the return of Danzig (now Gdansk) – the sea-port at the end of the Polish corridor which had been dominated by Nazis since May 1933 – to the Reich and the right to establish transportation lines across the Polish corridor to East Prussia. The Poles, unpopular both with both Eastern and Western Europe, bravely rejected these demands out of hand.

Poland was determined not to abandon Danzig to the Germans and support came from a surprising quarter: on 31 March 1939 Chamberlain announced to the House of Commons that should Germany clearly threaten Polish independence and were prompted to use force to resist, Britain and France would come to their aid. Britain had drawn a line in the sand in an attempt to make it clear to Hitler that he would no longer be able to expand into Europe on his own terms. In reality, however, there was not much Britain could do to save Poland.

As in France, the aftermath of Munich also encouraged the British Treasury to initiate increased armament expenditure. 1932–8 had been the locust years of British military spending. In 1919 Britain spent £604 million on its three armed services, by 1932 the figure had dropped to £101 million. Yet it was only in February 1939 that staff talks were initiated between Britain and France, and military planning began in April. By September 1939 British and French aircraft and tank turnout exceeded that of Germany, and by May 1940 France alone, contrary to contemporary belief, matched German output in aircraft production (with a new generation of combat aircraft: the Dewoitine, the Morane-Saulnier 406 and the Bloch 152). French tank output was higher also and of better quality than Germany's. Nonetheless, given the potential of the German economy, the singular purpose of Hitler's Cabinet and his determination to achieve a totally mobilized war economy by 1941/2, it was unlikely that the balance of armaments would remain in Britain and France's favour for long.

The development of radar, too, influenced the timing of the war. In 1937 work had begun to build a chain of 51 radar (Radio Direction Finding) stations around the British coast. While Göring dismissed radar as 'simply a box with wires', this early warning system was revolutionary and of decisive importance. Although incomplete, the radar stations were brought into continuous operation in the spring of 1939. In consequence, that year increasingly appeared the most opportune year to challenge the now global nature of the Nazi threat.

THE BRITISH EMPIRE AND HITLER, 1933–39

France welcomed a firmer British commitment to maintaining the territorial *status quo* in Europe in 1939, but British foreign policy did not have just Europe to worry about. It retained an 'imperial dimension' that affected all diplomatic calculations. As we have seen, the British Empire was larger during the 1930s than it had been in 1914. This was not simply because Britain 'inherited' parts of Germany's rather meagre empire at the Paris Peace conference, but because the Mandate territories were acquired in the Middle East. While supplying an increasingly valuable energy source – oil – they were proving costly to defend. In particular, political tension and military involvement dogged Britain's presence in Palestine from 1929 onwards, and problems in Iraq proved a further diversion. (France faced similar pressures in Morocco, Indo-China, Syria, Algeria and Tunisia).

Britain was caught in a paradox. The apparent source of its world power status – the Empire – was becoming a liability. British military power was stretched around the globe in order to protect it; and sometimes it was stretched so thin that Britain had to tolerate aggressive expansionism – Japan's incursion into Manchuria and later full blown war against China in 1937 – so long as its own trade links with its Empire, and especially India, remained secure. Even the imperial 'jewel' India was in political upheaval and a drain on British resources, and the White Dominions (Australia, Canada, New Zealand and South Africa) were becoming more significant in the formulation of British diplomacy. In South Africa powerful sections of opinion favoured Hitler.

After the First World War Britain's imperial allies were most unwilling to become embroiled in another European war so far from their own shores and Chamberlain had to cultivate carefully the support of Dominion cabinets for a potentially more interventionist European policy. His efforts received an important boost after the fall of Prague. From then on Australia and New Zealand were committed to British policy, although South Africa and Canada refused to be drawn into support of Britain until the eve of war. Until 1939, according to its Prime Minister, William MacKenzie King, Canada 'was resolved to maintain neutrality in war at any price'.

Britain was all too aware of the need to 'educate' the Dominions as to the relevance and reality of the European situation. By careful propaganda and by fostering a relationship of trust with the Dominion Prime Ministers, Chamberlain's 'management' of the Dominions was a success. But perhaps of greatest help in Chamberlain's efforts to secure Dominion support (and that of the United States) in the event of war, was the increasingly *global* nature of the National Socialist threat. By March 1939 Germany dominated all of Central Europe, while Hitler's allies, Italy and Japan, threatened the Mediterranean and the Far East.

THE ECONOMICS OF APPEASEMENT

The British government was more conscious than ever before of the cost of empire because of the relative decline of the British economy since 1914. Persistent unemployment, a reduced share in the world's export market and the decay of heavy industrial capacity (problems made more acute by the great depression), all underlined Britain's fall from grace as number one world power. The British industrial engine no longer appeared able to sustain a large and expensive defence commitment. Finding the money to pay for rearmament was made more acute by the increased social expenditures pledged by British governments of every political hue after 1918, and by the abolition of conscription from March 1920. The same was true of France, although French expenditure on armaments was proportionately higher than that of Britain in the 1920s. The late impact of the depression, however, meant that investment stalled at the same time as Germany began to rearm. By 1938 the German *Luftwaffe* was five times larger than the French air force. As we have seen, real progress on French rearmament only came after the Munich crisis.

Economic considerations in diplomacy and in the preparations for war played a more overt role on the road to the Second World War than they had before the 'Great War', a war which had brought home the cost of modern warfare. Budgetary preoccupations in Britain and France helped to determine the pace of rearmament and the timing of war. In Britain and France rearmament had to be speedy and efficient in order to prevent a balance of payments crisis in Britain and the collapse of sterling. Both British and French governments carefully targeted expenditure into the production of tanks and aircraft. There were political factors, too, that influenced rearmament. Good labour relations, especially with Britain's skilled workers, were needed in order to ensure that new weapons were delivered on time. The Conservative dominated National Government was never entirely confident of the 'responsibility' of British labour which, as elsewhere in Europe, remained affected by the widespread pacifism.

Economic bargains and deals entered diplomacy in a more calculated fashion than ever before as Britain and the United States came to believe that some form of 'economic appeasement' – providing Germany with economic concessions and economic satellites of its own – might work to assuage Hitler's expansionism. It was a strategy particularly favoured by those bankers and industrialists who invested and traded with the 'Axis' powers. Although profitable trading concessions were offered, Hitler and his cohorts were pledged to political annexation.

By 1938 Germany provided an average of 29 per cent of all imports into eastern and south-eastern Europe, largely thanks to Anglo-French concessions, and by 1939 German capital, as well as German goods, had replaced British and French imports into eastern Europe. Yet Hitler, Mussolini and the Japanese nationalists could not be bought off by economic concessions. Economic collapse had helped foster an aggressive nationalism across the globe, but economics by itself could not now solve the crisis.

THE FINAL CRISIS: POLAND, 1939

Europe's diplomatic crisis intensified with continued agitation of Nazi storm troopers on the streets of Danzig and continued German pressure on Poland. There was an astonishing new development also when the Ribbentrop and his Soviet counterpart, Vyacheslav Molotov, on the 23 August 1939 signed the Nazi–Soviet Pact. For Hitler the alliance was his 'trump card. Perhaps . . . the most decisive gamble of my life'. News that Germany and the USSR had reached a deal not to go to war with one another leaked the next day, although the fact that they had signed a secret protocol, giving Stalin a free hand in Finland, Estonia, Latvia, eastern Poland and Romania became apparent only later.

The Nazi–Soviet pact surprised the West. It should not have done. Britain and France, even during August 1939, never pursued an alliance with the Soviets with any degree of enthusiasm, nor, by now, did such an alliance offer Stalin any great advantages. Allied to Britain and France, the USSR might well have had to fight, whereas all that Hitler appeared to want was Soviet neutrality. Self-interest and the historic enmity between the capitalist powers and Communist Russia helped, therefore, to cement the unlikely alliance of two self-confessed enemies – fascism and Communism.

Poland was now encircled by hostile powers and *Der Führer* expectantly waited for news that Britain and France would abandon Poland as they had abandoned Czechoslovakia. Poland, on the other hand, was defiant, confident of Western assistance, especially when the Franco–British guarantee became a formal alliance on 25 August – unknown to them, the day before Hitler had planned to attack Poland. The re-affirmation of Franco–British support for Poland delayed Hitler's attack for five days during which time there was frenetic diplomatic activity, and meetings between Hitler, Ribbentrop and the British Ambassador to Berlin, Sir Nevile Henderson, sometimes degenerated into shouting matches. But neither side had anything to offer, although ironically, Britain showed renewed confidence that Hitler might back down at precisely the moment when Germany was mobilizing for war. At lunch on 31 August the British Foreign Secretary remarked that he had the 'first sight of a beaten fox'. At the same time in the Reich's Chancellery in Berlin was a buzz with the activity of Hitler's closest supporters. That evening Hitler signed his Directive Number One for the Conduct of War and at 4:45 a.m. on the morning of 1 September 1939, 'Operation Fishing' against Danzig had begun.

But neither France, Britain nor Britain's imperial and Dominion allies immediately issued declarations of war against Germany. Stunned incredulity typified the Western response to Danzig's destruction for although many had recognized that war over Poland was likely, this did not mean, in the words of the historian D. C. Watt, that 'in their hearts they had expected it'.[3] There followed two more days of furious diplomatic activity, mainly between Britain and France, with both powers making it clear that new negotiations would only be possible after a complete German withdrawal from Poland. The American President Roosevelt, Pope Pius XII, and the neutral 'Oslo group' of states (Belgium, Norway, Denmark, Sweden, Finland, the Netherlands and Luxembourg), also made vain attempts to secure peace in the final days before the outbreak of war. But the German government, with the possible exception of Göring, were not interested in peace. While the Polish ambassadors in London and Paris became frantic at Western inaction in the face of reports of the terrible atrocities committed in their homeland, public and parliamentarian pressure on the Cabinets of Britain and France grew. The British Cabinet met on the night of 2 September amid rumours that French resolve was weakening (there was some truth to this) and while a terrible thunderstorm raged, they agreed to issue Germany an ultimatum the following day: Sunday 3 September. No one at the meeting dissented from Chamberlain's conclusion that 'this means war'.

The British ultimatum expired at 11 a.m. that Sunday; the French ultimatum expired six hours later. The West was now at war with Germany, although there was little Britain and France could do to help the encircled and outmatched Poles. Hitler was flabbergasted by the news that they intended to stand by their guarantees to Poland. For the first time he had miscalculated the Anglo-French response and this time, unlike 1914, Germany had no plans for a general war. Until August 1939 Hitler had been able to fulfil his ambitions by negotiation or unresisted force, with his ultimate sights set on a racial war with the Soviet Union two or three years later. To Britain and France, however, 1939 seemed as good a time as any to confront Hitler's greed. On both sides of the channel, government was resolved. Indeed, Chamberlain's tactics of exploring every avenue of peace, which were so hastily discredited after 1939, had probably helped bring about national and imperial unity on the need to 'stand up' to Hitler – a potent memory in British politics after 1945. Public opinion in Britain was firmly behind the fight. For Chamberlain, however, the events of 1939 were a personal disaster. He did not remain in office for long and was quickly replaced by a man of a very different temperament who had long opposed appeasement: the Conservative Member of Parliament Winston Churchill. Britain and France now fought to preserve their power not only in Europe, but in the Mediterranean and Far East as well.

THE COURSE OF THE WAR, 1939–41

The cynical friendship treaty signed by Molotov and Ribbentrop in 1939 had promised to guarantee the Polish people 'a peaceful life in keeping with their national character'. These were empty promises, of course. The citizens of Danzig were the first to taste the horrors of the war. Every Pole that the Germans found was hunted down and beaten to death. Their bodies were then dumped into a mass grave and above it a wooden placard proclaimed: 'Here lies the Polish minority'.

The Poles fought bravely against overwhelming odds and managed to withstand the German onslaught for 17 days – their target had been two weeks. 'Operation Case White' against Poland quickly mobilized the three million German soldiers already amassed on the Polish frontiers under the age-old pretext of 'manoeuvres and exercises'. Strength of numbers, military technology and the confusion amongst Britain, France and Poland meant that only one-third of Polish troops were mobilized when the German invasion began, and a rapid German victory followed. The Soviet Union was not so quick off the mark. The Red Army moved to occupy Eastern Poland only on 17 September. By 1940, however, the possibility of Britain and France declaring war on the Soviet Union was no longer a threat – it had been one of the considerations which caused Stalin to delay before invading Poland – and Stalin greedily annexed Estonia, Lithuania, Latvia and Bessarabia to his Empire. Finland proved a more difficult 'morsel' for the Soviet empire to swallow. When the Russians began a military campaign against Finland in October 1940 they did not reckon with the Finnish army's ability to use the country's snowbound forests to its advantage. By the time victory came in March 1941, with large sections of British public opinion favouring the courageous Finns, the USSR had been forced to commit over a million men to defeat a force of only 175,000.

Meanwhile, the Polish people were forced into labour service for their Nazi occupiers and their land given to German settlers. It was a pattern of conquest intended to harness the productive resources of Western and Central Europe to enable Hitler to launch a war against Germany's 'true' racial and political enemy: the Soviet Union. After Poland, German attentions shifted northwards, however, to Norway and Denmark. Despite Hitler's anxieties and the substantial losses sustained by the German Navy, the battle for Norway lasted little more than six weeks (it capitulated on 10 June 1940). The fall of all of Scandinavia (bar neutral Sweden) to the Nazi-Soviet Pact did nothing to boost Anglo-French morale. The allied campaign to defend

Norway had been mismanaged – the RAF, for example, had used obsolete Gloucester Gladiators which lacked oxygen provision for their crews and lost all but one airplane. Thus far, Germany had enjoyed easy victories and still had to turn the might of its forces to confront the Allies in the West.

Britain, France, Belgium, the Netherlands and Luxembourg, unlike their Eastern and Northern European counterparts, had to wait for seven months until it was their turn on the German timetable. The period was nicknamed the 'phoney war' by the popular press because, while the civilian population waited for German bombs to fall, nothing appeared to happen except a large number of futile air-raid warnings which dragged them out of their beds for nothing. The frenetic preparations undertaken on the eve of war – the evacuation of children and mothers from urban areas, the introduction of rationing, the construction of large air-raid shelters and the family-sized Anderson shelter, the issuing of gas masks and the launch of vast barrage balloons into the air – signified that the British public, though apprehensive at the prospect of aerial bombardment, believed that the country was prepared. In France the terror of war, including land war, was no less and preparations for it less well advanced. In both countries the mood was sombre and serious. There were too many terrible memories of 1914 for it to be otherwise.

Preparations for war continued after 3 September 1939. New taxes were levied, cinemas and theatres, closed at first, re-opened under strict guidelines, censorship was introduced, armament production and conscription and the organization of labour stepped up, and the world's press corps waited to report the opening of the Western front. Indeed, the public were so thirsty for news that wild rumours of German espionage were commonplace. Military preparations, too, continued to escalate, although without orders for action, there was little for the troops to do except undertake training exercises. Morale declined and people began to wonder what kind of war this was. Some hoped against hope that the war would soon come to an end, perhaps because of an internal revolt against Hitler – a false hope which had been shared by Chamberlain in August 1939.

Few allied commanders believed that hostilities would soon end, particularly as Germany's military success soon rallied the German people behind Hitler. Yet Franco-British military co-operation was established in the Supreme Inter-Allied War Council, and by January 1940 the British Expeditionary Force had taken up its positions on the Franco-Belgian frontier after allied efforts to coax Belgium out of neutrality had come to naught. As in the First World War, the blockade of Germany was an important plank of the Allied strategy, although it was undermined by the willingness of some of Germany's neutral neighbours, notably the Netherlands, to become warehouses for produce intended for forwarding to Germany. The blockade was also weakened because the Allies allowed Italy to make considerable purchases abroad, including coal and raw materials, in the hope that they might yet prise Mussolini away from Hitler.

Throughout the Polish campaign, Hitler had instructed the army, the *Wehrmacht*, to exercise the greatest caution in the West, indeed to remain completely on the defensive. Until Germany was ready, Hitler ordered that 'any hostile initiative should come from Britain or France'. Thus, Germany could avoid, for as long as was practicable, the need to wage war on two fronts, and there was even the possibility that once Britain and France had witnessed the might of Germany's forces they would back down. The approach of winter, too, played its part. By October 1939, however, Hitler had altered his priorities and was anxious to wage war in the West. But autumn had given way to winter. Eleven times he gave the order to attack and eleven times poor weather forced him to cancel the order.

WAR IN THE WEST, 1940

The 'Phoney War' ended dramatically on 10 May 1940 with the launch of Hitler's 'Operation Case Yellow'. Countless discussions between Hitler and his generals – the latter fearing the strength of the Royal Navy, the RAF, and the resources of the British Empire and France would prove too great for Germany – had come to an end. The battle for Western Europe had begun and Hitler was proved right: victory was Germany's. Although the German war economy was not fully mobilized until 1942, in 1940 France's forces were poorly trained and demoralized, and its political leadership in disarray after Daladier resigned on 20 March, giving way to Paul Reynaud who struggled to form a majority. General Maurice Gamelin, who had put his trust in a defensive line named after him, complained of France's 'inferiority of numbers, inferiority of equipment, inferiority of method'. Only some of this was true. Gamelin and his general staff failed to see that Germany, leaving behind its Siegfried Line, would concentrate its attack on France through the Ardennes, not just via Belgium and the Netherlands. As a result France quickly capitulated to the German invaders with 500,000 British troops dispatched to France under the command of Lord John Gort (with a fine First World War record) unable to help their ally.

By 24 May 1940, ten days after the German attack had begun, Gort received orders to retreat across the Channel, and thus began the undignified British scramble from the Port of Dunkirk which at the time was turned from a devastating defeat for the Allied forces into a famed victory. 'Operation Dynamo' shipped British and Frenchmen from Dunkirk in small boats and the operation became the stuff of legend. Certainly, the firepower of the Luftwaffe, which had been so efficiently married with the German army in the battle for France, had limited effect on the beaches of Dunkirk. But France was now certain to be defeated (its army was outnumbered 2:1), and the British army had lost the bulk of its equipment and almost 70,000 men. Particular propaganda capital was made of the German occupation of Paris, widely regarded as the capital of modern civilization. On 22 June 1940,

Marshal Henri Pétain, who had succeeded Reynaud as Premier on 16 June, concluded armistice negotiations with Germany in the same railway carriage as Germany's humiliating armistice of 1918. With this final piece of theatre, Hitler's ambition to overturn the '*Schandvertrag*' of Versailles had reached its destructive conclusion.

Hitler's ambitions did not end here. Germany's generals and its people (who had shown little enthusiasm for war in 1939), were elated with the triumphs of 1940, and film footage of leading Nazis in Paris was used by Nazi Propaganda Minister Goebbels, a highly skilled propagandist, to demonstrate Nazi superiority. Film propaganda during the war, ranging from the subtle message of films like American-produced *Casablanca* (1942) to the more overt propaganda messages of German 'news reels', was more sophisticated than that of World War One. Civilians were not only able to offer their labour and their lives to wage 'total war' but they could now watch the results of their efforts on film. The world's 'dictatorships' and 'democracies' alike, were quick to exploit the media, and especially film, to maintain morale and to 'educate' their audience as to the cause and course of the war.

FROM THE BATTLE OF BRITAIN TO THE BATTLE OF THE BALKANS, 1940–41

By July 1940 Britain stood alone under the inspired leadership of Churchill, and with the potential resources of the British Empire ranged behind it – a fact of which Hitler and his generals often were more acutely aware than the British people. Preparations for the probable German invasion of the British Isles had begun early in the war. Windows were blacked out, and signposts were removed from roads, and in May Local Defence Volunteers, later called the 'Home Guard', and later still 'Dad's Army', was mobilized. But Hitler and his High Command were united in their belief that the invasion of Britain was 'an act of desperation', not an inevitable step on the road to dominating all Europe. Germany's real ambitions lay in Eastern Europe.

When Germany's half-hearted peace overtures to Britain came to naught, 'Operation Sea-Lion' (following Hitler's directive of 16 July 1940) was launched with Göring's Luftwaffe leading the assault. Göring boasted that 'by means of hard blows I plan to have this enemy, who has already suffered a crushing moral defeat, down on his knees in the nearest future.' But this was not to be. The carefully timed interception of incoming German aircraft, the ability of RAF pilots to learn 'on the wing' from their more skilled adversaries, good intelligence, the most important cryptographic, and the development of radar all contributed to Germany's defeat in the 'Battle of Britain'. So, too, did Germany's fateful decision, in August 1940, to send 100 aircraft on a bombing raid to London. This decision altered the whole course of the battle, for not only did the British order a retaliatory strike against Berlin which infuriated Hitler, but far more importantly, it diverted German attacks from Fighter

Command's bases in the South of England. Bombing Britain's industrial heartlands – Coventry, Liverpool, Birmingham, Glasgow, Leeds, Manchester and Belfast – set more difficult targets for the Luftwaffe. German bombing raids on Coventry had begun on 14 November and marked a new phase in air warfare. The centre of the medieval city, including its cathedral was set ablaze by incendiary devices. (After the war a cross would be fashioned of its charred roof-beams to become the moving centre point of a rebuilt and reconsecrated cathedral in 1962.) Using the blaze as a target, the raiders then dropped hundreds of tons of bombs on the city that also destroyed over one third of the city's housing, important factories and much of its transportation network.

The RAF was victorious in the Battle of Britain and German hopes that the bombing would cause British morale to collapse were mistaken, as were later British hopes that raids on Hamburg, Dresden and Berlin would prompt the capitulation of the German people. Britain was now determined to avenge the 23,000 lives taken in the Blitz. Churchill, a master of words, immortalized the 537 brave fighter pilots who had given their lives in the Battle, when 'so much (was) owed by so many to so few' and the film 'London Can Take It', made with authentic newsreel footage in 1940, glorified the nation's battle. But although this conflict was over in December 1940, battles at sea, in the Balkans and the Near East continued to rage. As Hitler's prime objective was to prepare Germany for racial war against the Soviet Union, he drained the material and labour resources of his conquests. Germany did not simply plunder obvious war resources: *The Times* newspaper reported that over eight million kilograms of butter had been removed from the Netherlands in the first weeks of occupation.

In the summer of 1940 Hitler also attempted to severely limit Britain's access to the Mediterranean and to improve German relations with the Balkan powers. But matters did not go according to plan. Franco, the 'Jesuit Pig' so carefully cultivated by Hitler, finally decided to abandon Spain's imperialist aspirations to Gibraltar and French colonies in North Africa, and informed the German Chancellor that Spain, exhausted by the civil war, would not enter the European War. After his 1940 meeting with the Spanish dictator, Hitler confided that he would rather have all his teeth pulled without anaesthesia than undergo such an experience again. This, plus only limited co-operation from Vichy and Italian suspicion of German ambitions, put paid to Hitler's aim to close off the Mediterranean to British ships.

But Hitler's frustration did not end here. While the German government worked to draw Romania, Hungary and Bulgaria into alliance with Germany (successful between April and June 1941), Mussolini launched an attack on Greece which threatened Hitler's entire strategy in the Balkans. The late Italian entry into the war in June 1940, extended the war to Yugoslavia, Greece, Bulgaria, Romania, Hungary, the Mediterranean and North Africa in the coming months. For Churchill the political and strategic reasons for intervening in Greece to counter attack the Italians were overwhelming and 'Operation Lustre' saw British troops shipped to Greece. Hitler, in the meantime, was not idle. He needed to secure the 'support' of Yugoslavia to enable German troops to reach Greece to aid the Italians and in preparation for the imminent invasion of the Soviet Union. As in the 1930s, he first tried diplomatic means, and when these proved fruitless he invaded Yugoslavia, successfully manipulating the Croat people against the Serbs in 'Operation Punishment'.

German troops had begun to attack Yugoslavia and Greece even before the British had time to work out their strategy. By 27 April 1941 German troops had entered yet another European capital: this time Athens. This made for great newsreel footage back home and crestfallen faces in London, especially when some 18,000 Allied soldiers had to be hastily withdrawn from Crete in another emergency evacuation. Churchill's instruction to 'keep hurling all you can' was to no avail. Although Hitler had been drawn into war in Greece by Mussolini, with its fall, Germany and Italy controlled most of the Mediterranean, their dominance only partially neutralized by the British navy. The German army had also secured the Balkans, now designated the 'cross-roads of Europe', in preparation for its assault against the Soviet Union, and now controlled the important oil-fields of Romania for the German economy.

Eastern Europe's traditional vulnerability to Russian and German ambitions was never more clear than during the Second World War. Any ethnic group which found itself on the wrong side of German or Russian ambitions, most obviously the regions with large Jewish populations, were especially vulnerable to the victimization and brutality. Some ethnic groups were so numerically small that a single act of war was apocalyptic. In April 1941, for example, German bombing of Yugoslavia devastated Zemun, the Gypsy quarter of Belgrade, destroying in one day a substantial portion of the entire Yugoslav Gypsy population. Patriotic hysteria, chauvinism and suspicion were also fuelled by war. In the First World War, stories of Jews signalling to German troops and acting as Habsburg spies were commonplace. In the Second World War Jews were again the most persecuted group in Eastern Europe suffering at the hands of natives and occupiers. But there were other internecine conflicts of which that between Serb and Croat was the most bitter, reaching its bloody climax in the 1940s when the fascist *Ustasha* movement declared a 'holy-war' of 'purification' against all non-Croats. Of the 2,300,000 military and civilian casualties in the Mediterranean area during the Second World War, more than half of them were sustained in Yugoslavia in a terrible war between Croats and Serbs. In both world wars, therefore, the same ethnic groups suffered disproportionate losses – Jews, Gypsies, Serbs, Poles, Ukrainians and Belorussians.

THE 'DESERT WAR', 1940-41

The outlook for the Allied forces was similarly bleak in Africa in 1941. The 'Desert war' in Africa, like Axis involvement in Greece, was triggered by

Mussolini's ambition to establish a Mediterranean Empire 'to the east and to the south, in Asia and Africa'. In August 1940, again without Hitler's prior approval, from his base in Ethiopia *Il Duce* launched a successful attack against British Somaliland. Italian troops outnumbered the British six to one and they made easy progress heading east towards Egypt. But Britain was determined to protect its strategic interests in the Mediterranean, and its access to the Suez canal and the precious oil resources of the Persian Gulf. On 8 December 1940, the British, led by General Sir Archibald Wavell, Commander in the Middle East, opened a surprise offensive and began to push the Italians back across the desert.

The Desert war highlighted that the Second World War, unlike its predecessor, was a war of movement, not of trenches. The extension of the conflict into Africa and the composition of the Axis and Allied forces emphasized the global character of the conflict – Italian troops were reinforced by indigenous forces from Ethiopia, Eritrea and Somaliland; the British army was supported by, amongst others, men from Somaliland, Sudan, Egypt, Kenya and later from India and South Africa.

The desert battles soon began to turn to Britain's advantage, and in less than three months the British took 113,000 Italian prisoners and 1,300 guns at the expense of 438 British dead. Mussolini's rhetoric about the creation of a new Roman Empire now looked like empty boasting. But at the same time as Churchill withdrew some of Wavell's men to help to defend Greece, Mussolini once again prevailed upon Hitler to bail him out. Hitler obliged. In February 1941 the Afrika Korps was hastily assembled. Under the command of Lieutenant–General Erwin Rommel, a man who had made his name commanding the 7th Panzer division in France, the Afrika Korps soon demonstrated its mastery of mobile operations against the Allied opponents. Nicknamed the 'desert fox', Rommel succeeded in pushing Allied troops back across the frontiers of Egypt and became Germany's first genuine war hero. An Australian garrison at Tobruk was cut off, inflicting, according to Churchill, 'one of the heaviest blows I can remember'.[4] As a result Wavell joined the ever lengthening list of military commanders sacked by Churchill. He was replaced by Field Marshall Claude Auchinleck.

Rommel's success opened up the tantalizing possibility of a German advance to Suez, Iraq and the Persian Gulf, but such prizes had to wait. It was now the turn of Hitler to divert resources to the Balkan campaign. In the heat and expanse of Africa supplies and reinforcements were even more critical in determining military success or failure than in Europe. By December 1941 Rommel was forced to withdraw to Tripolitania and the seige of Tobruk was temporarily lifted.

Despite such spectacular victories against an ill-equipped and ill-prepared Italian army, and victory over the German Luftwaffe in the Battle of Britain, the British Empire was in desperate straits in 1941. American material aid provided by the 'Lend-Lease' agreement passed by Congress on 11 March 1941 and signed formally by both countries on 23 February 1942, was vital to

Britain's survival. (Indeed, through the Second World War, international trading links of all kinds proved crucial to the Allies' cause.) In the Far East developments were equally grim. Already in July 1941, with the connivance of the Vichy French government in Saigon, Japan had absorbed Indo-China.

PEACE FOR SOME, 1939–41

From September 1939 until the summer of 1941, however, there were a number of nations intimately concerned with the outcome of war in the West, who at first chose to be isolated from it. The Soviet Union, the United States and Japan were important protagonists still waiting in the wings.

Stalin trusted neither the Axis nor the West. His prime concern was to keep the Soviet Union out of a major war, to consolidate the gains of the Five Year plans, and perhaps more important, to allow the Red Army to recover from the vicious bloodletting of the purges. Stalin certainly had good reason to distrust Hitler, the man who had expressed the ambition 'to cut a road for expansion to the East by fire and sword . . . and enslave the Soviet peoples'. Yet Stalin also had good reason to distrust Britain, France and the United States. The countries which had attempted to intervene on behalf of the White forces during the Russian Civil war, had been reluctant to recognize the legitimacy of the Bolshevik government, and had appeared to fear the menace of Communism as much, if not more than the menace of fascism, which had been typified by their failure to construct an international front to defend the Popular Front in Spain.

The United States and Japan, too, observed from the sidelines. The former, under the dynamic leadership of Franklin D. Roosevelt, chose a nationalist path to economic recovery. At the depths of America's depression, according to recent estimates over 25 million Americans were un- or under-employed and the collapse of the domestic economy made Roosevelt circumspect in foreign affairs. His caution was more than matched by the majority of American citizens who had grown 'gun-shy' of Europe: a widespread revulsion against foreign wars which had intensified in the wake of the First World War and criticism of America's failure to ratify the Treaty of Versailles and join the League of Nations by an 'ungrateful' Europe. During the 1930s the desire to isolate America grew. Neutrality legislation was passed in 1936 and 1937, with many Americans fearful that the United States would be infected by the social and political diseases which had swept Europe: a successful pro-Nazi party rally at Madison Square Garden in 1934 struck an icy chill in many hearts; subsequently, an American Legion commander in California demanded 'Down with all Isms!'.

Yet if the icy waters of the Atlantic appeared to protect America from the German menace, the USA faced a new threat to the West: Japan, with its enhanced economic and military capacity, and now hungering for an Empire. Its fragile liberal political tradition (established under the Meiji restoration of 1868), had collapsed under the strain of economic crisis, and the military gained increasing influence in government. In 1931 Japan sent troops to protect its economic interests in the Chinese territory of Manchuria and by 1937 the Japanese people were engaged in war against China. It was a development which threatened Britain and the USA, in particular.

By 1940 Japanese military operations had extended into Indo-China in the search for oil and other raw materials essential to military expansion and on the 7 December 1941, in a pre-emptive strike against the United States, Japan attacked Pearl Harbor in Hawaii and the Philippines. Within four months of this sensational attack the Japanese were complete masters of the whole of South-East Asia and much of the Pacific. The sinking of British as well as American ships gave Japan a naval supremacy which the Washington treaties of 1921 had never anticipated, and in air power also it was Japanese supremacy which made inevitable the fall of Hong Kong, Malaya, Singapore and the Philippines all by February 1942. Even India was now under threat. These Japanese victories, particularly the speedy capitulation of Singapore, triggered a lengthy debate on the future of British colonial rule, now that the Japanese had dealt a series of devastating blows to European authority. But the Japanese had also brought the Americans into the war.

The attack on Pearl Harbour ended American isolationism. The United States declared war on Japan, and the global spread of the conflict was complete when Hitler declared war on the United States. In many ways, American neutrality had already become a pretence by 1941. Munition supplies to Britain ('cash and carry' followed by 'lend-lease' schemes) and propaganda offensives through the media of film, radio and print, all served to illustrate the President's sympathies for Britain, sympathies cemented by the friendship of Roosevelt and Churchill. With American entry into the war, Britain no longer had to fight alone and Churchill was at last able to sleep 'the sleep of the saved and thankful'.

From 1939 until September 1941 the course of the world's second war had appeared to follow that of its predecessor: apart from the Sino-Japanese war, the conflict was concentrated inside Europe. Germany, as in 1914, now faced the prospect of a war on two fronts, while the United States entered the Second World War with the commitment to 'Europe First', despite the misgivings of men like US General Douglas MacArthur, who wanted to concentrate America's offensive against the Japanese in the Pacific. But with the bombing of Pearl Harbour in December 1941, the theatres of war in Western Europe, North Africa, the Balkans, the Soviet Union, at sea and in the air, linked to join Japan's struggle for dominance in the Far East, forming a continuous chain of conflict and destruction around the globe. This time, unlike World War One, the war was highly mobile. Characteristic of the ever accelerating pace of technological change in the twentieth's century, the development and improvement of aircraft, tanks and armed vehicles enabled well equipped and organized forces to sweep forward and engulf their opponent – as long as their supplies lasted, their communications remained cohesive and their organization strong and effective.

1941 TO 1943: TURNING POINTS

Before Pearl Harbor, Hitler's decision, contrary to the advice of his army leaders, to launch 'Operation Barbarossa' against the Soviet Union on 22 June 1941 exactly one year after the signing of the armistice with France at Compiègne, changed the whole direction of the Second World War, although it brought with it new conflicts and problems.

Singapore, the linch-pin of the Empire's defences in the Far East had fallen in February 1942 and on 21 June 1942 Tobruk finally succumbed to Rommel after a renewed offensive by the Afrika Korps. According to Churchill, it was 'one of the heaviest blows I can recall during the war'.[5] At sea, too, the British Navy suffered some terrible losses. The Germans were building U-boats (submarines) faster than they lost them, and in 1942 the Allies lost more ships, including enemy ships, than in the previous year, (the convoy system, radar and code-breaking skills eventually reduced the figures).

The Germans had made elaborate plans for the invasion of the USSR. Army generals who argued that an effective campaign against the Soviet Union would enable Germany to harness 75 per cent of the Soviet armaments industry found favour with the Führer. Those who counselled caution did not. Detailed plans were also drafted on the treatment of the Soviet population in the coming 'ideological war': Jews and Soviet Commissars were to be shot. When Germany attacked the Soviet Union without a declaration of war on 22 June 1941, echoing Napoleon's invasion of Russia, again almost to the day, Stalin, who had been warned by Britain, the United States and his own secret agents, was shattered. He did not appear in public until 3 July. Churchill, meanwhile, was quick to silence those who did not wish Britain to ally with the Communists:

> Can you doubt what our policy will be? We have but one aim and one single, irrevocable purpose. We are resolved to destroy Hitler . . . It follows, therefore, that we shall give whatever help we can to the Russians and the Russian people.

In reality, Anglo-American support for the Soviet Union amounted to very little until 1944. Stalin's repeated calls for the creation of a second front in Europe were impossible for Britain to meet, even with American help. Troops needed to be amassed, trained and supplied. Churchill's sometimes disingenuous remarks to Stalin on the timing of the Western Front stored up trouble, therefore, for the future. Britain did try to assist the USSR. Set against the terrible losses the Soviets endured, almost any quantity of British aid appeared paltry, although American Lend-Lease aid, carried in British ships which sustained heavy losses, comprised sophisticated equipment, such as radar and new radio technology the Soviets lacked. Without sufficient troops to invade continental Europe, the main hope for Britain and its Dominion allies lay with strategic bombing. But Bomber Command was without both the equipment and expertise to carry out a strategic offensive. Early airborne offensives also appeared to undermine the bombers' case: in

1941 it was estimated that over 50 per cent of British bombs were landing in open fields.

In that year, the Germans had a number of spectacular land victories inside the Soviet Union. By 16 July 1941 they had taken Smolensk, and by 19 September 1941 Kiev. The agricultural and industrial resources of the Ukraine thus fell into German hands; in the fall of Kiev alone, the Soviets lost 655,000 men, 884 tanks and 3,718 guns. From October to December there was a bitter battle for Moscow, and here the first signs of German fallibility appeared: their soldiers were exhausted and lacked sufficient materials and communications to sustain them. But while the infamous Russian winter worked against the Germans in 1941–2, Stalin often worked for them. He repeatedly undermined his generals' strategies and, like Hitler's 'Nero order' in 1945, called for 'fanatical resistance' from his troops in the face of overwhelming odds.

For those on the home front, however, and for large sections of the British public, Stalin appeared to be the author of the Soviet Union's victory in this 'Great Patriotic War'. Like many, a young Polish Jew, who had managed to escape the clutches of the occupying Germans in Poland, found inspiration in Stalin's speech to the people on 3 July 1941:

> he [Stalin] found some apt expressions to show how this time was not a matter of an ordinary war between two countries and two armies, but a trial of strength between two visions of the world, and how therefore the Red Army fought not only to defend its own soil, but the freedom of all peoples who 'groaned under the yoke of German fascism'.[6]

Churchill's speeches could inspire too, but his own position was far from easy.

By September 1942 the Germans had successfully countered the Soviet winter offensive, no thanks to directives pouring forth from the Führer's office, and by 10 September their 4th Panzer army was fighting on the streets of Stalingrad – the furthest point of German penetration. The Russians sought to hold the city with very limited numbers of men so that they could launch a counter-offensive on German lines around Stalingrad, and although the Germans captured much of the city and controlled most of the Volga river, the citizens of Stalingrad and the Sixty-second Russian army put up spirited and successful resistance in a bloody battle fought from house to house. The centre of the city was the battleground and its principal buildings, some of which changed hands as often as five or six times a day, were the tactical objectives. In the meantime, three Soviet armies made up of more than one million men, 14,000 heavy guns, 979 tanks and 1,350 aircraft, mounted a vicious onslaught. It was a spectacular victory. When the siege finally ended in February 1943, burning stumps of buildings and corpses piled high greeted the Russian liberators. The Moscow-based journalist Alexander Werth wrote of the new mood of the Russian people as news of the victory came in early February: 'No one doubted that this was *the* turning point of World War II.'

But it was the Soviet victory at Kursk, to the North East, which provided the USSR with more than a psychological victory over the Germans. The

Battle of Kursk, arguably the greatest tank battle in history, brought together more than two million men and three thousand tanks in ferocious fighting that began on 5 July 1943 and ended one month later on 6 August 1943. Hitler's elite forces – the SS *Totenkopf*, Adolf Hitler, *Das Reich* – all sustained heavy losses in one of the bloodiest battles of the war. Over 100,000 soldiers on the Axis side alone died and the battle marked the last general Nazi offensive on the Eastern Front. Stalin had conducted the engagement with meticulous efficiency. He had improved relations with his generals, and the USSR outnumbered and outgunned its German enemy. The tide had turned in Stalin's favour and his troops now pushed up towards Poland.

Beyond Europe the situation also began to improve for the Allies. Japan's expansion in the Far East was also checked in 1942, this time within reach of Australia. The Battle of the Coral Seas in May 1942 was followed in June by that of Midway Island, while in the West air attacks on Ceylon were repelled and Madagascar, still under Vichy control, was occupied by the British. Meanwhile, after the fall of Tobruk, General Bernard Montgomery ('Monty') took command of Allied troops in North Africa, breathing new confidence into an army sunk in despair after defeat. For Churchill the defeat was a particularly 'bitter moment' for defeat was 'one thing; disgrace another'.

The desert war had seen exceptional commanders, Rommel for the Axis, Wavell, Auchinleck and Montgomery for the Allies, play out a finely balanced encounter. After the humiliation of Tobruk, Churchill was determined on a victory in the field. That year saw the final defeat of the German-Italian Panzer army in the desert and the Battle of El Alamein was the centrepiece (November 1942). Rommel was defeated by both superior Allied numbers, resources and military intelligence, and by his own dwindling resources – German and Italian tanks and jeeps under the constant threat of an empty fuel tank. Britain lost a large number of forces at El Alamein but Montgomery had succeeded in halting the German advance. With the landing of American troops in the region in 'Operation Torch' that same month, the Allies were now in a position to tighten the net around the Axis forces in Europe.

The tide had turned in favour of the Allies but the war was by no means won. Divisions between Britain and the United States as to how to defeat Germany still needed to be ironed out: Britain favoured an attack from the Mediterranean, through Italy and the Balkans, to deliver the final blow to Germany. The United States, on the other hand, disagreed with what was condemned as Britain's 'periphery pecking' approach and remained determined to launch a full-scale invasion of France. Whereas this issue brought endless friction to Anglo–American relations, Churchill arrived in Moscow in the summer of 1942 to inform Stalin that there would be no second front in Europe that year, nor, in fact, was one very likely in 1943. The plain truth, although Churchill did not tell Stalin this, was that neither the British Empire nor the United States had sufficient trained manpower or ships to mount an effective campaign in Europe yet. No immediate end to the war was in sight, although the Allied victories had dealt an important blow to Axis morale. As a secret report of the German *Sicherheitsdienst* (security service) put it: 'A certain gloominess and anxiety exists among many people because they "cannot quite cope" with events any more and fear an unknown danger they cannot grasp.'

THE HOME FRONT

Hitler, Stalin, Roosevelt, Mussolini and Churchill, the principal wartime leaders, were amongst the most influential political leaders in the history of their nations in the twentieth century. They all gave strong and often uncompromising direction to their countries, although the policy decisions taken by Hitler ('Operation Barbarossa' and the Final Solution, for example), perhaps more than those of any other leader, determined the outcome of the war. For governments in the Second World War, as in the first, the principal task was to mobilize manpower and resources, balancing the needs of industry against those of the armed forces. In Britain and the Soviet Union this problem was especially acute in the early stages of the War.

During the Second World War, as in the First, failures in the war effort had an important impact on domestic politics, although the degree of public criticism permitted depended upon the character of the ruling regime. In Germany, Hitler's leadership went unchallenged. Italian political life, by contrast, was more complex. By 1942 the Italian Fascist party had begun to disintegrate from within. The factions and in-fighting which had long characterized Mussolini's regime grew increasingly bitter, particularly when the 'Petacci clan', the friends and family of Mussolini's mistress, Claretta Petacci, joined in the squabbling groups attempting to revive Italy's collapsing war effort. Four major anti-fascist parties also began to revive in 1942 – the Actionists, the Communists, the Socialists and the Catholics. Although these parties had yet to develop party organizations and manifestos, politicians who were to play an important role in Italy's post-war history, like the former Popular party leader and future Christian Democrat, Alcide De Gasperi, set about helping to destroy fascism and establishing a democratic political system for Italy.

The year 1942 brought the most serious political challenge to Churchill. The military failures of 1940–1, notably in Norway, Dunkirk, Greece, North Africa, were compounded in 1942 by news of the fall of Singapore and Tobruk. It was not Churchill's skill as a military commander, however, which was in doubt. In particular, the government was criticized from its management of the war economy and for its failure to help the Soviet Union. That summer Sir Stafford Cripps, Britain's former Ambassador to the USSR and a popular, young Labour politician, a barrister by occupation who had been expelled from the Labour Party before the war for supporting a Popular Front, challenged Churchill for the leadership of the British war effort. Neither his personal appeal – he was described as an *éminence beige* – nor the breadth of his political support was a match for Churchill. By November 1942 a Mass Observation report concluded that the public were 'completely disillusioned' with Cripps. Churchill's position was secure.

One of Britain's main difficulties was the short supply of munitions. Until December 1941 Britain had been heavily dependent upon supplies from an unreliable source: a United States President busy bending the rules of American neutrality. Businessmen were once again central in the struggle to marshal Britain's resources for total war. Learning the lessons of the First World War, the British this time quickly established that for every soldier there should be one worker in the defence industries and two more workers in the civilian economy producing food, clothing and other necessities for the war. These figures alone give some indication of the importance of the home front to the war effort. There were so-called 'reserved occupations'.

Miscalculating the proportion of workers to soldiers could be costly. In the Soviet Union, the excessive mobilization of troops in the front line in 1941–42, by drafting industrial workers and skilled defence workers into the army, seriously undermined the Soviet war economy at a time when German forces were marching across the Soviet Union's industrial heartland. As Hitler had stressed throughout the 1930s, managing the economy effectively was the key to winning the war. Yet despite Germany's extensive preparations in peace, the German economy was amongst the least efficient in war. This was partly due to the fact that Hitler had been planning for a large-scale war in 1941/2; war in 1939 prompted some hasty improvisations. Moreover, whereas the British war effort was comparatively well directed by a co-ordinated bureaucracy, strengthened by people from outside the pre-war Civil Service, Germany's war economy lacked such co-ordination. Regional administration under the *Gaus* resisted the centralized priorities of the war. There were also intense rivalries for resources and power amongst men like Göring, responsible for the aircraft ministry and a large corporation charged with its supply, and Walther Funk in charge of the civilian economy.

Göring claimed that 'no problem is so great that it could not be solved by a German'. Yet even the efforts of Albert Speer, a former architect with a flair for administration, appointed in February 1942 to co-ordinate Germany's war production achieved only mixed results. Speer, like Rathenau before him, believed in centralized, capitalist control and, with the full support of Hitler, he succeeded in more than doubling German war production in 1943. By the middle of 1943 it had more than trebled, although many of the weapons produced were of inferior quality to those of the Allies.

As during the 'Great' War, government extended its control over economy and people to new heights, and once again, the war provided an important stimulus to the development of the American economy. From 1940 to 1944 American manufacturing output increased by 300 per cent. Ingenious American businessmen used every opportunity afforded by the war to increase sales – Coca-Cola persuaded the American army that buying their drink was essential for morale – so even consumer industries prospered from the war.

Most Americans enjoyed an exceptional level of prosperity during the war, or so it appeared when compared to the deprivations of the Great Depression. The experience of the Second World War, in contrast to the experience of the 1930s, confirmed that capitalism could bring untold riches to the United States.

There was far more interest in far-reaching social reform in Britain than across the Atlantic, as was revealed to the world – and to Churchill – in the public recognition given to a long report published in November 1942, which became immediately known as the Beveridge Report, after its author, a long time civil servant and former Director of the London School of Economics, Sir William Beveridge. The report prepared far reaching schemes to provide post-war social security for all and was published by the BBC. It advertised its author too. He described its reception, which was also greatly publicized abroad, like 'riding on an elephant' through a 'cheering mob'. Although never a socialist, Beveridge was laying the foundations, as were later official White Papers, for a comprehensive social security system 'from the cradle to the grave'. The war fostered a feeling that all members of the community should be involved and on the same terms in post-war social policy. It also spotlighted the importance of 'fair shares for all', an objective realized in food rationing schemes devised under the leadership of Lord Woolton, a Food Minister who had been appointed from outside Parliament by Chamberlain, and who eventually became Churchill's Minister for Reconstruction – and later Chairman of the Conservative Party. It was the Labour Party, however, that benefited immediately after the European war ended from reconstruction schemes, when it won the general election of July 1945, the first for ten years.

While class barriers continued to remain, there was a growing determination as the War had gone on for far longer than anyone expected, to create a society where each individual could play his or her part for a common cause.

WOMEN AT WAR

Some propaganda was addressed to women, with the slogan 'Go To It' accompanying the slogan 'Fair Shares for All'. At the outbreak of war women across Europe were again warmly welcomed back into the work force. Based on the experience of the First World War, most countries recognized the importance of mobilizing women as soon as war began, yet it was only in the Soviet Union that the war prompted the state to announce that 'there are no longer so-called "male" professions'. Soviet women had shown that there was 'no profession that is beyond them'. In the rest of Europe women at war were employed in what were traditionally considered 'male' occupations – support services for the army, navy and airforce, farming, manufacturing, civil defence, driving buses, steering barges and even flying airplanes – but this, as during the First World War, did not mean that women remained in these occupations once war was over.

There was a tremendous variety in women's experiences of the war. Many went to work on the land. In Britain the Land Army was one of the more popular auxiliary services for women to join and they were also employed as farm labourers in France, Germany and much of Eastern Europe, with many more 'farming' unofficially to scavenge extra food and fuel for their families. Women made an important contribution to manufacturing, too. The proportion of women employed in industry varied greatly across Europe. By 1943 in Britain over seven million women were employed in the armed forces, civil defence and industry – responsible for almost two-thirds of manufacturing output. The Nazi government, too, attempted to bring more women into the labour force. By 1943 women made up 48.8 per cent of the German workforce – in Britain the figure was 36.4 per cent – and propaganda posters proclaimed, 'Earlier I buttered bread for him, now I paint grenades and think, this is for him'. But the Nazi party continued to emphasize the role of women as child-bearers. So, too, did the regime in Vichy France where the Vichy '300 Law' declared abortion to be a crime against society, the state and the race, and abortion thereby became an act of treason punishable by death.

In Nazi Germany there was another, uglier side to this pro-natalism, the party's conviction that racially and eugenically 'inferior' women must not be allowed to bear children. At the outbreak of war Polish and Russian women from the occupied territories who were conscripted into forced Labour were no longer permitted to return home when pregnant. Instead, they were encouraged or compelled to have abortions or to be sterilized, and those children which were born often fell prey to their employers, Himmler's race experts, or Nazi doctors. This was but a taste of plans for the occupied territories designed to reduce the number of children born. Worse was to come. Jewish and Gypsy women rounded up in concentration camps were subjected to sterilization experiments. Women were also involved in the killing – as nurses in the killing centres, as social workers, as doctors, as researchers and as camp guards.

The horrors of the Second World War – civilian bombing, mobile frontlines, occupation, resistance and, in some cases, combat – determined that the gulf of experience between men and women in this war was considerably less than it had been in the First World War. Nonetheless, in most countries as many women remained at home as came into the workplace. In part, this was because the state remained poor at recognizing that women required encouragement, by way of child-care, decent wage rates, and shopping facilities near their place of work. For women with young children the average working week of 12 hours a day for six days a week on top of looking after children, home and (sometimes) husband or elderly family members was too great a burden. It was also because some women did not want to work or their husbands disapproved.

But war-work brought additional, much welcomed house-keeping money, and for young single women, a more active social life (a British commentator was horrified to note that 40 per cent of single women now socialized in pubs). Sometimes there was even enough to provide women with a little freedom to spend money on themselves, although the work was not without its risks. An 18-year old volunteer recalled:

> It was putting the caps on the detonators of bullets. It was dangerous . . . the cordite used to fly about, fly up into your face. It caused a rash, impetigo, and it would come up in big lumps. Your eyes swelled up. We used to work seven (days or nights) a week. It was good money. I was earning £10 a week.

There are many such war memoirs. Lives were changed. As in 1918, at war's end few professions were feminized as a result of the war. In Western Europe women all but completely disappeared from the armed services, transportation (particularly women-drivers) and certain types of manufacturing. Only in the divided Germany and the USSR did the loss of men in the war ensure a strong demand for working women. The indications of change for women reflected changes in attitudes, particularly among women themselves. In 1945 many more married women were determined to remain in employment (traditionally most female employees were single), and most had an increased sense of self-worth as a consequence of their war-time experiences. But although across Europe politicians loudly praised the contribution of women to the war effort, they took considerably longer to legislate for change which recognized the economic value of women. Typical was the response of Ernest Bevin when women demanded equal pay to men (women worked for 50 to 70 per cent of men's wages) in the House of Commons:

> *Dr (Edith) Summerskill*: Even he admits my figures are right.
> *Mr Bevin*: I think your figure's perfect.

THE FALL AND RISE OF 'GREAT POWERS'

Britain's war experience was clearly set apart from the rest of Europe. Its land was not fought over, as in the Soviet Union, nor was it as extensively bombed as Germany, and apart from the Channel Islands, there was no occupation or resistance. The war did, however, emphasize the decline of Britain as a world power. Indeed, while the British Empire had stood alone in 1940, the experience was not enough to scupper new challenges to imperial unity. That the Empire was in crisis was clearly signalled by unrest in India and by Britain's dependence on the United States for financial aid. But while Britain's star was on the wane, the Soviet Union arose in the East as the world's latest great power.

The first year of 'the Great Patriotic War', which claimed over 20 million lives, brought terrible suffering to the USSR. Retreating in the face of the advancing German forces, the Soviets lost territories containing 63 per cent of all coal production, 68 per cent of pig-iron, 84 per cent of sugar, 38 per cent of grain and 60 per cent of pigs. Food shortages appeared within days of the outbreak of war – milk, sugar, fats were all very hard to come by – and even cabbage disappeared from the market place. Workers often walked four or five miles to and from work on an empty stomach, and housing conditions were pretty grim, usually without any heating. The USSR's most remarkable achievement during the war was to evacuate entire factories from the West to the Urals, Siberia, Kazakhstan and Central Asia. Moving these special defence industries was an essential foundation to the mobilization of the Soviet economy as a whole. This was effected very rapidly. The Soviet Union moved more than 44 per cent of its industrial production from civilian to military output between 1940 and 1942. By comparison Italy managed 15 per cent, Britain 38 per cent and Germany 29 per cent over the two years from 1939 to 1941. The short-term benefits were obvious, although when the war came to an end the Soviet Union struggled to rebuild its civilian economy and it was the only victor of the war 'to suffer a significant, long-lasting economic setback from World War II'.[7]

Winning the war after 1942 brought little relief for the Soviet peoples as the Germans carried out a policy of systematic destruction as they retreated, although the war went some way towards healing some of the divisions in Stalinist society prompted by the purges of the 1930s. But whereas these purges had effectively discriminated against particular social classes in the Soviet Union, under the impact of the war, belonging to a certain ethnic group now began to distinguish loyal workers from traitors. Volga Germans, Karachi, Kalmyks, Chechens, Ingushis, Crimean Tartars and others were shipped off to Siberia in a wave of Russian chauvinism which sought scape-goats and 'enemies within' to explain the early success of the Germans.

Other former enemies of the Soviet state fared better under the conditions of the Second World War. The Church and some artists discovered a new freedom as Stalin worked to sustain the morale of his people. In unoccupied Europe, maintaining morale was seen as the key to victory. In the United States posters of Rosie the Riveter claimed 'We Can Do It!', while in the USSR, a crab, complete with Hitler moustache, was shown crushed beneath the tracks of a Soviet tank. In occupied France, a different propaganda message was no more sophisticated with posters proclaiming: 'They (German soldiers) give their blood, You give your work!'.

The German people did not experience starvation to the same degree as the Soviet Union, although their standard of living was nevertheless substantially lower than that of Britain from 1939–47. Life in the cities was especially tough with food in short supply and, by the end of the war, many families were driven by allied bombs to living in cellars. As in Britain, the National Socialists attempted to provide their *Volk* (people) with an inspiring social vision, but plans drafted by Robert Ley, leader of the German Labour Front, came to naught under the demands of war. Instead, the Nazi vision became one of death and destruction. By 1941, the promised 'racial renewal' began to take place through genocide and subjugation. Hitler waged the war to provide *Lebensraum* for the German people, yet few understood what this concept meant. Scant numbers of Germans settled for long in occupied Eastern Europe and those who did – leading party members, large corporations – began to abandon their assets and plans for expansion into Eastern Europe in 1944 when it became clear that the dream of victory had become the nightmare of defeat. To his supporters Hitler's claim that 'in this war, not luck, but justice will finally triumph' appeared increasingly hollow.

RESISTANCE IN THE AXIS COUNTRIES

It was impossible to measure the degree of support or hostility Hitler's regime engendered during the war but active resistance amongst the population was low. As Speer noted, 'apathy . . . despite all the great triumphs' appeared to be the prevalent sentiment. Most were far too preoccupied with the task of daily survival. Under the ever watchful eye of the Gestapo, large-scale resistance was, at best, difficult. The experience of the 'White Rose' group, founded by brother and sister Hans and Sophie Scholl, illustrated the obstacles faced by organized resistance in the Reich. The group courageously printed leaflets which were distributed in Munich, Stuttgart, Frankfurt, Freiburg, Vienna and Hamburg. But their activities were short-lived. All members of the group were arrested, tried and executed. Sophie was 22 years old when she died. Carl Goerdeler, the former Lord Mayor of Leipzig, was representative of more elevated opposition to Hitler. He organized a daring attempt in July 1944 by officers and civil servants to assassinate Hitler, the so-called 'Officers Plot'. Such high level protest was directed more against the dishonour Hitler was heaping upon Germany during the war, than an attempt to stop murder in the concentration camps. In Italy resistance to the mass-murder of Jews in German-dominated Europe did come at a more senior level. Encouraged by the character of semi-official Italian life, diplomats, civil servants and administrators conspired against their orders to deliver Jews to the gas chambers. (See also p.296).

THE FINAL SOLUTION

It was unclear when the decision to murder Europe's Jews was taken by Hitler and his cabinet. War and the rapid conquest of Poland transformed the Jewish question as forced immigration schemes and plans to sell Jews for foreign currency were no longer an option. The war brought organizational chaos. To 'manage' the Jewish problem ghettos were created – the first of which was erected at Lódz (Litzmannstadt) in December 1939 – and compulsory labour, with the inevitable death of thousands, was introduced for all Jews. These steps gave momentum to what came to be called the 'Final Solution'. The killing process had already escalated during the war against the Soviet Union and, by the end of 1941, 'pressed' by problems of hygiene, food, accommodation and administration in the ghettos and labour camps, German policy towards the Jews had become one of full-scale annihilation. Six million European Jews alone, were murdered in the gas chambers of Auschwitz, Chelmno, Belzec, Sobibor and Treblinka.

The mentally and physically handicapped suffered too, in a Nazi euthanasia programme which liquidated over 70,000 mental patients between 1939 and 1941 to 'free' beds for those who could be 'cured'. While most Germans had heard rumours of horrors taking place in hospitals and in concentration camps, the full story came as a shock to many. A 17-year old German prisoner of war recalled:

> barely a week went by that the Americans did not show pictures of . . . the con-
> centration camps. Many of my fellow prisoners cried. Others, however, left the
> cinema after the film and laughed in the faces of American soldiers, because they
> believed the films were *Greuelmärchen* (horror stories), similar to the sophisticated
> propaganda they had been subjected to by Goebbels.[8]

The Holocaust, never forgotten, stands out in twentieth-century history, and there are many memorials to it.

PARTICIPATION AND RESISTANCE IN OCCUPIED EUROPE

Just as the First World War had shaken Europe from its belief in human 'progress', so the crimes of the Second World War worked to erode European claims to moral superiority over the rest of the world. In Nazi occupied Europe, the choice between participation or resistance was a painful one. The Polish poet, Czeslaw Milosz, went so far as to describe his country as a 'Gangster Gau' (the German–occupied Vistula basin bore the name Government – General, or G.G. for short), in which the entire Polish nation turned to criminal activities to survive the occupation.

Germany's occupation policy for Europe was by no means consistent. The Nazi occupiers wanted to exploit the economic and strategic resources of the Reich's new territories while imposing a new racial order. But different 'regions' were exploited in different ways, depending on how the territory was defeated, the strength of local Nazis and the character of the existing political structure. France, Belgium, Greece and Serbia were strategically important and so remained under military control. Holland and Norway, by contrast, had fledgling fascist parties which were allowed to establish powerless consultative cabinets (the most infamous was Vidkun Quisling's cabinet in Norway), while real power rested with a German Reichs-Kommisar. 'Native' fascists like Quisling, Anton Mussert in Holland and Léon Degrelle in Belgium were caught in a vicious spiral of concession to their Nazi occupiers – men who were much more extreme and ruthless than themselves. The local fascists provided the henchmen to do the Nazi's dirty work. They carried out raids and reprisals, rounded up and transported their compatriots to concentration camps, and even recruited volunteers to fight for Germany. Twenty-thousand supporters of Mussert served in the German army and the Grand Mufti of Jerusalem, head of the Moslem Supreme Council and the most prominent Arab in Palestine, recruited a Moslem Legion which paraded in Berlin alongside Bosnian or Soviet prisoners of war from Azerbaidzhan and Turkestan. The decision was to have a lasting impact on international relations in the Middle East. After the war, Grand Mufti Haj Amin Al-Hussaini went on to become the military governor of lands under Israeli occupation and a founder of the Palestinian National Movement; his wartime links to Hitler were never forgotten by successive Israeli generations. (The future leader of the Palestinian Liberation Organization, the PLO, Yasir Arafat, later fought under his command.)

Denmark, at first, was treated rather differently from the remainder of occupied Europe. King Christian X refused to go into exile and instead formed a national government to negotiate directly with the Nazis. The Danes were thus spared the degradation and horror of a Nazi occupation until 1943 when it became clear that here, as in Norway, there was little chance of home-grown Nazis mustering sufficient public support to take office. Occupied Western Europe as a whole, however, received better treatment than its Eastern counterpart, although here, too, the Nazis had their 'quislings'. In Hungary it was the Regent Horthy, in Croatia it was the fascist *Ustasha* party led by Ante Pavelič. Even in the Soviet Union the *Wehrmacht* sometimes received a warm welcome, notably from Estonians, Ukrainians, Armenians, Tartars, Caucasians and Moslems, who, if they did not join the German army, were taken prisoner by it in abnormally high numbers. Nonetheless, French, Danish and Norwegian men and women stood higher on the Nazi racial scale and so merited larger food rations and better conditions in their labour camps.

What of France – a country whose land mass, if not the size of its population, was equivalent to that of Germany? At first, only the Northern half of France was placed under military occupation, while the South-West region remained unoccupied to form Vichy France under the governorship of Pétain. It was on the other side of the English Channel in London that a former junior minister, Charles de Gaulle, took up the Free France cry. But not all Frenchmen and women shared de Gaulle's hostility to the Vichy government. Some inside France argued that Vichy was an opportunity to right the wrongs of earlier, weak French governments. Whatever their noble claims, the reality of Vichy France was an ugly one. Unlike the Netherlands and Belgium, where brave efforts were made to hinder the mass murder of their Jewish citizens, Vichy France had an appalling record of anti-semitism. After 1942 all of France was occupied by the Germans and the French Service d'Ordre Légionnaire co-operated energetically with France's occupiers.

But just as some people argued that collaboration with their Nazi occupiers was essential to national survival, the memory of efforts to resist the Germans was vital to national morale in the immediate post-war years. There was resistance to the Nazi occupation throughout Europe. It could be found in every country, but it was never unified or co-ordinated. The resistance fighters had much in common: a hatred of German and of foreign or local fascism, and their fierce patriotism. They also shared poverty: lacking weapons, money and trained personnel, and their sentiments and actions brought them into direct conflict with their compatriots, the collaborators, so that resistance often became civil war.

The early resistance to Axis occupation was passive – demonstrations in Wenceslas Square in Prague or at the Arc de Triomphe in Paris. Then came underground newspapers and leaflets, and direct action – sabotage and attacks on important figures, sometimes with the collusion of the Allies. But there was also enormous variety in European resistance, conditional on the character of the Nazi occupation, the local geography and history. In Norway military resistance was organized into a single group under the command of Norwegian Army General Otto Ruge. This, plus mountainous terrain created an effective, unified, guerilla unit, in sharp contrast to the resistance movements of Denmark and Holland, countries unsuitable for this type of warfare. Here resistance was restricted to acts of sabotage, rescuing Jews and collecting intelligence for the Allies. Resistance movements in Belgium and France, by contrast, planned and executed military operations. Belgium's 35 intelligence networks employing over 10,000 people became a vital part of the Allied war effort where the resistance movement, unlike in France, was unified under the control of the 'Secret Army'.

In France, organized resistance movements like the *ITLAIC Combat Liberation, Franc-Tireur, Front National* and *Organisation Civile et Militaire* played a vital role in defeating the Germans and opening a Western Front. French resistance increasingly formed competing splinter groups after June 1941 when the French Communist Party joined the resistance. Eventually, these groups were united under the command of General de Gaulle in 1942, but while they could fight together to defeat the Germans, peace-time political co-operation proved impossible.

In Eastern Europe the rivalry between Communist and non-communist resistance movements was fiercer than in the west because of the proximity of Soviet forces. Czechoslovak resistance from 1939, for example, was first led by the exiled President from France, but the defeat of France was a second 'Munich' for Beneš, and the Czech resistance was increasingly guided by Soviet directives. In Yugoslavia and Greece rugged terrain made guerrilla style resistance more practicable, but here, too, there was strong competition between non-communist and Communist groups. Yugoslavia's forces had capitulated quickly to the *Wehrmacht* in April 1941 (only 151 of the German invaders were killed). Draza Mihailovič was the only Serbian commander who escaped the demoralized collapse of Yugoslavia's forces and he took to the hills with his remaining troops, calling them *Chetniks* in memory of the struggle against the Turks. Within months these Serbian freedom fighters, who were loyal to the Crown, were in fierce competition with the Communist partisan forces led by the Communist Marshal Jusip Tito. The pan-Serbianism and monarchism of the *Chetniks* had little in common with the Croatian, Communist Tito bent on the creation of a federal South Slav state, and co-operation between the two groups proved impossible. The *Chetniks* came off second best, and Tito's political agenda and his struggle against the *Chetniks* and Croatian fascist *Ustasha* meant that Yugoslavian resistance, as in Greece and Romania, provoked civil war and revolution as well.

INTELLECTUAL AND SPIRITUAL RESISTANCE

In Eastern Europe Soviet-style Communism provided the intellectual backbone for many of the resistance movements. Elsewhere in Europe, and sometimes from exile, writers, artists and churchmen attempted to provide intellectual and spiritual support for those engaged in active and passive resistance. There was even an intellectual 'resistance' movement of sorts in Britain.

The need for security and unity in the face of the enemy imposed limits on the freedom of expression of leading British intellectuals. Although, as George Orwell noted, 'the British government started the war with the more or less openly declared intention of keeping the literary intelligentsia out of it', by 1943 almost every writer, 'however undesirable his opinions', was sucked into 'the B.B.C. or some other essentially literary job'. The contribution of writers like Orwell and J. B. Priestley, a superb broadcaster as well as writer of fiction, non-fiction and plays, to the British propaganda effort was impor-tant, but their official work sometimes rested uneasily with their socialist convictions. Orwell, for example, had a deep distrust of authority and the collectivist tendencies of the state at war. In his public broadcasts for a foreign audience, he, like Priestley, stressed that the war effort was to defend a 'unique island people' and expounded on the 'great' qualities of the British. Neither of them towed the government line. Both wanted the British workers to think positively of the future and the need to eliminate 'inefficiency, class privilege and the rule of the old'. The need for social justice was an especially popular message – so much so that in 1942 leading conservatives complained that too many left-wingers had been elevated to 'positions of eminence.'

The need to convey a positive vision of the future was also a powerful drive behind French intellectual resistance. In 1941 the French writer, Jean-Paul Sartre, born in 1905, released from a German prison camp, took a leading role in French intellectual resistance to the German occupation. Believing that writers were 'implicated' in the eras in which they lived, he urged his fellow countrymen and women to cease dwelling on the sins of the past and turn to the future, 'a future that they were still free to shape'. It was the main theme of his play, based on a Greek myth, *Les Mouches* (1943) translated into English in 1946 as *The Flies*.

Censorship in occupied France was strict, but not so strict as to prevent the publication of plays and books on classical and historical themes. Indeed, this tactic was also adopted in Germany to circumvent far harsher controls on censorship. As the editor of *Deutsche Rundschau*, one of the few Weimar publications which continued to be printed under the Nazi regime, explained: 'One criticized despots and crimes committed in all periods of history, illustrated with the figures of such tyrants to antiquity, Roman Caesars of the late Empire, Genghis Khan . . . and left the reader to draw the proper conclusions.'

In France and Italy there was also the underground press with *Combat*, *L'Humanité* and *Les Lettres Françaises* clandestinely published in Paris. The editorial board of *Les Lettres Françaises* included such authors as Sartre, Edith Thomas, Jean Paulhan and Albert Camus. In 1943 the circulation of the paper was over 12,000 and its readership many time higher as the paper was secretly passed from hand to hand. In common with anti-fascist writers across Europe, and those in exile, the paper sought to formulate a set of moral ideals opposed to fascism. Many of these politically radical intellectuals rallied to the defence of freedom of expression, freedom of conscience and the defence of human dignity. The paper also denounced writers who wrote in praise of their German occupiers. There were other French authors who counselled, not active physical and intellectual resistance, but stoic self-respect expressed in stubborn silence. Their call for passive resistance was typified in the novel by Vercors' (Jean Bruller) novel, *La Silence de la Mer* (the Silence of the Sea) and found echoes in the resistance writing of critics of Nazism who had remained in Germany after 1933. German poets and writers emphasized the notion that the German nation was a prisoner awaiting freedom that could only be earned through suffering. As Werner Bergenruen wrote:

> He who endures to the end
> is Crowned most truly
> No breadth of constancy is lost[9]

Opportunities for intellectual resistance in Germany were extremely limited. Hundreds of prominent German writers, poets, scientists, artists and musicians had fled Germany for Switzerland, Britain, America or the USSR in 1933. This group played an important role in 'educating' opinion outside Germany. Thomas Mann broadcast to the German people from Geneva, his son, Klaus published his memoirs and stories in the United States, as did their fellow artist and friend, the Austrian, Stefan Zweig. Life in exile was by no means easy. As Klaus Mann put it, 'in this world of nation states and nationalisms a man without a nation, a stateless person, has a difficult time.'[10] Of those who remained, many employed their skills in the service of the Reich. Typical was the vision of party functionary and author, Werner Beumelburg, who explained his mission to 'purify and shape the German destiny'. Nazi writers were also encouraged to write about military and heroic themes to stimulate wartime morale. Nonetheless, in Italy, where fascist censorship was never as strong as in Nazi Germany, the war marked an important turning point in intellectual resistance to fascism.

In Italy, the Second World War was unpopular from the outset. The number and output of resistance publications, such as the Milan based *L'Unità*, increased after 1940, and paintings like Renato Guttuso's, *Crucifixion*, depicted the suffering and futility of war. A number of leading writers, notably Elio Vittorini, broke with their fascist past, to criticize both the management of the war effort and the moral character of the government.

Italy's writers and artists did not receive much support from the Roman Catholic Church before 1943. Indeed, until his Christmas message of 1942 which denounced 'state worship' and 'racialism', Pope Pius XII was comparatively silent on the impact of fascist and Nazi policies in Europe. In 1940, however, he had allowed himself to used as a secret channel of communication between German conspirators against Hitler and the British government in the hope that this would save lives. For the most part, Roman Catholics believed that resistance to an immoral government must be passive and many of the clergy stressed the threat of the bolshevization of Europe. In 1944 Hitler, who hated Roman Catholics and despised Protestant pastors, threatened, 'I'm going to the Vatican right now. Do you think the Vatican bothers me? We'll grab it at once.' The Nazi Party Chancellor, Martin Bormann, argued that 'all influences that could impair, or even damage, the Führer's and the Party's rule must be eliminated.'

This warning to the Roman Catholic clergy and Protestant pastors came after a number of vocal protests against the party's euthanasia programme – the mass killing of people deemed 'degenerate' according to the 'eugenic' principles. Prominent among them was the bishop of Münster, Clemens August von Galen, who publicly denounced the euthanasia campaign as a 'violation of the fifth commandment' and filed a declaration to this effect with the police chief and the public prosecutor's office. This, amongst other complaints, helped to severely curtail the programme. There was no comparable protest about the murder of Jews.

Among the protestants Martin Niemöller was arrested and held in concentration camps, often in solitary confinement, while Dietrich Bonhoeffer, a leading anti-Nazi Lutheran pastor who chose to return to Germany from the United States of America in 1939, went further than many. He attempted to provide an intellectual and spiritual legitimation for active resistance in his writings, notably *Ethik* (*Ethics*, 1943). He was arrested in 1943 and was executed at Flossenburg in 1945. Niemöller's execution was ordered too, but was not carried out. Bonhoeffer's writings became well-known outside Germany, and his prison letters were published in 1951, *Wiederstand und Ergebung*, and translated into English four years later as *Letters and Pages from Prison*.

ALLIES ON THE OFFENSIVE, 1943–45

The last two years of the war witnessed a transformation, with Montgomery's victory at El Alamein effectively marked the beginning of Allied efforts to liberate Western Europe. 'Operation Torch' was the largest amphibious landing so far, and between November and May 1943 the Germans and Italians were evicted completely from North Africa. The reconquest of Sicily and Italy followed. It took 58 days to prepare the Sicilian landings and 38 days to achieve success. It was another 17 days before the Italian mainland was attacked. There was an almost immediate political result, for in July 1943 the first Fascist Grand Council to convene since 1939 deposed Mussolini and, in September 1943, the Italians made a separate peace. The subsequent Allied reconquest of Italy was by no means easy. Few Italian troops were like Private Angelo, hero of Eric Linklater's novel of the same name, who reflected, 'it has taken us a long time to lose the war, but thank heaven we have lost at last'. By December 1943 Allied troops were outside the monastery of Monte Cassino, and it was only in December 1944 that they reached the Dolomite mountains.

Hitler retained a warm enough regard for his Italian ally to send German parachutists to release Mussolini from his mountain prison on 13 October 1943 and release him in the North in Gargano. Unable to provide his people with an adequate explanation of why Italy or a part of it should remain at war and why there should be serious food, fuel and clothing shortages, he now forfeited popular support. Indeed, in public he increasingly blamed the Italian people for Italy's defeat and for their failure to appreciate his imperial dream. And in April 1945, just before Allied troops reached Milan, Mussolini and his mistress Clara Petacci were caught and summarily executed by Italian partisans.

It was not easy for Britain and the United States to formulate policies to deal with freed territories. They squabbled over whether an Italian government should be led by Marshal Pietro Badoglio, who had led Italian troops in Ethiopia and Greece, or dissident intellectual Carlo Sforza, who had been in exile since 1927. Badoglio, won out and remained as Premier until June 1944, and by then Italy, freed but fragmented, was divided on the issue of maintaining the monarchy. In the Balkans Britain and the United States had toyed with the notion of supporting the *Chetniks* in Yugoslavia, but in the end they decided to support Tito's Partisans because they were killing more Germans. In Albania, too, the Communist resistance movement led by Colonel Enver Hoxha was triumphant over the Republican resistance with important consequences for the character of post-war government.

With Greece threatening to disintegrate into civil war at the beginning of 1944, it was clear that Germany would not be easily defeated via this route. American determination to launch an invasion through France remained undiminished. They angrily dismissed British fears of a second Passchendaele or Dunkirk, and pointed to the advancing Soviet armies in the East to illustrate the mobility of the war and the need for a Western Front in France. By the end of August 1943 the Red Army was pushing through Bulgaria, by December 1944 it had reached Yugoslavia and was advancing through Czechoslovakia and in April 1945 the Eastern Front was in Königsberg (now

Kaliningrad) and Pillau in Eastern Poland (part of East Prussia before 1914, the territory was absorbed into Western Russia in 1945). Here the Red Army ran amok in an orgy of looting, rape and murder, and horror stories of the barbarous Red Army quickly spread.

Throughout the war Hitler and Stalin trumpeted that this great struggle was the supreme test of their respective political visions of the future. In reality, however, the war tested the resilience of their economies, the skill of their military leaders when they were allowed to do their job without the damaging interference of the dictators, the quality of their intelligence services, and the willingness of every family to sacrifice its menfolk in battle, their labour in war production, and their lives and homes to the enemy bombs.

The final stages of the war were accompanied by ever more numerous and terrifying bombing raids. To counter the failures of British bombing raids against Germany in 1940 and to prove the value of Bomber Command, Air Marshal (Bomber) Arthur Harris began to advocate saturation bombing: filling the skies with over 1,000 airplanes. Yet despite lavish claims massive, Allied bombing assaults appeared to do little to forestall increases in German industrial production during 1943–44. Nor did the terrible fire-bombing raids on Hamburg and Dresden (the latter described by Harris as 'more like fire-wood than human habitation') on the night of 13–14 February 1945, have much effect on German morale. Around 100,000 people are estimated to have died in Dresden which was bombed for 40 successive hours, although exact figures are hard to calculate since by that time the city was full of refugees fleeing from the Russians in the East. Little of the historic centre of one of Europe's most prized cities remained.

The character and impact of the bombing campaign remains controversial. Recent research suggests that Bomber Command's campaign against the German transport system in late 1944 contributed significantly to the collapse of the German war economy and war effort and that Bomber Harris should not be vilified for the decision to bomb civilians. Documents have come to light which make it clear that the strategy of attacking civilian population centres was advocated, not by Harris, but by the Chief of British Air Staff, Sir Charles Portal.[11] The peoples of 'Allied Europe' endured their own share of bombing terror in the closing stages of the war from Hitler's 'secret weapons': the V1 and V2 rockets. These weapons came too late to have a significant impact in the war, although the 9300 terrifying 'doodlebugs' which fell on London and the South, portents of the future, were designed to lower public morale.

American strategic attacks on the German aircraft industry had a great impact on the enemy and pointed the way forward for future military technology. Bombing cities mostly succeeded only in taking life: 25,000 were reported dead, 35,000 missing after the Dresden campaign. Behind the statistics lay individual human tragedies. For example, a young German woman recorded in her diary one grim story of a girl of 16 caught in an allied air raid on Berlin. She was standing atop of a pile of rubble, picking up the bricks one by one, dusting them carefully and throwing them away again. Apparently her entire family was dead, buried underneath, and she had gone mad.

The dead citizens of Rotterdam, Hamburg, London, Coventry, Dresden, Warsaw and Berlin are prominent among those still remembered as victims of enemy assaults. But other places, like Hull or Le Havres, suffered calamitously. Outside towns and cities, mistargeted bombs fell at random while women farming in the field made good target practice for passing fighter aircraft.

The 'second front', which Stalin had demanded for so long, was launched at last on 6 June 1944 when the Allied forces, under the command of the American General Dwight D. Eisenhower, born in Texas in 1890, landed at Normandy. Not all went according to plan. Allied landings on the Cotentin peninsula, for example, were a shambles, although this served to bemuse the Germans who were now entirely confused as to the Americans' true intent. Had the Germans reacted more effectively, the operation might have been disastrous for the Allies. As it was, however, Paris was liberated in less than three months, the prelude to the 'unconditional surrender' which the Allies had insisted upon. The German General Dietrich von Choltitz wisely disregarded Hitler's instructions to reduce Paris to 'a heap of rubble' and surrendered on 25 August 1944. On 19 March 1945 Hitler went even further, and issued his troops with a 'Nero order' to destroy everything in the path of the invader. Fortunately for Europe, this order too was ignored and sabotaged by leading Nazis, including Speer. Nothing could now save Germany from inevitable defeat. In April 1945 the German troops in the Ruhr surrendered. The SS resisted fiercely in the Harz mountains, but Hitler did not move out of Berlin to his mountain citadel of Berchtesgaden near the old Austrian border. The Red Army reached Berlin first on 22 April 1945, and eight days later Hitler and Eva Braun, married in the final days of the Reich, took their lives, as did some other Nazi leaders. It was the German Admiral, Karl Doenitz, who surrendered unconditionally on 9 May 1945.

The world war continued long enough in the Far East for the 'conventional' weapons, as they came to be called, to be abandoned in the search for peace. These weapons paled in their horror when set against the work of project 'Manhattan', the name by which the American programme to construct the world's first atomic bombs was known. The National Socialists had abandoned their work on nuclear weapons in 1942, believing that it would not bring dividends in time to help them win the war. American and British scientists, aided by émigrés from occupied Europe, pursued the quest and covertly developed their own 'secret weapon'. On 6 August 1945 a B–29 bomber, the 'Enola Gay', dropped a 14 kiloton uranium bomb on Hiroshima. The world had changed for ever. Nuclear technology, first employed not in Europe but in Japan, now could destroy more than towns, cities and thousands of the population. Ultimately it could destroy the earth.

ALLIED RELATIONS, 1943–45

With Germany defeated, tensions amongst the Allies, or the 'United Nations' as they had come to call themselves, burst out into the open. There had been some disagreement in Anglo-American relations over the conduct of the war, and especially over Britain's relations with its Empire, but these were nothing when set against the mounting frustrations in American relations with the Soviet Union. The mutual suspicion of the 1930s, greatly compounded by delay over the 'Second Front', the extent and character of the Soviet advance, and planning for the peace – particularly the vexed questions of what to do with Poland and Germany – was to replace the hot war which had ravaged Europe for six years with a Cold War which was to dominate political relationships for the next 45 years.

The Allies' wartime conferences at Casablanca in January 1943 and Teheran in November 1943 were genial affairs, and the Yalta conference in February 1945, ominous in retrospect, at the time appeared little different. Yet compromises arrived at there were dearly bought. It was clear that Stalin would not contemplate any return to the 1939 Polish frontiers or any future Polish government which was not dominated by Communists. There were also divisions over the shape of the future United Nations Organization, the new peace making agency which it was hoped would prevent any future war from breaking out. Frustration with the outcome of the Yalta Conference soon set in as it became apparent that the world's balance of power had shifted drastically in favour of the Soviet Union. It was now beyond doubt the greatest power in Europe.

Tension amongst the 'United Nations' were not eased when Japan unconditionally surrendered on 14 August 1945 after the Soviet Union had declared war on Japan on 8 August. Atomic bombs on Hiroshima and Nagasaki had sealed the fate of the Japanese Empire, and as one senior American recorded: 'the relief to everyone concerned when the bomb was finished and dropped was enormous.' But such relief as there was was short-lived. The last of the great wartime United Nations Conferences took place at Potsdam from 17 July to 2 August 1945, a short distance away from the ruined shell of Berlin. It was, however, a very different conference from Teheran or Yalta. Of the great war-time leaders only Stalin (along with Chinese nationalist President Chiang Kai-Shek) remained. Churchill had been replaced by Attlee, while Roosevelt's death had brought Harry S. Truman to the White House, and these new leaders now joined Stalin to discuss the perilous future of the world. Britain, Germany and France had been instrumental in causing two 'hot' wars which helped shape the twentieth century, yet they merely provided the stage for the Cold War. The principal actors in international affairs were now the Soviet Union and the United States, the former denied the secrets of 'the Bomb' and out of the (exclusively) American occupation of Japan.

The origins of the Cold War followed fast in the wake of the Second World War. It was not an 'inevitable' development any more than the

Second World War was the 'inevitable' consequence of the First, although it is difficult to see how East–West relations could have been anything other than troubled. The two world wars of the twentieth century began within 25 years of one another, and if the Cold War is included, Europe endured over 54 years of 'world war' in the twentieth century. But historians have, on the whole, eschewed the temptation to treat the two world wars as sequential chapters in one story.

The two world wars were different in their causes, origins and consequences. Kaiser Wilhelm II represented 'traditional' authority, as did in their different ways and policies the Romanovs of Russia and Habsburgs in Austria-Hungary. By contrast, Hitler's 'expansionism' was rooted in National Socialist thought, a confused but heady ideology, ushering in what Churchill called 'a new Dark Age, made more sinister, and perhaps more protracted, by the lights of perverted science.' Although the origins of the Second World War can only be fully understood if the diplomacy of other countries besides Germany is taken into account, German diplomacy can only be understood if National Socialist ideology, strategy and economics are brought into the picture. Hitler's foreign policy sprang from more than a desire to overturn the 'shame' of Versailles.

The Second World War proved not to be complete in itself. European history after 1945, very different from the history of the inter-war years, is inextricably related to the history of what happened between 1939 and 1945. There was no peace settlement as there had been in 1919. Nor was there any sense even of the provisional assurance of peace, despite the conditional surrender of the main defeated powers – Germany, Japan and Italy – and the creation of a new United Nations organization.

Notes

1. Quoted in R. J. Overy, *The Road to War* (1989), p.45.
2. R. Dell, *The Geneva Racket* (1941), p.8.
3. D. C. Watt, *How War Came* (1989), p.536.
4. W. S. Churchill, *The Second World War: The Grand Alliance*, Vol. III (1951), p.308.
5. *Ibid.*, *The Second World War: The Hinge of Fate*, Vol. IV (1951), p.343.
6. K. S. Karol, *Solik: Life in the Soviet Union, 1939–1946* (1986), p.76.
7. M. Harrison, 'The Soviet Union: the defeated victor' in M. Harrison (ed.), *The Economics of World War II. Six great powers in international comparison* (1998), p.293.
8. M. von der Grün, *Wie war es eignentlich? Kindheit und Jugend im Dritten Reich* (1981), pp.236–7.
9. W. Bergenruen, 'An die Völker der Erde', in W. Rose (ed.), *Modern German Lyric Verse, 1886–1955* (1960), p.185.
10. K. Mann, *Der Wendepunkt. Ein Lebensbericht* (1984), p.435.
11. R. J. Overy, *Bomber Command, 1939–1945*, (1997).

Chapter 10

FREEZING AND THAWING
POSTWAR EUROPE, 1945–1969

F or the people of Moscow peace officially began at 2 a.m. on the morning of 8 May 1945 when a salvo of a 1,000 guns was sounded. Some citizens cheered while others sobbed, recalling the loved ones who would never return. In London's Trafalgar Square crowds lit fireworks, sang songs and embraced, and beneath the Arc de Triumph General de Gaulle solemnly saluted the tomb of the unknown soldier before euphoric men and women swept away the barriers surrounding the tomb in enthusiastic celebration. In Germany, by contrast, news of the defeat was met in dumb, apathetic silence, despite Allied fears that zealous young soldiers would be reluctant to surrender arms.

For all of Europe, however, it did not take long for the pleasure of victory to be replaced by sobering recognition of the price to be paid for victors and vanquished alike. 'This noble continent', Winston Churchill proclaimed in neutral Switzerland in 1946, contained 'a vast quivering mass of tormented, hungry, care-worn and bewildered human beings' gaping at the ruins of their cities and scanning 'the dark horizons for the approach of some new peril, tyranny or terror'. Definitions of Europe now took on an institutional dimension as organizations appeared on a European and global level, dedicated to fostering understanding and co-operation between nations on economic, social and political issues.

Definitions of European geography changed too. Until the Cold War became the dominating feature of European life within three years of the Second World War, Europe was divided, as it was before 1939, into four distinct geographic regions: Northern Europe (Sweden, Denmark, Norway and Finland); Western Europe (including Ireland, Great Britain and France); Central Europe (including Germany, Italy, Greece, Austria, Hungary and Poland); and Eastern Europe (including Russia, the Ukraine and the Baltic states). Superpower rivalry and the political division of Europe in the Cold War changed all that. Central Europe effectively disappeared. Political alignment, not geography, determined that Northern Europe and, more particularly, large sections of Central Europe, notably Greece, Germany, Austria and Italy now all found themselves located in the West.

The following two chapters follow this division the treatment of events after 1950, with this chapter primarily concerned with Eastern Europe while the next chapter focuses on Western Europe. This artificial division of European history ends in Chapter 12. The tumultuous events of 1968 demonstrated both the social, cultural and economic limitations of European reconstruction, and the degree to which the fate of East and West remained profoundly intertwined. The end of the Soviet Union in 1991 ended many East/West divisions and the visit of President George W. Bush to Moscow in 2002 for both sides marked the formal end of the Cold War.

THE DAMAGE OF WAR

The Second World War had far outstripped its predecessor in the loss of life and property. This time, Britain and France had suffered less than in the First World War, with 350,000 and 620,000 victims respectively, but in central and Eastern Europe the loss of life had been enormous. Civilian deaths far outnumbered those of military personnel. Soviet losses were estimated at 20 million lives, while relative losses in Poland, Yugoslavia and Germany were even higher. Poland had sacrificed over six million men and women, Yugoslavia had sacrificed 1.7 million and Germany more than five million men and women. The racist character of the Nazi war effort had changed the composition of Europe's population for ever with significant consequences, too, for European culture and identity. In Poland, home to some 3.2 million Jews in 1939, nearly 90 per cent were murdered by the Nazis and their local collaborators; a similar proportion of the pre-war Jewish populations of the Ukraine and the Baltic states had also been murdered.

The infrastructure of Central and Eastern Europe had been damaged on an enormous scale. More than half of all livestock in Poland and Yugoslavia was destroyed and Eastern Europe's transportation network lay in ruins. Looting by the retreating Nazis and advancing Red Army also cost Eastern Europe dear. The total cost of German looting was estimated at around $20–25 billion, while Soviet looting, under the guise of 'justifiable reparations', was especially ruthless in European territories which had been allied to the axis powers – Bulgaria, Hungary and Romania. It was Soviet occupied East Germany, however, which suffered the most. As Charles Kindleberger, an American economist working for the reparations commission – and reparations were a contentious issue among the allies – recalled: while 'the United States was feeding its zone, and the British were feeding their zone as best they could . . . The Russians were looting their zone. It was really like a cow with the mouth in one zone and the udder in the other.'[1]

There was also physical destruction on a breath-taking scale. A mobile, mechanised war had been fought across Poland, Yugoslavia, Russia, Greece, Italy, northern France, Belgium, the Netherlands and Germany and heavy bombing had brought immense damage to almost every major European conurbation. Cities like Coventry, Rotterdam, and Warsaw had only one commodity in plentiful supply in 1945: rubble, the piles of which could be measured in acres or mountains, and buried beneath the rubble were homes, schools, hospitals, factories, shops and railway stations. For those living in the cities, eking out an existence amidst severe food and clothing shortages, the peace first brought further misery before it alleviated conditions. For many, the lack of adequate shelter was the greatest hardship of all. In Düsseldorf, for example, it was estimated that 93 per cent of dwellings were uninhabitable and Europe's urban housing shortage became acute with the approach of winter.

A RIVER OF REFUGEES

Around 50 million people had been expelled from their homes by the advancing armies, particularly those of the Soviet Union, and the search for shelter quickly entailed the greatest migration Europe had known for 1,500 years. Refugees fled in many directions, although the predominant flow was from East to West. Prisoners and forced labour seized by the National Socialists also began to stream from Germany once hostilities ceased. This group were known as Displaced Persons (DPs), waiting to be repatriated or to be given an immigration permit to begin a new life overseas. According to Allied estimates there were at least 25 million DPs from all over Europe in 1945, with the largest groups coming from the Soviet Union, France, Poland, the Netherlands, Belgium, Italy and Yugoslavia. Their shelter was often temporary and primitive, and their food supplies meagre; some DPs were even placed in Dachau, a former concentration camp, converted to house refugees. 'Why is it I smell all the time, wherever I turn, the reek of the Displaced Persons' Camp?', asked English novelist Evelyn Waugh, in his diary of November 1946.

Germans (*Volksdeutsche*) who had been lured eastwards in 1939 by the Nazi dream of an East European empire beat a hasty retreat in the face of the Red Army's advance. But so, too, did ethnic Germans who had been resident in Eastern Europe since the thirteenth century. Most dramatic were the population movements triggered by the westward expansion of the USSR into Poland by 1945. Poland, too, had moved west by some 120km (around 75 miles). Its new frontier with Germany was the confluence of the rivers Oder and Neisse. (The boundary became known as the Oder-Neisse line.) The move was intended to enhance Polish security – the reputedly militarist Prussian state now was dismembered with ancient German cities like Breslau, Danzig, Königsberg and Stettin given Polish names and absorbed into the republic – and to compensate Poland for the loss of lands and cities like L'vov (L'viv) to the east. The new arrangements still left Poland some 20 per cent smaller than it had been in 1919, whereas Allied-occupied Germany had shrunk by only 18 per cent.

The loss of these territories that had been Protestant since the Reformation also left Germany a much more Roman Catholic country than it had been before, and while Germany absorbed the refugees fleeing from its lost territories to the east with equanimity, this did not extend to a recognition of the Oder-Neisse line as the true frontier between Germany and Poland. Only in 1990, when East and West Germany were reunified, was the ambiguity resolved, a situation that suited the USSR throughout the Cold War because the uncertainty made Poland feel more dependent on Soviet support for its security.

The process of repatriation was not simple. Ukrainians and Latvians who had fought against the Red Army could not return home (some were forced to go back anyway), and thousands of Jews sought to flee Europe, although in 1947 the Jewish refugee ship, *Exodus*, laden with emaciated survivors of the death camps, ignominiously was unable to find safe harbour in Palestine or Europe. The main beneficiary of Europe's failure to make Jews feel welcome or secure in the wake of war's end was Zionism. It has been estimated that some 250,000 Jews fled Eastern Europe between 1945 and 1948, the vast majority of them helped by Zionist organizations who proved more efficient and adept at helping this desperate people than either the Allied powers or their relief organizations. In Germany, Austria and Italy, alone an additional 250,000 Jews were dependent for help on the United Nations Relief and Rehabilitation Agency (UNRRA), set up in 1943. The organization was overwhelmed by the scale of the problem.

When it came to establishing national boundaries in Central and Eastern Europe, the Anglo-American allies insisted that the transfers of populations be conducted humanely, but Stalin was not interested in such niceties. The motives behind the forced expulsions of Germans from these eastern territories was easy to understand: to prevent the emergence of a 'problem' German minority that had proved fatal for Poland and Czechoslovakia by 1939. Agreements signed between the Soviet Union and nations in Eastern Europe prompted waves of migration, as regions like northern Czechoslovakia, southern Bohemia and Moravia, once inhabited by three million Sudeten Germans, were now populated by Czechs and Slovaks. But there was also a new determination to achieve ethnic conformity and thereby, it was believed, national cohesion by expelling other minority groups from territories they had occupied, sometimes for centuries.

In February 1946 Czechoslovakia and Hungary signed an agreement which sanctioned the compulsory transfer of 200,000 Magyars out of Czechoslovakia into Hungary, and 200,000 Slovaks out of Hungary into Czechoslovakia. Particularly tragic was the fate of Poles living to the east of the Ribbentrop-Molotov line – the portion of Poland absorbed into the Soviet Union in 1939. Stalin made no secret of his intention to retain control of this territory, and despite Churchill and Roosevelt's best efforts to protect the four million Poles living there, Stalin forcibly resettled over two million of them into Western Poland by 1950.

Added to the struggle for shelter came the struggle for food. In 1946 over 100 million people in Europe were still sustained on only a diet of 1,500 calories a day (a calorific level which would guarantee weight loss for healthy Europeans today), and only 900–1,000 calories were allocated to Germans within British and American zones of occupation. Food shortages continued long after the fighting had ceased as crops went unplanted, unharvested or undistributed, shortages which were greatly exacerbated by the terrible winter of 1946–7. It would take time for Europe's agriculture and industry to recover. Even once the immediate physical shortages and transportation bottlenecks were cleared, Europe's overriding difficulty rapidly became earning sufficient foreign exchange to pay for food and other essential imports.

For the nations of Europe, which long had taken pride in their export industries, the war had caused substantial disruption. For fledgling post-war governments, troubled by inflation and widespread destruction, the need to revive international trade became imperative. As during the First World War, it was the American economy which had profited from Europe's warmongering. Sweden, Switzerland and Britain were among the only countries in Europe to export goods at anything like their pre-war levels. British export figures, invigorated by export drives and the restriction of supplies for the home market, were among the healthiest in 1945–6 even though they had fallen to 25–30 per cent of their pre-war figure. But in Eastern Europe many countries were unable to produce any exports at all.

THE LEGACY OF RESISTANCE AND COLLABORATION

In Germany 1945 was marked by *Die Stunde Null* (the zero hour) and the situation was critical: trains had ceased to run, banks were closed, there was no coal and hence no electric light, and there was little food. Without exports Europe, in effect, was unable to pay for its provisions, but its people still needed to eat. In seeking to provide food and other necessities UNRRA quickly found its resources intolerably stretched. In August 1945 the Soviet Union applied for $700 million to launch relief operations, but had to be content with $250 million for the two devastated republics of Byelo-Russia and the Ukraine. At the height of its far-flung activities UNRRA, a product of wartime co-operation, employed around 25,000 people outside as well as inside Europe. But by 1947 Europe's inability to pay for its food was to provoke an international crisis which had important and far reaching consequences for both diplomatic relations amongst European powers and for their links with the two 'superpowers' which now straddled the globe: the United States and the USSR.

In 1945 many well dressed and well fed American observers regarded European politicians and, indeed, European politics as morally bankrupt – a view shared by the Soviet Union. If the slaughter of the First World War had undermined Europe's confident belief in human progress, the Second World War eroded any vestiges of the implicit belief in Europe's moral superiority. In former German-occupied territories, the 'criminals' were the 'collaborationists', men and women who had worked for the Germans and their allies during the war: chief amongst them was Marshal Pétain, the 84 year-old 'supreme patriot' who assumed control of Vichy France and helped to create a corrupt, authoritarian state centred on his personal authority. Official Vichy documents began: *Nous, Philippe Pétain, chef de l'État.*

Clergymen found themselves on both sides of the collaboration/resistance divide. Those who had resisted the Nazis – such as Otto Dibelius who the Third Reich found a troubling presence in his Lutheran see of Berlin-Brandenburg – were now sought after for leading roles in the postwar church. Dibelius was appointed Lutheran Bishop of Hannover. Outside Germany, Eivind Berggrav, the Bishop of Olso who defied the Nazi quisling government in Norway became a revered figure in Protestant western Europe. But circumstances in France reflected the true complexity of the church's fate during the war. Implicated in the work of Vichy France, the postwar French government demanded that the Vatican remove some 40 bishops from their holy sees. But thanks to the intervention of General de Gaulle and the prominent role played by lower ranking churchmen in the French resistance, ultimately only five bishops were sacked.

The suspicion and iniquity which Vichy encouraged (movingly recounted in François Maspero's novel *Cat's Grin* published in 1988), had prompted around three to five million French men and women to denounce members of their town, village and even family. Now this was overtaken by a desire to punish the 'collaborators'. It is important not to exaggerate the degree of either collaboration or of resistance in France. While it is true that in some regions – notably the Dordogne, a tourist area of the future – resistance leaders took matters into their own hands, the French liberation government sanctioned only 746 executions after trial. There were, however, around 9,000 summary executions – rumours at the time put the figure closer to 100,000.

Inside Germany the prosecution of Nazi war criminals, which began in November 1945, was of a different order. The trials, held in the German city of Nuremberg, marked a new stage in the evolution of human rights. In 1789 the French declaration of the rights of man and of the citizen resounded and came to have a profound impact on domestic legal and political systems. Now after 1945, the term human rights began to take on a new meaning in a new institutional complex. A network of international law and practice began to develop around the idea that individuals possess human rights simply because they are human. The new ambition was that these rights be recognized by all humans and, if necessary, enforced by the international community, now a frequently used expression. This would take some time; and in 1945 itself the trials were designed as part of a de-Nazification process to remind all Europeans, not just the Germans, of the depths to which humanity could sink. Typical amongst the prosecution evidence in Nuremberg were excerpts from SS General Stroop's report on the razing of Warsaw:

> I . . . decided to destroy the entire Jewish residential area by setting every block on fire . . . Not infrequently, the Jews stayed in the burning buildings until, because of the heat and the fear of being burned alive, they preferred to jump down from the upper stories . . . With their bones broken, they still tried to crawl across the street into blocks of buildings which had not yet been set on fire.[2]

Many Germans felt shame, horror and anger at their former Nazi leaders, but they were also anxious to press on with the task of reconstruction, and took little interest in the trials of the war criminals.

There were times when existence itself was what mattered to them, as it did to many writers and artists of the period, for whom the expression 'existentialism' was coined. A stunned, dazed population spent their days trying to find food, clothing, shelter, and posting messages to bombed-out buildings in their efforts to be reunited with other members of their family. Reminders of Germany's inglorious past were unwelcome: war veterans, especially the wounded, were unable to find work when they returned home, while former concentration camp inmates were shunned.

Elsewhere in western Europe, former prisoners were treated to a similarly cool reception. Talk of the recent, inglorious past was avoided. As Jean-Marie Lustiger, a young Jewish survivor of Auschwitz who later went on to become Archbishop of Paris, remembered: 'What was quite extraordinary was that it was such a taboo subject that nobody spoke about it [life in the concentration camps] and nobody wanted to speak about.' Such bitter suspicion was not confined to local communities. It found a parallel in the mounting ill-will and division between east and west in international relations.

THE ORIGINS OF THE COLD WAR: THE VIEW FROM THE WEST, 1945–47

If the Cold War began with the deliberate Soviet decision to cut Europe in two, equally momentous was the decision by the Western powers to extend the division of Germany after 1945. The question of what to do with Germany had exercised the Americans, in particular, during the course of the war. Indeed, complaints were even voiced within Roosevelt's administration that too much attention was being devoted to planning for the peace, too little on waging the war. In 1944 the most influential proposal was that of Henry Morgenthau Jr., Secretary of State to the U.S. Treasury, who proposed that the world impose a punitive peace on Germany: it should be turned into a 'pastoral' country, with industrial assets like the *Kohlenpot* (coalpot) of the Ruhr given to France.

Such a retributive peace was not pressed for in the United States, but France and the Soviet Union were determined to extract recompense for German aggression. Like Stalin, General de Gaulle's strategy was designed to weaken Germany fundamentally by destroying all trace of centralized government, and he blocked attempts by the Allied council to treat Germany as whole. To some extent this reflected the different war experiences of France and the USSR to those of their 'anglo-saxon' Allies, but it was also a product of French and Russian attitudes to German history and the rise of Nazism. Thus, the four zones of military occupation soon became four distinct political units, each reflecting the political identity of its occupier.

By the end of 1945 peace settlements which threatened to debilitate Germany had been abandoned in favour of policies which increasingly placed the British, American and French zones of Germany at the heart of Western Europe's defence. So, where once the Allies, democratic and Communist alike, reeled in horror at the discovery of the concentration camps and were determined to enforce a policy of non-fraternization with the Germans, the need to manage Germany's mounting economic problems initiated a new response from the Western Allies. The abrupt ending of American Lend Lease in May 1945 had aggravated the situation.

While the State Department in Washington received sometimes exaggerated reports of the expansionist ambitions of the USSR – amongst the most famous and influential the so-called 'Long Telegram', 8,000 words in all, of George Kennan, counsellor to the U.S. Embassy in Moscow – conditions within Europe continued to deteriorate. Reconstruction loans granted from the new economic institutions set up at Bretton Woods in 1944, the International Monetary Fund and the International Bank for Reconstruction and Development (the World Bank), proved as inadequate as the efforts of UNRRA. But there was no agreement between Washington and Moscow as to how to handle Europe's desperate need for dollars to buy food and other essentials. By the time the foreign ministers of Germany's occupying powers met in March 1946, therefore, the Anglo-Americans and the Soviets were beginning to evolve largely incompatible plans for resuscitation. At this meeting, the disparate approaches of East and West were obvious, especially since the USSR and USA had begun to appeal directly to the German people for support against the other: the USSR offering a workers' republic; the USA offering a federal, liberal government to prepare for economic resuscitation.

A month before the representatives of the occupying powers met, it was in February 1946, too, that Churchill, in opposition, pre-empted the future hostility of 'the West' to the Soviet colossus, in his famous 'Iron Curtain' speech made in Fulton, Missouri:

> From Stettin in the Baltic to Trieste in the Adriatic, an iron curtain has descended across the continent . . . (Moreover), in a great many countries, far from the Russian frontiers and throughout the world, Communist fifth columns are established and at work in complete unity and absolute obedience with the Communist centre.

Churchill's words were condemned by Stalin in *Pravda* as a 'dangerous, calculated move' and his argument did not yet appeal to many Americans. There were many of the latter, indeed, who suspected that Churchill's 'scare-mongering' was born of Britain's desire to keep America involved in Europe. Inside the US administration there were many who still advocated sharing atomic technology with the Soviet Union, or who believed that the increase in international tension would harm world prosperity. Among those who urged greater conciliation between East and West, fearing that 'the tougher we get, the tougher the Soviets will get', was the influential journalist, Walter Lippmann, who argued that the doom-laden prophesies of Soviet expansionism were grossly exaggerated and that a political settlement for Central and Eastern Europe should be possible. In 1947 Lippmann's articles were published together in a book entitled *The Cold War* (September 1947), a term which was quickly assimilated into the world's political vocabulary.

Throughout 1946, however, there was no further progress on the still unresolved issue of how to treat Germany. For Truman's first US Secretary of State, James Byrnes, the one achievement of countless meetings with his Soviet counterpart, Molotov, was to establish that the latter thought American whisky as good as Russian vodka. The British Foreign Secretary, Ernest Bevin, too, had grown impatient with the Soviet Union. Much to the annoyance of the large British minority, which included many members of the Labour Party, who wanted a more independent, less pro-American orientated policy, Bevin was determined to place the blame for disagreement on the Kremlin and, in a display of unity with the Conservative party, Bevin joined Churchill before Parliament in calling the Soviet Union the main obstacle to peace and stability.

The need to ameliorate conditions in Germany while at the same time lightening the aid burden on taxpayers in Britain, France and the United States, was a further incentive to a speedy resolution of the German issue. Administrating Germany in separate zones was costly and trade between the different zones was handled as if it were trade between different states. In June 1946 the Americans suggested that the other occupying forces merge the zonal economies, but only the British accepted and a joint administration of the two zones, budded 'Bizonia', was in place by the end of the year. In September 1946 Byrnes had announced that the United States favoured 'the economic unification of Germany' and that if complete unification could not be secured, 'we shall do everything in our power to secure the maximum possible unification'.

Nevertheless, as the drain on the British Treasury continued, with extra burdens being borne outside Europe, too, in Palestine and in India, Britain could not maintain its role in Greece and Turkey. In March 1947 the United States stepped in to fill the gap left by Britain and introduced an extensive aid programme for Greece and Turkey pronouncing what was called at the time 'the Truman Doctrine'. It was a significant step on the way to Cold War, reflecting Kennan's conviction that the 'traditional and instinctive sense of Russian insecurity' made inevitable both Soviet domination of Eastern Europe and Communist ambitions over the remainder of the world'. Washington had become convinced that the Communist cancer was spreading, feeding on poverty and despair, and America should act to 'contain' this menace. 'Containment' was the Kennan word.

THE VIEW FROM THE EAST, 1944–46

In the West it was the interaction of the desperate conditions inside Germany and mounting unease about Soviet intentions amongst the western allies which increased the tension in East-West relations. In the East wartime developments helped Stalin's ambition to transform Eastern Europe into a pro-communist security zone for the Soviet Union. For many in war-torn Europe Communism was identified as a liberating, idealist creed, untainted by associations with the crisis of capitalism and liberal democracy in the 1930s, or with the barbarity of fascism in the 1940s. Indeed, many future Communist leaders – like the German Erich Honecker (1971–89) and the Czech Gustáv Husák (1969–88) – had impressive anti-fascist credentials having spent long years in fascist prisons. The extension of state control during the war also appeared to make communist-style government an appropriate choice for the massive effort of reconstruction which Eastern Europe would need once the war was over.

Although the application of Stalin's policies in Europe appeared inconsistent, his aim was not. Stalin was determined to establish as much of a security zone as possible for the USSR in Eastern Europe without provoking America, giving the Soviet Union time to 'catch up' with its rival superpower. Stalin did not establish Soviet control in Eastern Europe simply by right of conquest in 1945, but step by step, in response to political developments within each Eastern European country and to international events. By 1948 he was in exclusive control of most of Eastern Europe.

Stalin responded with caution when in the last year of the war armed Communist partisans, supported by popular front political movements, appeared capable of bringing Communist revolution to both eastern and western Europe: the Soviet leader did not wish to alienate his western allies and urged Communist partisans from the Balkans to France to abandon talk of popular Communist governments 'from below', and instead accept proposals to join post-war coalition governments as partners, sometimes even junior partners. Communists in France, Italy and, with considerable reluctance, in Greece did as they were told. But there were limits to his influence for already a popular Communist revolution 'from below' in Yugoslavia, led by Tito, had gone too far for Stalin to stop it.

The experience of democracy in Eastern Europe and in the Balkans during the inter-war years had been brief and desultory, but Stalin was by no means confident that all Eastern European countries would make a successful transition to Communism between 1945 and 1948. There was a clear distinction between countries like Poland, Romania and Bulgaria which Stalin placed under effective Soviet control from the moment the Red Army crossed their borders, and countries like Hungary and Czechoslovakia where the Soviet Union was content at first to allow the Communists·to have influence, but not complete control, in coalition governments.

Once again, as in the nineteenth century and during the Russian civil war (1918–21), Poland was central to Russia's strategic plans. The Polish people presented a sizeable obstacle to Stalin's forthright ambitions for Soviet security, with their historic hostility towards Russia, their vibrant Catholicism, the widespread opinions expressed by their vociferous government in exile and the public knowledge that it was Soviet soldiers who had murdered 15,000 Polish officers in the Katyn forest in 1943. Even Poland's Communists had a tradition of opposition to the Moscow line which first began with Rosa Luxembourg. In July 1944, therefore, Moscow acted decisively to ensure that political developments in Poland fell in their favour. In July 1944 the Lublin Committee, a communist-dominated group of Polish leaders drawn from the Polish resistance movement and subsequently groomed in Moscow, was established in Warsaw as the government of Poland in order to frustrate the aspirations of the London Poles who had conducted the fight against the Germans from exile. Here, as in Bulgaria and Romania in 1945, the intervention of the Red Army was decisive. Soviet control was now assured.

In Czechoslovakia and Hungary, however, where at the end of the war the Communists dominated the resistance movement and might have seized power immediately, there was a time lapse before they took over. Stalin, Churchill and Roosevelt had agreed in 1943 that coalition governments should be established across Europe in the aftermath of war and Stalin ordered Czech and Hungarian Communists to participate in 'Popular Front' governments as he did in the West. There was one important difference, however, in the instructions that he gave to Communists in Eastern Europe and their comrades in West. In Czechoslovakia and Hungary Communist militias were not disbanded and they soon became the basis of Communist army and security units. It was a further source of strength that they carefully took control of the powerful interior ministries.

Klement Gottwald, the Czechoslovakian Communist leader, obediently followed Stalin's instructions. Far from immediately asserting control over the 'national revolutionary committees' which had sprung up across Czechoslovakia, he sought instead to broaden the membership of these committees in 1945, bringing in other political parties. Meanwhile, Edvard Beneš, the Czechoslovak leader who had been exiled in London during the Nazi occupation, continued to have an influential voice in Czechoslovakian politics. In May 1946 free elections were held and the Communists won 38 per cent of the vote while the socialists secured a total of 51 per cent. This was a clear signal that the Communists would not acquire decisive political power.

Hungary as a defeated Axis power was more vulnerable to a Communist take-over, but even there Stalin acted swiftly in 1945 to stop Hungarian Communists from openly proclaiming that the 'dictatorship of the proletariat' was nigh and Hungary, too, had elections in 1945. The Communists and socialists achieved similar levels of support, but when the peasant dominated smallholders party secured 50 per cent of the vote for themselves, it was the British and Americans who made it clear that they preferred the stability offered by a coalition government. The Communists were quick to seize the advantage and in 1946 secured control of the interior ministry and exploited the growing conflict between the Left Bloc of socialists and Communists on the one hand and the smallholders party on the other. The result was that on new year's eve in 1946, the smallholders party resigned from government amid accusations that some of their senior leaders were involved in an extensive anti-Republican conspiracy. Having attacked conservative and centrist political groups with charges of 'anti-Sovietism' and 'pro-fascism' and driven them from government by what the Hungarian Communist leader, Mátyás Rákosi, later called 'salami tactics', it was now the turn of socialists to be cut off from power.

The same tactics had earlier been used in Bulgaria and Romania where there were fewer reasons to move cautiously. The much proclaimed popular front governments of Eastern Europe became caricatures of democracy – hiding behind their self-proclaimed status as 'People's Democracies' – as the Communists exploited their control not only of the interior ministries, but of the machinery of propaganda.

THE MARSHALL PLAN

Events in Western Europe encouraged Stalin to fortify the position of the Communists in Eastern Europe. By early 1947 the twin issues of a German peace treaty and economic unification became crucial as conditions across Europe continued to deteriorate. When the World Bank and International Monetary Fund opened their doors in the spring of 1947, France quickly borrowed to the hilt from both institutions, although neither had been created for such an eventuality, and in Germany miners in the Ruhr were so hungry that in the cold weather already dwindling levels coal production further declined. George Marshall, Truman's new Secretary of State, who had served as America's Chief of Staff during the Second World War, announced an extensive recovery plan to haul Europe to its feet. A massive aid package was offered to all European powers who were having great difficulty recovering from the war, particularly after the harsh winter that gripped the continent from 1946 to 1947. Congress and the American people gave the plan unprecedented support, although their approval was predicated, in part, on the fact that the European Recovery Plan, or Marshall Plan as it became known, embodied a long-standing tenet of American foreign policy: economic stability helps secure democracy. Self-interest also played its part. As both Truman and Marshall made clear, America's economic well-being was dependent upon the health of the European markets. The Marshall Plan was a bold and imaginative declaration. Costing the United States $13.7 billion, it injected a new confidence into the countries of Western Europe. Historians have argued about the extent to which the Plan made a crucial difference to countries whose economies were already improving, but the final report on the Plan in 1952 rightly pointed out that between 1947 and 1952 West European industrial production had risen by 64 per cent, aluminium production by 69 per cent and cement by 90 per cent.

The Soviet Union disliked both the character and the intent of the Plan in 1947 and (as the West had calculated) refused to participate. Although the Eastern European countries were desperate for economic assistance and both Czechoslovakia and Poland quickly assented to Marshall aid, they were forced by the Soviet Union to withdraw. Stalin came up with his own scheme: the Council of Mutual Economic Assistance or Comecon as it became widely known. By insisting that Communist Eastern Europe reject Marshall aid, these countries were thrown back on their own meagre resources making the resort to Soviet-style planned economics and coercive measures to manage their economies all the more likely. In reality, Comecon was not able to offer much help. The real transfer of sources was in the other direction: it has been estimated that between 1945 and Stalin's death in 1953, the USSR transferred resources out of Eastern Europe and into the Soviet Union on a scale comparable with Marshall plan aid to Western Europe.

Thanks to Americanization in the West and Sovietization in the East, in the first years after the war the economic, social and political histories of Western and Eastern Europe appeared set on increasingly divergent paths, although as events in the 1960s were to clearly demonstrate, their fate was still very much intertwined. Relations worsened when eastern bloc Communists, along with Communists from France and Italy who in their own countries had been marginalized from political power, were summoned to a meeting in Poland, where they were presented with the Kremlin's vision of a world which had 'repudiated the principles of international co-operation' and was now divided into two camps. In articulating this vision, the Soviets, of course, helped to make it a reality.

CZECHOSLOVAKIA

Europe's Cold War future in 1948 hinged on Czechoslovakia, the only country in Central Europe which at the end of 1947 had a genuine coalition government. To many people in the West it seemed like a bridge, democratic but within the Russian security zone, but the democracy would not last long. Disagreements between the socialists and Communists had grown increasingly acrimonious throughout 1947 (tension was also rife amongst the Communists); and in February 1948, in a bitter dispute over rates of pay for civil servants, ministers from the Slovak Democratic People's Party, the People's Party and the National Socialist party all resigned from the government. It was a grave tactical error. The Communists promptly called a number of large public meetings and set up Action Committees across Czechoslovakia to demonstrate popular support for Communism.

By March 1948, the Czechoslovakian cabinet was entirely Communist, apart from Jan Masaryk, Czechoslovakia's foreign minister and son of the founding President of Czechoslovakia, and even this semblance of political diversity did not last long. On 10 March 1948 he and a cabinet colleague were found dead after an apparent 'fall' from a high window. Masaryk's death shocked the west which immediately concluded that Masaryk had been pushed (the resonances of the 1648 defenestration of Habsburg officials in Prague offered tempting 'proof'), and further soured relations between east and west. In the aftermath of the coup all Czechoslovak political parties, including the Slovak Communist Party, were amalgamated within the Czech Communist Party. From February 1948 Czechoslovakia, like all the other countries of what was beginning to be thought of as an 'eastern bloc', was now under one party rule.

THE BERLIN BLOCKADE, 1948–49

Ideological difference was obvious in the new alignment, and the attempt to find practical, effective solutions to Europe's problems, was made more difficult. Nowhere was this more apparent than over the question of German currency reform in 1947–8. The Western powers had delayed as long as possible over the issue of monetary reform, recognizing its powerful political and economic implications: a western supported currency introduced into the trizonal area would create a completely separate economy from that of the Soviet zone, simultaneously undermining the value of the currency in the Eastern zone and, most important, contravening the agreement to treat all four German zones as a single economic unit. But with relations worsening between East and West, and with the imminent introduction of Marshall aid, something had to be done. It was in sudden and in secret. A new German mark was printed and introduced into Trizonia without warning in June 1948.

The result was a dramatic escalation in Cold War tensions. On 23 June 1948, in protest to what amounted to the creation of 'west' Germany, the Soviets began to blockade Berlin, a city which was divided into four occupied zones, but which lay deep within the Soviet zone. Stalin's action was typically ham-fisted. Rather than make the West more conciliatory, Stalin's blockade only served to convince those who had doubted alarmist prophesies of Soviet expansion, and hasten the creation of a West German Federal Republic. In a dramatic and resolute initiative, the Allies airlifted supplies to over two million stranded Berliners until May 1949 when the Soviet Union called off its blockade. British Air Commodore, Fred Rainsford, reflected on the irony of the operation: 'it was very odd that people like myself, who had been bombing Berlin a few years earlier, should now be intent . . . on keeping it alive.'[3]

AN END TO DIVERSITY:
EASTERN EUROPE, 1948–50

Stalin's vice-like grip over Eastern Europe tightened as relations between east and west deteriorated, and in 1948 the Cold War received new impetus from an unexpected quarter – the growing rift between Stalin and Tito. Until January 1948 Belgrade and Moscow had enjoyed excellent relations, although Stalin had disagreed with Tito's strategy of advancing Communism from below with widespread, popular support. The new Communist Information Bureau (Cominform), established in September 1947, and designed to bolster Communism in Eastern Europe and to impose some kind of ideological uniformity on the region, had its headquarters in Belgrade.

Yugoslavia had pressed full ahead with the implementation of a soviet style economy, collectivizing agriculture as early as July 1946, and introducing his first five-year plan in April 1947. Throughout 1947 Tito actively promoted Communism in Eastern Europe, including Greece, and bolstered his reputation further with a number of commercial treaties with Bulgaria, Hungary and Romania, raising the stakes in January 1948 by stationing Yugoslav troops in Albania to help defend Greek Communist bases. He did this, however, without the approval of Stalin who increasingly perceived Tito's independence as a threat to his authority. Tito publicly proclaimed that he looked forward to the creation of a Balkan federation of 'free Balkan peoples'. Such ambition was too much for Stalin and he could tolerate Tito's independence no longer. As Tito observed in 1950, 'the Russians are [not] prepared to accept anybody who is keeping a relationship with the other side . . . you have to be 100 per cent on their side.'

The consequences of the Tito-Stalin split were dramatic. The Soviet leader accused Tito and the Yugoslav Communist Party of operating semi-illegally, of failing to collectivize agriculture and, most significantly, of diminishing the status of the Communist Party and on 28 June 1948 Yugoslavia was expelled from the Cominform. Nor was that the end. By 1950 Stalin was contemplating a joint Soviet and Eastern European military action against Yugoslavia. He knew that he could count on the 'bloc'. Major General Béla Király of the Hungarian army made it clear, for example, that 'at the pleasure of Stalin, we would have marched against Yugoslavia'. The Yugoslavian republic was saved from this fate by the outbreak of the Korean war which diverted Stalin's attention to the most eastern tip of his empire.

For Tito, the outcome of the split was not all bad. He was able to press ahead with his conception of a planned economy and to improve Yugoslavian relations with the west, especially with the United States. In July 1948 frozen Yugoslavian assets in America, including over $47 million in gold, were liberated. Yet the impact of the Tito-Stalin split was not confined to Soviet-Yugoslav relations. The allegations levied against Tito were soon taken up elsewhere to ensure that Communist Parties would be loyal to Stalin. Allegations of 'Titoism' provided the grounds for purges which cost Wladyslaw

Gomulka his post as Communist Party leader in Poland, and in a spectacular show trial in Hungary, a former leader of the Hungarian Communist Party and Cabinet minister, László Rajk, confessed to spying for the Nazis, the United States, Britain *and* Tito. He and his 'accomplices' were executed on 15 October 1949. Rajk's conviction subsequently became the justification for all Eastern European countries to break diplomatic relations with Yugoslavia.

In Czechoslovakia purges concentrated on suspected pro-Titoists and Communists who had spent the war exiled in London. The trials quickly snowballed culminating in the trial of the 'Moscow Communist' and former party leader Rudolf Slánský in 1951 (the anti-semitic flavour of this purge reflected similar developments inside the USSR at this time), and in a sustained attack on the Catholic church which was to span many years. In Albania and Bulgaria, by contrast, the determination of some Communists to root out their pro-Tito comrades was not, on the whole, motivated by an unflinching loyalty to Stalin, but by long-standing, ethnic and national rivalries.

NATIONALISM AND COMMUNISM, 1948–56

In July 1946 Albania and Yugoslavia had signed a treaty of friendship, co-operation and mutual aid which, in practice, made Communist Albania a virtual satellite of its Yugoslav neighbour – Serbian was made compulsory in schools and Yugoslavian 'experts' were given key roles in the armed forces and government. It was not long, however, before the Albanians began to resent their vassal status, and Stalin's condemnation of Tito and the wave of anti-Titoist purges provided an excellent opportunity for anti-Yugoslav Albanian Communists, clustered around Enver Hoxha, to eliminate their pro-Yugoslavian comrades. Despite their credentials as 'internationalists', this dispute within the Albanian Communist Party amongst Albania's Communists was marked by all the historic enmity which had long characterized Serbian-Albanian relations. It was significant that the day of Yugoslavia's expulsion from the Comintern (28 June 1948) coincided with the feast day of St Vitus, patron saint of Serbia. Albania became the first Eastern European state to line up behind the Soviet Union in its crusade against Tito and its loyalty to Stalin was richly rewarded by the USSR: it received over $600 million in economic aid.

Some Bulgarian Communists were also happy to turn against their Yugoslav comrades who helped to accelerate the transition of the region to Communism. Bulgarian pride was wounded by the leading role taken by Yugoslavia's Communists in the region and were angered by their leadership's willingness to cede Bulgarian claims over Macedonia to Tito in his plans for a Balkan federation. After the Stalin-Tito split the anti-Serbian Communists in Bulgaria seized the initiative. In December 1949 Traicho Kostov, a leading Communist with well-known connections to the Yugoslavians was executed, and until the 1970s Bulgaria, unlike the sometimes wavering Albania, adopted a staunch pro-Soviet line which extended to contributing Bulgarian troops to the Soviet invasion of Czechoslovakia in 1968.

Communism did not banish or even repress nationalism in Eastern Europe for very long after the Second World War. Once the Communist Parties attempted to widen their appeal in the societies over which they governed, they resorted to traditional nationalist rhetoric. There was little attempt, for example, to protect ethnic minority rights to cultural and linguistic diversity within these multi-ethnic, Communist republics. Even Yugoslavia, which had a reasonable record in protecting the linguistic rights of Hungarians, Albanians and Gypsies, had few qualms in quashing demands from Croatia for the right to a separate language status.

STALINIZATION, 1948–53

The witch hunt for 'Titoists' in Eastern Europe, like the blood letting which had accompanied collectivization and industrialization in the Soviet Union during the inter-war period, helped to accelerate the region's transition to a Stalinist political and economic system. Any pretence of democracy was now abandoned as, in the haphazard and brutal style characteristic of Stalinism, the USSR imposed Soviet-style constitutions (which placed real power in the hands of the Politburo), and Soviet-style command economies on Poland, Czechoslovakia, Hungary, East Germany, Romania, Albania and Bulgaria. According to the principles of 'democratic centralism', the constitutions of Eastern Europe established a strict hierarchy of Communist party committees, soviets, bureaux, secretariats and congress, which were ultimately responsible to the politburo, and created an invisible relationship between party and state. The lower bodies in this hierarchy 'elected' the higher bodies, although they, in turn, were compelled to obey the decisions of the higher bodies.

This hierarchy explains the application of 'centralism'. But what of the party's claim to democracy which was based on the assertion that Communist society was free from 'class' or social conflict? It was a claim that is difficult to test statistically. While the empirical study of sociology was developing during the years of the Cold War, mainly to assist policy making, the Soviet political leadership was unwilling to permit the collection of economic or social data on income distribution, crime or social attitudes. This enabled it to affirm that since there were no conflicting interests, then the leadership could claim, logically if not truthfully, that the party leadership, described by the Yugoslav Communist Milovan Djilas as an elite, ruled in the interest of all.

In 1948 the limited nationalization of key industries which had taken place in the first years of Communist rule, was now replaced by sometimes idealistic, often irrational plans, to complete the industrialisation of Eastern Europe. Private ownership was abolished and the ownership of the means of the production rested with the Communist state as the representative of the working class. 'Democratic centralism' thus sought to concentrate economic, as well as political, power in the hands of the state, a fusion which underlined the unquestioned authority of the party. There were no longer any business-men or bankers to challenge the decisions of government. The party now claimed that it acted in the 'collective' interest. In practice, however, this was false, as the state primarily served the party offering such perks as better housing and education for their children. Most Soviet citizens benefited, however, from better education and better health services than Russia had ever known before.

In Eastern Europe old ruling classes, shop-owners, businessmen and artisans were soon erased as a command economy was introduced into the Soviet puppet states. Interestingly, the pace of nationalization reflected the strength of indigenous Communist Parties. In Yugoslavia and Albania, where Commun-ist Parties were in full control by 1945, and in Czechoslovakia's industrial heartland of Bohemia-Moravia, where the Communist Party was strong, the bulk of industry was nationalized by 1946. By this date 82 per cent of Yugoslavian, 80 per cent of Czechoslovakian and 84 per cent of Albanian industries were in state hands.

Nationalization in ex-enemy countries proceeded more slowly. In 1947 only 16 per cent of Bulgarian industry was under state control, while in Romania and Hungary the figures stood at 11 and 45 per cent respectively. Of this group, Hungary's advanced level of industrialization and its legacy of state intervention, eased its transition to full nationalization as the percentage of manual workers increased from 25 per cent to 50 per cent within 20 years. Private business was eliminated and the state lavished its attention on extra-vagant projects to enhance the prestige of Communism at home and abroad, like the new Hungarian steel town of Sztalinvaros.

By 1949 every Eastern European country had its own version of GOSPLAN, a soviet-style central planning office which professed its mission to rid the region of its ancient curse of technological backwardness. Despite these grand claims, the USSR also imposed a heavy burden of reparations upon its satellites. The burden of payments, mostly made up in deliveries of goods, fell upon Soviet-occupied Germany, Romania, Bulgaria and Hungary. The last of these, for example, supplied over 17 per cent of its very low national income in 1945–56 to the Soviet Union. These reparations payments ex-tracted from East Germany and Nazi Germany's former allies, some of which were made to Czechoslovakia, Yugoslavia, Poland and Greece, undoubtedly impaired reconstruction and prolonged human suffering.

Industrialization, nonetheless, was rapid, partly spurred on by the outbreak of war in Korea in 1950, but it came at a high price. The safety of workers and the environment were treated with cavalier disregard and working men and women discovered that the reality of the 'workers' state' was far removed from the Marxist rhetoric which accompanied its imposition. Women, for example, were overwhelmingly recruited into menial, low-paid occupations. The process of industrialization had other consequences for society. Whereas in 1945 most east Europeans lived in an agrarian setting, by 1960 urbanization had transformed the environment. Poland's urban population, for instance, had soared from 7.8 million to 14.4 million by 1960 – some 48 per cent of the country's total population.

Many of the region's great cities were giant building sites in the first years after the war thanks to the twin-fold pressures of reconstruction and industrialization, and although a few were lovingly restored to their former beauty, very many more were blighted by the construction of cheap and drab housing developments that rapidly became dilapidated. Aside from those deeply committed to the Communist Party and its goals, the process of industrialization and urbanization failed to generate any great sense of progress or achievement. For most people, freedom of movement and association was severely restricted and labour discipline was harsh. Although it was the spectacular show trials which captured public attention in Eastern Europe, most of the prison population were blue and white collar workers arrested for infringements of labour discipline amid the welter of suspicion and intrigue which accompanied Stalinization.

As in the Soviet Union, it was the collectivization of agriculture far more than the industrial five-year plans which provoked most popular discontent. The peasant was not just an important contributor to the economy of Eastern Europe: as in the nineteenth century, there was a 'traditional peasant' ideal tilling the land which remained at the centre of ethnic and national identity. Many of the indigenous Communist Parties, most notably in Romania, tried to turn a deaf ear on Moscow's entreaties for comprehensive collectivization, although there were benefits to be had from collectivizing 'dwarf' landholdings so that modern, efficient methods of farming could be used. By 1952 only Bulgaria could claim to have collectivized more than 50 per cent of arable land in the state sector. In Yugoslavia and Hungary only 25 per cent of land was collectivized, while in Romania the figure as low as 15 per cent. After Stalin's death in 1953 collectivization was slowed or even temporarily halted across all of Eastern Europe.

As in the Soviet Union of the 1930s, education and marxist culture were also placed high on the Communist agenda, partly out of conviction, and partly to replace the indigenous culture the Communists were doing their best to destroy. The Communist Party abolished all rival social and political organizations. Religious observance was not completely banned, but the Communists sought to depoliticize it by controlling churches' activities from Departments of Religious Affairs. They had a variety of names from the prosaic East German Secretariat for Church Affairs to the, more emotive, Romanian Department of Cults. On the whole the Communists found it easier to control religious observance in states where the Orthodox Christian Church dominated because there was some measure of state approval for the appointment of key priests in Romania, Bulgaria, Russia and Serbia. But in Roman Catholic states like Slovenia, Croatia, Slovakia, Poland, Lithuania and much of Hungary the choice of bishops – and hence the efforts of the Party to control the church – was an endless source of friction.

The smaller religious groups, like Baptists and Methodists, suffered more than the larger Orthodox and Catholic churches which continued to provide an important, alternative focus for social and political interaction. Meanwhile, Jews in Eastern Europe continued to find themselves singled out for 'special attention'. They were regarded as members of a national as well as a religious group and were registered as such on their identity documents. This made it easier to identify and to discriminate against them when it came, for example, to granting access to institutes of higher education.

Because the Communist states of Eastern Europe did subscribe to some notions of individual freedom, they grudgingly tolerated people's right to practise a religion provided it was done in private. This meant that prayers inside churches, synagogues and mosques were sanctioned. Nevertheless, life became especially tough for monks and nuns who were driven out of education as well as from hospitals and schools. Not all countries banned them. The Orthodox religion permitted only monks to become bishops so that Orthodox countries like Russia, Romania, Bulgaria and Yugoslavia had to tolerate monks. The Czechoslovak Communists were less tolerant. Monks were not banned but they were not allowed to wear habits, live in religious communities or accept novices. In effect, they could be monks but they could not behave like monks. In many countries the decline in the number of monks and nuns was gradual rather than dramatic. The famous Pochaev monastery in the Ukraine had only 146 monks left by 1961, and only 35 monks in 1981.

The loss of monks and nuns left important gaps in social, educational and health provision (particularly the care of the elderly and very ill) which the Communist state now had to fill. The party also discovered that people still wanted to perform rites to commemorate the great moments of life – birth, adulthood, marriage and death. Hopes that these rites would wither away under the logic of democratic socialism proved forlorn, so the Communist state began to invent *ersatz* rites to take their place. Baptism was replaced by a so-called naming ceremony, although many babies, as in the Ukraine, now received two rites instead of one. (Civil weddings were frequently followed by a religious service.) Alternative venues were created for these civil ceremonies: Palaces of the Babies, Wedding Palaces and Mourning Houses, for example. Aside from the, effectively compulsory, *Jugendweihe* (youth-consecration) ceremony instituted in East Germany, however, the attempts to generate popular new secular rites in Communist Europe failed. The power of rites lies in the sense of a shared culture, memory and community they evoke. The inventors of Communist rites found they were unable to compete with the potent resonance of centuries of organized religious practice.

The majority of Communist efforts to convince the people that all religion was superstition or invented to oppress the people focused on young people. As in Nazi Germany, the older generation was considered a lost cause. Holy books were banned from sale and religious topics were excluded from radio, film and, later, television. The state also set up atheist clubs, journals and museums to demonstrate that organized religion was cruel and based on mere superstition. The 'religious' artefacts displayed included whips, thumbscrews, reports of witchcraft or inquisitions, grubby 'miracle-working' objects and instruments of branding. These efforts largely failed. A more lasting impact was made by the decision to ban any religious education from schools and universities. Both schools and universities introduced classes in Marxism, and in both the curriculum was modified. Health-care provision in some areas improved, and high school and university attendance doubled as the youth of Eastern Europe were singled out for special attention. Aside from banning religion, the school curriculum was modified to reflect the Soviet world view more broadly. History teachers, for example, were instructed to teach that the Second World War began with Operation Barbarossa. The fever of Stalinism prompted some curious social experiments – rehousing the 'bourgeois' population of cities like Budapest and Prague in the countryside to provide accommodation for the new working class. To many, however, it seemed that the dictatorship of the Communist Party had simply been superimposed upon the dictatorship of the National Socialist party. Typical was the experience of Josef Skvorecky, dissident Czech novelist and keen saxophonist. He recalled Soviet censorship of jazz:

> New little Goebbelses started working diligently in fields that had been cleared by the old demon. They had their own little Soviet bibles . . . their vocabulary was not very different from that of the Little Doctor, except that they were, if possible, even prouder of their ignorance.[4]

THE DEATH OF STALIN AND THE DESTALINIZATION OF EUROPE, 1953–56

Until his death in 1953 Stalin continued to rule the Soviet Union with an iron hand, and celebrated his 70th birthday in 1949 with extraordinary pomp and ceremony. Vociferous propaganda depicted him as a benevolent father figure, the 'Saviour' of the USSR. He was now very rarely seen in public – only glimpsed on top of the Lenin Mausoleum on national holidays – and had made his last public utterance in 1948, but his grip on power remained terrifyingly undiminished. Purges directed against the military and party members in the 1930s were replaced in the post-war period by an overt political anti-semitism.

The first signs came in the autumn of 1946 with a series of press articles attacking 'Jewish nationalist deviations'. The attacks on Soviet Jews continued for the remainder of the decade, even as the USSR gave crucial assistance to the nascent Jewish state. But by 1948 the Soviet attitude to a Jewish state turned from support to hostility as it became clear that the best way to limit Anglo-American influence in the Middle East was to encourage Arab nationalism. Anti-semitic attacks in the USSR continued and reached their final, dramatic stage with the arrest, in January 1953, of a large number of Jewish doctors in the employ of the Kremlin. Then on 5 March 1953 all fears of a renewed purge dramatically evaporated, although state-sponsored anti-semitism continued for some time to come. Stalin was dead.

Stalin's death was followed by a period of collective leadership, at first under Georgi Malenkov, Lvarenti Beria and Nikita Khrushchev, but by 1957 Khrushchev had emerged as the new, undisputed leader of the USSR, the man who in 1954 had modified the powers of the security police (KGB) and who had brought previously uncultivated land under the Soviet plough (the 1954 Virgin Lands' campaign). Long before then, during his rise to the top he had established a reputation for innovation and 'reformist' projects, especially with regard to agriculture. Already in 1950-1, for example, he proposed that the Communist Party establish *agrogorods* (agri-cities) in the countryside. The broad sweep and the impractical ambition of this plan were to characterize Khrushchev's years as Soviet leader.

Khrushchev's reputation as a reformer helped him to secure his leadership and he became famous, not only among Communists, for his celebrated attack on Stalin during the 1956 Twentieth Party Congress, which condemned the old leader for, *inter alia*, using 'all conceivable methods to promote the glorification of his own person'. This attack on Stalin was primarily motivated by Khrushchev's desire to spur on the Soviet Union's cumbersome bureau-cracy into supporting economic reform and to modify the prevailing political mood to one conducive to reform, but it had ramifications far beyond the boundaries of the USSR.

Stalin's death briefly raised hopes across Eastern Europe that the pace and character of stalinization would be modified. Nowhere was this more so than in East Germany, which had been systematically fleeced by the USSR for reparations since 1945 – on average more than 25 per cent of all income derived from industrial production went in reparations to the USSR. Within three months of Stalin's death, however, these hopes were hastily dashed by the imposition of higher production quotas (in effect, a wage cut), on East German workers.

On 17 June 1953 East Berlin workers downed tools in protest, and this demonstration spread like wild-fire. Their numbers soon swelled by workers from outside the city. Some even marched across West Berlin to join them. This was an extraordinary demonstration of German workers' solidarity after, first, 12 years of Nazi, and then seven years of Soviet oppression. The East German state resorted to Red Army tanks to put down the demonstration and dozens of demonstrators were killed. Only a year earlier, Stalin had talked of the possibility of German re-unification in exchange for a 'neutral Germany', but the events of June 1953 effectively quashed any such proposals. The East Berlin workers' uprising had shown that Soviet control could be challenged, but not that it could be challenged successfully.

The problem for Communist leaders in Eastern Europe was that their slavish imitation of Stalin, which had once given their regimes a degree of legitimacy and security, became a liability once Khrushchev denounced Stalin. Events in Poland and Hungary in 1956 provided an acute example of the limits of Soviet control over its satellites. That year the threat of unmanageable unrest in Poland persuaded the Russian Politburo to reaccept as Prime Minister, Wladslaw Gomulka, whose loyalty, then and earlier, appeared to be first to Poland and then to the USSR. Gomulka succeeded in loosening Moscow's stranglehold over his country by reinstating workers' councils and securing some control over the deployment and command of Polish troops. Yet he did not attempt to reform the character of Communist government in Poland. His only aim was to modify Poland's strategic relations with the Soviet Union. The Stalinist style of government in Poland went unchallenged, and Moscow recognized that there was little to be gained by full-scale intervention.

Developments in Hungary, by contrast, were treated with less leniency by the Kremlin because they threatened the essential character of the Communist regime. After Stalin's death, political reform movements sprang into life across Hungary demanding improved living standards, an easing of collectivization and less secret police activity, and by November 1956 it had become clear to Moscow that the Hungarian Communist premier, a former mechanic from the city of Kapsovár, Imre Nagy, was unable and unwilling to control this new, independent political life. Hated secret police officials were lynched and some army units were reported to be supporting demonstrations against the Communist government. The Kremlin decided it must put down the unrest itself. Action followed quickly at a time when the West was divided by the Suez crisis, with the British and French governments in disagreement with the United States. The Red Army amassed over 2,000 tanks inside Hungary – the same number deployed by Hitler in 1940 against France – and on 4 November Budapest was attacked. Within a week of increasingly articulate resistance the uprising had been quashed. Over 3,000 people were killed, 2,000 were later executed – some estimates suggest that between 25,000 and 50,000 Hungarians were killed – and a further 20,000 fled abroad. Hungary's new Russian-appointed Premier, Janos Kádár, a Communist who had himself experienced life in gaol under the orders of the Hungarian Communists in the early 1950s, quickly reaffirmed Hungary's loyalty to Moscow and the Warsaw pact. He was to continue to exercise supreme power until his health began to fail in the 1980s.

The brutal counter-revolutionary suppression of the Hungarian uprising stunned the world. It also damaged the reputation of Russian Communists amongst their own comrades abroad in the East and West, despite the fact that in the aftermath of the bloodletting Eastern European Communist leaders showed a greater willingness to implement cautious reforms. Communist parties began to lose party members on a considerable scale in Europe, while Communist governments elsewhere shuddered at the crude display of Russian strength. Nonetheless, it added further strain to the already troubled relations between the Communist Russian 'bear' and the Communist Chinese 'tiger'.

THE COLD WAR AND THE WIDER WORLD, 1949–62

Although the origins of the conflict were obviously in Europe, it extended beyond Europe, producing hot wars elsewhere in the world. In Asia, for example, the British, French and Americans were already uneasy because of the long-feared Communist victory in China, where a People's Republic was proclaimed by the Communist Party leader Mao Zedong in September 1949. Encouraged by these events, Communists from North Korea invaded South Korea in June 1950. The United Nations passed a resolution demanding the North Koreans' immediate withdrawal (the Soviet Union was boycotting the UN at the time), and soon afterwards a United Nations Command was set up under US General Douglas MacArthur who was given orders to provide 'cover and support' for the South Koreans.

This intervention had important economic consequences in Europe as well as in Asia. In particular, it stimulated the economic revival of a former adversary – Japan. In all, some 45 UN member states provided assistance of some kind, with the USSR bitterly condemning their intervention. By July 1951 both sides began feeling their way to a truce, and it was a measure of the distrust which now permeated international relations that it took longer to sign a peace agreement than to wage war. It was only in 1955 that troops from America, and from China, which had joined the war on the side of North Korea, were finally withdrawn.

Some Cold War warriors, as they now considered themselves, like John Foster Dulles, who Eisenhower made Secretary of State when he became President of the United States in January 1953, two months before the death of Stalin, talked 'of taking the offensive in the world struggle for freedom and for rolling back the engulfing tides of despotism'. Other anti-Communists feared that localized wars would ultimately set the entire world ablaze. But the ethos of the Cold War meant that there could no longer be any localized defence structures: every conflict, no matter how small, could bring the possibility of Communist aggression.

This conviction soon became appended to another new, simplistic theory of Cold War relations: the 'domino theory' to explain the dangers of allowing the Communists any modicum of success. The theory claimed that if 'you have a row of dominos set up and you knock over the first one, and what will happen to the last one is that it will certainly go over very quickly'. The rationale, which underpinned American foreign policy in all parts of the world, involved more than defence. Dulles, in particular, was prone to talk of 'massive retaliation' in any international crisis, which to his critics seemed to imply the threat of nuclear power. This became one of the guiding elements in American and Western European foreign policy in south-east Asia, and provided the justification for super power intervention around the globe.

The intent of successive American administrations to 'contain' Communism was complicated by the dissolution of Western overseas empires after the Second World War. The former colonies of Britain and France, in particular, decided for the most part not to attach themselves to either side in the Cold War, but instead to adopt a distinct, non-aligned position. The Indian Prime Minister, Jawaharlal Nehru, leader of one of the world's most populous states took a leading role in the non-aligned movement, or 'third world' as it came to be known because it rejected the rigid Cold War division of the world split into two opposing ideological camps, which had little to do with their needs. At the same time the 'third world' leaders rejected neutrality as impractical (the Second World War illustrated the difficulty of containing war within national boundaries), and not necessarily appropriate for their needs. Rather, they wanted to influence world politics and economics by their non-aligned position.

At first, Western European governments were as cool towards this development as the United States and the Soviet Union, especially during the time of the Korean War which did not end until June 1953 – and only then with an armistice – but they came to appreciate the value of a third voice, albeit not always unison, in international affairs, especially as they were able to circumvent the non-alliance of some key states. In 1954, for example, Pakistan, Thailand and the Philippines all concluded military agreements with the United States, while Afghanistan became the first non-communist country to receive Soviet aid. The Cold War increasingly penetrated into 'third world' countries. It was here that after Korea (1950–3), hot wars erupted in, for example, Vietnam (1965–73) and in Angola (1975–89), one of the richest countries in Africa. During the 1950s alone financial aid and technical expertise were poured into Africa by both sides – some one billion dollars and 3,000 technical experts from the West alone.

The new role of Africa in international affairs was highlighted at the conference of non-aligned countries held in Bandung in April 1955 – a conference which originally had been designed to put Asia on the map. With Egypt, Libya, Sudan, Ethiopia, Liberia and Ghana represented amongst the 29 participants, the Bandung conference became the prototype for future Afro-Asian solidarity in the 1960s and 1970s. The 'Third World' had grown demonstrably larger. At Bandung, Russian and Chinese marxist representations in favour of 'liberation' and 'equality' made a favourable impression on Asian and African delegates, especially when set against past imperialisms, and the continued nationalism of the West. Bandung was more important, however, in that it established the basis for, and confidence in, Asian-African cooperation and laid the foundations for joint action at the United Nations, thus increasing Asian-African security and status in the world.

Indeed, the increasing importance of the non-aligned world, which included Tito's Yugoslavia, was well illustrated during the deterioration of Chinese and Soviet relations which culminated in a bitter Sino-Soviet split publicly announced to the world in 1961. Chairman Mao Zedong, began to press for the Soviet Union to use its military muscle to help their Communist friends to power throughout the underprivileged world, but the Soviet Union was less willing to engage directly in the possibility of open ended conflict with the West.

REFORMS IN THE SOVIET UNION, 1957–64

Combat in the Cold War was on a number of fronts – regional conflicts, the arms race, and the propaganda war – but in a war which saw no fighting in Europe, the underlying strength of the 'combatant' economies was crucial to determining its outcome. In the 1950s the economies of the United States and the recovery of the Western European bloc were undoubtedly stronger than their Eastern bloc rivals, though it was the Soviet economy which appeared to be growing at the faster rate. As Alexei Adzhubey, Khrushchev's son-in-law, recalled, 'children were even called *Dogonyat-Peregonyat*' (catch up and overtake) which became a popular boy's name.[5]

By the late 1950s, however, it was clear that official statistics in the USSR greatly overstated the growth of the Soviet economy. For one thing, Communist statisticians did not recognize inflation in the USSR, although it consistently ran at around three per cent and Communist managers over-estimated output on the plans to avoid punishment. Distribution networks were especially poor. Much of what was produced never reached its intended users, with perishable goods often rotting before they reached their, often desperate, customers. Not even the pioneering movement into space could hide such realities.

Recognizing that some reform was needed, Khrushchev sought to modify the economic system of the USSR so that individuals would be encouraged to work for themselves: he introduced new local and regional councils, brought new land into cultivation, and modified industrial output targets. He also planned to increase the supply of consumer goods, promising: 'give us time and we shall produce panties for your wives in colours which cannot be seen anywhere else'. He encouraged some political and public debate over economic reform, while insisting in what was a difficult balancing act that the Politburo should retain full authority over the Soviet Republics.

At first all appeared to go well, but by the early 1960s the reforms had begun to falter: meat production began to fall, the autumn of 1962 brought a calamitous corn harvest, and heavy price increases for the workers followed. This, plus the Cuban missile crisis (1961), served to undermine Khrushchev's authority. To defuse the growing crisis, he energetically set about – or so he claimed – to promote an 'Administration Reorganization' in the USSR. But further changes to Soviet agriculture and the continued stagnation of Soviet industry spelled the end for Khrushchev. In what was to become a time honoured tradition, (it befell President Gorbachev in August 1991), Khrushchev was removed from power while on holiday in 1964.

'REFORM' COMMUNISM
IN EASTERN EUROPE, 1957–68

Khrushchev's economic reforms and the emerging split between the Soviet Union and China in 1960–1 sponsored change in the economic systems in the Eastern bloc. Yugoslavia's independent route had already embraced foreign aid, and in 1965 Yugoslavia received special drawing rights from the International Monetary Fund (IMF) which enabled it to develop its steel and refinery capacity, to introduce the market to price and distribute goods, and to cultivate a tourist industry. East Germany, in constant search of Western European recognition, introduced limited economic reform and permitted the publication of long-banned books – Franz Kafka and T. S. Eliot, for example, were made available once more to an East German readership.

For Albania and Romania reform consisted of a radical change in their relationship with the USSR. Tiny Albania sided with China in dispute between Russia and China over the 'reformist' path inaugurated by Khruschev in the late 1950s, and Romania, under the leadership of, first, Gheorghe Gheorghiu-Dej and then Nicolae Ceausescu, negotiated the withdrawal of Soviet military advisers from Albania. It, too, remained neutral during the Sino-Soviet split, which peaked in 1961, and cultivated economic contacts with Western Europe. Poland and Bulgaria were largely out of step with this reformist trend, their tentative efforts at reform far surpassed by Hungary and Czechoslovakia.

Memories of 1956 determined that Hungary's reforms eschewed questions of political freedom and concentrated on economic issues. In 1968 the New Economic Mechanism was inaugurated which used the market to distribute goods and resources – it was dubbed 'goulash Communism' – but GOSPLAN continued to have considerable influence on planning for the future. In the 1960s it was only in Czechoslovakia that pressures for economic reform emerged alongside a vibrant, popular movement for greater democracy. Aspirations for change flowered when Alexander Dubček took office, in March 1968, with promises of elections and economic reform. Under Dubček police surveillance and censorship almost disappeared and the press was now filled with tales of torture in police cells and economic mismanagement. In a wave of reformist enthusiasm the newly liberated labour unions even offered unpaid work in 'Days for Dubček'.

This was too much for the USSR to swallow. Soviet troops, which had been on Warsaw Pact 'manoeuvres' inside Czechoslovakia, accompanied by comrades from East Germany, Poland, Hungary and Bulgarian units, invaded Czechoslovakia on 20 August 1968. Unlike the Soviet invasion of Hungary, there was little bloodshed in Czechoslovakia, although the psychological impact of Moscow's intervention remained profound. The 'Prague Spring', as this temporary thaw in USSR Communist control over Czechoslovakia was called, quickly withered and died as Soviet tanks rolled into Prague.

THE COLD WAR: CONFRONTATION AND DÉTENTE, 1957–69

The rise and fall of Khrushchev's buoyant confidence in the potential for reform within the Eastern bloc mirrored developments in the Cold War. The Soviet Union, whatever its economic problems on the ground, was the early leader in the race for space. In 1957 the Soviet launched *Sputnik* was the first artificial satellite in space (it was the size of a football); four years later, Yuri Gagarin became the first man to orbit the earth. More menacingly, though equally astonishing for the West, was the USSR's launch of the first Inter-Continental Ballistic Missile (ICBM) in 1957. Such technological successes provoked a new phase of Western rearmament, with British, French and American governments investing heavily in nuclear technology.

In 1961 overt Cold War hostility returned to Europe when, to stem the endless flow of East Germans migrating westward, the Soviets and East Germans erected barriers around West Berlin to prevent movement between the western sectors and the areas outside. The wall itself took months to build, and some East Berliners, desperate to escape, were willing to jump from high apartment blocks into the western sector. It was Churchill's 'iron curtain' brought to life. Indeed, the Berlin Wall quickly became a symbol of Soviet oppression throughout the world.

The Cuban crisis of the following year brought the world nearer to war than at any time since 1945. Khrushchev later noted that 'there began to be a smell of burning in the air'. President John F. Kennedy, elected Democratic President of the United States in January 1961, had failed in his early attempts to overthrow the left-wing government of Fidel Castro on the Caribbean island of Cuba and Khrushchev, seeing an opportunity to humiliate the young President, decided to build nuclear missile bases on Cuba. By blockading the delivery of the missiles to Cuba and standing firm, Kennedy forced Khrushchev to withdraw his missiles, and subsequent years saw a gradual improvement in East-West relations, even though the threat of 'mutually assured destruction' remained. Since Hiroshima the spectre of the bomb had hung over the world. Not only were scientists and defence ministries producing ever more numerous and ever more powerful nuclear weapons, but the potential, long-term effects of nuclear warfare, and indeed nuclear power, remained uncertain. There was a huge question mark – as well as an exclamation mark – in the mushroom cloud which represented the image of a bomb to a world which only the physicists could understand. After years of fearfully anticipating nuclear warfare, the world had stepped away from its brink in 1962.

The history of atomic and nuclear weapons in the post-war period illustrates the futility of American hopes in 1945 to keep this technology a secret. As J. Robert Oppenheimer, the American physicist involved in project Manhattan wrote, 'You cannot keep the nature of the world a secret'. It took other powers increasingly less time to catch-up on American weapon technology. The Soviet Union exploded its first atomic bomb in 1949 – four years after Hiroshima – but when, in 1952, the United States produced an even more terrifying nuclear weapon, the hydrogen bomb, the Soviets caught up within nine months.

By the 1960s, nuclear technology was not confined to the super-powers – Britain was committed to nuclear weapons as early as 1947, France exploded its first nuclear weapon in 1960, China in 1964 – and, for this reason, it was now in the interests of both superpowers to control the indiscriminate spread of nuclear technology. The Cuban missile, however, had a sobering effect. A telephone hot line (or in Russian red line) was installed between the Kremlin and the White House to ensure both parties could expedite talks and remain in contact for as long as possible during any future crisis, and careful diplomacy followed. There emerged a period of *détente* in East-West relations. The term had been used in the past, but now became exclusively associated with superpower relations to denote a new determination, first evident in the failed summit meeting between Khruschev and Eisenhower in 1955, to keep relations as harmonious as possible to preclude the risk of future nuclear war. Both parties began to recognize a commonality of interest. In 1968 the United States and the Soviet Union signed a nuclear non-proliferation treaty, but the rapid advance of technology for mass destruction demanded continuing action and a year later, coincident with the beginning of Strategic Arms Limitation Talks (SALT) between the two military giants, negotiations began to prevent the deployment of weapons of mass destruction on the sea bed.

In 1969 came an American triumph in space which symbolized the beginnings of 'victory' of the west over the east: on 21 July 1969, Neil Armstrong, gave a tremendous boost to American claims as the premier power in space by setting foot on the moon. In economic and military terms, too, Western Europe had developed a clear lead over the Eastern bloc. But it was a victory that had come at a tremendous price. Growth in the Soviet economy was faltering under the strain of arms manufacture – for ordinary citizens hardships included insufficient housing and few consumer products – and, for both Eastern and Western Europe, the military stockpiling had created the frightening military strategy of 'mutually assured destruction'.

While the societies of Eastern and Western Europe appeared to stand further apart by the late 1960s than they had in the 1940s in social, economic and political terms, their future remained inextricably interwoven. Not only did talk of a new era in relations between the superpowers have important consequences for the frontline of the Cold War – the division between Eastern and Western Europe – the growing prosperity, integration and harmonization of Western Europe posed important questions of the Stalinist states to the East, especially as they could not control of the flow of information in the airwaves of Europe, questions that were translated into challenges as the decade drew to a close.

Notes

1. C. P. Kindleberger, *The German Economy, 1945–47. Charles P. Kindleberger's Letters from the Field* (1988), cited in the introduction by Günter Bischof.
2. Quoted in J. Heydecker, *The Nuremberg Trials* (1962).
3. G. Partos, *The World That Came In From The Cold* (1993), p.25.
4. J. Skvorecky, *The Bass Saxophone* (1977), p.15.
5. G. Partos, *op. cit.*, p.121.

Chapter 11

RECONSTRUCTING EUROPE, 1945–1968

So long as eastern Europe ostensibly subscribed to Lenin's vision of workers' republics, called at first 'people's democracies', and so long as Soviet power held, the impetus to promote the integration of western Europe, exposed as it was to American ideas, economic methods, culture – and pressure – on an unprecedented scale, was fed by the Cold War. An important group of allied countries, and it was to grow in size, soon recognized their ultimate dependence on one another and on the fate of West Germany, a conviction that was enhanced further by the disintegration of overseas empires. Indonesia in 1945 was followed by India in 1947 and Indochina in 1954, each with its own history. There was also a sense of shared economic potential in Western Europe, particularly after 1958.

Politics in the colonial powers of the Netherlands, Portugal, Britain and France contrasted, but all were subject to similar influences after 1945. Inside Europe the ring of neutral countries on the periphery of Europe stayed independent as the 'iron curtain' which now divided Europe deprived countries, like France and Germany, of their traditional spheres of interest in the East. At all times there was a strong desire amongst many politicians in continental Western Europe to preserve and to assert 'European' values and interests, as distinct from those of the United States. Britain, however, which made much of its own values and interests, stressed its 'special relationship' with the United States even when the United States did not do so.

New definitions of Europe centred on institutions created to promote co-operation on practical issues, like the production of coal and steel and the reduction of trade barriers. Travel within Western Europe, for business and for pleasure increased as wealth within societies both grew, and was distributed more evenly. Europeans grew to know more about one another, but co-operation on questions of defence and foreign policy still proved difficult. The United States played an important supporting role. The first 20 years after the war saw democracy restored and consolidated in western, northern Europe and parts of southern Europe, with only Portugal and Spain standing apart. The constitutions of the democracies were remarkably similar to those before 1939, and some trends that had been evident after the First World

War continued after the Second, most apparently when it came to universal suffrage which finally became the norm. Women received the vote in France in 1944, in Italy in 1946, in Belgium in 1948 and in Greece in 1952. (Norway led the way in 1908.) Only in Switzerland did women have to wait for the vote – until 1971. By then relations both in and between western European nation-states had been reshaped significantly.

BRITAIN AND EUROPE, 1945–51

Why is it worth considering Britain apart from mainland Europe in 1945? The answer lies in Britain's unique position as the only major European power not to suffer defeat in the two world wars. Moreover, in 1945 it was hard to tar British democracy with the same discredited brush as democracy in France, Germany, Italy or Spain: the unwritten British constitution had proved more resilient than constitutions drawn up on the continent. There were parallels with 1815. The temper in many other societies was influenced by occupation as well as by war, and in the countries that Germany had occupied by the memories of collaboration as well as of resistance. There were strong Communist Parties in Western Europe, each looking east as well as west, except in Britain where the Communist Party had always been weak and where in July 1945 the Labour party won an historic, landslide election victory on a wide-ranging reform programme which included comprehensive health and social security measures. These had been proposed in wartime when the Beveridge Report had appeared. (See above, p.288.) There was also a Labour commitment to provide more and better housing and greater social equality and to nationalize coal, transport and the Bank of England, what was conceived of as the 'commanding heights' of the national economy. Nevertheless, there were some voters in Britain, as elsewhere, who were disenchanted with politics and politicians. One voter surveyed on the eve of the 1945 election described politicians as 'a lot of old fish wives'.

From late-1940s until the mid-1970s British 'fish-wives', whether Conservative, Liberal or Labour, shared a number of common, broad objectives relating to the role of government in society. Across the political spectrum (except for the extreme right), it was believed that government intervention would bring greater equality and wealth to the nation. In the language of the time, there was to be a 'welfare' not a 'night-watchman' state. The belief made for what became known as postwar consensus politics that lasted in Britain until the election of Margaret Thatcher in 1979. R. A. Butler, Minister of Education in the war-time coalition government was the 'architect of the new conservatism in the domestic field' and was Chancellor of the Exchequer when the Conservatives were returned to power in 1951, as he proclaimed that Britain was to become 'one single society or community in which all careers will be open to talent'.

In 1945 Prime Minster Clement Attlee's Labour government faced difficult tasks: the need to increase national income in order that the party's election promises could be met, and to transform Britain's relations with its empire, a matter of economics as well as principle. Its greatest challenge was to create a welfare state within a near bankrupt economy and, in large part, it succeeded, though only by maintaining 'austerity' which lost it votes. Within a year Labour had introduced 75 bills, a giant programme of nationalization (including the Bank of England, civil aviation, public transport, electricity and gas), and a far greater government commitment to providing social services. In 1946 the National Insurance Bill was passed insuring the nation's entire adult population in time of sickness, unemployment and retirement, and in 1947 the National Health Service quickly became the second largest item of government expenditure.

This was a programme widely admired and emulated across Western Europe, but criticized in the United States, which strained Britain's resources to the limit. The economy proved resistant to recovery, rationing continued, even extended beyond its wartime range, and essentials, particularly coal, were in short supply.

In 1947, the problems at home reached their climax during the bitterest winter of the century where near arctic conditions covered the nation in snow and brought economic life to an almost complete halt. Britain was forced to secure another substantial loan from the United States. Chancellor of the Exchequer, Hugh Dalton, by nature an optimist, saw ahead of him 'a looming shadow of catastrophe'. This domestic crisis helped to exacerbate further the crisis for British authority overseas. Britain voluntarily withdrew from India in August 1947 as the Labour party had long desired, but its withdrawal from armed intervention against the Communists in Greece and Turkey in March 1947 had ideological complications as did the creation of an independent Jewish state in Palestine, formerly a mandated territory. The Labour party was divided on this, and the problems, intractable, were left to the United Nations to resolve.

These changes to British foreign policy underlined the diminution of Britain's power relative to that of the two new superpowers, but Britain still retained important interests in the Middle East, Africa and South East Asia. Moreover, the indomitable British, demonstrated, by their role in the escalation of the Cold War, by cultivating of a 'special relationship' with the United States and by strengthening ties with the Commonwealth, that they still hoped to retain a powerful voice in international affairs. Britain also kept its own atomic weapons, although there were demands from the Left to dispose of them.

There were further economic crises, and when in 1949 the pound was devalued from \$4.03 to \$2.80 to the dollar the relative decline of Britain's economy to that of the United States was manifest. Nevertheless, notwithstanding American criticism, the reforms of the 1945 Labour government, in retrospect even more than at the time, constituted a remarkable achievement, exaggerating, a long–term shift of political power and influence within Britain itself.

RESTORING DEMOCRACY
TO WESTERN EUROPE, 1945–57

Like Britain, France continued to parade the outward trappings of great power status through its seat on the National Security Council of the United Nations and the possession of its empire, but defeat, occupation and economic collapse had reduced industrial production to one-third of pre-war levels and overseas trade was non-existent. After the short-lived leadership of de Gaulle, which ended in January 1946, a tripartite coalition of Communists, Socialists and the Christian Democrats (there was no Christian Democratic party in Britain) began to co-operate uneasily to create a constitutional framework for a new Fourth Republic. Within months, however, economic paralysis, fears over the true intentions of the Communists, and constitutional disputes (exacerbated by de Gaulle's outbursts), proved too much for 'tripartism'. The Communist members of the cabinet were sacked abruptly by the Socialist Prime Minister Paul Renardier in May 1947, and from 1947 until 1951 France once again experienced uneasy and transient cabinets formed by key individuals, among them Henri Queuille, Georges Bidault and René Pleven. This was the same version of democracy which had characterized French politics of the Third Republic of the inter-war years, although Bidault's Christian Democracy was a new force.

For all this turmoil, the extension of state management into the economy and society, brought dividends for many Frenchmen and women. The railway system recovered, so too did the automobile industry, while the Monnet plan in 1946, so-named after Jean Monnet, a former senior official of the League of Nations who had become head of the grandly named Plan for the Modernization and Equipment of France (*Commissariat du Plan*), eschewed widespread nationalization of industry, and instead set targets for key industries – steel, electricity, and cement production. Supported by American loans, it helped to foster growth, now as fashionable word as 'planning', within the French economy. And while the crisis of French imperialism and the tensions of the Cold War continued to plague hopes for stable government in France, as we will see, French reconciliation with West Germany and the creation of the European Economic Community in 1957 provided the basis for French domestic and foreign power in the final quarter of the twentieth century.

The conditions in Europe's smaller nations varied greatly after war's end. Switzerland and Sweden, both neutral during the war, faced few recriminations, and did not need to worry about reconstruction, while Spain and, to a lesser extent Portugal, in some respects dissimilar authoritarian dictatorships, stubbornly resisted democracy and were generally ostracized until the requirements of the Cold War determined a more co-operative Western approach towards them. The Benelux countries, devastated by occupation and the battle for liberation, struggled to revive. Rising inflation, a potent cause of instability in Europe after the First World War, was, once again, a danger to post-war recovery. In seeking to cope with this Belgium, which profited more than any other European country from its ownership of uranium deposits in the Congo, took the lead amongst former occupied nations. In October 1944, even before the country had been liberated, and before the first atomic bomb was dropped from the skies, Finance Minister, Camille Gutt, implemented drastic currency reform.

There were other problems. Notwithstanding Gutt's successful stabilization initiative, Belgium quickly began to suffer conflicts between its French-speaking Walloons, who held the levers of economic power, and the less industrialized Flemings, and these were to dominate much of its post-war history. The economy of the Netherlands was not as strong as its Belgian neighbour, but Gutt's currency reform in Belgium was emulated in the Lieftinck Reform of September 1945, supplemented by a policy of price control and continued rationing. Agriculture still played a crucial role in the economies of the Netherlands and Luxembourg, although the latter also maintained a strong steel industry thanks to rich iron ore deposits. All three nations – the Netherlands, Belgium and Luxembourg – were especially well placed, geographically, economically and politically, to play a key role in the forging of Western European co-operation in the 1950s and 1960s.

In the two defeated countries by then located securely in the west, Italy and Germany, the speed and success with which democratic politics had depended both on the pace of the allied invasion and the ability of the fascist state to withstand it. 'Normal' politics returned to Southern Italy as the Allies pushed north where the remains of the fascist state, once allied with Germany, now found its remaining territory invaded and occupied. Throughout 1944 Italian politics in the South were confused, with anti-fascist parties, each with a different champion among the Allies, unable to agree on how best to form a government and prepare for institutional change.

Democracy in Germany was first rekindled in free elections in the Bavarian village of Wohlmuttschüll in 1945, and by 1948 the Western zones of Germany were ready to create a Parliamentary Council to draft the *Grundgesetz* (basic law) which was to remain a provisional constitution until Germany could be reunited. In the meantime, the territories formerly governed by British, French and American troops became the Federal Republic of Germany (FRG) ruled under a liberal democratic constitution – with substantial powers over cultural, educational and religious matters delegated to Germany's states (*Länder*). Many of the political parties which had been active before 1933, notably the SPD, re-formed for the Republic's first elections in August 1949.

In Italy, as in France, with a more radical new constitution than any other European country, there was a weak post-war economy and a string of short-lived cabinets. In the aftermath of the defeat in war the Italian Communist Party (PCI), a strong force, played a very different role from that of Communist parties in other European countries. Its leader, Palmiro Togliatti, with strong links to Moscow, had argued that was impossible to effect a Marxist revolution in Italy because of the continued Allied presence (the Americans, in particular, sought to manipulate Italian politics to contain the Communists) and the lack of a revolutionary consciousness amongst the working class.

The Communists were to rue their mistake. The political opportunities of 1943–4 were not to come again. As Fausto Gullo, a PCI leader later recalled: 'we were all under the impression that the wind was blowing in our direction, and that therefore what was not achieved today, would be achieved tomorrow.' Terrified of the 'red peril', the Catholic church also played a role in containing the Communists before and after 1945. The Vatican loudly asserted that no Catholic could be a Communist, and the sentiment was reflected in religious practice by a number of clergymen. Cardinal Schuster of Milan, for example, instructed his clergy to withhold absolution (granted in the sacrament of Confession) from suspected Communists. So the Italian Communists only managed to retain political power by arranging a political pact with the new Christian Democrats, an alliance which robbed them of their working-class radicalism.

THE RISE OF CHRISTIAN DEMOCRACY

On 2 June 1946 a new era of democratic politics began in Italy with elections to a new constituent assembly and a referendum on whether Italy should become a republic. The monarchy did not survive, although far from presenting a consistent picture, the referendum and the elections demonstrated the deep divisions among the anti-fascist parties. The new Republic was split between a conservative, monarchist South and a radical, republican North. A new constitution, with a strong emphasis on regionalism, as opposed to the centralism of the fascist state, was formally introduced on 1 January 1948. The first new Prime Minister was 62-year-old Alcide de Gasperi, the first Catholic politician to become Prime Minister of a united Italy, and for most of the twentieth century Italian politics were to be dominated by Christian Democrats.

Christian Democracy was the new force in post-war Continental West European politics, supplanting the old Right. This was partly because in formerly Nazi-occupied Western Europe, conservatives and nationalists found themselves in an awkward position after 1945. Many of them, even when they were practising Christians of all denominations, had collaborated with, or worse joined, Fascist and Nazi movements. They gave way to key Christian figures who had been engaged in active resistance to National Socialism, whose influence was further enhanced when the post-war Churches set out to provide help to displaced peoples and the homeless. The assertion of Christian culture and morals in national politics was now believed, by many on the right to be the best hope in stemming the rising tide of socialism in the politics of democratic Europe.

The leftward shift in the politics of Eastern Europe, although encouraged at the barrel of a Soviet gun, was mirrored in western European politics.

When democracy was re-established in Norway, for example, and later in Austria socialist parties gained over 40 per cent of the vote, and while in France, Italy and Finland, socialist gains were less impressive, this, as we have seen, was because of the electoral appeal of the Communist Parties. When taken as a whole, the left did well here too. West Germany, however, was something of an exception. Given the dominance of the Social Democratic Party in German politics after the First World War, many, especially its leader Kurt Schumacher, believed that it would again dominate democratic politics in Germany. But the 70-year-old Adenauer, the former Mayor of Köln (Cologne) and a veteran of centre politics in Weimar, in 1949 became and then remained the Federal Republic's chancellor for 14 years.

The charisma and political skills of Adenauer, nick-named *Der Alte* (old man) who was 73 years old when he became Chancellor, a post he was to hold for the next 14 years, helped to explain the unexpected success of the newly formed Christian Democratic party. So, too, did the 'iron curtain' which divided German socialists and geographically separated the SPD from many of its former supporters in East Germany. (Unlike the old Catholic Centre party that died with the Weimar Republic, the new Christian Democratic Union or CDU – was an inter-denominational party with an emphasis on the shared values and culture of all Christian religions.) But most important was the fact that many voters believed that churches offered the best protection against what was now perceived by many as the strongest threat to stability and security – Communism.

It was, as one historian has put it 'perhaps not the rule of the Saints, but the rule of the Clericals'.[1] In de Gasperi's words, it was 'the sense of fraternity . . . the moving force of Christian civilization' (with a European base) which could reconcile human conflict. And while events in Czechoslovakia in 1948 confirmed the worst fears of all Christian Democrats, elections across Western Europe had demonstrated, by then, that Communism had lost ground. In such circumstances the 20 or so years after the war were a good time for organized religion in general and for the papacy, in particular, in democratic Europe. During the 1930s, the dictators had plagued church relations with their congregations (awkward questions about this period of religious history were to be raised again during the 1960s), and had damaged the reputation of organized religion in the wider world too. Now the contrast between the 'godless' states of Eastern Europe and the Western democracies gave the church renewed moral authority. So also did demands of reconstruction and recovery in the socially conservative 1950s when the values of organized religion were confidently asserted.

DEFENDING WESTERN EUROPE, 1947–54

Morals also were part of the reckoning as the larger powers of Western Europe thrashed out questions of financial and economic aid, and defence with the United States. Countries as diverse as Greece, the Netherlands, Belgium, Norway, Denmark, and Turkey were more spectators than participants in the negotiations, but for these countries and for other European nations which were unoccupied by the Red Army, the transition to peace was an absorbing challenge.

After it had become clear there would be no East-West co-operation over the issue of disarmament and that there had been no co-operation over Marshall aid, Western European governments became increasingly anxious to set up a formal defence structure to provide a secure environment in which European recovery could take place. Britain and France, in particular, wanted more than the vague American pledge to help countries under threat as set out in the Truman doctrine. The first important step in military co-operation came with the Treaty of Brussels between Britain, France and the Low Countries in 1948. This marked an advance in Western European co-operation, but the main focus of the treaty, that of thwarting 'a renewal by Germany of aggressive policy', was already outdated. Sweden, now a model social democracy, also made strenuous efforts to establish a similar security pact between the Scandinavian powers, but its efforts came to naught after neutral Finland withdrew from negotiations for fear of triggering the ire of the Soviet Union and the United States refused to supply any Nordic alliance with weapons.

By the end of 1948 British and French politicians, in particular, were calling for a military equivalent of the Marshall plan, and in 1949 they got what they wanted. In April of that year ten European powers joined the United States and Canada in signing the North Atlantic Treaty Organisation (NATO) in Washington. The ten were Britain, France, the Benelux states, Italy, Denmark, Norway, Iceland and Portugal. Unlike in 1919, the United States was this time convinced that its national security was tightly bound with that of Western Europe, and now co-operation between European countries on defence and foreign policy questions was conducted through the mediating influence of the United States. This was one of the reasons why Europe was to be slow in developing its own, distinctive presence in international politics and in nurturing initiatives designed to build a European defence network, separate from, if related to, institutions established by the United States in the aftermath of the Second World War.

In 1947 the American Central Intelligence Agency (CIA) had determined that the Soviet military threat to Western Europe was insignificant, but by 1949 a more apprehensive assessment of Soviet military potential was made and the pattern of the Cold War 'engagement' and the future arms race was thus established. NATO was proclaimed as 'an armour not a lance, a shield but not a sword' to afford security for Western Europe's reconstruction, and while it was dedicated to the principles of the UN charter, unlike the United Nations, it was regional, not global, in character and had substantial financial backing from the United States: the US Senate passed a vast programme of military aid to Western Europe, a day before news broke of the explosion of the first Soviet atomic bomb. The question of the holding and deployment of nuclear weapons was now at the heart of all dispositions of military power. By 1950 American nuclear bombers were based in Britain, and by 1954, when NATO's military build–up had begun in earnest, nuclear missiles and artillery were based across continental Western Europe.

With the arrival of Marshall aid, there was a further incentive inside Europe to co-operate through trade, expressed most notably in the creation of a Benelux customs union in January 1948. This highly successful example of regional co-operation was soon mirrored by similar groupings amongst other European nations: Sweden, Norway and Denmark formed a group to the North; in the Mediterranean there were rumours that Greece and Turkey were planning to form a customs union. These associations, it was hoped, would promote domestic recovery and afford smaller European nations a stronger voice in shaping their future. Meanwhile, as European links grew stronger, with politicians who were not Christian Democrat, like the Belgian Paul-Henri Spaak also determined to strengthen them, Europe's former 'great' powers were also dissolving long held imperial ties.

DECOLONIZATION, 1946–62

The Second World War, global as it was in its scale and in its aftermath, had contributed to a fundamental revision of relations between the colonial powers of Western Europe and the territories over which they held sway. The relative ease with which Britain and France ruled the waves in the nineteenth century now stood in dramatic contrast to their dependence upon America, and nowhere was the loss of power more clearly illustrated than in their imperial relations. Even before the Second World War had ended, however, there had been an Afro-Asian conference in industrial Manchester which drew up a declaration proclaiming that 'we are determined to be free . . . We will make the world listen'. Amongst those present were Kwame Nkrumah, later Prime Minister and President of Ghana, and Jomo Kenyatta, future President of Kenya. This declaration, and others like it, reflected the idea which was widespread even during the war, that since the Second World War was a truly global struggle, it would have global ramifications.

The wartime conferences of the Allies were marked by protests against colonialism, especially on the part of the United States which regarded Empire at best to be an archaic form of rule and at worst uneconomic and oppressive. It was at variance with the principles of self-determination first enunciated by Wilson at Versailles and repeated by Roosevelt in the 1941 Atlantic Charter. The Soviet Union, too, encouraged colonial struggles which its postwar propaganda, looking back to Lenin and Trotsky, was to describe as 'wars of liberation'. The transition to independence was traumatic for all involved and in some countries it produced bitter violence and turmoil. In the Dutch territory of Indonesia, for example, when a new republic was proclaimed on

17 August 1945, the Dutch government found it impossible to accept the proclamation without making uneasy compromises. It was not until the late summer and early autumn of 1949 that agreements were reached which enabled Indonesian independence to become a fact by August 1950.

By March 1946 the British government willingly rather than reluctantly had recognized that India had to be granted total independence from the Crown. The transfer of power was complete by August 1947, although the process unleashed deep hatreds between Hindus and Moslems as two new countries emerged: India and Pakistan. Burma followed – choosing to stay outside the Commonwealth, unlike India – in January 1948. Closer to home, the Republic of Ireland Act was passed on 18 April 1949 (this was not really 'decolonization'), although the 'Six Counties' of Northern Ireland remained part of the Union. The 'Commonwealth' in Africa was to be 'liberated' later, usually by agreement, the Gold Coast (Ghana) leading the way in 1957. The process of decolonization accelerated in east as well as west Africa during the 1960s. Meanwhile South Africa, having formulated and implemented through its largely Boer governments, an *Apartheid* philosophy of its own, withdrew from the Commonwealth in 1961.

France, like Britain, had begun to face some opposition to its colonial rule before the outbreak of war, but officials in Paris read these signs of protest as limited, and in 1945, France now freed from German occupation, was determined to retain significant parts of *France d'Outre-Mer*, the 'confetti' of the dispersed Empire of the French Republic, especially the territories of Indochina and, also closer to home, Algeria. The consequent wars of decolonization were amongst the longest and most brutal of the decolonization era. In 1945 France immediately returned to Indochina (which had been abandoned by the French and occupied by the Japanese during the war), and were quickly involved in expensive political and military operations which lasted until 1954. In northern Vietnam, Ho Chi Min had established a 'free state' with a strong Communist army and France's struggle, which ended with the fall of Dien Bien Phu in May 1954, became yet another 'frontier' in the Cold War, soon to drag in the United States with far-reaching consequences. Worse was to come for France with its *métropole*, the centre of the French Empire in Paris, when imperial rule in Algeria was directly challenged. Summed up in the popular slogan, '*Algérie, c'est la France*', Algeria was considered an integral part of the republic, a 'salt-water extension of France itself', and it was only after ten years of protracted conflict, which even challenged political stability on the French mainland, that Algeria became a sovereign state on 1 July 1962.[2] It was de Gaulle, returned to power in 1958, who made the transition possible.

PATTERNS OF MIGRATION

The process of decolonization reversed established patterns of migration between Europe and the wider world. Whereas in the nineteenth century,

Europeans had fled, or been forced from, their homelands in search of sustenance and security – only the already-wealthy or very ambitious dared to dream of more – in lands colonized by their governments. By the inter-war period these patterns of migration faltered as countries like America maintained paperwalls, erected late in the last century, to discriminate between migrants, and as glowing tales of the fortunes to be made overseas lost their shine. The process of decolonization, however, now sponsored new flows of migrants, this time into Europe as subjects, sometimes administrators, of former European empires secured and exercised their rights to settle in the mother-countries whose culture and values had formed the backbone of their education and aspirations.

Most of the French citizens in Algeria, the so-called *pieds noirs* (black feet), who numbered over one million people, moved to France after independence in 1962; their number swollen by a further one million immigrants who came to France from other parts of its former empire. Historical and cultural associations played a role. So, too, did language. Immigrants from former Dutch, French or British colonies, who spoke Dutch, French and English, were many of the most talented and enterprising people of their generation. Some were to find their ambitions and hopes thwarted, but their very presence and a later flow of immigrants, who on arrival spoke only their own indigenous language, changed for ever the cultural, political and economic environment into which they settled. The diversity of Europe acquired a new dimension.

As we have seen in chapter 10, the first large wave of migration within Europe after the war was politically motivated as people fled, or were forcibly moved, by Communist governments in Eastern Europe. By the 1950s, however, the movement of Europeans from East to West was supplanted by a new trend: migration from southern to northern Europe. The wealthier countries of Europe, including France, West Germany and the Benelux countries, as well as some private corporations, made bilateral agreements to import workers from the poorer countries to the south and east, including Italy, Turkey and Portugal. By 1969, for example, more than a million Portuguese worked outside their homeland in Europe, more than lived in all the Portuguese colonies combined. (It is important to remember that it was not possible for Western Europeans to live and work elsewhere in Europe without a lengthy, and often unsuccessful, process of application.)

The bilateral agreements were mutually beneficial: the richer countries gained cheap workers essential to their burgeoning economies and Europe's poorer regions exported the unemployment problem that blighted certain regions, such as southern Italy, and benefited from remittances sent home. Awkward questions about the status of these immigrants – were they guestworkers who were expected to go home, or fully paid-up citizens? – were side-stepped for several decades, only to surface with a vengeance after 1990. Even during the 1960s and 1970s, however, tensions over migration were evident already at the local level. Thanks to the understandable tendency for migrants to cluster together, like the Turkish communities established around Köln or the Algerians in Marseille, so that they could share information as well as social, cultural and economic resources, local politics were being shaped by debates on immigration before the topic emerged on a national level.

Britain was something of a special case. Migration into Britain during this period was at a lower level when compared to France or Germany, but, immigrants, who were mostly non-white, some like those from the Caribbean speaking English as their own language, were granted permanent citizenship rather than guestworker status. The case remained special even after restrictions were imposed, the first of them during the 1960s.

There were two groups of Europeans who obviously bucked this inward trend. The first were Britons who continued to migrate to areas of the former empire, notably the Commonwealth countries of Australia, New Zealand, Canada and South Africa, which promised a better standard of living than that available at home. And even in India there were more Britons living there during the 1960s than there were before independence. The second group were European Jews, drawn from all countries, to settle in what they considered to be their Jewish homeland in Palestine.

EUROPE AND THE MIDDLE EAST, 1945–68

Launched many decades earlier the Zionist aspiration to recreate Israel only emerged as a major force after 1944. Between then and 1948 British authority in the mandated territory of Palestine collapsed (see above, p.270). Already over-stretched in the inter-war period, the British authorities proved powerless in the face of a determined campaign by Zionist settlers in the territory against them (Jewish settlers, though totalling only some 650,000 were wealthier and far better organized than the million and a quarter Palestinians who lived there) and Zionist violence against Britons spilled out beyond Palestine's frontiers. In the autumn of 1947, for example, the underground Jewish terrorist organization, Irgun Zvai Leumi, led by one of the future premiers of the state of Israel, Menachem Begin, exploded bombs in British bases in Austria.

Tension over the region was heightened by bad-tempered exchanges between European governments over the fate of hundreds of thousands of Jewish displaced persons who were shunted around Europe until given a desperately needed home in Palestine (after 1939 Britain had banned Jewish immigration into Palestine to secure Arab support vital to its war effort). These events, alongside news of the mass extermination camps in occupied Europe mobilized support for the notion of a Jewish homeland around the world. Before the Second World War, the majority of European Jews regarded Zionism, with its injunction that Jews should abandon the diaspora and settle in a Jewish state of Israel, as extremist, impractical and, in the case of most Hasidic rabbis, contrary to the proper observance of the Jewish faith. But Hitler changed all that.

In 1947, pressure at home and abroad prompted Britain to withdraw from Palestine and by November 1947 a large majority of the United Nations agreed to carve Palestine into two separate states. But when the British mandate officially ended on 15 May 1948, David Ben-Gurion, Israel's first premier, pronounced the Jewish state independent and Israel was born. Within days, the five neighbouring Arab states of Egypt, Syria, Lebanon, Iraq and Transjordan invaded the new Israeli state (it is important to distinguish between the terms Jew and Israeli). But thanks, at this point, to the support of both the USSR and the United States, Israel rebuffed the invasion and armistice agreements were signed (none of the Arab states recognized Israel) which left Israel in control of 80 per cent of what had been Palestinian territory under the British mandate. (The remaining 20 per cent was absorbed into Transjordan, now renamed Jordan). The scenario of Arab attack followed by, first, a vigorous Israeli defence and subsequent territorial expansion, would be repeated again and again during the decades which followed.

As Palestinians fled, or were expelled from the territory, Jews now immigrated in considerable numbers from Europe and elsewhere around the world. Immigration from Western Europe's most prosperous countries was relatively limited. Between the years 1948 and 1966, 6,336 French Jews, 5,140 British Jews and some 3,047 Jews from Greece settled in Israel, although these figures exclude a large number of Jews who migrated to Israel only to return a few years later because they found the living conditions too harsh. The question of Jewish migration from Eastern Europe is more complex. By the 1950s Israel had fallen foul of the USSR as the latter attempted to curry favour with Arab opinion in the Cold War. As a consequence, Jews were no longer allowed to leave either the USSR or its satellite states in Eastern Europe. Even so, parts of Eastern Europe, formerly the heartland of the Jewish diaspora, saw Jews leave who had survived the war. Czechoslovakia and Bulgaria lost most of their remaining Jewish populations – in Bulgaria, over 33,000 out of a total population of 44,000 left between 1948 and 1949 alone.

The creation of Israel transformed relations in the Middle East, which were directly to affect Europe, and between the Middle East and the USA and the Soviet Union. While most western European Jews rejected the invitation to move to Israel, most of them took an active interest in Israel's welfare and its security. To this end, they sought to influence the policies towards the Middle East of the countries in which they lived. France, in particular, went on to develop a close relationship with Israel on defence, supplying important defence equipment, like Mystère and Mirage jet fighters – a relationship cemented by the migration of North African Jews from Algeria in France in the 1960s and 1970s.

Western European nation-states also had ties to the region through former colonial allegiances. But there was more than sentiment at work. Hard-nosed national interest played a role too. The Arab nations commanded a pivotal geographic position in the Cold War and a resource on which the prosperity and stability of the world's economy, especially its most industrialized nations, had come to rely: oil. In 1950 Western Europe was still able to meet more than 80 per cent of its energy needs from coal and other solid fuels, while oil formed only 14 per cent; by 1960 the proportions were 61 per cent and 33 per cent respectively. The days of 'carboniferous capitalism' were over.

The inability of Arab states to defeat Israel often triggered internal revolts in their territories. It is clear that the same problems that had made the British mandated territory of Palestine so vulnerable in 1948 – ethnic and territorial disputes, poverty and poor leadership – also afflicted the nation-states which had been created after the First World War. In March 1949 there was a military coup in Syria, while the leaders of two major Arab states, Iraq and Jordan, hitherto friendly to the 'great' powers in the West, now found themselves challenged by radical political groups and treated as imperialist collaborators who had no interest in, or sympathy for, their own people. Eventually, old leaders were replaced by a new, radical generation.

The disorderly end to European empire after the Second World War left one further legacy that was to plague Europe's relations with the Middle East. In 1967 Egypt and Syria, backed by the Soviet Union, which went so far as to provide pilots for their fighter planes, launched a new war on Israel. The outcome of the conflict which became known as the Six Day War was a spectacular victory for Israel that saw its aggressors rebuffed and its frontiers expanded. At first Israel's leaders did not intend to keep these 'occupied territories', hoping to use them as bargaining chips in negotiations with its neighbours. But no phone call from the Arab states came. The situation remained unresolved, but the war had done more than transform Israel into the dominant military power of the region. It also had a profound impact on European Jewry. Watched on television sets across Europe, it prompted many viewers to believe that they were about witness the mass murder of Jews akin to that ordered by Hitler. Thereafter, support for the state of Israel, be it political or financial, became a defining feature of Jewish identity around the world. Migrants from across Europe, when permitted, began to rise to significant levels for the first time.

POST-WAR IMPERIALISM

Some historians have argued that European imperialism lived on after decolonization, with continuing economic ties between former imperial territories that favoured the richer countries ('neo-colonialism') and with many people of the Third World adopting 'Western' forms of civilization which articulated traditional European values. The most obvious legacy was the resilience of the colonial 'languages', English and French being the most persistent, especially amongst the educated and powerful. Martiniquan born author Frantz Fanon in his book *Peau noir, Masques blancs* (*Black Skin, White Masks*), argued that the use of the French language distorted indigenous culture – he called it 'the zebra striping of my mind'. More positive critics of imperialism, on the other hand, stressed the educational and technological contribution made by the nineteenth-century conquerors. The first Prime Minister of India, for example, Jawaharlal Nehru, had been educated in England and inherited a relatively effective governmental structure from the Raj.

New appreciations of imperialism also led contemporary analysts to postulate that the Soviet Union, by annexing territories in Eastern Europe, and the United States, by exploiting the dependence of Western Europe and South American on American economic aid, was taking over the imperial mantle of the European powers. Indeed, some historians have argued that America's involvement in Western European reconstruction amounted to 'empire by invitation'. There were forces at work inside Western Europe, however, that contributed directly to its recovery and led it into the most prosperous period in its history, sharply distinguishing it from the 'Soviet Empire'.

ECONOMIC MIRACLES, 1949–68

The development of the Cold War, fast on the heels of the Second World War, had an important impact on the way Europe recovered. This time, the rejuvenation of Europe, after the first unsteady splutters in 1945–8, came quickly and durably, in a way that it had not done after 1919. By 1952 post-war reconstruction had largely been achieved. Nevertheless, once property and goods lost through war had been restored, this did not mark the end of the resurgent growth of European industry, as it had done after the First World War. It was rather the beginning.

Although Western European countries and the United States were at odds over the desire of the former to sustain higher levels of welfare provision than ever before – a goal which remained unaltered in the Christian Democrat and Conservative dominated Europe of the 1950s – the Americans 'sold' Western Europe the prospect of unprecedented levels of economic growth if Europeans were to enshrine the governing principles of mass production, scientific management and productivity into their management of the domestic economy.

During the 1950s the ethos of 'Americanization' which had begun to permeate Europe in the 1920s, spread widely, with English as its language. The United States tried to make the old world new and, in an unprecedented international propaganda offensive, the USA was held up to Europe as an inspirational model for growth, as the British author Graham Hutton put it in his book entitled *We Too Can Prosper* published in 1953. As in the inter-war period, however, the Europeans took what they wanted from the American model and discarded the rest. Intellectuals directed harsh words against consumerism, popular culture and language of the Americans, particularly in France.

In fact, growth was now faster in continental Europe, as it was in Japan, than in the United States, with unprecedented rates of growth of more than seven per cent a year. The reasons behind this sustained growth are still controversial, but of crucial importance, despite intellectual diatribes, was the emergence of a mass consumer market, driven by advertising, which created higher living standards and prosperity for all those in work. There was also a move towards bigger units as great corporations flourished often operating as an international force. Meanwhile, occupational trends established during the first half of the century continued: the numbers of farmers continued to dwindle (in Italy the proportion of workers employed in agriculture and fisheries fell from 43 per cent to 14 per cent) and the numbers of workers in the tertiary (service sector) expanded rapidly.

A social consensus, sometimes also known as the post-war settlement, which had emerged across Europe also contributed towards economic growth, notably in Italy, France and Germany. Its terms differed across Western Europe, but usually it involved an acceptance of social reform and a recognition of workers' rights. In sharp contrast to what had happened during the inter-war years, the democratic governments of Western Europe were able to secure at the same time economic growth and greater co-operation between employers and employed within the context of European peace.

GERMANY, 1949–68

The transformation of Germany in this period was undoubtedly the most dramatic example of a 'miracle', a *Wirtschaftswunder* (Economic Miracle). While East Germany was being transformed into a 'model' Communist state, the Federal Republic of Germany became the model of a modern capitalist liberal democracy. Under the leadership of Adenauer, the Republic, to the delight of the Americans and the disappointment of the British Labour Party, es-chewed the nationalization of the German economy in favour of the creation of a 'social market'. With the able assistance of Economics Minister, Ludwig Erhard, a strategy of low taxation, stable currency and liberal trade was followed. In consequence the Republic established favourable trading rela-tions with Northern, as well as with Western Europe, so that within a few years West Germany, with a rising of national income, had become a major exporter of industrial goods within the expanding multilateral trading system of the West. The CDU coalition government also succeeded in creating industrial management structures which incorporated trade unions into na-tional wage-bargaining process and drew workers participation on the factory management boards of individual enterprises. Workers in key industries like iron and steel, for example, were allowed a say (*Mitbestimmung*) in the man-agement of their companies. In both East and West Germany, fundamentally different though the regimes were, the German industrial worker, exploited and marginalized in Hitler's social vision, was made central to Germany's reconstruction. Yet as elsewhere in Western Europe, while there was a sense of accomplishment and direction, the fruits of the new prosperity were not distributed evenly. Pensioners and war widows, for example, fared less comfortably as Erhard's social market emphasized the role of workers and industrialists.

Demand for labour was high as the West German economy expanded. At first, demand for new workers was met by the eight or so million people who, as we saw in chapter 10, entered West Germany in the aftermath of the Second World War; by 1961 their numbers were swollen by an additional four million who moved from East to West Germany before the creation of the Berlin Wall in 1961. Consequently, it was only during the late 1950s and 1960s that West Germany took advantage of agreements to import workers from Italy, Greece, Spain and then later, Turkey and Yugoslavia. By the late 1960s the numbers amounted to some 400,000 workers a year. But these workers, although enjoying access to a variety of state benefits, were regarded, not as full citizens, but *Gastarbeiter* (guestworkers) who remained foreigners: they were expected to return 'home' and not to settle in Germany. Of course, many did, but it was only in the 1990s that serious questions about their status, and their integration into German society, were raised.

By the 1960s Germany had been plugged into the global system of banking and trade and had become both a formidable trading rival for Britain and France, and a serious competitor for the United States. Companies like Volkswagen cars, Bayer chemicals and Siemens electrics stood amongst the top ten multinational corporations in the world, their success marking a long overdue victory for those Germans who had advocated an 'internationalist' economic policy in the inter-war period, but whose ideas had gone untried. West Germany's formidable economic success, also restored a sense of confidence to the German people. Pension provision and the expansion of the network of social services continued to grow, unemployment stood at less than 1 per cent from 1961–3, and to complement this economic and social achievement, Adenauer aspired to follow in Chancellor Stresemann's footsteps by working to reintegrate Germany into the international community by joining NATO and reaching a rapprochement with France.

In 1963 Adenauer was replaced by Erhard, and both he and his subsequent successors continued to use social market strategies to govern West Germany. When the SPD's Willie Brandt, an exile from Nazi Germany, became foreign minister in a Grand Coalition (CDU/CSU and SPD), in 1966, it was foreign policy, therefore, not domestic policy which was altered dramatically as Brandt established a new, more conciliatory *Ostpolitik* (Eastern Europe foreign policy) which marked West Germany's coming of age. Brandt hoped to advance relations between East and West Germany by a series of small steps: commentators in the Democratic Republic dubbed it 'aggression in carpet slippers'. It was an initiative which he built upon during his tenure as

Chancellor from 1969 until forced to resign in 1974, in the wake of revelations that a member of his personal staff was a Communist spy.

Despite this and other intermittent spy scandals, the West German people now accepted East Germany as a separate entity. In Brandt's words there were 'two German states, one German nation' and this recognition brought the Federal Republic new trading partners in Eastern Europe and a deeper sense of political stability and permanence.

BEGINNINGS OF A EUROPEAN UNION, 1945–51

The evolution of the European Community (EC), as the various European collectives dominated by the European Economic Community (EEC) later came to be known, provided an important framework to ensure the commitment of the Federal Republic to West European, and not simply to German, prosperity and peace. Many different elements, political and economic, contributed to a step-by-step creation of the EC, its context set by international and domestic trends, by the prevailing balance of power, by economic and technical stability or change. So, too, did many personalities. The measures taken first by national politicians and later by officials of the EC acting in concert with national representatives integrated, partially at least, economic and social developments in Western Europe which largely were independent of the EC, and thereby served to strengthen the power of the community.

The idea of a European Union had emerged long before 1945, long, indeed, before 1789, but it was only after the First World War – which had exposed the reality of European relations as one of bitter, bloody conflict – that the campaign for a European Union had begun in earnest. The central-European intellectual, the Hungarian Count Coundenhove-Kalergi and the French foreign minister, Aristide Briand, were among the pioneers. During the Second World War Hitler sought to create some form of European union under German control, while the common experiences of resistance movements seeking to destroy him contributed to a sense, in its turn, of common European identity within national frontiers.

The post-war debate over European integration was opened by Churchill – then leader of the opposition in Britain – when, in a speech in Zürich in 1946, he proposed that a Council of Europe be established. It seemed as much of a clarion call as his Fulton speech denouncing the iron curtain and, in a climate of rising tensions between the superpowers, his proposal was seized upon by aspirants hoping to create a 'third force' – a united Europe – to match the United States and the USSR. Churchill subsequently launched a 'United Europe Movement' in London in May 1947, while France, with support from both the Left and the Right, established the 'Council for United Europe'. There was now a sense of a European Movement, expressed enthusiastically at a congress at the Hague in May 1948, which was described at the time as States General of Europe. The movement gathered momentum when the increasingly fashionable conviction spread that integration was a means to prosperity and security and an antidote to the demon of nationalism. Moreover, this approach attracted the warm support of the United States. There were divisions behind the scenes, however, between the federalists who thought of themselves as Europe's militants, and the nationalists. The federalists had erected a European Union of Federalists as early as December 1946.[3]

By the 1950s the 'European' debate was altered with the acceleration of the Cold War and the arrival of Marshall Aid in Europe. The notion of Britain championing a European 'third force' seemed hopelessly unrealistic in the face of Britain's near bankruptcy. It had been made all too clear that the countries of Eastern Europe, that had not been permitted to accept Marshall Plan aid, would be unable to join any such union. Nevertheless, there was a demand for new European institutions, and following the Hague Conference a Council of Europe, with a headquarters in Strasbourg, was established by the Treaty of Westminster in 1949. It had a committee of foreign ministers of the ten original members (Belgium, Denmark, France, the United Kingdom, Ireland, Italy, Luxembourg, the Netherlands, Norway and Sweden), with the Belgian instrumental in its creation, Paul Henri Spaak, appointed its President. A small minority of Western European powers had favoured a continental federation with a common parliament, cabinet and economic policy, but the ambitions of the Council of Europe were less sweeping, focusing on the maintenance of Europeans' political and civil rights.

For nations as diverse as Britain, Greece and Finland, the answer to any question of wider political or economic European union in 1951 was already a resounding 'No'. The British Labour government soon lost interest in Europe in the face of the Christian-Democrat dominance in Western European politics, Britain's imperial ties and the country's persistent economic problems which many feared would be exacerbated by a common market. Foreign Minister Ernest Bevin opted instead to cultivate a 'Special Relationship' with the United States. And when the 'European debate' shifted from political plans for a Western European union, towards suggestions for European economic co-operation, Britain still stood out. By contrast, the success of the OEEC, the European Payments Union (1950) to facilitate the transferability of currencies, and the creation of the Benelux Economic Union (Belgium, the Netherlands and Luxembourg), which aimed to free controls on 90 per cent of trade between the three countries, all pointed to the way of the future. Italy, France and the Benelux states, in sharp contrast to Britain and Denmark, sustained their enthusiasm for European co-operation as the old slogan of 'divide and conquer' gave way to 'unify and federate'.

France's commitment to European co-operation was especially important. In contrast to its inter-war policy towards Germany, France was now determined that the Federal Republic should be integrated into Western Europe. The French government's initiative was greatly assisted by Adenauer's staunch pro-West policies and by the warm support of the United States, anxious to create a strong and united Western Europe, able to defend itself and avoid the misfortunes which engulfed the continent in the inter-war period. It was Frenchman Jean Monnet who focused the vision. Enlisting the support of the then French foreign minister, Robert Schuman, he proposed what to him was a first step, a European Coal and Steel Community (ECSC) dealing with commodities crucial for Western European recovery and located in Europe's industrial heartland – the French province of Lorraine and the German Ruhr valley. The Schuman Plan, as Monnet's scheme came to be known, offered an enticing mix of potential economic benefits, with the ultimate ideal of European integration founded on Franco-German co-operation. The plan tapped into popular, majority support for the notion of 'functional co-operation'. This was a pragmatic, evolutionary approach to co-operation by which integration could be pursued on areas on common economic interest – the production of coal, for example.

The ECSC, formally created in Paris in 1951, was supported by the six European powers most committed to greater European co-operation, both economic and political: the Benelux countries, France, Germany and Italy (Britain, Europe's most powerful nation, first rejected membership, then became an associate member in 1954). The ECSC was an important innovation in the stimulation of coal and steel production – steel output increased by 50 per cent and industrial production expanded at twice the British rate during the ECSC's first five years. It was also a landmark in Western European history for the ECSC established the principle of supranational co-operation under which participating states had to cede authority to a European agency, restricted though it was to the production and sale of iron, coal and steel. A court to settle disputes amongst members was also set up along with an assembly which convened in the European Council's Chamber in Strasbourg.

From 1958–68 the economic resurgence of Western Europe was particularly impressive within the European Community and this success helped persuade countries of the community's potential benefits. Britain had opted for looser co-operation afforded by the European Free Trade Association (EFTA), created in 1960 with Britain, Denmark, Norway, Sweden, Switzerland, Austria, Portugal, and later Finland and Iceland, as members. By 1960 Western Europe's economy was booming. In that year alone Western Europe accounted for 58 per cent of world trade and for over two thirds of the globe's GNP. Moreover, Western Europe had also become the focus of the global security system (NATO), until Superpower tensions began to ease in the 1970s.

INSTITUTIONS OF THE COLD WAR

During the 1950s and 1960s, in both Eastern and Western Europe, the political and economic environment was stable for the first time in many decades, and hot wars outside Europe stimulated economic growth in the

West.[4] In consequence, despite the persistent fear that the 'third world war' lay just around the corner, the division of Europe seemed to be set by an inexorable logic which made it difficult, in part given American policy, to erode the ideological differences between Communists and non-communists. It was 'institutionalized' too by the growing numbers of organizations on either side of the iron curtain designed to co-ordinate economic and military activities inside the two blocs. In the East there was the Cominform, the Communist information bureau, interpreted by the West as a resurrection of the Comintern, dedicated to promoting Marxist revolution across the globe. In the West organizations of economic co-operation also advanced the segregation of Europe, the Bretton Woods institutions and, later, the EEC. It was in response to the creation and successful development of Western Europe that the USSR established the Council for Mutual Economic Assistance (CMEA), or COMECON as it became known in the West (1949), to provide economic assistance to Communist powers. Of course, the Soviet Union, unlike the United States, had no real aid to give, and in its early years COMECON, operating out of small, dingy offices in Moscow, concentrated instead on collecting reparations from East Germany, Romania and Bulgaria. After Stalin's death COMECON was remodelled to co-ordinate planning and production within the Soviet bloc as a whole and it also took on some responsibilities for military co-ordination in the East until the inauguration of the Warsaw Pact in May 1955.

The creation of military agencies, NATO and its Soviet equivalent, the Warsaw pact, formalized the military division of Europe between East and West. Founded in the same year that Yugoslavia was reconciled with the Soviet Union in the wake of Khrushchev's visit to Belgrade in 1955 and his new foreign policy of 'co-existence' with the West, the Warsaw Pact largely re-affirmed the military *status quo* in Eastern Europe. The Soviet Union continued to dominate the armed forces of the satellite countries – ostensibly they were there to discourage the imperialist West from invading – and the Pact was an attempt to integrate military command structures. The Pact also lent a spurious legality to the Red Army's effective occupation of Eastern Europe, in the words of the Hungarian Prime Minister, András Hegedüs, for its text gave 'at least in theory, an opportunity for the leaderships of these countries to take control of their armies.' Albania, Romania and Bulgaria did not have Soviet troops stationed on their soil, for their loyalty to the Soviet Union was unquestioned (though Albania was to drop out of the Pact in 1961). Yugoslavia, too, controlled its own military forces.

By 1960 Churchill's metaphoric iron curtain had become chillingly real as cultural and social contacts as well as diplomatic relations between East and West were infected by the suspicions and restrictions of the Cold War. It was during this period that a woman exclaimed to a Czechoslovak visitor who had just flown to Britain, 'I didn't know that was possible . . . I didn't realize that 'planes could fly so high as to go over the iron curtain.'[5] Yet, aside from the intrigue, popularized in stories like Graham Greene's *The Third Man*, made into an evocative film in 1949 by the British co-author of the screenplay and director of the film, Carol Reed, the Cold War had a number of unexpected spin-offs. It provided a 'system' of sorts which maximized peace and stability and minimized the chance of war within Europe.

FRANCE, 1960–68

The new spirit of co-operation in Western Europe was nowhere more clearly illustrated than in France, where internal developments fostered Franco-German reconciliation. Successive French governments, shaking off the uncertainty which had dogged their inter-war performance, favoured the West German style social market over the large-scale nationalization of industry and its industrialists and civil servants launched a drive for expansionist capitalism. By the 1960s it was clear Monnet's plan had kick-started French economic growth which reached unprecedented heights between 1967 and 1968 when French productivity rose by an astounding 10.4 per cent. The best indicator of France's newfound sense of purpose and optimism was the reversal of a trend which had plagued France's confidence in economic and foreign policy matters since the late nineteenth century: the country's birth rate began to rise dramatically. Throughout the 1950s and the early 1960s the French birth rate was over 18 babies per 1,000 of the population; in the 1930s it had been 14.9 per 1,000. It was hard to put the new trend down to the pro-natalist policies of the French state for these differed little from those which had failed in the inter-war period, as the government mounted educational campaigns urging couples to procreate. (One of the most famous featured a baby's face with the banner: 'It seems I am a socio-cultural phenomenon!) The real reasons underpinning young people's, and especially young women's, reluctance to have babies, were not effectively addressed by government policies. The French government, in common with most of Western Europe, failed to provide sufficient financial support, particularly when it came to childcare. The assumption remained that women would return to the hearth, abandoning their jobs, once they had children. The majority of European women either could not afford, or did not want, to leave their jobs. Increasingly, it also became clear that the economy needed its skilled, female workers. Governments continued to grapple with this problem for the rest of the century. As a consequence, the country was not freed from the need to import workers from the poorer regions of Europe, its former empire and beyond. By the early 1970s, France had immigration agreements with Spain, Portugal, Morocco, Senegal, Mauritania, Mali and the Ivory Coast, to name but a few.

As in Britain and Germany, this new prosperity was not distributed evenly throughout the nation, and it is important, therefore, not to exaggerate the sense of a permanent social equilibrium either in France or in Western

Europe as a whole during this period. *La France paysanne* continued to decline as did the fortunes of small shopkeepers and artisans. And as elsewhere in Western Europe, the prosperous new class in post-war France were the *cadres*, the executive or middle manager class, who were particularly comfortably placed in years of economic boom. Regional differences persisted too, for as an exasperated de Gaulle once reflected, 'How on earth does one govern a country which makes 265 different kinds of cheese?'

Political life in France reflected these mixed fortunes, riven as it was with instability and short-lived coalitions. This, plus the political crisis sparked by France's colonial struggle in Algeria, worked to return de Gaulle to power in 1958 after an absence of 12 years. He then set about devising a new constitution for France, and the new Fifth Republic that he created was an attempt to foster greater mainstream loyalty, minimize the representation of small or extremist parties, and above all, to demonstrate that the French government now controlled parliament rather than *vice versa*. More remarkably, Algerian independence was conceded in the Evian Agreements of 1962. By then the cost of Algerian autonomy was the death of 17,500 French people and over 200,000 Muslims.

At first President de Gaulle also insisted on a strong hand in French foreign policy. In an effort to re-assert French power after the loss of empire, he opened up relations with Russia, China and Eastern Europe, and the development of *Force de Frappe*, an independent nuclear deterrent also served to compensate the French military for their imperial losses. Although primarily motivated by the desire to liberate France from the role of twentieth-century victim to that of strong, independent regime in international affairs, de Gaulle was also anxious to articulate and preserve European, as distinct from British and American, interests in the Cold War. Most dramatic was his announcement on 7 March 1966 that France, while remaining a signatory of the Atlantic Pact, was leaving NATO. The military alliance was thrown into turmoil with the Americans particularly incensed, as the French, along with the rest of the Brussels Pact, had been relieved to see the United States sign the Atlantic Treaty back in 1949. It was ironic, too, given de Gaulle's claim to champion European interests, that the NATO headquarters had to be moved from Fontainebleau to Brussels now NATO forces were no longer welcome on French soil. But de Gaulle was a realist. He knew that ultimately Western Europe needed the United States to counterbalance the USSR. He sought to maximize French independence without permanently alienating America, and he succeeded in returning authority to French foreign policy and a sense of pride to the French people.

ITALY, 1951–68

Italy, too, enjoyed its own *miracolo economico* during these years. Despite constitutional weakness – some 48 different governments and 18 different premiers between 1945 and 1989 – there were unprecedented levels of economic growth in the mid-1950s and 1960s. Indeed, during this period of 'La Dolce Vita', the Italian economy grew more than any other major country in the world, including the USSR and Japan, with growth especially impressive in the production of automobiles (Fiat, Pirelli), of office machinery (Olivetti) and of the electrical industry. The remarkable growth of the Italian economy – in the 1950s and 1960s Italy's annual rate of growth was an average of 5.7 per cent – was surprising perhaps given Italy's poor economic record in the first half of the century when there was a chronic shortage of raw materials and a heavy dependence on food imports. Now the Italian people disproved critics who claimed Italian economic growth could only be secured by cheap labour and showed themselves to be amongst the most hard-working and inventive peoples in Europe.

As in the remainder of Western Europe, the state played an active role in generating economic growth, with 20–30 per cent of Italy's industry (including 60 per cent of all steel production) owned by the Italian state. Europe's burgeoning tourist industry in the first great age of civil aviation also played its part in firmly establishing prosperity in Italy. But, mimicking the trend elsewhere in Western Europe, the wages and the standard of living in Northern Italy comfortably equalled those of Europe's wealthiest regions, while the poor agricultural regions in the South became progressively more impoverished, their peoples fuelling the ranks of workers migrating north. Yet the drain of workers did not appear to dent the relatively buoyant growth of the Italian population. The total population rose from just over 46 million Italians in 1950 to just under 50 million ten years later. (The population of Catholic Ireland actually fell, from 2.9 million to 2.8 million over the same period of time.)

BRITAIN, 1951–68

The one nation to which the post-war settlement did not bring an ebullient sense of national prosperity and confidence was Great Britain. When the Conservatives returned to power in 1951 with Winston Churchill as Britain's 76 year-old Premier, there was no strong sense of change. Nor was there any new commitment to the future. Indeed, there was little alteration to the Labour Government's post-war settlement beyond the controversial de-nationalization of the iron and steel industries. The remainder of Labour's nationalization programme and of the, largely uncontentious, welfare state remained intact. The Conservatives continued to hold the reins of power from 1951 until 1964 with Anthony Eden succeeding Churchill in 1955, to be succeeded in turn by Harold Macmillan after a crisis which concerned not Europe but the Middle East. Despite Macmillan's claim in 1959 that 'most people have never had it so good' – for levels of education, housing and health provision had all increased – the period was marked by 'la maladie *anglaise*' (the English disease), self-doubt, sluggish economic growth (annual growth rates were amongst the lowest in West Europe at 2.7 per cent per annum), and a decline in international stature.

The Suez Crisis in 1956, which brought Macmillan to power, cruelly unmasked the reality of British power overseas. British governments had hoped that their claim to a 'special relationship' with the United States and their attachment to the Commonwealth would be sufficient to safeguard British interests in the Middle East and with it British world power status. Instead, the United States, the USSR and opposition parties at home were united in their condemnation of the independent action of Britain and France in attacking Nasser's Egypt (drawing dubious comparisons with the appeasement of the 'dictators' in the 1930s). The decline of John Bull's influence abroad was clear and provoked a run on the pound sterling in November 1956, Eden's resignation, and, when Britain decided to abandon the campaign, the alienation of France at a crucial period in the evolution of the European Community. The deep sense of national malaise which permeated Britain was compounded in the early 1960s, by numerous scandals which rocked political and governmental life – the Vassall, Philby and Burgess spy scandals and the exposure of Secretary of State for War, John Profumo, in a sex case (March 1963). Still more serious, however, was continued sluggish economic growth. The British economy was afflicted by what became known as 'stop-go' economics (deflationary policies, which, as soon as they were abandoned were followed by a steep rise in the level of inflation), with chronic symptoms of government overspending, and living on credit, involving regular, if unpredictable, balance of payments crises.

Government policies did not help the British economy, but they were not the root of the economic problem. This lay deeper. Britain was now among the 'disadvantaged' as a result of having been the world's first industrial power, and of having been among the victors in two world wars which had destroyed British assets and generated substantial overseas debts. Even its geographic assets now looked like liabilities. Its island status kept it apart from the centre of Europe; its high density of population entailed heavy economic costs in order to maintain an efficient infra-structure. During the 1960s Britain's most renown export was pop music – *The Beatles*, *The Rolling Stones* and *The Who* were hugely successful groups overseas.

Britain's relative decline as a world power was a challenge that was to face it throughout the rest of the twentieth century. Historians have proposed numerous explanations for it and debate still rages. The most telling interpretations centre on Britain's failure to invest sufficiently in its post-war manufacturing base, in its low level of investment in research and development relative to other European powers (as well as to the Japanese and Americans), in the negative influence of British trade unions on productivity levels, and in the 'amateurish', untrained calibre of British management. Some have argued that complacency was Britain's undoing. Unlike many countries in both Western and Eastern Europe, Britain did not ask any necessary questions of itself in the wake of the Second World War. It was not until the 1960s that institutions were questioned, and then it was mostly from the radical left.

It was only during the controversial 1960s, when Germany and Italy increased their exports six times more quickly than Britain, that Harold Macmillan and his Labour successor as Prime Minister, the pipe-smoking Yorkshireman Harold Wilson, reluctantly reached the conclusion in turn that trading with the Commonwealth and membership of the European Free Trade Association (EFTA) was no adequate alternative to membership of the EEC. And even then they both met with opposition from inside their own parties.

RECOVERY IN 'LITTLE' EUROPE

In the heady environment of capitalist boom, Britain's industrial rivals of the nineteenth century – France and Germany – now outstripped Britain's economic achievements, even though in both countries the radical left was stronger than in Britain. More humiliating, perhaps, was the unprecedented growth enjoyed by Western Europe's smaller powers, including Sweden, the Netherlands, Austria and Belgium. According to the Belgian economic historian, Herman Van Der Wee, the last of these, which had played an important part in early industrialization, developed a new style of mixed economy, which promoted central consultation between various 'social partners' – bankers, employers' organizations, organized labour, for example – with co-operation between the latter two groups especially effective in creating an atmosphere of social peace that was highly conducive to economic recovery. Later on, however, Belgium had to tackle the fact that many of its factories were in urgent need of modernization, since, as in Britain, it had been at the vanguard of European industrialization in the nineteenth century. Its mining industry, especially coal production, was old-fashioned and inefficient. By the early 1960s, the Belgian government grasped the nettle of modernization, albeit with mixed results.

Austrian economic performance followed closely in the wake of Germany. Sweden and the Netherlands also enjoyed considerable export-led growth, particularly once exports to Germany were revived in 1949. Low wages were also important, especially in the Netherlands where they helped to make Dutch goods competitive overseas, kept profits high and so sustained elevated levels of investment in the Dutch economy. Spain and Greece, on the other hand, began to make real economic progress at the beginning of the 1960s with the tourist industry which forged the way. Sunshine became a major economic asset, though the social costs of this development were to be high.

THE TREATY OF ROME AND AFTER

Emboldened by their strengthening economies, the Netherlands, Belgium and Luxembourg, the most consistent northern advocates of greater European co-operation during the inter-war period, launched a dramatic new initiative in 1955, led by Dutch Foreign Minister, Johan Beyen, who argued that if Europe of the 'six' were moving towards a common market through organizations like the ECSC, why not discuss the possibility of a European Common Market immediately? That same year the decision to explore this possibility was taken at Messina in Sicily, although the six member states of the ECSC proceeded with caution, with Britain watching from afar, confident that the common market scheme would collapse. Instead, by the 1957 treaties signed in Rome, the six had formed the European Atomic Energy Community (EURATOM) and the European Economic Community (EEC).

The EEC came into being on 1 January 1958. With its administrative centre in Brussels – a Commission with Vice-Presidents from each of the member states – the EEC seemed at first to lack much of the supranational authority enjoyed by the ECSC. By 1967, however, the EEC, EURATOM and the ECSC had merged together into a single European commission. Large nations appointed two commissioners each, small nations one, and they in turn supervised a staff that by 1970 numbered more than 15,000 men and women. Political, as well as economic, authority came to the EEC by accretion. It soon acquired a European Court of Justice (with the important brief to ensure that Community law had 'equivalent' effect on all member states) and an elected European Parliament, although the latter had little control over the operations of the Commission – for example, it could not sack an individual Commissioner.

The primary object of the EEC was to create a customs union with free and equal competition amongst its members. This would bring peace and prosperity to Europe and, for those who aspired to it, closer political union. It was hoped that greater economic co-operation would also foster political unity in social, foreign and defence policies of the member states – unity on foreign and defence policies, however, continued to elude the union into the twenty-first century. A full customs union was in place by 1968, an expensive Common Agricultural Policy (CAP) had been devised and implemented to protect farmers in the member states, average GDP growth rates of 5 per cent per annum had been reached, and a five-fold increase in the volume of trade between EEC members had been achieved.

Impressed by such obvious success, Britain, having first sought to foster a looser form of European co-operation with EFTA, made its first application to join the EEC in 1961. But disputes with General de Gaulle over defence and foreign policy served to scupper both this request in 1963 and a further application under a new government in 1967 – an exasperated American official complained at the time that de Gaulle was 'the most goddamn undealable-with human being that's ever existed.' However, de Gaulle's government was challenged in 1968 following student demonstrations, and after his resignation in 1969 the important resolution to widen the Community was taken at the EEC's Hague Summit that year. In the following year detailed talks on the enlargement of the Community began, with Britain,

Eire, Denmark and Norway. Only the Norwegian people went on to reject proposed membership, as they were to do again years later in 1994 and 2002.

Why had Britain's attitude changed? The decision to apply for membership tested the Labour party more than the Conservative party for many feared that it would cost British jobs and that Christian-Democrat Europe would work to compromise socialist initiatives in Britain. By 1967, however, it was all too clear that not only was the British economy growing less quickly than its continental counterparts, but that the British Commonwealth, long thought of as 'an alternative to Europe', was itself in crisis over the question of Rhodesia, which had, for the first time, brought the British government into conflict with a white minority regime over the issue of independence. (It was also the first rebellion by a British dependency since the eighteenth century). The leader of the Conservative opposition after 1964, Edward Heath, was a staunch pro-European, so that for Harold Wilson, sensitive to all currents of opinion, including business opinion, committing the Labour government to EEC membership would help steal Heath's electoral thunder. There was some urgency too in order to exert some influence over EEC policies, in particular CAP, which the British government considered to be poor economics and potentially damaging to the interests of British agriculture. Finally, Britain's potential participation in the EEC was warmly welcomed by the United States, while de Gaulle's veto itself encouraged popular enthusiasm to see it overturned. French *grandeur* had to be confronted, and this was an old task. Over the next 30 years, other countries in politically designated western Europe, notably to the North (Norway, Denmark, Finland and Sweden) and to the East (Austria) were facing the similar struggles over whether their economic, political and social destiny lay within the European Community or beyond it.

SPAIN AND PORTUGAL, 1945–68

The two countries of the Iberian peninsula remained relatively isolated from Western Europe during the 1950s and 1960s. The imperative of the Cold War had seen a gradual thawing of, in particular, Spanish relations with the West thanks to Spain's strategic position in the Mediterranean and its vehement anti-communism. But suspicions of, and distaste for Hitler's former ally Franco, remained. While the end of the Second World War returned democracy to much of Western Europe, Spain and Portugal continued to be governed by authoritarian leaders for all of the 1950s and 1960s. Both countries were relatively untouched by the Second World War, so by-passing the need to reconstruct their countries after 1945. But by the 1950s, the pressure to modernize and catch up with the economic and social advances evident elsewhere in Western Europe grew pronounced. Both countries moved to liberalize their economies. Economic growth soon ensued, but the development soon unleashed political tensions in their regimes which the dictators who had taken power in the 1930s – Franco in Spain and Salazar in Portugal – found increasingly difficult to master.

Since its victory in the Spanish Civil War in 1939, Franco's regime had doggedly maintained the divisions of Spaniards into the defeated and the victorious. The dictatorship strongly believed that any form of democratic politics would bring nothing but chaos and national disunity. This was a central tenet of the regime's educational and cultural policy. Franco governed Spain as a conquered territory, with the Spanish army acting as the instrument of social control. (The army did not do that well out of this arrangement: its equipment was old-fashioned and its capacity to defend Spain from any external threat was severely limited.) The regime also relied on prisons and concentration camps to suppress dissent, with the forces of the right fearing that if the repressive climate were relaxed, civil war might be renewed.

The Civil War had established networks of patronage that helped Franco to govern Spain. These networks formed different competing groups – members of the original Falange party, Catholics, monarchists, clergymen, regime families, technocrats – who were lumped together in a single party known as the *Movimiento*. As the Spanish economy expanded and modernized in the 1950s and 1960s, rivalries between the different groups in the *Movimiento* grew considerably. A significant step in Spain's economic and social development came in 1956 when industrial strikes and violent student unrest gripped the country. To quell the violence, Franco embarked on a programme of economic liberalization the following year. Planning still played an important role. The tourist industry, for example, benefited greatly from government designed plans incorporating tax concessions, building licences and government loans. Spain's economic growth, coupled with its application for associate membership of the EEC in 1962, created a political timebomb because this economic programme was accompanied by very little political change. The regime's brutal torture and execution of the Communist Julián Grimau in 1963 underlined its repressive nature to Spaniards and to the outside world alike. At the same time, the emergence of the Basque revolutionary separatist movement (the territory in Northern Spain that had long sought to assert its distinct cultural and linguistic identity), ETA (*Euzkadi Ta Azkatasuna*, 'Basque Homeland and Liberty') in the 1960s and its successful assaults on the regime's security forces was a sign Franco's regime was not invulnerable. By the early 1970s, the dictatorship was dying, although its oppressive grip on Spanish society was first to grow tighter before it finally relinquished its hold in 1981.

Events followed a similar pattern in Portugal. Economic growth came later to Portugal, stimulated only in the 1960s by the renewed vitality of Portuguese trading links with both members and former members of its empire that stretched from Brazil in the East, through Angola in Africa and Goa in India to Macau and East Timor in the Far East. The economic benefits of imperial ties, however, were offset by the cost of maintaining those ties and

Portugal fought expensive imperial wars, for example, in Angola after 1961. Important, too, to the Portuguese economy was the recovery of Western Europe as a whole which created a large market for Portuguese workers. The pace of change in 1960s Portugal was dramatic. It achieved an annual growth rate of some 3 per cent, with the production of clothing and fabrics soon outstripping Portugal's traditional exports of cork and wood-pulp. The expansion of industry and urbanization also triggered significant social change in Portugal's hitherto conservative and hierarchical society. In the past, most workers and farm hands were largely uneducated; in rural communities women were left to work the land as their menfolk sought employment overseas. But economic growth demanded a better education and a more mobile workforce, and gradually the poorer members of Portugal's society began to experience some of the pleasures enjoyed by Portugal's long-privileged middle and upper classes. The most visible indicator of the social change was the advent of the package tourist industry which marked the visible opening up of Portugal's hitherto closed society. As in Spain, however, the ruling oligarchy were able to ride the tide of economic and social change until 1974 when both leading industrialists and the military abandoned the regime because they was anxious to push the modernization and liberalization of the Portuguese economy further. At this point the regime also abandoned its embattled empire and turned its attention towards the European Economic Community where, it concluded, Portugal's future lay.

Notes

1. M. Clark, *Modern Italy, 1871–1982* (1984, 1990 edn), p.325.
2. R. F. Betts, *France and Decolonisation, 1900–1960* (1991), p.17.
3. For the post-war European story as seen by a committed federalist, see J-P Gouzy, *Les Pionniers de l'Europe Communitaire* (1968).
4. E. Shuckburgh, *Aspects of NATO: Political Consultation* (1960), p.1.
5. G. Partos, *The World That Came In From The Cold* (1993), p.25.

Chapter 12

TOWARDS A UNITED EUROPE, 1968–2002

The Cold War always highlighted the degree to which Europe was politically, socially, economically and culturally divided. But Europe was also united across the iron curtain by shared influences and events. On a human level this was represented by many Germany families who lived on both sides of the divide, although until 1989 only those in the West could visit family members in the East. It was much more difficult the other way around. In both countries social expectations were shaped by what was seen and heard about lifestyles in the other half of the country, elsewhere in Europe and in the United States. Life in the workplace was determined by regional and global, as well as local, policies and trends. While the Communist state made strenuous efforts to assert a new proletarian culture, as we saw in chapter 10, the outcome was ambiguous. Shared interests and influences with the West remained.

So, too, did the means by which culture was disseminated. Although available for the first time in the 1930s, television sets, like cinema black-and-white during the 1950s, were acquired by most people only in the 1960s. For those living close to the east–west border in Europe, pictures and sounds of what it was like to live in the West were beamed directly into people's homes in the East. As the Soviet style economy failed, especially when it came to fulfilling society's demand for consumer durables and fashionable clothing, so the appeal of western-style capitalism increased.

The 1970s and 1980s saw Eastern European governments attempt to remedy the growing shortcomings in their economic performance by opening and developing economic links with Western Europe and with the major international economic institutions, the International Monetary Fund, the World Bank, and the General Agreement on Tariffs and Trade (GATT). Yet economic change and the impact it had on society underlined the inflexibility of political structures in countries with Communist or rightwing authoritarian regimes to accommodate the process of change. In Spain, Portugal and Greece, as well as in Communist governed Eastern Europe, movements and parties that had clung to power, in some cases for almost 50 years, were finally deprived of it. When compared with the inter-war period and the first years after the Second World War, political change, when it came, was usually peaceful and moving in the direction of parliamentary democracy.

In Western Europe the guiding assumptions and ideals that had dominated reconstruction after the war were challenged by a new generation who imagined a different definition of, and a different future for, Europe. The year 1971 saw the end of the Bretton Woods system, and with it American leadership of financial relationships between countries. Europe would increasingly make its own way in the international economy as a new competitive spirit in Europe's financial and trading relations with the wider world emerged. As foreign policy crises complicated the global political and economic context, the assumptions of Keynesian economics that national policies of economic management could safeguard nation states from another Great Depression were severely challenged. The most significant indications that Europe was passing through the end of an era, came with two further endings: the collapse of Communism in Eastern Europe and the conclusion of the Cold War.

THE 'REVOLUTIONS' OF 1968

The political stability of the international system in post-war Europe until the early-1960s was remarkable when set against the first 45 years of the twentieth century. Yet it rested on assumptions which never went unchallenged. Nuclear deterrence, which kept the Cold War cold, always had its critics and their numbers increased during the 1960s. The global picture also became more relevant then as American and European pressure groups, often using militant tactics, demanded the extension of civil rights for Blacks (especially in the United States) and an end to the war in Vietnam. Urban riots broke out on both sides of the Atlantic triggered, in part, by the assassination of Black civil rights activist, Martin Luther King in April 1968, while the European media, more influential than ever before, came to suggest that the war in Vietnam could not be won. US strategists were surprised by a massive Communist offensive in January 1968, and this after the United States dropped more bomb tonnage on Vietnam between 1965 and 1967 than the Allies dropped on Europe during the Second World War.

In May 1968 in Europe, the universities were at the centre of demonstrations. The number of young people attending university in Western Europe had increased significantly as educational trends established in the nineteenth century continued. All children now attended primary school, most went to some form of secondary school and in the post Second World War period university education became the fastest growing educational sector. By 1970 there were more than four million university students in Europe.

Local and national issues shaped their protests, and some were also influenced by the events in Vietnam, but the greatest impetus for the demonstrations came from the expansion of the institutions of higher learning themselves. In

West Germany student numbers rose from 196,000 to 376,000 in the ten years before 1969; in France numbers went up from 202,000 to 615,000 over the same period. In these and other countries, the expansion in numbers was not matched by a commensurate increase in investment. The same number of staff were expected to teach a student body which had almost doubled in size, and university buildings, including student accommodation, deteriorated under the strain. (In Britain, this problem resurfaced alarmingly in the 1990s, at the same time as institutions of higher education across Europe faced new financial and cultural challenges.)

There was also a culture clash as young people, more numerous (the product of the postwar 'baby-boom') and from a greater variety of backgrounds than before, began to question the assumptions and structures than underpinned the, supposedly independent, institutions of higher learning. (Ironically most student leaders were the offspring of the privileged middle class capitalists they so vehemently denounced.) France was brought to a virtual halt in 1968 as students, condemning the 'hierarchical, authoritarian' methods of their professors, joined the French workers, who did not always welcome them, in the greatest general strike in European history: it involved nine million workers and lost 15 million working days. De Gaulle left Paris, but survived the crisis in 1969 and lost power only after proposed constitutional changes were rejected by the electorate in the same year.

The year 1968 proved to be explosive not only in Paris, but in Germany, where Frankfurt was the intellectual centre of a new, anti-capitalist critique articulated by philosophers, among them Herbert Marcuse, living in the United States. Ironically the phrase 'capitalist, military industrial complex' had first been used, in a more positive context, by US President Eisenhower. There was a terrorist streak in German and Italian protest. Thus, the German 'Baader-Meinhof gang' operated as a secret guerilla group, protesting, in particular, against American 'imperialism' and its German associates. It robbed banks and bombed military and civilian targets from 1970 to 1972.

Across the 'iron curtain' in Czechoslovakia there was a different pattern of protest in 1968, where student protestors had the support of a new, reforming Communist leadership led by Alexander Dubček, who became First Secretary of the Communist Party in 1967. The Prague spring of 1968, as this temporary thaw in Communist repression became known, prompted a flowering of artistic, as well as political, expression that was intolerable to the Soviet leadership in Moscow, and on 20 August Soviet troops marched into Czechoslovakia and moved to create a new Communist government that would follow Moscow's lead. The brutal repression of reform Communism in Czechoslovakia, combined with events in Hungary some 12 years before, firmly turned Socialists in Western Europe against Soviet-style solutions to the political and economic challenges they came to face in the 1970s.

For the time being, however, the confluence of European history was not sustained. Society in the West was not much changed as a consequence of the demonstrations. In the East, they had been suppressed. Even the universities, the centre of most European protests, were little altered by the demonstrations. Established patterns of privilege and hierarchy, for the most part, remained intact. Some 'reforms' were made but they were limited and controversial. In particular, demands for greater access and equality of treatment made by, and for, women students, were not met. In 1970 women still comprised only 23 per cent of the entire student body in West Germany. And while the figure was to rise in that and subsequent decades, women, and other so-called minority groups, continued to be under-represented, particularly at the most senior levels in university academic and management positions into the twenty-first century.

Some of the student leaders of 1968 returned to the political scene in both Western and Eastern European politics in the 1980s, with the Soviet leader Mikhail Gorbachev the most prominent among them. In 1998 they were to figure in Gerhard Schröder's Social Democratic government in Germany. Already in 1975 most of the Baader-Meinhof gang had been tried at the specially built Stammheim gaol and imprisoned, but their motivations and methods were echoed in the activities of the Red Army brigades in Italy, culminating in the kidnapping and murder in 1978 of Aldo Moro, the former Italian Prime Minister (1963–8 and 1974–6) and leader of the Christian Democratic party.

THE SOBERING SEVENTIES

During the 1970s any confidence in the post-war settlement all but disappeared. When the Republican President Richard Nixon, who had taken office in 1969, dramatically devalued the dollar two years later, it was clear that the American economy was in difficulties. Superpower status for the United States had come at a price and worse was to follow both for the United States and for Europe. Deteriorating international economic conditions meant a sharp drop in investment inside Europe and in demand for European products, and an unusual combination of inflation and unemployment ('stagflation') was generated. Again, there was a general international crisis, following the outbreak of war between Egypt, Syria and Israel in the Middle East in October 1973, which prompted the Arab nations to work together in a cartel (the Organization of Oil Producing Countries or OPEC) to raise the cost of oil. A subsequent quadrupling of oil prices fuelled inflationary pressures already at work in the European economy, which, taken together quickly ate away at European growth. The economic crisis, although very different from the Great Depression of the 1930s, forced Western European countries to become preoccupied with a great variety of social, economic and political challenges.

Meanwhile, some of the longer term implications of the Yom Kippur War, as the 1973 conflict became known, the last full-scale Arab-Israeli war in the twentieth century, were lost on Europe for many years to come. The war resulted in a spectacular, if costly victory for Israel (some 2,500 Israelis died as against some 5,000 Arabs) that saw the consolidation of the Israeli state in the territories occupied in 1967. In the aftermath of this war, unlike in 1948 and 1967, the Arab states surrounding Israel appeared to recognize that Zionism could not be defeated by force, a recognition that prompted Egypt to sign a negotiated peace with Israel in 1979, a move that led Palestinians to feel abandoned and isolated, and it was in this context that they embarked on a war of terror against civilian Israelis, organized by the Palestinian Liberation Organisation (PLO) and its leader Yasir Arafat.

The sense of isolation was short-lived. An Islamic revival was soon under way, fuelled by a desire to secure social justice, especially among younger people, and militant theology became a vehicle for political opposition at a time when the number of Muslims living in Western Europe had greatly increased and when the Soviet Union became disturbed by the Muslim presence inside and outside its borders.

When the Iranian Revolution of 1979 removed from power the pro-Western Shah of Iran after violent protests and strikes across the country, traditional Islamic dress, particularly the headscarf for women, became the main sign of protest. The inspiration behind the movement was Grand Ayatollah Ruhollah Khomeni, who had been living in exile in Paris and whose book *Islamic Government* published in 1971 argued that senior religious scholars should have the last word in running the state. He came to fill this role himself in Iran, enforcing Islamic law (the *sharia*) and waging a holy struggle (*jihad*) that was to transform relations within nation states that had large Muslim populations, and relations between those states and the wider world.

There was alarm, particularly in the United States (for Khomeni, the 'great Satan'), where there had been a dramatic internal crisis in 1974, when Nixon, threatened with impeachment after what became know as the Watergate scandal, resigned. And within Europe itself there were dramatic events also, including the fall from power in Britain in 1974 of Edward Heath, who had taken Britain into the European Community in 1973. He had found it impossible to deal with worker unrest, at its most serious in the coal industry, the traditional base of militant trade unionism. Economists in Britain and outside were agreed that, in the euphemistic language typical of their profession, European labour markets were among the most 'inflexible' in the world. What they meant was that thanks to unionization and rights accorded to workers in law, it was difficult either to pay workers less or, when necessary, sack them when economic conditions determined it was necessary to enable companies to maintain their profit margins while competing with cheaper labour available overseas.

The growth of large multinational corporations now enabled producers to shunt jobs from one country to another, a practice which was called (with no euphemism) 'social dumping', and industrialists resorted to it in increasing numbers when, in an effort to manage the spiralling costs of social security, governments moved some of these costs on to employers. Western European workers were warned that if they 'didn't wake up and smell the coffee' by agreeing to different terms and conditions of employment, their jobs would soon move to parts of the world where labour was cheaper and more compliant. Meanwhile, governments were paying out more in social benefits, which had greatly increased since 1945, than they received in taxation from businesses and wage earners. As a result they were borrowing more to tide themselves over, an expedient that made the levels of inflation gripping their economies all the more severe. A rising level of public debt could only be tolerated until it ran the risk of fatally undermining a country's national currency and its economy.

The pressures exerted by this process spelt the end of the postwar social settlement that had brought relatively high levels of employment, pay and social provision to the majority of European citizens. At first West Germany, the Netherlands and Austria fared better than Britain and France. Good labour relations between the government, employers and employees enabled the West German Socialist Chancellor, Helmut Schmidt, who had succeeded Brandt in 1974, to keep wages demands down and to control inflation before a further hike in oil prices came in 1979 and 1980 in the wake of the revolution in Iran, and a war between Iran and Iraq which began a year later. Unemployment now spiralled in West Germany and the Netherlands, too. The numbers of people seeking work there more than doubled.

In Britain, following decades of relatively lacklustre economic performance, the political landscape was transformed for good after the fall of Conservative Prime Minister Edward Heath, who was defeated in two general elections in the same year 1974, and the failure of two Labour governments, the first led by an exhausted Harold Wilson and the second by an equally beleaguered James Callaghan. British membership of the European Community was approved in a referendum of 1975, the first referendum in British history, but economic and social problems persisted, and after a 'winter of discontent', Margaret Thatcher, who had succeeded Heath as Conservative leader, became Prime Minister after the general election of 1979.

The need for 'flexibility' in the face of change raised important questions about the role of the state and about 'redundancy' in the economy. Those who advocated 'free market economics', and their numbers were rising in the Western Europe of the 1980s, argued that the state and unions should not be allowed to interfere in the operation of the market place. The cut and thrust of what people wanted to buy (demand) alone should determine the prices, incomes and level of business activity. Government or union interference (formerly regarded as mediation) in the relations between employers and workers, and between producers and consumers, was seen as a destructive and stultifying obstacle to the otherwise 'perfect operation of the market-place'. There was no 'social contract'.

Relations between states were also transformed as governments began to dismantle restrictions on the movement of capital and goods. (Similar steps were taken in Eastern Europe after 1990.) Trade barriers between Western European countries fell more quickly than those between Europe and the wider world. Most dramatic was the increase in financial transactions. In 1986, for example, the *daily* turnover of the London Eurodollar market, virtually unregulated by public authorities, was some $300 billion or some $75 trillion per year. This amounted to more than 25 times the value of world trade. Capital flows had come to dominate, and became increasingly separate from, trade-related payments.

Europe began to change what it produced and how it worked. While Europe's traditional heavy industries strove to become more adaptable, manufacturing industries, like car and household goods, moved into more sophisticated forms of production often based on robotics. Microchip technologies (see below, p.406) transformed the workplace, while research and development now played a central role in developing new products and new processes. The retreat of government from economic management was followed by privatization when industries previously owned by the state, including in Britain railway transportation and telecommunications, were now sold-off, in some cases to foreign owners. Not all governments followed the same policies – there were marked differences, for example, between Britain and France – but all faced the same challenges. Distance and location now became less important. At the same time, prolonged economic difficulties generated a new determination to effect greater European economic and monetary reintegration to protect the region from global shocks. By the mid-1980s the European Economic Community was reinvigorated and its membership swelled by newly established democracies in southern Europe.

DEMOCRACY IN SOUTHERN EUROPE, 1975–86

The economic crisis of the 1970s never seriously threatened democracy in Western Europe, while, for Spain and Portugal the 1970s marked the creation of liberal democracy after decades of authoritarian rule. As we have seen, both countries had prospered during the 1960s, which perhaps paradoxically, served to undermine, rather than to secure, the continuation of General Franco's strongly authoritarian dictatorship beyond his death in 1975. In his last years Franco attempted to pander to Spanish democrats without conceding real power, but after his death, it became clear that Spain's new 37 year-old King Juan Carlos, nominated by Franco, and his chosen Prime Minister, Adolfo Suárez, were committed to bringing democratic government to Spain as rapidly as possible. The first democratic elections for 40 years were held on 15 June 1977.

Amidst the euphoria, few appreciated the extent of the problems that lay ahead. The machinery and ethos of democratic politics had to be recreated almost from scratch. Remarkably, over 300 political parties sprang into life shortly before the elections. These were whittled down to four, and the electorate voted overwhelmingly for those of moderation. The chaos that Franco constantly warned would come from the reintroduction of democratic politics in Spain failed to materialize. More problematic, however, was the task of bringing both the army and the Basque separatists into the democratic fold. Over the four years from 1977 to 1981 repeated attempts by the military and ETA terrorists to subvert Spanish democracy failed. In November 1978, for example, a planned military coup code named Operation Galaxia, after the café in which the plan was hatched, fizzled out but not before a leader of the Civil Guard, General Juan Atarés Peña, publicly denounced the Spanish Minister of Defence as a 'freemason, traitor, pig, coward and spy'. A further attempt at military take-over in February 1981 also failed. Equally problematic for Spain's fledgling democracy was the economic stagnation that gripped the country as a result of both domestic upheaval and international conditions.

By the time of the elections held in February 1981, democratic politics in Spain were consolidated. Aside from the support of key industrialists and financiers, credit was also given to the press, courageous in its support of democracy. Equally deserving of praise were key politicians who had worked together, frequently putting narrow party interest aside, to protect democracy and the young king who had risked his life in the service of the constitution. The advent of democratic politics allowed cultural life to become open to new ideas and to diversify. Books previously banned on forbidden topics were now openly bought and sold. Music festivals that showcased styles of music long available in democratic Europe became hugely popular.

While Spain's transition to democracy was relatively orderly, despite attempted military coups and ETA terrorism, Portugal's was not. In April 1974 a group of army officers overthrew the dictatorship of Marcello Caetano (who had succeeded Salazar in 1968), and installed a junta under the Presidency of General Antonio de Spinola. The country was exhausted from a series of colonial wars in Africa, by the damaging rise in the price of oil, and a crisis over land ownership in the Alentejo, and Spinola soon lost power. In the face of militant left-wing groups (with the Communist party on the sidelines), the country owed much to General Antonio Ramalho Eanes who, from the Left, maintained order. Portuguese politics oscillated between left and right in inconclusive elections and unstable coalition governments in 1976, 1977, 1978 and 1979, although the country took the significant step in 1976 of electing the Socialist Dr Mário Soares as Prime Minister when the first free elections in fifty years were held. His was a minority government with Eanes as President, and Soares became President in 1986, to be re-elected, almost unopposed, to a second term in the Presidential palace in 1991.

Most of Portugal's remaining colonies became independent during this period, a transition that was remarkably peaceful given the years of bitter conflict that had preceded it, but there was to be a civil war in Angola and Mozambique. Inside Portugal, following further constitutional changes, designed to reduce the role of government in industry and agriculture, politics at last found a stable, if a little less colourful, middle ground, and in 1986 Portugal, along with Spain joined the European Community.

In Greece, which joined the Community five years earlier, there had been a chequered story of authoritarianism and freedom. Following the defeat of the Communists in the civil war of 1946–9 a rigid electoral system kept them on the margins of political life. The country's fragile democracy, divided between traditional monarchists and liberal modernizers, crumbled in 1967 when military officers, the 'Greek colonels', staged a coup. Political activity was banned and King Constantine was exiled. A republic was proclaimed in 1973, but a bungled attempt by the military junta to improve its popularity by asserting Greece's territorial claim over Cyprus, which had secured its independence from Britain in 1960, not only brought Greece into renewed conflict with Turkey, it also cost the colonels their power.

Constantine Karamanlis who had been Prime Minister before the coup, returned from self-imposed exile and became prime minister again from 1974 to 1980. Karamanlis, who went on to become President from 1980 to 1985, publicly avowed that his main aim as leader was to 'Europeanize the Greeks', a task which involved curbing the nationalism that had so long dominated political life. In 1981 Andreas Papandreou became Greece's first socialist Prime Minister, leader of the Panhellenic Socialist Movement (PASOK). He was defeated in the general election of 1989, by which time PASOK had created an extensive grass-roots organization. By the late 1980s, Greek democrats had demonstrated the veracity of their election slogan, 'We belong to the West!'

THE GROWTH OF INSTITUTIONAL EUROPE, 1970–86

By 1973 the EEC, with the entry of Britain, Ireland and Denmark, had already become the Europe of Nine, and with the accession of Spain, Portugal and Greece in 1986 it became a Europe of Twelve. The new members benefited greatly from the political credibility, investment and aid which European membership brought. Western Europe's largest industrial powers did not regard these new members as any threat to their dominance, but questions were inevitably raised by the potential demands they might make on the Common Agricultural Policy (CAP). The farm-sector was crowded and the CAP was to become highly contentious when huge food and wine stocks accumulated. Even more bitterly contested questions would be raised when the newly liberated countries of Eastern Europe bid to join the Union after 1990.

The production and distribution of products from the primary sector of the economy continued to be a major source of tension within the Community. It was riven not only by disputes over the CAP, but about fishing quotas and the allocation of the Regional Development Fund. After 1973 the British government had become the largest contributor to the Community's coffers while benefiting little from CAP, and Britain was an uneasy member of the Community throughout the 1970s and 1980s when there was little sense on the part of the public that substantial benefits had been gained. Tension also mounted over debates about how far the Community should widen its political activities. In 1974 the European Parliament was made an elected body, but talk of creating a 'citizens' Europe fell on fallow ground. So too did efforts to create a monetary union and to widen the Community's foreign policy brief. Members were encouraged to co-ordinate their foreign policies. It rarely happened. The most significant report of the 1970s, written for the Council by Léo Tindemans, Prime Minister of Belgium, discerned a lack of direction within the Community, but his recommendation for extending supranational powers were just as contentious as the CAP.

By the mid-1970s, West German dominance of the Community was a reality which France could no longer deny. Instead, a new Franco-German axis was forged, this time between the West German Chancellor Helmut Schmidt and the French President Valéry Giscard d'Estaing. Both were economists by background and, although their politics were different, both men were searching for new ways of stabilizing the international economy following the collapse of the Bretton Woods system. Their efforts met with opposition, particularly in Britain, where Callaghan remained uneasy about their proposal to create a new European currency (the ECU) and a new European Monetary System (EMS). Schmidt and d'Estaing had been assisted by the first (and only) British President of the European Commission, Roy Jenkins, a former Labour Chancellor of the Exchequer, but this did not help Callaghan. When the EMS came into operation in March 1979, Britain became a formal member of it, but did not take on the obligations of the ERM by fixing the value of sterling.

All this was confusing, but by the early 1980s the Community could boast some significant achievements. It now held comparable global economic importance to the United States, accounting for more than one-fifth of the world's trade, and its 320 million inhabitants were among the most prosperous in the world. Its economic and social agenda also evolved as the wellbeing of Community citizens was more broadly defined. In October 1972 it resolved to pursue action on environmental, scientific and social issues, and soon these activities mushroomed. Its economic success made it an attractive, lucrative market for Eastern Europe which Poland, Hungary, Romania and Yugoslavia were increasingly determined to exploit. Eastern Europe was now looking West, not East, for economic support but, with the deepening of Community relations, Western European countries continued to look largely to one another.

EASTERN EUROPE:
REFORM AND DECLINE, 1968–89

After 1968, the short-lived religious and political freedoms enjoyed in some parts of Communist Eastern Europe were submerged once more beneath the apparatus of what was still a Stalinist-style state. As in the Soviet Union, the Communist Parties in Eastern Europe continued to maintain a firm grip on power, despite rising popular disillusionment, by encouraging and exploiting social inequalities. Ideology was perverted as certain social groups, like skilled workers and 'card carrying' members of the intelligentsia, were given privileges. At the pinnacle of this social hierarchy were the *nomenklatura*, 'loyal communists' who were the backbone of the state. This pyramid of privilege, coupled with the party's monopoly of power (for no other political parties were allowed), along with ideological control and strict codes of censorship for the media and education, all made opposition difficult. The methods of the state police, largely operating in secret, ensured it was dangerous too.

Gradually, however, the need for economic reform came to subvert Moscow's claims to control over Eastern Europe. The symptoms of economic paralysis increasingly evident in the Soviet Union began to infect Eastern Europe. So, too, did the deteriorating global economic conditions that did much to undermine the established economic and social settlement in postwar Western Europe. With the flowering of détente in the Cold War in the 1970s and the obvious paralysis of Comecon, Eastern Europe increasingly imported Western technology and capital. Hungary was at the forefront of a new wave of economic reforms, building on the changes implemented in the New Economic Mechanism, to promote new economic contacts with the West. It was made a member of GATT in 1973, received most-favoured-nation trading status from the USA in 1978, and in 1982 joined the World Bank and the International Monetary Fund.

Membership of the Soviet bloc had been a persistent hindrance to trade and growth but Poland and Romania also advanced their commercial contacts with the West. By 1974 half of Polish and Romanian trade was with the West. Only Bulgaria balked at diluting its economic relationship with the Soviet Union. Although Bulgarian Communists cultivated trade with Middle Eastern and Mediterranean markets, they never weakened their economic links with Russia. In the short term this strategy paid off – Bulgaria was granted preferential access to Soviet credit and oil. In the long term, however, the uncompetitiveness and environmental destruction of Bulgarian industry fatally undermined the Communist Party in the 1980s.

Further fractures in the cohesion of the Eastern bloc were apparent in the ethnic tensions within Yugoslavia and growing labour unrest in Poland. Yugoslavia was first and most radical in its attempts to modify the workings of the command economy, but by 1975 business enterprises had over 273 billion dinars worth of unpaid bills and owed the same in unpaid loans. In 1983 the IMF stepped in to solve Yugoslavia's mammoth debt problems with a substantial debt re-scheduling package. Rampant inflation and labour unrest were also fuelled by ethnic tensions between Croats and Serbs, the prelude to what in the 1990s was to become civil war. In 1973 Croatian nationalists were put on trial, and in 1981, a year after the death of Tito, ethnic tensions between Albanians and Serbs in the republic of Kosovo boiled over once more. When Kosovo was placed under effective military rule it appeared that Tito's dream of a United Yugoslavia had died along with him.

But it was in long-suffering Poland that the first substantial political challenge to the Communist Party came. The causes of Poland's economic malaise were much the same as Yugoslavia's: massive foreign debts, barely perceptible levels of growth, rising inflation and, perhaps most importantly, a clear disparity between the grand claims of their Communist government to improve the living conditions of its workers and farmers and the grim reality. In 1980 demonstrations by industrial workers – an ominous development, for this group were the alleged 'vanguard' of the Communist revolution – were organized by the trade union Solidarity (*Solidarnosc*), founded at the Lenin shipyard in Gdańsk and led by Lech Walesa. The demonstrations threatened the Communist Party, but did not lever it from power. Instead, there followed a period of martial law imposed by General Wojciech Jaruzelski. This was ended in 1983, when an amnesty was granted to 35,000 political prisoners. The pressure to reform the economy increased and following further Solidarity-led strikes in 1988 the union was legalized in 1989. By then it was not merely Communism in Poland that was at stake, but the survival of the Communist order throughout Eastern Europe and the Soviet Union itself.

STAGNATION AND SENILITY IN THE SOVIET UNION, 1964–85

The Polish political philosopher, Leszek Kolakowski, once described reform Communism as 'fried snowballs' – changing the temperature dissolves the substance – for if the planned economy and the role of the Communist Party were diminished by reform, then the system was no longer Communist. Events in the Soviet Union after Khrushchev's fall reflected Kolakowski's view. Even unambitious reform was rejected in favour of maintaining the *status quo* and of fortifying the role of the military in Soviet life. In 1964 there was, once again, no obvious successor to the Soviet leadership. Gradually, however, Leonid Brezhnev, just like Khrushchev before him, marginalized his rivals. Twelve years younger than Khrushchev, he was General Secretary of the Communist Party from 1964 to 1982 and President of the Soviet Union from 1977 to 1982, the year of his death.

After his appointment as General Secretary there was little political change in the Politburo. Indeed, in his 18 years as leader, Brezhnev removed only nine individuals from it, whereas during the 'tempestuous' days of Khrushchev, 24 people were removed from the Politburo within nine years. Brezhnev, a Ukrainian by birth, had his own men, however, like Yuri Andropov, chief of the KGB from 1967 to 1982, who was to succeed him.

Under Brezhnev's cautious leadership, which brought no dramatic modifications of structure or policy, the most important development was the continued growth of the Soviet military arsenals, witness to one of the most substantial military build-ups in a country at peace in the twentieth century.

This was after Nixon became the first American President to recognize the Communist government of China when he visited Beijing in 1972, and his Secretary of State Henry Kissinger, had sought to secure a strategic arms limitation treaty with the Soviet Union (SALT I). 'Coexistence' suited both superpowers who, in a kind of fearful intimacy, now recognized areas of common interest, not least that of keeping nuclear weapons out of the hands of other nations.

The Cold War had thus eased into static postures and a well-rehearsed routine, with the occasional adventure, such as the Soviet Union's very costly invasion of Afghanistan in 1979. Maintaining the nuclear arms race, with East and West vying for technological and numerical supremacy in weapons over the enemy, had become the principal means of sustaining the Cold War, but huge arsenals not only imposed financial strains on the Brezhnev regime, it meant that the Soviet Union's cherished 'buffer-zone' of Eastern Europe was now irrelevant to Soviet defence needs. Western and Eastern Europe no longer held the centre stage in defence now that intercontinental ballistic missiles (ICBMs) could, in theory at least, wage war on one another's people directly – the USSR could bomb the USA without invading Western Europe first.

During the 1980s first the United States and, then, the USSR no longer enjoyed an easy confidence in the strategy of deterrence and when Ronald Reagan, who became President launched a new and immensely costly Strategic Defence Initiative (SDI) in 1983, a project which was nick-named after the hugely popular science fiction film trilogy of the 1970s 'Star Wars': it had an air of fantasy about it. At the same time, he launched a sharp verbal attack against the Soviet Union which he called an 'evil empire'.

Soviet opposition to Reagan's SDI was shared by many European countries, but it was only the Soviet Union which was feeling severe economic strain. Enhancing the authority and resources of the Soviet military had buttressed Soviet foreign policy, but the agricultural and industrial difficulties remained. Indeed, the Soviet military build up only served to exacerbate the chronic imbalance between the Soviet Union's heavy industrial output and the output of consumer products (known within the Politburo as the A/B debate).

The monstrous bureaucratic and economic structures, ostensibly created to benefit the working class, continued to oppress and exploit them as perks and privileges were showered upon party *apparatchiks* (agents of the state). Ultimately, stagnation under Brezhnev and his short-lived successors (Andropov, who died in 1984, and Konstantin Chernenko, who died in 1985), threatened the USSR as much as the failed reforms of Khrushchev. Change came only with the appointment of Mikhail Gorbachev as General Secretary of the Communist Party in 1985, when belatedly, the senile, the dying and the dead leadership of the preceding three Soviet leaders, was replaced by the drive of a representative of a long awaited 'next' generation. Born in 1931, he had been a member of the Politburo since 1980.

GORBACHEV'S 'PERESTROIKA' AND THE CRISIS OF COMMUNISM

Gorbachev was cut from a different cloth to that of his predecessors. He had no memory of the purges and little of the war. He was well educated, interested in reform and able as well as young. He took pride in the achievements of the Soviet Union as a superpower, but from the start expressed public concern that the slow down in Soviet economic growth would mean that it would no longer be a superpower in the year 2000. His candour was unprecedented. So, too, was his explanation of the Soviet Union's malaise: a decline of discipline, order and morality. This in turn had permitted corruption, privilege, 'breaches of the law, bureaucratism, parasitism, drunkenness, prodigality, waste and other negative phenomena' to run rampant.

At first Gorbachev believed that it would be possible simply to eliminate abuses and that the levels of production subsequently would climb. The task was far more difficult, although unlike his predecessors, he was not afraid to expose weaknesses. Indeed, his policy of *Glasnost* (openness) encouraged others to do likewise, arguing 'we shall not go under since we are not afraid to discuss our weaknesses and will learn to overcome them.' Debate now opened on hitherto 'closed' issues, like the role of women, the environment (especially after disaster struck at the Chernobyl nuclear power station in Kiev on 26 April 1986), and the existence and levels of crime.

The second Russian word to capture Europe's imagination on both sides of the Iron Curtain was *Perestroika* or reform. But while Gorbachev had energetically begun to assert the need for major reform, no major economic changes were implemented. Ultimately, this proved his undoing, although in 1987 he and Reagan, who had been re-elected US President with a massive majority in 1984, reached a historic agreement in 1987 to reduce their nuclear arsenals by four per cent, scrapping intermediate range nuclear missiles. In the same year Moscow's economic ministries were reorganized, but economic policy, governed by the 1986–90 four year plan – it was to be the Union's last – still remained heavily centralized, with elementary incentives for workers to increase their output. By the following year, the Politburo frankly admitted to the Communist Party that the USSR's economic problems were far worse than had been feared.

This news, rather than inspiring the party's reforming zeal, prompted the party's increasing fragmentation. On the Left, though the term is debatable, were those who believed the pace of reform was too slow: among them was Boris Yeltsin, born in the same year as Gorbachev and a future President of Russia and the Commonwealth of Independent States. On the Right were those who became increasingly distrustful of Gorbachev's reformist language, including Egor Ligachev who was to plot against him. By the summer of 1988 Yeltsin had been dismissed from the Politburo for his outspoken criticism of Gorbachev, while Ligachev was attempting to form a conservative alliance within the Politburo to block Gorbachev's policies.

Gorbachev was now under attack from all sides, and the June–July 1988 Special Party Congress saw the first open disagreements within the Communist Party since the 1920s. Meanwhile, tinkering with the command economy continued to be barren of results, and it was not until January 1989 that a major package of economic reforms was introduced: state enterprises were now allowed to sell some of their output on the open market and foreign companies could own Soviet enterprises. To many citizens of the Soviet Republics it appeared that this reform would make things worse not better, and supplies of meat and dairy produce began to fall as farm labourers preferred to cultivate their own plots for produce that they could sell at a substantial profit.

Arguably, Gorbachev's greatest domestic achievement was a political one: the country which had only ever enjoyed one democratic election (in November 1917), now called open elections. The 1989 election for the Congress of People's Deputies marked the beginning of this process. Although not truly democratic – 750 of the 2,250 seats were reserved for groups like the Communist Party and the trade unions – it marked the dawn of democracy for the Soviet Republics and the beginning of the end for the Soviet regime. To counterbalance the loss of control over Congress, Gorbachev created an executive Presidency for which he was the only candidate – there remained limits to the new spirit of openness in Soviet politics – but the step was not enough to keep him in control. In 1990–1 the pace of political change inside the Soviet Union further accelerated.

As the power and the authority of the central Communist Party institutions dwindled, Gorbachev seemed entirely unprepared for the demand for independence from 15 different Soviet Socialist Republics that constituted the Union. Demands for independence from Estonia, Latvia and Lithuania, territories absorbed after the Second World War, might have been anticipated, but, more problematic in the longer term were the aspirations for freedom expressed by states like the Ukraine, Georgia (Gorbachev's foreign minister was a Georgian, Eduard Schevardnadze) and Azerbaijan. A bitter conflict soon broke out in the last of these because the community of Armenians who lived in the Azerbaijani region of Ngorny Karabakh wanted, instead, to be incorporated into the Soviet Republic of Armenia. (The struggle was a foretaste of the even more violent and long-lasting war for independence waged in the 1990s by Islamic fighters representing the Muslim population of Chechenia.)

Gorbachev had no answer to the multi-ethnic and multi-lingual problems created by his reforms, and his handling of them served only to alienate further both conservative and liberal politicians. In August of 1991 an abortive coup by right-wing elements did little to enhance Gorbachev's dwindling popularity inside the faltering USSR, and he was saved only by the intervention of Yelstin. Briefly reinstated, he resigned on Christmas Day, 1991 and the following day what remained of the Soviet parliament dissolved the Soviet Union. Yeltsin went on to form a new decentralized Confederation of Independent States (CIS). COMECON too disappeared.

THE 'REVOLUTIONS' OF EASTERN EUROPE, 1989

The historian, Paul Kennedy found a ready audience in the East and West for his theory of 'imperial overstretch' – that the overextension of national resources overseas prompted the dissolution of 'empire' and decline at home.[1] Yet to understand the sequence of events in 1989 it is necessary to take account of the fact that the impetus for change had also swept across the Soviet satellites of Eastern Europe as it had the Soviet Union. Puppet governments began to unravel with surprising ease and speed, reported dramatically in the press and revealed on the television screen. It was clear that the Kremlin had made a conscious decision to allow events to run their course without intervention. To the people of East Berlin, who warmly praised Gorbachev for this courageous decision, this was liberation. Erich Honecker, leader of the Communist Party was replaced, and after a mass exodus of East Germans to West Germany (via Hungary) eventually the Berlin Wall came down on 9 November 1989.

The whole satellite system dissolved peacefully in 1989 as Gorbachev's foreign ministry spokesman, Gennadi Gerasimov, put it, the USSR now followed the 'Sinatra doctrine' in its relations with Eastern Europe. They had to find their 'own way' out of their troubles. Their Communist Parties, encouraged by Gorbachev, made earnest efforts at internal reform from 1988 until November 1989, but they were soon to meet the fate of Gorbachev. The spell of fear cast by Stalin had been broken, and this was formally recognized in October 1989 when the Soviet Union formally renounced the 'Brezhnev Doctrine', used to justify Soviet intervention in other Communist countries as a 'fraternal' gesture of solidarity. This brought the Cold War and Soviet domination of Eastern Europe to an end. The Warsaw Pact was dissolved on 1 July 1991.

At the time, the Communist Parties of Eastern Europe, particularly that of East Germany, appeared to surrender power with astonishing ease. The neutral stance of the Soviet Union had helped, but so, too, had widespread disillusionment with the 'moral' and 'economic' pledges of Communism. Jealous eyes cast upon the economic achievements of their Western European counterparts, and in central Europe Communist rule was decisively rejected and centre-right governments installed. In Czechoslovakia there was what was called a 'Velvet Revolution'. Further east, however, in Romania and Bulgaria, the transition was neither conclusive nor peaceful. In Romania, which had refused to behave as a Russian satellite, there were over 1,000 deaths as President Nicolae Ceausescu's security police made a brutal but short attempt to preserve his regime. He and his wife, to their surprise, were overthrown in a 'Christmas Revolution' seen on the television screens of the West through the transmissions of a Yugoslav broadcasting company. In Bulgaria Todor Zhivkov, who had been President since 1971, was ousted by his foreign minister, Petar Mladenov.

In the Baltic states of Estonia, Lithuania and Latvia which had been absorbed into the Soviet Union in 1940, after some tough talking, Moscow was forced to relinquish control. There had been ethnic violence before 1989 in the Soviet republics of Kazakhstan (December 1986), Armenia, Azerbaijan and Georgia (all in 1987). Now there was more of it. Old forces as well as new ones were released.

In 1987 Gorbachev had spoken of a 'common European house', a single cultural and historic entity 'from the Atlantic to the Urals' (a similar sentiment was pinned to the collapsed Berlin Wall in 1989: 'Stalin is dead, Europe lives'). But the years after 1990 witnessed the varied frameworks of European co-operation, both East and West, grow ever more strained in face of economic dislocation, political shortcomings, reawakened ethnic tensions and a comparatively uncertain international framework. To some it seemed that the 'frying snowballs' had jumped out of the frying pan and into the fire.

WESTERN EUROPE, 1979–92

Anxieties about the strength of existing economic, social and political structures were not only confined to Eastern Europe and the USSR in the 1980s and early 1990s. Prospects were not auspicious for Western Europe at the beginning of the 1980s, especially when, in the wake of the revolution in Iran in 1979 and war between Iran and Iraq which began a year later, oil prices were hiked up again, renewing the spectre of inflation and deep recession. There were threats too to heavy industrial capacity as Japan and the countries of the Pacific rim took the lead in meeting world demand for new electronic products. France was fascinated by the new microchip technology and Germany profited from it, but in Britain there was a mismatch between the available skills of its workforce and the demand for high-tech products. Worker productivity also remained relatively low.

Adaptability was necessary in Europe's traditional heavy industries, and increasingly in industries like car and household goods manufacturing where assembly line production was moving to more sophisticated forms of production, some based on robotics, the need for 'flexibility' raised important questions about 'redundancy' and the role of the state in the economy. Increasingly, free-market and monetarist economics (government intervention should be kept to a minimum while the supply of money in the economy was encouraged to become the determining factor affected performance) began to influence the economic policies of Conservative and Christian Democrat governments whose overriding objective was to reduce inflation. In Britain, which endured the most radical application of monetarist economics after 1979, hallowed policy objectives like full employment were discarded. In Germany, which was not immune from economic difficulties, Schmidt was replaced by Helmut Kohl in 1982. Both he and Margaret Thatcher were returned at subsequent elections – Thatcher in 1983 and the Centre/Right coalition under Chancellor Helmut Kohl in 1986. Kohl was to unite East and West Germany in 1990.

Only in France did the Left enjoy a sustained level of success with the election of François Mitterand as the first socialist President of the Fifth Republic. Although his claim to extensive socialist credentials, like his symbolic role in the 1944 liberation of Paris by leading an armed assault on the *Commissariat général aux prisoners de guerre*, rested uneasily with his rural, Catholic and conservative upbringing, and his employment and associations with the Vichy regime, he was, above all, a consummate politician, fighting four Presidential elections, and 23 other political seats at both national and local level in a political career which spanned from 1947 until 1995. He was in power for over 14 years thanks to his re-election in 1988 – a record in modern French history. In his writings Mitterand described himself as a man of the past who made 'an enormous effort to leap into the present'. Yet his political career was characterized by ambiguity and the primacy of retaining political power over ideological positions (as well as great personal courage), making him very much a man of the 1980s.

Spain, under Felipe González, and Greece, under the leadership of Andreas Papandreau, were more unequivocally socialist, but when compared with socialist governments in earlier periods of European history, little radical change was effected. Economic conditions were certainly an inhibiting factor. By 1986 there was some measure of economic recovery in all countries, socialist or not, induced less by government policy than by rearmament spending on the part of the United States, which under Reagan ran a considerable deficit throughout this period. Levels of trade increased again in a period of financial realignment and business mergers.

But there were other reasons to explain why politics, when compared to earlier decades, no longer appeared as a major force shaping European society. Instead, the 'globalization' of the world's economy became a new buzzword, with transnational corporations increasingly de-regulated and supported by information technology, crossing the boundaries of 'traditional', national economies and challenging the powers of government to control national developments.

THE ECONOMIC AND TECHNOLOGICAL TRANSFORMATION OF EUROPE, 1989–PRESENT

After the drama of 1989 Eastern and Western Europe, while subject increasingly to the impact of new technology, continued to enjoy or suffer widely differing fortunes. While Western Europe continued to face the challenge of vigorous competition, from both the United States and the Far East (although the economic collapse of the latter after 1997 provided something of a respite), life was much tougher to the East. Political liberation triggered the end of the planned economy, but early hopes that a sharp and swift exposure to market forces – so called 'shock therapy' – would facilitate the region's prompt and successful conversion to free market capitalism were soon dashed.

When the Cold War ended in 1989, Europe appeared transformed. Yet many of the problems and challenges Europe has faced since then can be traced directly first to the conflict that had gripped Europe for over 50 years, and, second, to the manner of its ending. Russia, in particular, struggled to make the transition to a market economy and democracy. The former, unassisted by any new counterpart of Marshall Aid, unleashed forces, notably the growth of organized crime (its own *Mafiya*) that constrained economic development and exacerbated social injustice.

Output fell dramatically across the region, dropping by almost 40 per cent between 1989 and 1995 in Russia, over 30 per cent in Bulgaria and Romania and in Hungary and Poland by some 18 per cent. Most people experienced a rapid reduction in their living standards as the positive benefits of the Communist system – health care and educational provision – now disappeared. Museums and galleries suffered. So also did publishing. Moreover, the environmental damage which caused rapid and crude industrialization, was now revealed for all to see. The environmental pressure group *Greenpeace* reported that fish caught in the Baltic Sea were so polluted that local residents said 'they already looked cooked'. In 1990 over 71 per cent of Polish drinking water was unfit for human consumption. Despite financial assistance from the IMF and the legions of economic advisers that trooped to the capital cities of Eastern Europe, there was no quick fix to be had. The region had to move from producing heavy industrial goods that no one wanted (this was relatively easy to achieve), attempting to create new consumer-orientated and service industries (a much more demanding task).

Personalities played a greater role in Russian political life than the new political parties and the surviving Communist party. The 1990s were dominated by Boris Yeltsin who, talented but erratic in his behaviour, was eventually replaced in 1999 after the Russian financial system had disintegrated in chaos, by a former KGB officer Vladimir Putin, little known outside Russia. In private many European leaders expressed disquiet at his KGB background, his relative youth, and the fact that he had come to power after a brutal ethnic war had been waged in Chechenia, but, rather than challenge his claims as a democrat, the Western approach towards his regime was one of pragmatism. He made visits to all Western capitals and entered into a number of joint schemes. Because of Russia's central position at the heart of the Eurasian continent, its huge nuclear arsenal, and the enormous amounts lent to the region by Western banks and financial institutions, the country continued to command a central role in European history. Doubts, however, remained about the Ukraine, internally divided between its East and West and run on authoritarian lines, and about Byelorussia, which retained a Communist President.

In Bulgaria and Romania political and practical constraints meant that economic privatization and the achievement of democracy proceeded at a slower pace than in Hungary, Poland and Slovenia, but this in itself sometimes facilitated recovery and growth. By 1995 output had recovered to 1989 levels in these three countries, and vigorous development was sustained in subsequent years. Links to the economies of Western Europe, especially to Germany, France, Italy, Austria and Scandinavia, became crucial. Patterns of trade and commerce thought lost to history re-emerged. These old connections, for example, played a significant role in the success story of Slovenia, the most 'Western', most undamaged and most affluent of the former Yugoslav republics. The country exploited its contacts with the more prosperous, neighbouring states of Austria, Hungary and Italy, and its economic achievement enabled the country to develop a stable multi-party political system that was the envy of the region.

Slovenia was a by-product of conflicts in the former Communist Republic of Yugoslavia which had profound repercussions for relations within and between European countries, in the West as well as in the East, more than ten years after the crisis first erupted. In September 1990, tension between Yugoslavia's competing ethnic groups, largely hidden since 1945, re-emerged to challenge all of Europe in much the way it had done in the years leading up to 1914.

Yugoslavia began to disintegrate when in September 1990, the Slovenians and then, a few months later, the Croats declared their independence. The dominant Serbian ethnic group refused to let them go and resorted to military force in efforts to maintain the integrity of the country. The desire for independence from the Yugoslav Federation was contagious and in February 1992, Muslims and Croats living in the Yugoslav state of Bosnia-Herzegovina voted in favour of independence (although Bosnian Serbs, who made up more than 36 per cent of the electorate boycotted the vote). In 1998–9 the problem spread to the state of Kosovo and also sparked a crisis in Albania in 1997.

The result was a vicious, bloody war that demanded a terrible price from the people of the former-Yugoslavia. Over a 100,000 lives were lost, around 3.5 million people were displaced and homes, farms and factories were destroyed. Concentration camps and 'displaced persons', last seen in Europe in the 1940s, reappeared in a new setting. Most alarming of all were concerted and highly organized efforts at 'ethnic cleansing', a new term for an old practice, the removal, by any means necessary, of individuals who did not belong to the ethnic group in control of a given piece of territory. Women, in particular, suffered terribly. There were comparisons not with the two twentieth-century world wars, but with the Thirty Years War of the seventeenth century.

New challenges also emerged in major countries in the West. Italian politics were rocked by corruption scandals in the mid-1990s that saw key individuals and political parties which had dominated its political life since 1945, notably the Christian Democrats, totally discredited in the mid-1990s. So, too, were the Socialists who had provided Italy's first Socialist Prime Minister, Bettino Craxi, who led a coalition between 1983 and 1987 which had improved the state of the Italian economy.

The most towering figure in European politics, the German Chancellor Kohl, who remained in power until 1998, eight years after the resignation of Margaret Thatcher, was discredited by his refusal to divulge full details of the sources of Christian Democrat funds. Thatcher's successor, John Major, in charge of a deeply divided party, having won one general election in 1995, was decisively defeated in a second general election two years later, when the press dwelt not on his leadership but on what became known as 'Sleaze'.

Two further trends became evident in Western European politics. In the late 1990s the coming to power of centre-left political parties and the rise of a 'Far Right'. By 1998 the 'Big Four' of Western Europe all had leaders who described themselves as socialists: Lionel Jospin in France – he had led his party for seven years in the 1980s and became Prime Minister in 1997, Gerhard Schröder in Germany who became Chancellor in 1998, and Tony Blair in Britain who became Prime Minister in 1997 after a landslide victory in a general election. There was to be a fourth socialist leader in Italy, Romano Prodi, a future President of the European Commission. In 1996 he became Prime Minister after an election victory of an 'Olive Tree alliance'.

All these leaders, and their parties, differed markedly from socialist governments of times past. Their determination to push down levels of taxation and spending on the welfare state was new. So, too, was their greater tolerance of rising inequality and the 'social exclusion' of the poorest groups evident in their countries. Yet there were significant differences between them as they coped with their parties and their countries. Blair, for example, was deliberately 'New Labour', learning from Thatcher and picking up where she left off. Uninterested in the history of 'old Labour', he seemed to his critics to be governing in American Presidential style, supported by what became known as 'spin'. Jospin, a former schoolmaster, was more dependent on socialist tradition, but he had to serve as prime minister under President Jacques Chirac, whose views were completely different from his own, and he resigned in 2002 after he and his party had been ignominiously defeated in a French Presidential election.

The growing sense of frustration and disillusionment felt by individuals and communities who were isolated from the dominant economic and cultural trends came back to haunt European politics at the end of the old century and in the first years of the new, and this accounted for the rise of the Far Right. In Austria Jörg Haider's Austrian Freedom Party enjoyed notable electoral success in 1998. So, too, did the Danish People's Party and the anti-immigrant Progress Party in Norway. In 2002 right-wing, largely xenophobic, parties won significant gains in France and the Netherlands. Jean-Marie Le Pen, no newcomer to politics, came second in his campaign for the office of President of France in 2002 and, far more eclectic, Pim Fortuyn's List in the Netherlands, enjoyed a notable degree of electoral success in national elections in May 2002. Ominously, the assassination of Fortuyn during the election campaign was an unprecedented event in Dutch politics.

The triumph of the Far Right was short-lived in France, where Chirac won the Presidential election of 2002 and in Austria where Haider's divided party lost heavily in the election of 2002. In Holland Fortuyn's party totally disintegrated. Nevertheless, demands for limited immigration and for tough controls to secure it remained vociferous at the local and the national level. Like religious fundamentalists, new right were opposed to any increase in the powers of the European Union.

INSTITUTIONAL EUROPE, 1986–PRESENT

It was continued fear of inflation and of the unpredictable ramifications of international finance that helped to explain the appeal of the European Community's European Monetary System (EMS), which had been established in 1979, and which, after the report of the Commission's most energetic President, Jacques Delors, in 1988, was to become the springboard for the full monetary union of the EC. Whereas during the 1970s countries had, for the most part, tried to solve their financial problems on their own, they now sought safety in numbers. Appointed in 1985, Delors, a socialist and a former French Minister of Finance was extremely active during his first two years as President, launching a number of co-operative initiatives with the French President until Mitterand's power was curtailed by the election of a Conservative government in France in 1986. Delors wanted to force the pace. Although he did not hold the fanatically federalist views that were ascribed to him by the British press for which 'federalism' became an increasingly dirty word, his language was very different from theirs and from Thatcher.

For him, as for any historian of the Community, the principal anchors of the system were the West German economy and the strong political partnership of France and Germany. Personalities were important here, too, as co-operation between Paris and Bonn in Brussels was enhanced by a political friendship which developed between Kohl and Mitterand. Despite their differing political loyalties, they were both fully committed to a European ideal as Thatcher obviously was not. So, too, were most politicians in Italy and Spain, and in Western Europe's smaller states.

In 1985, six months before Delors took over, a Community summit held in Milan set the agenda for the next phases of integration, and in February 1986 a Single European Act was signed (Britain and Denmark had a number of reservations) which, modifying some of the provisions of the Treaty of Rome, extended the legal authority of the EC into areas like the environment, technological co-operation and social policy. It was also agreed in 1985 and 1986 that a 'genuine common market' should be in force by 1992 with complete freedom of goods, capital and people across the Community. This had been one of the objects of the Treaty of Rome in 1970, and it had the full approval of Thatcher. The next step in the process came with the Maastricht Treaty ratified in 1992.

Deeper integration, it was argued, could create a unified economy as large, if not larger, than that of the United States, an economy which would better enable European producers to compete internationally. But between 1986 and 1992 Delors, re-elected as President in 1987, had embarked upon plans to move towards a single European currency with all that entailed, including a single monetary policy and the creation of a European Central Bank (ECB); and despite initial doubts in Germany as well as in Britain, a draft plan for European Monetary Union (EMU) and the Bank was accepted at meetings in Basel between September 1988 and April 1989. The draft plan was so strongly disliked and feared by Thatcher that she attempted to persuade the French to join her in refusal to recognize it. Yet the economic consequences of unification, followed by the opening up of membership of the Union to new members, set off contradictory forces that greatly influenced the next stages of European integration and diluted the kind of economic and political integration of which Delors and others had dreamed.

In September 1988 Thatcher made a speech to the College of Europe in Bruges in which she expressed bitter discontent with the policies being pursued by Delors, both in relation to EMU and a Social Chapter which he proclaimed to trade unionists in Stockholm in May 1988 and later, more ominously for her, to British trade unionists at their annual conference:

> We have not successfully rolled back the frontiers of the state in Britain only to see them re-imposed at a European level with a European super-state exercising new dominance from Brussels.[2]

She spoke too of 'a European conglomerate' and described it as folly to try to fit the notions of Europe into 'some kind of identikit European personality'. Delors, who made a speech in reply at Bruges almost exactly a year after hers, had never even implied this.

Britain joined the Exchange Rate Mechanism (ERM) of the EMS a few weeks before Thatcher resigned, and by then the unification of the two Germanies, which worried her, unleashed economic pressures that made European integration more difficult to achieve. At a conference in Maastricht in December 1991, attended by British Prime Minister, John Major, who faced an unenviable task, Mitterand, backed by the Italians, secured a firm commitment to create a common European currency by 1999 if the first target of 1997 was missed, and Major succeeded in purging from the Treaty references to 'federalism', which had figured as a goal in the first Dutch and in later drafts. As far as the Social Charter was concerned, Delors' *chef de cabinet*, Pascal Lamy, devised an ingenious compromise to avoid final deadlock. The charter was attached to the Treaty as a protocol, and member states could opt out. There was also a reference to 'subsidiarity'. Unwarranted intrusion by Brussels Commissioners into areas of national life was now forbidden.

Kohl emerged as Europe's power broker. And the change of the name 'Community' to 'Union', more than symbolic, echoed the word 'unification',

Kohl's great German triumph. Yet the economic pressures unleashed by West German efforts to integrate the East German *Länder* made West European integration more difficult to achieve. As West Germany pumped money into the east, its national deficit rose, causing interest rates to rise and the German economy to slide into the deepest recession of the entire post-war period.

A hike in German interest rates affected all the other members of the EMS, the forerunner to full monetary union in which member countries had to hold their currencies within fixed bands and adhere to strict rules governing their monetary policy, especially regarding the size of the national deficit. In the summer of 1992 the pressures on Brussels proved too much in the wake of a Danish referendum rejecting monetary union by a small majority. The rebuff was a stark reminder that voters could still derail the Union's project. Moreover, it prompted international financial speculators to pounce. Britain and Italy were the first to come under attack and, a day of high drama, 'Black Wednesday', demonstrated the limits of the nation state to protect its currency against a concerted attack by powerful financiers, prominent among them Georges Soros, an Hungarian-born investment banker, Britain popped out of the EMS on 16 September 1992. It was not to return.

During the months that followed speculative pressure switched from one currency to another. Italy, too, was forced out of the system but returned in 1996. Spain, Portugal and Ireland had to devalue their currencies, sometimes more than once, to stay in the EMS. Germany did not revalue the Deutschmark, and the value of the pound continued to fall. Only in the autumn of 1993 did the financial crisis come to an end. By then Denmark, in a second referendum, had ratified the treaty, but in Britain, Major, who won his first vote on Maastricht in the House of Commons with only a majority of three, had to assure British ratification in a vote of no confidence by threatening his party with a general election which he felt it would lose.

Unemployment levels in Europe began to fall after 1993, although structural unemployment and labour productivity remained a problem. Monetary co-ordination may have helped to rid continental Europe of the scourge of inflation that proved so destructive in the 1970s. The downside was that these steps also meant higher levels of unemployment and big cuts in public expenditure. Even then, it took the rest of the decade to lower budget deficits and interest rates to acceptable levels.

Expansion of the European Union added to the challenge. The Union acquired three new members in 1995: Austria, Finland and Sweden. The end of the Cold War had obviated the need for their strict neutrality, although the Norwegians and the Swiss rejected membership in order, so the successful 'No' campaigns argued, to better preserve their unique identities and freedoms. On 1 January 1999 the single European currency, comprising 11 member currencies, now called the Euro (names with historical resonance like the *Florin* were rejected), was launched on the international currency market.

The European Central Bank (ECB), based in Frankfurt, had responsibility for running the monetary policy of 'Euroland' countries – it was the first time a currency was launched without a government behind it, although governors of national banks offered a guiding hand – setting the interest rate for the Euro and controlling money supply through a variety of mechanisms. But the Euro remained a virtual currency, used only for bank transfers and electronic payments until 1 January 2002 when it was launched in coin and paper form. Each country's Euro coins looked different, using different national symbols, like the harp in Ireland for theirs.

Considerable disquiet remained about whether or not the Euro would be a successful currency, dependent as it was on the principles of German monetary policy-making, tough on inflation and depriving politicians in other countries of retaining any voice. France, in particular, sought an enhanced role for national governments in setting the priorities of monetary policy, but the launch of the Euro proper silenced many critics. The speed of the conversion, and the enthusiasm with which the new currency was embraced by most users, took many commentators by surprise.

Wider repercussions of the move for the European economy were soon felt. Consumers were now better able to compare prices across the Union. Where geography would allow, European shoppers had already become accustomed to crossing national frontiers in search of lower prices – Germany proving a popular choice for French consumers in search of a Euro bargain and British customers crossing the English Channel to France. In 2002, Britain, which had not joined the new EMS, had laid down economic criteria for joining, and had offered a referendum. There were strong British differences, political as well as economic, as to whether or not to join as there was on the obvious question of a single tax structure for the Union.

While the logic of economics and finance support the case rationale for a broader Union – an extension was strongly backed by Britain – so far it remained a Union of Western Europe alone. While many EFTA members have now joined, members of the former COMECON remain outside it. Bulgaria and the Czech republic, for example, both applied for membership of the Union in 1995 and 1996 respectively, yet to date access has been denied. With the end of the Cold War and the collapse of the Soviet Union, the politically imposed geography of the European Community had lost much of its rationale and the countries of Eastern Europe, isolated for so long behind the iron curtain, began to rebuild old links, drawn towards Western Europe by a powerful economic and political attraction. Most connections were made through private banks, companies and educational institutions rather than through governments. The state did not, despite Thatcher's warnings, played the major role.

Nor had the European Parliament, meeting in Strasbourg and Brussels, which held its first direct elections in June 1979. Elections are held every five years – there have been four elections since 1979. Yet the parliament acquired influence and authority through a series of treaties that have transformed it from a purely consultative body into a legislative parliament with powers similar to those of national parliaments. The European Parliament came to enjoy equal status with the Council of Ministers and, in the wake of the Treaty of Amsterdam signed in 1997, passed the majority of European laws. But the work that the European Members of Parliament (MEPs) do, and the complex legislative processes that underpin operations, continued to be opaque to most of the people who elected them. Allegations of corruption and of 'fat cat' lifestyles, like allegations of 'bureaucracy' in Brussels, haunted both the Parliament and the Commission, detracting from the considerable success the Union achieved in promoting economic integration and legal convergence. (In 1999 the entire European Commission was forced to resign because it was tainted by corruption.)

Meanwhile, the work of the European Court of Justice, sitting in Luxembourg, made a substantial contribution to the process of integration. As well as safeguarding treaties and the EU's legal order, the Court adjudicated disputes among member states, institutions and, not least, individuals. The European judges became the final arbiters of judicial processes that started in national courts, acquiring a reputation for adhering to the highest standards of impartiality. Some of the most important legal principles governing the European Union have been developed by the court, rather than by nation states bargaining over treaties. The most important of these principles was the supremacy of European Law: if EU and national law were in conflict, then EU law overrode national authority. National judges accepted this principle, and the work of the Court became one of the most tangible and visible ways of connecting the work of the Union to the lives of its citizens.

More generally, a commentator on West European politics writing in 1989 in the *Annual Review of Community Affairs* concluded that while the European Community had an 'untidy distribution of power' compared with 'existing federations', it already had 'many though by no means all, of the attributes of a mature sovereign state.'[3] There was no intimation in this survey that countries in the former Communist bloc would soon become involved in seeking to join it or that Britain and Denmark would stand out against what seemed to be an inevitable trend towards greater federalism. The future appeared no more problematic than the past. Yet some 13 years later, these issues are little closer to resolution. Similarly, an appeal by the American Secretary of State, James Baker, in December 1989 for a new relationship between the European Community and the United States and an address to the European Parliament in the same month by the Soviet Foreign Minister Eduard Shevardnadze have gone unanswered. Differences persisted, if not increased, on foreign policy. The extent of the Union's paralysis when it came to co-operation on defence and foreign policy issues became very obvious when the former Yugoslavia imploded in the face of violent ethnic conflict after 1991.

Since its origins in the 1950s, the convention of European co-operation was to leave foreign policy and security issues to intergovernmental co-operation, rather than to cede power to a supranational European authority.

(Although the European Commission also enjoyed the right to launch initiatives in foreign policy.) In effect, co-operation still only took place when nation-states were willing to work together, usually following the long established traditions of high politics. The conflict in Yugoslavia spiralled into a number of bloody wars in the territories of Croatia, Bosnia and Kosovo, rekindling old struggles before 1914, and demonstrated two things when it came to the possible formulation of a *European* foreign policy. First, violent conflict, including so-called 'ethnic cleansing' and genocide, was not confined to Europe's past or to distant lands – it now seemed possible anywhere within Europe's frontiers. Second, neither European nation-states nor Europe's supranational institutions were able to manage these developments. It took US intervention and leadership to bring a peace of sorts to the region with the 1995 Dayton agreement on Bosnia-Hercegovina.

While it would be wrong to claim that events in Yugoslavia, alongside rising evidence of the role of organized criminal gangs based in Eastern Europe in the illegal traffic of weapons and drugs, shocked the EU into action, co-operation on foreign and defence questions rose markedly after the 1990s. In 2002 it was building a military force of some 230,000 men and women, to be led by a new military staff based in the Council Secretariat. But the topic continued to touch on raw nerves, and old as well as new questions were raised. Should German troops, for example, be allowed to serve peacekeeping missions in Eastern Europe? How, if at all, did the Union reflect and relate the interests of members who are in NATO to the EU's non-aligned members, the latter including Austria, Finland, Sweden and Ireland? How would the United States respond to co-operative European action? When the Union managed to speak with one voice, as it did in May 2002 when it criticized US President George Bush Jnr's threat to wage war on an 'axis of evil' comprising Iran, Iraq and North Korea, it raised American ire. Indeed, Bush, with a limited knowledge of history, complained of European 'ingratitude' given that the US had been intimately involved in managing European security since 1945.

European statesmen floundered in the face of the crises, and there were differences of opinion within the Union and between the Union and NATO. Early German recognition of Croatian independence in 1991, for example, was heavily criticized by other major European powers: it encouraged demands for independence by other groups in Yugoslavia and affected Albania.

European countries, working in concert with members of NATO and the UN, used various diplomatic tools to try to resolve the crisis: the deployment of peacekeepers as military observers; the use of humanitarian and longer term economic aid to assist with the task of reconstruction; and, in the case of Kosovo in 1999, the use of overt military force to enforce peace. The deficiencies of international institutions created, and designed, for the Cold War was demonstrated by the fact that although the EU, the UN and NATO were all involved, the most dynamic organization was the 'Contact Group' comprising the USA, Russia, Germany, Britain and France – the so-called 'Great Powers' of late nineteenth and early twentieth centuries.

There were other echoes of history. Fifty years after the creation of NATO, this was the first time the organization deployed an airforce and army in Europe in a conflict that was billed as a 'humanitarian war'. After an extensive air campaign by NATO, Kosovo became a formal protectorate under the protection of the West. The problems of the region remained complex and in part unresolved, although steps were taken to ensure that individuals who committed war crimes in the territory were brought to justice. Criminal proceedings against Slobodan Milošević, began in the UN War Crimes Tribunal in The Hague, where the former leader of the Yugoslav Federation was charged with crimes against humanity for actions he authorized in Croatia and Kosovo, and for carrying out genocide in Bosnia. It was the biggest European war crime trial since the Nuremberg trials that followed the Second World War. Milošević rejected the authority of the Court as he had rejected appeals during the Yugoslav war to restrain Serbian forces in Kosovo.

Disquiet remained in Serbia, where critics of the procedures followed in transferring Milošević to The Hague argued that the trials of war criminals should take place before the Serbian people. His transfer had been made a condition of urgently necessary American financial aid. There was disquiet too in Europe and the wider international community over the small number of individuals who had so far been brought to book. The recriminations were widespread. There were complaints against French troops for allowing one wanted war criminal to escape, and in April 2002 after the Dutch government published a report on the massacre of some 7,000 Bosnian Muslim men and boys in the Bosnian Serb controlled territory of Srebrenica. The territory was ostensibly a NATO protectorate, but the battalion of lightly armed Dutch troops sent there to preserve the security of the 30,000 Bosnian Muslim community proved woefully inadequate to the task. The political fall out prompted the resignation of the entire Labour government, led by Wim Kok, who said his country's handling of the atrocity had been 'inexcusable'.

Considered more broadly, the war in Yugoslavia, alongside the US-led Gulf War waged inconclusively to liberate the Iraqi invaded territory of Kuwait in 1991, and the so-called 'War against Terrorism' launched by the US in the wake of the suicide bomb attacks on the World Trade Center in Manhattan and the Pentagon in Washington DC on 11 September 2001, brought out differences between European countries in their approach to global issues. The superpower power rivalry between the USA and the USSR was formally brought to an end when President Bush Jnr visited Moscow in the late spring of 2002, but he met with very different receptions when he visited Germany, France and Britain. Nor was there agreement between the great powers, who still thought of themselves as such, and the United States on how to deal with the serious Middle East crisis which continued to simmer through the summer of 2002. Afghanistan still remained disturbed, and there was the threat of nuclear war between India and Pakistan.

Meanwhile, issues like poverty and unequal development became more prominent on the diplomatic agenda, with the spotlight on Africa. During the Cold War, the world's poorer states, inside and outside Europe, only received attention from the more powerful when the latter wanted to tempt them onto their side. But the end of the Cold War rendered diplomacy more complex.

EUROPE AND THE WORLD, 1989–PRESENT

In retrospect, the history of Cold War Europe, perhaps paradoxically, stands out as the most prosperous period in Western European history. European integration had taken shape in human, not just economic terms, and Western Europeans, especially the younger generations, without losing all their differences, were better informed about each other than ever before. Cross border travel increased immensely. In 1950 there were 25 million global cross border tourist movements. By 1985 the comparative figure had risen to 333 million. No fewer than 45 per cent of tourist travel was within Europe. Added to this there was a three-fold increase in the number of foreign residents in Europe, and with it a cross fertilization of culture, customs and knowledge, if seldom, however, without strain.

In the wake of the Second World War Europe, both East and West, had also experienced the longest period of sustained peace in its history for many centuries, although it had been maintained by a balance of terror between two blocs. Some argued that a return to instability was, therefore, an inevitable outcome of the end of the Cold War. Others hoped that its end would revolutionize not only the way that European countries related to one another, but Europe's relations with the wider world. The UN, no longer paralysed by the East-West split, would give a more effective lead; the world's arsenals would be dramatically reduced; the ensuing 'peace dividend' could be spent on helping the world's poorer countries; and questions of environmental protection would rise to the top of the international agenda.

The word 'planetary' was in use as frequently as the word 'global'. More than a decade on from 1989 and into the new millennium, the dust had not yet begun to settle and evidence concerning the character of the post Cold War world remained contradictory. Complexity was another word that came into fashion. Threats now seemed to come from everywhere – suicide bombers could appear as dangerous as hostile nation-states. Above all, without the over-arching logic of the Cold War, it was more difficult to discern friend and foe. The threat of world war had receded, but had been replaced by an upsurge in conflict within individual countries. Europe faced serious challenges, within and beyond its frontiers, from the rising number of weak, sometimes even failed states, whose leaders were unable to control developments within their own territories. In particular, the continued Israeli occupation of the Middle East and the failure to create a state of Palestine caused concern, not least about domestic anti-semitism, in European countries with significant Muslim or Jewish populations.

It was in the 1960s and early 1970s that concern began to be expressed about the consequences of pollution on the world's environment, and the need to protect wild and cultivated flora and fauna. On a domestic level it spawned a number of political parties, like the Green Party in West Germany and counterparts elsewhere. Internationally the UN took the lead, sponsoring a conference on the Human Environment held in Stockholm in 1972. In the heady atmosphere created by the end of the Cold War, there was some optimism that the UN-sponsored Earth Summit convened in Rio de Janeiro in 1992 would trigger a breakthrough in international co-operation on the environment. The enthusiasm, however, proved short-lived as leading industrial nations continue to evade remedies that required a fundamental re-appraisal of the nature of consumption and production particularly, but not exclusively, in capitalist society. Europe stood out as the staunchest critic of America's record on environmental protection, and while there were variations of particular European countries' commitment to measures necessary to environmental protection, they provided an important lead on the topic in a global context.

At the same time there were significant changes at the level of European and global institutions. While the European Union failed to respond or responded only slowly to the clamour of Eastern European countries to join the Union or form a common foreign and security policy, the United States and NATO once more stepped in. Attempts were made to give new life to NATO, which appeared to have lost its role with the end of the Cold War. In 1994 the US agreed to grant membership to NATO to three former enemy countries, Poland, the Czech Republic and Hungary, who were formally welcomed into the alliance on 12 March 1999. Further expansion was achieved in 2002. Thus, with or without a Soviet threat, European governments looked to the United States, which, as in the war in Afghanistan in 2002, put more of its trust in bilateral or multilateral agreements than in joint NATO action.

Europe was also slow to take advantage of Russia's new willingness to co-operate within and beyond Europe under the Presidency of Vladimir Putin. Instead the Americans stepped in announcing, in May 2002, that the former superpower enemies signed an agreement on nuclear weapons intended to 'liquidate the legacy of the Cold War'. In the Strategic Offensive Reductions Treaty (START) Russia and the USA agreed to cut their nuclear stockpiles by two-thirds over the next two years, reducing their combined nuclear warheads from 12,000 to 4,000. The reduction was not enough to banish the spectre of 'Mutually Assured Destruction', but, coupled with an agreement to make Russia part of NATO's decision making process for the first time, the decision was crucial to the evolution of defence and foreign policy relations within and beyond Europe.

The UN, too, evolved after 1989. Its peacekeeping activities rose dramatically. So also did the number of countries who participated in those activities.

Meanwhile, the humanitarian concern that accompanied its creation during the Second World War became more evident and more central to its work. In particular, there was a new preoccupation with infringements of human rights. In 1997 Mary Robinson, a talented lawyer who had been President of the Irish Republic for the previous seven years, was appointed UN High Commissioner for Human Rights and served in that office until 2002, playing an important role with a high profile. She was prepared to take action in Europe and in other continents, including Africa, where ethnic violence in Rwanda had resulted in mass genocide in 1994 while Europeans and Americans alike looked on from a comfortable distance. In general, the UN and its agencies paid more attention to the world's poorer countries after the end of the Cold War than the European Union, although some European governments, notably the British, championed the cause of international debt relief. The North-South divide remained.

How capitalist and non-capitalist societies relate to each other is the key question in the context of 'globalisation', a term with widespread currency. And there are subsidiary questions. What is Europe? Do Europeans hold a distinct and coherent set of values? What is European culture? How far do the boundaries of Europe extend? Does it incorporate Russia and all former Soviet Republics? Is Turkey part of Europe? How should nation-states relate to the variety of ethnic groups within their territories? The study of history can help to inform the answers and facilitate, new, often multiple definitions of Europe in political, geographic, economics, cultural, linguistic and historical terms.

Notes

1. P. Kennedy, *The Rise and Fall of the Great Powers. Economic Change and Military Conflict* (1988), *passim*.
2. Cited in *The Times*, 21 September 1988, p.1.
3. P. Ludlow, *The Annual Review of European Community Affairs*, vol. 1 (Centre for European Policy Studies, 1990), p.xv.

Chapter 13

POST-MODERN?

The word 'post-modern' is only one of a number of words, they include 'post-industrial' and even 'post-history', that have the prefix 'post' attached to them. Like the others, the word 'post-modern', much in use, implies uncertainty as how 'to place' recent history in relation to past and future, but it sometimes goes further than this and seems to suggest that it is not worth trying so to place it. The adjective 'modern' and the noun 'modernity', examined in Chapter 5, were often used vaguely although they had complex histories behind them. The adjective 'post-modern' is even vaguer, and it too has behind it a complex history which post-modernists usually disdain to consider, let alone to chart. Like Chapter 5, this chapter bears no dates, but it passes beyond the millennium, which generated a huge literature of its own, and like Chapter 12 ends, as a history book should, with questions rather than with answers.

THE NEED FOR PERSPECTIVE

Another reason why this chapter has no dates is that each day news pours in, much of it instantly, much of it continuously, and in a 'media world' today and tomorrow count more than yesterday ('tomorrow is already here'). At the end of each week, each month, each year and each decade journalistic attempts are made to summarize it. There are also frequent public opinion polls (the questions require as much scrutiny as the responses) and in Britain and some other countries annual surveys both of social trends and of under-lying social attitudes. Such forms of accounting are as much a part of the picture as the news itself. Indeed, the Second World War, a great break in history, has been approached by the British historian Corelli Barnett in terms of an audit not of a chronicle. The need for managerial accounting, public and private, was a major demand of the 1980s and 1990s as productivity had been in the 1950s, not that either demand guaranteed good management. And in 2002 the profession of auditing was itself shaken by transatlantic scandals and with it what was now recognized as a global financial system.

It is difficult in such circumstances to secure any adequate sense of long-term perspective. And there are some writers, moreover, notably the French sociologist Jean Baudrillard, who have argued that because of the mass media flow it is already impossible to distinguish between 'social reality' and its simulation in the media, concluding that in the future it will be impossible to recognize or differentiate a long period of time. History is reaching a 'vanishing point' in a surfeit of information about events, including far-away events, that are too many to comprehend.[1] Meanwhile, 'vanishing' has acquired a double meaning. Ephemera (mobile telephone calls, fax messages, internet exchanges), often dealing with what were thought of as important matters, do not often make their way into historical archives.

A 'GREAT MUTATION': 'THE END OF HISTORY'?

Already, before the full implications of a continuing communications revolution were apparent – and it is now based on highly sophisticated and versatile digital technology – the then President of the American Historical Association, Carl Bridenaugh, described recent history in 1962 as 'the great mutation', an image used freely but appropriately after the atomic bombing of Hiroshima and Nagasaki and still highly relevant in 1962 when the hydrogen bomb lay in reserve. It had been used also in 1948 by another American world historian W. H. McNeill when he referred to 'a general mutation in perception and in production as revolutionary as that when power shifted from hunting to farming' in the days before recorded history began. And spanning the centuries three years before Bridenaugh, the American anthropologist Margaret Mead claimed that 'the gulf separating 1959 from 1943' was 'as deep as the gulf that separated the men who became builders of cities from Stone Age men'.[2] Old values had crumbled as the processes of daily life had changed.

Such judgements must always be studied critically, not least statements which are made by historians, for there have been many sharp breaks in the past, produced not only by new human inventions but by earthquakes, plagues and famines (and these continue) and by earlier population movements. There have always been prophets, too, who have proclaimed the end of an old order and the beginning of a new age, not least just before and just after the First World War. There was a change, however, during the 1960s when the sense of one planet was strengthened – it was seen for the first time from space in 1969 – and when 'futurology' became more sophisticated than it ever had been before in history, with some of the people hitherto called prophets now claiming to be social scientists. Models were devised, 'megatrends' were identified. Science and technology, often thought to be the great impulses behind all history, were directly related to human prospects sometimes in deterministic fashion. In the three short decades between now and the end of the millennium, Alvin Toffler warned in his best-seller *Future Shock*

(1970) 'millions of psychologically normal people will experience an abrupt collision with the future'.[3]

Nevertheless, for all the power of technology and for all the sophistication of the 'advance in social sciences', the last decades of the twentieth century were, as we have seen, characterized by surprises, economic, political and cultural, demonstrating that it is easier to forecast the advance of science and technology than the future of the economy, of politics or of culture, all of which have themselves become increasingly influenced by technology. In particular, the early collapse of the Soviet Union in 1989, the bicentenary year of the French Revolution, and with it the fall of the associated communist regimes of Central and Eastern Europe was seldom forecast. It seemed an 'unlikely' scenario to the authors of the illuminating *Europe 2000*, a co-operative study, launched by the European Cultural Foundation, which appeared in 1977; and it was only after it had happened that it was to be described by one writer, Francis Fukuyama – and he was not the first to do so – as 'the end of history'.[4]

The 'end of ideology' had been one of the key phrases of the 1960s, when there was talk of the convergence of conflicting political systems, and now, for Fukuyama, the victory of 'liberal democracy' in 1989, for so he interpreted it, constituted 'the end point of man's ideological evolution' and 'the final form of human government'. With it, he claimed, the Hegelian and Marxist sense of history as one single and coherent process disappeared. 'End of history' or not, the echoes of history were loud throughout all the changes from 1989 to 1992, and from 1992 to 2002 they were to grow louder both in the Balkans crisis and the continuing crisis in Israel/Palestine. The collapse of the Soviet Union and with it, most commentators as well as Fukuyama believed wrongly, the end of Marxism did not eliminate violence, international and domestic, from Europe. Nor was 'liberal democracy' assured. Anti-Semitism was not dead. Nor were racism and xenophobia. Marxism remained the operative ideology in China where Marxists adopted market models to fuel economic growth. It was impossible in 2002 to leave China out of any assessments of past, present and future.

Fukuyama argued that because history – in the sense that he defined it – had ended, 'the world-wide ideological struggle' that had called forth 'daring, courage and idealism' was over and would be followed by 'economic calculation, the endless solving of technical problems, environmental concerns and the satisfaction of sophisticated consumer demands'. There would be 'neither art nor philosophy, just the perpetual caretaking of the museum of human history'.[5]

Technical problems were not all solved, and while they remained unsolved they produced different kinds of consequential problems. 'Environmental concerns' generated struggle, with protesters breaking into international conferences and challenging international institutions. 'Economic calculation' was not simply a matter of arithmetic. The 'satisfaction of sophisticated consumer demands', now described as 'consumerism', was compatible with a widening of economic inequalities, so that free-market economics, often entrapped in jargon, remained challengeable. To add to other divides there was to be a 'digital divide' separating rich and poor and peoples at different 'levels of development'. Human history did not become a museum, and there were politicians who cared little about it.

If no new version of Marxism was advanced, in some countries, like Poland and Hungary, ex-Marxists were returned to power through the ballot box. They were not 'finished'. Finally, as has been shown in Chapter 12, Balkan nationalism remained a formidable force and there was no common European policy to cope with it.

The year 1989, for all its excitements, was not a good vantage point from which to survey past or future. Nor, indeed, is any single year, although an attractive attempt, one of several, to encapsulate the memory of 'our time' was made as long ago as 1977, the year of *Europe 2000*, when the first twin voyager spacecraft left Cape Canaveral in Florida on a probe into the far reaches of outer space, carrying with it a record of a two-hour message from Planet Earth to other planets and stars within the galaxy. It included speeches in 60 languages and 116 pictures, giving details of the twentieth-century environment and of twentieth-century science (among them the discovery by J. D. Watson and F. H. Crick in 1953 of DNA, the genetic code) and of older cultural achievements from the nineteenth-century past (among them a page of Beethoven's sheet music).[6]

CONTINUITIES AND DISCONTINUITIES

The end of the twentieth century was also the end of a millennium – and as a new millennium drew nearer, efforts were made to see the twentieth century as a whole and to give it a shape. Thus, the British Marxist historian Eric Hobsbawm, who in three volumes had charted world history since the French Revolution into the twentieth century, separated out three distinct periods within a 'short century', in contrast with the long nineteenth century – the first from 1914 to 1945, a period of war and depression, following a *belle époque*; the second from 1960 to 1989, a period of unprecedented prosperity, particularly in Europe; and the third, since 1989, a period of unresolved uncertainties, 'an age of anxiety', including an economic 'recession' that during the mid-1980s brought to an end a brief but hectic boom. Britain, without 'feeling good', fared better than its European competitors as it did in the first years of the twenty-first century, when all economies were 'fragile'.

The words 'great depression' remained reserved for the economic sequence which began with the Wall Street Crash of 1929, just as the words 'great war' remained reserved for the conflict that began in 1914. A key concept now was structural unemployment. How to deal with it was now conceived of as a difficult problem along with the reform of social security, made urgent as the population aged, and the reform of education. Neither seemed to have been reformed adequately within the framework of 'welfare states', a description which now lost its emotive power.

Such a historical schema focused too much, perhaps, on the middle years of the twentieth century which, like the middle years of the nineteenth century, were years of undoubted economic advance, when the future offered still better to come. In social and political terms, however, they saw many shifts of mood and preoccupation. As the contemporary English historian David Thomson put it in 1966, 'the supreme question confronting Europeans was whether . . . traditional resilience and . . . material advantages could be so combined, using intelligence and wisdom, to relegate Europe's internal contrasts and divisions to the function of cultural diversification and enrichment of life rather than to an intensifying of war-like jealousies and hatreds. Forces both of cohesion and of disunity still coexisted in a precarious balance.'[7] These words were written before Britain joined the European Community. Eleven years later, after it had joined, *Europe 2000* began with the words 'Europe has no idea where it's going but it's going there fast'. The book stressed the word 'anxiety', 'anxiety about the future, anxiety about the unknown'. Anxiety did not disappear after 1989.

In each of the three subdivisions of the century, if we divide it in that way, there were obvious 'anxieties' and 'precarious balances' – even in the brightly lit *belle époque* of the early pre-First World War century when the aristocracy, much of it in debt, and the power of money was displayed by new millionaires. A generation later the English poet of the 1930s W. H. Auden chose 'The Age of Anxiety' as the title of one of his poems, and during the 1930s there were many grounds for anxiety both for surviving sections of the aristocracy and respectable sections of the working class. Shadows of the last war criss-crossed ominously with the shadows of the next. It required rearmament and war to dispose of mass unemployment. It required war too to create a new apparatus for safeguarding peace. The League of Nations, based on Geneva, had collapsed before 1939: the United Nations Organization, created in 1945, with its headquarters in New York, was to face its biggest crises 50 years later. The most alarming international crisis of the 'middle years' was centred not on Europe but on Cuba. So, too, was the most significant war – in Vietnam.

As in all schemes of periodization by century or by decade, it is possible to trace continuities across the divides. Thus, despite the breaks associated with two world wars, there were obvious continuities between the 1890s and the 1940s, bridging what Margaret Mead described as 'the deep gulf'. Technical development continued to follow logically in the wake of the spread of electrical powers, of speeded transportation, and of 'mass communication'. The economic geography of the world did not then change drastically in its patterns of industry and trade. Nor did 'geopolitics', except (and it was a significant exception) through the rise of air power. The rule of empire, if challenged, persisted, and have-not countries without empires demanded a share in the imperial process. Social development continued to pivot on the developing relationship between 'masses' and 'minorities', of which there were many different kinds. These now included what had come to be called elites, including specialized elites of 'experts', 'meritocracies' who owed little to birth.

The word 'elite' was first used in its current sense by the Italian sociologist Vildredo Pareto in the first decade of the century, and it became as much of a key word as the word 'masses', an equally dangerous word to employ, with which it was originally bracketed. Both words carried with them nineteenth century baggage. Pareto was an economist as well as a sociologist, but he did not examine one other feature of twentieth-century change – a continuing (but not continuous) rise in consumer incomes, a precondition of a twentieth century *ism*, 'consumerism'. It was Britain's Minister of Food during the Second World War, Lord Woolton, appointed in 1940, a retailer by occupation and later Minister of Reconstruction, who talked most during the years of depression of the luxuries of yesterday becoming the necessities of today.

A society which was increasingly 'consumer-orientated' depended increasingly on 'mass production', the production of the assembly line, the system pioneered before 1910 (though not invented) by the American automobile manufacturer Henry Ford who significantly gave his name to an *ism*, even better known in the Soviet Union than in Britain, France or Germany. During the 1930s the great cinema comedian Charlie Chaplin, operating from the glamorous American centre of 'mass entertainment', Hollywood, had depicted assembly lines unforgettably in a film of 1936 significantly called *Modern Times*. (He also figured in the film *The Great Dictator*.) 'Consumerism' only turned into an *ism* a generation later – during the 1960s when 'Fordism' was already beginning to look out-of-date in an age of 'automation': robots were about to make their way into history in automobile factories like the great Fiat plant in Turin. In each phase in the history of production the ultimate appeal to the consumer depended on 'mass persuasion' – the 'arts' of advertising – and advertising of 'branded goods' had begun to flourish as early as the 1890s.[8]

Advertising, too, had its inherent logic, ensuring that within the longer movements of speeded-up time there were shorter up-and-down movements of the 'roller coaster' of fashion. Indeed, fashion was an essential facet of the process of mass persuasion which, with a time lag, became part of the political process also. Wherever it was used, it made for some confusion. What some people thought of as 'fads' – radio, for example, in the 1920s, developed for the home before the 'talkies' took over the cinemas, and in some countries financed by advertising – were new features of life which would remain dominant until new technologies emerged. More than entertainment was involved. News was presented in the cinema ('newsreels') as well as in the home, and in the 'age of television', which followed on logically, it seemed, in retrospect at least, as a new label for the 'age of broadcasting'; whatever people's political loyalties had been hitherto they were now subject to image refashioning. The 1960s was the crucial decade when fashion – in clothes (for example, jeans), in food ('fast food'), in drink (more wine), in travel (including mass air travel) and in education (More universities) – became a main preoccupation of the media. In the same decade the presentation of politics, including the politics of protest, identified briefly with student protest, was speeded up.

Until the 1960s there were continuities in conceptions of contemporary culture, linking it with the historic past before 1914, although Hitler's national socialists had launched a new and more terrifying *Kulturkampf.* The great names of 'high culture', collected from different historical periods, still stood out in all countries, east and west, and schoolchildren everywhere were expected to know at least the names of writers like Homer, Dante, Shakespeare, Cervantes, Molière, Hugo and Goethe. Knowledge of painters and sculptors was less common, and although the audience for music expanded significantly (thanks to radio and gramophone technology) this was still 'the age of the book'. For that reason alone, it was cultural treason when in the name of 'Action against the Un-German Spirit' students at the University of Berlin in May 1933 hurled into a bonfire books that seemed to subvert that spirit.

There had been intimations of this kind of behaviour in pre-1914 popular anti-Semitism, but now it was to be extended into other forms of ideological terror, ending with the burning not of books but of people. By the end of Hitler's 'Holocaust' six million Jews had been systematically murdered – with the help of doctors and 'scientists' as well as politicians and bureaucrats. The twentieth-century process was traced meticulously by Hannah Arendt in 1951, where in a great study of 'totalitarianism', the roots of which she traced, she insisted a generation before Fukuyama that 'every end in history necessarily contains a new beginning'.

THE CLIMAX OF THE 'MODERN'

By the 1960s in all parts of Europe, including post-Nazi Germany, literary 'modernism', discussed in Chapter 5, had been assimilated into the taught canon, with a number of writers being identified as makers of a 'modern movement', powerful enough to have survived both world wars and the rise and fall of Nazism. In parallel, the role of new avant-gardes – writers prepared to shock not to please – had been accepted by many devotees of 'high culture'. In literature James Joyce's *Finnegan's Wake*, published in 1939, a dream recounted in layers of wordplay, seemed to mark a climax: his earlier novel *Ulysses* (1922) had for long taken its place in the modern canon. Not all the key figures in the literary and artistic avant-gardes, many of whom had been active before 1914, had been politically to the left. T. S. Eliot, whose poem *The Waste Land* (1922) became a major modern text, was a conservative. Ezra Pound wrote and lived throughout the war in Mussolini's Italy.

The adjective 'modern' was vague enough to encompass aspects of Nazi art and of Fascist architecture in Italy. Moreover, it tapped 'other cultures' as well as the culture of 'the West'. In pictorial art, where all kinds of materials were now used as well as paint and canvas, there were influences even before 1914 from Japan, Polynesia and Africa. In music jazz made its way into Europe from the black world via the United States during the 1920s.

The Nazis attacked with equal bitterness jazz and the atonal music of Arnold Schoenberg and Alban Berg, while themselves venerating Wagner who in his lifetime had been hailed as the greatest of all modernists. And while they banned the music of Gustav Mahler and burned the novels of Thomas Mann along with those of Franz Kafka, the plays of Bertold Brecht and the works of Albert Einstein and Sigmund Freud, from time to time they looked back to Nietzsche, prophet of the 'modern European mind'. Many of the greatest figures in German 'modernism' fled from their own country (and later from Austria) during the 1930s in an exodus ('diaspora') which carried to other lands half a million Jews, among them Schoenberg, Brecht, Mann, Einstein and Freud. The fact that the exiles included scientists as well as writers and musicians was itself revealing. 'Our national policies will not be revoked or modified even for scientists', Hitler had told a scientist who dared to protest as early as 1933. 'If the dismissal of Jewish scientists means the annihilation of contemporary German science, then we shall do without science for a few years.'

In the Soviet Union, where socialism was thought of as a science, no one would ever have made such a statement. Yet versions of science which seemed to threaten state ideology were usually not tolerated in Moscow either. Nor was there any willingness to appreciate 'modern' tastes that were deemed, however absurdly, to be *bourgeois* – from 'impressionism' in painting to musical 'atonality'. Freud was anathema. Biology was less safe than physics. Even linguistics was not safe. After an initial phase of cultural experiment and innovation following the Revolution, much of it exciting, the Stalinist regime severely censored 'Western modernism' as a whole. A modern musician like Dmitri Shostakovich was never allowed to develop his music freely: his opera *Lady Macbeth of Mtsensk* (1930–2) had been dismissed as both 'formalistic' and 'decadent', although he regained favour in 1937 with his *Fifth Symphony*.

When the Soviet Union was at war with Germany from 1941 to 1945, Shostakovich's *Seventh Symphony* ('the Leningrad') was warmly welcomed in Britain, which now made much of cultural relationships between Russia and the West. There was an audience, too, for Maxim Gorky, who after a spell in exile had become first President of the Soviet Writers' Union. He was now read along with Dostoevsky and Tolstoy. Meanwhile, selected English 'classics' were published in cheap editions in the Soviet Union, as after the war were gramophone records of the great European composers of the past.

Such purposive 'cultural diffusion', associated as it was with a successful battle for literacy, represented a continuation of nineteenth-century aspirations as did much else in twentieth-century 'modernization'.[9] Yet the breakthrough from the past in the arts and in the physical sciences, which, as we have seen, had come in the name of 'modernity' in the decade before 1914, was continued during and after the end of the First World War. In 1915 in neutral Zurich, the city where James lived and died (and where Lenin lived in exile), the artistic and literary movement Dada, founded by a Romanian poet Tristan Tzara, but from the start consciously international, set out from a café base to deflate everything that was inherited from the past. Another Dada group was set up by Marcel Duchamps. Dada embraced everywhere the slogan of the Russian anarchist Mikhail Bakunin: 'destruction is also creation'.

In the wake of Dada, surrealist artists set out in the following decade to bring to the page or to the canvas the forces of the subconscious. The *ism* 'surrealism' had been coined by Apollinaire in 1917, and its disciples were guided in Paris (the word 'leader' was avoided) by André Breton who dreamed of a 'congress of intellectuals' that would 'distil and unify the essential principles of modernism'. The Spaniard Salvador Dali (1904–1989), who joined the Paris group in 1929, was disdained by Breton, but became the best-known of the surrealists, following a bizarre and totally unplanned career. He was to paint a *Last Supper* and a portrait of Queen Elizabeth II. A German surrealist, Max Ernst (1891–1976), who first exhibited in Berlin in 1916, pursued a very different path, moving through cubism, Dada and *frottage*, rubbing colour or graphite on paper laid over a textured surface, in the search to realize 'painting beyond painting', 'visual poetry'. In 1941 he migrated to the United States, which was to become the centre of late-twentieth-century abstract expressionism. The human figure was expelled from the canvas.

The writing of the history of twentieth-century art has depended much on the use of labels, like 'surrealism' and 'expressionism', the latter not the first *ism* to have been invented by its critics. Nevertheless, different painters followed their own course, sometimes drawing up common manifestos, selling through the same dealer, and whatever their 'school' exploring new techniques. One of the great pioneers of cubism, Picasso, whose paintings went through many phases, passed into general history with his Spanish Civil War painting 'Guernica' (1937) which depicted the destruction from the air of the Basque capital, Bilbao, and after 1945 with his 'doves of peace' which became the emblems of supporters of nuclear disarmament on both sides of the 'iron curtain'.

Influenced during the 1930s by the Spanish Civil War, and during the 1950s by the Cold War, both of them ideological struggles, in which significant numbers of artists, writers and musicians took part, they retained a sense of 'modernity' through into the late 1950s and early 1960s when the sense of the new was again reshaped. By then, dealers in and spokesmen for 'modernity' had acquired some of the trappings of an 'Establishment' in the educational, museums and arts world of 'the West'. Yet 'modern' artists, writers and musicians, many of them now dependent on agents, still stood self-consciously in what the American literary critic Lionel Trilling called an 'adversary position', hostile to 'modern *bourgeois* society'. They were opposed, therefore, both to 'mass culture', which seemed always to threaten them, and to 'middle-brow' culture, which seemed to represent the worst of all compromises. Those modernists who were favourable to Communism, if often critical of the Soviet Union, could extol 'the masses' while treating 'mass culture' as a form of manipulative commercialized contamination. Those modernists who were conservatives – and liberals – felt threatened by mass pressures, sharing the view expressed in 1938 by the Spaniard Ortega y Gasset that 'the mass crushes beneath it everything that is different, everything that is excellent, individual, qualified and serious'.

During the immediate postwar years, when the regularities of daily life had broken up, the most fashionable, if short-lived, philosophy in continental Europe was 'existentialism', another *ism* that was repudiated by some of the philosophers from whom it derived. It focused on immediate human choices and on their impact on other human existences. Its main literary spokesman was Jean-Paul Sartre, French philosopher, essayist and playwright, whose partner Simone de Beauvoir was an able and lively feminist. The roots of existentialist philosophy lay in pre-war Germany and in nineteenth century thought, and Kierkegaard, different though he was from the Marxist Sartre, was back in fashion after 1945. The mood shifted, however, as the war receded. What did not recede was the threat of the Bomb which itself carried with it a terrifying choice. Either/or. In fact, it proved prudent to hold the Bomb, not to make use of it. That was the lesson of the Cold War.

THE 1960s AND THE POST-MODERN

The shift of moods and styles during the late 1950s and the early 1960s was often associated at the time with talk of 'generation gaps'. In fact, differences of outlook within generations were as obvious as differences between generations. More significant were the influences originating in great cities, among them 'swinging London' and 'anti-conventional' Amsterdam and Copenhagen, and in universities which were growing in numbers and in size. There was as much talk in the 1960s and 1970s of 'exploding' cities as there was of generation gaps, and the most active European centres of militant student movements, which spread from one university to another, were Paris and Frankfurt. The media focused on them. They were news.

At a deeper level shifts in values were so great during the late 1960s that Peter Drucker, a shrewd observer of changes in the world of business, could write an influential book in 1969 called *The Age of Discontinuity*. It was during the 1960s also that the cluster of adjectives and *isms* beginning with 'post' began to be identified, among them 'post-modern', a term that was applied to art and architecture before it was applied to society. Drucker himself had used the word 'post-modern' in his *Landmarks of Tomorrow* (1957) which he subtitled 'a report on the new post-modern world'. In a 1965 edition he observed that 'at some unmarked point during the last twenty years we imperceptibly moved out of the Modern Age and into a new as yet nameless one'.[10]

For hostile critics the post terms include '*post mortem*'. There had always been a strand of cultural pessimism in the twentieth century, represented among historians by the much admired and much criticized German writer Oswald Spengler, whose *Der Untergang des Abendlandes* ('The Decline of the West') had appeared in 1918. For Spengler, indeed – and he was pessimistic about life as well as about culture – history was moving into its 'final stage' long before Fukuyama wrote of its end. And when a British historian, Arnold Toynbee, as ambitious as Spengler, surveying as Spengler did a global range of 'civilizations', used the word 'post-modern' in 1974, along with the word 'post-Christian', he too pointed to 'breakdown and disintegration'.

Pessimists were brushed aside, however, during the late-1960s by post-modern architects who celebrated a liberation from 'modernism', reacting sharply against 'Bauhaus' styles which, originating in 1919 with Walter Gropius (born in Berlin but exiled to the United States), had been carried across the Atlantic. Some architects and critics had assumed that the victory of func-tional modern architecture represented in the works of German-born Ludwig Mies Van der Rohe and Swiss-born Charles-Edouard le Corbusier was final and universal. It was not, although it was difficult to find any other label for the buildings of their successors than 'post-modern'. The adjective was used also in relation to religion and, if in brackets, in relation to science: in his *The Broken Image* (1964) Floyd Matson referred to the 'modern (or post-modern) image of the scientist as actor, as "participant observer" rather than detached spectator'. In literature brackets might have been used also: in painting and in building, in particular, in an essay of 1970 some figures previously thought of as 'modern', like Joyce, were now given a post-modern label.

In 1983 the Italian novelist and essayist Umberto Eco, born in 1932, who seemed aware of every cultural trend and who in his novel *Foucault's Pendulum* (1988) dealt with computers, traced the process which linked 'modern' and 'post-modern':

> The moment comes when the avant-garde (the modern) can go no further . . . The post-modern reply to the modern consists of recognizing that the past, since it cannot really be destroyed, because its destruction leads to silence, must be revisited but with irony, not innocently.

Eco's brilliant novel *The Name of the Rose* (1983), translated into most European languages, was set in the Middle Ages but even such an orienta-tion, which might have seemed natural in the nineteenth century was not completely new in the twentieth. The word *ricorso* was old and there had already been more than one twentieth-century return to the Middle Ages. An English medieval historian turned contemporary historian, Geoffrey Barraclough, suggested as early as 1955 that there were features of twentieth-century society that could be better understood in the light of medieval than of nineteenth-century history, while in 1978 the American writer Barbara Tuchman, who had written in depth of military blunders perpetrated during the First World War, called her study of the horrors of the fourteenth century *A Distant Mirror*, suggesting that the personalities, problems and events of that century clearly illuminate the twentieth century, a century of concentration camps and of curious cults and in its last phases a century of corruption and crime.

ELEVEN DISCONTINUITIES

During the 1960s, when there were more contemporary social critics looking ahead than looking backwards, it became common to identify at least 11 discontinuities between the nineteenth and twentieth centuries. Some still stand out in post-millennial perspectives.

(1) Decolonization and the pressures of a politically independent but still largely economically dependent 'third world', a new term of French origin, *le Tiers monde*, had transformed world politics, if not world economics. Large parts of that third world had no written history, but they now burst into late-twentieth-century history through Africa as well as through Asia, where there was a long history. Within that world, which was always more varied than it might seem on the surface, there were to be wide varieties of experience. It now became inadequate to write history in 'Eurocentric' terms.

(2) Pressures from within 'the first world' (an unarticulated concept) of hitherto deprived or suppressed minorities altered the styles and content of politics. Some of the deprived or suppressed were prepared to use the ballot box and the machinery of the 'welfare state', also a new term in the postwar world: others relied on action outside parliaments – strikes and demonstrations. Poverty was not abolished during the boom years of the mid-century, and some regions of Europe had income (and amenity) levels far below those of the most favoured, but poverty was now being interpreted differently, usually relatively, as general living standards rose.

(3) The drive for 'women's liberation', as we have seen, was not new but never before so explicit or so direct, intensified after 1960 as 'feminists' probed hidden assumptions about gender and in the name of 'consciousness raising' changed ways of thinking about it. Meanwhile, women's work full-time, and part-time, increased in volume and range, beginning in service occupations, like banking, but notable too in professions like the law. This entailed changes in family roles and, indeed – along with other changes, including contraception ('the pill' was first introduced from the United States in 1960) and abortion (first legalized in Britain, with stringent conditions, in 1967) – in the constitution of the family itself. What kind of a unit the family was – and could and should be – became a matter of political argument.

(4) Transistor radios, cheap and portable, were being used throughout the world during the 1960s, indispensable instruments (before satellites) in

news delivery (including propaganda) and in popular musical culture. The indispensable tool, the transistor, invented in 1948 – and later integrated circuitry – made it possible to compress all kinds of electrical equipment, including computers, into smaller and smaller space at lower and lower costs. The word 'electronics' was itself new in the 1950s. The result was what was already beginning to be thought of during the 1960s as a radically new 'information society' (the labels, including the French *Télematique* have subsequently multiplied). This had global as well as European implications. 'Information', a European Commission Green Paper published in 1984 began, 'is a decisive, perhaps the only decisive factor in European unification'.

(5) Different national attitudes towards communications development persisted, but there were signs in all countries of basic shifts in values associated with changing balances of work and leisure, particularly of both amateur and professional sports. In the 1960s the word 'sport' increasingly began to be used in the singular, and sportsmen, handled by agents, could now become 'celebrities'. Television focused on them as well as on the games they played.

(6) An erosion of the distinctions between 'high culture' and 'mass culture' was reflected not only on the screen but on canvas in 'pop art', a product, like 'op-art' of the late-1950s and early-1960s, and, above all, in sound. There was a combination of American and European influences, and not least in Eastern Europe 'pop music' had a powerful appeal during the 1980s. As the agency business thrived, there were new links between performers and advertisers. The study of the media and of 'popular culture' became a university subject in parts of Western Europe. So, too, did the study of 'sub-cultures', particularly those of 'youth'. The word 'lifestyle' became fashionable.

(7) In Western Europe 'counter-cultures' or 'alternative cultures' emerged, as they did in the United States, involving not only retreats into 'inner space', many drug-assisted, but new attitudes towards sex and violence. The number of people deemed 'misfits' rose, and there were links with crime. 'Travellers' were prepared to alienate others as they had been alienated themselves. Some developed forms of 'new age' religion, and this could spread. Bookshops now had sizeable sections devoted to 'the occult', sometimes placed side by side with equally sizeable sections on business and management.

(8) A highly planned (and costly) movement into outer space began in rivalry between the Soviet Union and the United States – and left the rest of Europe largely behind. It was to end in the 1990s with joint American-Russian co-operation. By then the sky was full of satellites traversing the Earth's orbit. It was not until 1975 that an 11-nation European Space Agency was set up to carry forward the earlier programmes of the European Space Research Organization, begun in 1962. Its headquarters were in Paris, its technical centre in Holland and its

operations centre at Darmstadt in Germany. Another European scientific venture was the European Organization for Nuclear Research, set up in 1954 with its centre straddling the French-Swiss border near Geneva.

(9) Despite or because of the Bomb, advances in quantum physics seemed less exciting from the 1950s onwards than advances in molecular biology, which raised new issues concerning life and death. So, too, did increased longevity, associated with developments in medicine (antibiotics) and (not least) in surgery (replacements and transplants). The proportion of over 65s in the population increased, and more attention was paid to the ageing process.

(10) Increased attention was paid to environmental issues identified by ecologists. The year 1970 was a landmark in the history of threatened ecosystems, during which the new emphasis on the environment became 'more than a phrase' and the first World Conference on the Human Environment was held in Stockholm in 1972. (See Chapter 12).

(11) The last discontinuity directly concerned people not resources. As Western Europe revived economically, and before it became computerized, countries became heavily dependent on immigration from outside their territories. Some immigration (for example Turkish and other male workers – *Gastarbeiter*, 'Guest workers' – employed in Germany) began as seasonal: others, like Caribbean and Asian immigration into Britain from its old Empire, was from the start more long-term. The *Gastarbeiter* had lower wages, little job security and no civic rights: the numbers and citizenship qualifications of British immigrants were restricted by government. In the middle years of the century it was Switzerland, however, not the bigger countries, which had the highest proportion of immigrant workers. (See Chapter 12).

There were many inter-relationships, logical and chronological, between these 11 discontinuities, and what might seem to be discontinuities had their origins long before 1945. For example, immigration issues had been raised during the first decade of the century when immigrants were sometimes being handled appallingly and there were Parliamentary debates in Britain in 1904 and 1905. The Bomb, which for one observer marked a break between one world and another, dividing the generations in a critical way, was the ultimate product of a revolution in nuclear physics that was one of the most remarkable intellectual achievements of the early-twentieth century – the dissolution of 'classical' Newtonian physics in the decade before 1914. (Einstein published five key papers in 1905, one of them setting out his special theory of relativity.) By 1925 A. N. Whitehead, a brilliant observer of what was happening not only in physics but in other sciences and in the arts, could conclude that 'the stable foundations of physics' had completely 'broken up'. 'The old foundations of scientific thought [were] becoming unintelligible. Time, space, matter, material, ether, electricity, mechanism, organism, configuration, structure, pattern, function, all require reinterpretation.' Quantum physics, which developed later, rested on what Werner Heisenberg described in 1927 in mathematical terms as a principle of 'uncertainty'.

After the Second World War, when the power of physics was demonstrated devastatingly, 'uncertainty' – like 'complexity' – was as apparent both during the 1960s at a time when economies boomed and during the uneasy 1970s when politicians were forced to confront the economic realities of an 'energy crisis' long in the making. Economics now seemed more relevant than sociology, a favourite subject of the 1960s, but there were sharp divisions on policy choices between economists and few insights concerning how to relate economics to other 'social sciences'. During the 1980s politicians in countries as different as Thatcher's Britain and Gorbachev's Soviet Union sought radical answers to old problems. The phrase 'enterprise culture' was coined in the short-lived boom in Britain from 1984 to 1987 which popularized the term, but the decade ended in the economic recession which severely hit both Germany and France and socialist Spain. By the late 1980s Britain had lost much of its industrial base, but welfare objectives were not completely abandoned. Ironically, when the European Community set them out in charter form, Britain, where the term 'welfare state' was first used, opting out. Cutting of taxes now became a major object of policy – along with control of inflation. 'Privatization' schemes were carried through both in Western and after 1989 in Eastern Europe, with as much rigour as 'nationalization' schemes had been carried out almost 50 years before. Meanwhile, and it became an essential part of the picture, some private multinational companies had revenues greater than that of most 'sovereign states'.

Before the break in European and world politics in 1989 there had been a sequence of international terrorist incidents, only the most dramatic of which, like hijacking, hit the headlines. Their numbers rose almost continuously from 125 in 1968 to 831 in 1987. Yet behind almost every one of them there was a historical legacy. The cause that moved many terrorists had its origins in Palestine, which had been made a British mandate after the First World War and which became the home of the new state of Israel after the Second World War. Another cause had its origins in Algeria. Internal sources of terrorism involved one of the oldest populations in Europe, the Basques, with one of Europe's oldest languages. In Ireland Britain was entangled in a distant religious past.

In the case of technology, which some of the terrorists learned to use, there were continuities also, thus rocketry had been conceived of in the early twentieth century by a Russian pioneer, Konstantin Tsiolhovski, who was born in 1857 and who lived long enough (until 1935) to serve the Bolshevik regime. It was new technology, however, the fourth discontinuity, that served, in a phrase of Alvin Toffler as 'the growling engine of change', ushering in a 'third age', the contemplation of which pushed many of its critics into 'new age' philosophies. There were also powerful writers who talked not of technology but 'technopoly'. It had a strong military dimension. The first aeroplanes to break the sound barrier and countries spending heavily on Cold

War weaponry determined the scale of late-twentieth century technology. In an age of satellites and missiles and attempts to provide new forms of defence through 'star wars', military expenditures rose higher than they ever had done in previous history. One of the key phrases of the 1960s — 'the capitalist, military, industrial system' or 'complex' — was popularized in the United States, where the 'system' was strongest and most challenged, but the Soviet Union, which was less able economically to embark upon increasing military expenditure, had a not dissimilar structured system. One of the leading 'new left' popularizers, Herbert Marcuse, came from Europe, a representative of the Frankfurt *Institut für Sozialforschung* (Institute for Social Research) which had been exiled *en bloc* from pre-war Germany. Marcuse, like the leader of the Frankfurt School, Theodor W. Adorno, criticized repression in the Soviet Union also, so that there was a lead-up to the events of 1989 in the 'capitalist' West, where Margaret Thatcher also claimed to have influenced the course of events in the East through 'selling' the merits of the free market.

There was still a regional as well as a national map of Europe in the early 1990s, and for all the continuing talk of a 'post-industrial society' there were still some regions in Europe which had been barely industrialized. The biggest geographic change was the linking-up of France and Britain by a new Channel Tunnel in 1994. Thatcher was present for the opening in May with Mitterand at Lille, first stop in France of the new Eurostar trains operating from November 1994. It was one sign of the limitations of the new project, which had first been attempted in the 1880s and which took seven years to complete, that the trains on the French side moved far faster along the track than on the British side.[11] Britain continued to be harassed by transportation problems, road and rail, in the early years of the twenty-first century. Indeed, transportation now rose to near the top of the political agenda.

TOWARDS THE MILLENNIUM AND BEYOND IT

The Channel Tunnel was not a millennial project, as many new projects, some of them as yet unrealized, were. There was still as much cross reference back to 1989 in 1994 than there was forward to 2000. The fall of the German Wall and the collapse of the Soviet Union 'settled' far less than it at first had seemed likely to do, and there were at least as many question marks about the future of Europe in the mid-1990s as there had been during the 1960s. The title of the successor to the scholarly *Daedalus* 1964 survey of Europe, published a generation later in 1994, was 'Europe Through a Glass Darkly'.[12] In 1992 an article in *The Times* called 'Interpreting the Treaty', complete with cartoon, had as its sub-heading in bigger print 'Key to understanding is hidden in the pages of European history'. When a bigger European Union, so designated in 1993, incorporated Austria, Sweden and Finland in 1995, there was already a long queue of other would-be members, and a meeting at Laeken in December 2001 concluded that Cyprus, Estonia, Hungary, Latvia,

Lithuania, Malta, Poland, the Slovak Republic and Slovenia 'could be ready by 2004'. Agreement was sealed at Copenhagen in December 2002. Europe was redefined, although Turkey, link with the Muslim world, against American wishes, was not among the new twenty-five. Even without it could Europe now retain 'cohesion' or, indeed, 'coherence'? The European Commission produced its first progress report on cohesion – 'unity, diversity, solidarity for Europe, its people and its territory' in January 2002.

By then a new millennium had come without settling anything either. There had been little sense of a new world in the offing as it approached, less, indeed, than there had been during the 1960s when *Europe 2000* provided a future reference point. 'Inventing the future' was out of fashion by 2002, and prophecies of the future, many of them odd, most of them drawn out of the past, were more common than forecast-based analysis. Nevertheless, preparations for millennial celebrations, the noun usually chosen, went ahead in all European countries during the late-1990s, the only anxiety being the possible impact of a millennial bug, described as a 'time bomb' which would affect computers, now essential to the working of economy and society.

Most fears were dispelled by the end of the first day of the new millennium, after London, Paris and Berlin vied with each other in pyrotechnic display. There was lavish television coverage. Yet not all was well. In France half-a-million householders were without electricity following Christmas storms, and an electronic scoreboard on the Eiffel Tower which had faithfully counted the days and hours to the year 2000 since 1997 failed five hours before the stroke of midnight. In London a new millennial dome was to stimulate as much – or more – controversy as delight. Control over its operations soon passed into the hands of a director who had worked with Disneyland.

Three major changes since 1989 were apparent in 2001 in what was now more generally thought of as a post-modern era that spanned two millennia. First, computerization had made possible an 'Internet' which opened up cyberspace to all its users, while at the same time drawing attention to new 'digital gaps' inside and between countries. There was a far more profound controversy about the impact of the Internet – in all countries – than there was in Britain about the Dome. Finland was in the lead inside Europe. Second; the Internet was a world-wide web. The adjective 'global' was now used more frequently than the adjective 'European'. 'Globalisation', not new, was re-shaping, it was said, not only economy and society but culture. 'Globalism Just Is'. Debating whether it was 'good' or 'bad' for 'humanity' sometimes, as at summit conferences, could lead to violence, as it did in Genoa and Seattle. Minorities were roused. Third, while there was global debate about 'sustainable growth' – the subject of a large international conference held in September 2002 not in Europe but in South Africa AIDS was scarcely mentioned – Europeans continued to live longer, their private histories merging in public history. On 11 September 2001 terrifying attacks by Islamic militants on the World Trade Centre in New York and the Pentagon in Washington DC seemed to suggest the beginning of a new age in global history, but despite war in Afghanistan and on 'terrorism' and increased religious tension, the world changed less than it had done even in 1989. 'Aids' was overlooked: Iraq entered the news again.

Probably the biggest change between 1989 and 2002 may have been scientific, suggesting, perhaps, that a new term might soon be substituted for 'post-modern'. Genomic research had led in 1992 to a Human Genome Project which released its data free on the world-wide web. It seemed a natural step in the wake of the discovery of the structure of DNA. Here was the newest of the new technologies, offering new leads into therapy – and much else – but posing further questions that would divide human beings rather than unite them. For Sir John Sulston, who led the British project, 'humanity' was given a new set of 'reminders'. The fact that any copy of the human genome differs only by one part in a thousand was a 'constant reminder that we are part of one family, part of one common thread that goes back to the origin of humanity'. Once more Fukuyama was on the trail. In *Our Posthuman Future* (2002) he argued that a convergence of scientific advances, the first of them the mapping of the genome makes it possible to remake human beings. Not only pain and disability could be eliminated, but even stupidity. It is a thesis that may be as suspect as *The End of History*, but its very enunciation is a sign of how different human beings and human culture were in 2002 from what they had been in 1789.

Notes

1. See M. Poster (ed.), *Jean Baudrillard, Selected Writings* (1988).
2. For the American context see E. N. Saveth (ed.), *American History and the Social Sciences* (1964).
3. A. Toffler, *Future Shock* (1970), especially ch.17, 'Coping with Tomorrow'. Toffler refers sideways to Margaret Mead.
4. Fukuyama's article 'The End of History' in *The National Interest* (1989) was written before the fall of the Wall. His book *The End of History and the Last Man* followed and appeared in a Penguin edition in Britain in 1992. For earlier description and discussion of the end of history, see L. Niethammer, *Post-historie: Has History Come to an End?* (1993).
5. *Ibid.*
6. For the discovery of the genetic code, see J. D. Watson, *The Double Helix* (1968).
7. D. Thomson, *Europe Since Napoleon* (1966 edn), p.946.
8. See G. Cross, *Time and Money: the Making of Consumer Culture* (1993).
9. The word 'modernization' was often used as uncritically as the word 'modern' to describe the impact of 'the West' on the non-European world. See, for example, I. R. Sinai, *The Challenge of Modernisation* (1964).
10. For a brief account of Peter Drucker's writings, which began with his stimulating *The End of Economic Man* (1939), see J. J. Tarrant, *Drucker* (1976).
11. For the Tunnel in historical perspective, see D. Abel, *Channel Underground* (1961) and for perceptive discussions of issues related to it, see ex-Ambassador N. Henderson, *Channels and Tunnels: Reflections on Britain and Abroad* (1987).
12. See also editions entitled 'Old Faiths and New Doubts: the European Predicament', *Daedalus* (Spring 1979) and 'Eastern Europe . . . Central Europe . . . Europe', *Daedalus* (Winter 1990).

FURTHER READING

R eaders should note that in all cases the place of publication is London
  unless otherwise stated.

The long period covered in this volume has stimulated an immense amount
of writing at all levels, much of it American. It reflects changes in the
approach to history as well as in the accumulation of documentary and other
evidence, visual and statistical. Much of the most searching interpretation is
to be found in historical periodicals, many of them deliberately 'revisionist' in
character. There are also, however, several series of useful paperbacks, for
example, *Documents and Debates* (general editor, J. Wroughton) and *Lancaster
Pamphlets* (general editors, E. J. Evans and P. D. King) which cover topics
like *Bismarck and German Unification* (D. Hargreaves, 1991) and *The Unification
of Italy* (J. Gooch, 1986).

The best general introduction remains D. Thomson, *Europe Since Napoleon*
(1957) which was revised in 1966 before its author's death. Its select bibliography is out of date, however, and much revisionist interpretation now has
to be taken fully into account. Compare from the same period G. Barraclough,
An Introduction to Contemporary History (1964).

For the period before this volume begins see its companion volume,
H. G. Koenigsberger, *Early Modern Europe, 1500–1789* (1987) and W. Doyle,
The Old European Order, 1660–1800 (1978). For the world setting, which
has changed dramatically in the twentieth century, see J. M. Roberts, *The
Pelican History of the World* (1980). For links with the twentieth century see
W. R. Keylor, *The Twentieth-Century World: An International History* (1984).
P. Kennedy examines the changing determinants in *The Rise and Fall of the
Great Powers, Economic Change and Military Conflict from 1500 to 2000* (1988).
See also A. W. Woodruff, *Impact of Western Man: A Study of Europe's Role in
the World Economy* (1967).

E. J. Hobsbawm has written an impressive trilogy on 'the long nineteenth
century' with revealing titles that reflect his approach: *The Age of Revolution,
1789–1848* (1962); *The Age of Capital, 1848–1875* (1975); *The Age of Empire*
(1987). The trilogy has been followed (after the world had developed differently from what Hobsbawm anticipated) by his *The Age of Extremes* (1994).
For more pluralistic interpretations by different authors see A. Briggs (ed.),
The Nineteenth Century (1970) and P. Flora *et al.*, *State, Economy and Society in
Western Europe, 1815–1975* (1983). For religion see H. McLeod, *Religion and
the People of Western Europe, 1789–1970* (1981).

Different countries have followed their own paths, and although there is a considerable literature on Germany's 'special way' (*Sonderweg*), it is clear that Britain, France and Italy followed 'special ways' also. See M. Fulbrook (ed.), *National Histories and European History* (1993). The implications for Germany are considered, but not settled, in D. Blackbourn and G. Eley, *The Peculiarities of German History: Bourgeois Society and Politics in Nineteenth-Century Germany* (1984) and R. J. Evans, *Rethinking German History: Nineteenth-Century Germany and the Origins of the Third Reich* (1987).

For individual countries see A. Briggs, *The Age of Improvement* (2000 edn); N. McCord, *British History, 1815–1906* (1991); H. Perkin, *The Origins of Modern English Society, 1780–1880* (1969); R. F. Foster, *Modern Ireland* (1988); W. Carr, *A History of Germany, 1815–1985* (3rd edn, 1987); C. A. Macartney, *The Habsburg Empire, 1790–1815* (1969 edn); R. A. Kann, *The Multinational Empire* (1950); D. Mack Smith, *The Making of Modern Italy* (1968); R. Carr, *Spain 1808–1939* (1966); R. Magraw, *France, 1815–1914: The Bourgeois Century* (1983); L. Kochan and M. Abraham, *The Making of Modern Russia* (1983 edn); J. K. Kerry, *A History of Scandinavia* (1979); D. Kirby, *The Baltic World, 1772–1993* (1995); N. Davies, *Heart of Europe: A Short History of Poland* (1986); and B. Jelavich, *The Establishment of the Balkan National States, 1804–1920* (1977).

There is a useful Open University course *What is Europe?* (AD 280) which has been produced by a course team drawn from different European countries. Volume I of the course material is called *The History of the Idea of Europe*, and the other three volumes are *Aspects of European Cultural Diversity*, *European Democratic Culture* and *Europe and the Wider World*. See also E. Bruley and E. H. Dance, *A History of Europe?* (1960); J-B. Duroselle, *Europe, A History of its Peoples* (English translation, 1990); D. Heater, *The Idea of European Unity* (1992); and H. Brugmans, *Europe: A Leap in the Dark* (1985). See also N. Davies, *Europe* (1996), a fascinating and provocative book which examines topics not dealt with in other general studies.

For regions within Europe see C. Harvie, *The Rise of Regional Europe* (1994) and R. Schulze (ed.), *Structural Change in Early-Industrialized Regions* (1993). There are many detailed studies of particular regions. See also H. C. Meyer, *Mitteleuropa in German Thought and Action* (1955).

L. Snyder, *Fifty Major Documents of the Nineteenth Century* (1955) is a useful brief collection of texts. See also R. R. Mowat, *Select Treaties and Documents, 1815–1916* (1932). For geography turn to *The Penguin Atlas of Recent History: Europe Since 1815* (1986) and for statistics to B. R. Mitchell, *European Historical Statistics, 1750–1970* (1978).

On population see L. Kosinski, *The Population of Europe* (1970) and W. R. Lee (ed.), *European Demography and Economic Growth* (1979); D. V. Glass and D. E. C. Eversley (eds), *Population and Social Change* (1965). Compare E. A. Wrigley and R. Schofield, *The Population History of England* (1981) and E. Hofsten, *Swedish Population History, Main Trends from 1750 to 1970* (1976). See also P. Hall, *The World Cities* (1966).

For migration see L. P. Moch, *Moving Europeans: Migration in Western Europe since 1650* (1993); C. G. Pooley and I. D. Whyte, *Migrant: Emigrants and Immigrants, a Social History of Migration* (1991); and for one special group of migrants E. H. Carr, *The Romantic Exiles* (1933). See also B. Porter, *The Refugee Question in Mid-Victorian Politics* (1979).

For an overview of the changing role of women, recently a much examined subject, see B. S. Anderson and J. P. Zinsser, *A History of Their Own: Women in Europe from Prehistory to the Present* (1988); A. Myrdal, *Nation and Family* (1968); J. Scott, *Women, Work and Family* (1978); and L. Tilly and T. McBride, *The Domestic Revolution: The Modernisation of Household Service in England and France, 1820–1920* (1976). For youth see J. R. Gillis, *Youth and History: Tradition and Change in European Age Relations, 1770 to the Present* (1974).

Chapter 1

REVOLUTION AND EMPIRE: EXPERIENCE AND IMPACT, 1789–1815

The best recent British study of the French Revolution is by W. Doyle, *The Oxford History of the French Revolution* (1989). There is a useful and brief survey of the often controversial issues raised before and during the revolutionary sequence by G. Lewis in *The French Revolution: Rethinking the Debate* (1993). Both books include bibliographies. C. Jones, *The Longman Companion to the French Revolution* (1989) provides a massive but manageable chronicle. For the most recent interpretation of the Revolution see the four volumes of *The French Revolution and the Creation of Modern Political Culture*, vol. I (1987) and vol. IV (1994) edited by K. Baker, vol. II (1988) by C. Lucas, and vol. III (1989) by F. Furet and M. Ozouf. See also R. Cobb, *The People's Armies* (1987), and P. Jones, *The Peasantry in the French Revolution* (1988). The most exciting book to appear in the bicentennial year of the Revolution was S. Schama, *Citizens* (1989). P. D. Sutherland, *France, 1789–1815, Revolution and Counter-Revolution* (1985) carries the story further intelligently and critically through the rise and fall of Napoleon. It includes a valuable bibliography. So too does P. McPhee, *A Social History of France, 1780–1880* (1992).

The best life of Napoleon is by G. Lefebvre, in English translation in two volumes (1969). P. Geyl, *Napoleon, For and Against* (1963) covers the arguments surrounding him at different times then and since. M. G. Hutt (ed.), *Napoleon* (1972) presents a collection of illuminating documents. See also J. Godechet, B. F. Hyslop and D. L. Dowd, *The Napoleonic Era in Europe* (1971). On Napoleon's wars see M. Glover, *The Napoleonic Wars: An Illustrated History, 1792–1815* (1979); G. Best, *War and Society in Revolutionary Europe, 1770–1870* (1982); D. Chandler, *The Campaigns of Napoleon* (1966); and G. Rothenberg, *The Art of Warfare in the Age of Napoleon* (1978).

Industrial change is covered in different countries in two volumes of the Fontana *Economic History of Europe*, edited by C. M. Cipolla – vol. 3, *The Industrial Revolution* (1973) and vol. 4 *The Emergence of Industrial Societies* (1973). D. S. Landes, *The Unbound Prometheus: Technological Change and Industrial Development in Western Europe from 1750 to the Present* (1969) is an invaluable and highly stimulating survey. See also T. Kemp, *Industrialization in Nineteenth Century Europe* (1969); C. Trebilcock, *The Industrialisation of the Continental Powers, 1780–1914* (1981); S. Pollard, *Peaceful Conquest, The Industrialisation of Europe, 1760–1970* (1981) and *The Integration of the European Economy since 1815* (1981); and A. S. Milward and S. B. Saul, *The Economic Development of the Economies of Continental Europe, 1780–1870* (1973). See also G. Gerschenkron, *Economic Backwardness in Historical Perspective* (1962).

For Britain see P. Matthias, *The First Industrial Nation: An Economic History of Britain, 1700–1914* (1969) and the still fascinating older French book by P. Mantoux, *The Industrial Revolution of the Eighteenth Century* (English translation, 1928).

For more recent studies of the cultural implications of industrialization see A. Briggs, *Ironbridge to Crystal Palace: Impact and Images of the Industrial Revolution* (1979) and *The Power of Steam* (1982). An earlier work of considerable historiographical importance, profusely illustrated, is S. Giedion, *Mechanisation Takes Command* (1948). For distinctive aspects of the cultural history of the French Revolution see F. Kennedy, *A Cultural History of the French Revolution* (1989); M. Carlson, *The Theatre of the French Revolution* (1966); M. Ozouf, *Festivals and the French Revolution* (1988); and A. Ribeiro, *Fashion in the French Revolution* (1966).

Comparative history is treated in J. Black, *Convergence or Divergence?* (1994); G. A. Williams, *Artisans and Sans Culottes* (1968); and P. O. Brien and C. Keydor, *Economic Growth in Britain and France, 1780–1914* (1978). For comparative history over time see A. D. Harvey, *Collision of Empires: Britain in Three World Wars, 1793–1945* (1992).

Chapter 2

ORDER AND MOVEMENT, 1815–1848

J. Droz, *Europe between Revolutions, 1815–1848* (1967) provides a brief introduction. See also A. Sked, *Europe's Balance of Power, 1815–1848* (1979); E. V. Gulik, *Europe's Classical Balance of Power* (1955); and P. Schroeder, *The Transformation of European Politics, 1763–1848* (1994). An older book by E. L. Woodward, *Three Studies in European Conservatism: Metternich, Guizot, the Catholic Church in the Nineteenth Century* (1929) is still worth reading. Compare the very different – not quite so old – book by H. Kissinger, *A World Restored: Metternich, Castlereagh and the Problems of Peace, 1812–1822* (1957), written before its author turned to diplomacy. For Metternich's personality and Austrian policies see E. Radvang, *Metternich's Projects for Reform in Austria* (1971) and A. Reinerman, *Austria and the Papacy*, 2 vols (1979, 1989).

For Germany see T. S. Hamerow, *Restoration, Revolution and Reaction: Economics and Politics in Restoration Germany (1815–1871)* (1958). For France see P. Pilbeam, *The French Revolution of 1830* (1971); D. Johnson, *Guizot* (1963); P. H. Hutton, *The Cult of the Revolutionary Tradition* (1981); M. Agulhon, *Marianne into Battle: Republican Imagery and Symbolism in France, 1789–1880* (1981); and F. L. J. Hemmings, *Culture and Society in France, 1789–1848* (1987). For Italy see K. R. Greenfield, *Economics and Liberalism in the Risorgimento: A Study of Nationalism in Lombardy, 1814–1848* (1934).

For nationalism as a force making for change see C. J. Hayes, *The Historical Evolution of Modern Nationalism* (1931), a dated but readable introduction to a complex subject; B. Anderson, *Imagined Communities: Reflections on the Origin and Spread of Nationalism* (1983); E. J. Hobsbawm, *Nations and Nationalism since 1780: Programme, Myth, Reality* (1990); J. Breuilly, *Nationalism and the State* (1985); A. D. Smith, *The Ethnic Origins of Nations* (1983); and, broad in its reference, E. Hobsbawm and T. Ranger (eds), *The Invention of Tradition* (1983).

For 'the city' see A. F. Weber, *The Growth of Cities* (1899); P. Hauser and L. Schnore (eds), *The Study of Urbanisation* (1965); E. Jones, *Towns and Cities* (1966); A. Briggs, *Victorian Cities* (1963); L. Chevalier, *Labouring Classes and Dangerous Classes in Paris During the First Half of the Nineteenth Century* (English translation, 1973); J. M. Merriman, *The Margins of City Life: Exploration on the French Urban Frontier, 1815–1851* (1991); and W. Sharpe and L. Wallack, *Visions of the Modern City* (1983).

For the 'middle classes' see P. Pilbeam, *The Middle Classes in Europe, 1789–1914* (1990) and for labour D. Geary, *European Labour Protest, 1848–1939* (1981) which carries the story of socialism beyond the revolutions of 1848. See also A. Mitchell and I. Deak, *Everyman in Europe: The Industrial Centuries* (2nd edn, 1981). For the origins of socialism see G. D. H. Cole, *A History of Socialist Thought*, 4 vols (1953).

R. Clagg, *The Movement for Greek Independence* (1976) deals with one of the first European movements that inspired and made for change. For the revolutions of 1848 see R. Price, *The Revolutions of 1848* (1988); F. Fejtî, *The Opening of an Era, 1848* (1948); L. B. Namier, *1848: the Revolution of the Intellectuals* (1945), a brilliant essay which now dates; M. Traugott, *Armies of the Poor* (1985); R. Stadelmann, *Social and Political History of the German 1848 Revolution* (1975); W. H. Sewell, *Work and Revolution in France: The Language of Labor from the Old Regime to 1848* (1980); and P. Ginsberg, *Daniele Manin and the Venetian Revolution of 1948–9* (1979).

Chapter 3

NATION BUILDING, 1848–1878

A valuable introduction to the diplomatic history of the period covered in this chapter and the next is A. J. P. Taylor, *The Struggle for Mastery in Europe, 1848–1914* (1954). The defeat of revolution and the development, by different means, of a new map of Europe is described in O. Pflanze, *Bismarck and the Development of Germany: the Period of Unification, 1815–1871* (1963).

For the Frankfurt Parliament see F. Eyck, *The Frankfurt Parliament, 1848–9* (1968) and for the European context W. E. Mosse, *The European Powers and the German Question, 1848–71* (1958). On the Crimean War and the 'destruction of the European Concert' see P. W. Schroeder, *Austria, Britain and the Crimean War* (1972). For two of the main contestants see O. Anderson, *A Liberal State at War, English Politics and Economics During the Crimean War* (1967) and J. S. Curtiss, *Russia's Crimean War* (1979). W. Baumgart, *The Peace of Paris* (1956) and W. E. Mosse, *The Rise and Fall of the Crimean System, 1855–1871* (1963) deal with the implications for the 'Concert of Europe'. See also W. N. Medlicott and D. K. Coveney (eds), *Bismarck and Europe* (1971); K. Bourne, *Victorian Foreign Policy, 1830–1902* (1970); and R. Hyam, *Britain's Imperial Century, 1815–1914* (1975).

For France see R. Price (ed.), *Revolution and Reaction, 1848 and the Second French Republic* (1975); P. McPhee, *A Social History of France, 1780–1880* (1992); and I. Collins (ed.), *Government and Society in France, 1814–1848* (1970). For the Second Empire see A. Plessis, *The Rise and Fall of the Second Empire, 1852–1871* (English translation, 1985); T. Zeldin, *France 1848– 1945* (1973) and (ed.), *Conflicts in French Society: Anticlericalism, Education and Morals in the Nineteenth Century* (1970). There is a revealing detailed study by D. Pinkney, *Napoleon III and the Rebuilding of Paris* (1975).

For Italy, L. Riall, *The Italian Risorgimento, State, Society and National Uni- fication* (1994) provides a useful chronology and sorts out the complexities of interpretation. See also H. Hearder, *Italy in the Age of the Risorgimento* (1983) and J. A. Davis and P. Ginsborg (eds), *Society and Politics in the Age of the Risorgimento* (1991); S. J. Woolf, *A History of Italy, 1700–1860, The Social Constraints of Political Change* (1979); and F. Coppa, *The Origins of the Italian Wars of Independence* (1992).

For three of the main figures in the mid-century story as seen by British historians, see A. J. P. Taylor, *Bismarck, the Man and the Statesman* (1955), D. Mack Smith, *Cavour* (1985), *Garibaldi* (1957) and *Cavour and Garibaldi, a Study of Political Conflict* (2nd edn, 1985) and for a British politician as seen by a British twentieth-century politician, see R. Jenkins, *Gladstone* (1995). The best biography of Bismarck (in translation in two volumes) is by L. Gall, *Bismarck: The White Revolutionary* (1990). See also F. Stern, *Gold and Iron: Bismarck, Bleichröder and the Building of the German Empire* (1971) and O. Chadwick, *The Popes and European Revolution* (1981).

Chapter 4

RIVALRY AND INTERDEPENDENCE, 1871–1914

For introductions to the period see J. Joll, *Europe since 1870* (1973); N. Stone, *Europe Transformed, 1878–1916* (1983); and C. L. Mowat (ed.), *The New*

Cambridge Modern History, vol. XII (revised edn), *The Shifting Balance of World Forces* (1968). A classic American study focusing on diplomatic detail is W. L. Langer, *European Alliances and Entanglements, 1871–1890* (1950 edn). It was followed by his further study *The Diplomacy of Imperialism, 1890–1902* (1965 edn).

For contrasting perspectives see J. Bartlett, *The Global Conflict, 1880–1970: The International Rivalry of the Great Powers* (1984); D. Calleo, *The German Problem Reconsidered: Germany and the World Order, 1870 to the Present* (1978); G. F. Kennan, *The Decline of Bismarck's European Order: Franco-Russian Relations 1875–1890* (1979); F. R. Bridge, *Austro-Hungary and the Great Powers* (1990); M. Beloff, *Imperial Sunset* (1961); J. F. V. Keiger, *France and the Origins of the First World War* (1983); and R. Bosworth, *Italy, the Least of the Great Powers: Italian Foreign Policy before the First World War* (1979).

See also P. Kennedy, *The Rise of the Anglo-German Antagonism, 1860–1914* (1980) and B. Porter, *Britain, Europe and the World, 1850–1892, Delusions of Grandeur* (1983).

For imperial Germany compare H.-U. Wehler, *The German Empire, 1871–1914* (1985) and R. J. Evans (ed.), *Society and Politics in Wilhelmine Germany* (1978). See also R. J. Evans (ed.), *The German Working Class, 1888–1933* (1982) and *The German Bourgeoisie* (1991). For Wilhelm II see J. C. Rîhl, *The Kaiser and his Court* (1995), and, dealing with questions of continuity, J. C. Rîhl (ed.), *From Bismarck to Hitler: the Problem of Continuity in German History* (1970).

For Italy see C. Seton-Watson, *Italy from Liberalism to Fascism* (1967). For France see R. D. Anderson, *France, 1870–1914, Politics and Society* (1977); D. Thomson, *Democracy in France since 1870* (1969 edn); and J. McManners, *Church and State in France, 1870–1914* (1972). For Britain see H. Pelling, *Popular Politics and Society in Late-Victorian Britain* (1968).

For labour politics see J. Breuilly, *Labour and Liberalism in Nineteenth-Century Europe* (1992); E. H. Hunt, *British Labour History, 1815–1914* (1981); K. Burgess, *The Challenge of Labour: Shaping British Society, 1850–1930* (1980); H. Pelling, *Origins of the Labour Party* (1965); R. Morgan, *The German Social Democrats and the First International* (1965); S. Edwards, *The Paris Commune, 1871* (1971); C. E. Schorske, *German Social Democracy, 1905–1917* (1955); W. Guttsman, *The German Social Democratic Party, 1875–1933* (1981); and J. L. H. Keep, *The Rise of Social Democracy in Russia* (1963).

For the military base of the Empire see G. Craig, *The Politics of the Prussian Army, 1640–1945* (1955); M. Kitchen, *The German Officer Corps, 1890–1914* (1968); and, in translation, four volumes of G. Ritter's *The Sword and Sceptre: The Problem of Militarism in Germany* (1969). For educational systems see as a lead-in D. K. Måller, F. Ringer and B. Simon (eds), *The Rise of the Modern Educational System: Structural Change and Social Reproduction, 1870–1920* (1987).

For the power of colonial empires see D. Fieldhouse, *The Colonial Empires: A Comparative Study from the Eighteenth Century* (1966). The technological and economic implications are well dealt with by D. R. Headrich, *The Tools of Empire: Technology and European Imperialism in the Nineteenth Century* (1981). For the dissolution of old European empires see A. Sked, *The Decline and Fall of the Habsburg Empire, 1815–1918* (1989). For the Russian Empire see H. Seton-Watson, *The Decline of Imperial Russia* (1960); H. Rogge, *Russia in the Age of Modernisation and Revolution, 1881–1917* (1983); and H. Kohn, *Pan-Slavism* (1960); and for the Ottoman Empire see W. W. Haddad and W. L. Oshsenwold (eds), *Nationalism in a Non-National State: the Dissolution of the Ottoman Empire* (1977) and M. Kent (ed.), *The Great Powers and the End of the Ottoman Empire* (1984).

Attempts at reform in the Ottoman Empire are dealt with by R. H. Davison, *Reform in the Ottoman Empire, 1856–1876* (1963). See also D. Kushner, *The Rise of Turkish Nationalism, 1876–1903* (1977). For change in Russia see M. S. Miller, *The Economic Development of Russia, 1905–1914* (1926); W. L. Blackwell, *The Industrialisation of Russia: An Historical Perspective* (1970); and, for the fascinating comparison with Japan, C. E. Black *et al.*, *The Modernisation of Japan and Russia: A Comparative Study* (1975).

There is an enormous literature on the origins of the First World War, written at different times and from different angles. For a summary see J. Joll, *The Origins of the First World War* (1984). D. C. B. Lieven, *Russia and the Origins of the First World War* (1983) is a notable recent contribution. The role of Germany is discussed, with very different conclusions, in H. W. Koch (ed.), *The Origins of the First World War* (1982).

For 'plans' see G. Ritter, *The Schlieffen Plan* (1958); P. M. Kennedy (ed.), *The War Plans of the Great Powers, 1880–1914* (1979) and E. Miller (ed.), *Military Strategy and the Origins of the First World War* (1985).

For the last stages in the making of war, see V. Dediger, *The Road to Sarajevo* (1966).

Chapter 5

MODERNITY

E. Weber (ed.), *Paths to the Present: Aspects of European Thought from Romanticism to Existentialism* (1960) provides an excellent, well-edited selection of documents. See also W. E. Houghton, *The Victorian Frame of Mind, 1830–1870* (1985), G. L. Mosse, *The Culture of Western Europe* (1963) and H. S. Hughes, *Consciousness and Society: The Reorientation of European Social Thought, 1890–1930* (1986 edn). For the lead into the twentieth century see S. Kern, *The Culture of Time and Space, 1880–1918* (1983).

Benedetto Croce's *History of Europe in the Nineteenth Century* (English translation, 1933), which provides the lead into this chapter, should be set within the framework of G. de Ruggiero, *The History of European Liberalism* (English translation, 1927). Compare J. Sheehan, *German Liberalism in the Nineteenth*

Century (1978) and J. P. Parry, *Democracy and Religion: Gladstone and the Liberal Party* (1986). See also J. Gray, *Liberalism* (1986).

For 'romanticism' and 'classicism', including 'neoclassicism', see the Royal Academy and Victoria and Albert Museum Catalogue, *The Age of Neo-Classicism* (1972); K. Clark, *The Gothic Revival* (1944); the classic study by M. Praz, *The Romantic Agony* (1933); the excellent brief introduction by L. R. Furst, *Romanticism* (1969); and A. K. Thorlby (ed.), *The Romantic Movement* (1966). For positivism see F. E. Manuel, *The Prophets of Paris* (1962).

P. Gay has written five huge volumes, each complete with impressive bibliographical notes. The first was *The Bourgeois Experience: Victoria to Freud – The Education of the Senses* (1984); the fifth was *The Pleasure Wars* (1998). The volumes reach down to 1914. See also his *Freud, A Life for Our Times* (1988). Compare A. Copley, *Sexual Moralities in France, 1780–1980, New Ideas on the Family, Divorce and Homosexuality* (1989).

Out of a huge literature on Darwin start with G. de Beer, *Charles Darwin* (1963) and L. Eiseley, *Darwin's Century* (1958). For its context and its implications see J. W. Burrow, *Evolution and Society* (1966), which focuses on England; L. L. Clark, *Social Darwinism in France* (1984); and A. Kelly, *The Descent of Darwinism: The Popularisation of Darwin in Germany, 1860–1914* (1981).

For technology see N. Rosenberg, *Perspectives on Technology* (1976); M. Kranzberg and C. W. Pursell (eds), *Technology in Western Civilisation* (1967); J. Beniger, *The Control Revolution: Technological and Economic Origins of the Information Society* (1986); M. Pearton, *The Knowledgeable State: Diplomacy, War and Technology since 1830* (1982); I. F. Clarke, *The Pattern of Expectation, 1644–2001* (1979); P. Anderson, *The Printed Image and the Transformation of Popular Culture, 1790–1860* (1991); and T. P. Hughes, *Networks of Power, Electrification in Western Society, 1880–1930* (1983).

For communications see M. Robbins, *The Railway Age* (1970); N. Faith, *The World of Railways* (1990); P. O'Brien, *Railways and the Economic Development of Western Europe, 1830–1914* (1983); J. Kieve, *The Electric Telegraph: A Social and Economic History* (1973); H. Perkin, *The Age of the Automobile* (1976); J. M. Laux, *The French Automobile Industry to 1914* (1976); H. O. Duncan, *The World on Wheels* (1926); C. E. Foyle, *A Short History of the World's Shipping Industry* (1933); C. Gibbs-Smith, *The Invention of the Aeroplane, 1799–1809* (1966); and, critical and constructive, D. Edgerton, *England and the Aeroplane* (1991). See also I. de Sola Poole (ed.), *The Social Impact of the Telephone* (1977); W. P. Joly, *Marconi* (1972); and R. N. Vyvyan, *Marconi and Wireless* (1974).

For the organizational shells within which technology and communications developed see W. Sombart, *The Quintessence of Capitalism* (1915); L. Hannah, *The Rise of the Corporate Economy* (1976); S. Rolfe, *The International Corporation* (1969); M. Wilkins, *The Emergence of Multi-national Enterprise* (1970); and A. Reichova, M. Lévy-Leboyer and H. Nussbaum (eds), *Multinational Enterprise in Historical Perspective* (1986). For links between economics and politics see J. A. Schumpeter, *Capitalism, Socialism and Democracy* (1943).

For the late-nineteenth century and early-twentieth century city see A. Sutcliffe (ed.), *Metropolis, 1890–1960* (1984). R. J. Evans, *Death in Hamburg: Society and Politics in the Cholera Years, 1830–1870* is a brilliant detailed study.

For *fin de siècle* perspectives see K. W. Swart, *The Sense of Decadence in Nineteenth Century France* (1964); F. Stern, *The Politics of Cultural Despair* (1961); and M. Teich and R. Porter (eds), *Fin de siècle and its Legacy* (1990). A brilliant study is C. E. Schorske, *Fin de Siècle Vienna: Politics and Culture* (1980). Compare H. Jackson, *The Eighteen Nineties* (1913). See also P. Pulzer, *The Rise of Political Anti-Semitism in Germany and Austria* (1963). For Nietzsche see W. Kaufmann, *Nietzsche* (1950). For anarchists see J. Joll, *The Anarchists* (1964).

The psychology of 'the masses' was a familiar topic in the late century. See G. Le Bon, *The Crowd: A Study of the Popular Mind* (1903). G. Lichtheim, *Marxism: An Historical and Cultural Study* (1961) is one of the many books that studies Marxist appeals to 'the masses'. The word 'mass' had a wider application too through changes in production, retailing, consumption and culture. See W. H. Fraser, *The Coming of the Mass Market, 1850–1914* (1981). For the early department store M. Muller, *The Bon Marché: Bourgeois Culture and the Development of the Department Store, 1869–1920* (1981) raises interesting questions. So too does R. Williams, *Dream Worlds: Mass Consumption in Late-Nineteenth Century France* (1982). See also A. Briggs, *Victorian Things* (1988). For 'mass leisure' see J. Walvin, *Leisure and Society, 1830–1950* (1978) and P. J. Graham and H. Weberhorst (eds), *The Modern Olympics* (1976).

For Press history see A. Briggs and P. Burke, *A Social History of the Media* (2001); R. Pound and G. Harmsworth, *Northcliffe* (1959); L. Brown, *Victorian News and Newspapers* (1985); A. J. Lee, *The Origins of the Popular Press in England, 1855–1914* (1976); and D. Read, *The Power of News: The History of Reuters* (1992).

For 'everyday life' and changing approaches to needs and wants (as expressed in food and drink) see J. Burnett, *Plenty and Want: A Social History of Diet in England from 1815 to the Present* (1966); S. Mennell, *All Manners of Food: Eating and Taste in England and France from the Middle Ages to the Present* (1985); R. E. F. Smith, *A Social and Economic History of Food and Drink in Russia* (1984); A. Corbain, *The Foul and the Fragrant* (English translation, 1986); and P. Goubart, *The Conquest of Water: The Advent of Health in the Industrial Age* (1989).

For art and design see M. Brion, *Art of the Romantic Era* (1966); Scottish National Gallery, *The Romantic Spirit in English Art, 1790–1990* (1995); P. Pool, *Impressionism* (1967); Metropolitan Museum of Art, *Impressionism, a Centenary Exhibition* (1974); J.-L. Daval, *Modern Art: The Decisive Years, 1884–1914* (1979); B. Denvir, *The Late-Victorians: Art, Design and Society* (1986); and R. D. Mandell, *Paris, 1900: The Great World's Fair* (1967).

For science see C. G. Bernhard, E. Crawford and P. Sorborn (eds), *Science, Technology and Society in the Time of Alfred Nobel* (1982). For medicine compare R. H. Skyrock, *The Development of Modern Medicine* (1947) and B. Inglis, *A History of Medicine* (1965).

Chapter 6

A EUROPEAN CIVIL WAR, 1914–1918

The major histories of the First World War are L. Hart's still authoritative *History of the First World War* (1972), first published in 1934, H. Strachan, *The First World War, Volume 1: To Arms* (2001) and N. Stone *The Eastern Front, 1914–1917* (1975). The most recent narrative survey of the conflict is by M. Howard, *The First World War* (2002). The studies of J. Kocka, *Facing Total War* (1984) and M. Ferro, *The Great War* (1973), translated respectively from German and French, are also useful, as is H. Strachan (ed.), *The Oxford Illustrated History of the First World War* (1998), T. Ashworth, *Trench Warfare, 1914–1918: The Live and Let Live System* (1980) and J. M. Bourne *Britain and the Great War, 1914–1918* (1989).

For greater detail on international politics and economic history during the war see D. Stevenson, *The First World War and International Politics* (1988), and G. Hardach, *The First World War, 1914–1918* (1987).

The impact of the war on society and literature has been dealt with by many writers in recent years. Some examples are A. Marwick, *War and Social Change in the Twentieth Century* (1974); J. Winter, *The Experience of World War I* (1989); R. Wall and J. Winter (eds), *The Upheaval of War: Family, Work and Welfare in Europe, 1914–1918* (1988), S. Pedersen, *Family, Dependence and the Origins of the Welfare State: Britain and France, 1919–1945* (1993), and J. Williams, *The Home Fronts: Britain, France and Germany, 1914–1918* (1972).

The study of how memories of the First World War were expressed and shaped subsequent European history became a topic of great interest to later twentieth-century historians. See P. Fussell, *The Great War and Modern Memory* (1975), J. Winter, *Sites of Memory, Sites of Mourning* (1995), M. Eksteins, *Rites of Spring: The Great War and the Birth of the Modern Age* (1989), F. Field, *British and French Writers of the First World War* (1991), and C. Coker, *War and the Twentieth Century: A Study of War and Modern Consciousness* (1994).

For women see C. M. Tylee, *The Great War and Women's Consciousness: Images of Militarism and Womanhood in Women's Writings, 1914–1964* (1990), M. R. Higonnet, J. Jenson, S. Michel and M. C. Weitz, *Behind the Lines: Gender and the Two World Wars* (1987) and D. Mitchell, *Women on the Warpath: the Story of Women in the First World War* (1966).

There is a considerable collection of memoirs of the First World War, the best known of D. L. George's voluminous six-volumes, *War Memoirs* (1933–6), and V. Brittain's *Testament of Youth: an autobiographical Study of the Years 1900–1925* (1979), first published in 1923, is an illuminating source.

For greater detail on individual countries see J.-J. Becker, *The Great War and the French People* (1985); F. Carsten, *Revolution in Central Europe* (1972), V. Berghan and M. Kitchen (eds), *Germany in the Age of Total War* (1981), R. Bosworth, *Italy and the approach of the First World War* (1983), J. Galantai,

Hungary in the First World War (1989) and N. Davies, *Heart of Europe: A Short History of Poland* (1984), and for the Ottoman empire see D. Fromkin's *A Peace to End All Peace* (1989).

The literature on the Russian Revolution is also vast. J. Reed, *Ten Days that Shook the World* (1919) is a highly readable eye-witness account by an American journalist, endorsed by Lenin. It appeared in a new illustrated edition in Britain in 1997 (Stroud, London and St Martin's Press, New York). The best of most recent studies are those by O. Figes, *A People's Tragedy. The Russian Revolution, 1891–1924* (1996), and R. Pipes, *The Russian Revolution 1899–1919* (1990) and *Russia under the Bolshevik Regime, 1919–1924* (1994). S. Fitzpatrick's *The Russian Revolution, 1917–1922* (1982) remains an excellent introduction. See also H. Shukman (ed.), *The Blackwell Encyclopedia of the Russian Revolution* (1994).

Chapter 7

A NEW ORDER? 1919–1929

The most recent accounts of the Paris Peace Conference include A. Sharp, *The Versailles Settlement* (1991); L. Ambrosius, *Wilsonian Statecraft: Theory and Practice of Liberal Internationalism during World War I* (1991); and M. Boemeke, G. D. Feldman, and E. Glaser (eds), *The Treaty of Versailles. A Reassessment after Seventy-Five Years* (1995). For contemporary accounts see H. Nicolson, *Peacemaking, 1919* (1933); F. Nitti, *Peaceless Europe* (1922); and J. M. Keynes, *The Economic Consequences of Peace* (1919). On the question of German guilt see A. Lentin, *Lloyd George, Woodrow Wilson and the Guilt of Germany* (1984), while B. Kent takes up the issue of war debts and reparations in *The Spoils of War: The Politics, Economics and Diplomacy of Reparations, 1918–1932* (1989).

S. Marks offers a useful, short survey of European diplomacy in this period in *The Illusion of Peace: International Relations in Europe, 1918–1933* (1976). P. Clavin, *The Great Depression in Europe, 1929–1939* (2000); D. H. Aldcroft, *From Versailles to Wall Street* (1977); and R. Munting and B. A. Holderness, *Crisis, Recovery and War: An Economic History of Continental Europe, 1918–1945* (1991) cover the economics.

Most histories of the Russian Revolution cover the Civil War, but for greater detail see E. Mawdsley, *The Russian Civil War* (1987). A. Nove, *An Economic History of the USSR* (1969 and third edition 1982), is an interesting account of the Soviet Union's economic development while M. McCauley gives a stimulating, documentary account of the war and how it changed the party in *The Russian Revolution and the Soviet State, 1917–1921* (1975).

The literature on Eastern Europe during this period in English is scant in comparison to its western counterpart. For the best examples see R. Okey, *Eastern Europe, 1740–1985* (1982); A. Polonsky, *The Little Dictators: the History of Eastern Europe since 1918* (1975), and, still most thorough, C. A. Macartney, *Independent Eastern Europe: A History* (1962). T. Masaryk in his *The Making of a State: Memories and Observations 1914–1918* (1927), gives an interesting, if lengthy, biographical account of the period.

C. Maier, *Recasting Bourgeois Europe: Stabilisation of France, Germany and Italy after World War I* (Princeton, 1975), offers the best comparative perspective on post-war stabilization. For individual nations see, on Britain, C. L. Mowat's *Britain Between the Wars, 1918–1940* (1955, fifth edition 1987); D. Reynolds, *Britannia Overruled: British Policy and World Power in the Twentieth Century* (1991); and, on the sunset and sunrise of British economy, *The Development of the British Economy, 1914–1990* by S. Pollard (1962, fourth edition 1992). For stimulating and recent accounts of British and French colonial relations during this period see P. J. Cain and A. G. Hopkins, *British Imperialism: Crisis and Deconstruction 1914–1990* (1993), and R. Betts, *France and Decolonisation, 1900–1960* (1991).

The history of the French economic crises in the 1920s is more accessible in English than its political history. The best of the former is S. A. Schuker, *The End of French Predominance in Europe: The Financial Crisis of 1924 and the adoption of the Dawes Plan* (1976). For foreign policy consult see J. Jacobsen, *Locarno Diplomacy: Germany and the West, 1925–1929* (1972). The best English introduction to French politics is J. McMillan's *Twentieth Century France: Politics and Society* (1985 and 1992). See also A. Adamthwaite, *Grandeur and Misery. France's bid for power in Europe, 1914–1940* (1995). For details of emergence of French right-wing see R. Soucy, *French Fascism: the first wave, 1924–1933* (1986). W. Fortescue has compiled a useful documentary study, *The Third Republic in France, 1870–1940* (2000).

D. M. Smith's *Mussolini* (1981), and A. Lyttelton's *The Seizure of Power: fascism in Italy, 1919–1929* (1973 and 1987), offer stimulating accounts of Italian politics. On Italian fascism's intellectual origins see A. James Gregor, *Young Mussolini and the Intellectual Origins of Fascism* (1979). The most commanding Italian history of the period is R. De Felice, *Mussolini il fascista* (1968). For comparisons between Germany and Italy, see R. Bessel (ed.), *Fascist Italy and Nazi Germany: Comparisons and Contrasts* (1996) and A. J. De Grand, *Fascist Italy and Nazi Germany: the 'fascist' style of rule* (1995). On Spain see G. Brenan's still useful *The Spanish Labyrinth: an account of the social and political background to the civil war* (1949 and 1950). The prolific output of R. Carr and P. Preston on Spain includes Carr's *The Civil War in Spain, 1936–1939* (1986), and Preston's *The Coming of the Spanish Civil War* (1978).

The literature of Weimar Germany is voluminous. R. Bessel, *Germany after the First World War* (1993); J. Hinden, *The Weimar Republic* (1984); D. Peukert's similarly titled *The Weimar Republic: the crisis of classical modernity* (1991); R. Bessel and E. J. Feuchwanger (eds), *Social Change and Political Development in Weimar Germany* (1981) are amongst the best. For greater detail on Germany's hyper-inflationary crisis see G. Feldman (ed.), *The Great Disorder: Politics,*

Economics and Society in the German Inflation (1993), and on culture P. Gay's entertaining *Weimar Culture: the outsiders as insiders* (1968).

Chapter 8

GUNS AND BUTTER, 1929–1939

P. Clavin, *The Great Depression in Europe, 1929–1939* (2000) is the only account to focus on Europe. C. Kindleberger, *The World in Depression, 1929–39* (1987) remains the best account of the crisis's global effects. B. Eichengreen, *Golden Fetters: The Gold Standard and the Great Depression, 1919–1939* (1992) and I. Drummond, *The Gold Standard and the International Monetary System, 1900–1939* (1987), detail the monetary side of the crisis.

M. Kitchen, *Europe Between the Wars* (1990) offers a comparative political survey of Europe in this period, while J. Jackson brings together a variety of themes in the edited collection *Europe 1900–1945* (2002). For a wealth of lively detail on politics, society and culture, see P. Brendon, *The Dark Valley. A Panorama of the 1930s* (2000). Still useful, too, are J. Schumpeter, *Capitalism, Socialism and Democracy* (7th edn 1987) and E. H. Carr, *International Relations between the two world wars* (1947). S. Salter and J. Stevenson, *The Working Class and Politics in Europe and America, 1929–1945* (1990) offer interesting accounts of the social and political impact of the crisis on Europe's working class. Unfortunately, no extensive comparative study of the middle class is yet available.

The depression also triggered debate about greater European unity. For early origins of the E.U. see P. M. R. Stirk (ed.), *European Unity in the Context of the Interwar Period* (1989). For the history of individual countries during the depression consult C. L. Mowat, *Britain Between the Wars 1918–1940* (1955); K. Robbins, *The Eclipse of a Great Power. Modern Britain, 1870–1975* (1983), J. Stevenson and C. Cook, *Britain in the Depression. Society and Politics, 1929–1939* (1994). The literature of the collapse of Weimar is vast. A good starting point is I. Kershaw (ed.), *Weimar: Why Did German Democracy Fail?* (1990) or D. Peukert, *The Weimar Republic* (1991). The treatment of inter-war France is slight by comparison, but important new additions are J. Jackson, *The Politics of Depression in France, 1932–36* (1985) and by the same author *The Popular Front in France* (1989). See K. Mouré, *Managing the Franc Poincaré. Economic Understanding and Political Constraint in French Monetary Policy, 1928–1936* (1991) for an important new account of French economic policy during this period. Detailed monographs of Eastern Europe during the depression are still scant. Those available include, F. L. Carsten, *The First Austrian Republic, 1918–1938* (1986), H. Rogger and E. Weber (ed.), *The European Right. A Historical Profile* (1966) and O. Rutter, *Regent of Hungary. The Authorized Life of Nicholas Horthy* (1938). For a summary of recent scholarship see M. Kaser's edited volumes *The Economic History of Eastern Europe, 1919–1975* (1986).

G. Brenan's *The Spanish Labyrinth* (1943) is a dated but fascinating explanation of the background to the Spanish civil war, as is F. Borkenau eye witness account of the war in *The Spanish Cockpit* (1937 and 1986). More recent scholarship is by R. Carr, *The Spanish Tragedy* (1986) and R. Fraser, *Blood of Spain. An oral history of the Spanish Civil War* (1986). Important, too, is the first complete study of Franco by P. Preston, *Franco. A biography* (1994). Good introductions to the topic include: F. Ribeiro de Menses, *Franco and the Spanish Civil War* (2001); A. Forrest, *The Spanish Civil War* (2000); and P. Preston, *The Coming of the Spanish Civil War* (2nd edn 1994).

Comparative studies provide an interesting insight into European fascisms. For an introduction, see M. Blinkhorn, *Fascism and the Right in Europe, 1919–1945* (2000) and P. Morgan, *Fascism in Europe, 1919–1945* (2002). The best detailed studies include; S. Payne, *A History of Fascism, 1914–1945* (1995); S. J. Woolf (ed.), *Fascism in Europe* (1981); and the still useful W. Laquer, *Fascism: A Reader's Guide* (1979). More focused comparisons of Italian and German fascisms are offered by A. D. De Grand, *Fascist Italy and Nazi Germany: the 'fascist' style of Rule* (1995) and R. Bessel (ed.), *Fascist Italy and Nazi Germany. Comparisons and Contrasts* (1995). For an illuminating contemporary documentation of the dominant ideologies see, M. Oakeshott, *Social and Political Doctrines of Contemporary Europe* (1940). (For further suggestions see chapter seven.) The antecedents of Fascist Anti-Semitism are explored by A. Lindemann, *Anti-Semitism before the Holocaust* (2000). Scholarship on the theory and practice of Nazism, sometimes treated as distinct from European fascism, is, needless to say, voluminous. I. Kershaw provides an invaluable aid to the historiographical disputes in *The Nazi Dictatorship* (1985, 4th edition, 2000). M. Burleigh has revitalized the field with his presentation of National Socialism as a 'political religion' in *The Third Reich. A New History* (2000). J. Noakes and G. Pridham offer documents and commentary in *Nazism, 1919–1945: a Documentary Reader* (1984). K. Bracher, *The German Dictatorship* is a celebrated account, as are those of J. Fest, *The Face of the Third Reich* (1972), F. Stern, *The Politics of cultural despair: a study in Germanic ideology* (1961) and, more recently, M. Burleigh and W. Wippermann, *The Racial State: Germany, 1933–1945* (1991). R. Overy, offers an excellent study of *The Nazi Economic Recovery, 1932–38* (2nd edition, 1996). The now classic study by E. Jäckel, on *Hitler's Worldview. A blueprint for Power* (1972) is a fascinating exploration of Hitler's ideas.

I. Kershaw's two volumed study of Hitler, *Hitler, 1889–1936: Hubris* (1991) and *Hitler, 1936–1945: Nemesis* (2000) have been hailed as a definitive biography of Hitler. A. Bullock's study, *Hitler and Stalin: Parallel lives* (1991) seeks to compare the German leader with his counterpart in the USSR. New archival materials from the former Soviet Union have also launched a number of revised studies on Stalinism. Amongst the best are those by S. Fitzpatrick, including an edited collection *Stalinism. New Direc-*

tions (2000) and the pioneering *Everyday Stalinism: Ordinary Lives in Extraordinary Times, Soviet Russia in the 1930s* (2001). Additional recent biographical studies to that of A. Bullock include, E. Radzinsky, *Stalin* (1997) and R. Brackman, *The Secret File of Joseph Stalin: A Hidden Life* (2001). For details of the terror see J. Getty, *The Road to Terror. Stalin and the destruction of the Bolsheviks, 1932–39* (1999) and R. Conquest, *The Harvest of Sorrow: Soviet Collectivization and the Terror-Famine* (1986). J. Brooks explores Soviet culture in *Thank you comrade Stalin! Soviet public culture from revolution to Cold War* (1999).

Chapter 9

FROM EUROPEAN TO WORLD WAR, 1933–1945

The fiftieth anniversary of the outbreak of the war prompted the publication of a number of new studies on the Second World War. D. Watt, *How War Came* (1989) and R. Overy, *The Road to War* (1989) are the best. P. Finney (ed.), *The Origins of the Second World War* (1997) offers an interesting perspective on recent historiographical debates and A. J. P. Taylor's controversial *The Origins of the Second World War* (1961) remains an excellent read.

For an economic perspective see the excellent collection of essays edited by M. Harrison, *The Economics of World War II. Six great powers in international comparison* (1998). For the economics of Britain's 'appeasement' of Hitler see G. Peden, *British Rearmament and The Treasury 1932–39* (1979). France's dilemma is well illustrated by A. Adamthwaithe, *France and the Coming of the Second World War* (1977) and D. Reynolds gives a fascinating account of Britain's increasing dependence on the United States in *Britannia Overruled* (1990).

For the story of *Mussolini's Early Diplomacy* see the book by R. Cassels (1970). M. Knox, *Mussolini Unleashed* (1982) provides valuable insight into Italy's imperial ambitions, while J. Steinberg, *All or Nothing. The Axis and the Holocaust, 1941–43* (1990) addresses a neglected area of Axis relations. P. Ginsbourg, *A History of Contemporary Italy. Society and Politics, 1943–1988* (1990) tells of Italy under Allied occupation.

R. A. C. Parker, *Struggle for Survival. The History of the Second World War* (1989) and M. Kitchen, *The World In Flames* (1990) are concise, well-written accounts of the war. R. Overy offers a pertinent and insightful appreciation of *Why the Allies Won* (1995), while G. L. Weinberg, *A World at Arms. A Global History of World War II* (1994) emphasizes the global character of the war.

M. Balfour, *Propaganda in War, 1939–1945* (1979) and M. G. Steinert, *Hitler's War and the Germans. Public Mood and Attitude during the Second World War* (1977) provide details as to propaganda efforts of the main belligerent. J. D. Wilkinson's study of *The Intellectual Resistance in Europe* (1981) is an important contribution to the study of wartime resistance and art. In contrast

P. Fussell, *Wartime* (1989), writes of the experience of soldiers and families in the war. For a cartoonist's eye view R. Douglas *The World War, 1939–1945: The Cartoonists' Vision* (1990).

For an insight into life under occupation and the social cost of the war see: W. Rings, *Life with the Enemy* (1982); M. Marrus, *The Holocaust in History* (1988); J. T. Baumel, *Double Jeopardy: Gender and the Holocaust* (1998); A. Mayer, *Why the Heavens did not Darken* (1990) and A. Marwick (ed.), *War and Social Change* (1988). The *Berlin Diaries of Marie 'Missie' Vassiltchikov* (1985) provide an unusual, well-written insight into life in Nazi Germany and the officer's plot against Hitler. The role of women in the war is explored by an ever growing number of authors. See P. Summerfield, *Women Workers in the Second World War* (1984) and *Reconstructing women's wartime lives: discourse and subjectivity in oral histories of the Second World War* (Manchester, 1998); M. Buckley, *Women and Ideology in the Soviet Union* (1989); D. Sheridan (ed.), *Wartime Women* (1990). See also A. Briggs, *Go to It* (2000), a study of Britain's civilian war effort, and S. A. Briggs, *Keep Smiling Through* (1975), an illustrated study of Britain's home front, and the comparative essays in A. Marwick (ed.), *Total War and Social Change* (1988).

Chapter 10

FREEZING AND THAWING POSTWAR EUROPE, 1945–1969

A. Bramwell (ed.), *Refugees in the Age of Total War* (1988); C. von Krockow, *Hour of the Women* (1992) a compelling account of life in defeated Prussia; and J. Skvorecky, *The Cowards* (1958; London, 1968) offer contrasting impressions of life in Eastern Europe after war's end. For greater detail on the treatment of Germany see A. Deighton, *The Impossible Peace: Britain, the Division of Germany and the Origins of the Cold War* (1990). N. Pronay and K. Wilson offer an interesting analysis on the 're-education' of Germany in *The Politican Re-Education of Germany and her Allies after World War II* (1985). For an introduction into the churches' role in the history of postwar Europe, see O. Chadwick, *The Christian Church in the Cold War* (1993). For bibliographical suggestions on Western Europe's economic, social and political reconstruction see chapter 11.

The literature on the Cold War is vast, offering a variety of interpretations as to its origins, course, and, more recently, its conclusion. Compare H. Feis, *From Trust to Terror* (1970); R. J. Maddox, *The New Left and the Origins of the Cold War* (1973); J. L. Gaddis, *The United States and the Origins of the Cold War, 1941–1947* (1972); and J. L. Gormly, *From Potsdam to the Cold War: Big Three Diplomacy, 1945–47* (1990). G. Partos makes lively use of interviews conducted since the iron curtain fell in *The World that Came in From the Cold* (1993).

For an account of life in the USSR before reform see: R. Pipes, *Russia under the Old Regime* (1974); R. Sakwa, *The Rise and Fall of the Soviet Union, 1917–1991* (1999); C. Linden, *Khrushchev and the Soviet Leadership: with an Epilogue on Gorbachev* (1966 and 1990); G. Hosking, *The Awakening of the Soviet Union* (1990); D. Lane, *Soviet Economy and Society* (1985); M. McCauley, *Politics and the Soviet Union* (1977).

The fall of the iron curtain has also allowed historians access to new documentary evidence on the history of Eastern Europe, enabling scholars to add details where before there was often conjecture. The best histories of Eastern Europe still include works written before 1989, see G. Schopflin, *Politics in Eastern Europe* (1981); S. White, J. Gardner and G. Schopflin, *Communist Political Systems: an Introduction* (1982); J. Rothschild, *Return to Diversity: a political history of East Central Europe* (1989); R. Okey, *Eastern Europe, 1740–1985* (1982); M. Roskin, *The Rebirth of Eastern Europe* (1991); and G. Swain and N. Swain, *Eastern Europe Since 1945* (1993). Recently published surveys include I. Bideleux and I. Jeffries, *A History of Eastern Europe. Crisis and Change* (1998). For further recommended books on Eastern Europe, see Chapter 12.

For greater detail on individual countries see J. Hoensch, *A History of Modern Hungary, 1867–1986* (1988); C. Cviic, *Remaking the Balkans* (1991); N. Malcolm, *Bosnia, a Short History* (1994); H. Ashby Turner Jr., *The Two Germanies since 1945* (1987); M. Balfour, *Germany: the Tides of Power* (1992); and N. Davies, *Heart of Europe: a short history of Poland* (1984).

Chapter 11

RECONSTRUCTING EUROPE, 1945–1968

Western Europe's reconstruction has been the subject of a number of excellent books. M. Hogan, *The Marshall Plan. America, Britain and the Reconstruction of Western Europe, 1947–52* (1987) and A. Milward, *The Reconstruction of Western Europe, 1945–51* (1984) offer contrasting accounts of the impact of Marshall Aid on European reconstruction. C. Maier (ed.), *The Marshall Plan and Germany. West German development within the framework of the European Recovery Programme* (1991) and D. Ellwood, *Rebuilding Europe. Western Europe, America and Postwar Reconstruction* (1992) are also important introductions to the subject.

For a comparative perspective on Western Europe's subsequent political history see: D. W. Urwin, *Western Europe since 1945: a political history* (1968, 5th edition 1997) and J. W. Young, *Cold War Europe. A Political History, 1945–1989* (1991). For a thematic treatment, see M. Fulbrook (ed.), *Europe Since 1945* (2001).

For a fascinating survey of the impact of the war on the world's most powerful economies, see M. Harrison (ed.), *The Economics of World War II:*

Six Great Powers in International Comparison (1998). Most books on post-war Europe touch on Western Europe's economic recovery, but for greater detail consult B. Eichengreen (ed.), *Europe's Postwar Recovery* (1995) and N. Crafts, 'The Golden Age of Economic Growth in Western Europe, 1950–1973', *Economic History Review*, 48:3 (August 1995). For Europe's place in the wider world, see H. James, *International Monetary Cooperation Since Bretton Woods* (1996). H. Van Der Wee, *Prosperity and Upheaval. The World Economy, 1945–1980* (1986) continues to be one of the most readable surveys. M.-S. Shulze has assembled an important collection of essays on Western European social and economic history in, M.-S. Schulze (ed.), *Western Europe. Economic and Social Change Since 1945* (1999).

Research by historians and sociologists into the consequences of Western Europe's 'economic miracles' for class relations in the post-war period can be uncovered in A. Carew, *Labour under the Marshall Plan* (1987); H. Machin (ed.), *National Communism in Western Europe: a third way to Socialism?* (1983); P. Weiler, *British labour and the cold war* (1988). W. Paterson has edited a number of books on this subject, including *Social Democracy in post-war Europe* (1974).

For a broader exploration of the relationship between the state and capitalism consult A. Shonfeld, *Modern Capitalism* (1965); R. Kuisel, *Capitalism and the state in modern France* (1981); M. L. Smith and P. M. R. Stirk, *Making the new Europe. European Unity and World War Two* (1991); and P. Hall, *Governing the economy: the politics of state intervention in Britain and France* (1986). For further details on individual nations see A. Ginsborg, *A History of Contemporary Italy. Society and Politics, 1943–1988* (1990); T. Stovall, *France since the Second World War* (2002); A. J. Nicholls, *The Bonn Republic. West German Democracy, 1945–1990* (1997); R. Carr and J. P. Fusi, *Spain. Dictatorship to Democracy* (1979, 2nd edition, 1991); P. Preston, *The Triumph of Democracy in Spain* (1986); D. Birmingham, *A Concise History of Portugal* (1993); P. Hennessy, *Never Again. Britain 1945–51* (1992); T. O. Lloyd, *Empire, Welfare State, Europe. The United Kingdom, 1906–2001* (2001); and R. Middleton, *The British Economy Since 1945* (2000).

The literature on the European Community grows ever larger. Amongst the best are works by W. Wallace including, *The Transformation of Western Europe* (1990) and his edited collection, *The Dynamics of European Integration* (1991). Also useful are D. W. Urwin, *The Community of Europe. A history of European Integration since 1945* (2nd edition, 1997) and S. George, *Politics and Policy in the European Community* (1985).

Chapter 12

TOWARDS A UNITED EUROPE, 1968–2002

Gorbachev's attempts at reform and the consequences of his failure are still being digested by political commentators and historians. For appraisals of Gorbachev before and after the collapse of the Soviet Union consult S. Kotkin, *Armageddon Averted. The Soviet Collapse, 1970–2000* (2001) and R. Sakwa who has put together a fascinating collection of primary materials on the topic in *The Rise and Fall of the Soviet Union, 1917–1991* (1999). S. White, A. Pravda and Z. Gitelman, *Developments in Russian Politics* (4th edition, 1997) and R. Pearson, *The Rise and Fall of the Soviet Empire* (2nd edition, 2002) are useful, and regularly revised, surveys. Recent biographies of Gorbachev include M. McCauley, *Gorbachev* (2000). For an insight into the impact of 'openness' on Soviet culture, A. Nove, *Glasnost in Action: Cultural Renaissance in Russia* (1989); F. Varese, *The Russian Mafia. Private Protection in a New Market Economy* (2001) is one of a number of studies to examine the emergence of the Russian mafia in the context of Russia's transition to a capitalist economy. G. Hosking, J. Avis and P. Duncan, *The Road to Post-Communism* (1992) were among the first to offer commentaries on life in the Commonwealth of Independent Republics. B. Gökay, *Eastern Europe Since 1970* (2001) and R. J. Crampton, *The Balkans Since the Second World War* (2002) offer fascinating insights into the recent history of Russia's near neighbours.

The history of Western Europe since 1970 is still best accessed through national histories. For Germany, see A. J. Nicholls, *The Bonn Republic. West German Democracy, 1945–1990* (1997) and D. Childs, *The Fall of the GDR* (2001); for Greece, see D. H. Close, *Greece Since 1945* (2002); for France, see R. Gildea, *France Since 1945* (2002); and A. Guyomarch, H. Machin, and J. Hayward, *Developments in French Politics* (2nd edition, 2001) and for Spain, P. Heyward, *The Government and Politics of Spain* (1995). For an eye-witness account of the dramatic events of 1989 see T. G. Ash, *We the People: the Revolution of '89 witnessed in Warsaw, Budapest, Berlin and Prague* (1990).

As most historians tend to treat the period after the Second World War as a whole, the bibliographical notes for chapters 10 and 11 should also be consulted.

Chapter 13

POST-MODERN?

Most of the key texts are referred to – and cited – in the text of this chapter. The literature concerning it is massive. In particular, see S. Freud, *Civilisation and its Discontents* (1929); U. Apollonio, *Futurist Manifestos* (1973); J. Ortega y Gasset, *The Revolt of the Masses* (1930); H. Arendt, *The Origins of Totalitarianism* (1951); J. Ellul, *The Technological Society* (English translation, 1969); S. Giner, *Mass Society* (1976); N. Wiener, *The Human Use of Human Beings: Cybernetics and Society* (1954); A. Toffler, *Future Shock* (1970) and *The Third Wave* (1980); J. Naisbik and P. Aburdeen, *Megatrends* (1990); S. Nora and A. Minc, *The Computerization of Society* (1980); H. Pagels, *The Dream of Reason: The Computer Technology and the Rise of the Society Complexity* (1989); and N. Postman, *The Surrender of Culture to Technology* (1992).

For 'the end of ideology' see D. Bell's book with that title (1960) and for 'the end of history' F. Fukuyama, *The End of History and the Last Man* (1989). See also D. Bell, *The Cultural Contradictions of Capitalism* (1976); T. Roszak, *The Making of a Counter Culture* (1970); D. Kumar, *Prophecy and Progress: The Sociology of Industrial and Post-Industrial Society* (1978); D. Harvey, *The Condition of Postmodernity: an Enquiry into the Origins of Cultural Change* (Oxford, 1989); and S. Connor, *Postmodernist Culture* (1989).

For capitalism – and the economic background of change – see A. Shonfield, *Modern Capitalism, The Changing Balance of Public and Private Power* (1965); and H. van der Wee, *Property and Upheaval: the World Economy, 1945–1980* (1986). For links with politics see S. Berger (ed.), *Organising Interests in Western Europe: Pluralism, Corporatism, and the Transformation of Politics* (1981); W. N. Lindberg, *The Political Dynamics of European Integration* (1963); and A. S. Milward, *The European Rescue of the Nation State* (1992). On risk, chance, and the prospects of human survival see M. Douglas and A. Wildavsky, *Risk and Culture* (1982); I. Hacking, *The Taming of Chance* (1990); R. Falk, *The Endangered Planet* (1973); and W. A. McDougall, *The Heavens and the Earth: A Political History of the Space Age* (1995).

There have been many books dealing with the rise of 'consumerism' and its various modes of expression, particularly American. See G. Cross, *Time and Money: The Making of Consumer Culture* (1993) which includes a useful bibliography; S. Ewen, *Captains of Consciousness: Advertising and the Social Roots of Consumer Culture* (1976); R. Willett, *The Americanization of Germany, 1945–1949* (1992); R. F. Krisel, *Seducing the French: the Dilemma of Americanization* (1990); K. A. Kaplan, *Rocking Around the Clock. Music Television, Post-modernism and Consumer Culture* (1987); H. Lefebvre, *Everyday Life in the Modern World* (English translation, 1979).

For art and architecture see *Post-Impressionism* (Royal Academy, 1979–80); E. F. Fry, *Cubism* (1966); H. Richter, *Dada* (1965); B. Hinz, *Art and the Third Reich* (1979); D. Cooper, *Cubism and the Cubist Epoch* (1971); *Art and Power, Europe Under the Dictators, 1930–45* (Hayward Gallery, 1995); L. R. Lippard, *Pop Art* (1966). See also B. Hillier, *The Style of the Century* (1983) and C. Jencks, *Post-Modernism, The New Classicism in Art and Architecture* (1987).

For the media see A. Smith, *The Shadow in the Cave* (1973); D. Dayan and E. Katz, *Media Events: The Live Broadcasting of History* (1992); A. Smith (ed.), *Television: An International History* (1995); G. J. Mulgan, *Communication and Control* (1991); and A. Briggs and P. Burke, *A Social History of the Media From Gutenberg to the Internet* (2002).

For science see R. Mendelsohn, *Science and Western Domination* (1974); C. Sagan, *The Demon-haunted World: Science as a Candle in the Dark* (New York, 1994); J. D. Watson, *The Double Helix* (1999 edn); C. Dennis, R. Gallagher and J. Watson (eds), *The Human Genome* (2001); and J. Sulston and G. Ferry, *The Common Thread* (2002).

For population see E. S. Woytinsky, *World Population and Production* (1953) and R. W. Hiorns (ed.), *Demographic Patterns in Developed Societies* (1980); for migration C. G. Pooley and I. D. Whyte, *Migrants, Emigrants and Immigrants: A Social History of Migration* (1991); and for cities P. Hall, *The World Cities* (1966) and M. Dogan and J. D. Kasarda, *The Metropolis Era*, 2 vols (1988).

For the end of the century and the millennium see N. P. Gardels (ed.), *At Century's End: Great Minds Reflect on Our Times* (La Jolla, 1996); A. Briggs and D. Snowman (eds), *Fins de Siède, How Centuries End* (1996); and P. Kennedy, *Preparing for the Twenty-First Century* (1993).

INDEX

The index covers Chapters 1–13 but not the 'Bibliographical Essay'. Titles of books, journals, newspapers and pictures are in *italic e.g. Avanti!* (newspaper) 223, as are words in foreign languages e.g. *Action Française* 253, 248. Locations in **bold** indicate a definition or an explanation e.g. *beaux moments* **13**. The locations of illustrations are given in *italic* followed by *illus.* e.g. alliances, hardening 117, 130, *138–9 illus.* All 'battles' and 'treaties' appear under the headings 'Battles' and 'Treaties' respectively. The following abbreviations are used: '19thC' for 'nineteenth century'; '20thC' for 'twentieth century'; 'WWI' for 'World War One'; and 'WWII' for 'World War Two'.

Hardenberg, Karl August, 43

Hardy, Thomas, 198

Harmsworth, Alfred, 135

Harris, Arthur 'Bomber', 301

Hartung, Fritz, 29

Haussman, George, 154

Haut Brion (Bordeaux), 37

haute bourgeoisie, **60**

Haydn, Franz Joseph *Deutschland Über Alles*, 103

Hayes, Carlton J. H., 114

Hazlitt, William

health statistics, 64

Heath, Edward, 367, 368, 360

Hébert, J. R., 23

Hecker, Friedrich, 75

Hegedüs, András, 354

Hegel, Georg Wilhelm Friedrich, 7, 25, 60

Heine, Heinrich, 55–6, 154

Heligoland, 46, 123

Helmholz, Herman von, 157

Helvetic republic (Switzerland), 27

Hemingway, Ernest, *A Farewell to Arms* (1929), 198

Henderson, Nevile, 272

Herat, 130

Herder, J. G., 59

Herriot, Edouard, 208, 247

Hertz, Heinrich, 157

Herzl, Theodore, *Jewish State* (1896), 153

Hesse-Cassell, 56, 87, 134

Hetairia Philike, **57**

Hindenburg Programme, **191**

history, 37, 67, 144–6, **148**, 394

History of Munitions (1922), 236

Hitler, Adolf, 207, 244, 255, 298, 300, 299, 303. *See also* Germany, National Socialism

  Beer Hall putsch, 216

  Chancellorship, 252, 254

  European agenda, 265–6

  goals, 254

  ideological terrorism, 400

  interest group politics, 245–6

  marriage, 301

  personal power consolidated, 255

  Viennese influence, 152

  Weltanschauung (world view), 257

Hitler Jugend, 256

Hobsbawm, Eric, 397

Hobson, J. A., 116, 128

Hofmannstahl, Hugo von, 161

Hollywood, 157, 232

Holstein, Friedrich von, 123, 138, 139

Holy Alliance (1815), 46, 55, 57, 70

Holy Roman Empire, 32

homosexuality, 164

Honecker, Erich, 313, 378

Hoover Moratorium, **240**

Horta, Victor, 162

Horthy, Nikolaus, 216, 294

Hoxha, Enver, 299, 319

Hrushevsky, Mikhail, 214

Hugenberg, Paul, 252

Hughes, Stuart, *Consciousness and Society*, 165

Hugo, Victor, 54, 58, 148, 159

  Hernani (1830), 149

Huguenots, 5

Human Genome Project, 411

Human Rights, 393

Humboldt, Wilhelm von, 43

Hundred Days, 39, 45

Hungary

  Arrow Cross, 252

  fascism, 253

  Independence Party, 191

  nationalities & nationalism, 84, 111

  nobility, 71

  punitive peace, 210

  revolutions, 216–17, 326

  Stalinization, 320, 321, 322

  WWII, 294

Husák, Gustav, 313

Hutton, Graham, *We Too Can Prosper* (1953), 347

Huxley, T. H., 150

Iberian peninsula, 33

Ibsen Henrik, 16, 162, 164

  John Gabriel Borkman, 162

  The Master Builder, 162

Il Risorgimento (newspaper), 73, 93

Illyrian coast, 26

immigration, 387, 407

imperialism, 116

  and European politics, 129–30

  motives, 126–7, 128–9

  post WWII, 346–7

  use of term, 125

Impressionism, 151–2, 156

Imrédy, Béla, 251